Why do you need this new edition?

8 good reasons why you should buy this new Second Edition of *Visions of America*!

1. New with this Second Edition: *Visions of America* works in tandem with the innovative website, *MyHistoryLab*, helping you learn more in your history course (www.myhistorylab.com). *MyHistoryLab* icons connect the main narrative in each chapter of the book to a powerful array of resources, including primary source documents, analytical video segments, multi-media tutorials, and more. A *MyHistoryLab Connections* feature now appears at the end of each chapter, capping off the study resources for each chapter. *MyHistoryLab* also includes both an eText and Audio Book of *Visions of America*, so that you can read or listen to your textbook any time you have access to the Internet. For even greater flexibility, you may download the eText to an iPad® using the free Pearson eText app.

2. New with this Second Edition: *Visions of America* now uses the latest *New MyHistoryLab*, which offers the most advanced Study Plan ever. You get personalized study plans for each chapter, with content arranged from less complex thinking—like remembering facts—to more complex critical thinking—like understanding connections in history and analyzing primary sources. Assessments and learning applications in the Study Plan link you directly to the *Visions of America* eBook for reading and review.

3. New with this Second Edition: the *New MyHistoryLab* course for *Visions of America* offers more than 100 powerful Closer Look learning applications developed by the authors of the textbook. These engaging on-line applications will help you learn to think critically about the past, which is essential to doing well in your history class.

4. Also in the *New MyHistoryLab* course for *Visions of America*, the text authors have created Critical Visions videos for each chapter of the book. In these videos the author highlights the most important themes and questions explored in the chapter. View the videos to get more out of your reading of each chapter, and watch them later to refresh your understanding of the material before classes and exams.

5. A new feature in this Second Edition of *Visions of America* is the Envisioning Evidence sections that appear in fifteen of the chapters. Each Envisioning Evidence uses charts, graphs, maps, or illustrations to discuss and highlight the kind of materials that historians use to illuminate and analyze the past. Among the topics covered in this new feature are: the eighteenth-century slave trade (Chapter 3), a comparison of military strength of the North and South during the Civil War (Chapter 13), and interpreting public opinion polls during the Great Depression (Chapter 22).

6. The pedagogical framework of the Second Edition of *Visions of America* has also been strengthened by the addition of Learning Objective Questions at the start of each chapter. These questions help you identify the most important themes and topics as you work through the chapter.

7. The Second Edition of *Visions of America* covers numerous new topics in the thematic features that appear in every chapter—Competing Visions, Images as History, and Choices and Consequences. Among these new topics are: reactions to the French Revolution in the early Republic (Chapter 6), the freeing of slaves during the Civil War (Chapter 13), and the annexation of the Philippines in 1898 after the Spanish-American War (Chapter 19).

8. To improve the narrative presentation of the Second Edition of *Visions of America*, the authors and editors have reviewed each line of the text and made numerous significant changes to enhance the strengths of the First Edition.

VISIONS *of* AMERICA

VISIONS *of* AMERICA

SECOND EDITION

A History of the United States

VOLUME 2 • SINCE 1865

Jennifer D. Keene
Chapman University

Saul Cornell
Fordham University

Edward T. O'Donnell
College of the Holy Cross

PEARSON

Boston Columbus Indianapolis New York San Francisco Upper Saddle River
Amsterdam Cape Town Dubai London Madrid Milan Munich Paris Montréal Toronto
Delhi Mexico City São Paulo Sydney Hong Kong Seoul Singapore Taipei Tokyo

Editorial Director: Craig Campanella
Editor in Chief: Dickson Musslewhite
Executive Editor: Ed Parsons
Development Editor: Gerald Lombardi
Editorial Project Manager: Alex Rabinowitz
Supplements Editor: Emsal Hasan
Editorial Assistant: Emily Tamburri
Director of Marketing: Brandy Dawson
Senior Marketing Manager: Maureen E. Prado Roberts
Marketing Assistant: Samantha Bennett
Senior Managing Editor: Ann Marie McCarthy
Senior Project Manager: Debra A. Wechsler
Senior Operations Manager: Mary Fischer
Operations Specialist: Alan Fischer
Cover Design: Laura Gardner and John Christiana

Interior Designer: Laura Gardner
AV Project Manager: Mirella Signoretto
Cartographer: Peter Bull Art Studio
Cover Art: Immigrants: Picture History/Newscom; First Vote:©Bettmann/CORBIS; Native-American Woman: The Granger Collection, NYC; Operating a hand drill: Library of Congress; Soldier in Iraq: STEFAN ZAKLIN/EPA/Newscom
Director of Media and Assessment: Brian Hyland
Media Editor: Andrea Messineo
Media Project Manager: Tina Rudowski
Full-Service Project Management: Melissa Sacco
Composition: PreMediaGlobal USA, Inc.
Printer/Binder: Quad/Graphics
Cover Printer: Lehigh-Phoenix Color/Hagerstown
Text Font: Minion Pro Regular

Credits and acknowledgments borrowed from other sources and reproduced, with permission, in this textbook appear on appropriate page within text (or on page C-1).

Library of Congress Cataloging-in-Publication Data

Keene, Jennifer D.
  Visions of America : a history of the United States / Jennifer D. Keene, Saul Cornell,
Edward T. O'Donnell. — 2nd ed.
    p. cm.
  Includes bibliographical references and index.
  ISBN-13: 978-0-205-09266-6 (combined vol.)
  ISBN-10: 0-205-09266-7 (combined vol.)
  ISBN-13: 978-0-205-09267-3 (v. 1)
  ISBN-13: 978-0-205-09268-0 (v. 2)
  1. United States—History—Textbooks. I. Cornell, Saul. II. O'Donnell, Edward T.
III. Title.
  E178.1.K24 2012
  973—dc23

                   2011041966

10 9 8 7 6 5 4 3 2 1

Combined Volume	Volume 1 à la carte
ISBN 10: 0-205-09266-7	ISBN 10: 0-205-19327-7
ISBN 13: 978-0-205-09266-6	ISBN 13: 978-0-205-19327-1
Instructor's Review Copy	Volume 2
ISBN 10: 0-205-19244-0	ISBN 10: 0-205-09268-3
ISBN 13: 978-0-205-19244-1	ISBN 13: 978-0-205-09268-0
Volume 1	Volume 2 à la carte
ISBN 10: 0-205-09267-5	ISBN 10: 0-205-19329-3
ISBN 13: 978-0-205-09267-3	ISBN 13: 978-0-205-19329-5

PEARSON

Dedication

To our parents, who imbued us with a love of history; our spouses, who have learned to share this passion; and our children, present and future students of American history.

Brief Contents

Contents

CHAPTER 14 Now That We Are Free: Reconstruction and the New South, 1863–1890 **404**

CHAPTER 15 Conflict and Conquest: The Transformation of the West, 1860–1900   **438**

CHAPTER **18** Creating a Democratic Paradise: The Progressive Era, 1895 –1915   **530**

CHAPTER **23** World War II: Fighting the Good War, 1939–1945   **684**

Maps

Charts, Graphs, and Tables

Envisioning Evidence

Images As History

Competing Visions

Choices and Consequences

About the Authors

Jennifer D. Keene

Saul Cornell

Edward T. O'Donnell

Jennifer D. Keene is a Professor of History and chair of the History Department at Chapman University in Orange, California. Dr. Keene has published three books on the American involvement in the First World War: *Doughboys, the Great War and the Remaking of America* (2001); *The United States and the First World War* (2000); and *World War I: The American Soldier Experience* (2011). She has received numerous fellowships for her research, including a Mellon Fellowship, a National Research Council Postdoctoral Award, and Fulbright Senior Scholar Awards to Australia and France. Her articles have appeared in the *Annales de Démographie Historique, Peace & Change, Intelligence and National Security*, and *Military Psychology*. Dr. Keene served as an associate editor for the *Encyclopedia of War and American Society* (2005), which won the Society of Military History's prize for best reference book. She works closely with the Gilder-Lehrman Institute, offering Teaching American History workshops for secondary school teachers throughout the country.

Saul Cornell is the Paul and Diane Guenther Chair in American History at Fordham University in New York. Professor Cornell has also taught at the Ohio State University, the College of William and Mary, Leiden University in the Netherlands, and has been a visiting scholar at Yale Law School. He is the author of *A Well Regulated Militia: The Founding Fathers and the Origins of Gun Control* (Langum Prize in Legal History) and *The Other Founders: Anti-Federalism and the Dissenting Tradition in America, 1788–1828* (Society of the Cincinnati Book Prize), both of which were nominated for the Pulitzer Prize. His articles have appeared in the *Journal of American History, the William and Mary Quarterly, American Studies, Law and History Review*, and dozens of leading law reviews. His work has been cited by the U.S. Supreme Court and several state Supreme Courts. He lectures widely on topics in legal and constitutional history and the use of visual materials to teach American history.

Edward T. O'Donnell is an Associate Professor of History at the College of the Holy Cross in Worcester, Massachusetts. He taught previously at Hunter College, City University of New York. He is the author of *Ship Ablaze: The Tragedy of the Steamboat General Slocum* (Random House, 2003) and the forthcoming *Talisman of a Lost Hope: Henry George and Gilded Age America* (Columbia University Press). His articles have appeared in *The Journal of Urban History, The Journal of the Gilded Age and Progressive Era, and The Public Historian*. He is also very active in the field of public history, curating exhibits and consulting at institutions such as the Lower East Side Tenement Museum and the New York Historical Society. Since 2002, he has worked with more than fifty Teaching American History grant programs across the country, offering lectures and workshops for middle and high school teachers.

Supplements for Instructors and Students

FOR QUALIFIED COLLEGE ADOPTERS

Name of Supplement	Supplements for Qualified College Adopters
MyHistoryLab	MyHistoryLab (**www.myhistorylab.com**) **The moment you know** Educators know it. Students know it. It's that inspired moment when something that was difficult to understand suddenly makes perfect sense. Our MyLab products have been designed and refined with a single purpose in mind: to help educators create that moment of understanding with their students.
Instructor's Resource Manual with Test Bank	Available at the Instructor's Resource Center, at **www.pearsonhighered.com/irc**, the Instructor's Resource Manual with Test Bank contains chapter overviews, key points and discussion questions, suggested assignments and information on audio-visual resources that can be used in developing and preparing lecture presentations. The Test Bank includes multiple choice and essay questions that are both general and text specific. It also contains brief answers to all the questions in the textbook—learning objective questions, crawl questions, review questions, and questions for analysis.
Annotated Instructor's eText	Contained within MyHistoryLab, the *Annotated Instructor's eText for Visions of America (Second Edition)* leverages the powerful Pearson eText platform to make it easier than ever for teachers to access subject-specific resources for class preparation. The *AI eText* serves as the hub for all instructor resources, with chapter-by-chapter links to PowerPoint slides, content from the Instructor's Manual, and to MyHistoryLab's ClassPrep engine, which contains a wealth of history content organized for classroom use.
PowerPoint Presentation	Available at the Instructor's Resource Center, at **www.pearsonhighered.com/irc**, the PowerPoint presentations are text specific and available for download. The PowerPoint slides to accompany Visions of America (Second Edition) include an outline of each chapter and full-color images, maps, and figures from the textbook. All images from the textbook have corresponding teaching notes that provide background information about the image and teaching strategies.
MyTest	Available at **www.pearsonmytest.com**, MyTest contains a diverse set of over 2,300 multiple choice, true-false, and essay questions, with a test bank that supports a variety of assessment strategies. The large pool of multiple choice questions for each chapter includes factual, conceptual, and analytical questions, so that instructors may assess students on basic information as well as critical thinking. The MyTest program helps instructors easily create and print quizzes and exams. Questions and tests can be authored online, allowing instructors ultimate flexibility and the ability to efficiently manage assessments anytime, anywhere! Instructors can easily access existing questions and edit, create, and store using simple drag-and-drop and Word-like controls.
Retreiving the American Past	Available through the Pearson Custom Library (**www.pearsoncustom.com, keyword search | rtap**), the *Retrieving the American Past* (RTAP) program lets you create a textbook or reader that meets your needs and the needs of your course. RTAP gives you the freedom and flexibility to add chapters from several best-selling Pearson textbooks, in addition to *The American Nation, 14/e*, and/or 100 topical reading units written by the History Department of Ohio State University, all under one cover. Choose the content you want to teach in depth, in the sequence you want, at the price you want your students to pay.

Name of Supplement	Supplements for Students
MyHistoryLab	MyHistoryLab (**www.myhistorylab.com**) **The moment you know** Educators know it. Students know it. It's that inspired moment when something that was difficult to understand suddenly makes perfect sense. Our MyLab products have been designed and refined with a single purpose in mind: to help educators create that moment of understanding with their students.
CourseSmart	**www.coursemart.com** CourseSmart eTextbooks offer the same content as the printed text in a convenient online format—with highlighting, online search, and printing capabilities. You **save 60% over the list price** of the traditional book.
Books à la Carte	Books à la Carte editions feature the exact same content as the traditional printed text in a convenient, three-hole-punched, loose-leaf version at a discounted price—allowing you to take only what you need to class. You'll **save 35% over the net price** of the traditional book. **Vol. 1 - ISBN: 0205193277; ISBN-13: 9780205193271; Vol. 2 - ISBN: 0205193293; ISBN-13: 9780205193295**
Library of American Biography Series	**www.pearsonhighered.com/educator/series/Library-of-American-Biography/10493.page** Pearson's renowned series of biographies spotlights figures who had a significant impact on American history. Included in the series are Edmund Morgan's *The Puritan Dilemma: The Story of John Winthrop*, B. Davis Edmund's *Tecumseh and the Quest for Indian Leadership*, J. William T. Youngs, *Eleanor Roosevelt: A Personal and Public Life*, John R. M. Wilson's *Jackie Robinson and the American Dilemma* and Sandra Opdycke's *Jane Addams and her Vision for America*.
Penguin Valuepacks	**www.pearsonhighered.com/penguin** A variety of Penguin-Putnam texts is available at discounted prices when bundled with *Visions of America*, 2/e. Texts include Benjamin Franklin's *Autobiography and Other Writings*, Nathaniel Hawthorne's *The Scarlet Letter*, Thomas Jefferson's *Notes on the State of Virginia*, and George Orwell's *1984*.
A Short Guide to Writing About History, 7/e	Written by Richard Marius, late of Harvard University, and Melvin E. Page, Eastern Tennessee State University, this engaging and practical text helps students get beyond merely compiling dates and facts. Covering both brief essays and the documented resource paper, the text explores the writing and researching processes, identifies different modes of historical writing, including argument, and concludes with guidelines for improving style. **ISBN-10: 0205118607; ISBN-13: 9780205118601**
Longman American History Atlas	This full-color historical atlas designed especially for college students is a valuable reference tool and visual guide to American history. This atlas includes maps covering the scope of American history from the lives of the Native Americans to the 1990s. Produced by a renowned cartographic firm and a team of respected historians, the Longman American History Atlas will enhance any American history survey course. ISBN: **0321004868; ISBN-13: 9780321004864**

MyHistory Lab

The Moment You Know

Educators know it. Students know it. It's that inspired moment when something that was difficult to understand suddenly makes perfect sense. Our MyLab products have been designed and refined with a single purpose in mind—to help educators create that moment of understanding with their students.

The new MyHistoryLab delivers **proven results** in helping individual students succeed. It provides **engaging experiences** that personalize, stimulate, and measure learning for each student. And, it comes from a **trusted partner** with educational expertise and a deep commitment to helping students, instructors, and departments achieve their goals.

A **personalized study plan** for each student, based on Bloom's Taxonomy, promotes critical-thinking skills, and helps students succeed in the course and beyond.

Assessment tied to every video, application, and chapter enables both instructors and students to track progress and get immediate feedback—and helps instructors to find the best resources with which to help students.

The **Pearson eText** lets students access their textbook anytime, anywhere, and any way they want. Just like the printed text students can highlight relevant passages and add their own notes. For even greater flexibility, students can download the eText to an iPad® using the free Pearson eText app. And, students can even listen to their text, streaming **full chapter audio** on their computers.

Closer Look tours walk students through maps, images, and key primary sources in detail, helping them to uncover their meaning and understand their context.

Author Video Lectures with Pearson history authors help students achieve a deeper understanding of key topics and themes. These narrated clips feature documentary images that capture students' attention.

Class Prep collects the very best class presentation resources in one convenient online destination, so instructors can keep students engaged throughout every class.

Key Supplements

Annotated Instructor's eText

Contained within MyHistoryLab, the *Annotated Instructor's eText* for *Visions of America, Second Edition,* leverages the powerful Pearson eText platform to make it easier than ever for teachers to access subject-specific resources for class preparation. The *AI eText* serves as the hub for all instructor resources, with chapter-by-chapter links to PowerPoint slides, content from the Instructor's Manual, and to *MyHistoryLab's* ClassPrep engine, which contains a wealth of history content organized for classroom use.

Instructor's Manual

The Instructor's Manual contains chapter overview, lecture supplements, discussion questions, suggested assignments, and research resources for each chapter, including both general and text-specific content. It also contains brief answers to all the questions in the textbook—learning objective questions, question crawl, review questions, and questions for analysis—along with the text of the questions themselves.

PowerPoint Presentation

The PowerPoint slides to accompany *Visions of America, Second Edition,* include an outline of each chapter and full-color images, maps, and figures from the textbook. All images from the textbook have corresponding teaching notes that provide background information about the image and teaching strategies.

MyTest Test Bank

Containing a diverse set of over 2,300 multiple choice, true-false, and essay questions, the MyTest test bank supports a variety of assessment strategies. The large pool of multiple choice questions for each chapter includes factual, conceptual, and analytical questions, so that instructors may assess students on basic information as well as critical thinking.

CHAPTER

14

((•—[Hear the Audio File on myhistorylab.com

◉—[Watch the Video *Critical Visions, Chapter 14*

Now That We Are Free

Reconstruction and the New South, 1863–1890

The Civil War ended in April 1865, concluding the bloodiest and most divisive conflict in American history. The period that followed came to be known as Reconstruction for several reasons. Most obviously, the name called to mind the need to rebuild the war-torn South. It also referred to the effort to reestablish the Union torn apart by secession. Finally, it indicated the need to remake Southern society in the wake of slavery's destruction.

The complexities and challenges of this last goal are evident in Winslow Homer's 1876 painting, *A Visit from the Old Mistress*, which depicts ex-slaves being visited by their former owner. The elegant clothing worn by the "Old Mistress" suggests she has money, but clearly the relationship between the women has changed significantly in the wake of emancipation. To begin with, the mistress has come to visit the former slaves in their home, suggesting a diminishing of her status and power relative to them. The scene also lacks any sense of the affection that plantation owners always assured themselves existed between slaves and masters. Indeed, the three African American women eye the mistress warily. One of them even chooses to remain seated in what surely would have been considered a show of contempt. The old order was gone, but what would replace it remained unclear in the aftermath of the war.

Americans entered the Reconstruction period facing the profound questions raised by war and emancipation. Could whites and former slaves live together in peace and mutual respect? What rights were the freedmen entitled to, and who would guarantee these rights? The different answers articulated by freedmen and white Southerners revealed sharply divergent visions of the future and led to a bitter struggle to define the meaning of freedom. "Verily," observed ex-slave Frederick Douglass, "the work does not end with the abolition of slavery, but only begins."

"Never before had I a word of impudence from any of our black folk, but they are not ours any longer."

SUSAN BRADFORD, observing the defiant attitude among former slaves on her Florida plantation, 1865

Preparing for Reconstruction

Long before the Emancipation Proclamation took effect on January 1, 1863 countless thousands of enslaved Africans took advantage of the chaos produced by the war to liberate themselves. Their actions raised a host of questions about what rights the freedmen would be entitled to, including land ownership and voting. Lincoln and his advisers preferred to wait until the war was won before addressing these questions, but actions taken by the freedmen to assert their rights and secure their liberty forced the Lincoln administration to develop policies during the war that ultimately shaped postwar Reconstruction.

Emancipation Test Cases

Even before the Emancipation Proclamation took effect, the federal government realized that it needed to enact policies regarding the growing numbers of freedmen in areas of the South occupied by the Union army. These policies varied by region and were shaped by local customs and the attitudes of freedmen and white officials. As such, they amounted to test cases for the coming debate over Reconstruction. Three of these test cases revealed both the promise and the conflict surrounding emancipation.

The first test case began when federal forces seized the Sea Islands off the coast of South Carolina in November 1861. They found a vast system of cotton plantations, but no planters. The latter had fled, leaving behind 10,000 slaves, who moved quickly to establish new lives based on their understanding of freedom. While clearly posed, "Planting Sweet Potatoes" (**14.1**), shot by a New Hampshire photographer visiting a regiment from his state stationed on one of the islands, captured one fundamental way in which ex-slaves expressed their freedom. Rejecting cotton, a crop they associated with slavery, they planted crops of their own choosing, such as sweet potatoes and corn for local consumption. Freedom for the African Americans of the Sea Islands

meant a future as independent farmers living free of white control.

Many Northern whites who arrived after the military takeover, however, brought with them a different vision of the future for the Sea Islands. Convinced that Sea Island blacks should resume their labors on cotton plantations—not as slaves but as paid wage earners—federal officials chose not to grant land to the freedmen. This decision was driven in part by the sincere belief that subsistence farming on small tracts of land was backward, harmful to the long-term

14.1 Freedmen in the Sea Islands Cultivating Sweet Potatoes, 1862
Most freedmen refused to grow cotton, considering it a symbol of slavery. They grew sweet potatoes and other crops, such as corn, primarily for their own consumption.

How did freedmen define freedom in the Sea Islands?   **Read** the **Document** *Charlotte Forten, "Life on the Sea Islands"*

interests of the freedmen and also by the racist notion that African Americans could not handle freedom responsibly without the guidance of white employers. Consequently, they auctioned the land off to the highest bidder. Northern investors bought most of the land, hired freedmen as wage laborers, and resumed cotton cultivation.

A second test case unfolded on Davis Bend, the Mississippi plantations owned by Confederate President Jefferson Davis and his brother Joseph. Before the Civil War, they had tried to make Davis Bend a model slave-labor community, where slaves received better food and were granted considerable autonomy. The Davis brothers hoped other planters would follow their example and thus refute the abolitionist argument that slavery was inhumane. Instead, Davis Bend became a model of a very different sort of ideal, one that vividly demonstrated what freedmen could achieve if granted land and autonomy. When General Ulysses S. Grant arrived and found the former slaves running the plantations, he ordered federal officials to lease land to the freedmen. Unlike the freedmen of the Sea Islands, the African American residents of Davis Bend did not have to contend with Northerners seeking to reassert white control over the land and impose a wage labor system. As a consequence, by 1865 Davis Bend residents had established their own local government and cleared a profit of $160,000 in cotton sales.

A third and far larger test case for emancipation policy began in Louisiana and was eventually extended up the Mississippi Valley affecting some 700,000 former slaves. Soon after Union forces seized New Orleans in April 1862, army officers established a policy to guide the transition from slavery to emancipation. As in the Sea Islands, the policy reflected the racist belief among Northern whites that African Americans could not responsibly handle their freedom and therefore needed strict rules of conduct and work. Blacks were required to remain on their plantations, working as wage laborers bound by one-year contracts. Those wishing to travel, even for short distances, required a pass from the plantation owner. Runaways and resisters, as depicted in this 1864 drawing (**14.2**), would be forcibly returned to their plantations. Offsetting these harsh provisions was a ban on corporal punishment for plantation labor. Freedmen bitterly opposed the new system, arguing that it rendered them nearly

14.2 Freedmen Forcibly Returned to Their Plantations, 1864 Violators of the Reconstruction plan were deemed "vagrants" and forcibly returned to their plantations.

Why did Union officials define freedom for former slaves so narrowly in Louisiana?

powerless under the authority of their former masters. In New Orleans, home to the South's largest free black population before the war, African Americans began to demand equal rights for all freedmen, including the right to vote and hold office. Although their efforts failed, they sparked a national debate over freedmen's rights that would dominate Reconstruction.

The experiences in the Sea Islands, Davis Bend, Louisiana, and elsewhere during the war created conflicting visions regarding the rights of freedmen, land redistribution, and the authority of ex-slave owners. Yet emancipation also revealed the optimism of the freedmen and their commitment to defend their newly won freedom and make the most of it.

Lincoln's Ten Percent Plan

Even as the Civil War raged, President Lincoln had begun to formulate an official Reconstruction policy. In keeping with his moderate political views before the war, Lincoln proposed a moderate Reconstruction policy. As he suggested so eloquently in his second inaugural address, he intended to deal with the defeated South "with malice toward none" and "charity for all" to "achieve and cherish a just and lasting peace among ourselves…." He believed that extending lenient terms to the South would convince Confederates to surrender sooner and speed the healing process necessary for the good of the Union. Vengeance, he held, would only delay Reconstruction. It might even inspire defeated Confederate soldiers to form renegade bands of insurgents to wage a war of terrorism for years to come.

> ### "A more studied outrage on the legislative authority of the people has never been perpetuated."
>
> Wade-Davis Manifesto denouncing Lincoln's veto of the Wade-Davis Bill

In December 1863, Lincoln issued his Proclamation of Amnesty and Reconstruction, also known as the **Ten Percent Plan**. Intended to establish Southern state governments, the plan pardoned all Southerners (except high-ranking military officers and Confederate officials) who took an oath pledging loyalty to the Union and support for emancipation. As soon as 10 percent of a state's voters took this oath, they could call a convention, establish a new state government, and apply for federal recognition.

Radical Republicans Offer a Different Vision

Lincoln's lenient plan enraged many Radical Republicans. In July 1864, Radical Republican leaders Senator Benjamin Wade of Ohio and Congressman Henry W. Davis of Maryland cosponsored the Wade-Davis Bill, a Reconstruction program designed to punish Confederate leaders and destroy the South's slave society. Southerners could reestablish new state governments only after a majority of a state's voters signed an "ironclad" oath declaring they never aided the Confederate army or government. Southerners who served as high-ranking army officers or government officials would be stripped of their citizenship, including the right to vote and hold office. The former Confederate states would be readmitted only after a long period of punishment and a clear demonstration of their commitment to the Union, emancipation, and freedmen's rights.

Lincoln quietly pocket vetoed the bill. Furious, Radicals sought to replace him as the Republican Party presidential nominee in 1864. Although the effort failed, it exposed the deeply divided opinions regarding Reconstruction.

Lincoln and his fellow Republicans did manage to find common ground on two issues. In late January 1865, at the urging of Lincoln's administration, Congress passed the Thirteenth Amendment, abolishing slavery. The measure ended any ambiguity over the Emancipation Proclamation, abolishing slavery everywhere in the United States and offering no compensation to former slaveholders. By year's end 27 states, including eight former Confederate states, would ratify the amendment.

In March 1865, Congress established the Bureau of Refugees, Freedmen, and Abandoned Lands. Known simply as the **Freedmen's Bureau**, it became an all-purpose relief agency in the war-ravaged South, distributing food, providing emergency services, building schools, and managing confiscated lands. It represented the first attempt by the federal government to provide social welfare services and quickly became the bedrock institution for implementing Reconstruction policy.

What advantages did Lincoln see in a moderate Reconstruction policy?

Read the **Document** *Carl Schurz, "Report on the Condition of the South" (1865)*

The Fruits of Freedom

 Many Southerners were stunned by the response of their slaves to freedom. Clinging to self-serving paternalistic notions of the plantation as one big family under the benign authority of the master and planter, they were taken aback when their slaves refused to obey their orders or exhibited anger or disrespect toward them. Susan Bradford, a young woman living on a Florida plantation, wrote in her diary that she was "hurt and dazed" when one of her former slaves refused to prepare a dinner for her mother. "Tell her if she want any dinner," sneered the free woman, "she kin cook it herself." "I believed that these people were content, happy, and attached to their masters," wrote one South Carolina planter in 1865, unable to comprehend why slaves abandoned their masters "in [their] moment of need." It would be the first of many such shocking experiences for whites, who never imagined that slavery might one day be abolished.

Freedom of Movement

Even before the guns of the Civil War went silent, African Americans had begun to explore the meaning of their freedom and formulate their own vision of a reconstructed postwar South, both of which included unrestricted mobility. Under slavery, movement was sharply limited, and few slaves ventured far from their plantations. In the chaos of war, however, and later with official emancipation, African Americans hit the road. Many did so to escape the plantations that were home to their former masters and countless bitter memories. Others simply reveled in free and unfettered movement. They wandered for the pleasure of it with no particular destination in mind. As these advertisements (**14.3**) from the *Colored Tennessean*, Tennessee's only African American–owned newspaper, indicate, many freedmen also journeyed in search of loved ones sold away years before.

African American mobility led to a sharp rise in the black population of Southern cities. In contrast to rural life, black settlements in cities offered more varied job opportunities, albeit nearly always menial, difficult, and low paid. Urban life also provided freedmen access to strong black institutions such as churches, charities, and newspapers.

Southern whites reacted to black mobility with both alarm and disdain. Just as former slaves equated freedom with mobility, their former masters saw in it a shocking reminder that the old order was gone. As a consequence, in one of the first expressions of resistance to black freedom, white Southerners passed vagrancy laws intended to restrict African American mobility.

Forty Acres and a Mule

Many freedmen also tried to become landowners. If travel was a symbolic expression of their new freedom, land was freedom in concrete form. Land, the freedmen believed, would give their freedom meaning by providing an independent living, free of planter control.

The idea that freedmen would receive land in addition to their freedom originated during the war. As Southerners abandoned their plantations before the advancing Union army, ex-slaves often took control, partitioned land, and planted crops. Freedmen defended these extralegal actions as simple justice, citing the generations of unpaid labor that they and their ancestors had performed on farms and plantations. "The property which they [former slaveholders] hold," asserted a group of freedmen, "was nearly all earned by the sweat of our brows."

14.3 Freedmen Searching for Loved Ones Sold Away during Slavery These classified advertisements in the August 12, 1865 *Colored Tennessean* were just two of thousands published in mainly black-owned newspapers during Reconstruction. They vividly highlight the efforts of freed-men to overcome one of slavery's harshest legacies.
[*Source:* (t) ICHi-36218; Information Wanted: Of a man by the name of Elias Lowery McDermit; Nashville, Tennessee; 1865; Creator - "The Colored Tennessean"; (b) ICHi-36219. Saml Dove wishes to know of the whereabouts of his mother; Utica, NY. Aug 5 1865. Looking for his mother, Areno and his sisters and brother.]

> **INFORMATION WANTED**
> OF A MAN BY THE NAME OF ELIAS LOWERY McDERMIT, who used to belong to Thomas Lyons, of Knoxville, East Tennessee. He was sold to a man by the name of Sherman about ten years ago, and I learned some six years ago that he was on a steamboat running between Memphis and New Orleans, and more recently I heard that he was somewhere on the Cumberland river, in the Federal army. Any information concerning him will be thankfully received. Address Colored Tennessean, Nashville, Tenn. From his sister who is now living in Knoxville, East Tennessee.
> je24-1m]   MARTHA McDERMIT.

> SAML. DOVE wishes to know of the whereabouts of his mother, Areno, his sisters Maria, Neziah, and Peggy, and his brother Edmond, who were owned by Geo. Dove, of Rockingham county, Shenandoah Valley, Va. Sold in Richmond, after which Saml. and Edmond were taken to Nashville, Tenn., by Joe Mick; Areno was left at the Eagle Tavern, Richmond
> Respectfully yours,
> SAML. DOVE.
> Utica, New York, Aug. 5, 1865-3m
>
> U. S. Christian Commission, Nashville, Tenn., July 19, 1865.

> "Give us our own land and we take care of ourselves; but without land, the old masters can hire or starve us, as they please."
>
> A South Carolina freedman speaking to a Northern journalist, 1865

To bring order to these unofficial acts of confiscation, General William T. Sherman issued in early

Read the **Document** *James C. Beecher, "Report on Land Reform" (1865, 1866)*

Why did freedmen believe they were owed land?

1865 Special Field Order No. 15. It announced that 400,000 acres of abandoned land from northern Florida to the South Carolina Sea Islands would be distributed to freedman in 40-acre plots. Weeks later Congress established the Freedmen's Bureau, authorizing it to rent to freedmen 40-acre plots of confiscated and abandoned land, along with a mule. By June some 40,000 freedmen lived on land distributed by Sherman, while thousands more rented plots under control of the Freedmen's Bureau.

Whether they owned land or worked as farm laborers for wages, African Americans used their freedom to change the way they worked. They often refused to work in gangs under overseers because it reminded them of slavery. Instead they preferred working independently, under the direction of elder family members. Many African American women left the field to work in their homes and care for children.

African Americans and Radical Republicans wanted land redistribution programs, popularly known as "forty acres and a mule," enacted across the South. Before long, however, their optimism would give way to bitter disappointment as nearly all the land was returned to its original white owners.

Uplift through Education

Along with land, freedmen sought education as an essential element of their freedom. Laws prohibiting the education of slaves had left most freedmen illiterate. But if they learned to read and write, they could conduct their own legal and business affairs, acquire better-paying jobs, read newspapers, and participate more fully in politics.

General O. O. Howard, the first head of the Freedmen's Bureau, also viewed education as an essential goal of Reconstruction. Working with charitable societies and African American leaders, the Freedmen's Bureau helped build 3,000 schools across the South that by 1870 served 150,000 students of all ages. By 1875, literacy among freedmen jumped from 10 percent to 30 percent (and 52 percent by 1900).

In the early years of Reconstruction, educated single white women from the North like the Cooke sisters (14.4) made up the majority of the teachers in these schools. Often sponsored by Northern charitable societies, they saw themselves as missionaries dedicated to the uplift of the freedmen. The journal that published this image in 1866, *Frank Leslie's Illustrated Weekly,* shared this vision. Note how the artist depicted the children in spotless attire with all of them focused on their studies.

That the vision of these teachers and their sponsors went beyond merely teaching ex-slaves to read is shown in this image (14.5) of a brief biography of African American poet Phillis Wheatley. Published in 1866 by a Boston Christian organization, it demonstrates an effort to inspire ex-slaves' quest for education and independence by instilling pride in African American achievement.

Educating freedmen, however, proved no easy job. Southern whites often put up fierce resistance

14.4 The Misses Cooke's School Room, Freedman's Bureau, 1866
The Cooke sisters moved from the North to Richmond, Virginia to run one of hundreds of Freedmen's Bureau schools established across the South.

14.5 Education and Inspiration
Some Northern charitable societies, like the Boston Tract Society, published and distributed books to both teach reading and inspire African Americans.

to African American education, especially in more remote areas. One report in 1865 described the hardships teachers faced: "Compelled to live on the coarsest diet … subjected to the jeers and hatred of her neighbors … swamped in mud—the school shed a drip, and her quarters little better; raided occasionally by rebels, her school broken up and herself insulted, banished, or run off."

The Freedmen's Bureau and Northern aid societies also established more than a dozen black colleges, including Howard in Washington, D.C., and Hampton in Virginia. One of their most immediate goals was to train black teachers. By 1870, African American teachers outnumbered white teachers in freedmen's schools. Many freedmen teachers became community leaders and ran for political office. At least 70 former teachers won seats in Southern state legislatures during Reconstruction.

The Black Church

The vast network of black churches established during Reconstruction provided an even greater source of community leadership. Black churches had existed in the South before the Civil War, but most were part of larger white congregations and subject to strict white control. Southern whites usually insisted that white ministers lead black congregations to ensure that preaching never challenged slavery and white domination.

When the war ended, countless African American congregations of Methodists, Baptists, Presbyterians, and other sects separated from white ones. They resented their inferior status in white-controlled churches and longed to practice a more emotional, expressive worship style disdained by whites. Most important, they wanted black clergymen who could address their spiritual and social needs.

Often churches assumed a central place in the lives of freedmen. Religious services provided spiritual and psychological support for blacks' daily struggles. Churches also ran schools and provided charitable services to the community. As this illustration (**14.6**) of a freedmen community at Trent River, North Carolina, demonstrates, African Americans built a church in the center that doubled as a schoolhouse and meeting place. Churches also offered African Americans a degree of self-government, electing members to serve as trustees and on committees overseeing parish life and budget management. African American women, in particular, filled numerous roles, planning events, raising money, and running programs such as temperance societies. Like their white counterparts, African American churches also sponsored countless initiatives, such as burial societies, fraternal organizations, and youth groups.

With the church taking so prominent a place in African American life, black ministers, like black teachers, assumed major leadership roles. White hostility convinced most ministers to concentrate on building up their communities from within. Still, many ministers entered politics to advance the cause of black equality, including more than 100 elected to Southern state legislatures during Reconstruction. Reverend Richard H. Cain, for example, went to Charleston, South Carolina, in 1865, where he assisted at a black church. Two years later he served as a delegate to the state constitutional convention, followed by terms in the state senate and U.S. House of Representatives.

African Americans' response to emancipation showed that they understood freedom as more than simply an end to slavery. Freedom included the right to free movement and travel, to labor for themselves under conditions of their own choosing, on land granted to them by the government. It meant self-improvement through education and self-help organizations. It meant establishing their own institutions and building their own communities. It also meant full civil and social equality with whites, including the right to vote and hold office.

14.6 The Black Church Anchors Freedmen Communities
African Americans organized thousands of churches across the South to address both their spiritual and social needs. In the freedmen settlement of Trent River, North Carolina, a simple structure served as a church, school, and meetinghouse (from *Harper's Weekly*, June 9, 1866).

How did the black church become such a vital institution in freedmen communities?

The Struggle to Define Reconstruction

As freedmen in the South worked to define, protect, and extend their freedoms, political leaders in Washington, D.C., debated how to reconstruct the South. The debate revealed sharply divergent visions of the postwar South's social, political, and economic order. Radical Republicans wanted to replace the old slavocracy with an interracial democracy protected by federal authority. Conservatives sought to limit Reconstruction to granting ex-slaves freedom and opposed proposals to distribute land and grant full equality to ex-slaves. Moderates held the balance of power in deciding most of these questions, but they lacked a clear vision of the postwar South and made their decisions in response to events as they unfolded.

The Conservative Vision of Freedom: Presidential Reconstruction

Andrew Johnson, who became president after Lincoln's assassination in April 1865, was a complicated man. Although he once owned slaves, like many other poor whites from the backcountry of eastern Tennessee, he grew up deeply suspicious of the planter aristocracy. As a politician, he gained a wide following among poor farmers for his populist criticism of planter power. He opposed secession and was the only senator from a seceding state who did not withdraw from the Senate in early 1861. Lincoln appointed Johnson governor of Tennessee after the state came under Union occupation. In 1864, Republicans sought to appeal to Southern unionism and picked Johnson as Lincoln's vice presidential running mate.

Initially Johnson indicated he intended to deal harshly with the South. He spoke of punishing ex-Confederates for their "treason." He also talked of the need to assist former slaves in their transition to freedom. Radical Republicans, who shared these views, were thrilled.

But their joy was soon replaced by anger. First, despite his harsh anti-planter rhetoric, Johnson

was a bitter racist who abhorred the notion of black equality. Committed to maintaining white supremacy, Johnson outlined in May 1865 a lenient policy toward the South designed to rapidly re-establish Southern state governments and restore the Union. It offered pardons, amnesty, and the return of all confiscated property to Southerners who took an oath of allegiance to the Union. Former Confederate leaders and planters possessing more than $20,000 in personal wealth, however, would have to apply to him personally for a pardon.

> "We have turned loose … four million slaves without a hut to shelter them or a cent in their pockets.… This Congress is bound to provide for them until they can take care of themselves."
>
> Congressman THADDEUS STEVENS, December 18, 1865

Second, Johnson set out the terms for readmitting ex-Confederate states to the Union. As soon as Johnson appointed a temporary governor, a state could then convene a constitutional convention of elected delegates (chosen only by those citizens granted amnesty or pardons). If the convention ratified the Thirteenth Amendment, renounced secession, repudiated all Confederate debts, and held elections for state office and Congress, Johnson would recognize the state as a fully reconstructed member of the Union.

With Congress out of session, Johnson's plan faced little formal opposition. By the fall of 1865, all but a few planters and high-ranking ex-Confederates had been pardoned and had

What was Andrew Johnson's primary motivation in devising his lenient Reconstruction policy?

 View the Closer Look Competing Visions: Federal Authority and Equal Rights

restored to them virtually all their lands, including the vast tracts of land that had been set aside in 40-acre plots for freedmen. In December, with all 11 former Confederate states having established new governments under his terms, Johnson announced the Union was restored, and Reconstruction was over.

Johnson's actions outraged Northern Republicans, including moderates. This political cartoon (**14.7**) shows Johnson accepting bags of cash from a former Confederate (depicted as the devil) in exchange for a pardon, while a "Pardoned Reconstruction Rebel" in the lower left kills "Union men and freedmen." Three developments in the supposedly "reconstructed" South stoked Republican discontent. First, many of the state constitutional conventions had failed explicitly to ratify the Thirteenth Amendment; some even demanded financial compensation for the loss of their slaves. Second, and even more galling, in the state elections in November 1865, Southern voters elected dozens of ex-Confederate

officials and army officers. Among them was Alexander Stephens, former vice president of the Confederacy, chosen to represent Georgia in the Senate. Third, new Southern state governments, beginning in late 1865 with Mississippi and South Carolina, passed laws known as **Black Codes** to limit the civil and economic rights of freedmen and create an exploitable workforce. Observing these developments less than a year after the end of the Civil War, many Northerners wondered if the great conflict had been fought in vain. Had hundreds of thousands died to defeat the Confederacy only to see its leaders quickly resume power? Had slavery been abolished only to be replaced with a similar system of unfree labor?

One of the most common Black Codes (first established in Mississippi in 1865 and then replicated across the South) established the vague charge of "vagrancy"—having no regular home or employment—as a pretext for controlling freedmen. (See *Competing Visions: Demanding Rights, Protecting Privilege*.) Any freedman who

14.7 Johnson's Leniency Angers the North
Johnson's pledge to punish the South ("Treason must be made odious") is ridiculed in this 1866 political cartoon. His sweeping pardons of ex-Confederate leaders and planters and easy terms for readmission of Southern states provoked anger in the North.

What events in the South in 1865–1866 angered Northern Republicans?

Competing Visions
DEMANDING RIGHTS, PROTECTING PRIVILEGE

In the aftermath of the Civil War, one question dominated the minds of Americans North and South: Now that slavery was abolished, what would be the status of the freedmen? While newspaper editors, clergymen, and members of Congress debated the issue, white and black Southerners set out to answer the question themselves. As you read the following documents, one from a convention of freedmen and the other from the state legislature of Mississippi, consider the starkly contrasted visions for the future of Southern society. Why do the freedmen feel compelled to say they bear no ill will toward their "former oppressors?" Why do Mississippi legislators define vagrancy in such vague terms?

"Address to the Loyal Citizens and Congress of the United States of America," Proceedings of the Convention of the Colored People of Virginia, Held in the City of Alexandria, August 2, 3, 4, 5, 1865.

We, the delegates of the colored people of the State of Virginia … solemnly declaring that we desire to live upon the most friendly and agreeable terms with all men; we feel no ill-will or prejudice toward our former oppressors; are willing and desire to forgive and forget the past, and so shape our future conduct as shall promote our happiness and the interest of the community in which we live …

We must, on the other hand, be allowed to aver and assert that we believe that we have among the white people of this State many who are our most inveterate enemies; who hate us as a class, who feel no sympathy with or for us; who despise us simply because we are black, and more especially, because we have been made free by the power of the United States Government …

We claim, then, as citizens of this State, the laws of the Commonwealth [of Virginia] shall give to all men equal protection; that each and every man may appeal to the law for his equal rights without regard to the color of his skin; and we believe this can only be done by extending the franchise, which we believe to be our inalienable right as freemen, and which the Declaration of Independence guarantees to all free citizens of this Government and which is the privilege of this nation. We claim the right of suffrage:

1st. Because we can see no other safeguard for our protection.

2nd. Because we are citizens of the country and natives of this State.

3rd. Because we are as well qualified to vote who shall be our rulers as many who do vote for that purpose who have no interest in us, and do not know our wants.

Mississippi legislators in December 1865 enacted the first "Black Codes" to limit the freedoms of African Americans. Defining vagrancy in such vague terms allowed white Southerners to arrest freedmen at will and to curtail their freedom of movement. These measures were quickly copied in the remaining ex-Confederate states.

Section 1. All rogues and vagabonds, idle and dissipated persons, … persons who neglect their calling or employment, misspend what they earn, or do not provide for the support of themselves or their families, or dependents shall be deemed and considered vagrants, … and upon conviction thereof shall be fined not exceeding one hundred dollars, with all accruing costs, and be imprisoned … not exceeding ten days….

Section 5…. In case of any freedman, free negro or mulatto shall fail for five days after the imposition of any or forfeiture upon him or her for violation of any of the provisions of this act to pay the same, that it shall be, and is hereby, made the duty of the sheriff of the proper county to hire out said freedman, free negro or mulatto, to any person who will, for the shortest period of service, pay said fine and forfeiture and all costs …

Colored Men's Convention 1869.

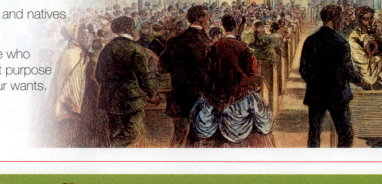

What is significant about the freedmen's use of the term citizen?

Read the **Document** *"Address of the Colored State Convention to the People of the State of South Carolina" (1865)*

hit the road seeking new opportunities could be arrested as a vagrant and fined. If a freedman could not pay his fine, he could be hired out for a time to a local plantation owner willing to pay his fine. As this drawing (**14.8**) dramatically shows, in some cases the contracts for such labor were auctioned off to local planters. The artist intended to conjure in the minds of Northerners a grim scene reminiscent of a slave auction, suggesting that one of the war's chief accomplishments, emancipation, was being undermined. Some Black Codes required that the children of "vagrant" freedmen be forced to accept apprenticeships that bound them to an employer until age 21. Others coerced blacks to sign long-term work contracts as proof of employment, a practice that left them at the mercy of employers who were not required to pay them for work performed if they quit before the contract expired. Other laws restricted freedmen to renting land only in rural areas (to keep them on plantations), prohibited ministers from preaching without a license,

outlawed interracial marriages, and barred blacks from serving on juries.

Congressional Reconstruction and the Fourteenth Amendment

Republicans in Congress vowed to block Johnson's rapid and lenient Reconstruction program for both idealistic and practical reasons. Excepting emancipation, none of the Republicans' goals for changing Southern society had been accomplished, and the former slavocracy appeared poised to resume power—a result certain to revive the Democratic Party. A slower process of Reconstruction would allow the Republican Party to take root in the South, especially if African Americans were granted the right to vote, as many Radicals like Congressman Thaddeus Stevens of Pennsylvania demanded.

The confrontation began in January 1866 when Congress reconvened. Republicans first refused

14.8 *The Black Codes in Action* Unable to pay his fine for "vagrancy" as defined in the Black Codes of Florida, a freedman is auctioned off. The high bidder won the right to a freedman's labor for months or years.

How did Black Codes calling for freedmen to sign labor contracts curtail their freedom?

14.9 *Race Riot in Memphis*
White mobs, unrestrained by police, killed 46 blacks in Memphis, Tennessee on May 1–2, 1866. News of the atrocities, conveyed in images such as this one, stoked Northern opinion against Johnson's lenient Reconstruction policies.

to admit the senators and representatives from the former Confederate states Johnson had declared reconstructed. Next, they established the Joint Committee on Reconstruction, a body that gathered evidence and testimony from hundreds of witnesses detailing widespread lawlessness and violence against freedmen and their white allies in the South.

To counteract Southern resistance and the oppression of freedmen, Congress passed two bills. The first expanded the powers of the Freedmen's Bureau and authorized it to continue operations for two more years. The second, the Civil Rights Act, declared African Americans and all persons born in the United States (except Native Americans) citizens. It also defined the rights of all citizens regardless of race—for example, the right to sue and to make contracts. Taking direct aim at the Black Codes, the law prohibited state

governments from depriving any citizen of these "fundamental rights." Johnson, infuriated at Congress's rejection of his Reconstruction program and determined to thwart efforts to establish racial equality, vetoed both bills.

Congress overrode the vetoes and the bills became law, but by June 1866, Republicans decided bolder action was necessary. Johnson remained opposed to freedmen's rights, and violence against blacks was on the rise in the South. The worst incident (**14.9**), was a race riot in Memphis, Tennessee, on May 1–2 that left 46 blacks, many of them Union army veterans, and two whites dead. This drawing from *Harper's Weekly*, a widely read publication that favored freedmen's rights, was intended to arouse anger in the North over Southern intransigence and support for congressional action. The Civil Rights Act was an unprecedented piece of legislation,

How did the Civil Rights Act promote equal rights for all Americans, regardless of race?

Read the **Document** *Charles F. Johnson and T. W. Gilbreth, The Memphis Riot (1866)*

but its supporters knew that it could easily be overturned by a future Congress. An amendment, on the other hand, became a permanent part of the Constitution.

On June 13, 1866, Republicans passed the **Fourteenth Amendment** to the Constitution. Its five main provisions radically redefined the role of the federal government as the guarantor of individual civil rights. First, it declared all persons born or naturalized in the United States as citizens, a definition that necessarily included all freedmen. Second, all citizens were entitled to "equal protection of the laws" of the states where they lived. Third, states that denied adult male citizens, including African Americans, the right to vote would have their representation in Congress reduced. Fourth, all high-ranking former Confederates were prohibited from holding public office, unless pardoned by act of Congress. Fifth, it repudiated the Confederate debt (thus punishing those who lent money to the Confederacy) and prohibited financial compensation for ex–slave owners.

Johnson greeted the unprecedented amendment with an unprecedented response: He went on the campaign trail to urge its defeat. Hoping to make the midterm state and congressional elections in November 1866 a referendum on the amendment, Johnson and his allies played on white racism, conjuring up images of racial equality and racial intermarriage to alarm Northern whites. Republicans responded in kind, portraying Johnson and the Democrats as traitors who waged war on the Union. Republicans won a sweeping victory in November. Northern voters, although still leery of racial equality, rejected Johnson's lenient form of Reconstruction because it required too little of Southerners and restored planter rule.

Republicans Take Control

Emboldened by their legislative and electoral success, congressional Republicans moved to take complete control of Reconstruction policy. In March 1867, Congress passed the first of four Reconstruction Acts. They divided the South (except Tennessee) into five military districts, each governed by a military commander empowered to restore peace and protect individuals, especially freedmen. As soon as order was established, the ex-Confederate states could begin a new, stricter readmission process. The act called for elections to select delegates to state constitutional conventions—elections that permitted African American men to vote, but barred Southerners who had served in the Confederate government and army. The new state constitutions drawn up by these conventions had to allow universal male suffrage, regardless of race. As soon as a state's voters approved the new constitution, the state could hold elections to fill government offices. Finally, if Congress approved the state's constitution and the state legislature ratified the Fourteenth Amendment, the state would be readmitted to the Union.

Two years after the end of the Civil War, the federal government had finally adopted a clear Reconstruction plan. The delay was understandable, given Lincoln's assassination and the lack of precedent. Yet delay granted Southerners time to recover from the war and mount an effective resistance to federal intervention.

> ## "The President has no power to control or influence anybody and legislation will be carried on entirely regardless of his opinion or wishes."
> Republican Senator JAMES W. GRIMES, Iowa, January 1867

President Johnson promptly vetoed the Reconstruction Acts, but the Republican Congress passed them again over his veto. Some of the more radical Republicans grew so embittered by the president's actions and words that they attempted to remove him from office. When Johnson dismissed Secretary of War Edwin Stanton in August 1867, Republicans charged him with violating the Tenure of Office Act, a constitutionally dubious measure they had passed in March. It required the president to seek congressional approval before removing a cabinet official. The House voted to impeach the president, charging him with 11 offenses. The trial began in March 1868 and after two months of heated debate and accusation, the Senate failed—by one vote—to convict Johnson and remove him from office.

Johnson was saved by some moderate Republicans who feared setting a bad precedent if a politically motivated campaign succeeded in removing a president from office. Many moderate Republicans also considered Johnson's likely replacement, Senator Benjamin Wade, far too radical. They also knew Johnson had less than a year left in office.

View the Map Interactive Map: Congressional Reconstruction

Why did moderate Republicans decide not to remove Johnson from office?

Implementing Reconstruction

As Congress engaged in its impeachment struggle with President Johnson in 1867–1868, the Reconstruction Acts took effect. A coalition of African Americans, poor up-country whites, and economically ambitious merchants (many originally from the North) and white planters formed the Republican Party in the South. They seized the opportunity presented by the congressional Reconstruction program and dominated the process of electing state governments and gaining readmission to the Union. The task would not be easy, especially as their different goals conflicted with each other and with those of most white Southerners, who would clearly oppose—politically, economically, and violently—any attempt to establish what they called "Negro rule."

14.10 The Hated Scalawag Scalawags became despised figures in the popular Southern mind. Here a scalawag is depicted as an opportunist seeking political power by manipulating the black vote.

The Republican Party in the South

The process of remaking state governments under the Reconstruction Acts fell to the Republican Party in the South, an organization comprising three distinct and in some cases antagonistic groups: Northerners who settled in the South, white Southerners, and former slaves. Northerners who moved south after the war were derided as **carpetbaggers** by white Southerners. The term suggested they were poor opportunists who carried to the South only a cheap suitcase, or carpetbag, which they intended to fill with plunder garnered from Southerners still reeling from the war. In reality most were middle class, often former Union soldiers or merchants, ministers, artisans, and professionals who viewed the South as a region of opportunity where they planned to settle permanently. Others came as idealistic relief workers, sent by Northern charitable and religious societies, intent upon aiding ex-slaves in their transition to freedom.

The Republican Party in the South also contained many white Southerners. Most white Southerners referred to them derisively as **scalawags** and considered them traitors to their region and race, men eager to accrue riches and power by manipulating black voters (**14.10**). Most scalawags came from the less developed backcountry regions of the South, especially eastern Tennessee and Kentucky, northern Alabama and Georgia, and western North Carolina. Like carpetbaggers, they believed that the Republican Party offered them and their region the best chance for economic betterment. Most did not, however, embrace on the idea of racial equality.

Former slaves made up the largest (about 80 percent), most significant segment of the South's Republican Party. Empowered with the vote by the Civil Rights Act of 1866 and Reconstruction Act of 1867, African Americans turned out in huge numbers in late 1867 to vote in elections held to select delegates to state constitutional conventions. For supporters of black suffrage, this extraordinary moment—persons only recently considered property now exercising for the first time the right to vote—was captured in

Why did many Northerners move south after the Civil War?

> "But be sure to vote for no Southern men that was a rebel or secessionist; for, if you do, you are pulling them hemp to hang yourself with."
>
> R. I. CROMWELL, advising his fellow freedmen, *New Orleans Tribune*, April 25, 1867

14.11 Casting Their First Votes
For supporters of racial equality like the Northern publication *Harper's Weekly*, whose cover featured this drawing, the large turnout of black voters in the 1867 elections was exhilarating.

this *Harper's Weekly* drawing (**14.11**). The dignified scene depicts three voters who symbolically represent a spectrum of blacks that includes common laborers, educated blacks who were free before the war, and Union army veterans. Most African American Republican leaders came from the second group. They tended to come from the North and possessed more wealth and education than the average freedman.

The three factions of the Republican Party—carpetbaggers, scalawags, and freedmen—formed an uneasy alliance as they came together to reestablish Southern state governments. Nonetheless, their combined votes in the 1867 elections for delegates to state constitutional conventions led to a sweeping Republican victory. White Republicans, even though they comprised only 20 percent of party membership, won most of the seats. But freedmen won 265 seats overall and a majority of seats in South Carolina and Louisiana.

Creating Reconstruction Governments in the South

Republican delegates soon drafted new constitutions for former Confederate states according to the guidelines established by the Reconstruction Acts. In a few states, notably Virginia and Texas, conservatives delayed the process for more than a year. But by the end of 1868, seven Southern states had ratified new constitutions, created new governments, and been readmitted to the Union.

These Republican governments achieved remarkable results. To begin with, they represented a revolutionary advance in the status of the freedmen. Held as slaves and denied citizenship only a few years before, African Americans now enjoyed

the right to vote and hold office. Between 1869 and 1901, 22 African Americans would serve in Congress (20 representatives and 2 senators). More than 600 would win seats in state legislatures and to other state offices.

While embittered white Southerners decried what they termed "Negro rule," statistics show that white Republicans held a far greater share of offices than blacks. No African American was elected governor, and no state legislature ever had a black majority (the South Carolina lower house briefly had a black majority). What white Southerners really objected to was Republican rule

View the **Closer Look** *First Vote*

How did African American voting affect the political situation in the South in 1867–1868?

and what it stood for: African American equality and empowerment.

Republican-controlled Southern state governments also achieved several significant reforms. In contrast to the tightfisted governments of the antebellum era, they funded public works projects, built hospitals and orphanages, and founded public school systems. They also enacted more equitable tax codes and passed laws to help indebted farmers keep their land. Opponents of Republican rule denounced these initiatives (and the higher taxes needed to fund them) as wasteful and poorly managed. Fundamentally, they objected to their social and racial implications, since many of the projects were designed to aid the poor and freedmen.

But the charges of corruption, mismanagement, and debt lodged by the opponents of Reconstruction governments were not entirely groundless. The rapid expansion of government services and expenditures caused many states to run up large deficits. It also created opportunities for graft and bribery which some Reconstruction legislators took advantage of.

Democratic opponents railed against these abuses as alleged evidence that blacks were incapable of holding office and that their white allies were

14.12 Linking the Democrats to Secession and Civil War This political cartoon from a pro-Republican periodical sought to demonize Democrats Horatio Seymour and Francis Blair by reminding voters that their Democratic Party was the party of Southern secessionists.

interested only in plunder. In reality the corruption in Southern state governments paled in comparison to that found in the North. New York's Tammany Hall political machine, for example, under William "Boss" Tweed, stole more than $20 million from 1869 to 1871. Moreover, the spending by Southern state governments on social programs looked large only compared to the paltry expenditures on education, health care, and public works before the war. Nonetheless, charges of corruption and excessive spending, coupled with increased taxes, diminished support for the Southern Republican governments and created an unfavorable impression in the North.

> ## "We cannot vote without all sorts of threats and intimidations. Freedmen are shot with impunity."
>
> ### Report of a Republican official, 1868

The Election of 1868

By summer 1868, there was little doubt whom the Republican Party would nominate for president. General Ulysses S. Grant enjoyed widespread popularity across the North and among Southern Republicans for defeating Robert E. Lee and ending the Civil War. Grant conveyed a tone of moderation in a time of partisan and sectional acrimony. "Let us have peace," became his campaign slogan.

Democrats, still weak in the aftermath of the war and the disenfranchisement of many ex-Confederates, faced an uphill battle against Grant. Note how this political cartoon (**14.12**) "'Tis But A Change of Banners" from a pro-Republican journal sought to link the Democratic nominees for president Governor Horatio Seymour of New York and for vice president Francis Blair of Maryland with both secession and postwar racial violence. But as this racist Democratic campaign song makes clear (**14.13**), Seymour ran an aggressive campaign designed to arouse fears that the Republican Party and black suffrage threatened the rights of white Americans. Republicans, his campaign claimed, must be prevented from spreading the disastrous experiment in black political empowerment to the North.

Running on a message of political moderation, fiscal responsibility, and an even-handed approach

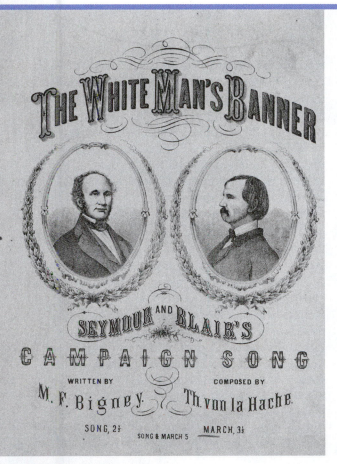

14.13 The Politics of Racism
The campaign of Democratic Party nominees Horatio Seymour and Francis Blair appealed to white voters' racism though the nominees' speeches, campaign literature, and songs such as this one, "The White Man's Banner."

to Reconstruction, Grant won 214 electoral votes to Seymour's 80. The popular vote, however, was much closer: 53 percent for Grant, 47 percent for Seymour (**14.14**). This outcome reflected three things. First, it indicated the wide appeal of Seymour's blatantly racist message to conservative whites in both North and South. Second, it showed how vital the freedman vote was for the Republican Party. Grant received nearly 500,000 African American votes, but won by only 300,000 votes. Third, it revealed the effectiveness of violence as a weapon in electoral politics. A reign of terror unleashed by violent whites before the election, especially in Georgia and Louisiana, kept thousands of black voters away from the polls.

The Fifteenth Amendment

After the 1868 election, congressional Republicans decided that black suffrage required an explicit constitutional guarantee. Black male suffrage was implied in the Fourteenth Amendment's phrase, "all male citizens," but with Southern resistance

on the rise, many Republicans argued that another amendment was necessary to guarantee unequivocally the right of African Americans to vote.

Women's rights activists agreed, but many also argued for universal suffrage—the vote for all adult citizens regardless of race or gender. Bitterly disappointed over the reference to only "male citizens" in the Fourteenth Amendment, feminists, such as Elizabeth Cady Stanton and Susan B. Anthony, demanded that any subsequent amendment include women.

This demand was opposed by former abolitionists and Radical Republicans, including fellow feminists like Lucy Stone and Frances Harper, who argued that gaining the vote for African American men was a higher priority. Including women, they argued, would doom the amendment because the nation was not ready for such radical change. The cause of women's suffrage could be taken up immediately after black suffrage was secured. Stanton and Anthony rejected this reasoning, leading to a twenty-year split in the women's rights movement. Most Republicans in Congress, however, agreed with Frederick Douglass's assertion that this was the "Negro's Hour," and they drafted the **Fifteenth Amendment** to read succinctly: "The right of citizens of the United States shall not be denied or abridged by the United States or by any state on account of race, color, or previous condition of servitude."

Passed by Congress in late 1869 and ratified in 1870, the Fifteenth Amendment presented a striking contradiction. It established a revolutionary experiment in interracial democracy, something no other slave society, such as those in the Caribbean or

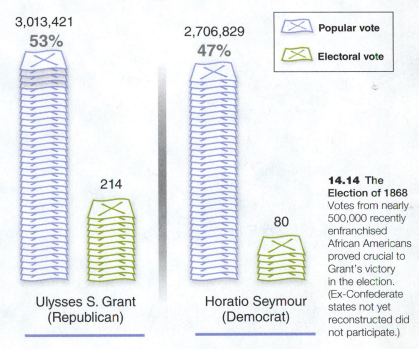

3,013,421
53%

2,706,829
47%

Popular vote

Electoral vote

214

80

Ulysses S. Grant
(Republican)

Horatio Seymour
(Democrat)

14.14 The Election of 1868
Votes from nearly 500,000 recently enfranchised African Americans proved crucial to Grant's victory in the election. (Ex-Confederate states not yet reconstructed did not participate.)

Why did some women's rights activists oppose ratification of the Fifteenth Amendment?

Latin America, did so soon and so completely after emancipation. Yet its spare wording left wide open the possibility that states could devise clever ways to deny blacks the right to vote that did not directly invoke "race, color, or previous condition of servitude."

The Rise of White Resistance

The secret white terrorist organizations that first arose in 1866 and that wrought havoc in parts of the South during the 1868 election grew bolder and more violent by 1870–1871, especially during election season. Known by various names, including the White Brotherhood, Knights of the White Camelia, and especially the Ku Klux Klan, they functioned in much the same manner. As illustrated in a popular Northern newspaper (**14.15**), Klansmen often operated at night, wearing hoods, robes, and other regalia to hide their identities and terrify their victims. Blacks (and occasionally carpetbaggers and scalawags) targeted for "punishment" were beaten and frequently killed. Some had their crops or homes burned or their mules killed. Klansmen also targeted symbols of black self-improvement and independence, such as black churches, businesses, and schools.

Klan terrorism served many purposes. For the poor whites who made up the bulk of Klansmen, the violent suppression of African Americans provided the psychological reassurance that they were not at the bottom of the social order. For white elites who approved of and often assisted the violence, it prevented a political alliance between poor whites and blacks. It also maintained a large, exploitable workforce for plantations and industry by keeping African Americans powerless and poor. Klan violence also discouraged African American voting and thus threatened the Republican Party in the South.

In response to surging violence in the South, Republicans in Congress, with strong support from the Grant administration, passed several Enforcement Acts in 1870 and 1871, outlawing "armed combinations" that deprived anyone of their civil or political rights. The Justice Department vigorously enforced these laws across the South, arresting and prosecuting thousands and weakening significantly the Klan and similar organizations by 1872. Although the Enforcement Acts demonstrated that federal authority could effectively protect the rights of freedmen, they also revealed the vulnerability of freedmen should the federal commitment to Reconstruction ever wane.

14.15 *Another Victim of the Klan* Terrorist violence by white vigilante groups soared in the early 1870s. In this scene from Moore County, North Carolina, a freedman pleads for his life, surrounded by Klansmen in full regalia.

Why did groups like the Klan indulge in anti-black violence?

Read the **Document** *Hannah Irwin Describes Ku Klux Klan Ride (Late 1860s)*

Reconstruction Abandoned

By the end of Grant's first term in office in 1873, supporters of Reconstruction and freedmen's rights could look with satisfaction at the many extraordinary changes that had taken place in the South. Yet ominous signs suggested Reconstruction was in trouble. Despite the crackdown on the Klan, white Southerners increasingly demonstrated their commitment to seizing power and imposing a new form of servitude on African Americans. Northerners, by contrast, seemed less and less willing to support a vigorous Reconstruction policy. Slowly, from 1872 to 1877, the extraordinary experiment in interracial democracy and progressive government in the South was dismantled in favor of oligarchy and white supremacy.

Corruption and Scandal

A major factor in the pullback from Reconstruction was a series of corruption scandals that plagued the Grant administration. Grant himself was honest, but also politically naive and given to a hands-off style of leadership that gave officials in his administration unusual independence. Many of them took advantage of Grant's trust to enrich themselves through illegal schemes.

For example, in the 1869 "Black Friday" scandal, Wall Street titans Jay Gould and Jim Fisk conspired with Grant's brother-in-law to corner the gold market. The plan failed but not before hundreds of innocent investors were ruined. In the Credit Mobilier scandal, Grant's vice president and several high-ranking members of Congress took bribes from the company involved in the completion of the government-subsidized Union Pacific Railroad. In the so-called "Whiskey Ring" scandal, Treasury Secretary Orville E. Babcock made a fortune by illegally allowing whiskey distillers to avoid paying excise taxes. In yet another scandal, Secretary of War William W. Belknap accepted bribes from companies engaged in corrupt activities on Indian reservations.

With so much negative publicity stirred up by corruption scandals, Grant's administration took steps to minimize political controversies. To secure his reelection and keep the Republican Party in power, Grant adopted a more conservative approach to Reconstruction, by now a frequent source of rancor in Washington.

In summer 1872, for example, Grant lobbied Congress for and then signed into law the Amnesty Act, granting a general pardon to all but a few hundred former Confederate leaders. Now eligible to vote and hold office, these planters and ex-Confederate army officers and officials wasted little time in reasserting their authority.

Republican Disunity

The retreat from Reconstruction in the 1870s was also hastened by growing dissention within the Republican Party. Many Republicans, including some former Radicals, began to question the wisdom of maintaining a strong federal role in the affairs of Southern states. Some argued the fundamental goals of Reconstruction—citizenship, civil rights, and suffrage for the freedmen—had been accomplished. There was, they believed, a constitutional and moral limit to what the federal government could do for the freedmen. Now was the time for freedmen to use their new rights to elevate themselves economically, socially, and politically.

Other Republicans argued for an end to Reconstruction for less idealistic reasons. Even though some of them had been abolitionists before the war and advocates of freedmen's rights in the first years that followed, they now considered Reconstruction a failure. These Liberal Republicans, as they came to be called, had grown tired of the political strife produced by debates over freedmen's rights.

> "It seems to me that we are drifting, drifting back under the leadership of the slaveholders. Our former masters are fast taking the reins of government."
>
> GEORGE M. ARNOLD, African American Republican

Read the **Document** *Credit Mobilier/Union Pacific Railroad Scandal Testimony of C.P. Huntington (1873)*

How did the scandals of the Grant administration undermine Reconstruction?

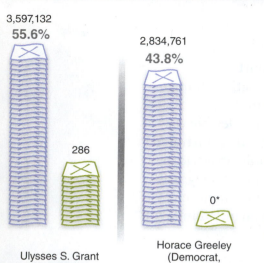

3,597,132
55.6%

2,834,761
43.8%

286

0*

Ulysses S. Grant
(Republican)

Horace Greeley
(Democrat,
Liberal Republican)

☒ Popular vote

☒ Electoral vote

* Greeley died before the
electoral college met and
therefore received no votes

14.16 The
Election of 1872
Ulysses Grant easily
won reelection when
opposed by a weak
candidate, Democrat
Horace Greeley.
Scandals and
economic turmoil
soon undermined
his popularity and
power.

They also worried about the growing power of the federal government.

Liberal Republicans also expressed disgust over the corruption and mismanagement of Southern Reconstruction governments. They accepted the argument of Southerners that freedmen and their white allies were incapable of honest and effective government. No one embodied this dramatic change of heart more than Horace Greeley, the progressive editor of the *New York Tribune*. Once the outspoken champion of abolition and freedmen's rights, by the early 1870s, he advocated returning the South to white rule. Blacks, he wrote in 1870, were a "worthless race," who would rather accept charity than help themselves. Their Reconstruction governments were based on "ignorance and degradation." A similar transformation from a progressive to a reactionary view of Reconstruction was revealed in the political cartoons of Thomas Nast (see *Images as History: Political Cartoons Reflect the Shift in Public Opinion*).

The Election of 1872

The dissatisfaction of Liberal Republicans reached full bloom in summer 1872. Disturbed by the prospect of Grant being renominated for a second term, they broke with the Republican Party and held their own convention in Cincinnati where they nominated Greeley for president. A divided Democratic Party also endorsed Greeley.

But the election of 1872 proved disastrous for Greeley and his backers. The public viewed Greeley as an eccentric who during his long career in public life had supported many fringe causes such as vegetarianism, spiritualism, and utopianism. Greeley's call for an end to Reconstruction and reconciliation between North and South also repelled many Northern voters who still associated Southerners and the Democratic Party with secession and civil war.

In Grant's sweeping victory over Greeley (**14.16**), Republicans had good reason to cheer. The Democrats' and Liberal Republicans' call for

ending Reconstruction and returning the South to white rule had been rejected. Moreover, the Grant administration's crackdown on the Klan had allowed African Americans unprecedented freedom to vote. Still, Northerners and Republicans in Congress were not prepared to support federal intervention in the South indefinitely. As new pressing issues emerged after 1872, support for Reconstruction rapidly eroded.

Hard Times

The American economy had boomed after the Civil War. Hundreds of thousands of new businesses were established. These included massive factories that employed hundreds, in some cases thousands, of workers. Aiding this economic growth was the dramatic expansion of the railroad and telegraph systems and increased availability of capital through banks and stock sales.

The booming economy encouraged businesses to expand and investors to take bigger risks. When these trends reached a critical point in late1873, a panic on Wall Street ensued. Some of the nation's most prominent financial houses and banks went bankrupt. As credit became scarce, businesses began to fail. Hundreds of thousands of workers lost their jobs. By early 1874, the nation's economy had plunged into a deep depression that lasted until 1877.

The Panic of 1873 directly affected Reconstruction. As hard times set in, the fate of the freedmen became less of a concern to Northerners. Economic issues like currency reform and the tariff took precedence over civil rights and white vigilante violence against freedmen. The public, declared one Republican, is tired of hearing about Southern violence against the freedmen: "Hard times and heavy taxes make them wish the 'everlasting nigger' were in hell or Africa." The public expressed its discontent in the congressional elections of 1874 by voting in a Democratic majority in the House for the first time since the war.

The Return of Terrorism

Reconstruction was also undone by a resumption of violence waged by white terrorist groups like the Klan. As the Grant administration bowed to political pressure to reduce federal intervention in Southern affairs, advocates of white supremacy seized the opportunity. In one notorious incident in 1873, a large band of heavily armed whites overran

Images as History
POLITICAL CARTOONS REFLECT THE SHIFT IN PUBLIC OPINION

One of the nation's most skilled and popular political cartoonists in the Reconstruction era was Thomas Nast. An immigrant from Germany, he landed a job in 1861 at *Harper's Weekly,* the nation's leading journal of politics and society. Nast's artistic talent, combined with *Harper's* vast circulation, soon turned him into one of the most influential illustrators of his day. As a staunch Republican and Unionist, his drawings during the Civil War were as intensely patriotic and pro-Lincoln as they were anti-Confederate.

After the war, Nast's widely distributed cartoons continued to shape Northern opinion about Reconstruction and freedmen's rights. Cartoons like *And Not This Man?* (August 5, 1865) proclaimed the dignity and humanity of the freedmen and their moral right to full citizenship and suffrage. In *This is a White Man's Government* (September 5, 1868), he stressed the violent intent of white Southerners to reclaim power and the necessity of federal authority in carrying out the goals of Reconstruction.

Nevertheless, Nast's cartoons eventually reflected the growing disillusionment of Northern Republicans regarding Reconstruction. While he rejected the Liberal Republican call to end Reconstruction, Nast nonetheless expressed the fear that African Americans were incapable of responsible government. Note the contrast between his earlier depictions of freedmen and that in *Colored Rule in a Reconstructed (?) State (March 14, 1874).*

"Columbia," an early symbol of America and democracy, advocates black suffrage. The globe is actually a nineteenth-century ballot box.

By showing African Americans in Union Army uniforms, Nast sought to remind Americans that blacks had earned the right to full citizenship through their service and sacrifice (note the missing leg) in the war.

And Not This Man?

A freedman wearing a Union Army uniform is crushed beneath an Irish immigrant (left), a white supremacist ex-Confederate (center), and a Northern capitalist (right). Nast saw these three groups as members of an opportunistic alliance.

A ballot box, representing the freedman's claim on citizenship and voting rights, has been kicked aside.

This is a White Man's Government

Reflecting Nast's disillusionment, "Columbia" chastises African American political leaders.

In 1874, frustrated with what he saw as inept and selfish African American political leadership in the South, Nash changed his depiction of blacks from noble individuals worthy of citizenship to racist caricatures.

Colored Rule in a Reconstructed (?) State

Why are political cartoons so popular and effective?

Colfax, Louisiana and slaughtered over 100 African Americans.

Just as in the late 1860s, white vigilante violence had two goals: to strip away the freedmen's hard-won rights and prevent them from voting and holding office. This effort peaked in Mississippi in 1875 when armed groups of whites closely allied with the Democratic Party waged a campaign of terror that came to be known as the **Mississippi Plan**. Through threats, beatings, and killings, they delivered an unambiguous message: blacks and their white allies who dared vote Republican risked their lives. But the Grant administration rejected Governor Adelbert Ames's request to send troops to keep the peace and protect the polls.

Not surprisingly, more than 60,000 Mississippi voters—nearly all black and Republican—stayed away from the polls on Election Day. Democrats swept to victory and took control of the state legislature for the first time since the Civil War. Immediately they threatened Governor Ames with impeachment and forced him to resign. The success of the Mississippi Plan in intimidating black voters and demolishing the Republican Party is indicated in this 1876 image, *Of Course He Wants to Vote the Democratic Ticket* (**14.17**). The artist shows the ruthless character of the white supremacy movement and the vulnerability of freedmen left without federal protection.

Other Southern states soon employed their own version of the Mississippi Plan. One by one the remaining Reconstruction governments

14.17 The Mississippi Plan in Action In much of the South, violence kept most freedmen away from the polls. Here a freedman is threatened with death unless he votes for the Democratic Party.

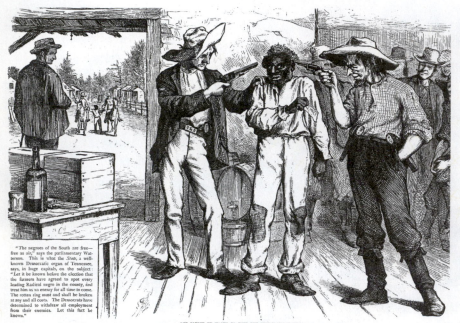

"The negroes of the South are free—free as air," says the parliamentary Watterson. This is what the *State*, a well-known Democratic organ of Tennessee, says, in huge capitals, on the subject: "Let it be known before the election that the farmers have agreed to spot every leading Radical negro in the county, and treat him as an enemy for all time to come. The rotten ring must and shall be broken at any and all costs. The Democrats have determined to withdraw all employment from their enemies. Let this fact be known."

"OF COURSE HE WANTS TO VOTE THE DEMOCRATIC TICKET!"
DEMOCRATIC "REFORMER." "You're as free as air, ain't you? Say you are, or I'll blow yer blank head off!"

fell to a new class of political leaders known as **Redeemers**. As the name suggests, they cast themselves in almost biblical terms as saviors of Southern society. By 1876, only South Carolina, Louisiana, and Florida remained under Republican control—largely because of the presence of federal troops. The removal of these troops in 1877 opened the way for the complete "redemption" of the former Confederacy and the restoration of white supremacy.

Defenders of Reconstruction and the rights of freedmen in Congress were appalled at the rising tide of Redeemer oppression. In response they managed one final measure to bolster the rights of freedmen, the **Civil Rights Act of 1875**. It required that state governments provide equal access in public facilities such as schools and allow African Americans to serve on juries. The law was largely ignored, and in 1883 the Supreme Court ruled it unconstitutional.

The End of Reconstruction

The final blow to Reconstruction occurred as the result of the presidential election of 1876. With the Democratic Party reinvigorated by gaining a majority in the House in 1874 and control of most Southern state governments by 1876, a close election was expected. The Democrats nominated Samuel J. Tilden, governor of New York and a well-known reformer. Republicans nominated Ohio governor and Civil War veteran Rutherford B. Hayes. The issues centered on political corruption, the failed economy, and of course, Reconstruction.

On Election Day Tilden received 250,000 more popular votes than Hayes (**14.18**). But the electoral vote—which actually determines the victor—was unclear. Voting irregularities in South Carolina, Louisiana, and Florida left both sides claiming victory—and the 19 electoral votes at stake in those states (one electoral vote was also in dispute in Oregon). Tilden needed to be declared the winner in only one of these four states to win a majority of electoral votes and thus the presidency. Hayes needed to win all three Southern states plus the Oregon vote to put him one electoral vote ahead of Tilden and into the White House.

Both sides refused to budge, and a constitutional crisis loomed. Eventually they agreed

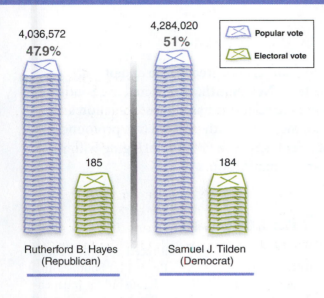

4,036,572
47.9%

4,284,020
51%

Popular vote

Electoral vote

185

184

Rutherford B. Hayes
(Republican)

Samuel J. Tilden
(Democrat)

14.18 The Election of 1876
In one of the most controversial presidential elections in U.S. history, Samuel B. Tilden won the popular vote (4,284,020 to 4,036,572), but lost the electoral vote to Rutherford B. Hayes, 185 to 184.

March 2, 1877, the commission issued its decision, known as the **Compromise of 1877.** By a vote of eight to seven, the 15-member commission awarded all 20 disputed electoral votes to Hayes, giving him a 185 to 184 electoral vote victory over Tilden.

Democrats denounced the "stolen election." Yet the result proved beneficial to the party. Hayes's presidency was weakened by the aura of illegitimacy (detractors referred to him as "his fraudulency"). More important, as part of a behind-the-scenes deal, he oversaw the final steps in the dismantling of Reconstruction. By the end of 1877, the last federal troops were removed from the South, and as the map (**14.19**) indicates, the last Reconstruction governments fell to Democratic Redeemers.

14.19 The Readmission of Southern States and Return of White Rule
Most former Confederate states were readmitted to the Union under the direction of Republican-controlled state governments. But as the dates in parentheses indicate, in most cases, conservative white Democratic governments soon seized control.

to abide by the decision of a bipartisan commission. The commission authorized an investigation and heard testimony. Behind the scenes members of Congress and party leaders conducted intense negotiations. On

Military Districts established under Reconstruction Act of 1867

1870   Date of readmission to the Union

(1871)   Date of reestablishment of conservative white government

The New South

The optimism with which white Southerners greeted the end of Reconstruction gave rise to the term **New South**. It reflected the South's development of a new system of race relations based on segregation and white supremacy. Even more so, the New South pointed to a profound economic transformation that swept across the region, bringing with it a boom in manufacturing, railroad construction, and urbanization.

Redeemer Rule

The Redeemer governments that took control of Southern states by 1877 represented a new ruling oligarchy. Before the war a small and powerful class of planters dominated Southern politics. Now, in the aftermath of Reconstruction, a new elite took control. Although some were planters and former planters, most were men who drew their wealth and power from a new Southern economy based on industry, finance, commerce, and railroad construction.

As men of business their politics reflected the dominant conservative economic theory of the era, which argued that the best form of government was small, frugal, and pro-business. Accordingly, Redeemer governments slashed taxes and spending on social programs and public education created during Reconstruction.

Redeemer politics also championed a return to white supremacy. The return of one-party (Democratic) rule in most Southern states resulted in a steady decline in office holding by African Americans and Republicans. Intimidation and violence also led to a marked decrease in black voting across the South. Despite these setbacks, however, African Americans in many Southern states managed to vote and hold office in appreciable numbers into the 1880s and 1890s.

Redeemer rule did not go unchallenged. In several states anger among poor farmers coalesced into full-fledged political challenges to oligarchic rule, inequitable taxation, and cuts to social programs. These insurgents denounced the new elite as "Bourbons" (the name of the former French royal family), a derogatory term that implied aristocratic ambitions. In Virginia, for example, a coalition of Republicans and disaffected Democrats called Readjusters turned out the Redeemer government in 1879. All of these challenges to Redeemer rule, however, ultimately failed.

The Lost Cause

Southerners after 1877 embraced not only Redeemer rule, but also an image of the prewar South as an ideal society and the Confederate bid for independence a valiant Lost Cause. Southerners clung to this image because it provided them with a psychologically soothing explanation for why they lost the war. According to the Lost Cause idea, Confederate society was more virtuous than the North and its soldiers braver, but the South lost because the Yankees possessed overwhelming advantages in population, industry, arms, and ruthlessness. Defeat, while bitter and painful, was also a glorious martyrdom for a people and a way of life.

Southerners expressed this interpretation of the war as a glorious, yet ill-fated campaign in poems, plays, songs, speeches, sermons, and books. One of the most popular Lost Cause poets was Rev. Abram Ryan, a Catholic priest from Norfolk, Virginia. Many of his poems, such as "The Conquered Banner," became required recitations among white Southern schoolchildren for decades. These works by Ryan and others stressed courage, glory, duty, sacrifice, and the need for true Southerners to honor their Confederate heroes forever. As Ryan put it in one of his poems:

> But their memories e'er shall remain for us,
> And their names, bright names, without stain for us;
> The glory they won shall not wane for us,
> In legend and lay
> Our heroes in Gray
> Shall forever live over again for us.

The Lost Cause carried with it an obligation to keep alive the memory of Confederate glory. Southerners built elegant battlefield cemeteries to inter the war dead and monuments to celebrate Confederate victories. White Southern women, many widowed by the war, played a major role in these efforts,

What groups constituted the political leadership of the New South?

Read the Document R. B. Buckley, Confederate Song, "I'm a Good Old Rebel" (1866)

founding organizations such as the Ladies Memorial Association (1867) and the United Daughters of the Confederacy (1894). Southerners also erected thousands of statues honoring Confederate soldiers, including legends like Generals Robert E. Lee, Stonewall Jackson, and Nathan Bedford Forrest. The photograph (**14.20**) demonstrates how enthusiasm for the Lost Cause only grew the further the Civil War receded into history. Lee had discouraged efforts to raise monuments to the Confederate cause, but soon after he died in 1870, they sprang up across the South, including this monumental rendering unveiled in Richmond in 1890. Thousands turned out for the dedication of the heroic statue by French sculptor Antonin Mercie and to hear Colonel Archer Anderson laud Lee for his "courage, will, energy …

fortitude, hopefulness, joy in battle … [and] unconquerable soul." Nothing that day, certainly not the speeches or Lee's triumphant pose, recalled the fact that Lee had lost the war.

But the Lost Cause legend served a second purpose beyond helping Southerners cope with their defeat in the war. It celebrated a nostalgic vision of the prewar South that supported their arguments for a resumption of white rule and African American subservience. Through literature, art, and music, Southerners (and some Northerners) fashioned romantic depictions of the "Old South" as a harmonious paradise where benevolent masters treated loyal, contented slaves with kindness, where chivalrous Southern gentlemen protected delicate, charming women, and where everyone revered tradition, family, and the Bible. Yet even as they glorified slavery, the proponents of the Lost Cause downplayed its importance as a cause of secession. The real issue, they insisted, was "states' rights" and attempts by Northerners to run roughshod over them in the 1850s.

The Lost Cause thus presented Southerners as victims of misguided and unjustified Yankee aggression who, in the wake of devastating war and humiliating Reconstruction, ought to be left alone to run their own affairs. The overt racism and self-serving depictions of slavery in Lost Cause rhetoric and imagery served to justify a resumption of white rule and the return of African Americans to the status of powerless, exploitable laborers.

The New South Economy

Even as Southerners revered the Lost Cause and Old South, their new leadership steered the region's economy into an industrial future. In the 1870s and 1880s, they joined with Northern entrepreneurs who settled in the South during Reconstruction to develop a modern, market-oriented, and diversified economy. This effort entailed not simply the establishment of banks, textile mills, and railroads, but also the celebration and spreading of capitalist values, such as hard work, risk taking, thrift, and the profit motive.

14.20 Celebrating the Lost Cause As the commemorative ribbon indicates, this monument to Robert E. Lee was erected in the former Confederate capital of Richmond, Virginia in 1890. It was one of thousands of monuments to the Confederacy erected across the South.

View the **Image** *Cotton plantation, United States of America*   How was the Lost Cause a useful myth for Southerners?

14.21 Celebrating the New South
The Atlanta Exposition of 1895 offered a great opportunity for boosters of the New South to showcase the region's newly diversified economy.

The leading figure in this movement to establish a New South economy was Henry Grady, editor of the *Atlanta Constitution*. Beginning in the mid-1870s, in editorials and speeches, he proclaimed industrialization as the solution to the South's devastated postwar economy. His message inspired many Southerners, especially those who had never been part of the planter elite, to start businesses, invest, and support pro-business policies. Grady also convinced many Northerners, to invest in New South enterprises.

The vast expansion of manufacturing represented the most stunning change in the New South. Drawn by low taxes, cheap labor, ample water power, proximity to cotton supplies, and the absence of unions, textile manufacturers moved their operations from New England to the South,

especially the Carolinas. By 1900, the South had become the nation's leading producer of textiles. A similar transformation occurred in the tobacco industry, as the South went from merely producing raw tobacco to become the nation's leading producer of finished tobacco products like cigarettes.

Another significant aspect of the New South economy was the lumber and furniture industry. New South entrepreneurs took advantage of the region's tremendous forest reserves and new technologies, such as rotary saws and dry kilns, and an expanded railroad system, and soon made the South the leading producer of lumber. In Mississippi alone the number of lumber mills jumped from 295 in 1880 to 608 in 1899. The furniture industry likewise boomed in the New South, especially in places like High Point, North Carolina, where a single factory opened in 1889, followed by 30 more over the next decade.

Industry also flourished in the lower South. Birmingham, Alabama had only a few hundred residents when founded in 1871, but its position at the junction of two major railroads and nearby deposits of coal, iron, and limestone soon attracted iron and steel factories and the nickname, "Pittsburgh of the South." By 1890, the South produced 20 percent of U.S. iron and steel. As this promotional poster (**14.21**) makes clear, the booming and increasingly diverse economy of the New South was the central theme of the 1895 Atlanta Exposition. Here "Liberty" carries in her left arm a cornucopia filled with symbols of traditional Southern products like cotton and sugar, but also steel and iron. Note the imagery at the bottom that suggests the Civil War–and all its destruction and lingering controversies—is long gone.

As in the North the expansion of industry in the South relied on the existence of a large pool of cheap labor. But unlike the North, where millions of immigrants made up much of the workforce, the South relied on a rising population of poor white farming families pushed off the land by indebtedness, falling crop prices, and crop failure. In the rare

> "The growth of the iron interests of the South during the last few years has been the marvel of the age, attracting the attention of the entire business world."
>
> New South booster, M. B. HILLYARD, 1887

instances where African Americans secured industrial employment, it was usually in the most menial, dangerous, and poorly paid jobs.

Southern workers earned wages 50 percent lower than their Northern counterparts, revealing the limited success of the New South economy in overcoming the region's poverty and social problems. Despite decades of impressive growth in industry, mining, and railroads, the South in 1900 lagged far behind the North in virtually every category of economic and social progress. Most Southern industry, for example, was small scale and focused on low-skilled labor, including growing numbers of child laborers. Per capita incomes in the South remained stagnant from 1880 to 1900.

Other indications of backwardness and under-development abounded. The infant mortality rate far exceeded the national average. And because Redeemer governments had slashed per pupil spending in public education to half the average in the North, the South led the nation in illiteracy; its high school graduation rate was one-third that in the Midwest.

The Rise of Sharecropping

The limitations of the New South economy was most vividly revealed in the preponderance of Southerners engaged in agriculture. The region's economy remained fundamentally tied to the production of cash crops, particularly tobacco, sugar, rice, and of course, cotton. Only 6 percent of the Southern workforce in 1900 was employed in manufacturing.

The condition of Southern farmers, both white and black, deteriorated sharply between 1875 and 1900. While cotton production soared, the price plummeted, from 18 cents per pound in the early 1870s to 5 cents per pound in 1894. Shrinking profits forced many Southern farmers to forfeit title to their land and became tenant farmers. Some

14.22 Poverty and Independence
Sharecropping condemned most African Americans to poverty, but it also helped to free them of immediate white control. No longer confined to slave cabins, they also worked on their own, free of white oversight and coercion.

rented land for a set fee which left them free to grow whatever crops they desired. But most tenant farmers resorted to the sharecropping system, whereby they received the right to farm a plot of land in exchange for rent paid in the form of a share (generally one-third to one-half) of the harvest. By 1900, more than 70 percent of the South's farmers (white and black) earned their living in this manner.

Sharecropping granted African Americans a measure of independence. White landlords generally allowed their tenants to control their own time and to set their own work routines. The people in this photograph (**14.22**) are poor and live in a ramshackle house, but like most sharecroppers they work as families free of direct white supervision. Freedmen cherished this independence, given their experience in slavery of gang labor under the brutal control of overseers. And yet, as a closer look at this image shows, a well-dressed white man is in the background—probably the landlord who arranged for the photograph to be taken. Sharecroppers were not slaves, but as this photograph makes clear, they lived under the control of their white landlords.

Read the **Document** *James T. Rapier, Testimony before U.S. Senate Regarding the Agricultural Labor Force in the South (1880)*

How did sharecropping provide limited independence to freedmen?

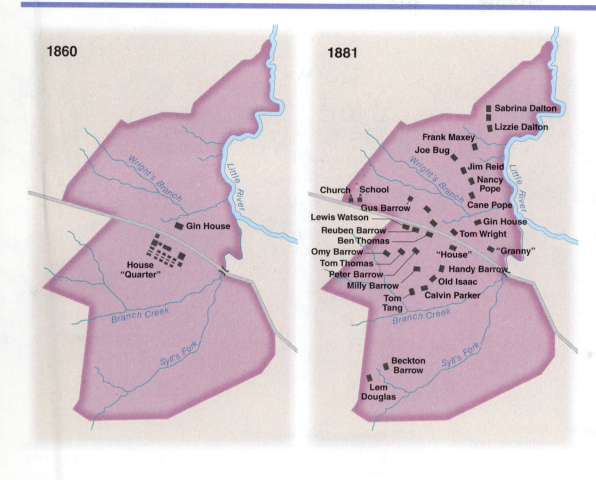

14.23 Moving from Slavery to Freedom: The Barrow Plantation, Oglethorpe County, Georgia, 1860 and 1881
Under slavery the Barrows confined their slaves' housing to a narrow section of the plantation. Sixteen years after emancipation, African Americans on the plantation, living beyond the immediate oversight of the Barrows, established a church and school.

The transformation from the tightly controlled plantation system to the relative independence of sharecropping can be seen in this map (**14.23**) of a Georgia plantation. The 1860 map shows the Barrow Family Plantation before the abolition of slavery. Note the layout of the slave quarters—in tight rows clustered within sight and earshot of the master. Seeking maximum control over their enslaved laborers, the Barrows kept them close at hand.

Twenty-one years later, many of the Barrow's former slaves and their descendents still lived on the plantation. But as the 1881 map indicates (see 14.23), the relationship between the Barrows and their workers had changed considerably, reflecting a sharp conflict in visions regarding the social order in the postwar South. Initially the Barrows had tried, like so many other former slave owners, to limit the freedom of their former slaves, hiring them as wage workers bound by annual labor contracts and trying to coerce them into accepting gang labor under an overseer. The freedmen, however, resisted and eventually negotiated to work as tenant farmers. By 1881, most ex-slaves lived in separate households scattered on the former plantation, working as sharecroppers

on 25- to 30-acre farms. The 1881 map also indicates the presence of two key institutions of African American freedom—a church and a school. Within the narrow limits allowed by hostile whites, freedmen enjoyed privileges they had been deprived of under slavery.

Nonetheless, tenancy exploited the freedmen. Landlords demanded they grow cash crops like tobacco, wheat, and especially cotton. Because they often needed to buy seed, tools, and animals on credit (usually on unfavorable terms) from their landlords or local suppliers, most tenants found themselves in a condition of ever-mounting debt which prevented them from moving to better land or to a landlord offering better terms. It also exposed freedmen to economic reprisals should they try to vote or stand up for their rights.

Jim Crow

Although life in the New South for most African Americans meant poverty and exploitation as sharecroppers, some managed to achieve a measure of economic success. Despite racism, poverty, and a hostile white business community, they bought property and started small businesses. Some of these endeavors blossomed into large, prosperous enterprises. For example, in 1898 two African American men in Durham founded the North Carolina Mutual and Provident Insurance Company. By 1907, the company boasted more than 100,000 policy holders. Other African Americans took advantage of the many black schools and colleges established during Reconstruction to enter the professions as teachers, professors, lawyers, doctors, nurses, and ministers. These members of a black middle class worked almost exclusively in segregated settings providing services to their fellow African Americans.

How did the poverty and indebtedness associated with sharecropping curtail the freedom of African Americans?

View the Map *Atlas Map: The Rise of Tenancy in the South (1880)*

These educated and relatively affluent African Americans provided leadership and direction for their communities, building social networks of churches, fraternal societies, and self-help organizations. The directors of the aforementioned North Carolina Mutual and Provident Insurance Company, for example, used their financial resources to support schools and establish a hospital, bank, and library to serve the black community of Durham. As *Heroes of the Colored Race* (**14.24**) suggests, middle-class blacks also cultivated pride in the accomplishments of African Americans after emancipation. This lithograph was published in 1881 for sale to African Americans. Note its emphasis on education and the role of African Americans in the Civil War and later as members of Congress.

But in the late 1870s and early 1880s, Southern political leaders began to create a social and legal system of segregation and disenfranchisement that came to be called Jim Crow (named for a derogatory black character in a popular minstrel show). They understood that as long as some African Americans possessed civil, economic, and political rights, especially the right to vote, white supremacy was called into question. Redeemer politicians also recognized that stoking racial animosity protected their privileged status as a ruling elite by deflecting the frustration and anger of poor Southern whites away from them and onto African Americans.

The Jim Crow system consisted of three main elements: segregation, disenfranchisement, and violence. The goal of segregation was to foment racial divisions by separating African Americans from as many aspects of everyday life as possible. Initial efforts focused on barring African Americans from hotels, restaurants, and railroad cars. Blacks denounced these violations of their constitutional rights-especially the Fourteenth Amendment-and challenged them in court.

But a conservative Supreme Court sharply restricted the authority of the Fourteenth Amendment and its guarantee of equal protection. In *Hall v. DeCuir* (1878), for example, the Court

HEROES OF THE COLORED RACE.

declared unconstitutional a Louisiana law prohibiting racial discrimination on steamboats because the vessel was engaged in interstate commerce (running routes between Louisiana and Mississippi), which only Congress could regulate. Five years later, in the Civil Rights Cases, the Court declared the 1875 Civil Rights Act unconstitutional, asserting that the Fourteenth Amendment did not empower Congress to outlaw racial discrimination by private individuals and organizations. The ruling cleared the way for private individuals such as hotel owners and institutions such as men's clubs to bar African Americans, but left standing the right of Congress to prohibit discrimination by state government institutions. As explained in *Choices and Consequences: Sanctioning Separation* (page 434), this issue came before the Court in an 1896 case, *Plessy v. Ferguson.*

Hand-in-hand with segregation came the effort to eradicate black political power by circumventing the Fifteenth Amendment. Violence and intimidation in the 1870s had reduced black voting and office holding significantly, but not completely. In Mississippi, for example, black voter turnout averaged 39 percent in the 1880s. But rising fears over the voting power of both blacks and disgruntled poor whites led Redeemer

14.24 *Heroes of the Colored Race* African Americans kept alive their hopes for a better future by cultivating an appreciation for their history.

((•— **Hear** the **Audio** *The Black Laws by Bishop B.W. Arnett, pamphlet excerpt*

What role did the black middle class play in the Jim Crow South?

Choices and Consequences

SANCTIONING SEPARATION

In 1890, Louisiana required separate cars for black and white passengers on all railroads in the state. To challenge the law, an African American carpenter named Homer A. Plessy bought a first-class ticket on the East Louisiana Railroad and sat in the whites-only first-class car. As expected he was arrested. Plessy argued before a local judge named John H. Ferguson that the law violated the Thirteenth Amendment's prohibition of slavery and the Fourteenth Amendment's equal protection clause. Ferguson ruled in favor of the railroad, stating that separation did not violate Plessy's rights, a decision upheld by the state's Supreme Court. When Plessy appealed to the U.S. Supreme Court, the justices considered three major options:

Choices

1 Refuse to hear the case and thus not render a judgment on the constitutionality of segregation, letting stand the Louisiana State Supreme Court decision.

2 Rule in favor of Plessy and declare Louisiana's segregation law unconstitutional.

3 Reject Plessy's appeal and uphold Louisiana's segregation law as constitutional.

Continuing Controversies

How should African Americans respond to the imposition of Jim Crow laws?

Black leaders in the 1890s were divided over the best strategy to oppose segregation. Booker T. Washington, the nation's most prominent African American leader, argued that efforts to overturn segregation were doomed to failure due to black Americans' lack of political and economic power (see Chapter 18). Instead he recommended blacks focus their energy and resources on self-improvement, especially in education, a strategy that would one day empower them to challenge segregation. Founding member of the National Association for the Advancement of Colored People (NAACP), W. E. B. Dubois, rejected this policy and insisted that African Americans keep up a sustained legal and political effort to end segregation. Ultimately it was Dubois's vision and NAACP attorneys that ended legalized segregation. In *Brown v. Board of Education of Topeka* in 1954, the Supreme Court overturned *Plessy* and rejected the concept of "separate but equal."

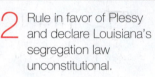

JIM CROW LAW.

UPHELD BY THE UNITED STATES SUPREME COURT.

Statute Within the Competency of the Louisiana Legislature and Railroads—Must Furnish Separate Cars for Whites and Blacks.

Washington, May 18.—The Supreme Court today in an opinion read by Justice Brown, sustained the constitutionality of the law in Louisiana requiring the railroads of that State to provide separate cars for white and colored passengers. There was no inter-

Decision

On May 18, 1896, the Supreme Court by a vote of 7 to 1 chose the third option and rejected Plessy's claim that the law violated his constitutional rights. The Thirteenth and Fourteenth Amendments, argued the majority, were never intended to establish full social equality of the races. Furthermore, legal separation of the races, a doctrine subsequently known as "separate but equal," was constitutional so long as states provided equal facilities. The lone dissenting justice, John Marshall Harlan, blasted the majority opinion, declaring the law a racist violation of the nation's "color-blind" Constitution.

Consequences

In sharply limiting the Fourteenth Amendment's equal protection provisions, the court allowed state governments to establish separate schools, hospitals, parks, theaters, restaurants, and public transportation across the South. The decision also opened the way for segregation laws aimed at Mexicans in the Southwest and Asians in California. In practice "separate but equal" proved only half accurate as segregated facilities were indeed separate, but never equal in terms of funding, staffing, and supplies.

How did the Supreme Court play a role in the imposition of segregation?

politicians to commence a program of disenfranchisement.

Given the sparse and direct language of the Fifteenth Amendment, the proponents of disenfranchisement needed to devise laws that deprived African Americans of the right to vote without making specific mention of "race, color, or previous condition of servitude." In 1889, Tennessee became the first of many Southern states to enact a poll tax, an annual tax imposed on all adult citizens in the state. Those who failed to pay it could not vote. As the image (**14.25**) of a Florida poll tax receipt for 1900 shows, the tax of $1 was low enough so that most white voters like Henry R. Nicks could pay it, but high enough to disenfranchise thousands of impoverished African Americans. Most states also required that all unpaid poll taxes from previous years be paid off before a citizen could vote, meaning that a black man who had fallen behind in his taxes for five years would need to pay $5 before entering a polling place.

In 1890, Mississippi enacted a poll tax and an additional measure to facilitate disenfranchisement: the literacy test. It allowed state and local officials to bar from voting anyone who failed a literacy test. It usually required a potential voter to read a complicated section of the state constitution and explain its meaning—a provision aimed at excluding African Americans given their low levels of education. Most Southern states soon adopted similar tests.

In the mid-1890s, Southern states added a third disenfranchisement policy, the so-called grandfather clause. It guaranteed the vote to anyone, even if they could not pass a literacy test, if their grandfather had been eligible to vote before 1867. Since no African Americans could vote before 1867, they were the only ones subject to literacy tests.

14.25 Disenfranchisement through the Poll Tax
Because H. R. Nicks, a white man in Hernando County, Florida, in 1900, could pay his poll tax of $1, he was eligible to vote. Mired in poverty, many African Americans could not afford the fee and lost their right to vote.

Adding to the effectiveness of the segregation and disenfranchisement movements was a stepped-up campaign of violence against African Americans. Vigilante groups across the South composed largely of poor whites, but often aided by local law officers and prominent citizens, launched an unprecedented wave of beatings, humiliations, and murders intended to intimidate blacks and "put them in their place." Often an unsubstantiated accusation of rape or murder brought out a community's lynch mob, but many killings were prompted by minor incidents of alleged disrespect such as arguing with a white man. Lynchings in the 1890s soared to an average of 187 per year, or roughly one killing every two days.

By 1900, these disenfranchisement policies had reduced overall black voting in the South by 62 percent. In some states black voting was effectively eliminated. In Louisiana, for example, the number of black voters dropped from 130,334 in 1896 to 1,342 in 1904—a reduction of 99 percent. Thousands of poor whites were also disenfranchised, reducing the total white vote by 27 percent by 1900. White supremacy had triumphed.

1863–1865

The Ten Percent Plan
Lincoln proposes moderate terms for readmission of Southern states

Thirteenth Amendment (Ratified 1865)
Abolishes slavery in every state

1866

Ku Klux Klan founded
Groups of armed white vigilantes wage campaign of violence to suppress freedmen's rights

Fourteenth Amendment (ratified 1868)
Defines citizenship to include African Americans and guarantees equal protection before the law

1867–1868

The Reconstruction Acts
South placed under military rule and freedmen guaranteed voting rights

Progressive state governments take power in South
Freedmen wield their newly won right to vote and hold office

Republicans impeach Johnson
Reflects the divisive politics of Reconstruction

1869–1871

Fifteenth Amendment (ratified 1870)
Establishes the right to vote for all male citizens regardless of "race, color, or previous condition of servitude"

Enforcement Acts passed
Empowers Grant administration to weaken Ku Klux Klan and like groups

North Carolina elects first Redeemer government
Signals a return to white supremacy in the South; other Southern states soon follow

CHAPTER REVIEW

Review Questions

1. Why did African Americans want land? How did they justify their claims to plantation lands?

2. Why did Reconstruction become violent? How did Congress and the Grant administration try to curb the violence?

3. How did feminists react to the Fifteenth Amendment? How did this affect the women's rights movement?

5. Why did Reconstruction end?

6. What was the Lost Cause? What purposes did it serve in the post-Reconstruction South?

7. Who were the "Bourbons" and what was their vision for the New South?

Key Terms

Ten Percent Plan Pardoned all Southerners (except high-ranking military officers and Confederate officials) who took an oath pledging loyalty to the Union and support for emancipation. As soon as 10 percent of a state's voters took this oath, they could call a convention, establish a new state government, and apply for congressional recognition.   **408**

Freedmen's Bureau Relief agency for the war-ravaged South created by Congress in March 1865. It provided emergency services, built schools, and managed confiscated lands.   **408**

Black Codes Laws designed by the ex-Confederate states to sharply limit the civil and economic rights of freedmen and create an exploitable workforce.   **413**

Fourteenth Amendment Drafted by Congress in June 1866, it defined citizenship to include African Americans, guaranteed equal protection before the law, and established the federal government as the guarantor of individual civil rights.   **417**

Carpetbagger White Southerners' derogatory term for Northerners who came south after the war to settle, work, or aid the ex-slaves. It falsely suggested they were penniless adventurers who came south merely to get rich.   **418**

Scalawag White Southerners' derogatory term for fellow whites considered traitors to their region and race for joining the Republican Party and cooperating with Reconstruction policy.   **418**

Fifteenth Amendment Constitutional amendment passed by Congress in 1869 providing an explicit constitutional guarantee for black suffrage.   **421**

Mississippi Plan Campaign of violence and intimidation waged by armed groups of whites closely allied with the Democratic Party that drove Republicans from power in the Mississippi state elections of 1874. Copied by other Southern states.   **426**

Redeemers Name for white Southern political leaders who successfully returned their states to white Democratic rule in the mid-1870s. The name was intended to depict these leaders as saviors of Southern society from rule by freedmen, scalawags, and carpetbaggers.   **426**

Civil Rights Act of 1875 Passed by Congress in 1875, it required state governments to provide equal access in public facilities such as schools and to allow African Americans to serve on juries. In 1883 the U.S. Supreme Court ruled it unconstitutional.   **426**

Compromise of 1877 Resolution of the disputed presidential election of 1876 that handed victory to Republican Rutherford B. Hayes over Democrat Samuel J. Tilden. Democrats agreed to the deal in exchange for patronage and the continued removal of federal troops from the South.   **427**

New South Optimistic phrase white Southerners used to describe the post-Reconstruction South, reflecting the South's development of a new system of race relations based on segregation and white supremacy and pointing to a profound economic transformation that swept across the region.   **428**

1872–1873

Amnesty Act
Pardons and restores full political rights to most ex-Confederates

Panic of 1873
Begins four years of severe economic depression that weakens Northern support for Reconstruction

1874–1875

The Mississippi Plan
Violence by white terrorist groups keeps thousands of blacks from voting. Restores the Democratic Party to power

Second Civil Rights Act passed
Guarantees equal access to public facilities and affirms the right of blacks to serve on juries

1876–1877

Compromise of 1877
Republican Rutherford B. Hayes becomes president; Republicans promise to remove federal troops from the South. End of Reconstruction

1883–1889

Civil Rights Act of 1875 Declared Unconstitutional
Clears the way for adoption of Jim Crow policies across the South

Tennessee enacts first poll tax
Sharply reduces black voting; adopted by other Southern states. Followed by literacy test and grandfather clause

MyHistoryLab Connections

Visit www.myhistorylab.com for a customized Study Plan that will help you build your knowledge of *Now That We Are Free.*

Questions for Analysis

1. How did former slaves make use of their new freedoms?

📖 **Read** the **Document** *Charlotte Forten, "Life on the Sea Islands", p. 406*

2. Why did some Americans believe the federal government was obligated to assist the freedmen?

🔍 **View** the **Closer Look** *Competing Visions: Federal Authority and Equal Rights, p. 412*

3. What changes did Republican governments bring to Southern society?

🔍 **View** the **Closer Look** *First Vote, p. 419*

4. How did the system of sharecropping sharply limit the freedom of African Americans?

📖 **Read** the **Document** *James T. Rapier, Testimony before U.S. Senate Regarding the Agricultural Labor Force in the South (1880), p. 431*

5. What role did violence play in establishing white supremacy in the New South?

((•)) **Hear** the **Audio File** *A Georgia Lynch Law, p. 435*

Other Resources from This Chapter

((•)) **Hear** the **Audio File** *The Black Laws by Bishop B.W. Arnett, pamphlet excerpt, p. 433*

📖 **Read** the **Document**

- *Carl Schurz, "Report on the Condition of the South" (1865), p. 408*
- *James C. Beecher, "Report on Land Reform" (1865, 1866), p. 409*
- *"Address of the Colored State Convention to the People of the State of South Carolina" (1865), p. 414*
- *Affidavit of Former Slave Enoch Braston (1866), p. 415*
- *Charles F. Johnson and T. W. Gilbreth, The Memphis Riot (1866), p. 416*
- *Hannah Irwin Describes Ku Klux Klan Ride (Late 1860s), p. 422*
- *Credit Mobilier/Union Pacific Railroad Scandal Testimony of C.P. Huntington (1873), p. 423*
- *Blanche K. Bruce, Speech in the Senate (1876), p. 426*
- *R. B. Buckley, Confederate Song, "I'm a Good Old Rebel" (1866), p. 428*

🔍 **View** the **Image** *Cotton plantation, United States of America, p. 429*

🔍 **View** the **Map**

- *Interactive Map: Congressional Reconstruction, p. 417*
- *Atlas Map: The Rise of Tenancy in the South (1880), p. 432*

👁 **Watch** the **Video** *Video Lectures: The Schools that the Civil War and Reconstruction Created, p. 410*

((●—[Hear the **Audio File** on **myhistorylab.com**

◉—[Watch the **Video** *Critical Visions, Chapter 15*

Conflict and Conquest

The Transformation of the West, 1860–1900

Most Americans envisioned the conquest and transformation of the West as a tale of triumph. In John Gast's 1872 painting, *American Progress,* the goddess Liberty glides westward, stringing telegraph wire and holding a book, symbols, along with the distant railroad, of the civilization and new technology that would soon tame the wilderness. Beneath her, Gast depicts farmers and pioneers intent on taking advantage of the West's bountiful resources. Turned into a lithograph, it was advertised as worthy of hanging in both "the miner's humble cabin" and the "stately marble mansion of the capitalist." Publishers put the image on the cover of a popular guide to the West, *The New Overland Tourist and Pacific Coast Guide.*

Before 1840 most Americans viewed the lands west of the Mississippi as a great, untamed, and dangerous wilderness of rugged terrain, extreme temperatures, wild animals, and hostile Native Americans. But beginning in the 1840s, an ever-growing number of farmers, miners, ranchers, entrepreneurs, and adventurers moved west, aided after 1869 by the completion of the transcontinental railroad and soaring demand for Western products and resources.

Gast's celebratory scene reveals, doubtless unintentionally, the bitter conflict that accompanied the transformation of the West. On the painting's left border, a cluster of Native Americans flee before the advancing whites. Above them a herd of buffalo likewise make their escape. Gast's matter-of-fact portrayal of the seizure of Indian land and the near extinction of the buffalo reflected the nation's enthusiasm for "progress" and the inability—or unwillingness—to confront the human and environmental costs associated with it.

By 1900, the West had been radically transformed. Networks of railroads and telegraph lines crisscrossed the landscape, as did millions of miles of fencing that marked the boundaries of farms and ranches. Western cities like San Francisco and Denver rivaled their Eastern counterparts. Perhaps even more remarkable than the appearance of these new aspects of Western life was the disappearance of others. By 1900, the American government had confined hundreds of independent Native American tribes that had once lived in virtually every corner of the West to reservations. Gone, too, were the millions of buffalo from the plains and, in areas of intensive mining, large sections of once pristine mountain landscape were defaced. The conquest of the West between 1865 and 1900 included many stories of success, achievement, and undeniable progress, but it was far more complex, violent, and tragic than Gast's dreamy vision suggests.

> "The destiny of the American people is to subdue the continent—to rush over this vast field to the Pacific Ocean . . . to change darkness into light and confirm the destiny of the human race . . . Divine task! Immortal mission!"
>
> WILLIAM GILPIN, *The Central Gold Region*, 1859

Natives and Newcomers

Inspired by visions of unlimited opportunity and measures of Congress like the Homestead Act, westward migration increased dramatically after the Civil War. Contrary to the popular notions of a vacant landscape, much of the West was home to hundreds of thousands of Native Americans. Their many languages, lifestyles, and religious practices made for a rich cultural landscape, but also conflict with the rising numbers of newcomers.

Congress Promotes Westward Settlement

In 1862, Congress passed three major bills to facilitate settlement of the trans-Mississippi West, the vast region of the United States west of the Mississippi River. The Morrill Land Grant College Act of 1862 created a system whereby funds raised by the sale of public land went toward establishing colleges specializing in agricultural, mechanical, and technological education. Far more significant, however, was the **Homestead Act**. It provided 160 acres of free land to any settler willing to live on it and improve it for five years. Farmers with more capital could buy the land for $1.25 per acre after living on it for only six months. Those who took advantage of the program included immigrants, landless farmers from the East, single women, and ex-slaves. By making available more than 600 million acres of public land to be settled and farmed, the Homestead Act touched off the largest migration of people ever within the United States. Advertisements and promotional literature produced by land companies and railroads convinced many people to head West to acquire homesteads. Like this image (**15.1**), which ap-

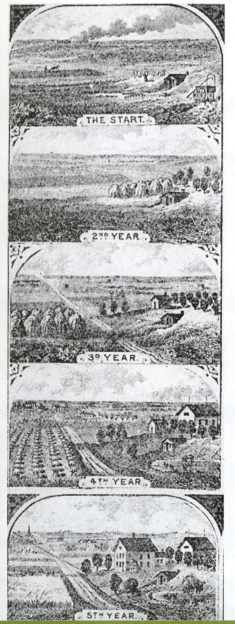

peared in a Czech language magazine, these enticements promised rapid success. Note the year-by-year progression that begins with a barren farm and humble house. By the fourth year the landscape features not only a substantial house and flourishing farm, but also trees, a road, and more homes, suggesting that the loneliness of life on the plains will be short-lived. One year later a church steeple appears, further suggesting the development of a community and all the blessings of civilization.

But the actual results of the Homestead Act varied widely by region. On the Great Plains and the lands farther west—regions with a harsh climate, poor soil, inconsistent supplies of water, and limited access to transportation—farmers who participated in the Homestead Act often went bankrupt. By contrast, the act worked well in the northern and central portions of the Midwest, where the soil and the climate were favorable to farming.

Some people prospered from the Homestead Act in ways not intended by Congress. Many "homesteaders" were actually speculators who claimed their 160 acres with the intention of selling them for a quick profit in a few years. Larger enterprises like railroads and real estate companies accumulated vast land holdings by buying out farmers who failed or paying people to file homestead claims and then buying the land from them. The Homestead Act did indeed attract farmers to the West, but by 1900, only 52 percent of original homestead claimants had acquired legal title to the land.

The third major piece of legislation passed by Congress in 1862 to promote Western development, the Pacific Railway Act, created two corporations to build the **transcontinental railroad** spanning the continent. The Union Pacific was to build west

15.1 Homesteads and the Promise of Success in the West
The B. and M. Railroad paid for this advertisement, which appeared in a Czech magazine. Its six panels showing extraordinary year-by-year progress of a typical homesteading family were intended to draw settlers to Nebraska.

Why did the Homestead Act have uneven results?   ▶️ **Read** the **Document** *Homestead Act of 1862*

from Omaha, Nebraska, across the Plains and the Rockies to meet the Central Pacific, which was to build from California through the Sierra Nevada Mountains. To help the railroad corporations raise capital to pay for the road, Congress granted them ten square miles of land (in a checkerboard pattern with the federal government retaining ownership of the remaining sections) for every mile of track completed. The law also granted the railroads cheap loans and cash subsidies for each mile of track laid.

It took six years of low-paid, hard, and dangerous work by huge gangs of workers, especially Irish and Chinese, to complete the project. Scores were killed. On May 10, 1869, a grand ceremony marking the union of the two lines took place at Promontory Point, Utah. At the appointed moment, Leland Stanford, president of the Central Pacific, drove a symbolic golden spike into place, joining two rails, one placed by a team of Chinese workers and another by an Irish crew. Telegraph wires attached to the sledge hammer and spike sent a signal across the nation, announcing the

long-anticipated news: the continent had been spanned. Keenly aware of the historic nature of the event, railroad officials staged this iconic photograph (**15.2**) showing the workers and locomotives of the Union Pacific and Central Pacific. It soon appeared in numerous publications, often as a lithograph. Conspicuously absent from the photograph, however, are any of the thousands of Chinese workers who labored on the Central Pacific.

The Diversity of the Native American West

As this map of the trans-Mississippi West (**15.3** on page 442) shows, white settlers heading west encountered Native Americans belonging to hundreds of different tribes that comprised some 360,000 persons. That number was significantly lower than it had been a century earlier, reflecting the impact of earlier European contact, starting with the Spanish, French, and Russians, that brought conflict and

15.2 The Continent Spanned Conscious of the historic significance of the event, workers and officials of the Union Pacific and Central Pacific railroads pose for a photograph while celebrating the completion of the transcontinental railroad in 1869.

Why did the federal government provide land and loans to the companies that built the transcontinental railroad?

15.3 The Major Tribes of the Trans-Mississippi West
More than 360,000 Native Americans, constituting some 500 tribes, lived west of the Mississippi River.

devastating disease. Most Indians had lived there as far back as anyone could remember, while some had come from the East only decades earlier during the many forced removals (see Chapter 8).

Before the arrival of Europeans, dozens of Native American tribes in what is now California lived in villages as small bands of hunters and gatherers. These include the Hupa, Karok, Northern Paiute, Pomo, Wintun, and Yuki peoples. Their way of life was first disrupted in the late eighteenth century when the Spanish established a line of Christian missions on the Pacific coast running north from San Diego. While thousands of Indians lived beyond the reach of the missions, many were gradually transformed by the Spanish into an exploited class of laborers, converted to Christianity, and absorbed

into Spanish colonial society. Even greater change followed the discovery of gold in northern California shortly after the U.S. government seized the territory in the Mexican War. Waves of white fortune seekers soon arrived and drove the Native Americans off their lands. This violence, along with the starvation and disease that followed, killed thousands of Indians (see Chapter 12).

Present-day Arizona, New Mexico, and west Texas also fell under Spanish colonial rule in the seventeenth and eighteenth centuries. But because this region was dry and remote, it attracted few Europeans. Its native inhabitants, therefore, retained core elements of their culture despite Spanish rule and the presence of Catholic missionaries. Indeed, missionaries managed to gain converts only

What was the impact of European contact with
Indians in the trans-Mississippi West before 1850?

by blending Christianity with local customs and traditions.

One major group, descended from the ancient Anasazi people, included the Hopi, Zuni, and Rio Grande Pueblo tribes. They lived in settled farming communities in western New Mexico and eastern Arizona, growing corn, beans, and cotton, and herding sheep. They also traded with neighboring Mexican ranchers, exchanging their decorative pottery and woven cloth for manufactured products such as hoes and tools.

Eastern New Mexico and western Texas harbored more tribes, including the Jicarilla Apache and Navajo. Like the Pueblo, they lived in relative isolation from Spanish missions and thus retained much of their traditional religion, language, and culture. Before the sixteenth century they had lived much like the Pueblos, but their adoption of horses and, for the Navajo, sheep which had been brought to America by the Spanish, transformed them into more migratory peoples. The Navajo tended large flocks of sheep, following them on their seasonal migrations. Sheep provided food, but also wool, which Indian women wove into cloth. Navajo silversmiths also produced beautiful jewelry.

The Pacific Northwest, comprising present-day Washington, Oregon, and northern California, was home to thriving native societies such as the Chinook, Salish, Yurok, and Shasta. Living in large villages, they divided their time between growing vegetables, hunting in the lush forests for bear, deer, and moose, and fishing along rivers and the ocean shore. Highly skilled in woodworking, the men produced excellent canoes for fishing and elaborate totem poles. Women wove intricate baskets that were both beautiful and practical. Many of these tribes enjoyed a rich material life that was offset by their custom of *potlatch*—a ceremony during which rich tribe members gave away many of their possessions as an act of competitive benevolence and a demonstration of superior status.

Native American Tribes of the Great Plains

While Native American tribes could be found in virtually every corner of the West, the largest group—constituting nearly two-thirds of all Native Americans in the West—lived on the **Great Plains**. This vast open territory stretched from present-day Missouri to the Rocky Mountains and from North Dakota to Texas. In the northern half (the Dakotas, Idaho, Minnesota, and Montana) lived tribes such as the Flathead, Blackfeet, Crow, Arapaho, Northern Cheyenne, and Sioux. Tribes in the southern Great Plains (present-day Nebraska, Kansas, Oklahoma, Texas, and New Mexico) included those relocated from the East during the so-called Trail of Tears ordeal (Cherokee, Choctaw, Creek, Chickasaw, and Seminole; see Chapter 8), as well as Pawnees, Comanches, Kiowas, Southern Arapahos, and Cheyenne.

The Plains tribes varied culturally, but many shared a similar tribal structure. Most tribes consisted of bands of about 300–500 related men and women, each governed by a council that welcomed community involvement in decision making. The Comanches, for example, divided their population of 7,000 (ca. 1870) into 13 bands.

Religious beliefs and practices varied among the Plains tribes, but most shared important fundamental elements, beginning with the worship of one primary god whom the Sioux called *Wakan Tanka* (the Great Spirit). Plains Indians also believed in spirits found in everything in creation, from the earth itself, to plants, animals, stars, the moon, and sun, and they considered certain places, such as burial grounds, sacred. A shaman deemed *wakan,* or blessed, led religious ceremonies, healed the sick, and even decided where to hunt.

Many Plains tribes lived in settled villages near rivers where they tended fields of corn, beans, and squash; fished; and hunted game, including bear, deer, and buffalo. Trade with white settlers, explorers, and trappers since the eighteenth century had allowed them to procure guns, kettles, and tools. These sedentary tribes included the Wichitas of northern Texas and Oklahoma, Pawnees of western Kansas, the Dakota Sioux of Minnesota, the Mandans of North Dakota, the Omahas of Nebraska, the Osages of western Missouri and Arkansas, and the Arikawas of South Dakota.

Although essential aspects of this Plains lifestyle had changed little over the centuries, some of the largest tribes took to using horses by the eighteenth century and adopted a migratory lifestyle. These included the Crow, Blackfeet, Cheyenne, Arapaho, Comanche, and Lakota Sioux. The horse allowed the Plains tribes to follow the seasonal migrations of the buffalo, whose

What is significant about the diversity of Native American life in the trans-Mississippi West?

population stood at 30 million in 1800. This scene, *Buffalo Chase over Prairie Bluffs,* (**15.4**), painted in 1844 by George Catlin, who traveled extensively among Indian tribes in the West from the 1830s to the 1850s, reveals both the drama of the buffalo hunt and the extraordinary horsemanship of Plains Indians. It also shows the centrality of the buffalo in Plains Indian culture, for the hunters' clothing, jewelry, spear tips, and bridles are made from buffalo parts. Other uses for the buffalo included flesh for food; skin for teepees and blankets; horns and hooves for glue; bones and tendons for weapons; hair for rope; teeth for ornaments; and dried dung for fuel.

The military advantages of the horse and the material wealth provided by the buffalo led these migratory tribes to become the dominant powers on the Plains, allowing them to exact tribute from weaker sedentary tribes. But reliance on the huge migratory beasts also meant that tribes, such as the Lakota Sioux in the north and Comanche in the central Plains, traversed enormous tracts of land during their annual migrations, a practice that increasingly brought them into conflict with whites eager to acquire land. It also increased conflict between rival tribes, such as the Lakota Sioux and Crow, as white settlement forced tribes into closer contact.

While not all Native Americans were warlike, the culture of most Plains Indians glorified battle. Warriors aspired to earn reputations as brave hunters and fighters. Warfare between tribes to control land and access to game consisted of small skirmishes where the goal was not so much to kill their opponents as to steal their horses (a measure of a tribe's

15.4 Plains Indians Hunting the Buffalo
This 1844 painting by George Catlin shows Native Americans hunting the buffalo, which they relied on as a major source of food, clothing, tools, and fuel.

> **"I was famous as a hunter…. I gave the [buffalo] calves that I killed to the poor that had no horses. I was considered a good man."**
> SITTING BULL

wealth and power) and drive them from the field. Individual warriors earned fame and respect by "counting coup," or touching an enemy with one's hand or weapon. Respect was also earned through acts of charity. Sitting Bull of the Lakota Sioux, for example, became chief of his tribe both because of his success as a warrior and his generosity.

The Great Westward Migration

In the late 1840s, after the Mexican War and the discovery of gold in California, a steady flow of settlers into the trans-Mississippi West commenced. By the mid-1850s, thousands annually traversed the 2,000-mile Oregon Trail that stretched from Missouri to Oregon. What attracted them was a torrent of pamphlets, books, articles, and photographs produced by publicists and boosters, many employed by railroads and land companies, celebrating the West as a region of wealth and opportunity.

Several groups led this migration westward. One was the recently freed slaves who hoped to secure new lives as independent farmers, free of the poverty and violence in the South. One of these ex-slaves, Henry Adams, who became a land promoter after emancipation, helped more than 20,000 other black "**Exodusters**" move in the "Exodus of 1879" from the South to farms in Kansas. This image from *Harper's Weekly* (**15.5**) captures the hope this movement inspired. Note the contrast the artist draws between the "old style" of African American migration (a desperate escaped slave hiding from a passing steamboat) and "the new" (well-dressed ex-slaves arriving at their destination by steamboat). The name Exodusters reflected the belief that, like the Israelites in the Bible's Book of Exodus, they were heading

How did the introduction of horses change the lifestyle of some Plains Indians?

View the **Map** *Atlas Map: Western Migration, 1850–1880*

for a "promised land." The inclusion of a black veteran of the Union army symbolizes the fulfillment of the promise of emancipation won during the war. Unfortunately many Exodusters settled on poor land and lacked the capital to establish successful farms. As a result only about one-third stayed. The rest moved on or returned to the South.

Native-born whites constituted a second, much larger segment of the westward migration. Many were Eastern and Midwestern farmers who sought larger plots of land, either through purchase or by the Homestead Act, and opportunities for upward mobility. Others came to work in railroad construction or mining. In addition, many westward migrants were white soldiers who had been stationed in the West and elected to stay and settle after their terms of service expired.

One distinct subgroup of native-born whites migrants were the Mormons. Joseph Smith had founded this religious sect in upstate New York in 1830. But violent persecution—Smith was killed by a mob in Illinois in 1844—prompted the Mormons to head west in 1846 in search of an isolated homeland that could ensure their security and survival. They eventually chose a valley in Utah near the Great Salt Lake, territory then under Mexican rule. After the United States acquired the region following the Mexican-American War, Congress created the Utah territory in 1850 (see Chapter 12), and by 1865 some 20,000 Mormons lived in the region under a form of theocratic local rule where the church controlled most property, businesses, and

public services. Gradually, as more non-Mormons moved to Utah and federal officials condemned the sect's practice of polygamy (a practice the Mormons officially banned in 1896), the church took a less prominent role in public life.

Joining Exodusters, Mormons, and native-born Americans in the great migration into the trans-Mississippi West were more than two million immigrants. They were drawn by the same desire for free, or at least inexpensive, farmland or to find work in mines, on railroads, or in the rapidly expanding economies of Western towns and cities. Over time large concentrations of particular ethnic groups emerged. For example, 30 percent of Minnesota's population in 1880 was foreign-born, including more than 66,000 Germans, 62,000 Norwegians, and 39,000 Swedes. Drawn by jobs in the copper mines, thousands of Irish immigrants settled in Butte, Montana. By 1900, it was the most Irish city in America.

15.5 Seeking a Better Life in the West In response to poverty and mounting violence in the South, more than 20,000 African Americans known as "Exodusters" migrated to Kansas in 1879–1880 to acquire homesteads and start new lives as independent farmers.

"[I]f you strike off into the broad, free West, and make yourself a farm from Uncle Sam's generous domain, you will crowd nobody, starve nobody, and . . . neither you nor your children need evermore beg for Something to Do."
HORACE GREELEY, Editor, *New York Tribune*, 1867

As in the East, increased ethnic and racial diversity and economic competition in the West led to tension and conflict that occasionally exploded into raw violence. Frequently victims of the violence were Chinese immigrants. By 1880, California was home to 75,132 Chinese, while 30,000 more lived elsewhere in the West. But as this drawing (**15.6**) from *Harper's Weekly* shows, anti-Chinese racism surged in the 1870s and 1880s as white laborers accused the Chinese of taking jobs and lowering wages. In this attack in 1885 at Rock Springs, Wyoming, whites killed 28 Chinese miners. Two years later white laborers massacred at least 34 Chinese miners in Hells Canyon, Oregon.

15.6 Anti-Chinese Violence Surges in the West
In the 1870s and 1880s, Chinese workers in the American West faced hostility and violence from whites. In this incident at Rock Springs, Wyoming in 1885, whites killed 28 Chinese miners.

Railroads and land companies played a key role in promoting immigration to the West, sending agents to Europe and advertising there to encourage migration, sometimes by entire villages, directly to the West. Railroads brought more than two million immigrants to the trans-Mississippi West between 1870 and 1900. "California, Cornucopia of the World" (1883) was one of countless posters that railroads placed in Eastern seaports to attract newly arrived immigrants (**15.7**). The competition among Western states for settlers is indicated in the phrase "without Cyclones or Blizzards," a clear attempt to make California more appealing than the Plains states like Kansas. Also significant is the claim of "Room for Millions of Immigrants," since only one year earlier Congress, with heavy lobbying from California, passed the Chinese Exclusion Act that barred Chinese immigration to the United States.

15.7 The Railroads Promote Westward Settlement
Railroads placed promotional posters such as this one from 1883 in Eastern cities to entice settlers to head west to settle on land owned by the railroads, much of it acquired in land grants from the federal government.

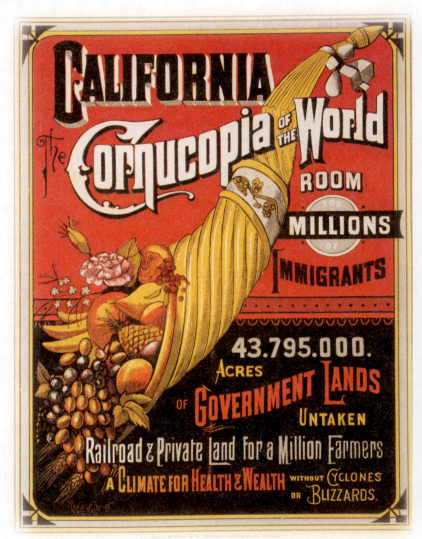

Why did railroads promote the migration of immigrants to the West?

The Economic Transformation of the West

While many Americans were inspired to migrate westward by notions of Manifest Destiny, the primary motivation was economic—a search for land and work. As a result, economic development was the chief driving force behind the profound transformations of the West after 1865. By 1900, four major industries—the railroad, farming, ranching, and mining—had fundamentally reshaped the region. These industries employed millions of workers and supplied some of the essential needs of consumers and industry in the East and internationally. Such progress, however, was accompanied by labor exploitation, environmental damage, and conflict with Indians.

The Railroad Fuels Western Development

Between 1860 and 1900, the country's agricultural output soared. The number of farms in the United States grew from two million to six million, with most of the growth taking place in the West. Agricultural output increased from $1.6 billion in 1860 to $4.3 billion in 1900.

Several factors account for this agricultural boom. New technologies such as the steel plow and mechanical reaper dramatically increased the acreage a farmer could till. The establishment of many agriculture schools, most funded by states and the federal government, led to advances in fertilization, irrigation, crop rotation, seed selection, and the care of livestock.

One of the biggest factors underlying this boom in agriculture was the spread of the railroad. As the map

(**15.8**) shows, the transcontinental railroad marked only the beginning of a vast transportation network of both major east-west railroad lines, such as the Atlantic and Pacific Railroad and the Northern Pacific Railroad, and countless smaller feeder railroads. This growing network opened up more and more western lands for farming, allowing farmers in once remote areas to sell their grain in the national market. The railroad also benefited many non-farmers, opening up Western lands for mining and ranching and providing employment for thousands who built the lines

15.8 The Spread of the Railroad Government loans and land grants helped spread a railroad network across the nation, facilitating economic development and settlement in the West.

Railroads in operation
— by 1870
— by 1890

How did the railroad shape western economic development?

and later gained employment as firemen, engineers, switchmen, mechanics, dispatchers, and clerks.

Railroads also transformed the West by promoting urban growth. Many Western cities like San Francisco, Portland, and Denver, were significant centers of trade before the arrival of the railroad. Once connected to the national rail network, however, they boomed into major metropolises. Their economies diversified as demand for construction, food, transportation, and retail opened up new opportunities for entrepreneurs. By 1890, the West was more urbanized than any region in the United States except the Northeast. Between 1860 and 1890, for example, Denver's population rose from 2,600 to over 100,000, while Omaha, Nebraska's soared from less than 2,000 to over 140,000. Like their Eastern counterparts, Western cities struggled with urban problems, including crime, disorder, corruption, poor public health, inadequate water, and ethnic tensions.

Hard Times for Farmers

While the overall trend in this period was one of expansion and profit, the reality for many farmers was struggle, frustration, and failure. To begin with, farmers faced unpredictable weather patterns. Farmers on the Plains, for example, enjoyed unusually high levels of rainfall between 1878 and 1886, leading them to think this was the norm and encouraging still more farmers to acquire homesteads. But a return to dry conditions and occasional drought after 1886 caused widespread hardship and failure. Other threats came from swarms of insects such as grasshoppers that attacked crops.

Farmers also struggled with wild fluctuations in prices for their crops from year to year. A plentiful harvest of wheat or corn often meant a glutted market and low prices. In the 1880s, wheat farmers on the Plains saw prices fall due to competition with less expensive wheat grown in Russia, South America, Canada, and Australia. Sudden drops in prices pushed many farmers into foreclosure because most carried high levels of debt

to finance the purchase of land and equipment such as harvesters, plows, and windmills.

These conditions favored larger farms, revealing a significant flaw in the original Homestead Act: in the more arid regions of the West the 160-acre allotment was too small for profitable farming. By the 1880s, so-called bonanza farms of 1,000 acres or more became increasingly common in the Dakotas and California. With more capital, these large enterprises could better afford the expensive equipment needed for plowing, sowing, and harvesting.

On top of all these challenges were the loneliness and drudgery of life on the Plains. As this photograph (15.9) of the four Chrisman sisters standing by their sod house in Custer County, Nebraska, illustrates, life on a Western farm was often Spartan. Sod houses and dugouts cut into hills lacked even the most basic amenities like running water and glass windows. Apart from occasional trips to town, church, court sessions, and harvest fairs, opportunities for social interaction were rare since farmers usually situated their homesteads far apart. The Chrisman sisters developed a strategy that diminished their isolation and allowed them to fulfill the Homestead Act's requirement that they live on their land to receive full title to it. Beginning with Lizzie's homestead claim in 1887 and Lutie's in 1888, the two younger sisters took turns living on the homesteads, keeping their sisters' company, helping on the farm, and waiting until they were old enough to file their own claims. Hattie eventually did, but all the homestead plots were gone by the time Jennie Ruth came of age.

To improve the lot of American farmers, a former clerk in the Department of Agriculture named Oliver

15.9 Homesteading on the Plains
Western farmers received 160 acres of free land through the Homestead Act, but success required years of hard work and sacrifices such as living in crude sod houses. This one, in Nebraska, was owned by one of the four Chrisman sisters shown here.

What challenges did Western farmers face?

View the **Closer Look** *Thirty-Three Horse Team Harvester*
Watch the **Video** *Video Lectures: "The Urban West"*

H. Kelley founded in 1867 the Patrons of Husbandry, or **Grange**. This social and educational society was dedicated to alleviating the problems faced by farmers by promoting fellowship, fraternity, and education. Grangers, as they were called, shared ideas about farming through a newsletter and attended lectures by traveling experts. Local chapters opened across the nation, and by the early 1870s, the organization had several hundred thousand loyal members.

The Grange was transformed into a powerful political movement during the economic depression triggered by the Panic of 1873. Hundreds of thousands of farmers faced ruin as prices plummeted, while their creditors demanded payment for loans, and railroads charged high prices to transport their produce to market. In their desperation they created Granger Parties, which in 1874 won control of the legislatures of Illinois, Wisconsin, Iowa, and Minnesota and gained significant influence in others. They enacted "Granger Laws," some of the earliest regulations of banks and corporations, especially railroads. These measures set maximum rates for transporting or storing grain and banned abusive practices such as offering preferred customers special rates. Grangers tried, as this 1873 cartoon (**15.10**) indicates, to convince Americans not involved in farming to recognize the threat posed to them by uncontrolled railroad power. As a "Consolidation Train," a name suggesting monopoly, pulls cars labeled "extortion," "bribery," "usurpation," and "oppression," a Granger warns unsuspecting citizens of their impending doom.

Railroad magnates denounced these limitations on their power and profit as unconstitutional and sued. The Supreme Court, however, in two key cases in 1876 (*Munn v. Illinois* and *Peik v. Chicago and Northwestern Railway*) ruled that state legislatures had the legal authority under the Constitution to regulate commerce, including especially commerce between states.

Despite this legal victory, the Granger movement faded when the depression lifted and farm product prices rose in the late-1870s. The Democratic and Republican parties also added pro-farmer planks to their platforms that made the Granger parties seem less necessary.

The Cattle Kingdom

Another key emerging sector of the Western economy was cattle ranching. When the United States annexed Texas in 1845, millions of longhorn cattle (introduced to Central America in the sixteenth century by the Spanish) roamed the range, raised mainly for their skins and tallow. But as Americans developed a taste

15.10 Warning of the Perils of Monopoly The Grangers saw themselves as reformers trying to warn the American public about the growing danger of powerful railroads to the survival of democracy and individual liberties.

for beef in the 1860s, ranchers envisioned the great profits to be made if they could get their cattle to Northern markets. A longhorn that cost $4 in Texas could be sold for $40 on the Northern market.

Beginning in 1866 and lasting two decades, Texas ranchers began the first of the annual **Long Drives** of more than 1,000 miles to bring the cattle to market. Ranchers Charles Goodnight and Oliver Loving drove thousands of cattle from Texas to Colorado, prompting many imitators. In 1867, another cattle entrepreneur, Joseph McCoy, established a stockyard, hotel, bank, and office in a small Kansas town along the Kansas-Pacific Railroad. Advertising heavily, he quickly turned Abilene, Kansas for a time into the premier cattle drive destination. By the late 1870s, more than 600,000 longhorns arrived per year to be sold and transported by rail to Chicago and other destinations for slaughter.

Over time the need for the drives diminished as rail lines were extended from Kansas into Texas and entrepreneurs established large cattle ranches close to railroads in states such as Kansas, Nebraska, Wyoming, and Colorado.

The period of the great cattle drives lasted only 20 years, but it established the cowboy as an enduring icon of the Old West. Nineteenth-century dime novels, paintings, books, and plays (and in the twentieth century, films) depicted cowboys as paragons of manliness, independence, and courage who spent most of their days battling fierce Indians and driving cattle (see 15.21 on page 464) and nights in raucous saloons playing poker, brawling, and gun fighting. But the life of a cowboy was far more difficult and

View the **Closer Look** *Railroad Routes, Cattle Trails, Gold and Silver Rushes*

Why did Western farmers resent the railroads?

complicated. Cattle drives exposed them to harsh weather that included searing heat, flash floods, and deadly blizzards. Cowboys' wages averaged only about $1 a day—or less if the price of beef fell—and they survived on a relentless diet of meat, beans, and coffee. They worked from dawn until dusk and then served a shift guarding the cattle at night against rustlers and Indians.

Moreover, American cowboys were a far more diverse lot than the popular images depicting them as exclusively white men would indicate. Approximately one-third of cowboys in the American West were nonwhite, the largest group being Mexican *vaqueros*. Indeed, much of the equipment, clothing, techniques, and culture of the American cowboy derived from Mexican and Spanish traditions. This borrowing is evident in the many items associated with cowboys that bear names derived from Spanish. For example, the word *cowboy* itself is a direct translation of the Spanish term *vaquero*, while other terms such as lariat (*la reata*), chaps (*chaparejos*), and wrangler (*catallerango*) are anglicized versions of Spanish words.

African Americans comprised the second-largest group of nonwhite cowboys. The eight black cowboys shown in this 1880s photograph (**15.11**) worked on the ranch of Thomas Jones (shown standing) in Texas. One of the most famous black cowboys was Bose Ikard. Born a slave in Mississippi in 1847, he was taken to Texas where he became a skilled cowboy. Freed by the Civil War, he played a key role in the first Long Drive led by Goodnight and Loving.

Ranching held out the prospect of great profits, but ranchers faced big challenges. In the early 1870s,

15.11 African American Cowboys Despite the popular image of cowboys as white men, many were African American and Hispanic.

the invention of barbed wire soon ended open-range ranching and the long drives, as farmers enclosed their land to protect crops from cattle hooves. Cattle ranchers also clashed with other livestock enterprises, such as sheep herders, over access to water and grazing lands. These conflicts frequently led to violence and even widespread hostilities known as "range wars." Ranchers, like farmers, also were vulnerable to extremes of weather, losing cattle to scorching heat and drought and freezing cold and snow. They also suffered from rapid expansion of the ranching industry in the mid-1880s and consequent flooding of the cattle market that caused a collapse of beef prices, bankrupting many ranchers.

Fortunes Beneath the Ground: The Mining Booms

While many Western adventurers found fortune and failure in railroads, farms, and ranches, still others tried their luck underground in the many mining districts that emerged in the West. The second great Western mining boom, after California in 1849 (see Chapter 12), began in 1859 with the discovery of gold in Colorado and silver in Nevada. The Comstock Lode, as the Nevada site was called, yielded an astonishing $400 million in silver in the next 20 years.

As with most mining booms, the initial wave of small-time prospectors garnered only modest profits. The real fortunes came in the succeeding years as heavily capitalized and incorporated enterprises established mining operations to extract the ore that lay deep underground. Among the titans who

How did the reality of cowboy life differ from that presented in popular culture?

View the **Map** *Atlas Map: The New Economy of the West, 1850–1893*

accrued stupendous fortunes were four Irishmen—John Mackay, Jim Fair, James Flood, and William O'Brien—known collectively as the "Silver Kings." They bought a controlling interest in a mine many declared "spent" and virtually worthless. Yet in 1873, their miners hit the greatest silver vein of them all, the Big Bonanza, that eventually yielded more than $100 million. Most fortune seekers, however, earned modest livings as wage earners working in the mines, while others flocked to the resulting boomtown, Virginia City, to work in construction, dry goods stores, and saloons. Thousands of women in Virginia City found work in hotels, laundries, and restaurants. Unfortunately, low wages and a lack of a family network to fall back upon forced many women to become prostitutes.

Other discoveries of gold, silver, copper, lead, and zinc, followed in Colorado, Montana, Idaho, Wyoming, and the Dakotas. As in Nevada, the initial prospectors eventually gave way to larger, more sophisticated industrial operations that possessed the capital to invest in the technology needed to dig deep shafts, extract the ore from rocks, process it on site, and ship it by rail to market. Like Eastern industrialists such as Andrew Carnegie and John D. Rockefeller, these corporations often integrated their resources with the means and methods of production to maximize profits (see Chapter 16). The industrial revolution was not merely an Eastern phenomenon.

The Environmental Legacy

Economic development in the trans-Mississippi West led to countless success stories of enterprising and risk-taking individuals who established farms, ranches, mines, and small businesses, or who simply found lucrative employment in the region's many urban centers. But such development often came at the expense of the natural environment.

Mining, for example, came in many forms, but in nearly every case it left behind a badly scarred landscape. Open-pit mining of the Mahoning iron ore mine in Minnesota's Mesabi Range eliminated vast tracts of forest and created massive gouges in the land (15.12). These changes shattered the local ecosystem and choked surrounding waterways with muddy runoff water. Hydraulic mining, or the use of high-pressure water streams to wash away soil and gravel, created similar problems.

Ore processing often used toxic chemicals to separate ore from rock or other materials. Miners simply dumped them into rivers or open fields, where they eventually seeped into the water table and throughout the ecosystem.

The arrival of ever-growing numbers of humans in the West altered the delicately balanced Western ecosystems. On the Great Plains, for example, hunting and other human activity led to the eradication or near eradication of elk, bear, wolf, and buffalo populations. Conversely, settlers introduced foreign animals and plants that, lacking natural predators, spread rapidly and disrupted the balance of the ecosystem. For example, cheatgrass, accidentally introduced to the West from Asia in the 1890s, quickly spread over millions of acres, wiping out or diminishing other flora and greatly increasing the incidence of wildfires.

Farming in arid areas of the West, through the use of deep-cutting steel plows that loosened hard-packed dry soil, contributed to significant topsoil erosion. Vast herds of livestock had a similar effect as their grazing eliminated the grass whose roots held the soil in place. Likewise the practices of the timber industry led to deforestation, the loss of habitat for many animal and plant species, and without trees to shield the soil from heavy rainfall, erosion.

Some Americans decried this environmental damage, but most viewed the West through the lens of Manifest Destiny, seeing it as a place of limitless resources provided by God for the enjoyment and enrichment of human beings.

15.12 The Price of Unchecked Economic Development Western states bowed to the powerful and profitable mining industry, leaving its practices unregulated. As a result, methods such as open-pit mining led to serious environmental damage.

View the **Closer Look** *Competing Visions: Preservation versus Exploitation*

How did human settlement and economic development alter the Western environment?

Native Americans under Siege

Westward expansion benefited many Americans, but it devastated Native Americans. They faced a relentless tide of white settlers who possessed both superior weaponry and a belief that they had a higher claim to Western land. White settlers also enjoyed the support of the federal government and army. The result for Native Americans in the last third of the nineteenth century was broken treaties, devastating wars, relocation to reservations, and forced assimilation.

15.13 Promoting an Image of Indian Savagery
This 1853 sculpture by Horatio Greenough promoted the idea among white Americans that Native Americans were violent savages.

15.14 Seeing Savagery
Greenough's image became so widely known that a dime novel artist easily adapted it to a Daniel Boone story.

Mounting Problems for Native Americans

In 1851, as it became clear that the traditional government policy of simply forcing tribes into the West was no longer viable because of increased white migration into the region, Congress passed the Indian Appropriations Act. It set aside vast tracts of the Oklahoma Territory as reservations for dozens of Native American tribes. That same year the U.S. government, the Sioux, and other Plains tribes signed the first Treaty of Fort Laramie. In exchange for declaring nearly all of the central and northern Great Plains off limits to white settlement, the tribes agreed to allow whites to pass unmolested along the Oregon Trail as they moved westward. But the lasting peace that government officials and tribal leaders hoped the treaty would secure did not materialize. Tension and violence between white settlers and Native American tribes only increased in the coming years.

One of the most serious problems Native Americans faced in resisting Euro-American incursion onto their lands was the racism of white Americans that characterized Indians as backward, pagan, violent savages who lacked a rightful claim to the lands they occupied. As *Competing Visions: Inevitable Progress or Unjust Invasion?* makes clear, many Americans believed their own culture was vastly superior and viewed Native Americans as obstacles to national progress that must be removed. These notions originated in the colonial period, but greater contact and conflict between whites and Indians after 1850 led to a proliferation of largely negative depictions of Native Americans in newspapers, magazines, songs, plays, and works of art like *The Rescue,* by sculptor Horatio Greenough (**15.13**). Commissioned by the federal government and placed at the entrance to the U.S. Capitol in 1853, the scene drew on the many sensationalized stories and paintings of white settlers, especially women, being kidnapped, raped, and murdered by Native Americans. But Greenough departed from the traditional depictions and introduced a towering, dominant white settler. Note the contrasts in the men's size, demeanor, and clothing. "I have endeavoured," Greenough explained, "to convey the idea of the triumph of the whites over the savage tribes." By 1874, the scene had merged with the life of the famous pioneer and icon of frontier masculinity, Daniel Boone (**15.14**). Both images proclaim Indian savagery and justify white domination, a message that eventually resulted in the sculpture's removal from public view in 1958.

Competing Visions

INEVITABLE PROGRESS OR UNJUST INVASION?

THE GREAT WEST

As more and more Euro-Americans moved westward in search of land and opportunity, they came into conflict with the region's Native American inhabitants. As you read these documents from 1877, the first by an Englishman William Blackmore and the second by the famous Sioux Chief, Sitting Bull, consider the sharply different ideas expressed over which group had the higher claim to the land and which culture brought a more moral and enlightened notion of how to treat it. How does Blackmore make the extinction of Native Americans seem natural and inevitable? What message does this notion convey to white Americans? How does Sitting Bull express the Native American vision of nature and access to resources? How does he criticize the vision of whites like Blackmore?

William Blackmore, Introduction to Richard Irving Dodge, *The Plains of the Great West and Their Inhabitants* (1877)

All authorities who have investigated the subject are unanimous in predicting that the Red Men are a doomed race. The … Indians will as surely disappear before the progress of the more energetic and aggressive Anglo Saxon, as sure as the snows of winter melt away before the summer sun.

But sad as the fate of the Red Man is, yet, even as philanthropists, we must not forget that, under what appear to be one of immutable laws of progress, the savage is giving place to a higher and more civilized race. Three hundred thousand Red Men at the present time require the occupation of an entire continent as large as Europe, in order that they may obtain an uncertain and scanty subsistence by the chase. Ought we, then, to regret if in the course of a few generations their wigwams, tepees, and mud lodges, rarely numbering more than one hundred in a village, are replaced by new cities of the West, each equaling, perhaps, in magnificence, in stately structures, and population (exceeding that of all the Indians), either in St. Louis or Chicago? Or if in supplanting less than 300,000 wandering, debased, and half-naked savages, we can people the self-same district with a population of many tens of millions of many prosperous and highly civilized whites?

. . . in a few years the only reminiscence of the Red Men will be the preservation of the names of some of the extinct tribes and dead chiefs in the nomenclature of the leading cities, counties, and States of the Great West.

Sitting Bull, Speech at the Powder River Council, 1877

Behold, my friends, the spring is come; the earth has gladly received the embraces of the sun, and we shall soon see the results of their love! Every seed is awakened, and all animal life. It is through this mysterious power that we too have our being, and we therefore yield to our neighbors, even to our animal neighbors, the same right as ourselves to inhabit this vast land.

Yet hear me, friends! we have now to deal with another people, small and feeble when our forefathers first met with them, but now great and overbearing. Strangely enough, they have a mind to till the soil, and the love of possessions is a disease in them. These people have made many rules that the rich may break, but the poor may not! … They claim this mother of ours, the Earth, for their own use, and fence their neighbors away from her, and deface her with their buildings and their refuse. They compel her to produce out of season, and when sterile she is made to take medicine in order to produce again. All this is sacrilege.

This nation [of whites] is like a spring freshet; it overruns its banks and destroys all who are in its path.

We cannot dwell side by side. Only seven years ago we made a treaty by which we were assured that the buffalo country should be left to us forever. Now they threaten to take that from us also. My brothers, shall we submit? or shall we say to them: 'First kill me, before you can take possession of my fatherland!'

View the **Map** *Atlas Map: Native Americans, 1850–1896*

Why did many white Americans believe they had a right to take lands inhabited by Native Americans?

> "Women and children were killed and scalped, children shot at their mothers' breasts, and all the bodies mutilated in the most horrible manner. . . . Colonel J. M. Chivington all the time inciting his troops to their diabolical outrages."
>
> MAJOR EDWARD WYNKOOP, testimony before congressional committee investigating the Sand Creek Massacre

White hostility to Native Americans shaped government policy, especially when it came to signing and honoring treaties. Invariably, it seemed, federal officials negotiated treaties with tribes that promised to permanently fix the boundaries of their hunting grounds and places of habitation, only to find soon thereafter that whites, hungry for land, had begun settling there. Rather than enforce the terms of the treaty and force the removal of white settlers, the government inevitably revised the treaty to further shrink designated Native American lands.

This combination of white settlers' desire for land and disregard for Native Americans' rights, and the efforts of Native Americans to resist white encroachment, led to repeated outbreaks of violence. One of the worst incidents was the Sand Creek Massacre. On November 29, 1864, angered by sporadic attacks on settlers by Native American tribes in Colorado, a military outfit under Colonel John M Chivington raided a peaceful encampment of 800 Cheyenne at Sand Creek. With most of the Cheyenne men off hunting, Chivington's force slaughtered more than 200 Indians, mostly defenseless women and children, mutilated their bodies, and returned to Denver with their scalps.

Native Americans also confronted epidemics of diseases such as smallpox and measles—diseases that they possessed little or no resistance to. While the worst devastation had taken place in previous centuries during initial European contact (see Chapter 1), epidemics continued to kill thousands. For example, a smallpox outbreak in the Pacific Northwest in 1862 killed some 12,000 Indians. The widespread abuse of alcohol, a commodity obtained

15.15 Evidence of Extermination This mountain of buffalo skulls gathered by a fertilizer company attests to the scale of wanton killing of buffalo in the 1870s and 1880s.

How did negative stereotypes of Native Americans influence government policy?

View the **Closer Look** Railroad and Buffalo

through trade with whites, further compromised Native American health.

Additionally, long-standing animosities among tribes prevented Native Americans from developing a united front against the U.S. Army. White officials took advantage of these divisions to obtain help from one tribe, in the form of guides and even soldiers, against another. Disunity *within* tribes also contributed to this problem, as individual bands guarded their autonomy and resisted the idea of centralized tribal authority. For example, in 1863 leaders of the Nez Perce tribe split over whether to sign a treaty that would confine them to a reservation.

The Plains tribes' dependence on the buffalo left them particularly vulnerable in the 1870s. Railroad companies, disdainful of the large herds that occasionally disrupted the passage of trains, hired gunmen to kill buffalo. Entrepreneurs made buffalo robes fashionable in the East, thereby encouraging hunters to kill still more buffalo. The army soon recognized the strategic value of wiping out the great herds to undermine the independence of the Plains tribes and force them to stay on reservation lands. The scale of extermination was staggering. In this photograph (**15.15**), workers at the Michigan Carbon Works prepare thousands of buffalo skulls for processing into fertilizer, glue, and other products. The buffalo population, estimated at 30 million in 1800, plunged to only a few thousand by the early 1880s creating a crisis for the Plains Indians who depended on them.

The technological disparity between Indians and white settlers left the latter at a great disadvantage. Euro-American settlers and soldiers alike were heavily armed with modern rifles. The army also had early machine guns (called Gatling guns) and heavy artillery. While many Native American tribes had long ago acquired firearms, they never produced guns and ammunition and remained dependent on whites for them. The telegraph also allowed the army to communicate over great distances about troop movements and Native American military activity, and request supplies and reinforcements.

Wars on the Plains

Despite its lack of commitment to honoring them, the federal government nonetheless signed many treaties in the late 1860s hoping to bring peace to the West and allow continued settlement by whites. Treaties were drawn up and signed with the Apache, Cheyenne, and Arapaho in 1865, the Kiowa, Comanche, and Apache in 1867 (the Medicine Lodge Treaty), and the Sioux (the second Fort Laramie Treaty) in 1868. The latter treaty ended Red Cloud's War (1866–1868), a conflict that erupted when the army announced plans to build forts along the Bozeman Trail in the Wyoming and Montana territories to protect white migrants drawn by the discovery of gold in Montana. It guaranteed to the Sioux ownership of the Black Hills and land and hunting rights in South Dakota, Wyoming, and Montana. It also explicitly barred white people from these lands. "From this day forward all war between the parties to this agreement shall forever cease," declared the treaty in words that would soon prove false. "The government of the United States desires peace, and its honor is hereby pledged to keep it."

Despite these measures, continued violation of treaties by white settlers who ventured onto Indian lands and bands of Indians who refused to accept confinement on reservation lands led to increased bloodshed. The Red River War broke out in 1874 on the southern plains in present-day Texas, Oklahoma, and Kansas when bands of Kiowa, Comanche, southern Cheyenne, and southern Arapaho, angered over the federal government's failure to uphold its obligation to provide adequate supplies and keep whites off the reservation land (the army actually organized buffalo hunting parties that devastated local herds), left the reservation and raided white settlements. Led by General Philip Sheridan, the army crushed the rebellion by the spring of 1875, thereby ending Native American resistance on the southern plains.

By then the primary conflict had shifted to the northern plains. The discovery of gold in the Black Hills of South Dakota in 1874 touched off a flood of white fortune seekers into the region that was indisputably (as stipulated in the 1868 Fort Laramie Treaty) territory granted exclusively to Native American tribes. Rather than keep white trespassers out, however, the federal government demanded the Sioux vacate their Red River hunting grounds and return to their reservations. When the tribes refused to comply, the army launched an offensive.

In the late spring 1876, the Seventh Cavalry, led by a young and vainglorious lieutenant colonel named George Armstrong Custer, closed in on a large band of Cheyenne, Sioux, and Arapaho warriors, including the well-known Crazy Horse and Sitting Bull, near the Little Bighorn River in

Read the **Document** *Chief Red Cloud's Speech*

How did the dependence of the Plains Indians on the buffalo weaken their ability to resist the loss of their lands?

Montana. Eager to earn fame and believing there were only a few hundred Indian warriors when in fact the number was closer to 2,000, Custer attacked before the rest of the army (and other officers who might overshadow him) arrived. The **Battle of Little Bighorn** quickly disintegrated into one of the most devastating defeats ever suffered by the U.S. military as Custer and more than 250 of his men were killed.

Although the battle was an overwhelming triumph for the Sioux, Cheyenne, and Arapaho, it quickly proved a hollow victory. As this cartoon (**15.16**) published in the *New York Graphic* a few weeks after the battle demonstrates, the Eastern media ignored Custer's blundering and instead depicted him and his men as valiant victims and demanded vengeance. Note the artist's blunt depiction of Indians as savage, semi-animal beings in stark contrast to the two white soldiers, one a heroic victim and the other a coolheaded executioner. The caption, "The Right Way to Dispose of Sitting Bull and His Braves—What the Country Expects of General Sheridan," was a not-so-subtle assertion of the popular belief that the government was showing too much leniency toward Native Americans who resisted white expansion. Responding to this pressure, the government expanded military action in the Black Hills and forced the Sioux and other defiant tribes onto reservations.

15.16 The Negative Fallout from Little Bighorn
After the Sioux, Cheyenne, and Arapaho Indians defeated Custer and the Seventh Cavalry in the Battle of Little Bighorn, negative press coverage hardened white attitudes toward Native Americans. This image appeared in the *New York Graphic* (August 15, 1876) with the caption, "The Right Way to Dispose of Sitting Bull and His Braves—What the Country Expects of General Sheridan."

War and Conflict in the Far West

Farther west, native tribes encountered similar problems. During the last third of the nineteenth century, the states and territories west of the Rockies also were growing. The mining and railroad industries, the economic centerpieces of that

How did the victory over Custer and his men ultimately prove costly to the Plains Indians?

region, required a great deal of land—land long occupied by Native Americans. Just as on the Great Plains, the tribes on the West Coast and in the intermountain West faced an encroaching white population that considered the land theirs for the taking.

In 1876, following the massacre of Custer and the Seventh Cavalry, army and government officials increased pressure on tribes to move to reservations. One such group targeted was a portion of the Nez Perce tribe that lived on the northwestern plateau of Idaho, Oregon, and Washington. In 1863, most of the Nez Perce had agreed to move onto a reservation, but about a quarter had refused. Led by Chief Joseph, about 750 Nez Perce (500 of them women, children, and elderly non-combatants) fled the region to escape the army. Over the ensuing four months, they engaged in an epic flight of 1,400 miles, hoping to cross into Canada. Despite their small numbers and dwindling supplies, they defeated the army in several battles and came within 40 miles of the Canadian border before they were forced to surrender to the army and to life on a reservation.

Similar scenes of final military resistance played out in the Southwest. An Apache warrior named Geronimo had emerged in the 1860s and 1870s as a fearless opponent to encroaching Euro-American and Mexican settlers. Captured in 1874, Geronimo and some 4,000 Apaches were sent to a reservation at San Carlos, Arizona. The grim life on the reservation led him to escape and resume his campaign of resistance. He surrendered in 1884, but in 1885 and again in 1886, Geronimo escaped with a few warriors and their families and eluded capture for months. These escapades added to his already legendary status, but he eventually surrendered for good in 1886, ending the last significant Native American resistance.

In the 1880s and 1890s resistance to exploitation and abuse also erupted in the Southwest among Hispanos (descendants of Spanish colonists) and Mexicans. Euro-American settlers who arrived in New Mexico in the mid-nineteenth century eventually gave rise to a powerful ruling class of politicians, landowners, and ranchers. Many allied themselves with powerful gangs that provided protection and intimidated (and sometimes killed) their rivals. Poor Hispano and Mexican farmers often bore the brunt of these ruling Euro-Americans' ruthless tactics and hunger for land. When officials began to sell off to speculators and ranchers what had long been used as common grazing lands, the poor farmers resisted. The most famous of these resistors were *Las Gorras Blancas*, or The White Caps, a secret militant vigilante group of Mexican men who in the late 1880s and early 1890s wore white masks and cut fences on lands taken over by speculators. They also destroyed railroad bridges, buildings, and crops.

In Pursuit of a Solution

While most Americans expressed little concern over the fate of Native Americans in the West, a few did protest. One of the first was Helen Hunt Jackson. Inspired by an 1879 lecture by Susette La Flesche and her uncle, Chief Standing Bear, relating the plight of the Ponca tribe to an audience in Connecticut, she began speaking and lobbying on behalf of Native Americans. In 1881, she published *A Century of Dishonor*, a book that chronicled in searing detail the misguided and murderous treatment of Native Americans by the U.S. government. The book prompted Congress to appoint a commission to study Indian affairs and seek a new and more humane policy.

> **"Hear me, my chiefs! I am tired. My heart is sick and sad. From where the sun now stands, I will fight no more forever."**
>
> CHIEF JOSEPH, shortly after his surrender in 1877

Another influential reformer garnered a wide audience as an authentic spokesperson for the Native Americans. Sarah Winnemucca, the granddaughter of a Northern Paiute chief, had received some education from white families in Nevada and California and worked as a translator for the army. In the late 1870s, her lectures in the East demanding more humane treatment of the Paiutes and other tribes brought her to the attention of reformers. Winnemucca tried to gain credibility among whites by presenting herself as an "Indian Princess," an image firmly established in American popular

Read the **Document** *Helen Hunt Jackson, from "A Century of Dishonor" (1881)*

Why did Native Americans resist the government's demand that they settle on reservations?

culture by the mid-nineteenth century, notably in the story of Pocahontas (see Chapter 2). In her posed portrait (**15.17**), hardly anything in her costume, especially the crown and bag embroidered with a cupid and bow and arrow, resembles traditional Paiute clothing and jewelry. Nonetheless, in an era when the political and social opinions of women, especially Native American women, were largely ignored, Winnemucca's strategy brought extensive and respectful press coverage of her speeches and eventually her book, *Life Among the Paiutes: Their Wrongs and Claims* (1883). "In the history of the Indians," wrote one reporter in 1885, "she and Pocahontas will be the principal female characters."

Both Jackson and Winnemucca promoted education for Native Americans, but with different goals in mind. Jackson represented the reformers who believed it the duty of the government to elevate Native Americans from "savagery" by educating and assimilating them into white Euro-American society. In particular they advocated the establishment of boarding schools for Indian children and the eventual dissolution of reservations (see *Choices and Consequences: Forced Assimilation Versus Cultural Preservation*). In contrast, Winnemucca believed in formal education, but not at the expense of eliminating Native American culture. She believed that Indian children could become educated and productive Americans, while retaining the core of their culture and traditions.

Jackson's ideas prevailed among reform-minded legislators in Congress concerned about the plight of Native Americans, especially Senator Henry L. Dawes. In 1887, Congress passed the **Dawes Severalty Act** to break up the reservations

15.17 Speaking Out for Native-American Rights Sarah Winnemucca, a member of the Paiute tribe in California, drew attention to the injustices being suffered by Native Americans through a speaking tour of the Eastern United States and the publication of a book.

> "For shame! For shame! You dare to cry out Liberty, when you hold us in places against our will, driving us from place to place as if we were beasts."
>
> SARAH WINNEMUCCA, *Life Among the Paiutes: Their Wrongs and Claims* (1883)

and assimilate Native Americans into the dominant white Christian American culture. The plan offered Native American heads of household allotments of 160 acres of reservation land (with smaller amounts going to those unmarried or under age 18) to encourage them to become independent family farmers. Remaining reservation lands would be sold off and the profits set aside for tools and education. Native Americans who accepted these terms could apply for U.S. citizenship. To prevent speculators from defrauding Indians, land allotments would be held in trust for 25 years before full ownership was conferred.

The Dawes Severalty Act (and subsequent related laws) was born of high ideals and good intentions, but it proved devastating to the Native Americans it was intended to help. The program was rife with flaws, beginning with the allotment of land that was often of poor quality, making successful farming difficult if not impossible. It also included restrictions on

Why did reformers like Dawes believe the break up of reservations would benefit Native Americans?

Read the Document *Autobiographical Narrative by Zitkala-Sa on Her First Days at Boarding School in Indiana (1900)*

Choices and Consequences

FORCED ASSIMILATION VERSUS CULTURAL PRESERVATION

The Dawes Severalty Act of 1887 stipulated that revenue generated from the sale of reservation lands be applied to the education of Native American children. As with the land allotment plan, the principal motivation of people like Dawes and reformer Helen Hunt Jackson was to assimilate Indians into American society, which they believed would be facilitated by providing vocational training to enhance their job prospects. But the act did not specify what kind of education ought to be provided, and so Congress and the Bureau of Indian Affairs faced a choice.

Choices

1 Establish reservation-based schools offering a traditional public school curriculum, while allowing Native Americans to maintain their culture and language.

2 Establish reservation-based schools offering a traditional public school curriculum, while requiring a higher degree of assimilation (especially learning English).

3 Establish off-reservation boarding schools committed to eliminating all vestiges of Native American culture.

Decision

The government chose to establish off-reservation boarding schools. The model was the Carlisle Indian Industrial School in Carlisle, Pennsylvania. Established in 1879, it operated on the simple, but brutal principle of "kill the Indian, save the man." As the "before and after" photographs indicate, Native American children sent to boarding schools were required to cut their hair, wear American clothing, take an American name, and speak only English. Some schools made conversion to Christianity a top priority.

Consequences

Removal from families and fellow Native Americans on their reservations caused many children to suffer psychological trauma. Many also suffered from physical abuse, malnutrition, and poor health care. About one in seven ran away, and many committed suicide. Still, by 1902, 25 federally funded boarding schools, and many more private ones, operated in 15 states with 6,000 students.

Continuing Controversies

What was the long-term impact of the boarding schools? Along with the trauma inflicted on generations of children, it hastened the demise of Native American culture, including the disappearance or near disappearance of many languages. Native American groups have filed lawsuits against the government and the churches that ran the schools and demanded formal apologies.

Before-and-after photos of Chiricahua Apache children at the Carlisle Boarding School, circa 1890.

▶ **Read** the **Document** *Secretary of Interior's Congressional Report on Indian Affairs (1887)*

What assumptions about Native American culture influenced the boarding school program?

hunting, further limiting options for participants. Despite safeguards, white speculators and scammers found ways to con Native Americans out of their allotted land long before the 25-year term. The act also allowed, as indicated by the poster (**15.18**), the government to sell land deemed "surplus" to white settlers. This poster touts the high quality of the estimated 350,000 acres being offered for sale in 1910. As the map (**15.19**) shows, by the time the Dawes Act was replaced in 1934, two-thirds of Native American reservation land had been lost.

15.18 Selling off Reservation Lands
This advertisement issued by the federal government in 1911 vividly illustrates the Dawes Severalty Act in action as it exuberantly proclaims a sale of 350,000 acres of Indian land.

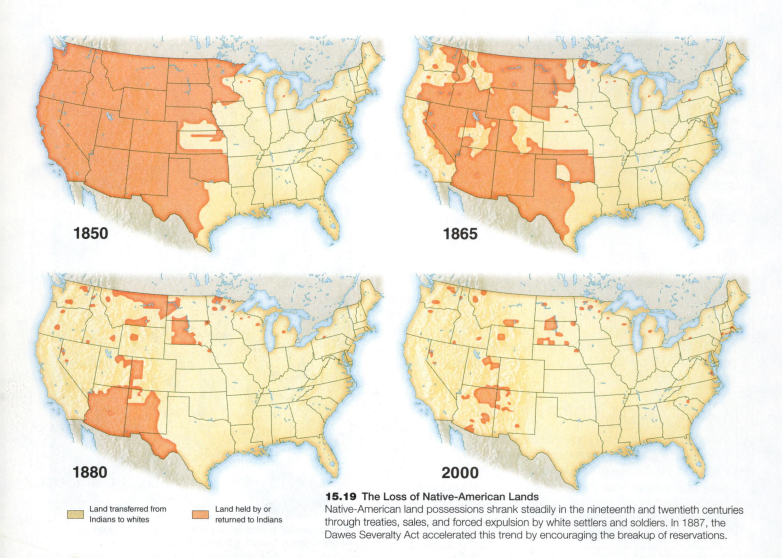

1850

1865

1880

2000

15.19 The Loss of Native-American Lands
Native-American land possessions shrank steadily in the nineteenth and twentieth centuries through treaties, sales, and forced expulsion by white settlers and soldiers. In 1887, the Dawes Severalty Act accelerated this trend by encouraging the breakup of reservations.

Land transferred from Indians to whites

Land held by or returned to Indians

How did the Dawes Act play a key role in the loss of Native American land?

Resistance and Romanticism

The surrender of Geronimo in 1886 symbolized the end of significant armed resistance by Native Americans to the Euro-American settlement of the trans-Mississippi West. Nonetheless, a revival movement called the Ghost Dance, offered one final chance to reverse the fortunes of Native Americans. When that effort was brutally crushed by the army at a place called Wounded Knee, Native Americans turned to more subtle and enduring efforts to preserve their tribes, families, and culture.

At the same time, white Americans continued to fashion a pleasing image of the West as a place of adventure, heroism, individualism, and opportunity. This image found its way into art, literature, music, and popular culture in the twentieth century. Yet historians and activists have offered a corrective to this romantic image that takes into account the experiences of Native Americans, Mexicans, and women, and the impact on the environment.

Persecution and Persistence

The last major form of resistance to the Euro-American conquest of the West emerged in the late 1880s. The Ghost Dance movement originated in the 1870s, but did not become widely popular until a Northern Paiute shaman named Wovoka began preaching a message of Native American revival based on a vision he had experienced during a total eclipse of the sun in 1889. In this vision, which he related to his followers, a great flood scoured the land clean of all white settlers, leaving behind Indians who had remained true to traditional teachings and a renewed herd of buffalo. Wovoka told his followers to perform the Ghost Dance, a ritual ceremony where participants donned special shirts and danced in a circle until brought to an ecstatic state that they believed drew to them the spirits of ancestors who would protect them from the white man's bullets.

The hopeful message of the Ghost Dance spread rapidly among Native Americans from the Rocky Mountains to the Great Plains, alarming federal officials who feared it contained the seeds of rebellion. The director of the Pine Ridge Reservation in South Dakota ordered Sitting Bull arrested. When he resisted, the police shot him dead. Two weeks later, on December 29, 1890 the army confronted about 300 Sioux Ghost Dancers at Wounded Knee Creek in South Dakota. When one of the Indians accidentally fired his gun, the soldiers attacked and massacred more than 200. This photograph (**15.20**), "The Medicine Man Taken at Wounded Knee, S.D.," conveyed the brutality of the event. The date of January 1, 1891, on the photograph indicates that bodies were left unattended for days before being interred in a mass grave. Note the rifle placed on the body by a soldier, so that the photographer could present an image of a hostile Indian. It was not the bloodiest clash between Native Americans and the U.S. Army, but the **Wounded Knee Massacre** symbolized the brutality associated with the conquest of the West.

The end of armed conflict did not mean an end to resistance for Native Americans. In the coming

15.20 Massacre at Wounded Knee In an incident that symbolized American brutality toward Native Americans, soldiers killed between 200 and 300 Sioux at Wounded Knee, South Dakota, after a tense standoff over the Ghost Dance movement.

Read the **Document** *Accounts of the Wounded Knee Massacre*

Why was Wovoka's message so appealing to Indians and so frightening to military officials?

decades, as they struggled with the loss of tribal lands, the cultural erosion caused by the boarding schools, and high levels of poverty and alcoholism, Native Americans found ways to preserve their culture, including languages, artistic forms, and religious beliefs. They did so by maintaining traditions within families and establishing informal methods of passing on traditions from one generation to the next. As a result, when a Native American rights movement emerged in the 1960s and 1970s, it included a commitment to reaffirming and strengthening traditional Native American cultures.

Creating Mythical Heroes and Images

The story of the American West has long been the object of romanticism and myth. The image of the West as a place of high adventure, heroism, rugged individualism, and endless opportunity developed with the first enthusiastic reports of Western explorers such as Lewis and Clarke (see Chapter 7). But this image really flourished after 1850 as more migrants and journalists headed west and sent back to the East countless letters and dispatches describing the West's wide-open lands, roaring rivers, and majestic mountains, as well as the heroic struggles of pioneers against weather and hostile Indians. Eventually writers turned to fiction, especially a new genre known as the "dime novel."

The first Western dime novels appeared in the 1860s and their subjects—characters like cowboy Deadwood Dick and his rough and ready girlfriend Calamity Jane—soon became pop heroes. So too did Buffalo Bill. Stories based on the legendary exploits of a real Western scout, buffalo hunter, and Pony Express rider named William "Buffalo Bill" Cody first appeared in a newspaper and then in dime novel form as *Buffalo Bill, King of the Border Men*. When it sold well, its author (and many imitators) wrote hundreds more Buffalo Bill stories.

Cody grew famous but he earned no royalties from the novels. To capitalize on his fame, he created in 1883 "**Buffalo Bill's Wild West**," a circus-like production that purported to show audiences the thrilling and harrowing life on the frontier, replete with huge reenactments of cattle drives and clashes between Indians and cowboys, and exhibitions of marksmanship,

cattle roping, and riding. Immensely popular, it grew more elaborate every year, eventually topping out at 400 horses and 650 cowboys, Indians, musicians, and support staff. Over time Cody added big-name stars like the famous sharpshooter Annie Oakley and even the Sioux chief Sitting Bull.

Most Americans, indeed, much of the Western world, viewed the West, through Buffalo Bill's performances, as a place of heroism, optimism, gallantry, and success (see *Images as History: Annie Oakley*).

The West in Art and Literature

Western imagery and ideas also shaped American art and literature. Mark Twain, whose real name was Samuel Langhorne Clemens, emerged in the late nineteenth century as one of the first American novelists generally unaffected by European mores. Twain headed west in the early 1860s seeking adventure and wealth in Nevada's Comstock Lode mines. The result was his classic book *Roughing It* (1872). Based on his experiences of the wild life in Virginia City, Nevada, the book fit in with the evolving Western tradition of the yarn or tall tale. Twain's major works, *The Adventures of Tom Sawyer* (1876) and *The Adventures of Huckleberry Finn* (1884), were set along the earlier frontier of the Mississippi River and both contained Western themes of adventure, individualism, and a desire to escape the constraints of modern society for a purer, more authentic world. When Huck Finn sets out at the end of the book to start life anew, he heads for the West. Many subsequent writers like Owen Wister and Zane Grey popularized this vision of the West, especially the figure of the cowboy as the embodiment of American manliness, decency, courage, and common sense.

In addition to writers, artists popularized a heroic image of the West. One of the most famous was Frederic Remington. Raised in the east, Remington eventually made his way West where he worked a variety of jobs before becoming a newspaper artist covering battles between the army and Native Americans. Drawing upon earlier Western artists like George Catlin (see 15.4), he painted, drew, and sculpted vivid scenes of Western life. Most were vignettes of the lives of unknown cowboys, Native Americans, and soldiers.

Why did the West become such a popular topic in entertainment and literature?

Images as History

ANNIE OAKLEY

Two years after William Cody launched his Wild West show, he hired a woman who became one of his most celebrated performers. Born and raised not in the West, but in Ohio, Annie Oakley was a gifted sharpshooter. She had been taught to shoot at a young age and killed game to earn money for her struggling family. At age 16 she beat a professional in a sharpshooting match. She soon married the man and joined him on stage. In 1885, they joined Buffalo Bill's Wild West.

For 16 seasons Oakley thrilled audiences with her marksmanship. She shot cigarettes from her husband's mouth and coins from his fingers. She blasted an endless succession of glass balls thrown in the air.

She hit a target behind her by holding a mirror in one hand and shooting over her shoulder with the other. No one could match the "peerless lady wing shot."

But as this photograph and virtually every one she posed for show, an essential part of Oakley's appeal lay in her image as an ideal frontier woman who combined Victorian femininity and rugged, almost masculine, strength.

Oakley's adoring public was not put off by her entry into the traditionally male world of guns and horses because she presented a pleasing and reassuring feminine persona. In so doing Annie Oakley, the woman from Ohio, played a key role in shaping the evolving mythical image Americans held of the Old West.

Oakley's dual image as both feminine and tough is captured in her facial expression. In all of her studio portraits, she presents herself as beautiful and composed, but unsmiling, to emphasize her grit and fearlessness.

While Oakley radiated a beguiling feminine charm (she entered the show ring skipping and blowing kisses to the audience), this hand-on-hip pose was masculine and expressive of the manly self-assuredness that audiences associated with cowboys.

Conforming to Victorian mores about proper behavior for women, Oakley always wore a dress and rode side saddle.

Her many medals were intended to lend her authenticity, as if to say that although she was a performer, her skills as a shooter were real.

Oakley's outfit was modeled on the cowboy's, but with exceptions to emphasize her femininity. Unlike the oblong cowboy hat, hers had a broad round brim. She set it on the back of her head to reveal her face and ladylike curls.

She always appeared with a gun, a central icon of how Americans in the late nineteenth century understood the West. It was a symbol they associated almost entirely with men.

Annie Oakley poses for one of her many studio portraits depicting an idealized image of a frontier woman.

What traits did Annie Oakley portray to present an ideal woman of the West?

One exception was Lt. Col. George A. Custer, whom Remington helped make into a hero after the Battle of Little Bighorn. Charles Russell, a cowboy-turned-artist, also emerged as a leader of Western art, producing works that often depicted more sensational and imaginative scenes than Remington's. Both men played a central role in creating the iconic image of the American cowboy. Russell's 1897 painting (**15.21**) is typical of most depictions, showing skilled and fearless cowboys roping a bull.

Historians Reinterpret the American West

Another key influence on the way Americans came to develop a particular image of the West was the work of historian Frederick Jackson Turner. In 1893, he published an essay, "The Significance of the Frontier in American History," that focused on a recent announcement by the Census Bureau (based on data compiled from the 1890 census) that the American frontier was "closed," that is, the United States was essentially "settled" from coast to coast. He argued in what historians came to call the **Frontier Thesis** that the frontier had played a vital role in shaping the American character and American institutions. The frontier's importance began with the first settlers along the Eastern seaboard during the colonial period and continued in every succeeding generation as it pushed farther and farther west. This seemingly endless supply of land created widespread opportunity for upward mobility. The demands of the frontier, Turner argued, forced Americans to develop a spirit of rugged individualism and innovation. Frontier life also fostered values such as equality and democracy because success was determined not by one's background but rather by one's ability to work hard, sacrifice, and command the respect of others.

Turner's thesis proved enormously influential. Generations of Western historians based their writing and research on his ideas about the frontier. His influence also spread well beyond Western history—indeed, well beyond the study of history itself. Some American politicians and policy makers reacted to the apparent closing of the frontier in the 1890s by embracing imperialism to acquire new lands and markets that might make up for the absence of new places to conquer within the United States (see Chapter 19).

During the second half of the twentieth century, a new generation of historians challenged Turner's thesis. One of the leading figures in this "new Western history" movement is Patricia Nelson Limerick who in 1987 published *The Legacy of Conquest: The Unbroken Past of the American West*. Just as Turner's article was a product of the optimism and anxiety of late-nineteenth-century American society, Limerick's book offered an interpretation that reflected the fact that she was a woman raised in the 1960s, a time of social ferment, when historians began to focus more on racial, ethnic, and gender issues. Consequently she brought a far more critical eye to her study of the West than Turner.

While Turner had depicted white Euro-American settlers as triumphing over such "obstacles" as a stubborn landscape and "a fierce race of savages;" historians like Limerick present a far more complicated story. They emphasize, for example, that Native Americans had inhabited the West for thousands of years before the arrival of Europeans and thus had a legitimate claim to the land. Viewed from this perspective, the story of westward migration was one of violence, exploitation, and conquest. New Western historians also stress the diversity of the West, seeing it as a meeting place of Native Americans, Euro-Americans, immigrants from Europe and Asia, African Americans, Mexicans, and Hispanos who contributed to and shaped a Western

15.21 The Making of an American Icon
Artists such as Charles Russell, who painted this scene, *The Herd Quitters,* in 1897, played a central role in promoting the cowboy as a symbol of the West and the West as a place of heroism, daring, and manly individualism.

How have new Western historians changed the way many Americans understand the history of the West?

Read the Document *Frederick Jackson Turner, The Significance of the Frontier in American History (1893)*

15.22 Reinterpreting the History of the West
After more than 125 years of commemorating only Custer and his men, in 2003, the site of the Battle of Little Bighorn added an Indian Memorial to honor the Native Americans who fell there.

culture that was not simply "white." Finally, these historians study the environmental impact of westward economic development.

This new way of seeing the history of the West in recent years has had an impact beyond the history books. Hollywood films on Western themes also began to change. In the classic Western epics of the 1940s and 1950s, cowboys were heroes, fighting Indians who terrorized innocent white settlers. Beginning in the 1990s, filmmakers began to present a more complicated view of westward settlement, lawlessness, and white-Indian conflict. *Dances with Wolves* (1990), for example, presented Native Americans in sympathetic terms. *Unforgiven* (1992) presented the West as a place of violence, lawlessness, failure, desperation, and corruption, where the line between good and evil is not at all clear. Many more such films followed.

This reassessment of the West's history has also changed the way museums and public memorials present key chapters in American history. Nowhere is this more apparent than at the site of the 1876 Battle of Little Bighorn. For more than a century following the battle, the site memorialized Custer and his men as heroic martyrs who died in the cause of Western settlement. Named the Custer Battlefield National Cemetery it featured a memorial to the Seventh Cavalry and some Indian scouts on Last Stand Hill. Native Americans, who, of course, won the battle, were ignored. But the influence of new Western history and Native American activism led to the renaming in 1991 of the site as the Little Bighorn Battlefield National Monument and in 2003 the unveiling of the Native American memorial shown here (**15.22**). Only 100 yards from the Seventh Cavalry monument, it features three bronze outline sculptures representing Sioux, Cheyenne, and Arapaho warriors who participated in the battle. Its official theme is "Peace through Unity," but it also represents a growing awareness that for far too long Americans relied on an incomplete and overly simplistic understanding of the history of the American West.

Why are Native Americans so committed to reshaping the interpretation of historic sites like Little Bighorn?

1862–1866

Homestead and Pacific Railway acts passed
The first distributes millions of free land to settlers; the second starts construction of the transcontinental railroad

George Perkins Marsh publishes *Man and Nature*
A widely read book that warns of environmental damage due to unrestricted exploitation of western resources

Sand Creek Massacre
Soldiers in Colorado massacre two hundred Indians

1866–1867

First "Long Drive" of cattle from Texas to the Great Plains
Leads to the rapid expansion of ranching industry in the West

The Grange Movement founded by Oliver Kelley
Becomes a powerful pro-farmer political movement by 1874 in western states

1868–1874

Second Fort Laramie Treaty signed
Guarantees the Sioux ownership of the Black Hills and additional land and hunting rights in South Dakota, Wyoming, and Montana

John Gast paints *American Progress*
Widely reproduced, the painting presents an enthusiastic vision of westward expansion and Manifest Destiny.

Gold discovered in Black Hills
Leads to escalating conflict as white miners move onto land reserved to Native Americans in the Second Fort Laramie Treaty

1876–1877

The Battle of Little Bighorn
Defeat of Lt. Col. Custer and Seventh Cavalry hardens white attitudes toward Native Americans

The flight of the Nez Perce fails
Symbolizes both Native American resistance to reservation policy and its ultimate failure

CHAPTER REVIEW

Review Questions

1. What was the significance of railroad building to the West as a region and to its peoples?

2. What challenges did American farmers face in establishing successful farms in the West?

3. What significant industries, including agriculture, developed in the West, and how were they linked to the economy of the Eastern United States?

4. What critical factors led to the conquest of Native American tribes and their forced relocation to reservations?

5. Why did U.S. officials favor forced assimilation for Native Americans in the late nineteenth century? How did they implement it?

6. Why did Americans embrace a romanticized vision of the American West in the late nineteenth century? How close was this image to reality?

Key Terms

Homestead Act Passed in 1862, it provided 160 acres of free land to any settler willing to live on it and improve it for five years; promoted massive westward migration.   **440**

Transcontinental railroad A line spanning the continental United States. Congress helped the Union Pacific and Central Pacific railroads build it by providing land grants, cash incentives, and loans.   **440**

Great Plains Vast open territory stretching east to west from present-day Missouri to the Rocky Mountains, and north to south from North Dakota to Texas.   **443**

Exodusters More than twenty thousand ex-slaves who in 1879 left violence and poverty in the South to take up farming in Kansas.   **444**

Grange Originally founded in the fall of 1867 by Oliver H. Kelley as a social and educational society for farmers, it became a major political force in the Midwest in the mid-1870s.   **449**

Long Drive The annual cattle drives of more than 1,000 miles from Texas to the Great Plains that started in 1866 and established the ranching industry in the West.   **449**

Battle of Little Bighorn Lt. Col. George A. Custer and the Seventh Cavalry are wiped out by a force of Cheyenne, Sioux, and Arapaho warriors on June 25, 1876; hardens white attitudes toward Native Americans.   **456**

Dawes Severalty Act 1887 law that started the breakup of reservations by offering Native Americans allotments of 160 acres of reservation land to encourage them to become independent farmers.   **458**

Wounded Knee Massacre U.S. soldiers open fire on a group of Sioux Indians on December 29, 1890, killing between two hundred and three hundred.   **461**

"Buffalo Bill's Wild West" A circuslike production begun in 1883 that helped create a romantic and mythological view of the West in the American imagination.   **462**

Frontier Thesis Historian Frederick Jackson Turner's 1893 theory that extolled the positive role the frontier had played in shaping the American character and consequently American institutions.   **464**

1879–1881

Exoduster movement begins
To avoid violence in the South, thousands of ex-slaves migrate to Kansas, Nebraska, and Colorado to take up homestead farming

Helen Hunt Jackson publishes *A Century of Dishonor*
Brings national attention to the brutal and dishonest treatment of Native Americans

1883–1886

William Cody launches "Buffalo Bill's Wild West"
This hugely popular traveling show romanticizes the story of westward settlement

Apache resistance leader Geronimo surrenders
Ends the last major Native American military opposition to the U.S. military

1887

Dawes Severalty Act passed
Begins breakup of reservations and promotes boarding schools to encourage farming and assimilation

1890–1893

Wounded Knee massacre
Soldiers open fire on a gathering of Sioux, killing as many as three hundred

Frederick Jackson Turner publishes his frontier thesis
Bemoans the closing of the frontier, arguing that it had exerted a major influence on American values, ideals, and institutions

MyHistoryLab Connections

Visit www.myhistorylab.com for a customized Study Plan that will help you build your knowledge of *Conflict and Conquest*.

Questions for Analysis

1. How did Congress promote westward migration and settlement?

> **Read** the **Document** Homestead Act of 1862, p. 440

2. What role did immigration play in the peopling of the trans-Mississippi West?

> **View** the **Map** Atlas Map: Immigration, p. 445

3. How did the dependence of the Plains Indians on the buffalo make them vulnerable to white settlement?

> **View** the **Closer Look** Railroad and Buffalo, p. 454

4. What was the goal of Indian boarding schools?

> **Read** the **Document** Autobiographical Narrative by Zitkala-Sa on Her First Days at Boarding School in Indiana (1900), p. 458

5. How did historians help shape the mythical image of the West?

> **Read** the **Document** Frederick Jackson Turner, The Significance of the Frontier in American History (1893), p. 464

Other Resources from This Chapter

Read the **Document**

- *Chief Seattle, Oration (1854), p. 452*
- *Chief Red Cloud's Speech, p. 455*
- *Helen Hunt Jackson, from "A Century of Dishonor" (1881), p. 457*
- *Secretary of Interior's Congressional Report on Indian Affairs (1887), p. 459*
- *Accounts of the Wounded Knee Massacre, p. 461*

View the **Closer Look**

- *Thirty-Three Horse Team Harvester, p. 448*
- *Railroad Routes, Cattle Trails, Gold and Silver Rushes, p. 449*
- *Competing Visions: Preservation versus Exploitation, p. 451*

View the **Image** Ho for Kansas!, p. 445

View the **Map**

- *Atlas Map: Western Migration, 1850–1880, p. 444*
- *Atlas Map: The New Economy of the West, 1850–1893, p. 450*
- *Atlas Map: Native Americans, 1850–1896, p. 453*

Watch the **Video** Video Lectures: "The Urban West", p. 448

((•⊷ **Hear** the **Audio File** on **myhistorylab.com**

◉⊷ **Watch** the **Video** *Critical Visions, Chapter 16*

Wonder and Woe
The Rise of Industrial America, 1865–1900

This scene of industrial discontent, *The Strike* (1886) by artist Robert Koehler, was inspired by the great railroad strike of 1877. Set in an unidentified industrial town, it captures a moment of confrontation as workers pour out of a factory to gather outside the office of their employer. Unlike most scenes of labor unrest painted or drawn in the late nineteenth century, Koehler presented these workers as sympathetic characters, painting each as an individual rather than as nondescript members of a mob. Many wear square hats popular among various skilled trades, suggesting that these are more established workers. They appear as hardworking and hard-pressed men voicing their anger to the employer, perhaps over a wage cut or layoffs, through the spokesman at the bottom of the stairs.

Yet the painting is fraught with tension and an atmosphere of impending violence. Note, for example, the worker in the foreground stooping to pick up a rock. Maybe he is doing this merely as a dramatic show of anger, but perhaps he fully intends to throw it. Note also the scene to his left where a woman tries to calm down another angry worker. Again, it is not clear that she will succeed. And what about the employer? He appears to be listening patiently to the workers' representative, but whether he will accede to their demands is unclear (his stiff, emotionless bearing suggests he will not).

The uncertainty in the painting over both what is about to happen and which side—workers or employer—is in the right illuminates a central theme in American society as it experienced rapid industrialization in the late nineteenth century. By 1900, the Industrial Revolution had transformed the United States from a predominantly agricultural nation that ranked well behind Britain, Germany, and France to the world's most formidable industrial power.

While many Americans celebrated the Industrial Revolution for the unprecedented material wealth and progress it brought, others grew disturbed by some of the grim consequences of industrialization, especially the immense power accrued by big businesses and capitalists and the growing number of workers living in squalid slums. The result of these conflicting visions was an intense debate—much of it vividly captured in Koehler's painting—over the proper role of government in regulating the economy, the rights of workers to form unions and strike for better wages and working conditions, and the impact of growing disparities of wealth on America's republican traditions.

> "This association of poverty with progress is the great enigma of our times…. It is the riddle which the Sphinx of Fate puts to our civilization, and which not to answer is to be destroyed."
>
> HENRY GEORGE, *Progress and Poverty*, 1879

The Emergence of Big Business

16.1 The Industrial Revolution by the Numbers During the second half of the nineteenth century, every area of the economy produced enormous increases in output and value. Huge population increases helped to drive industrial and farm output.

America's huge supplies of key raw materials, its rapidly growing urban workforce, and its tradition of imposing few restraints on business enabled industrialization to boom after the Civil War. The railroads quickly emerged as the first big business, followed by steel and petroleum. All three industries pioneered in establishing modern business practices, but they also drew increasing criticism as Americans worried about their extraordinary power.

Sources of the Industrial Revolution

Compared to most of Western Europe, the United States was a relative latecomer to the Industrial Revolution, which made its rise to industrial supremacy by 1900 even more astonishing. Every statistical comparison between 1860 and 1900, from factory production to railroad mileage, told the same story of phenomenal growth that saw the Gross National Product rise 171 percent (**16.1**).

Several factors combined to allow the United States to surpass all other industrialized countries by 1900. First, the nation possessed enormous quantities of two essential ingredients for rapid industrialization: raw materials and cheap labor. Vast deposits of coal in Pennsylvania, West Virginia, and Kentucky, for example, provided a seemingly inexhaustible supply of inexpensive fuel to fire steam locomotives and factory machinery. Other plentiful resources included iron, lead, copper, silver, gold, wood, cotton, and oil. Cheap labor came from two sources. Record levels of immigration (see Chapter 17) in the late nineteenth century pushed the number of foreign-born to one in five American workers (two in five in manufacturing and mining) by 1910. Millions of American-born workers also moved from rural settings to manufacturing centers in search of new opportunities. Many women and children, both immigrant and native-born, also entered the paid workforce.

		1860	1900	% Increase
	Population	31,450,000	76,212,000	142.3
	Farms	2,044,000	5,737,000	180.7
	Value of Farms	$6.64 billion	$16.60 billion	150.0
	Factories	140,500	510,000	263.0
	Value Factory Production	$1.9 billion	$13 billion	584.0
	Industrial Workers	1.3 million	5.1 million	292.3
	Patents Issued	4,589	95,573	1982.7
	Coal	20 million tons	270 million tons	1250
	Lumber	10 billion board ft.	40 billion board ft.	300
	Cotton	3.8 million bales	10.1 million bales	165.8
	Oil	500,000 barrels	45,824,000 barrels	9064.8
	Railroads	30,000 track miles	193,000 track miles	543.3
	Steel	13,000 tons	10,382,000 tons	79,761.5
	Gross National Product	$7 billion	$19 billion	171.4

How did human migration foster American industrialization?

The relentless development and adoption of new technology also furthered industrialization in the United States. Inventors flooded the U.S. Patent Office with applications, raising the number from an average of 1,000 per year in the 1850s to 20,000 per year in the 1890s.

Some notable inventors, such as George Eastman (Kodak camera), William S. Burroughs (adding machine), Isaac Singer (sewing machine), Alexander Graham Bell (telephone), and Thomas Edison (incandescent light bulb, phonograph, motion picture camera, mimeograph machine, and more) became business giants. Less well known were the many women, immigrant, and African American inventors who filed thousands of patents in this period. For example, Jan Matzeliger, an immigrant of African and Dutch heritage from South America, invented a machine that simplified the most difficult and time-consuming step in making shoes (**16.2**). Although much of shoemaking had become mechanized by the 1880s, the difficult "lasting" process—attaching the upper portion of a shoe to the sole—could be done only by hand. Matzeliger's lasting machine (patented in 1883) was a complex device, yet was easy for unskilled workers to operate, allowing manufacturers to boost production while slashing costs.

Government policy also boosted American industrialization. The federal government and the states extended substantial support to railroad projects that totaled almost 180 million acres in land grants and $500 million in loans and tax breaks (see Chapters 13 and 15). Public officials, in an argument later used to justify government support for the interstate highway system and the Internet, defended this largess by arguing that railroads generated economic growth that benefited everyone from travelers to farmers to manufacturers. High federal tariffs that raised the price of imported goods, thereby helping domestic manufacturers, also promoted industrialization.

Yet the government also facilitated industrialization by inaction. Public officials, business leaders, and conservatives subscribed to the philosophy of **laissez-faire** (French for "let do," or "leave alone"), which argued that the government should impose no restraints on business, including workers' demands for laws to regulate the hours of work, safety conditions, and wages. Government officials also ignored reformers' demands for an income tax and laws curbing cutthroat business

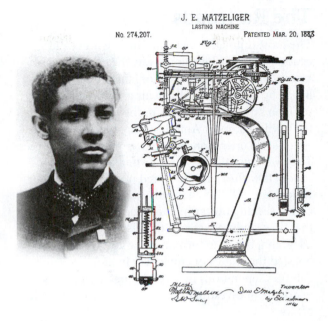

16.2 The Matzeliger Lasting Machine Jan Matzeliger's complex sewing machine wiped out jobs for skilled shoe "lasters," who had hand-stitched shoe tops to soles, but allowed for a huge increase in mechanized shoe production.

practices. As Thomas Nast's political cartoon vividly shows (**16.3**), business and government leaders argued that government interference harmed the American economy, depicted here as a woman weighed down by government-imposed burdens such as income taxes, laws (regulations), and "ideal" money (money not backed by gold). The closed shop and idle ship in the background and the vultures circling overhead all suggested these policies would kill the economy. Widespread support for laissez-faire among lawmakers left capitalists to operate in a market free of the restraints of government regulation.

16.3 Defending Laissez-Faire This 1878 cartoon warns that government interference with the economy threatens the well-being of the nation.

Read the **Document** *Thomas Edison, The Success of the Electric Light (October 1880)*

How did government officials defend the practice of making huge land grants to the railroads?

The Railroads

The most dramatic change in the late nineteenth-century industrial economy was the emergence of large corporations, business organizations established by a group of individuals and owned by people who buy shares of stock in the company. Before the Civil War, most American manufacturers were small-scale operations with fewer than 25 employees. They were usually privately owned and sold their products within a few hundred miles of where they were made. All this changed after 1865, as entrepreneurs, seeking bigger markets and greater profits that they could now reach thanks to the railroad and telegraph, began to form massive corporations that boasted thousands of employees in a single factory complex, operations in several states, and millions of dollars of investment capital raised from the sales of stock.

The original big businesses were railroads, and they played a key role in transforming the United States into an industrial power. In 1865, scores of small railroad companies operated throughout the Northeast and Midwest and, to a lesser extent, the South. Comprising 35,000 miles of track, they serviced small areas and established their own standards for things such as track gauge (the distance between the rails). Nearly all suffered from financial instability and poor management. But by 1900, this haphazard system had developed into a massive, consolidated, and integrated national railroad network of 193,000 miles dominated by just seven large corporations.

Railroads grew at such a ferocious pace because they could be built almost anywhere, creating a transportation network no longer confined to meandering rivers and expensive, slow-to-construct canals that often froze in winter. The railroad also offered another great advantage: speed. People, mail, and goods traveling by stagecoach might, on a good day, cover 50 miles. A steam locomotive pulling many times more people, mail, and goods could cover the same distance in less than two hours. And after the completion of the first trans-continental line in 1869 (see map 15.8), the railroad offered service from coast to coast.

The quicker and cheaper transportation offered by the railroad benefited the national economy. Railroads opened new areas of settlement, enticing farmers to settle on nearby land (often sold to them by the railroad), confident that they could get their produce to market. Shopkeepers, artisans, laborers, and railroad employees (one million by 1900) settled in towns that sprang up along the tracks. In turn they became consumers of finished goods brought by the railroad from Eastern manufacturers. The railroad industry also contributed to the national economy by consuming large quantities of iron, steel, coal, and wood.

Fierce competition among railroads initially led to the rapid expansion of lines. By the 1870s, many railroads tried to diminish competition by buying out rivals, leading to the creation of giant corporations such as the Pennsylvania Railroad and the New York Central Railroad. Both owned thousands of miles of track in many states, employed tens of thousands of workers, and handled millions of dollars in investment capital and revenue.

Modern Business Practices

The success of the large railroad corporations led to the modernization of business practices in two important ways. First, railroad corporations showed other types of businesses the advantages of incorporating and issuing stock. Stock sales allowed corporations to raise capital to expand the business (for example, to buy new and more efficient equipment, or a rival company). If the company earned a profit, stockholders benefited from an increase in the value of the stock (which they could sell for a profit) and sometimes by earning dividends. Stockholders played no direct role in running a company; a professional management team performed that

> "Railroad time, it appears, is to be the time of the future. And so, people will now have to marry and die by railroad time. Ministers will preach by railroad time, and banks will be required to open and close by the same time. The sun is no longer the boss of the job."
>
> *Indianapolis Sentinel, 1883*

How did railroad grants both reflect and promote national economic growth?

Watch the **Video** *Video Lecture: Mastering Time and Space: How the Railroad Changed America*

function. But stockholders also enjoyed "limited liability": If the company failed they were not liable for any of its debts or obligations; they stood to lose only their shares. By the 1870s, many companies involved in manufacturing, mining, communications, and finance had incorporated.

Second, the sudden emergence of huge railroad corporations encouraged the development of modern, sophisticated management practices. Chief among these practices was standardization. For example, in 1883, the nation's major railroads established the four time zones that are still in use today. This decision helped to combat the problem of irregular "local time" (for example, when local time in New York City was 12:00 p.m., it might be 11:55 a.m. in Philadelphia and 11:47 in Washington, D.C.) that often led to costly accidents between trains sharing a single track or crossing at a junction.

Similarly, the development of standardized equipment like couplers, signals, and brakes allowed for easier operation and maintenance of a railroad's growing fleet of rolling stock. In 1886, the railroads also established a standard gauge for track of 4 feet 8.5 inches, thereby eliminating costly delays caused by the need to transfer cargo from one train to another wherever tracks of two different gauges met. As this drawing (**16.4**) indicates, many Americans viewed standard gauge as bringing both economic and political benefits to the nation, since it promised to create both a more efficient railroad system and greater unity between the less developed South (see Chapter 14) with the rapidly industrializing North. The banner "The Last Spike of Our Commercial Union" likens the event to the 1869 completion of the transcontinental railroad.

To oversee these vast commercial operations—the largest in the world—executives of the major railroads, such as Jay Gould, Tom Scott, and Collis B. Huntington, developed complex hierarchies of superintendents, managers, and clerks and new systems of accounting, advertising, information management, and pricing. Other big businesses, such as steel, oil, manufacturing, and retailing, soon copied these organizational practices, making them the norm in most large corporations.

Rising Concern over Corporate Power

Americans greeted the astonishing spread of the railroad with mixed feelings. Many agreed with poet Walt Whitman, who celebrated the railroad

as "the modern emblem of motion and power—the pulse of the continent." They delighted in the benefits of inexpensive and speedy travel and increased access to finished goods in new mail order catalogs.

Yet many Americans worried about the larger implications of the railroad. This cartoon depicting

16.4 Celebrating the Standard Gauge, 1886
In this imagined scene Northerners and Southerners celebrate the adoption of a standard rail gauge as a measure destined to bind the country together economically.

What advantages did standardization bring to business?

16.5 Demonizing the Monopoly Americans grew increasingly worried about the rising power of railroads, and the largest were often criticized as monopolies that strangled their competition.

tions further tarnished the railroads' image and fueled concerted efforts to curb their power. Although few critics raised the issue at the time, later generations decried the railroad for its role in hastening the defeat of the Plains Indians and the near extermination of buffalo, on which they depended (see Chapter 15).

Growing anxiety and anger over the abusive practices of many large railroads eventually compelled reformers to seek tighter regulation of the industry. Given the immense power and wealth of the railroad and politicians' reluctance to regulate business, reform faced many setbacks. Farmers, bitterly opposing the high rates charged by railroads to transport and store agricultural commodities, led the first significant effort to curb laissez-faire business practices. Known as the Grange (see Chapter 15), it led a successful political movement in the 1870s to pass numerous laws regulating prices and outlawing unfair business practices.

Andrew Carnegie: Making Steel and Transforming the Corporation

Of all the new things produced by the explosion of industrial output after 1865, none was more important than steel. Much stronger than iron, steel became the essential ingredient in the transformation of America into an industrial society, allowing for the construction of the railroad and telegraph networks and tall buildings called "skyscrapers." Steel also enabled the construction of huge factories, filled with powerful machinery—made from steel, of course. Sharp, durable, and deep-cutting steel plows and mechanical reapers accelerated the commercialization of American agriculture. More accurate and powerful, and thus more deadly, weapons made of steel also altered modern warfare. Steel, in short, was as influential and revolutionary a substance in the late nineteenth century as silicon (used to make computer chips) was to become in the late twentieth.

Steel was important in still another way, for it brought to prominence the single most influential big businessman of the era, Andrew Carnegie. Carnegie's success was all the more remarkable because of his humble origins. Born in Scotland in 1836, he immigrated to America with his family at age 12. Settling in Pittsburgh they struggled to earn a living. Young Carnegie dropped out of school and worked

the Southern Pacific Railroad as a ravenous octopus (**16.5**) expressed their concern. The railroads and the fabulously wealthy men who ran them (shown in the eyes of the octopus) wielded immense power. The artist labeled the octopus a **monopoly**, a popular term to describe the control of an industry or market by one corporation. Was such unchecked power vested in the hands of so few people, worried the critics, compatible with the nation's republican principles? Many feared it was not—especially when they learned that railroad executives routinely bribed state legislators, members of Congress, and cabinet officials. Revelations of stock manipulation, price gouging of farmers and manufacturers, exploitation of workers, shoddy construction, and unsafe opera-

Why did many Americans come to see railroads as potential threats to democracy?

🔍 **View** the **Image** *Modern Colossus of (Rail) Roads (1879)*

in a textile factory where he earned just $1.20 per week. Bright and ambitious, he took night classes in accounting, taught himself telegraphy, and worked for Western Union. In 1853, Pennsylvania Railroad regional supervisor and future company president, Thomas A. Scott, hired the 17-year-old as his personal telegrapher and eventually private secretary. In this capacity, Carnegie learned every detail of the modern business practices that the railroad was developing. He also became rich by investing in railroads, factories, and, increasingly, the iron and steel industries.

In 1870, while running a successful company that built steel bridges, Carnegie decided to move entirely to steel production. He built his own steel works and, drawing on his knowledge of railroad management, followed obsessively one fundamental business principle: reducing production costs to the lowest possible level.

To achieve this goal, Carnegie hired the brightest executives, accountants, managers, scientists, and engineers. He also invested heavily in the latest technology. He was the first U.S. steelmaker to invest in the breakthrough Bessemer-Kelly process, a method of making exceptionally strong steel quickly and at low cost (in part due to reducing the need for skilled metalworkers).

Carnegie's focus on cost control led him to pioneer what is known as **vertical integration**, the organization of a business by which one company controls all the main phases of production, from acquiring raw materials to retailing the finished product. Other industrial magnates who came to dominate their industries opted for a **horizontal integration**, a model where they bought out many companies producing the same product to eliminate competition and achieve greater efficiency (**16.6**). To provide a steady supply of cheap coal, iron, and other essential raw materials that steel production depended on, Carnegie bought mines, smelting operations, railroads, and ships.

Finally, Carnegie pursued cutthroat practices to battle rival steel producers. Carnegie slashed his prices to levels that bankrupted his competitors, allowing him to buy them out and gain a greater share of the market. Like many other industrialists, he also signed secret deals with railroads, securing lower transportation rates for his steel than his competitors charged. Most of these tactics were legal at that time, but many critics considered them abusive.

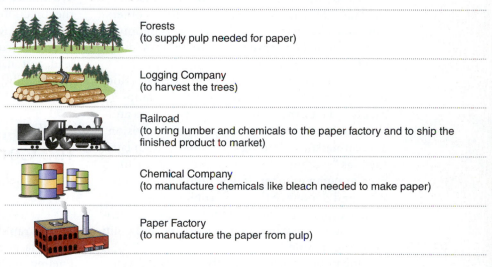

VERTICAL INTEGRATION Seeking to bring under one company the many different products and processes that go into the making of paper, Company A has acquired forests, logging companies, railroads, and chemical companies, as well as paper manufacturing plants. The advantages in this system are lower prices for and greater control over supplies of essential materials (such as wood pulp from trees).

Paper Company A Acquires

Forests
(to supply pulp needed for paper)

Logging Company
(to harvest the trees)

Railroad
(to bring lumber and chemicals to the paper factory and to ship the finished product to market)

Chemical Company
(to manufacture chemicals like bleach needed to make paper)

Paper Factory
(to manufacture the paper from pulp)

HORIZONTAL INTEGRATION Seeking to gain the largest share of the market for paper products, Company B has acquired five more paper manufacturing companies. The advantage of this system is that Company B can generate more revenue from the added production and sales of paper products. It can also lower costs by eliminating redundant operations like advertising, marketing, and accounting in the acquired companies in favor of single operations covering these functions. Because of its increased size, the company can also lower costs by striking deals with suppliers (wood pulp, chemicals, etc.) eager for its business.

Paper Company B Acquires

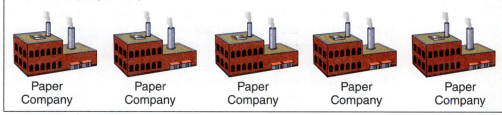

Paper Company   Paper Company   Paper Company   Paper Company   Paper Company

16.6 Horizontal Integration versus Vertical Integration
Industrialists pursued two strategies when seeking to expand their corporations. With vertical integration they sought to minimize costs and increase control of production by acquiring different kinds of companies involved in the chain of production. Through horizontal integration they attempted to reduce competition by acquiring their competitors.

Read the **Document** *Interstate Commerce Act*

What policies contributed to Andrew Carnegie's success in business?

The result of Carnegie's business policies was astonishing, bringing annual profits to $40 million by 1900. By then Carnegie Steel was the largest corporation in the world, with more than 20,000 employees and operations in many countries. Carnegie's success was part of the larger story of the "age of steel." By 1900, the U.S. steel industry employed 272,000 workers who produced 10.4 million tons of steel—an output more than twice that of its nearest rivals, Germany and Great Britain.

Rockefeller and the Rise of the Trust

Carnegie was the most famous industrialist in the late nineteenth century, but countless others developed key parts of the American economy. They included entrepreneurs like Philip Armour and Gustavus Swift (meat-packing), James B. Duke (tobacco products), George Eastman (Kodak camera), and Cyrus McCormick (farm equipment). Like Carnegie these industry leaders and thousands more succeeded by combining vision and ruthlessness, leading the public to both laud them as "captains of industry" who offered an ever-growing number of new products and services and denounce them as "**robber barons**," greedy capitalists who grew rich by devious business practices, exploitation of workers, and political manipulation.

One industrialist frequently denounced as a robber baron was John D. Rockefeller. His rise to dominance in the oil industry resembled that of Andrew Carnegie. Through relentless cost-cutting, acquisition of new technology, hiring top-notch managers and scientists, and making secret deals with railroads to undermine his competition, Rockefeller's Standard Oil company controlled 90 percent of the nation's oil-refining capacity by 1879. Unlike Carnegie, Rockefeller initially expanded his interests via horizontal integration (16.6), focusing almost exclusively on buying or building oil refineries. Later he followed Carnegie's vertical integration model, purchasing oil fields, railroad cars and warehouses, pipelines, and barrel factories.

Rockefeller's chief contribution to the rise of big business was the invention of two new forms of corporate management: the trust and the holding company. Like many industrial magnates, Rockefeller

paid lip service to the ideal of competition, but privately he believed competition between rival companies was wasteful and led to market instability. Because so-called pools—secret deals between ostensibly rival companies to set production limits to keep prices high and award each participant a certain share of the market—inevitably failed, Rockefeller devised the trust.

Unlike pools, which lacked any legal basis and thus carried no penalty for cheating, **trusts** were legally binding arrangements that brought many companies in the same industry under the direction of a single board of "trustees." To join a trust, a company turned over to a board a majority of its stock in exchange for trust certificates, which guaranteed it a share of the profits. Rockefeller's Standard Oil Trust, for example, consisted of 40 companies under the direction of a nine-member board of trustees selected by Rockefeller himself. As profits soared, dozens of trusts in other industries, such as sugar, lead, cotton, and oil, were formed, although not all successfully.

"Honest labor never rusts: up with labor down with trusts."

Banner in 1889 Boston Labor Day Parade

The rapid emergence of giant trusts, as with the rise of large railroads, alarmed many Americans. Fueling this concern was the unwillingness of Congress and the Supreme Court to curb the power of big business. In 1886, the conservative Supreme Court declared that state railroad commissions did not have the authority to regulate railroads because only Congress had the right to regulate interstate commerce (*Wabash, St. Louis & Pacific Railway Co. v. Illinois*, 1886). In a separate case (*Santa Clara County v. Southern Pacific Railroad*, 1886), the Court also declared that corporations were "de facto persons" and thus subject to all the protections under the Fourteenth Amendment. No state or local government, therefore, could impose limits on corporations "without due process of law"—in other words, approval by conservative federal courts.

The next year in 1887, Congress attempted to curb the power of the railroads by establishing the Interstate Commerce Commission (ICC) and making pools and rebates (special discounts by railroads

---

Why did big business find trusts so useful and attractive?   🔍 **View** the **Image** *John D. Rockefeller Cartoon (1901)*

to favored customers) illegal. But the ICC proved weak and ineffective, especially in the face of a conservative Supreme Court. Of the 16 cases that resulted when railroads challenged a ruling by the ICC between 1887 and 1905, the Court sided with the railroads 15 times.

Big business also benefited from enormous political influence in Congress. In this damning 1889 cartoon from the popular magazine *Puck*, *The Bosses of the Senate* (**16.7**), the bloated trusts, are clearly in charge. Congress was all too willing to do the bidding of corporate interests. Note that the doorway marked "People's Entrance" is boarded shut while a much larger "Entrance for Monopolists" is wide open. Note too the bitter conclusion that big business has subverted American democracy: "This is a Senate of the monopolists, by the monopolists, and for the monopolists."

The fate of the **Sherman Anti-Trust Act** of 1890 seemed to verify this conclusion. It was originally proposed to empower the Justice Department to prosecute any illegal contract, combination, or conspiracy among corporations that was designed to eliminate competition or restrain free trade. In other words the act made trusts illegal. But months of lobbying by corporate interests influenced Congress to word the final version of the act so vaguely that it was essentially unenforceable. As a result, the Justice Department prosecuted only 18 antitrust cases between 1890 and 1904.

Rockefeller's other major corporate management innovation—the holding company—replaced the trust in the 1890s as the preferred big business model. The holding company was a huge corporation that bought and ran other corporations by purchasing their stock. Rockefeller's idea caught on immediately because it offered protection from the Sherman Act and allowed for the creation of enormous corporations, many of which exercised near monopoly control of the market. Corporate mergers occurred at an astonishing pace. By 1900, one percent of corporations controlled 33 percent of the nation's manufacturing output, a figure that rose to 44 percent by 1910. The same was true of the railroads. In 1900, seven colossal railroads controlled two-thirds of the nation's track mileage. Big business, despite the best effort of reformers, was here to stay.

16.7 The Political Power of the Trusts Reformers criticized trusts for their power to bribe and bully Congress to pass favorable legislation. Here, a meek-looking Congress sits under the domineering gaze of the bloated trusts.

Why did efforts to curb the power of trusts fail?

Creating a Mass Market

 Railroads, oil refineries, textile factories, and steel mills were the most vivid symbols of the industrial era, but production was only one part of the story. Equally important was consumption—getting the public to purchase the growing array of the national economy's new products. Advertising would play a crucial role in creating a consumer culture, as would the department store and mail order catalogs.

The Art of Selling

To promote consumption, businesses developed sophisticated advertising techniques and marketing strategies. Many hired psychologists and other experts to develop advertising campaigns that appealed to both consumers' fears and their desires. Ads for toothpaste and deodorant, for example, stoked the public's fears about bad breath and body odor, while those for pianos and fine clothing played to desires to appear sophisticated and wealthy. Advertisers also cultivated brand loyalty through catchy slogans and impressive claims. The makers of Ivory Soap, for example, touted their product's healthful qualities with the impressive, but ridiculously exaggerated, claim that it was "99 $\frac{44}{100}$ % Pure." Recognizing the value of celebrity, some manufacturers hired famous entertainers and athletes to endorse their products and allow the use of their pictures in ads. The underlying idea of advertising—spending a portion of a business's profits to generate more profit—soon became a standard business principle. Spending on advertising jumped accordingly, from $50 million in 1867 to more than $500 million by 1900.

As advertising caught on among manufacturers and retailers, competition led to increasingly complex and sophisticated advertisements. Gone were the days from before the Civil War when advertisers relied exclusively on a few bold headlines in a newspaper or magazine and some accompanying text touting a product's quality and price. With so many advertisements jamming the pages of these media, and adorning roadside signs, sides of buildings, and grocery store windows, a product's advertisement had to be eye-catching, convincing, and memorable. Advertisers experimented with new styles and sizes of type, developed catchy slogans, and enlisted celebrities and "experts" like doctors to vouch for their product. Once developments in print technology made it possible and affordable, they focused increasingly on images to sell their products.

Shopping as an Experience: The Department Store

With the emergence of advertising came the department store. Irish immigrant Alexander Turney Stewart established the first department store in New York City in 1846. Stewart and the entrepreneurs who copied his idea built giant stores that offered a huge selection of goods for sale usually organized into different "departments." Customers also found a small army of clerks ready to assist them and fixed prices that eliminated uncomfortable negotiations. Retailers also offered attractive policies such as the money back guarantee and free delivery.

By the 1870s, customers, increasingly called "shoppers," flocked to department stores not only for the selection, price, and convenience but also for the experience. Retailers had discovered that it was not enough to offer the finest products at good prices. Shopping had to be a pleasurable experience, so merchants built palatial, richly decorated "emporiums," an impressive Latin term meaning a store

> "You can now buy your pins, your outing shirts, your wines, your prayer books, your Indian clubs, your pianolas, your false teeth, your automobiles, … [and] your spectacles … in the same place."
>
> *The Wall Street Journal*, 1903

that displayed a large variety of merchandise. One of the first merchants to do so was John Wanamaker, who transformed a Philadelphia railroad depot in 1876 into a massive and opulently decorated store called the Grand Depot.

Rival stores soon sought to outdo each other in size and splendor, and customers came to look forward to store openings. On September 12, 1896, for example, 150,000 New Yorkers paraded through the new Siegel Cooper store on opening day. This new "shopping resort," as the *New York Times* called it, employed 8,000 clerks and cashiers and 1,000 drivers and packers. It offered not only a huge selection of merchandise but also conveniences such as telegraph and long-distance telephone services, foreign currency exchange and stock trading, and a dentist office. As this photograph (**16.8**) of the central lobby shows, the store also wowed shoppers with its lavish interior. Note the marble columns, high, decorative ceilings, and the statue in the center of "The Republic," a copy of the one carved by the renowned American sculptor Daniel Chester French for the 1893 World's Fair in Chicago.

The success of the department store led some retail entrepreneurs to expand their operations to large regions or even the whole country. The most noted figure in this field was Frank W. Woolworth, whose "five and dime" stores specialized in low prices rather than opulence. He opened his first store in Utica, New York, in 1879. By 1911, he owned more than 600. Like their big business counterparts in manufacturing, Woolworth and other national retailers found that with size came advantages. Because he bought huge quantities of goods, Woolworth received big discounts from wholesalers and manufacturers that allowed him to sell his merchandise at low prices.

Bringing the Market to the Frontier

Some entrepreneurs realized that despite advertising and the growth of department stores, a massive retail market remained untapped: rural America. Living on farms or in small towns far from cities, these potential customers had money and desire to spend but lacked access to consumer goods. In 1872, Montgomery Ward set out to change that. If rural America could not get to a department store, he would bring it to them—in the form of a single broadsheet offering two dozen items for sale by "mail order."

16.8 Shopping as an Experience Large retailers in cities built lavishly appointed shopping palaces to attract customers. The Siegel-Cooper store in New York City opened with great fanfare in 1896.

View the **Closer Look** *"Testing" Clark's O.N.T. Spool Cotton*

Why did retailers spend so much money to build lavish stores?

Ward steadily expanded his list of offerings. By 1884, his broadsheet was now a catalog featuring some 10,000 items. By this time a rival mail order company run by Richard W. Sears and Alvah C. Roebuck had begun operation. Eager to reach this new market, established department stores like Macy's in New York, Jordan Marsh in Boston, and Marshall Field's in Chicago brought out their own mail order catalogs.

The reach of corporate retailing beyond urban centers and into rural America (where most Americans lived until 1920) marked the emergence of a mass market. Whereas Americans had long shared a common language and republican political culture, they now developed a shared consumer culture. Exposed to the same advertising images and appeals, millions of Americans in different parts of the country began to adopt the same fashions, develop the same habits (cigarette smoking, for example), and purchase the same newfangled contraptions, including more than one million bicycles a year in the 1890s.

Selling to the World

As the nation's industrial production soared to unprecedented heights, manufacturers searched for new markets for their goods. The United States had long been an exporter of agricultural products like cotton and wheat, but the leading trend after the Civil War was the export of manufactured goods. The total value of exports rose between 1870 and 1900 from $450 million to $1.5 billion, with the percentage of manufactured goods rising from 15 to 32 percent.

In addition to selling produce and goods overseas, American business interests also began to invest heavily in business ventures in foreign countries. By 1897, Americans had invested $635 million in overseas mines, plantations, oil wells, and increasingly, manufacturing plants ($94 million). By the 1890s, the Singer Sewing Machine Co. was an international corporation (16.9). With factories in Scotland and the United States, Singer sold its machines throughout the world. Note how the advertisement's text, "The Singer Seam unites Two Continents," and angelic female figures suggest that the company is pursuing humanitarian as well as capitalist goals. Farm equipment giant, International Harvester, likewise opened factories in Canada and Sweden.

The globalization of the American economy brought many benefits to workers, consumers, and investors. But it also contributed to the growing sentiment in the 1890s that the United States needed to become an imperial power to protect overseas investments and ensure that markets in Asia, Africa, and Latin America remained open (see Chapter 19).

16.9 The Globalization of American Industry Like many large American firms, the Singer Sewing Machine Co. became an international corporation by the 1890s, selling its machines throughout the world.

How did advertising promote the development of a national consumer culture?

The World of Work Transformed

 The huge industrial enterprises built by Carnegie, Rockefeller, and others ultimately depended not on their individual genius but on the collective labors of American workers. As the number and size of factories grew in the late nineteenth century, so did the industrial workforce expanding from 1.3 million workers in 1860 to 5.1 million in 1900. Many of them faced hardships: long hours, low pay, dangerous conditions, and frequent downturns in the economy. Workers responded by forming unions, staging strikes, and protesting the surging power of business as a threat to democracy.

The Impact of New Technology

New industrial technology greatly increased manufacturing output, but it also changed the status of industrial workers. New machines produced more goods in less time and required mostly low-skilled labor to operate. Machinery transformed shoemaking, for example, from a skilled trade in the 1820s to a low-skill factory occupation by the 1860s. The same was true in the garment and textile industries. Because they could easily replace low-skilled labor, employers could pay low wages and demand long hours. They could also simply fire or replace workers who complained or failed to keep up the pace with other unskilled workers.

This trend occurred unevenly across industrial America. For example, in building trades like carpentry and bricklaying, new technology did little to undermine the position of skilled craftsmen. In other settings new technology created new opportunities for some workers. Some found well-paid skilled work as mechanics, while others became foremen and floor managers who oversaw the work of unskilled operatives. These more fortunate workers often enjoyed far higher wages, shorter hours, and better treatment than the unskilled.

Nonetheless for many workers new industrial technology eliminated their skilled jobs in favor of unskilled ones. Just as shoemaking changed from a skilled trade in the 1820s to a low-skill factory occupation by the 1860s, so did the garment and textile industries. In these settings, employers enjoyed increasing power over their employees for the simple reason that unskilled workers were easily replaced.

Hard Times for Industrial Workers

New technology was but one of many difficulties confronting industrial workers in the age of industrialization. Most workers complained about long hours and low wages. Although averages for both varied by industry and region, workers often toiled 12 hours a day, six days a week, for wages that barely covered basic living expenses. By some estimates wage earners in the late nineteenth century made $400–500 per year, when living decently required a minimum of $600–800. Working-class families made up the difference by sending their children to work, taking in boarders, and bringing in "home finishing" work, performed by women and children, such as sewing buttons on new shirts.

Compounding the precarious economic position of wage earners was the instability of the industrial economy. Severe depressions (1873–1877 and 1893–1897) and recessions interrupted periods of prosperity and economic growth and brought widespread business failure and high unemployment lasting years. The severe depression of the 1870s, for example, resulted in the loss of more than a million jobs and nearly 50,000 businesses. Those who did keep their jobs often found their wages slashed and hours increased by employers desperate to remain solvent or ruthless enough to take advantage of rising job competition between the employed and the unemployed.

The monotony of industrial work also added to the difficulties wage earners faced. Many jobs required a laborer to perform the same task repeatedly, such as pulling a lever on a metal stamping machine. Workers felt, in the words of one machinist in 1883, that they were becoming "part of

Read the Document *Technology and the Shoe Industry in Fincher's* Trade Review (1864)

How did new technology weaken the independence of skilled workers?

the machinery," a state of affairs they found "very demoralizing."

The industrial workplace was also extremely dangerous. Every year between 1880 and 1900, 35,000 workers (on average) were killed on the job and another 500,000 injured. This carnage resulted in part from the monotony of factory work, which led mind-numbed workers to make mistakes or fall asleep. But most injuries stemmed from the factory owners' negligence. With no laws compelling them to make their workplaces less lethal, few industrialists were willing to pay for safety devices or procedures. Not until the early twentieth century did most states begin enacting laws requiring compensation be paid to injured workers or the families of killed workers (see Chapter 18).

Another disturbing trend was the sharp rise in child labor. Before the Industrial Revolution children of farmers and artisans performed all sorts of work that contributed to the family economy—but always under the supervision of a parent or relative. Children working in industry, however, left their homes to work in factories and mines under the supervision of a manager rather than a parent. Between 1870 and 1900, the number of children younger than 16 working for wages—usually a fraction of those paid adults—skyrocketed from 700,000 to 1.7 million. Children as young as seven toiled long hours in dangerous conditions in mines and factories, at jobs that exposed them to dangerous and unhealthful conditions. The boy in this photograph (**16.10**) lost his arm while operating a power saw in a box factory. Many states passed laws prohibiting child labor, but they rarely enforced them.

Exploitation, Intimidation, and Conflict

Central to the transformation in the lives workers ushered in by industrialization was the increasing power exercised by employers in the workplace. Since profit was their paramount goal, employers imposed strict discipline on their workers. clock dominated the workplace, as employers demanded workers begin and their day (with a few short scheduled breaks) at precise times. Workers who arrived late or took unauthorized breaks were fined or fired. Some factories forbade workers to talk to one another—or even to whistle.

16.10 The Price of Child Labor Because they could pay children less than one-half the wages of an adult, employers hired more children in the late nineteenth century, depriving them of education and often exposing them to industrial hazards.

> ## "I make about three dollars a week, and my sister—she is only six years old—she does not make as much, sometimes a dollar a week, sometimes more."
>
> An eight-year-old child laborer, New York, 1871

Enforcing these new rules was an increasingly important figure in the industrial workplace: the manager or foreman. In sharp contrast to the early nineteenth-century preindustrial economy, few workers now ever saw, let alone spoke to, their employer. Instead, they dealt with managers or foremen hired to run a factory as efficiently and profitably as possible. This meant pushing workers to meet production goals and firing those who could not keep up or caused trouble. Many foremen came from working-class backgrounds and treated workers fairly, but others could be abusive, especially to workers of a different ethnic background. Female workers were particularly vulnerable to abuse. In this drawing from 1888, the foreman in a garment factory shakes his fist at a weary woman, urging her to work faster (**16.11**). In the larger inset, the overworked woman sprawls on a bed in a dingy tenement. That this image ran under the sensational title *The Female Slaves of New York* in a popular newspaper that often expressed hostility toward workers indicates the notoriety the foreman had achieved in the garment industry by the late nineteenth century.

Workers also found it difficult to organize labor unions. The first major effort to build a national labor movement after the Civil War began in 1866 when William Sylvis, a charismatic iron molder, founded the National Labor Union (NLU). A federation of independent craft unions, the NLU sought to unite skilled workers nationwide to secure demands such as a federal law establishing the eight-hour day and a federal department of labor. Its membership topped 300,000 (nearly all native-born white men in skilled trades)

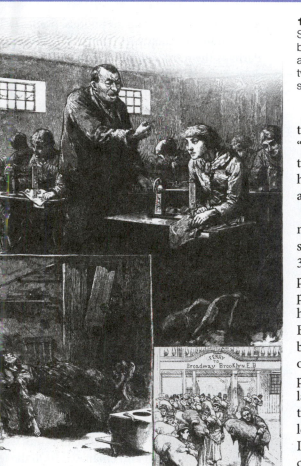

16.11 Exploiting Female Workers
Shop floor foremen and managers became increasingly important as workplaces grew bigger. As demands for productivity grew, female workers were especially vulnerable to abusive foremen. The threat of overwork to the health of women is emphasized in the two insets. One depicts workers carrying heavy bundles of work home while another shows an exhausted laborer collapsed on her bed.

than a few weeks. Strikers, one worker attested, "have had nothing to combat capital with except their empty stomachs, while the capitalists have had unlimited financial resources and have been able to starve the workingmen into submission."

Rising worker frustration and anger led to more strikes and violence. Between 1881 and 1905, six million American workers participated in nearly 37,000 strikes. One particularly bitter incident took place in Pennsylvania. In response to the abusive policies of coal mine bosses in the 1860s, miners had formed a union called the Workingmen's Benevolent Association (WBA). Many of its members were Irish immigrants, some of whom, drawing on the tradition of secret societies that resisted oppressive landlords in Ireland, formed a clandestine labor organization known as the Molly Maguires that carried out acts of intimidation, vandalism, violence, and murder against foremen and managers. In 1874, mine owners set out to destroy the WBA by convincing the public that it was one and the same as the Molly Maguires. Within a year this campaign resulted in more than 50 arrests and numerous convictions—many on questionable testimony and with little or no evidence. Twenty alleged Molly Maguires were hanged for murder, including ten on a single day, June 21, 1877. Note how in this drawing (**16.12**) public officials created a powerful public spectacle to emphasize the men's guilt and, aware that

16.12 The Pageantry of Execution
On June 21, 1877, "Black Thursday," Pennsylvania officials staged carefully planned executions of ten convicted miners known as Molly Maguires.

by 1869. But Sylvis's sudden death that year weakened the NLU, and the depression of the 1870s wiped it out.

Most employers saw unions as threats to their profits and freedom to run their businesses as they wanted. Many hired spies to expose labor organizers so they could fire them and put them on **blacklists**, lists of workers that employers in a town or industry refused to hire because they were considered trouble-makers. During strikes, employers routinely hired replacement workers, and enjoyed the support of local officials who ordered policemen to drive away or arrest pickets gathered outside a workplace. If a labor dispute went to court, an employer could normally count on a favorable ruling by a judge or jury. On top of all this, workers faced one over-riding problem—few unions had the resources to support striking workers for more

Why were employers so hostile to labor unions?

most of the region's miners were Catholic, their sinfulness.

Three weeks later, on July 14, 1877, the largest nineteenth century strike in the world erupted. The "Great Uprising" of railroad workers began in Martinsburg, West Virginia, and quickly spread to Baltimore, Philadelphia, Pittsburgh, St. Louis, Chicago, and other cities. The strike involved thousands of workers, and violence emanated from both sides. In Pittsburgh, for example, soldiers opened fire on striking workers and their families, killing 25 and wounding 29. Enraged strikers and their supporters attacked the troops and destroyed all of the Pennsylvania Railroad terminal's buildings and other property.

The mainstream press criticized the railroads for slashing workers' wages, but most dismissed labor activism as illegal, ill-informed, and un-American. (See *Competing Visions: The Legitimacy of Unions*.)

While workers faced hostility from employers, politicians, and journalists, they also had to contend with animosity within the ranks of labor that often hindered their ability to organize. Deep hostility often existed between skilled and unskilled workers, who frequently saw little in common with each other. Workers were also riven by disputes arising from different ideologies, including varieties of socialism, a theory that rejected capitalism and advocated common ownership of private property and greater social and economic equality. They also argued the persistent question of whether workers' interests were best

served by pressuring the major political parties or by forming an independent labor party.

Perhaps the most significant divisions among workers centered on race and ethnicity. A rising tide of immigration in the late nineteenth century increased the ethnic, racial, and religious diversity of an already diverse workforce, making it more difficult to unite them in common cause. For example, when hard times hit during the depression of the 1870s, anti-Chinese sentiment among American workers soared, leading to the Chinese Exclusion Act in 1882 barring Chinese immigration to the United States. As the cartoon (**16.13**) from *The Wasp* demonstrates, Chinese workers were blamed for taking jobs from Americans. The artist depicts a 12-armed Chinese worker, drawn in racist caricature, laboring maniacally at a dozen tasks while young American-born workers stand idly near a factory. One of the workers is being hauled away by a policeman, implying that unemployment has led him to a life of crime.

African American workers also faced racist hostility from white workers, especially when they began moving to Northern cities in the 1890s. Much of this hostility stemmed from the widely held racist beliefs of the day including the concept that all whites were superior to blacks. But it also emanated from the fear that African Americans would take jobs from white workers—a fear exacerbated when employers occasionally used black workers as strikebreakers.

16.13 Hard Times Fuel Anti-Chinese Racism
During the depression of 1873–1878, workers blamed high unemployment on Chinese immigrants, whom they accused of working long shifts for low wages.

Read the **Document** *Chinese Exclusion Act*

Competing Visions

THE LEGITIMACY OF UNIONS

Although conflict between workers and their employers often centered on wages and hours, it also occurred over the legitimacy of labor unions. Many Americans denounced unions as illegal, foolish, and un-American. The editor of *Scribner's Monthly*, writing after the 1877 Great Uprising of railroad workers, reflects this view as does the image from *Puck*. Workers and their advocates like John Swinton, editor of a pro-labor newspaper in New York, offered a different vision of labor unions as vital organizations that protected workers from the exploitation. Why did employers find unions so objectionable, even dangerous? What benefits did workers see in unions?

Scribner's Monthly (October 1877)

And now that it is over, it is a good time to ask once more what good has come from this strike, and what good has come of any strike. The laws of nature which, after all, govern the laws of trade … can never be overcome or circumvented by a strike. Labor will always command its value—no more, no less…. Strikes are always mistakes; they are often crimes.

The day of the inauguration of trades unions and labor organizations in this country was a day the blackest and fullest of menace to the popular prosperity and peace that ever dawned upon the nation. They have been an unmitigated curse to employers and employed alike. The nature and purpose of these organizations are simply outrageous. They have been despotic toward their own members, oppressive toward the class in whose interest they pretend to have been established, impertinent and intermeddling. They have assumed the right to control property and business in which they had no more right than if they lived in the moon. There should be in the good sense of the great mass of laborers a reaction against this wretched crime, and this stupendous foolishness.

John Swinton's Paper (January 27, 1884)

There are many who cannot understand why Trades Unions exist here. They have heard them described as alien to the American craftsman, causing strikes, and raising ill-feeling generally between … employer and employe[e].

In the present state of industry, Trade Unions are a necessity, recognized as such by the great majority of intelligent workmen, … and securing for their members a partial degree of protection without which they would sink into depths as yet unfathomed.

There is a hue and cry against the Unions as agencies that provoke strikes. In nine cases out of ten, strikes are made necessary by circumstances over which the Unions have no control whatever; sometimes they are a protest against unendurable reductions in wages … sometimes by unjust conduct on the part of bosses or corporations. No Union to-day orders a strike that can be avoided by reasonable means; no Union orders a strike without full consideration of the subject and after a fair vote….

But we are told that no strike ever brings any advantage to the strikers … This is a mistake that cannot be made by any one who has observed the results of strikes either in the United States or in any other country….

But strikes often fail,—yes, it is true. Capital often triumphs in the conflict with labor,—true again. Yet capital would be even harsher and more exacting than it is, if it were not for the protest of the strike, and the warning that it gives. The wages which, in many industries, are but little above the living point, would be put down and kept down to the starvation point, if the men accepted with submissive spirit every reduction of wages, and all the severe terms that capital tries to enforce.

This Puck magazine cartoon from the mid-1880s portrayed labor union officials as tyrants who hurt the interests of workers.

Women Employed in Offices	19,000 / 503,000
Women Employed as Saleswomen	7,462 / 142,265

■ 1870 ■ 1900

16.14 Rising Numbers of Women in the Paid Workforce
Economic necessity and a desire for greater independence brought millions of women into jobs outside the home.

New Roles and Opportunities for Women

Economic necessity brought millions of women into the paid workforce. Whereas just 13 percent of women worked outside the home in 1870, 20 percent did so by 1900. Nearly all these women were single and younger than 25. Domestic service (cooking, cleaning, and childcare in the homes of middle- and upper-class families) remained the leading occupation for wage-earning women in this period, but many also took on factory work, especially in the garment and textile industries. Like their male counterparts, women factory workers labored at repetitive tasks for long hours in unsafe conditions—but for only half (or less) the wages of men. Employers justified this disparity by claiming women worked merely for extra money, whereas men worked to support whole families and therefore deserved higher pay. In fact, many working-class families depended for their survival on the earnings of wives and daughters. Factory owners simply paid them less because women were powerless to prevent it.

The emergence of modern corporations requiring armies of secretaries, clerks, and stenographers, combined with the invention of the telephone, adding machine, and typewriter, created new opportunities for educated, native-born, white women (**16.14**). Teaching, social work, and, as indicated in the graduation photograph of the Philadelphia School for Nurses (**16.15**), nursing emerged in the late nineteenth century as almost exclusively female professions. Although these fields represented new opportunities for women, they were deemed appropriate because they drew on what was widely believed to be women's "natural" role as nurturers. The pageantry evident in this photograph, especially the bright white and highly professional looking uniforms, the elegant setting of the Philadelphia Academy of Music, and the presence of Red Cross founder Clara Barton (seated at center), indicates the high reputation the profession had achieved by 1900.

Regardless of the level of work, social custom dictated that women leave the paid workforce soon after they married (only five percent of married women worked outside the home in 1900). Of necessity, working-class women continued to earn money to support their families. Only now they did so from within the home by taking in boarders, laundry, and "piece work," which paid by the piece rather than by the hour.

Many more African American women, more out of economic necessity than custom, remained in the paid workforce even after marriage. In urban areas in both the North and South, many worked as domestic servants in white homes, cooking, cleaning, doing the laundry, and caring for children. These jobs required long hours and paid low wages, but racist hiring policies in industry and other sectors of the economy left African American women with few options.

16.15 Women Find Opportunities in Nursing
These graduates of the Philadelphia School for Nurses, with Red Cross founder Clara Barton at center, were among the thousands of young women in the late nineteenth century who became nurses.

Why did more women enter the paid workforce?

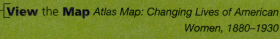

View the **Map** Atlas Map: Changing Lives of American Women, 1880–1930

Conflicting Visions of Industrial Capitalism

 As the Industrial Revolution unfolded in the late nineteenth century, Americans of all classes, occupations, and regions felt its impact. For many it was an age of wonder, marked by a succession of new inventions, ideas, and possibilities. Yet one did not have to look far for signs of anxiety, fear, and discontent. Numerous critics offered a different vision of society, emphasizing the growing poverty, gaps between rich and poor, and inequality.

Capitalism Championed

Many Americans in the late nineteenth century celebrated industrial capitalism. Proponents noted that every year American industry produced more consumer goods, from inexpensive clothing in a dizzying array of colors and styles to exciting new products like phonographs and bicycles. It also generated new forms of transportation that allowed people, including the poor, to travel to new and different places. In farming industrial technology led to stupendous annual harvests, falling food prices, and a more varied diet for the average American, whose life expectancy rose from a mere 38.3 years for white men in 1850 to 50 years by 1910. The telegraph, telephone, and steam-powered printing press allowed for the unprecedented spread of information and literacy (aided by an expanded public school system). And despite unrest, depressions, and strikes, real wages for the average worker rose 50 percent between 1860 and 1900 (74 percent for skilled workers and 31 percent for unskilled). To these optimists industrial capitalism meant progress.

Of the enthusiastic champions of the new industrial order, none was more fervent and influential than Andrew Carnegie. He offset his hard-driving corporate style with a carefully constructed public image designed to set him apart from many of his fellow industrialists who angered the public with arrogant pronouncements. The shipping and railroad magnate Cornelius Vanderbilt, for example, once brushed aside the suggestion that his business practices violated the law by saying, "Law! What do I care about the law? Ain't I got the power?"

In countless speeches and articles in prominent magazines, Carnegie defended the status quo and emphasized its virtues. Rejecting the claims of critics that industrialists like him were greedy, abusive monopolists, he insisted they were visionaries who built key industries that brought immeasurable benefits to Americans, including jobs for workers and products that improved the quality of life. Granted, Carnegie explained in what he came to call the "Gospel of Wealth," he and other entrepreneurs had grown fabulously rich, but this was a necessary and beneficial result of a free economy. Without the hope of future riches, business leaders would not have the incentive to seek new opportunities, take risks, and develop new products.

> "I can hire one half of the working class to kill the other half."
>
> Financier and railroad magnate
> JAY GOULD

Carnegie and other champions of big business also emphasized that industrial fortunes could be—and increasingly were—used to fund philanthropic projects such as schools and libraries. In the 1880s and 1890s he emerged as the nation's most ostentatious philanthropist. In 1901 he sold his steel empire to financier J. P. Morgan for $400 million and then donated most of it to various causes, including thousands of public libraries. For a man who was both conservative and optimistic, libraries appeared the perfect form of charity because they

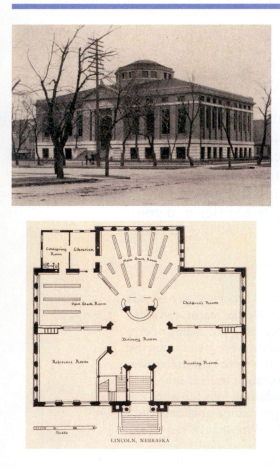

16.16 The Carnegie Library and Floor Plan in Lincoln, Nebraska As a symbol of the virtue of industrial capitalism and the spirit of individual uplift, steel magnate Andrew Carnegie funded nearly 1,700 public libraries in America. The exterior designs reflected the popularity of classical styles circa 1900. The interiors emphasized the industrial values of order and efficiency.

provided ambitious, hard-working, and intelligent people opportunities to better themselves, instead of handouts. This Carnegie library (**16.16**), built in Lincoln, Nebraska, in 1901, typified the more than 2,500 (1,689 in the United States) libraries funded by Carnegie between 1886 and 1929. Communities awarded a library were allowed to pick their own architectural style. Most, like Lincoln, opted for some variation on the popular neoclassical style. But Carnegie and the staff that oversaw the program insisted that library interiors stress efficiency and order—the values reflected in the design of his steel factories. Note how the floor plan allowed for a single centrally located librarian (seated at the curved desk in the center) to monitor all the neatly organized spaces devoted to reading, children, reference, and stacks.

When Carnegie and other defenders of industrial capitalism were asked about the growing problem of poverty amid such progress, they pointed to what they claimed was the greatest virtue of a capitalist economy: the self-made man. As Carnegie's own life story seemed to attest, anyone, regardless of birthplace, family, education, or poverty, could climb the ladder of success. Success was not guaranteed, noted Carnegie. But for those who possessed self-discipline, intelligence, frugality, and diligence and who avoided liquor and debt, the future was bright.

Aiding Andrew Carnegie and other optimists in spreading this ideal of the self-made man was Horatio Alger. A former minister, Alger wrote more than 100 young adult books, beginning with *Ragged Dick* in 1868. All featured similar plots that told the story of a young boy, often a bootblack or a delivery boy, who lived a life of poverty and irresponsibility on the mean streets of a big city. Through the intervention of a "respectable" man, the boy discovers that he need only end his prodigal ways and pursue education and opportunity to enjoy the good life. Alger sold millions of books, and imitators churned out similar publications, including the popular *Fame and Fortune* magazine (**16.17**). As this cover shows, each issue offered dramatic "stories of boys who make money" by exhibiting honesty, diligence, and courage.

Not all conservative defenders of industrial capitalism shared Alger's rosy vision of a society where anyone willing to work hard, save money, and avoid liquor could find success. They subscribed to a theory known as **social Darwinism**, a corruption of Charles Darwin's biological theory of natural selection (later termed "evolution"). British philosopher and sociologist Herbert Spencer took Darwin's central idea that in evolution, plants and animals that are able to adapt to changing conditions survive, while those that cannot become extinct, and tailored it to fit his idea of modern industrial society as "survival of

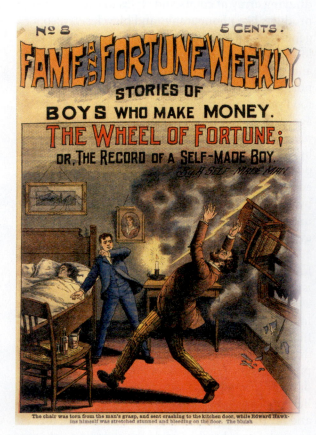

The chair was torn from the man's grasp, and sent crashing to the kitchen door, while Edward Hawkins himself was stretched stunned and bleeding on the floor. The bluish

16.17 The Promise of Success Taking their cue from the success of Horatio Alger's success in writing scores of young adult novels, many imitators published similar books and magazines preaching that reward and respectability could be won if only one worked hard, told the truth, and helped the less fortunate.

Why was the self-made man idea so popular in the age of industry?

Read the Document *Herbert Spencer, Social Darwinism (1857)*

Read the Document *Horatio Alger, Ragged Dick*

> **"What a blessing to let the unreformed drunkard and his children die, and not increase them above all others…. How wise to let those of weak digestion from gluttony die, and the temperate live. What benevolence to let the lawless perish, and the prudent survive."**
>
> *The Christian Advocate* (N.Y.), 1879

the fittest." The wealthy and powerful were the "fittest," people endowed with innate intelligence, strength, and the adaptability that enabled them to succeed in the competitive world of business. And the poor? They were the "unfit," men and women consigned by nature to failure, misery, and early death. To impose government regulation on business, social Darwinists argued, was both immoral and impractical, an affront to the laws of nature and God. They also attacked any initiatives public or private to alleviate the plight of the poor because they would promote the survival and growth of the unfit population with devastating consequences for society.

Capitalism Criticized

Despite these confident assertions on the morality and virtue of laissez-faire industrial capitalism, critics decried the widening chasm between rich and poor. While some 4,000 Americans had become "millionaires" by the early 1890s, millions of others lived in poverty, or perilously close to it. A tour of any city provided ample evidence of what some called the "haves and the have nots," a concern vividly captured in this 1876 image (**16.18**) from a popular magazine. Its caption, "The Hearth-Stone of the Poor," and accompanying article pointed out that many of the poor, unlike the wealthy family on the left, had no warm fireplace around which to gather on cold nights. Instead, like these children, they gathered around outdoor steam vents to keep warm. Note how the wealthy

parents fail to notice the shivering children as they pass.

Many commentators in this period focused on the profound extremes of wealth and poverty found in two New York City neighborhoods: Fifth Avenue and Five Points. In the former neighborhood were the homes of the Stewarts, Vanderbilts, Astors, Morgans, and Carnegies. They patronized the opulent Metropolitan Opera House, entertained each other at lavish balls and dinners, and summered in their 50-room "cottages" in coastal retreats like Newport, Rhode Island. Just a few miles downtown was a notorious district called the Five Points. In this neighborhood and the surrounding Lower East Side district, nearly one million people lived in tiny, airless tenement apartments with no running water or toilets. Their neighborhoods had no parks, and the streets were filled with filth due to irregular street cleaning.

Reformers, ministers, and social critics began to question whether American democracy, with its ideals of equal rights and individual freedom, could endure under such inequality and enslaving poverty. For example, a self-taught political economist named Henry George wrote *Progress and*

16.18 The Growing Gap between the Haves and Have-Nots
This image, *The Hearth-Stone of the Poor* from the popular magazine *Harper's Weekly* (February 12, 1876) captured the growing concern among Americans over the growth of poverty amid rising levels of wealth.

Why was the theory of social Darwinism so attractive to the wealthy and successful?

Poverty, an influential book that addressed one of the central questions of the age: Must industrial and technological progress be accompanied by increased poverty? If so, he warned, American democracy was doomed. George claimed that the monopolization of resources, especially of land, by powerful elites was to blame for the era's growing social inequality and class conflict. Few people understood or supported George's unorthodox solution (a "single tax" on land values), but his vivid diagnosis of the rising clash between labor and capital and his vision of a more equitable social order gained him an enormous following in the 1880s and turned *Progress and Poverty* into a bestseller.

Edward Bellamy achieved similar fame as a critic of laissez-faire capitalism with his novel *Looking Backward, 2000–1887*. Published in 1887, it told the story of Julian West who, like Rip Van Winkle in another era, falls asleep in 1887 and awakens in 2000. To his astonishment he finds American society transformed into a socialist utopia. The class conflict, poverty, and economic inequality of the late nineteenth century are gone. The government controlled the economy, eliminating destructive competition and providing a comfortable living for all citizens. Bellamy's book became a bestseller, and his largely middle-class followers established nearly 500 clubs to spread its message.

Power in Numbers: Organized Labor

Less famous, but more influential than critics like George and Bellamy, were the protests of those most buffeted by the Industrial Revolution: workers. Through the pages of labor newspapers and in speeches at worker rallies—and in actions such as strikes—American workers articulated a sharp critique of the new industrial order. A few were socialists, but most supported the broad ideals of a free market economy. Their protest stemmed from the growing conviction that greedy monopolists, in league with unscrupulous politicians, had seized control of the economy and bent it toward their own advantage. As a result, argued workers, they received a shrinking portion of the wealth they created, while working longer hours in increasingly inhumane conditions. Try as they might, these workers claimed, the upward mobility celebrated by

Andrew Carnegie and Horatio Alger was less and less attainable.

Unsettled and angered by their declining power in the face of big business, American workers renewed their efforts to organize labor unions. In 1869, Philadelphia garment cutters formed The Noble and Holy Order of the **Knights of Labor (KOL)**, an organization that called for many of the same reforms as the NLU, but added a long list of radical, even utopian, goals. For example, it advocated replacing the existing competitive industrial system with an economy based on cooperation. In addition, unlike the NLU's emphasis on craft workers, the KOL was an industrial union open to all workers, including unskilled wage earners, immigrants, and eventually women and African Americans. Its leaders believed that fundamental social change was impossible unless this broad spectrum of workers joined forces.

To overcome employer hostility, the organization adopted a policy of strict secrecy that necessitated holding meetings in clandestine locations. This requirement, however, combined with the depression of 1873–1877, hindered its growth. By 1879, it counted just 10,000 members, most in Pennsylvania. But two key developments that year propelled the KOL to become the world's largest industrial union. First, the national economy recovered, providing wage earners with a measure of economic security that allowed them to form and join local unions in huge numbers. Second, a young machinist named Terence Powderly became the KOL's leader, or Grandmaster Workman. Powderly was a superb organizer and gifted orator who in 1882 abolished the KOL's secrecy rule, a decision that made it possible to recruit thousands of new members and fend off accusations from employers, politicians, and religious leaders that the KOL was a sinister and conspiratorial organization.

Membership soared to 42,000 in 1882 (on its way to an eventual peak of more than 700,000 in late 1886). What drew many workers to the organization was the KOL's sharp critique of laissez-faire capitalism and emphasis on economic justice and democracy. Its constitution decried, "the recent alarming development and aggression of aggregated wealth" by industrialists, bankers, and stock speculators, warning that it would soon lead "to the pauperization and hopeless degradation of the toiling masses." (See *Images as History: Why Fear Big Business?*)

What conditions led to rapid membership growth in the Knights of Labor?

Read the **Document** *Henry George, "Progress and Poverty"*

Images as History
WHY FEAR BIG BUSINESS?

As large corporations emerged in the Gilded Age (the late nineteenth century period of rapid economic growth), many Americans grew concerned about their power and influence. Some focused on the fact that large corporations and the immensely powerful men that ran them, people like John D. Rockefeller and William H. Vanderbilt, operated beyond the control of laws and democratic institutions. Did this not mean, they asked, that the republic was in danger? How could a democracy—a society governed by the will of the people—retain its legitimacy when big business exercised so much power and answered to no public officials and no voters? Other Americans focused on the plight of the worker under such a system. How could workers resist the power of large employers to slash wages, increase hours, and ignore safety issues? Could the United States endure as a republic if these citizens were reduced to desperate poverty while a few wealthy families reveled in luxury? These concerns are on full display in this vivid political cartoon from *Puck Magazine*.

Big business and monopoly are depicted as a knight, a symbol of European aristocracy and the antithesis of republicanism. His plume carries the word, "arrogance." Note how this figure stands in sharp contrast with the much smaller, humble worker.

The artist represents the horse of "monopoly" as a huge golden locomotive. Railroads were the original big businesses and the largest corporations. They were also at the center of the era's biggest corruption scandals and strikes. In contrast, the shoeless American worker sits on a scrawny horse labeled "poverty."

This huge, seemingly endless, crowd symbolizes the American people, who clearly outnumber the handful of capitalists on the left. Observe how small the people are compared to the industrialists. Note too how most of the crowd looks anxious or angry at what is happening (some shake their fists) and how some of the children appear malnourished.

In a section labeled "Reserved for Capitalists," sits a collection of the nation's most powerful businessmen, including Cyrus Field, William H. Vanderbilt, and Jay Gould. Note the joy they seem to take in seeing the American worker destroyed.

THE TOURNAMENT OF TO-DAY.—A SET-TO BETWEEN LABOR AND MONOPOLY.

One of the most significant aspects of this image is its source. Subscribers to *Puck* were overwhelmingly middle- and upper-class. This shows that the rising fear of big business in the Gilded Age was not confined to low-wage factory workers. It was shared by a large cross-section of the American people.

The vast disparity in power is captured in the weapons brought to the fight. The knight holds a shield labeled "corruption of the legislature," suggesting corporate titans' ability to bribe state and federal elected officials to ensure laws favorable to business. In his other hand he holds a lance labeled "subsidized press," indicating the power of big business to buy favorable coverage in the newspapers. The lowly worker, in contrast, holds only one weapon: the strike.

These sentiments and spirit of protest inspired workers in New York City, many of them KOL members, to establish the Labor Day holiday in September 1882. The organizers took care to present workers as orderly and dignified, marching in almost military fashion (**16.19**). Yet they also held aloft signs voicing their grievances ("Abolish Contract Labor" and "8 Hours to Constitute A Day's Work") and announcing their intent to reclaim their influence in the political system ("Vote for the Labor Ticket"). Others proclaimed the importance of workers ("Labor Creates All Wealth" and "Labor Pays All Taxes"), and in an age of growing economic inequality, reminded the spectators of key American principles ("All Men Are Created Equal"). The annual Labor Day holiday quickly gained popularity. By 1886, it was a national event, and in 1894, President Grover Cleveland signed a law establishing Labor Day as a holiday for all federal workers.

Another significant aspect of the KOL's vision, albeit one that was not embraced in every part of the country, especially the South, was its inclusion of African American workers as members. Many in the KOL's leadership argued that the union must include all workers, including blacks, because employers would inevitably use them against organized labor to break strikes and lower wages. This same argument for inclusion led the KOL to allow women members. As a result, in an era when labor unions were almost exclusively the domain of white men, in 1886, ten percent of the KOL's membership was women and another ten percent was African American.

Many workers also joined the KOL because it emphasized practical goals. Its constitution called for the eight-hour workday, equal pay for men and women, the establishment of state bureaus of labor, and the prohibition of child and convict labor. The KOL also gained enormous support among workers because it led successful strikes. But the decision to strike was difficult and risky. (See *Choices and Consequences: To Strike or Not to Strike?*)

Most strikes in this period were small and local, but on several occasions the KOL enjoyed success on a grand scale. In 1885, KOL-affiliated railroad workers won a strike against the Wabash Railroad, owned by financier Jay Gould, a man widely despised and

16.19 Establishing Labor Day
In 1882, workers in New York City held the first local Labor Day celebration. It soon became a national holiday.

Why did so many workers find the Knights of Labor appealing?

View the **Map** *Interactive Map: Organizing American Labor in the Late Nineteenth Century*

Choices and Consequences

TO STRIKE OR NOT TO STRIKE?

Most strikes in the late nineteenth century failed, but the surge in labor activism and the emergence of the Knights of Labor in the 1880s boosted confidence among workers that strikes could succeed. In the summer of 1881, the hundreds of male shoemakers in the Knights Local Assembly 64 successfully opposed a wage reduction by the Mundell Company in Philadelphia. Management then imposed a rate cut on its female shoemakers. One of the workers, Mary Stirling, urged the workers, men and women, to strike until the company rescinded the wage cut. The workers at the Mundell Company considered essentially three major options:

Choices

1 Fearing for their jobs male and female workers refuse to strike.

2 Seeking to protect their recent victory, the men remain on the job while the women walk out.

3 Recognizing their mutual interests in opposing wage cuts for all workers, the male and female workers agree to strike together.

Decision

Inspired by the KOL motto, "an injury to one is the concern of all," the 700 men and women of the Mundell factory decided on option 3, walking out at Mary Stirling's urging. The strike lasted weeks, during which time the female workers formed their own KOL local assembly—even though the union did not yet enroll female members. Strikers organized pickets, rallies, and fundraisers to help pay for food and rent.

Consequences

The Mundell Company, facing lost profits and pressure to settle from other factory owners who feared worker unrest, rescinded the wage cut. The victory boosted the confidence of the workers and the reputation of the KOL locally. Within three years the shoe industry alone had 11 local assemblies that managed to win many struggles with employers over wages, firings, and work rules. Even more important, later in 1881, Mary Stirling attended the national convention of the KOL and convinced the organization to admit women. By 1887, ten percent of the KOL's 700,000 members were women.

The Mundell Shoe Company was one of the nation's leading footwear manufacturers in the late nineteenth century

Continuing Controversies

How should organized labor deal with the rising number of women in the workforce?
The admission of women into the KOL did not end the opposition of many American workers to the rights of women to work and join unions. They continued to argue that keeping women out of the workforce would open up jobs for men and raise overall wages. When the KOL fell apart in the 1890s, the status of women in the labor movement fell with it. The American Federation of Labor, the organization that succeeded the KOL, admitted few female members until well into the twentieth century.

What made strikes so risky for workers?

feared by workers. Elsewhere the KOL popularized the boycott, the organized effort to discourage customers from patronizing a business engaged in anti-labor activity, as an effective labor tactic less costly and risky than a strike.

As the KOL's membership and influence grew in the mid-1880s, it alarmed employers, politicians, and conservatives, who feared its radical rhetoric of class conflict and demands for economic reform. They denounced Powderly and other KOL leaders as radical socialists bent on promoting violence and class warfare. Although both accusations were false, they made many Americans, including many wage earners, leery of the KOL and of organized labor.

The Great Upheaval of 1886

Fear of the KOL in particular and the labor movement in general peaked in 1886. On May 1, 340,000 workers across the country staged a one-day work stoppage to bring attention to their demand for the eight-hour day. Three days later a far more serious

incident occurred that would hurt the labor movement for decades. Outraged by the killing of striking workers outside the McCormick Reaper Works in Chicago, the city's radical labor leaders called a mass meeting in Haymarket Square on May 4. When 300 policemen moved in to disperse the crowd, a bomb exploded amid their ranks. The enraged police attacked the crowd with guns and batons. In less than 20 minutes, seven policemen lay dead (most, an investigation would show, from shots fired by fellow officers) along with four workers. The press quickly dubbed the incident the **Haymarket Riot**, and especially when accompanied by images such as this one (**16.20**), the incident stoked vehement opposition to organized labor. Note the placement of the dead policemen in a sort of martyrs' pantheon above a riot scene depicting "murderous rioters" being gunned down.

The next day, as hysterical headlines across the nation proclaimed that revolution was at hand, Chicago police arrested eight men, all self-proclaimed anarchists, and charged them with

16.20 The Haymarket Incident, 1886
The Haymarket incident sparked a nationwide backlash against organized labor. Newspapers ran images like this one, in which martyred policemen hover over a scene where, "murderous rioters" are gunned down.

What role did the press play in promoting a negative impression of labor unions?

Read the Document George Engel, "Address by a Condemned Haymarket Anarchist" (1886)

murder. After a hasty trial in which even the prosecution conceded that no one had seen the men throw a bomb, all were convicted. Seven were sentenced to death and one to life imprisonment. Four were hanged; one committed suicide in his cell. In 1893, Illinois elected a pro-labor governor who pardoned the remaining three, declaring they had not received a fair trial. Haymarket created a climate of fear and provided justification for officials across the nation to crack down on the labor movement. Throughout the spring and summer of 1886, hundreds of labor activists were arrested—100 in New York City alone. In response workers across the nation formed labor parties and ran candidates for offices from city councilor to governor. Most candidates lacked the money or experience to win, but there were notable surprises. For example, Chicago's United Labor Party polled 25,000 votes (of 92,000 cast) and elected a state senator and seven state assemblymen. In Milwaukee, the People's Party elected a mayor, a state senator, six state assemblymen, and a congressman. In one of the most widely watched contests, Henry George, the reformer and author of *Progress and Poverty,* finished a close second in the mayor's race in New York City—out polling Republican Theodore Roosevelt, who finished a distant third.

However, the unity and hope expressed by workers at the polls in November 1886 were soon undermined. First, the tumult of 1886 brought to the fore the dissatisfaction of many skilled workers within the KOL. Deeming the organization too strike prone and too influenced by socialists and radicals (who after Haymarket brought organized labor unwanted criticism), 25 unions of skilled workers convened in Columbus, Ohio, in December 1886 and founded the American Federation of Labor (AFL). The more radical activists within the

KOL also grew dissatisfied with Powderly's leadership, decrying his growing opposition to strikes and political action. Anti-labor hysteria in the press and legal repression following Haymarket further weakened the labor movement. Membership in the KOL dwindled rapidly, from 700,000 in 1886 to only 100,000 by 1890.

National leadership of the labor movement after 1886 fell to the new AFL. Comprised exclusively of unions of skilled workers and led by cigar-maker Samuel Gompers, the AFL shunned the KOL's idealistic goal of industrial cooperation. Instead, it accepted capitalism and the wage system and focused on what it termed "pure and simple" goals: higher wages, shorter hours, and job security.

The AFL also refused to organize unskilled workers, arguing that they were too weak and unreliable. They similarly excluded (with a few exceptions) women, African Americans, and recent immigrants. The AFL grew to 1.6 million members by 1904. However, its narrowed vision and conservative approach to the labor question would leave the growing numbers of less-skilled industrial workers without a national voice until the 1930s.

These divisions within the labor movement reflected the dramatic and often controversial changes industrialization brought to the United States after 1865. Many Americans prospered in this period, but others found themselves working in dangerous factories for long hours and meager wages. As a result, this period was marked by vigorous debates about economic justice, social equality, and the proper role of government in regulating the economy and protecting the rights and well-being of its most vulnerable citizens. These debates that would continue into the next century.

1866–1868

William Sylvis founds the National Labor Union
First significant effort to organize workers nationally

Horatio Alger publishes
Ragged Dick
First of one hundred "rags to respectability" novels popularizing the ideal of the self-made man

1873–1876

The Panic of 1873
Begins four years of severe economic depression

Wanamaker opens Grand Depot in Philadelphia
Sets standard for lavish department stores in an era of increasing consumerism

1877

The "Great Uprising" railroad strike
Massive strike spreads to several cities. Clashes between workers and police and soldiers leave dozens killed and millions of dollars in damage

1878–1879

Terence Powderly elected Grandmaster Workman of the Knights of Labor
Transforms KOL into a powerful industrial union with 700,000 members by 1886

Henry George publishes
Progress and Poverty
The bestseller gives voice to the anxiety over growing social inequality

CHAPTER REVIEW

Review Questions

1. What strengths did the United States possess in terms of resources, culture, technology, and public policy that facilitated industrialization after 1865?

2. Why were the Supreme Court and Congress so slow to curb the power of big business?

3. How was advertising transformed after 1865? How did it affect the Industrial Revolution?

4. Why did American workers have such a difficult time uniting to oppose abusive and exploitative employers?

5. How did industrialization create new opportunities for women? How and why were these opportunities limited?

6. Why did the Knights of Labor expand in the 1880s? Why did it collapse almost as suddenly?

Key Terms

Laissez-faire (French for "let do" or "leave alone") A philosophy that argued that the government should impose no restraints on business.   **471**

Monopoly The control of an industry or market by one corporation.   **474**

Vertical integration Business organization where one company controls the main phases of production of a good, from acquiring raw materials to retailing the finished product.   **475**

Horizontal integration Business organization where one company buys many other companies producing the same product to eliminate competition and achieve greater efficiency.   **475**

Robber barons A pejorative name for big business leaders that suggested they grew rich by devious business practices, exploitation of workers, and political manipulation.   **476**

Trust A legally binding deal bringing many companies in the same industry under the direction of a board of "trustees."   **476**

Sherman Anti-Trust Act Authorized the Justice Department to prosecute any illegal contract, combination, or conspiracy among corporations that eliminated competition or restrained free trade.   **477**

Blacklist A list of workers that employers in a particular town or industry refused to hire because they were considered troublemakers.   **483**

Social Darwinism The belief that the principles of evolution, which Darwin had observed in nature, also applied to society. Advocates argued that individuals or groups achieve advantages over others as the result of biological superiority, an idea expressed as "survival of the fittest."   **488**

Knights of Labor A labor organization founded in 1869 that in the 1880s accepted workers of all trades and backgrounds and became the world's largest industrial union   **490**

Haymarket Riot A violent incident touched off when a bomb exploded amid a group of policemen as they broke up a peaceful labor rally in Chicago's Haymarket Square on May 4, 1886.   **494**

1882

John D. Rockefeller creates the first trust
Becomes a key feature of modern business organization and target of social critics

Workers in New York City establish Labor Day
Reflects strengthening of labor movement and protest against growing inequality and exploitation

1883–1884

Railroads establish standard time zones
Reflects power of railroads and the trend of standardization in business. In 1886, they establish a standard track gauge

Knights of Labor wins strike against Wabash Railroad
Gains publicity and credibility for the KOL, leading to a surge in membership

1886

Police and workers clash in Haymarket
Leads to nationwide crackdown on labor union activism

The American Federation of Labor founded
Workers in skilled trades separate from Knights of Labor

1889–1890

Andrew Carnegie publishes "The Gospel of Wealth"
Popularizes the belief that opportunity and upward mobility are available to all in an industrial society

Sherman Anti-Trust Act passed
Reflects popular mood that big business must be restrained; weak, and ineffective

MyHistoryLab Connections

Visit www.myhistorylab.com for a customized Study Plan that will help you build your knowledge of *Wonder and Woe.*

Questions for Analysis

1. **Why did many Americans come to fear large corporations like railroads?**

   🔍 **View** the **Image** *Modern Colossus of (Rail) Roads (1879), p. 474*

2. **How did the introduction of new technology impact American workers?**

   📖 **Read** the **Document** *Technology and the Shoe Industry in Fincher's Trade Review (1864), p. 481*

3. **How did industrialists champion industrial capitalism?**

   📖 **Read** the **Document** *Andrew Carnegie, "Wealth," p. 487*

4. **How did critics of industrial capitalism argue that it threatened the republic?**

   📖 **Read** the **Document** *Henry George, "Progress and Poverty," p. 490*

5. **What challenges did workers face in trying to organize unions?**

   🔍 **View** the **Map** *Interactive Map: Organizing American Labor in the Late Nineteenth Century, p. 492*

Other Resources from This Chapter

📖 **Read** the **Document**

- *Thomas Edison, The Success of the Electric Light (October 1880), p. 471*
- *Interstate Commerce Act, p. 475*
- *Massachusetts Bureau of Statistics of Labor, from "The Working Girls of Boston" (1884), p. 482*
- *Chinese Exclusion Act, p. 484*
- *Herbert Spencer, Social Darwinism (1857), p. 488*
- *Horatio Alger, Ragged Dick, p. 488*
- *George Engel, "Address by a Condemned Haymarket Anarchist" (1886), p. 494*

🔍 **View** the **Closer Look**

- *Images as History: Advertising and the Art of Cultivating Anxiety and Desire, p. 478*
- *"Testing" Clark's O.N.T. Spool Cotton, p. 479*

🔍 **View** the **Image** *John D. Rockefeller Cartoon (1901), p. 476*

🔍 **View** the **Map** *Atlas Map: Changing Lives of American Women, 1880–1930, p. 486*

👁 **Watch** the **Video** *Video Lecture: Mastering Time and Space: How the Railroad Changed America, p. 472*

Becoming a Modern Society

America in the Gilded Age, 1877–1900

Hundreds of thousands of people, including President Chester A. Arthur and countless dignitaries, participated in the joyful ceremonies marking the opening of the Brooklyn Bridge on May 23, 1883. As this painting of the event demonstrates, Americans in the late nineteenth century celebrated the onset of the urban age. An astonishing sight and the very embodiment of the modern age, it was the world's largest suspension bridge, a style made possible by the one product that in many ways defined the industrial revolution—steel. The bridge's designer, German immigrant John Roebling, emphasized this transition to the modern age by using a stark contrast: he constructed the bridge's twin towers out of the ancient building material (stone) and formed them into gothic archways, a style reminiscent of the great medieval cathedrals of Europe.

The Brooklyn Bridge embodied the new urban and industrial era beyond its cutting-edge technology and symbolic design. Workers who were either immigrants or the children of immigrants constructed the bridge. By connecting the nation's largest city (New York) and third largest city (Brooklyn), a prelude to their consolidation into one city in 1898, the new bridge also symbolized rapid urban growth. Finally the bridge hinted at the emergence of a new, more independent American woman. When Washington Roebling (who had succeeded his father as chief engineer) fell gravely ill in 1872, his wife, Emily Warren Roebling, spent the next 11 years as the project's onsite manager.

The enthusiasm that marked the bridge's opening masked the grave problems that rampant urban growth entailed. Indeed, the era's name, the **Gilded Age**, reflected this notion that the amazing achievements of the period were like a thin gold layer that covered many unresolved social problems. The sections of New York and Brooklyn connected by the bridge, for example, were vast working-class immigrant districts beset by high rates of poverty, crime, and disease. Equally unseen in the glow of the fireworks was the rising discontent among American workers over exploitation by employers and alienation from an unresponsive political system. Indeed, dozens of men had died during the bridge's construction, and more than once the workers went on strike. These sentiments and those of hard-pressed American farmers in the heartland would explode in the 1890s, leading to the emergence of the People's Party. The party eventually faded away, but not before establishing a reform agenda that would shape the Progressive Era (1900–1920).

"The day seems brought distinctly nearer when the nation, equipped with the latest implements furnished by science, shall master and use as never before its rich domain."

REV. RICHARD STORRS, speech at the opening of the Brooklyn Bridge

The Rise of the City

The United States experienced explosive urban growth in the second half of the nineteenth century. Industrialization and mass immigration transformed older cities, such as New York and Philadelphia, and newer ones, such as Denver and Chicago, into major metropolises. Their growth was often chaotic and attended by significant increases in crime, poverty, and epidemics. City political machines grew powerful, providing relief to the vulnerable and promoting urban growth, but earning a reputation for corruption.

To the Cities

The urban population of the United States grew at an astonishing rate between 1860 and 1900. In 1860, one in five Americans lived in urban areas—by 1900, two in five. In that same period the number of cities with populations greater than 100,000 soared from 9 to 38. Among these were New York (3.4 million), Chicago (2.7 million), and Philadelphia (1.3 million). Seventy-eight other cities had 50,000 or more inhabitants by 1900.

Much of this new urban population came from rural areas within the United States. As agriculture became more mechanized (see Chapter 15), thereby lowering demand for farm labor, men migrated to urban areas. Similarly, the rise of American manufacturing eliminated the need for rural women to make clothes and other household goods, leading many to seek economic opportunity in cities. These men and women found an array of job opportunities in the city, from low-paid work as factory operatives, laborers, and servants to more desirable positions as skilled artisans and clerks. They also were faced with the challenge of adjusting to an utterly new lifestyle.

Another rural-to-urban internal migration involved African Americans seeking to escape the poverty, racism, and violence of the Jim Crow South (see Chapter 14). Drawn by word of better jobs and greater freedoms, some 300,000 migrated to northern cities between 1890 and 1910. Chicago's African American population jumped from 15,000 in 1890 to 110,000 in 1920. This marked the beginning of what became known as the Great Migration, the relocation of some 7 million African Americans from the South to the North between 1890 and 1970.

However, the greatest source of urban population growth was mass immigration from Europe, with significant numbers also from Latin America, the Caribbean, and Asia. Before 1880, most immigrants to the United States came from Britain, Ireland, Germany, and Scandinavia. Thereafter, the sources of immigration shifted to nations in Southern and Eastern Europe such as Russia, Italy, Greece, and Austria-Hungary (**17.1**). All told, the United States accepted 28 million newcomers between 1860 and 1920.

As with all immigrants before and since, some of these newcomers chose immigration to escape poverty, warfare, political and religious

17.1 Immigration to the United States, 1880–1920
Before 1880, most immigrants to the United States came from Northern and Western Europe, but after 1880, most were from Southern and Eastern Europe.
[*Source:* U.S. Bureau of the Census.]

	1880–1889	%	1890–1899	%	1900–1909	%	1910–1919	%
Austria-Hungary	314,787	6.0	534,059	14.5	2,001,376	24.4	1,154,727	18.2
German Empire	1,445,181	27.5	579,072	15.7	328,722	4.0	174,227	2.7
Greece	1,807	.1	12,732	.3	145,402	1.8	198,108	3.1
Ireland	764,061	12.8	405,710	11.0	344,940	4.2	166,445	2.6
Italy	276,660	5.1	603,761	16.3	1,930,475	23.5	1,229,916	19.4
Russia	182,698	3.5	450,101	12.7	1,501,301	18.3	1,106,998	17.4
Scandinavia	761,783	12.7	390,729	10.5	488,208	5.9	238,275	3.8
United Kingdom	810,900	15.5	328,579	8.9	469,578	5.7	371,878	5.8
Totals	**5,248,568**		**3,694,295**		**8,202,388**		**6,347,380**	

Why did so many people flock to American cities?   **Read** the **Document** *Adna Weber, "The Growth of Cities"*

persecution, and natural disasters. But most were drawn by the promise of economic opportunity and upward mobility in America. Some migrated to rural areas and became farmers, but most headed for America's cities with their ever-expanding number of jobs in industry, construction, service, and entrepreneurship.

Cities already characterized by ethnic, racial, and religious diversity brought by earlier immigrants and African Americans saw their diversity reach unprecedented levels. By 1910, immigrants and their American-born children comprised an astonishing 78.6 percent of New York's 4.8 million residents. Chicago (77.5 percent), Milwaukee (78.6 percent), San Francisco (68.3 percent), and most medium-to-large cities boasted similarly astoundingly numbers. Overall, the foreign-born comprised 14.8 percent of the national population in 1910.

Emergence of Ethnic Enclaves

These new immigrants, like the Irish and Germans before them, soon formed concentrated ethnic enclaves. Often they moved into neighborhoods previously dominated by immigrants who had arrived before the Civil War. As a result in New York, for example, the Lower East Side enclaves of Little Ireland, Little Germany, and Little Africa became by the 1890s Little Italy, Chinatown, and the Jewish East Side. This process of ethnic succession is captured in a World War I memorial plaque affixed to the façade of the Church of the Transfiguration on New York's Lower East Side (**17.2**). A community of native-born Americans built the church in 1801 as the English Lutheran First Church of Zion, but they sold it in the 1840s to Irish Catholics who renamed it Church of the Transfiguration. In the 1890s, a massive influx of Italians and outflow of Irish to other parts of the city turned the neighborhood into Little Italy and Transfiguration into a mostly Italian Catholic church. (Mother Elizabeth Cabrini, later canonized a saint, worked in the church caring for Italian immigrants.) The plaque provides a snapshot of the transformation from Little Ireland to Little Italy. Of the twenty names of parishioners who died in World War I,

seventeen are Italian and only three—Donahue, Durkin, and Kane—are Irish. Today the neighborhood is part of Chinatown and most of the parishioners are Chinese.

Immigrant groups formed ethnic enclaves in part because they faced hostility and discrimination from Americans and other immigrant groups. But the primary cause was their recognition that grouping together enhanced their chances of success in America. Italian immigrants in Chicago's Little Italy, for example, enjoyed the comfort and practical benefits of residing among people who spoke their language. There they could find help getting a job from an immigrant aid association, fellowship in an Italian fraternal society, or solace in an Italian Catholic church. They also found things that reminded them of home: Italian food, books, newspapers, churches, theaters, and opera houses.

A closer look at these enclaves revealed that they usually comprised smaller units composed of people from a particular region or village of their home country. New York's Jewish East Side, for example, included large concentrations of Jews from Hungary, Romania, Galicia, Russia, and the eastern Mediterranean. Italians in Boston's North End clustered on certain streets depending on whether they came from Sicily, Campania, the

17.2 Evidence of Ethnic Succession
This 1919 plaque lists 17 Italian and three Irish names, indicating that the neighborhood once known as Little Ireland had become Little Italy.

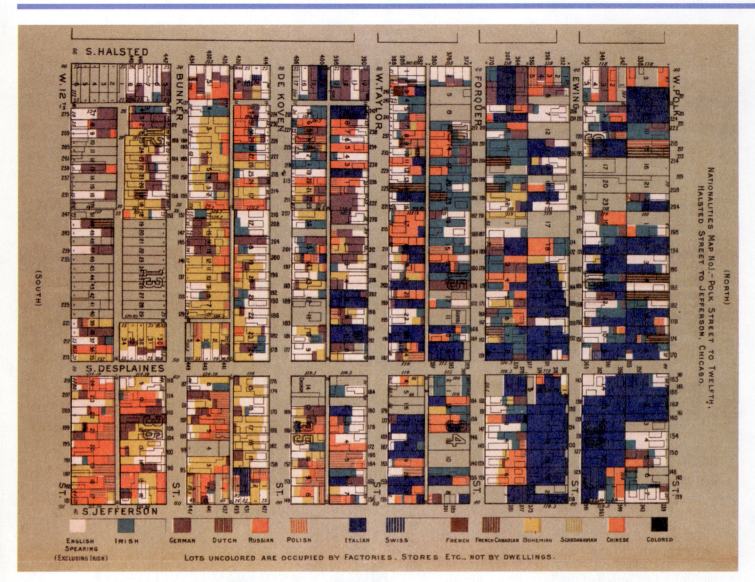

ENGLISH SPEAKING (EXCLUDING IRISH) | IRISH | GERMAN | DUTCH | RUSSIAN | POLISH | ITALIAN | SWISS | FRENCH | FRENCH CANADIAN | BOHEMIAN | SCANDINAVIAN | CHINESE | COLORED

LOTS UNCOLORED ARE OCCUPIED BY FACTORIES, STORES ETC., NOT BY DWELLINGS.

17.3 Mapping the Diversity of Ethnic Chicago
This 1895 map of the 12-block area surrounding Hull House demonstrates the diversity of the immigrant neighborhood. [*Source*: ICHi-51283; Hull House—map of Nationalities in Chicago; Chicago (Ill.); n.d.; Creator- Hull House. Nationalities Map No. 1—Polk Street to Twelfth, Halsted Street to Jefferson, Chicago.]

Abruzzi, or Liguria. Yet as this 1895 map (**17.3**) of the neighborhood surrounding Chicago's famous Hull House, which provided that city's immigrants with social and educational services, demonstrates, even immigrants in ethnic enclaves shared their neighborhoods with people of diverse origins. This twelve-block section of the city included immigrants from Ireland, Germany, Italy, Russia, Poland, Switzerland, France, Canada, Bohemia, Scandinavia, China, and the Netherlands, not to mention African Americans.

The Troubled City

Many Americans in the late nineteenth century saw cities as exciting places filled with opportunity, cultural diversity, entertainment, and new technology such as electric lighting and skyscrapers. Yet many more viewed cities as places of crowding,

turmoil, filth, and despair. Both images were accurate, but the latter generated the most commentary and concern. One of the most striking features of modern urban life was the emergence of densely packed "slums." In one ward on New York's Lower East Side in 1890, population density reached 334,000 people per square mile, numbers never seen before in history. Most people living in these densely packed districts were immigrants who worked for low wages as day laborers and factory operatives. Few men earned enough money to support their families. So they relied on their wives and children to produce additional income (see Chapter 16).

Squalid housing exacerbated the poverty of urban workers. **Tenements**, or multiple family dwellings of four to six stories housing dozens of families, became the most common form of housing for poor city dwellers by the 1860s. Most tenement apartments consisted of just two or three dimly lit and poorly ventilated rooms.

Tenement districts in every city suffered from high rates of disease and death, much of it caused when drinking water became contaminated by bacteria due to primitive sewage systems. Another source of disease was horses. In 1900, New York's 120,000 horses dropped six million pounds of manure on the streets every day. In most cities, as shown in this photograph (**17.4**), street cleaning was inadequate in working-class neighborhoods. Note that in this filthy working-class street in New York, vendors sell all manner of goods on the sidewalks, including food. These conditions contributed to frequent epidemics. In Chicago in 1891, for example, 2,000 people died from typhoid fever and 4,300 from bronchitis and pneumonia. Every year in Chicago in the early 1890s, 10,000 to 12,000 children under the age of five died.

Despite the dreadful condition of many tenements, the surging population of American cities kept the demand for housing high, causing rents to rise continually. In New York an 1883 survey of bricklayers, among the city's best-paid workers, determined that they paid 28 percent of their annual income to their landlords. Another survey a few years later revealed that cloak makers, another skilled group, devoted 38 percent of their income to

rent. As a result evictions for falling behind in rent were common. New York averaged more than 16,000 evictions per year in the early 1880s and more than 23,000 by 1892.

> **"Thousands of small houses and cottages arranged for one family are now packed with a family in each room."**
>
> **Chicago Board of Health report**

Late-nineteenth-century cities also suffered from high rates of crime, especially in the tenement districts. Some crime was driven by poverty or despair. Women, for example, usually turned to prostitution as a last resort to survive. Immigration also increased crime, because it resulted in a disproportionately high population of young single men (typically an age cohort with higher than average crime rates). The overall growth, diversity, and mobility of urban populations also contributed to increased crime because these populations fostered anonymity and undermined the ability of communities to prevent potential criminal activity.

17.4 Mired in Muck Late-nineteenth-century American cities, especially in working-class neighborhoods, had public health problems because of inadequate street cleaning.

The Political Machine—"Boss Rule"

Another unsettling feature of urban life, in addition to poverty, crime, and disorder, was the emergence of **political machines**. Most often associated with the Democratic Party, these organizations became powerful in nearly every large American city by mobilizing large blocs of working-class and immigrant voters while developing favorable relationships with real estate and business interests. Some machines controlled small sections of big cities. Martin Lomasney, for example, was the "boss" of Boston's Eighth Ward. Others, such as New York's Tammany Hall, ruled the entire metropolis by the 1860s. By the late nineteenth and early twentieth centuries, several machines extended their power to the state level.

> ### "Tammany Hall bears the same relation to the penitentiary as the Sunday school to the church."
> #### A reformer, 1876

Several trends coincided to account for the rise of political machines in American cities. The spread of universal white male suffrage in the 1820s (see Chapter 8) meant that political success depended less on a candidate's family name or wealth than on his ability to whip up enthusiasm and get out the vote on Election Day. Rapid urban growth also produced unprecedented opportunities for politicians and their machines to reward supporters with construction contracts and jobs such as police officers and building inspectors. Machines also garnered support from immigrants by denouncing nativism and stymieing anti-immigrant legislation such as proposals to deny public jobs to the foreign born. Finally, the growing numbers of the poor provided a needy constituency, for which the machines supplied not only jobs but also a range of services and favors, including cash handouts, payments for funerals, legal assistance, and seasonal giveaways of turkeys at Thanksgiving and bags of coal in winter. Recipients of machine largesse and charity were expected to vote for its candidates.

The emergence of political machines horrified many wealthy and native-born Americans. They found rule by the foreign-born threatening and the rough and corrupt style of bosses offensive. One aspect of machine politics, however, aroused especially bitter criticism: the policy of no-questions-asked charity.

Political machines acquired and retained power not only by providing services to their constituents but also, as suggested by this political cartoon of boss William Tweed, the notoriously corrupt head of Tammany Hall, by intimidating voters and engaging in election fraud (**17.5**). This image shows that the ballot "box" in many cities was actually a transparent glass ball that allowed the political machines' "shoulder hitters" to intimidate voters by letting them know they were watching to see how they voted. The motto "In Counting There Is Strength" refers to the machines' tactic of using the police and boards of elections to manipulate the vote count to ensure victory for their party. Equally important was the money machines garnered by selling patronage jobs, demanding kickbacks from city contractors, and collecting protection fees from a vast economy of vice the machine-controlled police allowed to flourish. Reformers railed against the machine, but consistently failed to defeat it.

17.5 Winning By Any Means Political machines often resorted to voter intimidation and election fraud. As the motto "In Counting There Is Strength" suggests, vote counts were manipulated to ensure victory.

"THAT'S WHAT'S THE MATTER."
BOSS TWEED. "As long as I count the Votes, what are you going to do about it? say?"

How did political machines gain the support of working-class and immigrant voters?

Read the **Document** Lincoln Steffens, The Shame of the Cities
View the **Closer Look** Competing Visions: How Best to Help the Poor?

A Search for Solutions

The dark side of urbanization in the late nineteenth century prompted a wide range of competing views and responses. Some Americans concluded that the real problem of urban poverty and the troubling crime, disease, disorder, and corruption that accompanied it was the urban poor, in particular, the foreign-born. Their solution was heightened nativism and a demand to restrict immigration. Other Americans, however, worked to develop government agencies to address the emerging challenges of urban life. Still others established private institutions like settlement houses that reflected a new attitude toward the immigrant poor.

17.6 Fear of Foreigners on the Rise Decrying the so-called "new immigrants" from southern and Eastern Europe as bearers of unwanted habits and ideas, nativism surged in the Gilded Age.

The Nativist Impulse

The rise of the modern American city was accompanied by a revival of nativism, or anti-immigrant views and sentiments. Suspicion of and hatred for the foreign-born had flared up during the Know-Nothing movement (see Chapter 12) in the 1850s, which targeted Irish and German immigrants, especially those who were Catholics. In the Gilded Age nativism targeted the so-called new immigrants, or those coming from Southern and Eastern Europe. As this 1899 image (**17.6**) illustrates, nativists decried newcomers as bearers of a wide range of unwanted habits and ideas. The immigrant, shown here in a racist caricature of Eastern Europeans, carries according to his labels poverty, anarchy, superstition, intemperance, and Sabbath desecration (working or recreating on a Sunday). Note Uncle Sam's disdainful reaction and the sarcastic inscriptions on the gateway—"admittance free," "walk in!" and "welcome"—meant to convey nativists' anger over what they considered lax immigration laws. As slums grew larger and strikes (often involving many foreign-born workers) became more violent, nativists called all the more loudly for the sharp restriction of immigration. One of the most prominent was Josiah Strong, a Midwestern minister whose 1885 book, *Our Country:*

Its Possible Future and Present Crisis, warned the nation against the immigrant menace.

In 1882, Congress responded to pressure by American workers and passed the Chinese

📖 **Read** the **Document** *Josiah Strong, "Anglo-Saxon Culture Under Siege" (1885)*

Why did nativists oppose immigration?

Exclusion Act (see Chapter 16), which barred Chinese immigration to the United States. In 1887, nativists who were especially fixated on the dangers posed by Catholic immigration formed the American Protective Association (APA) to lobby for immigration restriction. The organization grew to 500,000 members by the end of 1893. Its main base of strength was middle-class Protestants in the Midwest, but chapters also sprang up in most cities in the East.

> # The city has become a serious menace to our civilization.... It has a peculiar attraction for the immigrant....Here is heaped the social dynamite; here roughs, gamblers, thieves, robbers, lawless and desperate men of all sorts, congregate; men who are ready on any pretext to raise riots for the purpose of destruction and plunder.
>
> JOSIAH STRONG, *Our Country: Its Possible Future and Its Present Crisis* (1885)

In 1890, Congress made oversight of immigration a federal responsibility and established immigration depots in most major ports to weed out and reject immigrants with incurable diseases, radical beliefs, criminal backgrounds, or so little money and skills they seemed likely to swell the ranks of the urban poor. The largest and most famous of these facilities, Ellis Island in New York harbor, opened in 1892.

Many nativists considered this new system too lenient and called for additional restrictions on immigration. In 1894, several Harvard graduates founded the Immigration Restriction League to lobby for a literacy test for all would-be immigrants (requiring they demonstrate the ability to read and write in any language). Presidents Cleveland, Taft, and Wilson vetoed immigrant literacy test bills, but Congress overrode Wilson's veto, and it became law in 1917.

A Different View: Urban Reforms

While some Americans believed urban poverty, crime, disease, and overcrowding could be eliminated simply by restricting immigration, others developed a range of innovative policies and institutions to solve, or at least minimize, these problems. To meet the problem of rising crime, most cities followed the lead of New York, when in 1845 it replaced the traditional night watch of a few untrained and unarmed men with a paid professional police department. Large cities also disbanded their volunteer fire companies and invested in new fire-fighting technology, such as steam pumpers, and adopted tougher building codes.

More dangerous to a city than fire—at least to its inhabitants—were the frequent outbreaks of cholera, diphtheria, typhoid fever, and other maladies. Drawing on increasing knowledge about germ theory, cities established boards of health and took steps to improve water quality, waste removal, and street cleaning.

The latter half of the nineteenth century also witnessed a movement to build urban parks to provide the beauty and serenity of nature and offer wholesome and healthy recreation space (as opposed to alleys and saloons) for all. New York's Central Park, built in the 1850s and 1860s, proved so successful that nearly every large city commenced its own park projects. Because most of the grand parks were located far from the slums, however, reformers in the 1890s pushed urban governments to condemn blocks of tenements and build parks within working-class neighborhoods.

Urban reformers also expanded public education. Compulsory education laws (usually requiring schooling until age 14) and a massive building campaign saw public school enrollments surge from 6.9 million to 17.8 million between 1870 and 1910. Millions more students attended parochial schools established by the Catholic Church. This effort reflected the traditional belief that education made for a productive and informed citizenry. But as the photograph (**17.7**) of children reciting the Pledge of Allegiance illustrates, advocates also saw expanded urban public schooling as a means of Americanizing the immigrant masses, teaching them English and respect for democracy and the law. The pledge was first published in a youth magazine in 1892 to promote patriotism and civic pride among school children on the eve of the 400th anniversary of

Christopher Columbus's arrival in the New World. Educators quickly made its recitation a daily ritual in schools across the country. This earlier style, which required people to end the pledge by extending their arms out straight, was abolished in the 1930s because of its similarity to salutes used in fascist Germany and Italy.

Capturing a New View of Poverty

Reformers in the Gilded Age also developed a new way of thinking about poverty and its causes. Most Americans held to the traditional view that poverty was caused by personal or moral failures such as laziness or drunkenness. The poor, as Horatio Alger and others argued so persuasively in popular literature (see Chapter 16), needed only to abandon their dissolute ways and seize the opportunities for success that abounded in American life.

But reformers began to challenge this view of poverty by arguing that factors beyond their control made people poor. A key figure in this new outlook was photojournalist Jacob A. Riis, who emigrated from Denmark to New York in 1870. After spending his first years in America in poverty, he gained a foothold in journalism. By the mid-1880s, he had earned a reputation as a reporter covering the city's crime beat. But Riis was troubled by the poverty and suffering he saw and decided to publicize it to gain public support for reforms. In 1887, he started taking photographs of

17.7 Promoting Loyalty and Patriotism Advocates saw public education as a means of Americanizing the urban immigrant masses. Soon after its introduction in 1892, educators made the Pledge of Allegiance a daily ritual in schools.

Read the **Document** *Jacob Riis,* How the Other Half Lives

Why was the Pledge of Allegiance adopted in the 1890s?

slum life to spark public awareness, and by 1888–1889, he began showing his photographs while giving lectures before reform societies and church groups. Spurred by the positive reaction to these talks, especially to the photographs (see *Images as History: Seeing the Poor*, page 509), he wrote the book *How the Other Half Lives: Studies among the Tenements of New York*, which he published in 1890. Books providing shocking accounts of prostitution, drunkenness, and violence in America's slums had appeared as early as the 1840s, but Riis's book was different and it caused a sensation.

Living among the Poor: Settlement Houses

Riis was not alone in promoting a more progressive and sympathetic view of poverty and remedies to it. In the early 1880s, middle-class and college-educated women began establishing in immigrant neighborhoods **settlement houses**, or institutions dedicated to helping the urban poor by providing a wide range of social and educational services. Jane Addams and Ellen Gates Starr founded the most famous and influential settlement house, Hull House, in Chicago in 1889. Born to wealthy Illinois families, they had met in college and toured Europe together in 1888, where they were inspired by a visit to Toynbee Hall, a settlement house in London's poor East End. There they saw educated, wealthy young men enter the East End to assist the poor. They vowed to establish a similar institution in Chicago.

With financial backing from wealthy reformers, Addams and Starr rented an old mansion on Chicago's Near West Side. The neighborhood was overwhelmingly foreign born (see 17.3) and its residents lived in dreary, run-down tenements. It also suffered from poor sanitation and high rates of crime. Unlike socially conscious elite women of earlier generations who simply raised money for the poor or lobbied the state legislature for laws against child labor, Addams, Starr, and the many women workers they attracted to Hull House chose to live among the poor to get to know them and understand their needs—even learn from them.

The staff at Hull House first offered educational classes in literature and art. When these proved popular, they began to teach more practical subjects, such as cooking, sewing, hygiene, civics, the English language, and vocational training. They also opened their doors to fledgling labor unions, recognizing the vital role unions could play in raising the earnings of workers, especially the foreign born.

Within a decade Hull House was a flourishing institution offering an array of services to the poor of Chicago. Addams and other Hull House workers like Florence Kelley also became activists to prod city authorities to improve tenement laws, increase street cleaning and garbage removal, and expand public education. They also lobbied state officials for laws against child labor and for improved factory safety. Hull House was not the first settlement in America, but it soon became its most famous, inspiring hundreds of successful imitators (400 by 1910), including Denison House in Boston (1889) and Henry Street Settlement in New York (1893).

The White City

The optimistic vision of modern urban life articulated by reformers like Jane Addams and Jacob Riis found vivid expression in the **City Beautiful Movement**. Taking form in the late 1880s, it brought together architects, landscape architects, and urban planners who believed the many problems afflicting American cities could be ameliorated, even eliminated, through the comprehensive planning and grand redesign of urban spaces. City Beautiful proponents like Daniel Burnham and Frederick Law Olmsted argued for the creation of large parks and public squares linked by grand boulevards. They also emphasized classical architectural styles for both public and private buildings.

Burnham, Olmsted, and others first demonstrated these ideas at the 1893 Chicago World's Exposition, a grand celebration of the 400th anniversary of Christopher Columbus's arrival in the New World in 1492 and of Chicago's recovery from its devastating fire in 1871. Like the many world's fairs that preceded it, the Chicago Exposition celebrated technology, culture, and commerce. It contained thousands of exhibits on science, machinery, art, history, ethnic heritage, music, and theater. But its greatest significance was its impact on architecture, design, and urban planning. Given nearly 700 acres of waterfront property along Lake Michigan on which to erect buildings, Burnham and the extraordinary team he assembled, including landscape architect

Images as History

SEEING THE POOR

In 1890, Jacob Riis published a shocking exposé, *How the Other Half Lives,* of the dreadful conditions in which the poor lived. But unlike most Americans writing about urban poverty in that era, who attributed these problems to the moral failures of the poor, Riis argued that the poor were *victims* of unhealthy and unregulated tenements for which they were forced to pay most of their earnings. Adding to the book's impact were his photographs and drawings made from photographs. His carefully composed photograph, "An Italian Rag-Picker in Jersey Street," shows the woman's desperate situation.

Sandro Botticelli, *Madonna and Child* (c. 1470)

Riis convinced many of his readers that the growing numbers of impoverished slum dwellers were trapped in circumstances beyond their control largely due to unhealthy and expensive tenement housing. He called for improved tenements that would free the poor from their debilitating circumstances and allow them the chance to succeed. As a result of *How the Other Half Lives* and other books, not to mention magazine articles and speeches, many cities passed tougher laws regulating room size, windows, running water, and toilets.

The ladder suggests her "apartment" is little more than a dingy, windowless basement room with only one piece of furniture (the chair on which she sits).

Riis presents her not as filthy or drunk; despite the dreadful circumstances, she and her baby wear clean clothes.

Riis often included babies and innocent-looking children in his photographs to prompt the viewer to wonder—and worry—about their fate if the plight of the poor was not alleviated.

The man's hat on the wall prompts the viewer to wonder if this desperate woman has a husband or has been abandoned.

Although poor this woman is a hard worker. A rag picker collected discarded rags and other fabric (note the sacks), laundered them on a stovetop tub, and then sold them to paper manufacturers for pennies per pound.

The mother's heavenward gaze was intended to spur sympathy among middle- and upper-class viewers by conjuring up the familiar religious imagery of the Madonna and Child.

Jacob A. Riis, "Italian Mother and Her Baby in Jersey Street" (1889) [*Source:* Jacob A. Riis "Italian Mother and Her Baby in Jersey Street", in the home of an Italian rag-picker, Jersey Street, circa 1890. Museum of the City of New York, The Jacob A. Riis Collection (#157)]

How did Jacob Riis's portrayal of the poor differ from traditional notions of poverty?

17.8 The
White City
Designed by some
of the nation's
leading architects,
Chicago's White City
consisted of 14 main
buildings designed
in the Beaux-
Arts style, set in
landscaped grounds
featuring waterways
and reflecting pools.

Frederick Law Olmsted and architect Louis Sullivan, developed a master plan that called for landscaped grounds featuring waterways and reflecting pools.

Around the waterways, (**17.8**), Burnham placed 14 main buildings designed in the Beaux-Arts style, which emphasized logic, harmony, and uniformity. The Court of Honor buildings, shown in the image, lined the Grand Basin that formed the centerpiece of the exposition grounds. Covered in shimmering bright white stucco, the buildings of the White City astonished the estimated 27 million visitors who entered through the main gates.

Yet as this image indicates, Burnham and his team sought not simply to wow the public with grand architecture. They wanted to showcase the potential glory of the modern city. All cities could be—should be—as impressive as the White City. All that was needed were civic leadership and enlightened urban planning. This grand vision never fully caught on, but many of the City Beautiful ideals and concepts exhibited in the White City influenced a generation of urban planners and architects committed to making American cities more beautiful, healthy, and efficient.

How did the White City reflect an optimistic vision of urban life in the future?

New Habits, Roles, and Lifestyles

The development of vast working-class districts was but one aspect of a broad trend that reshaped urban life in the late nineteenth century. Urban and suburban growth also led to the development of middle-class and elite residential neighborhoods and urban central business districts dedicated almost exclusively to commerce. Middle-class neighborhoods increasingly reflected the new values of the urban middle class, including a growing interest in leisure activities. The growth of leisure time allowed women to take on significant roles in public life through memberships in socially and politically active clubs.

The New Urban Landscape

The evolution of mass transit systems like horse cars steam railroads, and trolleys, led to explosive urban growth and specialized districts dedicated to specific functions. Most cities, for example, developed central business districts where almost no one lived. Instead the high-value real estate in downtowns from Baltimore to Chicago to San Francisco was dedicated to commerce: banks, department stores (see Chapter 16), and the offices of corporations, accountants, lawyers, and other professionals. Each day mass transit systems carried thousands of shoppers and workers to central business districts from sections of cities now dedicated almost exclusively to residential use, or from residential neighborhoods just beyond the city limits.

Soaring real estate values and new technology led to another distinct feature in central business districts: skyscrapers. Before the Civil War few buildings exceeded six stories, but the invention of the elevator and new building materials like cast iron and steel led to ten- and twelve-story buildings by the early 1880s. The big breakthrough came in 1885 with the completion of the Home Insurance Building in Chicago. It was remarkable not for its height (ten stories), but for its internal steel skeleton that allowed for thin walls and large windows. This first true skyscraper led to a boom in tall building construction in downtowns across the country. By 1900, Lower Manhattan alone featured 12 buildings of 300 feet or more in height.

Equally significant, although less dramatic, than the upward reach of city skylines was the outward sprawl of urban areas due to mass transit. Suburbs, or residential communities established just beyond a city's boundary but connected to the urban center by

mass transit, boomed in the Gilded Age. This cover image (**17.9**) from an 1874 real estate publication renders the great commercial metropolis of Chicago in the background while touting the immense tracts of surrounding land as ideal for suburban development. Note the many sets of tracks for trains and trolleys, suggesting the ease with which commuters could travel to and from work in the dirty, loud, and crowded city. Suburbs attracted middle-class

17.9 Spreading Outward
Fast and inexpensive transportation systems in cities led to the development of separate and distinct urban areas. This image from the cover of an 1874 real estate publication shows the densely settled commercial and residential districts of Chicago surrounded by vast stretches of land being developed into commuter suburbs. Note the many sets of train and trolley tracks.

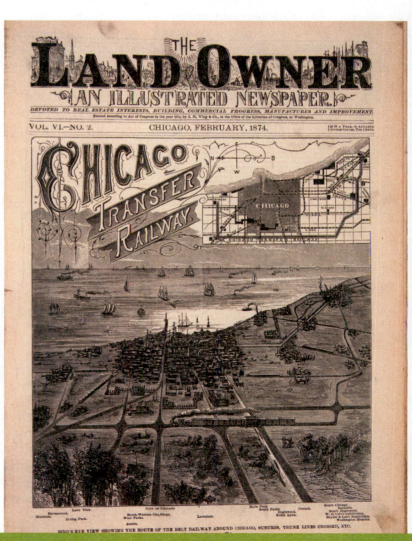

families that could afford to buy a house and pay the cost of commuting to the city for work. Middle-class families found suburbs attractive for their serenity, cleanliness, and greenery—aspects that stood in sharp contrast to the crime, disease, violence, and noise of the inner city. Given the prevalence of racist and nativist attitudes in Gilded Age American society, suburbs also attracted people unwilling to live with immigrants and African Americans.

> ## "Since water hems in the business center on three sides and the nexus of railroads on the south, Chicago must grow upward."
>
> Real estate columnist, *Chicago Tribune*, 1888

The creation of middle-class communities of like-minded people of similar ethnic and religious backgrounds fostered the development of new middle-class values, tastes, and social patterns. Middle-class families had fewer children and higher incomes than their working-class counterparts. Greater wealth and fewer mouths to feed allowed them to purchase an ever-increasing array of consumer products, most often by women who rode trolleys or commuter lines to the central business district. Many of these products were everyday items that came with increasingly recognizable names like Ivory Soap and Coca-Cola. Others were more substantial, such as small pianos that could be purchased on credit. The popularity of pianos in the late nineteenth century reflected not merely the rising wealth of middle-class families, but also the increased leisure time they enjoyed and their desire to develop refined tastes.

New Roles and Expectations for Women

Lower birth rates and a growing trend for hiring servants to perform duties like cooking, cleaning, and laundry left middle-class women with more free time. The dominant notions about gender roles, however, emphasized the need for women to remain in the home, focusing on creating a moral and nurturing environment for their husbands and children. According to this view the outside world of business and politics was the male sphere, full of corruption,

dishonesty, immorality, and violence that threatened virtuous womanhood.

Yet two trends in the late nineteenth century led directly to new, more public roles for middle-class women. The first was a rise in education, especially at the college level. By 1900, women constituted nearly 20 percent of college graduates, up from just 13 percent in 1890. Education allowed women, if only temporarily, to leave the domestic sphere to interact with other young women and encounter emerging ideas about women's rights. Not surprisingly, nearly every leader in the women's rights movement in the late nineteenth century had attended college.

The second was the increased involvement of women in clubs dedicated to charity and social reform. The General Federation of Women's Clubs, established in 1890, counted 160,000 members in more than 500 clubs by 1900. The largest and best known organization was the Women's Christian Temperance Union (WCTU). Activism in clubs gave women the opportunity to exert political influence, build leadership skills, and learn from networks of other activist, reform-minded women.

By the 1890s, many of these activist women joined the women's suffrage movement to obtain voting rights for women. The movement had split into rival factions in 1869 in the debate over the Fourteenth Amendment (see Chapter 14), but in 1890, they reunited to form the National American Woman Suffrage Association (NAWSA). It helped win suffrage in states like Colorado (1893) and Idaho (1896) and then, after considerable struggle, for all women with the ratification of the Nineteenth Amendment in 1920 (see Chapter 18).

Racism led white women to exclude black women from their clubs and the suffrage movement. Nonetheless, African American women established their own clubs to pursue goals such as temperance and women's suffrage. Most of these clubs affiliated with the National Association of Colored Women, an umbrella group. Some black women pursued goals of particular concern to African Americans. Ida B. Wells launched a national campaign against lynching in the 1890s that drew many African American women and men into public activism for reform, especially civil rights.

By the 1890s, Americans had begun to use the term "**New Woman**" to describe middle-class women who pursued higher education, engaged in political activism, delayed marriage, and bore fewer children. The New Woman had a distinct look, donning the clothing, hair style, and air of the so-called Gibson Girl. A creation of illustrator Charles Dana Gibson in 1890s popular magazines, the Gibson Girl was tall and beautiful, with a tightly cinched waist that accentuated her bosom and with hair piled high on her head.

Offsetting these traditionally feminine characteristics, however, was an outgoing, even mischievous spirit that reflected the greater independence and activism of younger American women. Symbolic of this attitude was the degree to which young women took part in the great national enthusiasm for bicycling in the 1890s. Note the striking contrast between these two images.

The first from 1886 (**17.10**) shows a traditional Victorian-era wife in formal attire being carried as a passenger by her husband. The second image, an 1896 advertisement poster for the Stearns Bicycle Company (**17.11**), shows a self-confident and carefree woman in the Gibson Girl style breezing along on her own bicycle. Many conservative Americans condemned the bicycling craze as unnatural and immoral because it allowed young women and men the freedom to pedal off unchaperoned, away from the watchful eyes of parents and other guardians of respectability.

17.11 The New Woman
Many Americans saw a connection between the growing independence, activism, and outgoing spirit of young women and their participation in the national enthusiasm for bicycling in the 1890s.

17.10 The Traditional Woman
Reflecting Victorian values, this conservatively dressed woman in 1886 enjoys a bicycle ride only as the passenger of her husband.

View the Map Atlas Map: Changing Lives of American Women, 1880–1930

What was new about the "New Woman"?

> "Bicycling has done more to emancipate women than anything else in the world. I stand and rejoice every time I see a woman ride by on a wheel. It gives women a feeling of freedom and self-reliance."
>
> SUSAN B. ANTHONY, 1896

17.12 Selling Celebrity
The booming tobacco industry created the original baseball cards to capitalize on the value of sports celebrity endorsements for their products.

New Forms of Leisure and Popular Culture

As industrial life created sharp distinctions between time spent at work and time doing everything else, Americans in the Gilded Age developed the concept of leisure time. This trend was at the heart of the labor movement's persistent demand for the eight-hour day as both a call for shorter hours of toil and an insistence on the right to leisure time. Many city dwellers spent their leisure time in informal activities in their neighborhood, such as walking about, playing games in streets and local parks, and socializing with their neighbors. For many working-class men, the local saloon was the preferred place of leisure.

Increasingly popular, however, were more formal leisure opportunities such as amusement parks and organized spectator sports. Amateur, semiprofessional, and professional baseball teams, for example, drew large crowds. Entrepreneurs soon saw baseball as a business, despite its reputation as the "national pastime." They built large baseball stadiums near streetcar lines and sold patrons not merely tickets but also food, beer, trinkets, and scorecards. By the 1880s, baseball stars like Mike "King" Kelly and Adrian "Cap" Anson were high-paid celebrities. Corporations, especially the booming tobacco industry, quickly realized the value of celebrity endorsements for their products and in the 1880s created the original baseball cards like the one shown here (**17.12**). To legitimize tobacco use, companies such as Old Judge portrayed players like Kelly as ideal men—the perfect blend of athletic masculinity and refined, almost gentlemen-like bearing. In an era when the press rarely reported on the bad behavior of athletes or politicians, few Americans could have known that the real Mike Kelly was a violent alcoholic who would drink himself to death in 1894 at age 37.

Other spectator sports also enjoyed great popularity in the late nineteenth century. Professional boxing, horseracing, track and field competitions, and bicycle races drew large crowds to venues such as Madison Square Garden in New York City, the Chicago Coliseum, and the Boston Arena. By the 1890s, college football games in Boston, New York,

OLD JUDGE & GYPSY QUEEN CIGARETTES

How did commercial interests shape the new forms of leisure in the Gilded Age?

Read the **Document** *Coney Island Frolics*

Philadelphia, and Chicago often drew more than 50,000 fans. Baseball, football, and other urban spectator sports proved consistent money-makers for promoters, but they also attracted criticism from ministers and public officials who decried the violence, alcohol consumption, and gambling associated with them and the trend to play them on Sundays.

Competing for the attention of the American with increased leisure time on his or her hands was a burgeoning theatrical entertainment industry. By the late nineteenth century, the typical city resident could choose from a vast array of entertainment forms on stage. In ethnic neighborhoods, for example, Old World productions like Italian melodramas based loosely on operas and Yiddish comedies drawn from Eastern European traditions flourished.

Elsewhere in the city in more mainstream venues, people flocked to musical comedies, a distinctly American innovation pioneered by the duo of Edward Harrigan and Tony Hart. They were succeeded by others such as George M. Cohan and Irving Berlin, whose popular songs like "Give My Regards to Broadway" and "Alexander's Ragtime Band" became enduring hits.

Also popular was vaudeville, a kind of variety show featuring a series of acts by entertainers from jugglers, musicians, acrobats, and family routines, to singers, wild animal acts, ribald comedians, and scantily clad women. With its low admission fees and democratic approach, vaudeville was geared for the masses. At its peak circa 1900, vaudeville shows drew two million patrons a day. Many of the great American stage and film performers from the early twentieth century, such as James Cagney, Mae West, and Al Jolson, began their careers in vaudeville.

Wealthier and better-educated city residents rejected vaudeville and the more raucous forms of musical comedy as undignified and coarse. Instead they went to opera houses to hear European music and to what they considered legitimate theater to see productions of Shakespeare and the classics.

While these varied forms of entertainment were developed and popularized in large cities, they quickly spread via published sheet music and touring companies to communities across the nation. The result was the beginning of a national popular culture, one that would flourish more fully with the arrival of movies, radio, and television in the twentieth century.

Lifestyles of the Rich and Famous

Another feature of urban life that became a defining feature of the Gilded Age (so much so that it gave the era its name) was lavish displays of wealth. Dubbed "conspicuous consumption" by sociologist Thorstein Veblen in 1899, this trend featured the construction of opulent mansions in elite urban districts such as New York's Fifth Avenue, Chicago's Lake Shore Drive, and San Francisco's Nob Hill, as well as in exclusive summer retreats like Newport, Rhode Island. Wealthy families like the Vanderbilts and Astors competed to see who could throw the most extravagant balls, weddings, and parties.

> ## "There is many a palace in Europe that would hide its diminished roof beside the sheer luxury of Fifth Avenue homes."
> EDGAR SALTUS

One of the most famous was a ball hosted on March 26, 1883 by Alva Vanderbilt, wife of tycoon William K. Vanderbilt, to celebrate the opening of their new $3 million mansion on upper Fifth Avenue. The elite of New York arrived in costume (**17.13**). Many dressed as Marie Antoinette, Queen Elizabeth, and Louis XV. This choice of an ostentatious royal theme reflected the belief by the nation's wealthy elite that they constituted an American aristocracy—a notion that ran counter to the longstanding American fear and loathing for such undemocratic pretensions (see Chapters 4 and 5). Labor activists and social critics castigated the ball and high society's rejection of republican simplicity, but Mrs. Vanderbilt's guests paid no heed. They reveled past dawn in a party that cost $250,000—in an age when an average worker could expect to earn less than $700 per year. By the mid-1880s, most newspapers featured "society" columns that devoted extensive coverage to the lives of the wealthy.

While Americans followed the exploits of the rich with a certain wonder, the public would accept only so much extravagance before expressing

How did varied forms of leisure reflect class differences?

revulsion. That finally occurred in February 1897, when the Bradley Martin family hosted a $400,000 party in which 800 guests arrived in costumes depicting European royalty. One society reporter described "a gorgeous, superb, and wonderful spectacle." But in 1897, when the nation was suffering from a severe depression, public criticism of the ball erupted, including indignation from public officials, clergymen, and workers,. The Bradley Martins fled to Europe and settled permanently in England, ending the days of diamond-necklace party favors.

> ## "[Y]ou rich people put next to nothing in the collection plate, and yet you'll spend thousands of dollars on Mrs. Bradley Martin's ball."
>
> Sermon of a minister outraged over the Bradley Martin Ball

17.13 Imagining an American Aristocracy
Wealthy Americans in the Gilded Age competed to throw the most expensive and decadent balls, weddings, or parties. At Mrs. William K. Vanderbilt's 1883 ball, New York's elite arrived in costumes depicting figures of European royalty.

How did the great displays of wealth in the Gilded Age represent a break with America's republican traditions?

Read the **Document** *Thorstein Veblen, excerpt from The Theory of Leisure Class*

The Challenge from Below

The revulsion expressed over the Bradley Martin Ball in 1897 reflected rising discontent. Many farmers and industrial workers felt exploited by powerful corporations. When they turned to elected officials to address these problems, they found them unresponsive. Most politicians remained committed to a laissez-faire philosophy, which argued against government intervention in the economy. As a result the period was marked by some of the most bitter and violent strikes in American history and by the rise of a third party comprised mainly of farmers, workers, and reformers—the **People's Party**—to challenge the Republicans and Democrats.

Out of Touch Politics

Popular enthusiasm for politics reached extraordinary heights in the Gilded Age. Indeed, American voters turned out in astonishing numbers, averaging 79 percent between 1876 and 1896 (as compared with between 50 and 60 percent in recent decades). Despite such intense interest, politicians made little progress in resolving the major issues that dominated national politics in this period. This political stalemate stemmed from several factors. First, as indicated in (**17.14**), the electorate was evenly divided between the two major parties, resulting in remarkably close presidential elections. For example, the five presidential elections between 1876 and 1892 were decided by tiny margins of 1 to 3 percent. Indeed, in 1876 and 1888, the candidate with the highest popular vote total lost because his opponent tallied more electoral votes. No incumbent president won reelection, and only twice (Republicans, 1889–1891 and Democrats, 1893–1895)

17.14 Deadlocked Presidential Politics in the Gilded Age With an electorate evenly divided between the two major parties, Gilded Age politics were often marked by stalemate on key issues.

Year	Candidate	Party	Popular Vote	Electoral Vote
1876	**Rutherford B. Hayes***	Republican	4,036,298 (48%)	185
	Samuel J. Tilden	Democrat	4,300,590 (51%)	184
1880	**James Garfield**	Republican	4,454,416 (48.5%)	214
	Winfield S. Hancock	Democrat	4,444,952 (48.1%)	155
1884	**Grover Cleveland**	Democrat	4,874,986 (48.5%)	219
	James G. Blaine	Republican	4,851,334 (48.2%)	182
1888	**Benjamin Harrison***	Republican	5,439,853 (47.9%)	233
	Grover Cleveland	Democrat	5,540,309 (48.6%)	168
1892	**Grover Cleveland**	Democrat	5,556,918 (46%)	277
	Benjamin Harrison	Republican	5,176,108 (43%)	145
	James B. Weaver	People's	1,041,028 (9%)	22

Winner in bold

* = winner despite losing popular vote

Read the **Document** *Mary Elizabeth Lease, "The Popular Crusader" (1892)*

Why were election results in the Gilded Age so close?

did one party control both houses of Congress and the presidency.

Political inaction in the Gilded Age also reflected the conservatism of most politicians who clung to longstanding political traditions that celebrated small, nonintrusive government, especially at the federal level. For many leaders government regulation of business appeared socialistic and harmful to both the economy and republican principles. Political paralysis stemmed from the power of corporate interests to use huge donations to political parties and bribery of lawmakers to stymie legislation they deemed harmful to their interests. For example, big business interests blocked efforts to lower the tariff because a high tariff protected their manufactures from foreign competition.

The record for 1890, the year Congress took up the big issues of tariff, currency reform, and corporate regulation, provides a particularly vivid example of this ineffective political system. Support for corporate regulation reflected rising concern from many

17.15 Liberty Suffocated by Big Business This 1889 Thomas Nast cartoon captured the concerns of many, that trusts threatened democracy, equality, and liberty by monopolizing the necessities of life.

corners of American society. Industrial workers saw themselves as victims of corporate power that demanded long hours of dangerous toil for low wages. Many other Americans, as suggested by this 1889 Thomas Nast cartoon, *The Rising of the Usurpers and the Sinking of the Liberties of the People* (**17.15**), viewed trusts as a threat to democracy and equality. By monopolizing the necessities of life, trusts literally threatened to smother American liberty. The Sherman Anti-Trust Act of 1890 promised to empower the federal government to crack down on business practices that diminished competition (see Chapter 16), but opposition from pro-business legislators weakened the law to such a point that it did little to slow the growth of big business. Indeed, the 1890s saw record numbers of mergers, and big business used the Sherman Act to weaken labor unions by arguing that strikes amounted to restraint of trade.

In 1890, Congress also took up the contentious issue of currency reform to determine what constituted the proper basis for American currency. Advocates of "hard money," which included most Republicans, businessmen, and the wealthy, argued for basing currency solely on the amount of gold in the U.S. Treasury. They opposed issuing paper money, popularly known as "greenbacks," or minting more silver coinage, arguing that it contributed to inflation and lowered interest rates. "Soft money" proponents like farmers, workers, and Democrats, however, argued that the supply of gold, and thus of a currency based exclusively on it, was insufficient to meet the needs of an expanding commercial economy. They advocated the issuance of greenbacks and expanded coinage of silver, which was more plentiful than gold. More money in circulation would lead to inflation, but debtors, especially farmers, welcomed inflation because it promised to raise the prices of their goods and diminish the burden of their debts. In 1890, they supported the Sherman Silver Purchase Act, which required the Treasury to purchase 4.5 million ounces of silver every month and issue notes (paper money) redeemable in either silver or gold.

Republicans opposed the bill but wanted a higher tariff. Democrats opposed a higher tariff, arguing that it amounted to a huge subsidy paid by American consumers to business. Both sides therefore compromised, and both the silver act and a higher tariff became law. Neither bill, however, had the desired effect. The higher tariff caused consumer prices to surge producing widespread discontent. The silver program caused the price of silver to fall, so most of the people holding the notes redeemed them for gold, which depleted the nation's gold reserves and contributed to the Panic of 1893 and four years of severe depression.

The one notable exception to the politics of stalemate was a civil service law to open certain government jobs only to those who demonstrated their competency on a civil service exam rather than those who merely possessed strong political connections. Neither party favored the law, since it threatened to undermine their ability to reward friends and campaign contributors. It took the assassination of President James A. Garfield in 1881 by a frustrated and apparently deranged office seeker to pass the Pendleton Act in 1883, which placed ten percent of federal jobs under civil service.

The People's Party

Anger against the political system's corruption and failure to act on critical issues like corporate regulation and currency and tariff reform gradually produced a popular reaction. In the late 1870s, **farmers' alliances,** successors to the Granger movement (see Chapter 15), formed to alleviate the plight of farmers beset by rising costs and falling prices for their products. The Southern Farmers' Alliance (1877) and Northern Farmers' Alliance (1880) grew in the 1880s to a combined membership of more than five million. Excluded by the segregationist doctrines of the post-Reconstruction South, black farmers formed the Colored Farmers' Alliance in 1886 and soon had more than 1.25 million members.

The alliances argued that the economic woes of the American farmer were due to exploitive bankers who charged farmers exorbitant interest rates for farm mortgages, to railroads that charged them extortionate rates to transport farm produce to market, and to commodity brokers on Wall Street, who bought their crops at rock bottom prices and then resold them at many times the original price paid. To combat this injustice, the alliances promoted the establishment of cooperatives that combined the buying and selling power of farmers to gain them better prices for their produce and lower rates for loans and crop insurance. They also promoted education on agricultural topics.

In 1889, the Northern Farmers' Alliance and Southern Farmers' Alliance united to form the National Alliance. One year later, convinced that the only way to combat the power of the monopolies and trusts was to transform the National Alliance into a political movement to elect pro-farmer candidates to office, delegates gathered in Ocala, Florida, and drew up a manifesto listing their grievances and proposed reforms. That fall National Alliance-backed candidates won complete or partial control of 12 state legislatures and elected 6 governors. They also sent 50 representatives and 3 senators to Congress. Because most of these men were Democrats, Republicans lost control of the House. These victories convinced many National Alliance activists like Ignatius Donnelly of Minnesota and Tom Watson of Georgia that they needed to form a third party and run a slate of candidates in the 1892 presidential contest.

A National Alliance convention in St. Louis in early 1892 led to the formal creation of the People's Party (its followers would be known as "Populists") and the adoption of a platform that emphasized the plight of the American farmer and worker at the hands of greedy businessmen and corrupt politicians (see *Competing Visions: Progress or Peril?*).

By now the People's Party movement had begun to alarm the leaders of the mainstream political parties. Worried about the party's potential to determine the winner in 1892 by taking votes from them, the major parties launched a campaign to discredit the Populists. In this political cartoon (**17.16**), which appeared on the cover of *Judge*, a pro-Republican magazine, the artist ridicules the Populists as a "patchwork" of strange and dangerous political and ideological movements like socialism and prohibition. The balloon's basket, labeled "Platform of Lunacy," carried the party leaders, depicted as eccentric fools.

In July 1892, the Populists nominated Union Army veteran James B. Weaver for president and Confederate veteran General James G. Field of Virginia for vice president. Their convention adopted a platform aimed at the following: eliminating monopolies (abolition of national banks and government ownership of railroads and telegraphs); protecting small producers (free silver coinage and "sub-treasuries" to store surplus farm produce during times of low prices and to allow farmers to borrow money against it at low interest); strengthening democracy (the popular election of U.S. senators and the referendum and initiative); and promoting fairness (a graduated income tax to make the rich pay more of the tax burden). To create a national base of support among all struggling people, not just

Competing Visions
PROGRESS OR PERIL?

Americans in the Gilded Age interpreted the economic, political, and social developments of the era in very different ways. Some looked about them with enthusiasm at the sight of a nation growing in size, wealth, population, and international prestige. President Benjamin Harrison, in his inaugural address in 1889 reflects this optimistic view. Other Americans, however, especially many farmers and industrial workers who sympathized with the People's Party, expressed alarm and dismay over the state of the nation. What key signs of progress and national strength does President Harrison cite? What dangers to American ideals such as equality and democracy do the authors of the People's Party Platform identify? How do we account for these starkly different visions?

President Benjamin Harrison, Inaugural Address, March 4, 1889

[O]ur growth has not been limited to territory, population and aggregate wealth, marvelous as it has been in each of those directions. The masses of our people are better fed, clothed, and housed than their fathers were. The facilities for popular education have been vastly enlarged and more generally diffused. The virtues of courage and patriotism have given recent proof of their continued presence and increasing power in the hearts and over the lives of our people. The influences of religion have been multiplied and strengthened. The sweet offices of charity have greatly increased.... We have not attained an ideal condition. Not all of our people are happy and prosperous; not all of them are virtuous and law-abiding. But on the whole the opportunities offered to the individual to secure the comforts of life are better than are found elsewhere and largely better than they were here one hundred years ago.

No other people have a government more worthy of their respect and love or a land so magnificent in extent, so pleasant to look upon, and so full of generous suggestion to enterprise and labor. God has placed upon our head a diadem and has laid at our feet power and wealth beyond definition or calculation. But we must not forget that we take these gifts upon the condition that justice and mercy shall hold the reins of power and that the upward avenues of hope shall be free to all the people.

I do not mistrust the future. Dangers have been in frequent ambush along our path, but we have uncovered and vanquished them all. Passion has swept some of our communities, but only to give us a new demonstration that the great body of our people are stable, patriotic, and law-abiding.... The peaceful agencies of commerce are more fully revealing the necessary unity of all our communities, and the increasing intercourse of our people is promoting mutual respect....

Platform of the People's Party, July 4, 1892

[W]e meet in the midst of a nation brought to the verge of moral, political, and material ruin. Corruption dominates the ballot box, the Legislatures, the Congress, and touches even the ermine of the bench. The people are demoralized ... The newspapers are largely subsidized or muzzled, public opinion silenced, business prostrated, homes covered with mortgages, labor impoverished, and the land concentrating in the hands of capitalists. The urban workmen are denied the right to organize for self-protection, imported pauperized labor beats down their wages, a hireling standing army, unrecognized by our laws, is established to shoot them down, and they are rapidly degenerating into European conditions. The fruits of the toil of millions are boldly stolen to build up colossal fortunes for a few, unprecedented in the history of mankind; and the possessors of those, in turn, despise the Republic and endanger liberty. From the same prolific womb of governmental injustice we breed the two great classes—tramps and millionaires.

... A vast conspiracy against mankind has been organized on two continents, and it is rapidly taking possession of the world. If not met and overthrown at once it forebodes terrible social convulsions, the destruction of civilization, or the establishment of an absolute despotism.

We have witnessed for more than a quarter of a century the struggles of the two great political parties for power and plunder, while grievous wrongs have been inflicted upon the suffering people. We charge that the controlling influences dominating both these parties have permitted the existing dreadful conditions to develop without serious effort to prevent or restrain them. Neither do they now promise us any substantial reform....

How did the People's Party platform reflect the concerns of farmers and industrial workers?

17.16 Discrediting the Populists Concerned about the potential of the People's Party to determine the outcome of the 1892 presidential election, the major parties ridiculed them as a "patchwork" of dangerous political and ideological movements like socialism and prohibition.

farmers, the platform also expressed sympathy with industrial workers.

In the end, the People's Party was no match for the established parties. Democrat Grover Cleveland won the election with 46 percent of the vote to Republican incumbent, Benjamin Harrison's 43 percent. Yet Weaver garnered more than one million votes (9 percent) and won Kansas, Colorado, Idaho, and Nevada. Results on the local and state levels were even more impressive, as Populists elected almost 1,500 candidates to state legislatures, three governors, and five senators and ten representatives to Congress.

People's Party leaders hoped to build on this achievement in 1896, but they faced severe challenges. In 1892, the party had performed poorly among Midwestern farmers and industrial workers who stayed with either the Republicans or Democrats. In addition, a campaign by conservatives to equate support for the People's Party with attacks on white supremacy severely weakened the party in the South.

Industrial Conflict and Depression

Events soon highlighted the unchecked power of big business and the severe consequences of a laissez-faire economy. Many People's Party activists hoped the anger and suffering produced by the Homestead strike and Panic of 1893 would prompt workers and farmers to reject the mainstream political parties and join the Populists. Workers at the Homestead Steel Works, a mammoth plant near Pittsburgh owned by Andrew Carnegie, for years enjoyed a strong union (the Amalgamated Association of Iron and Steel Workers), high wages, and decent living conditions. But in 1892, Carnegie decided to rid the company of the union to cut costs by introducing labor-saving machinery and reducing wages. To protect the public persona of a benevolent capitalist that he had worked for years to develop (see Chapter 16), Carnegie went on vacation in Scotland, leaving his hard-nosed business partner, Henry Clay Frick, to do the dirty work.

On June 29, Frick announced a lockout and closed the mills. After a week the standoff turned violent when

workers exchanged gunfire with heavily armed professional strikebreakers of the Pinkerton Detective Agency, whom Frick had brought by boat to the Homestead complex. Six strikers and five Pinkertons were killed. The national press gave extensive coverage to the strike, and its tone was surprisingly pro-worker, probably due in part to the Pinkertons' negative reputation. Carnegie, despite his attempt to separate himself from the conflict, drew some of the harshest criticisms. His critics challenged his reputation as the great philanthropist who handed out libraries to communities in the United States and Europe by depicting him as a two-faced hypocrite who funded his philanthropic largesse by grinding down his workers with wage cuts (**17.17**).

But the tide of public opinion soon shifted against the strikers, for on July 23 anarchist Alexander Berkman burst into Frick's office and shot him. Remarkably Frick survived the assassination attempt. Even though Berkman had no connection to Homestead workers, his actions brought widespread condemnation upon the strikers. In September state officials arrested 33 members of the union's leadership and charged them with treason against the state. On November 20, 1892, with nearly all the jobs at Homestead filled by replacement workers, the union ended the strike.

Six months later, on May 5, 1893, a financial crisis rocked the nation, leading to the most severe economic depression in American history

17.17 Carnegie's Reputation Takes a Hit
The Homestead strike tarnished Carnegie's image as a benevolent capitalist and friend of labor. This cartoon from the July 9 issue of the Utica, New York, *Globe* accuses him of being a two-faced hypocrite, who funded his philanthropy by cutting his workers' salaries.

Why did critics accuse Carnegie of hypocrisy during the Homestead Strike?

to that time. Within a year the Panic of 1893 led to the failure of thousands of farms and businesses, including almost 200 railroads and 600 banks closed, throwing millions out of work and pushing the unemployment rate to 20 percent. The depression produced two vivid images of the widespread suffering endured by millions and the unwillingness of public officials to do much about it. The first came from an Ohio Populist named Jacob Coxey, who called for the government abandon laissez-faire and create public works projects such as building roads to alleviate mass unemployment and stimulate the economy (programs the federal government adopted in the Great Depression of the 1930s). To draw attention to this idea, he organized 100 unemployed men in Massillon, Ohio, to march to Washington, D.C. (the first such march on the capital). Setting out on March 25, 1894 **Coxey's Army**, as it came to be known grew in size as as various groups joined along the route. As this photograph (**17.18**) and nearly every other one taken of the march shows, Coxey and his followers sought to portray an image of patriotism, earnestness, and moderation. Dressing as decently as their poverty permitted and marching with dozens of American flags, Coxey and his men rejected the accusations of their critics that they were violent radicals determined to attack the government. Rather, they asserted, theirs was a campaign to save the republic from the trusts and laissez-faire policies.

Most of the men and women who joined Coxey walked for only part of the march to Washington. Nonetheless, about 600 accompanied him when he entered the nation's capital on April 30, 1894. Denied entry into the Capitol, Coxey delivered an impassioned address on its steps.

> We stand here to-day in behalf of millions of toilers whose petitions have been buried in committee rooms, whose prayers have been unresponded to, and whose opportunities for honest, remunerative, productive labor have been taken from them by unjust legislation, which protects idlers, speculators, and gamblers.

Coxey and other activists were arrested for "disturbing the peace" but convicted only for walking on the Capitol lawns. Other groups of unemployed workers staged similar protest marches, but all met with frustration and inaction.

17.18 Coxey's Army Emphasizes Its Patriotism Aware that critics denounced them as violent radicals, Coxey and his "army" of protesters emphasized their patriotism and moderation by marching with American flags.

Read the Document *Jacob S. Coxey, Address of Protest (1894)*

What did Coxey and his followers want from the federal government?

A second image of government indifference to widespread suffering arose in Chicago. The World's Columbian Exposition had opened on May 1, 1893, just four days before the panic on Wall Street. The fair's emphasis on American progress and prosperity, symbolized by the opulence and beauty of its huge complex of white neoclassical buildings, soon stood in stark contrast to the growing despair of the city's tenement districts a few blocks away. When the fair closed in October, thousands of homeless people moved into the vacant buildings that had only recently housed elaborate displays of prosperity. That winter of 1893–1894, 60,000 Chicagoans per day received a free meal from soup kitchens and missions.

Some of the hardest hit workers during the depression were employees of the Pullman Palace Car Company, located just outside Chicago. Founded by George Pullman in 1867, the company manufactured luxury railroad cars. Pullman was an idealist who believed that workers and employers could work together in harmony for mutual benefit. Acting on this idea he established the town of Pullman in 1880, a **company town** built and owned by the Pullman corporation for its employees, who rented homes and patronized stores owned by the company. As this 1881 depiction of the town demonstrates (**17.19**), Pullman, like Carnegie, prided himself on being a model capitalist, who earned a vast fortune but still managed to provide a decent living for his workers.

> "We are born in a Pullman house, fed from the Pullman shop, taught in the Pullman school, catechized in the Pullman church, and when we die we shall be buried in the Pullman cemetery and go to the Pullman Hell."
>
> Pullman worker

This sensibility informs the drawing of Pullman's vision of the future town (since it was still under construction in 1881) as a model community of neat houses, schools, churches, stores, open spaces, and, of course, the factories that made it all possible.

So long as the company remained profitable, its employees considered themselves fortunate. But the depression in 1893 hit the railroad industry hard, and Pullman laid off hundreds of workers and announced a wage cut of 30 percent for the rest. On top of this devastating news, workers learned that Pullman would not reduce their rents, which were deducted automatically from their paychecks. Some workers soon began receiving checks for less than one dollar per week to cover the cost of food, heat, and clothing.

On May 11, 1894, Pullman's hard-pressed workers went out on strike. After a six-week standoff during which Pullman refused to negotiate, Eugene Debs, the leader of the American Railway Union (ARU) announced all of the union's 125,000 members across the country, as an act of solidarity with the Pullman workers, would refuse to handle Pullman cars. Within days the **Pullman strike** caused the nation's railroad system to slow to a crawl.

The heads of more than two dozen railroads moved to support Pullman and break the ARU by hiring thousands of strikebreakers and pressuring

17.19 Capitalism and Community
George Pullman's vision of himself as a benevolent capitalist was captured in these plans for Pullman, a company town of neat houses, schools, churches, stores, open spaces, and factories.
[*Source*: i38519. Sepia illustration showing the town and factories of Pullman, with Index to Works on lower left and Index to Town on lower right.]

Why did the Pullman workers strike?

Read the Document *Address to 1894 Convention of American Railway Union by Jennie Curtis*

Governor Richard Altgeld, to send in the state militia. When he refused out of sympathy for the strikers and a desire to avoid violence, the railroads asked President Grover Cleveland to send federal troops (see *Choices and Consequences: The Pullman Strike*).

The Election of 1896 and Political Realignment

The turmoil caused by the depression and Pullman strike greatly affected the 1894 off-year elections. Dissatisfaction with Cleveland's administration hurt the Democrats, who lost their brief hold on both houses of Congress. The shift in power meant more stalemate for the next two years, with a Republican Congress opposed by a Democratic president.

The election of 1896, however, led to a major realignment in political affiliations among the American people. Republicans nominated former Congressman and Governor of Ohio William McKinley for president and affirmed their conservative commitment to the gold standard and a high tariff. The Democrats nominated a young and dynamic congressman from Nebraska, William Jennings Bryan. Just 36 years old, Bryan had earned a reputation for stirring oratory against the tariff and in support of free silver. The latter issue held great symbolic importance in the middle of the depression. Silver was the metal of the common man, argued its supporters, while gold was the metal of elites. In speeches, pamphlets, songs, and images, People's Party activists had convinced millions of Americans that free coinage of silver (putting more money into circulation and thus lowering the value of the dollar backed exclusively by gold) would both end the depression and curb the monopolies and trusts. Recognizing the popularity of this policy, delegates at the Democratic Party convention made free silver a key plank in the party platform.

Bryan then delivered one of the most famous speeches in American history, in which he argued that average Americans were being crucified on a "cross of gold," forced upon them by Wall Street and big business. Capturing this theme, this campaign poster (**17.20**) included the text of the famous speech (framed by silver coins) and ribbons bearing two of its most memorable

17.20 For Silver and the People
The Democratic Party emphasized Bryan's commitment to workers and farmers through his advocacy of free silver and his promise to protect Americans from being crucified on a "Cross of Gold."

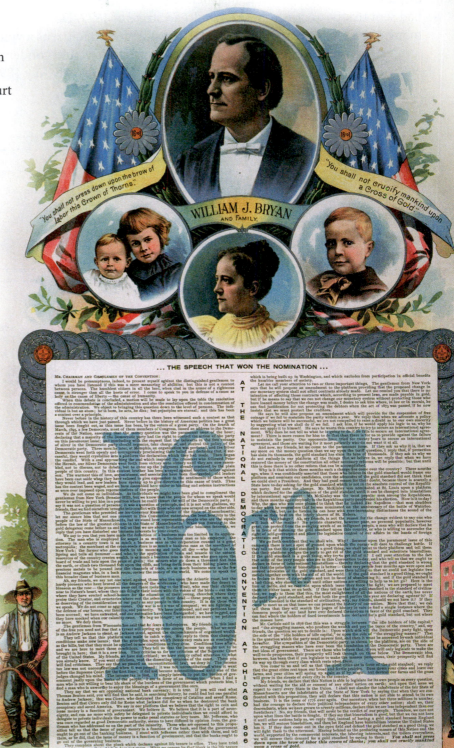

📖 **Read** the **Document** *William Jennings Bryan, "Cross of Gold" Speech (1896)*

Why did silver hold such political significance in the late nineteenth century?

Choices and Consequences

THE PULLMAN STRIKE

Grover Cleveland was not the first president to face the choice of whether to send federal troops to quell a labor dispute. Andrew Jackson had dispatched troops in 1834 to end a strike by canal workers. Rutherford B. Hayes had sent troops to crush the great railroad strike of 1877. Despite these precedents, Cleveland was aware that many considered the use of the army against American citizens a violation of the key republican principles of limited federal power. He also worried that the public would condemn such use of federal power if violence ensued as it had in 1877. He spent days in late June and early July 1894, consulting with advisors and mulling over his options.

Choices

1 Take no action, allowing Illinois and its pro-labor governor to handle the matter.

2 Intervene as a neutral and insist that both sides negotiate an equitable settlement.

3 Send in the army to break the strike and allow the railroads to use strikebreakers to operate the trains.

Continuing Controversies

When is using federal troops in a strike compatible with republican principles?

Subsequent presidents, including Woodrow Wilson, also ordered military intervention during labor disputes. In 1916, the National Security Act empowered the president to federalize a state's National Guard to quell a disturbance like a natural disaster, riot, or strike. The two most notable uses of this law, however, came in 1957 (Little Rock, Arkansas) and 1963 (Tuscaloosa, Alabama) to enforce federal desegregation orders.

Decision

Despite misgivings Cleveland was a pro-business conservative. He authorized Attorney General Richard Olney, a man with extensive ties to the railroad industry, to obtain a court injunction declaring the ARU boycott of Pullman cars a "conspiracy in restraint of trade" that unlawfully blocked the U.S. mail. When the union defied the injunction, Cleveland ordered the army to end the boycott and get the trains moving again. Debs and other ARU leaders were arrested.

Federal troops sent by President Cleveland to break the Pullman strike escort the first meat train out of the Chicago stockyards.

Consequences

Cleveland's decision touched off violence. Workers destroyed railroad property, and soldiers killed 13 workers and wounded scores more. The boycott collapsed in mid-July and with it the ARU. The Pullman strike ended in early August in complete defeat for the workers. Public opinion, however, turned against Pullman for his obstinate refusal to negotiate with his workers. A government investigation later criticized him and argued that labor unions and government regulation were needed to curb corporate power. Yet in 1895, the Supreme Court (*In re Debs*) upheld the use of injunctions to end strikes.

How did President Cleveland justify using federal power to break the Pullman strike?

lines: "You shall not press down upon the brow of Labor this Crown of Thorns" and "You shall not crucify mankind upon a Cross of Gold." A youthful Bryan flanked by his wife and children tops the poster, while images of a worker and farmer flank the speech text.

That left the People's Party facing a dilemma. Most of its activists had expected the Democrats to follow the Republicans and support the gold standard, leaving the silver issue to the Populists. Now the People's Party had to decide whether to nominate their own candidate and divide support for the silver issue with the Democrats, or, as was common practice among small parties in the nineteenth century, to nominate Bryan as their candidate, a move that would diminish their standing as an independent party concerned with issues other than silver. In July the People's Party nominated Bryan. But they nominated their own candidate for vice president, Populist leader Tom Watson of Georgia.

Rejecting a longstanding tradition that considered campaigning by presidential candidates unseemly, Bryan embarked on one of the most remarkable campaigns in American history, traveling more than 18,000 miles through 27 states and delivering more than 600 stump speeches to three million people.

Bryan's campaign generated a lot of commentary and excitement, but not enough votes on Election Day. McKinley, backed with an unprecedented amount of corporate money, won with 51 percent of the vote to Bryan's 47 percent. The most significant outcome of the contest was a new and enduring political alignment. The Republican Party became dominant in the Midwest and Northeast and dominated national political power for the next three decades. Republicans would portray themselves as the party of economic prosperity (the economy recovered under McKinley) and international power. The Democrats became the party of the South and West. They retained the Populist belief that government needed to do more to secure the well-being of the average citizen and limit the power of big business. Given its base in the South, however, the Democratic Party also upheld a states' rights philosophy that protected white supremacy.

The People's Party disintegrated after 1896, but many of its core ideas, such as the graduated income tax and the direct election of U.S. senators, remained popular and were eventually adopted during the next two decades, a period known as the Progressive Era.

> "If they dare to come out in the open field and defend the gold standard as a good thing, we will fight them to the uttermost. Having behind us the producing masses of this nation and the world, supported by the commercial interests, the laboring interests and the toilers everywhere, we will answer their demand for a gold standard by saying to them: 'You shall not press down upon the brow of labor this crown of thorns! You shall not crucify mankind upon a cross of gold!'"
>
> WILLIAM JENNINGS BRYAN

1871

Boss Tweed's corruption ring exposed
Shows the rising influence of political machines in cities and efforts to limit their power

1874–1877

Women's Christian Temperance Union established
An early indication of growing women's activism in the Gilded Age

The Southern Farmers' Alliance established in Texas
Reflects growing discontent of American farmers that eventually leads to the formation of the People's Party

1882–1883

Charity Organization Society founded
Founded by wealthy reformers who feared that too much charity was actually harming the poor

The Vanderbilt Ball
A lavish exhibition of "conspicuous consumption" attended by the richest families in America

The Pendleton Act becomes law
Intended to diminish nepotism and corruption, it required Civil Service exams for 10 percent of federal jobs

1885

The Home Insurance Building completed in Chicago
Considered the world's first skyscraper, it signaled the transformation of the modern urban landscape.

Josiah Strong publishes, *Our Country*
A best-selling book written in an alarmist style, it warned Americans that cities and immigrants posed a grave threat to the republic.

CHAPTER REVIEW

Review Questions

1. Why did cities grow in the late nineteenth century?

2. Who supported political machines and why? Why did reformers dislike political machines so much?

3. How did the approach to poverty by reformers like Jacob Riis and Jane Addams differ from traditional approaches?

4. How did the roles and expectations for middle-class women change in the Gilded Age? What social and economic developments made this possible?

5. What were the primary grievances of people who supported the People's Party? How did they propose to resolve them?

6. What was the long-term impact of the 1896 election?

Key Terms

Gilded Age The name for the period 1877–1900 that suggested the amazing achievements of the period were like a thin gold layer that covered many unresolved social problems.   **498**

Tenement Multiple family dwelling of four to six stories housing dozens of families that became the most common form of housing for poor city dwellers by the 1860s.   **502**

Political machine Powerful urban political organization that mobilized large blocs of working-class and immigrant voters and often engaged in corrupt and illegal activity.   **504**

Settlement house Institution established in cities beginning in the 1880s and dedicated to helping the poor by providing a wide range of social and educational services.   **508**

City Beautiful Movement A movement begun in the 1880s that advocated comprehensive planning and grand redesign of urban space to eliminate pollution and overcrowding.   **508**

New Woman A phrase used to describe young women in the 1890s and early 1900s that reflected their rising levels of education, economic independence, and political and social activism.   **513**

People's Party A third party effort launched in 1890 by a coalition of farmer organizations, reformers, and labor unions and dedicated to curbing corporate power and increasing the voice of the masses in politics.   **517**

Farmers' alliance Organization in the 1870s and 1880s dedicated to helping farmers struggling with rising costs and falling crop prices by advocating farmer cooperatives and laws to regulate banks and railroads.   **519**

Coxey's Army A protest march from Ohio to Washington, D.C., organized by Jacob Coxey in 1894 to publicize demands for the federal government to alleviate the suffering brought on by the Panic of 1893.   **523**

Company town A town built and owned by a corporation and rented to its employees, reflecting both the corporation's desire to help their workers and to control them.   **524**

Pullman strike A bitter strike that began on May 11, 1894, at the Pullman Palace Car Company and soon spread nationwide, paralyzing the railroad system. President Cleveland sent in federal troops and broke the strike.   **524**

1887–1889

American Protective Association founded
Signals a rise in anti-immigrant sentiment

Hull House founded in Chicago
Settlement house movement provides a wide range of social services to poor and immigrants city dwellers

1890

Women's suffrage activists form NAWSA
Brings together two separate women's organizations to concentrate on securing the vote for women

Jacob Riis publishes *How the Other Half Lives*
A shocking exposé of urban poverty that builds support for reform measures

Sherman Anti-Trust Act passed
Reflects growing concern over corporate power, but fails to curb it

1892–1893

People's Party established
A coalition of farmers, workers, and reformers committed to curbing the power of big business

The Homestead strike
A bitter and highly publicized defeat for workers

Columbian Exposition opens in Chicago
Celebrates American progress and promotes cleaner, healthier, and more beautiful cities

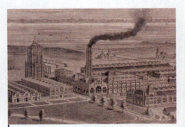

1894–1896

Coxey's Army marches on Washington, D.C.
Economic depression prompts many to demand relief by the federal government

The Pullman strike
President Cleveland breaks the strike by sending in federal troops

Election of 1896
Republican William McKinley defeats Democrat William Jennings Bryan

MyHistoryLab Connections

Visit www.myhistorylab.com for a customized Study Plan that will help you build your knowledge of *Becoming a Modern Society*.

Questions for Analysis

1. **What role did immigration play in the rise of large cities?**

   View the **Closer Look** *Immigration to the U.S. 1870–1915, p. 501*

2. **Why did political machines grow so powerful in the late nineteenth century?**

   Read the **Document** *Lincoln Steffens,* The Shame of the Cities, *p. 504*

3. **How did reformers offer a new interpretation of the causes of poverty?**

   Read the **Document** *Jacob Riis,* How the Other Half Lives, *p. 507*

4. **What led to the emergence of new forms of leisure in the Gilded Age?**

   Read the **Document** *Coney Island Frolics, p. 514*

5. **What did Populists identify as major threats to American values like democracy and equality?**

   Read the **Document** *The People's Party Platform (1892), p. 521*

Other Resources from This Chapter

Read the Document

- *Adna Weber, "The Growth of Cities," p. 500*
- *George Waring, "Sanitary Conditions in New York" (1897), p. 503*
- *Josiah Strong, "Anglo-Saxon Culture Under Siege" (1885), p. 505*
- *Proposal to Buffalo, New York, Park Commission (1888), p. 506*
- *Jane Addams,* Twenty Years at Hull House, *p. 508*
- *Susan B. Anthony, "The 'New Departure' for Women" (1873), p. 512*
- *Thorstein Veblen, excerpt from* The Theory of Leisure Class, *p. 516*
- *Mary Elizabeth Lease, "The Popular Crusader" (1892), p. 517*
- *N.A. Dunning, ed., Alliance's Vision of Community (1891), p. 519*
- *Jacob S. Coxey, Address of Protest (1894), p. 523*
- *Address to 1894 Convention of American Railway Union by Jennie Curtis, p. 524*
- *William Jennings Bryan, "Cross of Gold" Speech (1896), p. 525*

View the Closer Look

- *Competing Visions: How Best to Help the Poor?, p. 504*
- *The Bowery at Night, p. 511*
- *Republican Campaign Poster of 1896, William McKinley, p. 527*

View the Map

Atlas Map: Changing Lives of American Women, 1880–1930, p. 513

Source: Victor Joseph Gatto/ Museum of the City of New York

Creating a Democratic Paradise
The Progressive Era, 1895–1915

Female employees of the Triangle Shirtwaist Factory, many recently arrived from Italy and Eastern Europe, worked on sewing machines 6 days a week, 12 hours a day, making blouses. On March 25, 1911, a fire engulfed the top floors of the building that housed the factory in New York City's Lower East Side. As bundles fell to the street, onlookers below assumed that workers were throwing their best cloth out the window to save it. They soon realized their mistake. Female workers were jumping by twos and threes to escape the flames. In the end, 146 women and men perished.

The memories of this horrific scene never left 18-year-old Victor Gatto, who stood on the corner and watched as women plunged directly onto the pavement. In 1944 Gatto, a self-taught artist, painted *Triangle Fire: March 25, 1911.* His painting depicted a woman plunging to her death past unprepared firefighters atop ladders too short to reach the victims above. On the ground indifferent police officers stand near the neat row of shroud-covered corpses that lined the sidewalk.

By the time Gatto provided this visual indictment of the government's inability to protect workers, Americans' expectations of their government had radically changed. This new vision took hold during the Progressive Era, partially in response to events like the Triangle Shirtwaist Factory Fire. In Gatto's painting the immense stone buildings tower above the lifeless workers, the artist's way of representing the complete domination of big business over labor at the beginning of the twentieth century. On the day of the fire, employers had locked the workshop doors from the outside to prevent the women from stealing materials or leaving early. With the doors bolted and flimsy fire escapes collapsing under the weight of fleeing workers, the windows offered the only means of escape for the rest.

To many Progressive Era reformers, the Triangle Shirtwaist Factory Fire illustrated the tragic consequences of capitalist exploitation and the government's lack of interest in the plight of workers. Middle-class activists championed an array of reforms that envisioned using local, state, and federal governments to protect Americans from the greed and indifference of big business. Their agenda aroused considerable criticism, but Progressives, aided by three reform-minded presidents, Theodore Roosevelt, William Howard Taft, and Woodrow Wilson, found enough common ground to construct cross-class alliances that sought to end exploitive business practices and class conflict. Progressive-led coalitions also tackled pressing political and social issues. From the mid-1890s to the mid-1900s, Progressives transformed the role of government in American society and laid the foundation for the liberal reform movements of the twentieth century.

"We have reached the point in our history when we realize that the nation has tremendous social, economic, and industrial problems."

THEODORE ROOSEVELT, 1912

The Progressive Impulse

The tide of reforms that swept across America at the turn of the twentieth century had its roots in a range of middle-class concerns. Middle-class dismay over the dismal living and laboring conditions for most working-class people turned to alarm as strikes and the appeal of socialism increased. The Progressives had unprecedented success building alliances that transcended class and political party affiliation, winning the support of three consecutive presidents. Dramatically reshaping the nation within a decade, the Progressive vision of an activist government that used regulation to safeguard the public challenged the prevailing laissez-faire notion that the government should not interfere with market forces.

The Angst of the Middle Class

At the dawn of the twentieth century, middle-class Americans looked around the nation and did not like what they saw. The upper 2 percent of the population controlled the nation's banks and industry. Even worse during the Gilded Age (see Chapter 17), they flaunted their prodigious wealth by leading pleasure-filled lives replete with mansions, yachts, and private art collections. The upper class embraced an ethos of individualism that made each man responsible for his and his family's wealth or poverty. "Failures which a man makes in his life are due almost always to some defect in his personality, some weakness of body, mind, or character, will, or temperament," proclaimed John D. Rockefeller, the billionaire titan of Standard Oil. In the nineteenth century many middle-class Americans had uncritically echoed these same sentiments. Increasingly, however, these words rang hollow as the middle class watched the rich discard the tenets of self-discipline, frugality, and charity that had prevented individualism from turning into outright selfishness.

Big business came of age at the turn of the century, as huge conglomerates began to dominate the economy. Smaller businesses, many run by middle-class proprietors, found it increasingly difficult to compete with these immense corporations. From 1897 to 1904 a wave of business mergers reduced 1,800 firms to just 157 in key economic sectors. Leading captains of industry vertically integrated businesses to control the production and distribution of their products from start to finish (see Chapter 16). Industrialists also integrated horizontally to eliminate competition from companies manufacturing similar items. Through such measures Rockefeller created the Standard Oil Trust and eventually produced and distributed 90 percent of refined oil in the United States, giving him the sole power to set prices for consumers and making him the richest man in the country.

American factories employed a large wage-earning working-class population whose members had little chance of improving their circumstances, no matter how hard they worked. More than half (**18.1**) of the nation's population toiled at manual labor in mines, factories, docks, and farms owned by others. Low wages, seasonal layoffs, sickness, and workplace accidents created a life filled with insecurity for most workers. "Father, does everyone in America live like this?" asked an 11-year-old Russian Jewish immigrant, "Go to work early, come home late, eat and go to sleep? And the next day again work, eat, and sleep?" For most of the nation, the answer was a painful "yes."

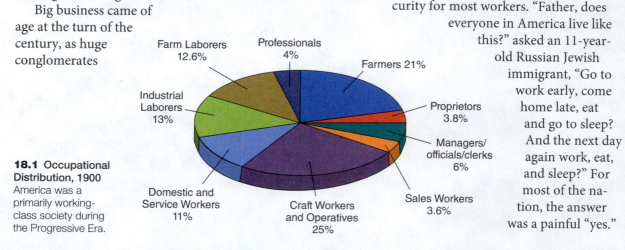

18.1 Occupational Distribution, 1900 America was a primarily working-class society during the Progressive Era.

Farm Laborers 12.6%
Professionals 4%
Farmers 21%
Industrial Laborers 13%
Proprietors 3.8%
Managers/officials/clerks 6%
Domestic and Service Workers 11%
Craft Workers and Operatives 25%
Sales Workers 3.6%

Large corporate bureaucracies also employed middle-class clerks whose ranks grew from 4 percent of the working population in 1900 to 8 percent by 1920. Most earned enough to maintain an acceptable middle-class lifestyle, but the middle class worried that the growing divide between the "haves" and "have-nots" put them in a precarious position. Press reports focusing on the dire living and working circumstances of the working class aroused middle-class sympathies, but fear motivated them to act as well.

The popularity of radical political ideologies, unions, saloons and dancing halls within working-class neighborhoods—each in its own way offering the promise of a better, easier life—alarmed the middle class. The classless paradise without private property championed by working-class radical leaders horrified most middle-class professionals, who owned their own homes and businesses. This 1912 image of state militia confronting a parade of striking textile workers in Lawrence, Massachusetts, underscored the reality that strikes often turned violent

(**18.2**). This photo's suggestion of an imminent clash between troops enforcing martial law and defiant workers offered visual evidence to middle-class Progressives that class tensions were tearing the nation apart. While sympathetic to labor unions' demands, middle-class Progressives valued law and order. They wanted to find a way to end both industrialist exploitation and the steady stream of strikes that disrupted their daily lives.

Progressives aspired to change other aspects of working-class culture as well. They deplored what they saw as the twin evils of drink and prostitution rampant in working-class neighborhoods. In the Progressive imagination the relentless pursuit of pleasure by both the upper class and the working class signaled the overall moral decay of American society.

The Progressive Vision

Glaring problems on both sides of the class divide—an idle and exploitive upper class on one side and an increasingly radicalized and impoverished working class on the other—threatened the middle-class vision of what life in America should offer. *Progressivism*, a broad term used to describe a shared philosophical approach rather than a formal organized movement, provided an answer to this threat.

Like the Populists (see Chapter 17) and Socialists, Progressives formed their own political party to advance their agenda. Theodore Roosevelt, for example, made a failed bid to regain the presidency by running as the candidate of the short-lived Progressive (Bull Moose) Party in 1912. Mainly however, Progressives, built cross-class political coalitions that transcended party lines. Lacking the wealth that the upper class possessed, or the sheer numbers that gave the working class tremendous economic clout, the middle class needed the support of other classes for their reforms to succeed.

Women played a particularly visible and active role in Progressive causes. Female settlement house workers (see Chapter 17) and women's civic club members, usually white, middle class, and college educated, embraced the notion of "municipal housekeeping," the Progressive conviction that women could not adequately protect their children without help from the government. Female trade unionists agreed, but they also wanted to empower female

18.2 Troops and Striking Workers Face Off, Lawrence, Massachusetts 1912 When the governor proclaimed martial law to prevent mass union rallies, protesting workers took to the streets carrying large American flags. Middle-class Progressives hoped their reforms would end strike-related violence, like the mayhem threatening to unfurl in this scene.

workers by organizing unions to improve wages and working conditions. Tragedies like the Triangle Shirtwaist Factory Fire brought these diverse female factions together, even winning support from appalled upper-class women. In the wake of the fire, this cross-class female coalition focused on bolstering city safety regulations, but only the labor activists emphasized the need for unions to end employer exploitation.

One particularly effective cross-class female alliance lobbied for legislation to ensure that mothers had clean, disease-free milk for their children. These women succeeded in their quest for local laws that prevented distributors from using chalk to make dirty milk appear white. They successfully rallied for mandatory pasteurization to kill germs, and for milk to be transported in refrigerated containers. Female-led reform campaigns also injected new energy into the suffrage movement.

> ## "Children need pure milk and good food, good schools and playgrounds, sanitary homes and safe streets."
>
> A female trade-union activist on why women needed the vote

Many middle-class female Progressive reformers and working-class labor organizers became convinced that without the right to vote, women lacked an essential tool they needed to keep themselves and their families safe. The National Woman Suffrage Association (NWSA) achieved notable successes between 1910 and 1917, winning the right to vote in Washington, California, Arizona, Kansas, Oregon, and New York. Defeats in other states, however, convinced the NWSA to seek a constitutional amendment guaranteeing all women the right to vote, a campaign that succeeded in 1920 (see Chapter 20).

In a general sense the Progressives wanted to turn America into a middle-class paradise where economic security, education, health, and civility flourished. The tradition of Christian charity also helped shape the Progressive agenda. In the 1880s, Protestant ministers like Josiah Strong began preaching the Social Gospel, the religious belief that Christians had a responsibility to create an ethically sound and morally upright society. The settlement house movement, begun in the spirit of Christian charity, became the incubator for strategies

Progressives developed to attain these goals. As they confronted the problems of the poor at Hull House, a settlement house in a Chicago immigrant neighborhood, Jane Addams and Florence Kelley articulated the middle-class values that would form the cornerstone of the Progressive ethos.

Foremost among these was an emphasis on how the environment, as well as individual traits, shaped the lives of the poor. Progressives argued that poor living and working environments created many of the social problems troubling the nation. Exhibiting a typical Progressive faith in the scientific method, Addams and Kelley compiled a statistical portrait of disease, over-crowding, and crime in their Chicago neighborhood that helped Hull House devise solutions to these problems.

Improving sanitation and garbage collection, creating playgrounds for children, eliminating saloons, limiting the hours spent at work, reducing workplace accidents—these were all ways to improve the environment in working-class neighborhoods so that individuals could flourish. Personal responsibility also remained a bedrock principle for Addams and Kelley. While offering more respect for immigrant cultures than many past reformers, Addams and Kelley still believed strongly in teaching immigrants the importance of thrift, temperance, and self-discipline—lifestyle changes that some immigrants resisted.

Finally, Progressives embraced a new vision of governmental power, one that Americans from many different walks of life challenged. Their notion that governmental regulation should protect workers and curtail the excesses of big business put them at odds with industrialists and unions. Industrialists embraced the laissez-faire ethos that they had the right to control their businesses as they saw fit without government interference. Unions also viewed potential government intervention with unease, mindful that during labor conflicts the government usually sided with industrialists. Labor leaders preferred using collective action, including strikes, to win concessions from industrialists. To socialists, who wanted to nationalize all major industries, the Progressive emphasis on regulation was too timid. Essentially the Progressives sought the middle ground between these competing views. They wanted to establish a balance that avoided the excesses of unfettered laissez-faire economics, unending class conflict, or complete government control of the economy. Their aim was notable—the creation of a socially just, capitalist America.

Reining in Big Business

When three consecutive presidents—Theodore (Teddy) Roosevelt, William Taft, and Woodrow Wilson—embraced components of the evolving Progressive reform agenda, Progressivism entered the mainstream with a vengeance. What to do about big business aroused considerable debate within Progressive circles. Progressives held competing visions of whether to regulate, dismantle, or accept the trusts, making it hard to rally public opinion around one clear solution. Presidents Roosevelt, Taft, and Wilson devised differing regulatory and antitrust strategies to reform business practices, and openly disagreed on how to tackle the problem. Curtailing big business's access to the nation's environmental riches also provoked debate. Did business have the right to fully exploit the country's forests and water, or should these resources be preserved?

Roosevelt's Trust-Busting

Roosevelt enthusiastically supported turning the government into a "steward of the public welfare." While serving as New York City police commissioner from 1895 to 1897, Roosevelt had become friendly with pioneering photojournalist Jacob Riis (see Chapter 17). "The midnight trips that Riis and I took" to the tenements, Roosevelt later acknowledged, showed him "what overcrowding means, some hot summer night." Roosevelt's feats during the 1898 Spanish-American War made him a national hero, catapulting him into winning the New York governorship. In 1900, President William McKinley selected Roosevelt as his running mate for his successful reelection bid.

On September 5, 1901, anarchist Leon Czolgosz shot McKinley with a pistol wrapped in a handkerchief while the president was shaking hands at the Pan-American Exposition in Buffalo, New York. When McKinley died eight days later, the 42-year-old Roosevelt became the youngest president in American history. A robust man who appeared to be in perpetual motion dictating letters, lecturing visitors, playing tennis, or having pillow fights with his younger children in the White House, Roosevelt captured the public's affection. When Teddy Roosevelt saved a bear cub during a 1902 hunting expedition, a toymaker felt inspired to name a new children's toy after him, and so the teddy bear was born.

Like many Progressives Roosevelt believed that the country stood at a crossroads—either reform or face the end of democracy. He established his credentials as a Progressive reformer, and won public approval, by mediating the 1902 coal strike and filing suit against the Northern Securities and Standard Oil Trusts.

On May 12, 1902, 140,000 northeastern Pennsylvanian miners walked off their jobs. They demanded an eight-hour day, a 20 percent wage increase, and recognition of their United Mine Workers (UMW) union. The mine owners refused to negotiate. "'The public be damned,' appears to be their motto," decried one Illinois newspaper as coal shortages forced factories to close, and the poor began cooking food with oil-soaked asbestos.

President Roosevelt viewed the miners' predicament sympathetically. "I strongly favor labor unions," he declared. "If I were a wage worker in a big city I should certainly join one." Fearing widespread suffering and urban riots, Roosevelt threatened to use troops to take over the mines unless the owners agreed to let a government commission fashion an agreement. For the first time a president had stood up publicly against big business, winning him accolades in union circles. The resulting resolution reduced miners' hours from ten to nine and awarded them a 10 percent pay hike without forcing the owners to recognize the union. "I wish the capitalists would see," the president privately remarked, that the government-ordered compromise "is really in the interest of property, for it will save it from the danger of revolution."

Roosevelt also joined the Progressive campaign to remove the stranglehold that some trusts had on parts of the economy. In 1902, journalist Ida Tarbell began publishing a multipart series, "The History of the Standard Oil Company," in *McClure's Magazine*, a popular and influential middle-class news periodical. In her scathing critique Tarbell detailed the illicit deals that John D. Rockefeller had made with railroad companies to build his oil trust. Secret rebate agreements meant that Rockefeller paid considerably less than his competitors to ship oil. Many could not even get the railroads, which feared incurring Rockefeller's wrath, to transport their oil. Tarbell had firsthand experience with Rockefeller's cut-throat practices: They had bankrupted her father's oil business. She was convinced that Rockefeller's tactics would drive other small producers out of business, leaving a handful of industrialists in control of the economy.

The titans of industry offered a competing vision. There was nothing wonderful about economic competition, Rockefeller contended. Destructive price-cutting drove down wages, over-production created depressions, and duplication of services wasted valuable resources. Rockefeller defended his railroad agreements as beneficial to all concerned. Standard Oil got lower rates while the railroads received guaranteed freight. Preventing too much oil from flooding the market stabilized prices and kept men in all oil-related industries profitably employed. The richest man in America also disputed claims that trusts made economic advancement impossible for average Americans, noting that he needed intelligent and skilled men to run his subsidiaries.

President Roosevelt agreed with much of Rockefeller's assessment. "The corporation has come to stay," he conceded, acknowledging that the nation benefited from the economies of scale that "good" trusts offered. Nonetheless, Roosevelt maintained, the government needed to break up "bad" trusts when consolidation threatened the public interest. The president soon singled out the Northern Securities Trust for dissolution, earning a reputation for trust-busting by taking steps to break up the monopoly.

In 1901, the financier J. P. Morgan had joined with two other powerful trust-builders, James J. Hill and E. H. Harriman, to form the Northern Securities Trust. The new transportation conglomerate meant "that you can ride from England to China on regular lines of steamships and railroads without once passing from the protecting hollow of Mr. Morgan's hand," announced journalist Ray Stannard Baker. With his eye on the 1904 presidential election, Roosevelt filed an antitrust suit charging the Northern Securities Trust with violating the 1890 Sherman Anti-Trust Act. A shocked Morgan rushed to the White House to broker a deal with the president. "If we have done anything wrong, send your man to my man and they can fix it up," suggested Morgan, an offer for a backroom deal that Roosevelt refused. In 1904, the Supreme Court upheld a Justice Department order to dissolve the Northern Securities Trust into independent railroad companies, earning Roosevelt public acclaim. After Roosevelt easily defeated the lackluster Democrat Alton B. Parker to win reelection in 1904, one newspaper called him "the most popular man that has come into public life within recent times."

Standard Oil was next. In 1906 the Justice Department filed suit claiming that the trust had violated the Sherman Anti-Trust Act. This political cartoon (**18.3**) depicts Standard Oil as a frenzied octopus that has consumed the entire oil industry. Tentacles grasp overweight steel and copper businessmen in suits on one side and steamboats on the other, symbolizing how Standard Oil's control of the supply and price of oil strangled transportation and manufacturing industries. In the caricature state legislatures and Congress have succumbed to the monster's strength, and a leg now reaches for the White House.

When the Supreme Court finally ordered Standard Oil to dissolve in 1911, the justices avoided a blanket ruling that all trusts were illegal. The Court instead invoked a "rule of reason," stating that only unreasonable restraints of interstate trade violated the law. The Court's ruling aptly described ex-president Roosevelt's own trust-busting philosophy. Roosevelt launched highly visible assaults on the Northern Securities and Standard Oil Trusts. He did nothing, however, when Morgan bought Andrew Carnegie's steel empire in 1901 to create U.S. Steel, a trust that employed nearly one million workers.

Roosevelt balanced trust-busting with regulation to ensure that big business behaved responsibly. He strengthened the Interstate Commerce Commission (ICC), created in 1887 to address Western farmers' criticism of high railroad freight rates and rebates (see Chapter 17). By 1900, Supreme Court rulings

---

What competing visions did Roosevelt, the Supreme Court, and leading industrialists offer on the trust issue?

Read the **Document** *Louis Brandeis, from* Other People's Money and How Bankers Use It *(1913)*

18.3 Standard Oil's Tentacles In this political cartoon Standard Oil is an octopus, consuming everything in its path.

had essentially stripped the ICC of real authority. During his second administration, Roosevelt reinstated the power of the ICC to regulate railroad monopolies, convincing a reluctant Congress to pass the 1906 Hepburn Act. Four years later the Mann-Elkins Act further bolstered the rate-setting powers of the ICC and put the telegraph and telephone communication industries under its purview as well.

Taft and Wilson: Competing Progressive Visions

Having promised not to run again for president in 1908, Roosevelt helped his secretary of war, William Howard Taft, secure the Republican nomination.

Roosevelt believed that Taft would continue his efforts to create a stronger, regulatory federal government. The Democrats countered by nominating the fiery William Jennings Bryan for a third time (see Chapter 17), trying to siphon Progressive votes away from a tepid Taft. Roosevelt's tireless campaigning for his chosen successor undercut Bryan's claim that he was the only real Progressive in the race. The Republican campaign slogan, "Vote for Taft now, you can vote for Bryan anytime," reminded voters of Bryan's two previous attempts to win the presidency and portrayed him as a perennial loser. Taft won easily, handing Bryan his worst electoral defeat.

Once Taft became president important philosophical differences between Roosevelt and Taft emerged. Like Roosevelt, Taft had to work with a divided

Republican party that controlled Congress. Roosevelt had sided with the Progressive faction, while Taft gravitated to the conservatives. Unlike Roosevelt Taft viewed the president as an executor of law and protector of existing social institutions, not someone who spearheaded new reforms. A stickler for the law, Taft proved less willing than Roosevelt to make any distinction between good and bad trusts, filing more antitrust cases over four years than Roosevelt had in eight. Taft's decision to file charges against U.S. Steel enraged Roosevelt, who saw it as a personal attack on his earlier choice to leave this "good" trust alone.

Unhappy with his successor Roosevelt decided to run for president again in 1912. When Roosevelt's bid for the 1912 Republican nomination failed (the party renominated the incumbent Taft), Republican Progressives bolted and formed the short-lived Progressive (Bull Moose) Party, which nominated Roosevelt as their presidential candidate. The split in Republican ranks offered the Democrats an opportunity to capture the presidency for the first time since the election of 1892. They nominated New Jersey Governor Woodrow Wilson, a Virginia-born politician with Progressive ideals. In contrast to the divided Republican Party, Wilson's candidacy kept the Southern base happy and prevented Progressively inclined Northern Democrats from joining the Progressive Party.

18.4 1912 **Presidential Election Results** Strong third-party challenges from the Progressive Party and Socialists split the national vote four ways, but Democrat Wilson prevailed to win the presidency in 1912.

Taft, Roosevelt, and Wilson supported different degrees of federal activism, competing views that gave voters a clear choice in the election of 1912. Taft was willing to zealously enforce existing Progressive reforms but had no intention of initiating new ones. Roosevelt embraced a governing philosophy that he called "New Nationalism," a vision that emphasized increased federal regulation and widespread political reform. In contrast to Roosevelt, who wanted to regulate but not destroy big business, Wilson's "New Freedom" promised to restore a competitive marketplace where small businessmen and farmers thrived.

The 1912 slate also included Socialist Party candidate Eugene V. Debs, a railway trade union leader who had become a socialist after being jailed during the Pullman Strike of 1894 (see Chapter 17). Formed in 1905 the Socialists had won numerous local elections and grown to over 100,000 dues-paying members. Roosevelt, Taft, and Wilson believed that with regulations in place (although each favored different amounts of regulation), capitalism would operate more fairly. Debs offered a competing view. He proposed transferring ownership of existing railroad, oil, and steel trusts to the government to ensure fair prices and wages. Government-run monopolies would be the first step toward ending the free-market system altogether.

Most voters agreed that the time had come to reform how the economy operated, but they overwhelmingly chose Progressivism over Socialism. Wilson won the presidency in 1912 (**18.4**) by a landslide in the Electoral College, while receiving only 41.9 percent of the popular vote. Roosevelt came in second with 27.4 percent of the popular vote, followed by Taft's 23.2 percent. Over 900,000 Americans, 6 percent of the electorate, voted for Debs. Nearly 70 percent of those who voted cast their ballots for Wilson or Roosevelt, a resounding public endorsement of Progressive principles and reforms.

Once he entered the White House, President Woodrow Wilson went beyond trust-busting to weaken monopolies. He accepted the Democratic orthodoxy of cutting the tariff so foreign businesses could market lower-priced goods in the United States, thereby creating a more competitive marketplace where smaller businesses could thrive. By 1913, most industrialists had dropped their longstanding opposition to lowering the tariff. The heads of Singer Sewing Machines, Eastman Kodak, and U.S. Steel believed that other nations would reciprocate, allowing American captains of industry to conquer foreign markets as well. Wilson offset the lost tariff

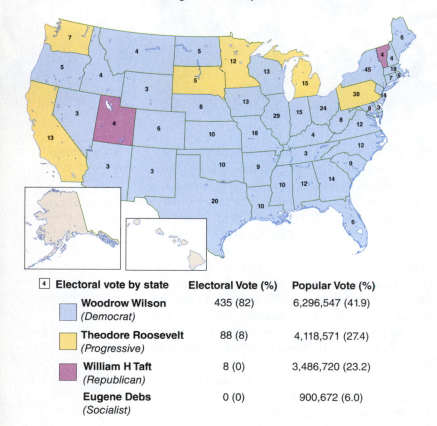

4 Electoral vote by state	Electoral Vote (%)	Popular Vote (%)
Woodrow Wilson (Democrat)	435 (82)	6,296,547 (41.9)
Theodore Roosevelt (Progressive)	88 (8)	4,118,571 (27.4)
William H Taft (Republican)	8 (0)	3,486,720 (23.2)
Eugene Debs (Socialist)	0 (0)	900,672 (6.0)

What clear philosophical differences separated the four candidates in the 1912 presidential election?

revenue (which the government needed to fund its operations) with the first federal income taxes, now constitutional thanks to the newly ratified Sixteenth Amendment (1913). Only people making more than $4,000 a year paid federal income taxes (less than one percent of the population) at a time when many workers felt lucky to make $1,000 a year.

Wilson also tried to help small businesses by improving the flow of credit. Most small and big businessmen agreed with Wilson that the time had come to reform the country's chaotic banking system. They vividly remembered the Panic of 1907 when financial giant J. P. Morgan had used his own funds and those of other bankers to shore up the national banking system. The nation's 7,000 banks operated with complete independence, issuing all forms of currency, some backed by gold and silver, others backed by government bonds. No centralized authority existed to expand or contract the currency supply as the economy demanded, or to move money around the country to stave off panics.

Conflicting visions soon arose over whether private financiers or the government should control the nation's financial institutions. Southern and Western Populists wanted a federally run banking system that would destroy the Wall Street "money trust." Eastern bankers likened government oversight to socialism. After much debate Congress passed the **Federal Reserve Act** (1913), creating a federally run Federal Reserve to serve as a "banker's bank" that held a portion of bank funds in reserve to help member banks in time of crisis. The Federal Reserve also set rates for business loans and issued a new national paper currency.

Wilson beefed up federal regulation of trusts as well. In 1914, the **Clayton Anti-Trust Act** prohibited interlocking directories, the practice of setting up shadow companies that appeared to compete but were actually run by the same board of directors. The law exempted trade unions from prosecution under the 1890 Sherman Anti-Trust Act, eliminating a tactic that businessmen had used to undercut the labor movement. The Federal Trade Commission (1914) had the power to order companies to cease unfair trading practices, although its decisions were subject to court review.

Preservation versus Conservation

Roosevelt, Taft, and Wilson prescribed differing amounts of regulation and federal activism to rein in the trusts. Business's access to the nation's forests, water, and minerals provoked another set of competing visions within Progressive circles. In 1867, John Muir suffered an eye injury that caused temporary blindness while working as a mechanic. After his eyes healed Muir walked 1,000 miles from Indianapolis, Indiana, to the Gulf of Mexico to rejuvenate his spirit. Like Muir, Roosevelt had turned to the revitalizing power of nature while recovering from personal tragedy when he retreated to his North Dakota ranch in 1884 after both his mother and 22-year-old first wife died on the same day in their New York City home. In 1903, President Roosevelt went camping with Muir in Yosemite, an area of the California Sierra Nevada Mountains filled with spectacular waterfalls, massive rock formations, and Giant Sequoia trees nearly 200 feet high and 3,000 years old. A photo of the pair on Glacier Point (**18.5**) before Yosemite Falls, the largest waterfall in North America, commemorated the trip. The two men dominate the frame, suggesting the power they had to decide the fate of such national treasures. This moment of unity was fleeting. Despite their mutual love of unspoiled forests, Muir and Roosevelt became formidable opponents who embraced different environmental visions.

Muir was a preservationist who championed preserving nature in its unspoiled state as a refuge for a "tired, nerve-shaken, over-civilized people." He accused businessmen of ravaging forests, polluting water, and destroying meadows with little regard for the long-term social costs of ruining the environment. Muir's condemnation resonated well with members of the middle class, who wanted to escape the

18.5 President Roosevelt and John Muir in Yosemite, 1903 Despite their camaraderie during a camping trip, Roosevelt and Muir embraced competing environmental visions.

How did Wilson's economic vision and policies differ from those pursued by the Roosevelt and Taft administrations?

18.6 *Chief and his staff*, 1904 This image of Crow warriors riding away into the mist captured the prevailing sentiment that Indian cultures were on the verge of disappearing.

Taft fired Pinchot in 1910, Roosevelt and his Progressive followers took it as a sign that Taft had abandoned conservation, deepening the split between the two former colleagues.

Environmentalists expressed great admiration for Native Americans' ecologically friendly farming and hunting practices, fueling mainstream curiosity about Indian cultures at the turn of the century. In 1900, photographer Edward Curtis began a 30-year multivolume ethnographic project entitled *The North American Indian*, which recorded images of 80 different Indian civilizations. Many Indians willingly participated in Curtis's photography project, proud of the beautiful portraits he took of them in their best festive dress. Curtis wanted to capture the variety and richness of Native American cultures before they completely disappeared. Considering himself a friend to the Indian, Curtis believed (like most of his generation) that to survive Native Americans needed to assimilate into mainstream American society. Curtis often photographed groups of Indians riding off into the distance (**18.6**) to symbolically convey the notion that, as Curtis wrote, "the Indians as a race, already shorn in their tribal strength and stripped of their primitive dress, are passing into the darkness of an unknown future."

Neither preservationists nor conservationists had any interest in reversing official policies of forced assimilation that divided collective reservation lands into individual farms, banned native languages, and sent Indian children to white-run boarding schools (see Chapter 15). Preservationists inadvertently hastened the demise of some Indian cultures by enticing Americans to visit national forests. Tourism undercut Indians' access to traditional hunting grounds so that their economic survival increasingly depended on selling crafts to tourists and charging them to see performances of native dances.

stress of urban life with holidays in the pristine wilderness. His influential writings led to the 1890 establishment of Yosemite as a national park and the creation in 1892 of the Sierra Club, an environmental group dedicated to preserving wilderness.

Muir's antibusiness message fit well with the Progressive determination to put the social good ahead of individual self-interest. Roosevelt agreed that a few unscrupulous entrepreneurs should not unfairly consume what belonged to the entire nation. To this end Roosevelt created 5 national parks, 18 national monuments, and bird reserves that placed millions of acres off-limits to development. The president parted company with Muir, however, by choosing to regulate, not ban, public access to other federally controlled lands, waterways, and mineral deposits. Roosevelt embraced a conservationist vision that tried to balance two goals: meeting present economic needs and conserving natural resources for future generations. When the U.S. Forestry Service Director Gifford Pinchot allowed timber companies to harvest trees in designated areas, the new regulations enraged both preservationists, who wanted all economic development to cease, and Western businessmen, who demanded unfettered access to federally controlled forests.

Taft was sympathetic to Western complaints that Roosevelt had overstepped his authority. When

How did Americans disagree about the environment during the Progressive Era?

View the **Closer Look** *Images as History: Envisioning a Vanishing Race*

Competing Views on Transforming the Workplace

In 1900, the United States earned the questionable distinction of being one of the most strike-torn nations in the world. To end class conflict and introduce more social harmony, Progressives wanted to transform the workplace into an environment where workers labored a reasonable number of hours in safe conditions for decent wages. Industry and labor each presented a competing view that challenged the Progressive vision as they sought the upper hand in their decades-long class struggle.

Capitalist Visions of Industrial Harmony

Industrialists differed on how to rid the workplace of labor conflicts that interfered with the smooth operation of their businesses. The National Civic Federation brought together moderate industrialists and labor union leaders dedicated to seeking industrial peace through compromise. Ohio Senator Mark Hanna, who made his fortune in coal, argued that industrialists should turn labor into "the ally of the capitalist, rather than a foe." In return for a few minimal concessions, factory owners could demand that union leaders discipline their membership and keep workers on the job, thus ending the constant strife that permeated the industrial sector.

Hanna's voice was a decided minority. Most industrialists refused to compromise their authority. Staunchly antiunion they employed a host of methods to undercut unions. If forced to accept a union, they insisted upon an "open shop" that let workers choose whether to join a union, then used intimidation to stop workers from enrolling. Industrialists hired private security forces to spy on workers, fired identified union members, and put them on blacklists that prevented union members from getting another job. During strikes factory owners expelled families from company-owned housing and hired substitute workers (called scabs) to replace striking workers. To protect union members from these discriminatory industrialist policies and build strength, labor organizers fought to establish a "closed shop," which required all workers in the same company to join the union.

Other industrialists embraced benevolence to dissuade workers from organizing. Welfare capitalism, the notion of using benefits to gain workers' loyalty, aimed to improve worker morale and weaken interest in unions. Some large firms instituted free medical care, pensions, kindergartens, and even baseball leagues, but these services typically evaporated at the first sign of economic downturn. Unions did not want to leave it up to the employer to decide whether to offer benefits. They preferred using collective bargaining to negotiate a contractual agreement between workers and their employers that established such benefits as a permanent right.

The drive for efficiency, a goal that many Progressives shared, was another way that industrialists undercut workers' collective power. Henry Ford's innovations in automobile manufacturing demonstrated how industrialists could boost profits by reducing manufacturing costs. The son of a prosperous Irish immigrant farmer in Dearborn, Michigan, Ford built his first car in 1896 in a shed behind his Detroit home. Forming the Ford Motor Company, Ford introduced the Model T in 1908, a moment when 515 separate companies were manufacturing automobiles. Ford standardized parts and constantly improved machinery—innovations that let him produce more cars for less money. Ford passed these savings on to consumers, lowering the price of his "car for the great multitudes" from $825 in 1908 to $345 in 1916. By then Ford had captured half the market for new cars.

In 1914 Ford created headlines by offering male factory workers a five-dollar daily wage for nine hours of work (extended to female and male office employees two years later). Ford paid twice the standard wage rate, because he recognized that the common practice of paying workers subsistence wages limited the markets for many consumer goods. Ford wanted his workers to be able to afford his automobiles. Working nine instead of ten hours a day, Ford reasoned, reduced fatigue-induced mistakes and worker

"The men do their work and go home—a factory is not a drawing room."

HENRY T. FORD on his rule prohibiting workers from talking to each other as they assembled automobiles

18.7 The Assembly Line
Ford's innovative mass production techniques included a well-lit and ventilated environment that relieved workers of backbreaking tasks. The assembly line also deadened the mind, as constant routine movements eliminated the need for decision making.

turnover, giving the company a loyal and experienced workforce. The moving conveyor belt in Ford's assembly lines (**18.7**) meant that workers no longer had to lift or move the chassis as they assembled a car. Ford admitted that he "could not do the same thing day in and out," but he condescendingly believed that the average worker "wants a job in which he does not have to think." To keep workers focused and productive, Ford prohibited sitting, talking, singing, or whistling in his factories. Fearful of losing their jobs, workers only dared to criticize Ford's iron control over the production process in private.

Ford's five-dollar/nine-hour-day came with strings attached. Ford instituted many reforms that Progressives sought because they made business sense, but he staunchly resisted government regulation and attempts to organize a union, retaining the right to make his own factory rules. Ford also firmly subscribed to industrialists' long-standing belief that they had the right, and the duty, to interfere in the private lives of their employees. For Ford this meant offering benefits only to employees who met certain moral criteria. Married men, for instance, had to live with their families. Thirty investigators working for Ford's Sociological Department visited workers' homes and sometimes imposed other requirements, such as mandatory English classes for immigrants. Gambling, excessive drinking, or having sexual relations with a prostitute were all grounds for dismissal. A Ford Motor Company investigator had to verify that a male worker was morally upright (and not trying to organize a union) before he and his family could move into a spacious two-story home built by the company.

How much did Ford's innovations and paternalism benefit workers?

Read the **Document** Frederick Winslow Taylor, "A Piece-Rate System" from The Principles of Scientific Management (1911)

Progressives valued efficiency and expertise, and Frederick Winslow Taylor took the drive for efficiency further than Ford by popularizing **scientific management**, the effort to use scientific knowledge to maximize output and profit. Taylor used stopwatches to evaluate how long each part of the manufacturing process should take. He then outlined the steps laborers should replicate to lay bricks without any wasted energy, and determined the perfect shovel size and the exact amount of rest workers needed to lift the maximum amount of pig iron each day. After establishing the optimal time and method for a specific task, Taylor argued, industrialists could then fine or fire unproductive workers who failed to maintain an acceptable pace. Taylor admitted that his system, dubbed "taylorism," intentionally eliminated workers' independence and creativity. Each man, he asserted, must "grow accustomed to receiving and obeying directions covering details, large and small, which in the past have been left to his individual judgment."

Working-Class Labor Activism

The working class had long fashioned its own solutions to surviving difficult living and working conditions. Fraternal associations assisted those who lost their jobs or needed to bury a loved one, while urban political machines (see Chapter 17) secured voters' loyalty by helping families endure personal tragedies such as fires or illness. Meanwhile unions tried to negotiate better wages and shop floor rules for dues-paying members, but organizing the working class so it could speak with one voice proved impossible. Ethnic and racial prejudices kept the working class fragmented. Italian strikebreakers, for instance, had few qualms about walking across a picket line manned by Slavic strikers. The craft-based American Federation of Labor (AFL), led by Samuel Gompers, organized only skilled, mostly white workers, refusing to let unskilled laborers, women, or blacks into its unions. Only a handful of industrial unions like the UMW and International Longshoreman's Union adopted a big umbrella approach that organized all workers in one industry into the same union.

Middle-class Progressives supported many union goals but deplored their methods. Strikes continually disrupted normal life by shutting down railroad lines, street cars, and coal mines.

Government regulation, they maintained, would improve workers' lives and ensure that the economy functioned smoothly. Nevertheless, many unions remained skeptical about relying on the government to solve their conflicts. The AFL preferred using its collective economic power to force industrialists to negotiate. Its members had unhappy memories of what happened when state or federal officials intervened in labor conflicts, as during the 1894 Pullman Strike.

The Roosevelt administration occasionally chose to aid labor, but Progressive Era courts nearly always favored industrialists. In 1908, the Supreme Court stopped workers from launching sympathy strikes or boycotts to support fellow workers, labeling them "restraints of trade" barred under the 1890 Sherman Anti-Trust Act, a law originally intended to curtail the creation of business monopolies. Another 1908 decision allowed employers to fire workers who joined unions. Reducing government interference in labor conflicts therefore remained the AFL's primary goal.

Radical trade unionists rejected the AFL vision of working within the free market system. The **Industrial Workers of the World (IWW)**, formed in 1905, envisioned "one big union" that welcomed all workers regardless of sex, race, ethnicity, or skill, which would one day take over all means of production in the United States. "It is the historic mission of the working class to do away with capitalism," declared the founders of the IWW, whose members were nicknamed "Wobblies." The founding group included 75-year-old Mother Mary Jones, a tireless white-haired organizer for the UMW, and William D. "Big Bill" Haywood, an organizer for the Western Federation of Miners. Their drive to abolish private property and formal government struck many Progressives as anarchy. Government harassment of the IWW limited its formal membership to around 10,000.

The Progressives' Limited Progress

Employers had traditionally held employees responsible for workplace accidents, maintaining that workers knowingly accepted all job-associated risks. Carelessness caused most mishaps, they argued. Progressive organizations undertook detailed sociological studies to refute these self-serving generalizations. Lewis Hine's photographic investigation into the lives of injured Pittsburgh workers

18.8 An Injured Pittsburgh Worker Portraits of maimed workers helped generate a groundswell of support for state workers' compensation laws.

suggested that few were responsible for their accidents. This young man (**18.8**) had his leg crushed when he fell under a coal car in a Pittsburgh coal mine. The company paid the hospital expenses for his amputation, but nothing else. In the image a nicely dressed passerby avoids making eye contact with the injured boy who stands idle on the street, suggesting that the well-off preferred to ignore the plight of disabled workers. The boy's tidy appearance reveals an effort to maintain personal dignity while relying on private charity to survive. Studies like Hine's convinced many states to establish worker compensation programs that provided employer-funded disability payments and medical care to injured workers. As a result employers began paying more attention to workplace safety.

The drive to limit hours for male workers was less successful. Employers had traditionally maintained that as property owners they had the sole power to decide the terms of employment. In the 1874 Slaughter-House cases, the Supreme Court had ruled that a state could not deny individuals control over their own labor. Industrialists claimed that this decision granted individual workers the constitutionally protected right to negotiate wages, hours, and workplace rules. According to this line of reasoning, state laws or unions that tried to impose restrictions on individual workers violated their right to control their own labor.

The Supreme Court, however, proved willing to abridge this right to protect public health and safety. In 1898, the Court upheld an eight-hour day for Utah miners, deciding that guarding the health of workers engaged in a dangerous occupation served the public interest. Progressives failed in their efforts to extend these protections to the entire workforce. In *Lochner v. New York* (1905), the Court ruled that unless long work hours directly jeopardized workers' health, the government could not abridge an employee's freedom to negotiate his own work schedule with his employer. This decision is explored more fully in *Choices and Consequences: Regulating Workers' Hours.*

Miserable and unsafe working conditions also persisted. The Colorado mining town of Ludlow sat along the Purgatory River, a telling name that suitably described what working in a mine was like. In Ludlow, the Rockefeller-owned mining company paid miners $2 a day in company-issued currency (called scrip) redeemable only in the company-run store. The mining company required that workers live in company-owned housing, and claimed no responsibility for accidents that killed 200 miners between 1904 and 1914.

In 1913, 12,000 miners, mostly Italian, Greek, and Serbian immigrants, went on strike to protest these conditions and demand company recognition of their UMW union. When the company expelled the strikers and their families from their homes, the workers erected tent cities in the nearby hills. After armed company detectives failed to dislodge the miners, the Colorado governor sent in state troops, whose wages Rockefeller agreed to pay. The **Ludlow Massacre** ensued on April 20, 1914 when troops set fire to one striking miners' camp, and thirteen women and children suffocated to death in a shallow underground shelter where they had sought refuge.

Throughout the nation outraged laborers temporarily put their ideological divisions aside to stage protest marches in every major city. The UMW issued "a call to arms," and hundreds of neighboring miners flooded into Ludlow to defend their comrades against the state militia. Faced with the prospect of all-out class war, the governor requested federal troops, and President Wilson immediately complied. Federal intervention left the union in tatters and Rockefeller free to run his mining town as he saw fit. Incidents like these convinced many unions that the Progressive proposal to rely solely on the government to solve their problems was not the answer. Throughout the twentieth century union folklore and songs used the memory of Ludlow to inspire workers to organize.

How effective were the different strategies that Progressives and unions employed to reform the workplace?

View the **Image** *Logo for the Industrial Workers of the World*

Choices and Consequences

REGULATING WORKERS' HOURS

Most city residents, especially tenement-dwellers who did not have ovens, bought their bread from bakeries. Bakers worked long hours in hot, poorly ventilated kitchens, sleeping and washing where they baked bread. In 1895, New York State passed a law that set sanitary standards and limited bakers to ten hours of work per day, 60 hours per week. Joseph Lochner, a bakery owner in Utica, challenged the law after New York fined him $50 for making an employee exceed these limits. The Supreme Court faced three choices when it heard the case in 1905.

Choices

1 A state could use its police powers to protect workers' health and safety.

2 A state could not limit an individual's right to buy or sell labor in nonhazardous occupations such as baking.

3 States had the right to enact any laws not expressly forbidden by the Constitution to promote the general well-being of society.

Decision

The Court ruled 5 to 4 that the Fourteenth Amendment, which declared that "no state shall … deprive any person of life, liberty, or property without due process of the law," prevented states from using their police powers to regulate work that did not imperil the health or safety of the public.

Consequences

The decision curtailed Progressives' attempt to use regulation to transform the workplace. During the subsequent 32-year "Lochner" era, the Court struck down maximum hour, minimum wage, and child labor laws if no clear risk to the public existed. Dismayed Progressives noted that many state laws restricted an individual's ability to buy or sell labor, such as mandatory school laws or Sunday closures, to promote the general welfare. They also accused the Court of ignoring the disproportionate power that employers wielded over workers to set the terms of employment.

Continuing Controversies

Should the government limit work hours or set a minimum wage?
Lochner remained the law of the land until 1937, when the Supreme Court ruled that it was "reasonable" for Washington State hotel owners to pay female hotel maids the state-mandated minimum wage because the state had a right to protect its residents. Defining an acceptable standard for work and pay has been controversial ever since. Is a reasonable day's work six, eight, ten, or twelve hours? Does it matter if the work involves strenuous physical labor or is sedentary? Is it better for unions to negotiate the terms of employment or for the government to step in? How does regulating hours of work or setting a minimum wage hurt or benefit the general public? These are questions that Americans have debated for more than 70 years.

Lochner bakery

What competing views existed concerning a state's right to regulate the workplace?

Protecting Women and Children

Progressives never convinced unions to give up strikes, but together they demanded laws protecting women and children. Relying on mountains of sociological data and heart-rending photographs, female activists helped secure protective legislation that reduced the hours women worked and kept children in school longer. Working-class men offered more resistance when female reformers tried to make temperance the law of the land.

Women at Work

In 1908, Curt Muller, a laundry owner in Portland, Oregon, challenged a recent state law granting a ten-hour workday for female laundry workers. In making his case before the Supreme Court, Muller followed the same line of reasoning used in the *Lochner* case, arguing that the law deprived his workers of their right to control their own labor. He disputed the reformers' claim that scrubbing all day in a hot, wet workplace posed a serious risk to laundry workers' health. In its unanimous 1908 **Muller v. Oregon** ruling, the Supreme Court upheld maximum hour laws for female workers, accepting lawyer Louis Brandeis's argument that protecting women's reproductive health served the public good. "As healthy mothers are essential to vigorous offspring, the physical well-being of woman becomes an object of public interest and care in order to preserve the strength and vigor of the race," the Supreme Court declared.

Reactions to the ruling among women were mixed. Middle-class Progressive reformers and female trade unionists celebrated it as a victory for female workers, unperturbed by the Court's emphasis on the biological inferiority of women to men. Feminists who believed in total equality were disappointed with the ruling, creating a fissure in the women's movement that soon widened into an open split. The male-dominated AFL embraced the decision,

18.9 Carry A. Nation Portrait and Hatchet Pin
Carry A. Nation cultivated her notoriety as a Bible-toting, ax-wielding saloon smasher by selling portraits and pins to her admirers.

believing it reduced employers' incentive to hire women instead of men. As if to prove this point, Muller responded by firing his female workers and hiring Chinese men to take their place.

Cross-class alliances between middle-class and working-class women flourished around other efforts to help working women. In 1898, the National Consumers' League (NCL) formed to coordinate local consumer boycotts of department stores that mistreated their female clerks. The NCL made the long hours and low pay endured by female working-class clerks the responsibility of every middle-class female shopper. The group soon expanded its boycotts to include stores that sold clothing made in sweatshops or with child labor. Compiling "blacklists" of stores to boycott was illegal, so the NCL instead worked with female garments' unions to create "white lists" of shops with equitable labor policies where socially conscientious women could shop without remorse.

Stamping Out Vice

Local and state reformers also took aim at alcohol, believing that prohibition would improve women's lives by reducing domestic violence and bolstering family income. The Woman's Christian Temperance Union (WCTU; see Chapter 17) viewed the saloon as a haven for gambling, prostitution, corrupt city political machines, and excessive alcohol consumption. The WCTU crusade took a surprising turn on June 6, 1900, when a deeply religious 64-year-old woman named

Why did the campaign for maximum work hour laws succeed for women, but fail for men?

Carry A. Nation strode into a southwestern Kansas bar with a bag of bricks and smashed the liquor bottles, glassware, and mirrors, then calmly left. Nation's tactics were extreme, but many Progressives shared her sense of urgency. Drinking was on the rise in America. From 1885 to 1900, beer consumption nearly doubled from 590 million to 1.2 billion gallons. Hundreds of inspired "Home Defenders" throughout the nation organized similar attacks on neighborhood bars, hoping to convince their communities to go dry. As her fame grew, Nation raised funds by selling miniature hatchet pins, her new weapon of choice (**18.9**), along with photos of herself holding her bible and hatchet. She spent time in jails from New York to Los Angeles publicizing the temperance cause before collapsing on a stage in 1911 and dying shortly thereafter.

Working-class men resolutely defended their freedom to drink, and many upper-class men were reluctant to give up a pleasure-based lifestyle that included ready access to alcohol. Attacking on multiple fronts the nonpartisan Anti-Saloon League, founded in 1893, and the WCTU established an effective coalition that included Progressives, rural Americans, and industrialists. Prohibitionists linked ridding the nation of alcohol to the broader Progressive desire to eliminate the corrupting influences of big-city political machines. Saloons, temperance advocates maintained, served as the headquarters where dishonest city politicians paid immigrants for votes and dispersed favors to supporters. Temperance advocates drew rural folk into the movement by addressing their concerns about the growing cultural influence of urban pleasures and the beer-drinking immigrants who lived in the cities. Molding their message to appeal to industrialists, temperance advocates blamed saloons for contributing to the nation's labor troubles by giving unions a place to meet and recruit.

Working through churches in the South and the West, the Anti-Saloon League and WCTU urged supporters to focus on making their state or county "dry" by banning the sale of alcohol. The "Prohibition 1904 and 1917" map (**18.10**) traces the rapid success of this strategy as the number of dry states grew from three to 23. Many western women had already secured the right to vote, and they flocked to approve prohibition in large numbers.

> ## "You refused me the vote and I had to use a rock."
> CARRY A. NATION explains her saloon-smashing ways

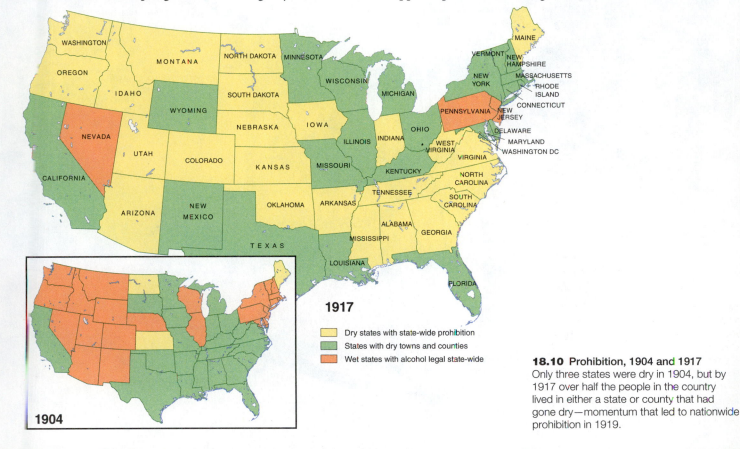

1917

- Dry states with state-wide prohibition
- States with dry towns and counties
- Wet states with alcohol legal state-wide

1904

18.10 Prohibition, 1904 and 1917
Only three states were dry in 1904, but by 1917 over half the people in the country lived in either a state or county that had gone dry—momentum that led to nationwide prohibition in 1919.

Read the **Document** *Report of the Vice Commission, Louisville, Kentucky (1915)*

What diverse concerns about alcohol helped the temperance movement gain momentum?

Restoring Childhood

18.11 "Models of 1898"
The middle class believed that children should engage in healthy and creative play, not work in dangerous and dreary factories.

Middle-class Americans believed that childhood should be devoted to education and play, not work. This advertisement (**18.11**) from an 1898 Sears and Roebuck catalog portrayed the type of idyllic childhood that many middle-class families tried to give their children. In the ad an immaculately dressed young girl rides joyfully in the sunshine on a new bicycle, a portrait of health and happiness. The reality for working-class children offered a stark contrast. Census records revealed nearly 1.75 million children ages 10 through 15 worked in factories full time, a figure that did not include children employed in home sweatshops or on family farms.

To Progressives child labor epitomized the greed of employers who eagerly sent children into mining crevices where adults could not fit, used children to harvest crops in the Midwest, or dispatched an army of small

Models of 1898

Manufactured by Sears, Roebuck & Co. Inc. Chicago.

What does this advertisement reveal about middle-class ideals of childhood?

boys to hawk newspapers in northern cities. Organized labor joined this crusade, certain that child labor drove down adult wages. Industrialists offered a competing vision, arguing that jobs provided valuable training for working-class children who needed to learn the importance of punctuality and hard work to become successful adult workers.

Many working-class families shared employers' beliefs that their children should work. In Chicago Hull House cofounder Jane Addams discovered that most immigrants, having worked themselves as children, found nothing wrong with putting their own children to work. "A South Italian peasant who has picked olives and packed oranges from his toddling babyhood, cannot see at once the difference between the outdoor healthy work which he has performed in the varying seasons, and the long hours of monotonous factory life which his child encounters when he goes to work in Chicago," she noted, adopting the Progressive tendency to gloss over the drudgery of farm work.

Rather than banning child labor, working-class parents often preferred making factories safer places for their children to work. They were not hard-hearted, but pragmatic. Child labor provided one-tenth of family income in the early twentieth century, and a family's survival often depended on children's meager wages. Recently arrived immigrant men, especially unskilled, non-English speakers, realized with dismay that their English-speaking children were more apt to be hired than they were. Children in these families became the breadwinners, while their fathers stayed at home. This reversal of normal family relations often created tensions within working-class households. "I left Europe and I was a man, and here I am a what?" lamented one Russian Jewish immigrant.

The drive to end child labor gained momentum when the National Child Labor Committee formed in 1904 to lobby for state and federal laws prohibiting child labor. The group hired photographer Lewis Hine to help them build a scientific, legal, and moral case against child labor. In one photo-story, Hine paired images of children who worked in two textile mills owned by the same company. The company's mill in Huntsville, Alabama, hired children as young as eight years old, Hine noted, while Massachusetts law prohibited the Lowell factory from employing children under the age of 14. The National Child Labor Committee presented such regional discrepancies as evidence that the nation needed a federal child labor law. *Images as History: Exposing the Evils of Child Labor*, page 550, explores Hine's images more fully.

The pervasiveness of child labor in the South particularly troubled him. In 1900, nearly 25 percent of the workers in Southern textile factories and cotton mills were white children ages 10 to 16. Some reformers viewed child farm work as a healthier alternative to long days in a factory. Hine disagreed. "The sunshine in the cotton fields has blinded our eyes to the monotony, overwork and the hopelessness of their lives," he wrote.

In 1916, President Wilson signed a law banning the interstate sale of products made by child labor that protected only about 150,000 industrial child laborers out of nearly 1.75 million. Two years later the Supreme Court sided with a father who argued that the law deprived him of his parental right to control his sons' labor and declared the law unconstitutional. Progressives responded by trying to amend the Constitution. In 1924 Congress approved an amendment giving the federal government the power to regulate child labor, but southern opposition to any curtailment of states' rights prevented its ratification. A nationwide ban on child labor did not come until the 1930s, when the Court upheld a New Deal federal child labor law.

Ultimately child labor declined as states began to mandate school attendance. Embracing the notion that all children had the right to an education, local women's groups pushed hard to ensure that their neighborhood schools received appropriate funding, provided free books, offered kindergarten, paid teachers adequately, and were equipped with satisfactory fire escapes. Throughout the Progressive Era school enrollments, the number of days in a school year, and money spent per pupil all rose.

Other Progressive endeavors also aimed to improve the lives of working-class children. The allure of pleasure and hunger at home sometimes became too strong for children, who resorted to stealing to meet their needs. "Most of these premature law breakers are in search of Americanized clothing and others are only looking for playthings," Jane Addams maintained. Some, she pointed out, were simply "eager to take home food or fuel which will relieve the distress and need they so constantly hear discussed." Reformers spearheaded the creation of a juvenile criminal system that focused on rehabilitating young offenders.

To keep young children safely off the streets when their parents went to work, Progressive activists established urban playgrounds with adult supervisors. To divert female teenagers from tempting dance halls and male adolescents from saloons or brothels, Progressives created local boys and girls clubs that included organized sports teams and art classes. Not every child appreciated becoming the object of reform. "I can't go to the playgrounds now," complained one 11-year-old boy. "They get on me nerves with so many men and women around telling you what to do."

Images as History
EXPOSING THE EVILS OF CHILD LABOR

Trained as a sociologist, photographer Lewis Hine took nearly 5,000 photographs as a staff photographer for the National Child Labor Committee from 1908 to 1918. Hine visited factories, canneries, textile mills, farms, and mines snapping photos and recording the experiences of each child, evidence the Committee used to argue that full-time work damaged children's health, deprived them of an education, and ruined their childhood. Hine often posed as a factory inspector or salesman to gain access to factories or mines. When a factory owner guessed his real purpose and refused to let him in, Hine took pictures of child laborers arriving at daybreak or leaving covered in grime. He carefully recorded the children's names, ages, and stories to counter industrialists' accusations that he staged his photos.

His notes for this image of a young girl tending machines in a South Carolina cotton mill read, "Sadie Pfeifer, 48 inches high, has worked half a year. One of the many small children at work in Lancaster Cotton Mills." Are Hine's photographs best understood as historical evidence, propaganda, or both?

Sadie Pfeifer was a spinner in a South Carolina cotton mill, charged with repairing breaks or snags as the machines spun the cotton into yarn or thread.

The electric lights indicate her long hours, beginning before daybreak and extending after dark.

The closed windows helped the factory maintain the hot and humid conditions that prevented thread from breaking.

The long row of machines underscores how much work she had to manage on her own, dangerous work that could cost her a finger.

The photograph does not convey the deafening noise that left some workers partially deaf.

The adult supervisor in the background represented Sadie's future and underscored her subservient position in the mill.

Lewis Hine, "Sadie Pfeifer, Lancaster Cotton Mills, South Carolina"

How did the composition of this photograph reinforce Hine's message about child labor?

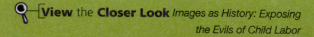

View the **Closer Look** *Images as History: Exposing the Evils of Child Labor*

Wise beyond their years, these tough-looking newsboys emulate their elders by learning to enjoy pipes and cigarettes. Newsboys also gambled, swore, and began visiting houses of prostitution at shockingly young ages.

Camaraderie among newsboys helped make a difficult and lonely job more enjoyable.

This photo of hardened newsboys warned that lacking a proper education, these boys contributed to the moral breakdown of society.

By innocently buying a daily paper from one of the hundreds of newsboys who hawked newspapers on city corners from dawn to dusk, the middle class helped perpetuate an insidious form of child labor.

Lewis Hine, "Newsies Smoking on a Monday Morning, St. Louis, Missouri, 1910"

The National Child Labor Committee distributed Hine's "Making Human Junk" poster nationwide to send the message that child labor ruined individual lives and hurt the entire society.

Appealing to middle-class self-interest, this poster suggested that sickly child workers contaminated the materials used to make clothing for the middle class.

Hine directly refuted industrialists' claims that work benefited children. "The object of employing children is not to train them, but to get high profits from their work," he wrote.

The poster showed a group of healthy children entering a harsh and dangerous factory environment where they were powerless to control their own fates.

Long days in the mill turned children into broken pieces of industrial "junk" that factory owners discarded, burdening society with their care.

Lewis Hine, "Making Human Junk"

Did these images offer similar or different reasons to oppose child labor?

Reforming the Government

Progressives recognized that passing laws governing the workplace or protecting women and children was not enough. Ensuring their enforcement through the establishment of regulatory agencies required reforming how local, state, and federal governments functioned. Only then could the government become a positive force in workers' lives. Socialists agreed that the government should act, but ultimately wanted to give state and national governments control of all major industries.

Containing Socialism

Progressives discovered an unexpected ally in their drive to turn the government into a guardian that actively protected the public. Both Progressives and socialists championed the creation of city-run utilities to provide streetcar service, gas, water, and electricity. Progressives viewed such arrangements as an efficient way to deliver reliable, fairly priced public services to city residents, prevent disruptive strikes, and improve conditions for utility workers. Socialists believed that municipal-run utilities would become the opening wedge that led to eventual public ownership of railroads, mines, and banks.

In 1904, the novelist and socialist Upton Sinclair lived with workers in Chicago for nearly two months, learning firsthand about their work in the meatpacking industry. This experience became the basis for his novel, *The Jungle*, which told the story of a Lithuanian immigrant family, who came to America full of hope only to discover crushing poverty and horrific working conditions. Sinclair wanted his exposé to convince Americans that socialism offered the only way to end the rampant capitalist exploitation that ground down the working class. Instead readers focused on his vivid descriptions of rotten meat, workers' fingers, and rat excrement being tossed into the hopper to produce the sausage that Americans enjoyed each morning for breakfast. When a federal investigation confirmed Sinclair's account, the public demanded federal regulation to ensure that the nation's meat supply was safe. Faced with plummeting meat sales, packing-house owners understood that government certification of their meat as disease-free could help them regain consumer confidence. The Meat Inspection Act (1906)

> ## "I aimed at the public's heart, and by accident I hit it in the stomach."
>
> ### UPTON SINCLAIR laments America's reaction to his novel, *The Jungle*

gave federal inspectors the authority to condemn meat unfit for consumption and established federal sanitary standards for meatpacking plants.

Reformers also wanted manufacturers of patent medicines to list their ingredients. Lydia E. Pinkham's Vegetable Compound, a widely popular patent medicine, circulated advertising cards (**18.12**) with images of rosy-cheeked children to create the impression that the company used the purest ingredients in its syrup. The flipside of this card touted the medicine as "a positive cure for all those painful complaints and weaknesses so common to our best female population," including headaches, depression, ovarian troubles, and menopause. In 1906, the **Pure Food and Drug Act** levied fines for mislabeling food or medicine. To their dismay many female temperance advocates who had avidly consumed Lydia E. Pinkham's Vegetable Compound discovered that it contained 15 percent alcohol.

Ultimately the Progressive vision of government oversight prevailed over the socialist view of complete government control. Most cities balked at direct ownership of public utilities, preferring to create regulatory boards that set rules for the private companies that continued to run streetcars or gas lines. The subsequent improvement in city services reduced the appeal of socialism in many working-class neighborhoods.

Ending Government Corruption

Progressives knew that meaningful regulation required eliminating corruption within all levels of government. For an enticing bribe, city officials often

18.12 Marketing Lydia E. Pinkham's Vegetable Compound
Ads for the patent medicine promised to cure practically every ailment and restore youthful vigor.

In the absence of a comprehensive social welfare system, the patronage-based ward system gave many working-class urban residents a way to survive hard times.

On the state level Progressives tried to reduce the power of corrupt political parties. Many states eliminated the practice of handing voters different colored ballots marked "Republican" or "Democrat" to stuff into the ballot boxes as party officials looked on. The secret ballot removed the threat of payback or shunning if one broke with the neighborhood party boss. Instead of letting party leaders choose candidates, some states introduced direct primaries that allowed party members to pick the candidates. A reform measure called the "initiative" provided a way, usually by gathering signatures on petitions, for the electorate to introduce legislation before state legislatures. The referendum put legislative proposals on the ballot, letting the voting public decide whether a measure became law. Finally, the recall used special elections to remove unpopular or corrupt officials from office before their term expired. Wisconsin, one of the most Progressive states, adopted all these measures under the leadership of Governor Robert Lafollette.

proved willing to look the other way when businesses broke the law. Political parties sometimes stole elections, creating fictitious lists of voters that let individuals use multiple aliases to vote as often as they liked.

Progressives disagreed over how to eliminate corruption. One answer was to get rid of politicians and instead rely on nonpartisan commissions of experts or city managers to run city services. Over 400 municipalities turned to commission-style governance, an approach that reflected the broad faith placed in expertise during the Progressive Era. Other Progressives replaced the ward system that let each neighborhood select its own councilman with city councils elected at large. Voters expected their ward representative to "bring home the bacon," patronage that Progressives felt encouraged parochialism and corruption. Impoverished working-class residents offered a competing vision. Their ward representatives provided needed job opportunities or relief. *Envisioning Evidence: The Family Economy* (page 554) illustrates the hand-to-mouth existence for many working-class families.

In 1906, journalist David Graham Phillips detailed the close ties between big business and federal senators in a series of magazine articles entitled "The Treason of the Senate." Phillips viewed this alliance as threatening to "the American people as any invading army could be." Roosevelt charged Phillips with exaggerating the extent of corruption and urged the "men with the muckrakes" to avoid stirring up needless controversy. Roosevelt's rebuke gave a new nickname to investigative journalists, "**muckrakers**." Subsequent corruption scandals solidified public support for the **Seventeenth Amendment (1913)**, which enabled voters, rather than state legislatures, to elect federal senators.

What reforms did Progressives introduce to improve the democratic process?

Envisioning Evidence
THE FAMILY ECONOMY

Stiff employer resistance to labor unions and the unions' tendency to organize only skilled workers meant that few workers could use collective bargaining to increase their wages. Instead, working-class families relied on themselves or, if the main breadwinner fell ill, on community charities to survive. This working-class family's expenses outweigh the income of one male wage earner, a common problem. Less than 3 percent of married women worked outside the home, but wives supplemented the family income by doing laundry for others or taking in boarders who paid for a room and meals. Putting children to work (at the expense of their schooling) helped families make ends meet even though children earned much less than adults. This responsibility never ended for some. Adult children continued to contribute to their family's financial well-being by delaying marriage or supporting aging parents who could no longer work.

	Monthly 1891 budget for a married laborer with a baby. Monthly income: $23.67	Monthly 1892 budget for a married accountant with no children. Monthly income: $66.50	
Food	$6.51	$13.22	The average laborer ate a more monotonous and less nutritious diet than a white-collar professional—consuming less meat, prepared foods (canned and dry goods), fruits, vegetables and sweets.
Rent	$9.02	$9.88	
Furniture	$3.61	$0.30	
Taxes and Insurance	$3.32	$7.11	Buying life insurance from a local fraternal organization ensured that if the father died, the laborer's family could afford his funeral and survive in the short term.
Utilities	$2.94	$4.99	
Sundries	$1.09	$2.10	
Liqour and Tobacco	$0.66	$0.42	The accountant drank and smoked less than the worker, leading to charges that the poor squandered their money.
Medicine	$0.29	$0.27	
Clothes	$0.21	$0.19	The similar amounts paid for rent do not mean comparable living circumstances. The accountant's higher transportation costs indicate that he lived farther out of town, probably in a new suburb. The worker lived close to work, nearer to industrial pollution. High demand for tenement apartments meant landlords often charged laborers exorbitant rents.
Dry Goods	$0.16	$2.45	
Postage	$0.10	$0.00	
Transportation	$0.08	$1.71	The accountant had an extra $23.33 a month to save, or give to his aged mother, along with $931 in household goods (including musical instruments and jewelry) that he could sell if necessary.
Reading Material	$0.00	$0.53	
Total Expenses	$27.99	$43.17	This working-class family's expenses outweigh the income of one male wage-earner, a common problem. Less than 3 percent of married women worked outside the home, but wives supplemented the family income by doing laundry for others or taking in boarders who paid for a room and meals.

Source: *Michigan Bureau of Labor and Industrial Statistics.* Tenth Annual Report of the Bureau of Labor and Industrial Statistics (Lansing, MI: The Bureau, 1893), pp. 1043-1047.

What do these budgets reveal about urban lifestyles?   View the **Closer Look** *Envisioning Evidence: The Family Economy*

Accepting Separate but Equal

The Progressive campaign to remake the government into a champion of the common man did not include challenging the legal edifice constructed in the wake of the Supreme Court's 1896 "separate but equal" ruling in *Plessy v. Ferguson* (see Chapter 14). By 1900, southern states had rushed to pass laws that formally segregated every public facility from railroad waiting rooms to cemeteries, parks, beaches, and water fountains. Use of poll taxes and literacy tests to disenfranchise blacks also exploded. When southern-born Woodrow Wilson took office in 1913, he let the heads of federal agencies segregate their offices.

African American leaders cultivated their own reform impulse during the Progressive Era. Unlike white Progressives black leaders had little faith that government would solve their social problems. The most prominent African American of the Progressive Era, Booker T. Washington, instead embraced self-help as the best way to end poverty among African Americans. Born a Virginia slave in 1859, after the Civil War Washington developed an almost fanatical desire to get an education, arriving penniless at the doorstep of Virginia's Hampton Institute, a vocational high school founded in 1868 to educate freed slaves and Indians. He passed his entrance exam—sweeping a floor—with flying colors. Hampton taught practical skills such as brick-making, blacksmithing, and shoemaking along with more traditional academic subjects like reading and math. This staged photograph (**18.13**) of a Hampton Institute carpentering class, taken 20 years after Washington attended, encapsulated the school's educational philosophy. The photo underscored that these perfectly groomed, hard-working, and well-trained students had the skills they needed to advance step-by-step up the ladder (in this case staircase) of success.

18.13 Hampton Institute Students Building a Staircase, 1900 Black educators distributed images of tidy black students working industriously to counter stereotypes that portrayed blacks as lazy or dangerous.

How does this photograph convey the Hampton Institute's educational philosophy?

Washington followed the Hampton model when he established his own school in 1881, the Tuskegee Institute in Tuskegee, Alabama. A captivating orator, Washington popularized the notion that blacks should focus on economic advancement first, politics and civil rights later. Washington's apparent willingness to accept social segregation, as long as blacks and whites worked together toward their common economic goals, won him a large white following. Roosevelt even invited him to dine in the White House, the first African American to ever receive this honor—an invitation that provoked howls of protest throughout the South. Washington's private behavior, however, was often at odds with his public persona. Publicly he reassured whites that most blacks had little interest in demanding equality as long as they could prosper economically. Privately Washington helped fund court challenges to *Plessy v. Ferguson* and sent his own children to northern white colleges.

Washington believed that American race relations would gradually improve. Methodist Bishop Henry McNeal Turner offered a competing vision, telling blacks to immigrate to Africa. Black journalist Ida B. Wells-Barnett also disagreed with Washington. Rather than striving to prove their economic worth to whites, Wells-Barnett urged African Americans to use boycotts to win equal treatment from white-owned railroads. She also advocated armed resistance to lynch mobs. "A Winchester rifle should have a place of honour in every black home, and it should be used for that protection which the law refuses to give," she declared. Wells-Barnett began lobbying for a federal anti-lynching law after a white mob in Memphis, Tennessee, lynched three friends of hers who had opened a grocery store that drew customers away from white businesses. With her life threatened Wells-Barnett moved to Chicago, where she worked with Jane Addams to prevent the segregation of city public schools and continued her anti-lynching campaign.

The most powerful challenge to Washington's vision came from the northern-born sociologist W. E. B. Du Bois, the first African American to attend Harvard University. Du Bois argued that individuals should receive the education that best suited them, regardless of their race. He emphasized that the African American community needed an educated elite of professionals and teachers, the so-called "Talented Tenth." Economic progress was not possible without the right to vote, Du Bois contended, pointing out that discriminatory laws made it difficult for black sharecroppers or craftsmen to get ahead. *Competing Visions: Seeking Racial Uplift* offers more detail on the debate between Washington and Du Bois. In 1909, Du Bois joined with Wells-Barnett and Jane Addams, among others, to establish the National Association for the Advancement of Colored People (NAACP). This interracial civil rights organization demanded an immediate end to racial discrimination, beginning a decades-long struggle for racial justice that would eventually overturn Jim Crow laws in the 1950s and 1960s.

Few white Progressives followed Addams's lead in denouncing racial discrimination. Most northern Progressives remained content to let the South handle the "race problem" as it saw fit. They essentially chose social peace over racial justice, asserting that segregation would quell racial conflict. "Good fences make good neighbors," declared southern Progressive leader Edgar Gardner Murphy.

> ## "In all my teaching I have watched carefully the influence of the toothbrush, and I am convinced that there are few single agencies of civilization that are more far-reaching."
>
> BOOKER T. WASHINGTON, noting the importance of personal discipline, hygiene, dress, and decorum to racial advancement

What alternatives did critics of Booker T. Washington offer to improve life for African Americans?

Watch the Video Video Lecture: The Conflict Between Booker T. Washington and W.E.B. DuBois

Competing Visions

SEEKING RACIAL UPLIFT

In 1895, Booker T. Washington delivered his most famous speech, "The Atlanta Cotton States and International Exposition Address," before an audience that was composed mostly of Southern whites. The speech proposed a compromise that accepted social segregation in return for white support of blacks' economic advancement. In 1903, W. E. B. Du Bois accused Washington of sending blacks down a path that ensured their permanent enslavement to white America. How does Washington take into account the racially hostile climate that prevailed in the South during the Progressive Era? Is Du Bois's criticism of Washington accurate?

In this passage from his 1895 "Atlanta Exposition Address," Washington outlines his plan for racial progress and peaceful race relations.

Our greatest danger is that in the great leap from slavery to freedom we may overlook the fact that the masses of us are to live by the productions of our hands, and fail to keep in mind that we shall prosper in proportion as we learn to dignify and glorify common labour and put brains and skill into the common occupations of life…. No race can prosper till it learns that there is as much dignity in tilling a field as in writing a poem. It is at the bottom of life we must begin, and not at the top.

In all things that are purely social we can be as separate as the fingers, yet one as the hand in all things essential to mutual progress…. Nearly sixteen millions of hands will aid you in pulling the load upward, or they will pull against you the load downward. We shall constitute one-third and more of the ignorance and crime of the South, or one-third its intelligence and progress.

The wisest among my race understand that the agitation of questions of social equality is the extremest folly, and that progress in the enjoyment of all the privileges that will come to us must be the result of severe and constant struggle rather than of artificial forcing. No race that has anything to contribute to the markets of the world is long in any degree ostracized. It is important and right that all privileges of the law be ours, but it is vastly more important that we be prepared for the exercises of these privileges. The opportunity to earn a dollar in a factory just now is worth infinitely more than the opportunity to spend a dollar in an opera-house.

Charles Keck, *Booker T. Washington Lifting the Veil of Ignorance*

In this excerpt from his book, *The Souls of Black Folk* (1903), Du Bois explains why Washington's ideas would not work.

Mr. Washington distinctly asks that black people give up, at least for the present, three things,—
   First, political power,
   Second, insistence on civil rights,
   Third, higher education of Negro youth,
and concentrate all their energies on industrial education, the accumulation of wealth, and the conciliation of the South….

Is it possible, and probable, that nine millions of men can make effective progress in economic lines if they are deprived of political rights, made a servile caste, and allowed only the most meager chance for developing their exceptional men? If history and reason give any distinct answer to these questions, it is an emphatic *No*. And Mr. Washington thus faces the triple paradox of his career.

1. He is striving nobly to make Negro artisans business men and property-owners; but it is utterly impossible, under modern competitive methods, for workingmen and property-owners to defend their rights and exist without the right of suffrage.
2. He insists on thrift and self-respect, but at the same time counsels a silent submission to civic inferiority such as is bound to sap the manhood of any race in the long run.
3. He advocates common-school and industrial training, and depreciates institutions of higher learning; but neither the Negro common [elementary] schools, nor Tuskegee itself, could remain open a day were it not for teachers trained in Negro colleges, or trained by their graduates.

His doctrine has tended to make the whites, North and South, shift the burden of the Negro problem to the Negro's shoulders and stand aside as critical and rather pessimistic spectators; when in fact the burden belongs to the nation.

View the **Closer Look** *Competing Visions: Seeking Racial Uplift*

Was Washington a sell-out, as Du Bois implies, or a master strategist?

1901–1902

McKinley assassinated, Roosevelt becomes president
Progressivism gains presidential advocate

"The History of the Standard Oil Company" published
Exposé of oil trust stokes interest in trust-busting

1903–1904

Roosevelt and Muir camp together in Yosemite
They later champion competing conservationist and preservationist visions

Northern Securities Trust dissolved
Earns Roosevelt reputation as a trust-buster

1905

Lochner v. New York
Stymies Progressive effort to mandate set working hours and wages

Socialist Party of America and IWW formed
Unlike Progressives, Socialists and IWW emphasize working-class solidarity over reform

1906

Pure Food and Drug Act and Meat Inspection Act passed
Establishes new regulatory role for the federal government

"Treason of the Senate" exposé
Reveals close ties between senators and big business

Review Questions

1. What social problems did middle-class Progressives identify at the beginning of the twentieth century? How did their solutions differ from those embraced by socialists and laissez-faire industrialists?

2. Why did the Progressive notion of an activist, regulatory government create controversy on both the right and the left?

3. How did visual images and investigative journalism transform Americans' views of poverty and corruption?

4. What role did government, including presidents, the Supreme Court, and state and local governments, play during the Progressive Era?

5. In what ways did the Progressive reform agenda succeed? How did it fail?

Key Terms

Federal Reserve Act (1913) The act creating a federally run Federal Reserve to serve as a "banker's bank" that held a portion of bank funds in reserve to help member banks in time of crisis, set rates for business loans, and issued a new national paper currency.   **539**

Clayton Anti-Trust Act (1914) The act prohibited interlocking company directories and exempted trade unions from prosecution under the 1890 Sherman Anti-Trust Act.   **539**

Scientific management The effort to use scientific knowledge to secure maximum output and profit.   **543**

Industrial Workers of the World (IWW) This group envisioned "one big union" that welcomed all workers regardless of sex, race, ethnicity, or skill, which would one day take over all means of production.   **543**

***Lochner v. New York* (1905)** A Supreme Court ruling that unless long work hours directly jeopardized workers' health, the government could not abridge an employee's freedom to negotiate his own work schedule with his employer.   **544**

Ludlow Massacre (1914) Colorado state troops set a striking miners' camp ablaze, killing thirteen women and children, an act that outraged laborers throughout the nation.   **544**

***Muller v. Oregon* (1908)** The Supreme Court upheld maximum hour laws for female workers because protecting women's reproductive health served the public good.   **546**

Pure Food and Drug Act (1906) Law levied federal fines for mislabeling food or medicine.   **552**

Muckrakers Progressive Era term for investigative journalists who wrote exposés on government and business corruption.   **553**

Seventeenth Amendment (1913) A constitutional amendment that enabled voters, rather than state legislatures, to elect federal senators.   **553**

CHAPTER REVIEW

1908–1909

Lewis Hine begins photographing child laborers
Nationwide campaign to ban child labor fails

Muller v. Oregon
Upholds maximum work hour laws for women

1911–1912

Triangle Shirtwaist Factory Fire
Shocking tragedy confirms need to reform workplace

Supreme Court announces "rule of reason" in breaking up trusts
Makes distinction between good and bad trusts

1913

Wilson allows federal agencies to racially segregate their offices
Reflects lingering impact of *Plessy v. Ferguson*

Sixteenth and Seventeenth Amendments ratified
Congress authorizes first federal income taxes and popular election of senators

1914

Ford announces nine-hour/five-dollar workday
Secures competitive advantage through benefits and assembly lines

Ludlow Massacre
Reveals potency of class conflict during Progressive Era

MyHistoryLab Connections

Visit www.myhistorylab.com for a customized Study Plan that will help you build your knowledge of *Creating a Democratic Paradise*.

Questions for Analysis

1. **What interpretation did this painting offer of the 1911 Triangle Shirtwaist Factory Fire?**

   View the **Closer Look** *Triangle Fire: March 25, 1911, p. 534*

2. **Why did these photographs arouse controversy?**

   View the **Closer Look** *Images as History: Envisioning a Vanishing Race, p. 540*

3. **How did Taylorism transform the workplace?**

   Read the **Document** *Frederick Winslow Taylor, "A Piece-Rate System" from The Principles of Scientific Management (1911), p. 542*

4. **What insights does Sinclair offer on workers' lives and food safety?**

   Read the **Document** *Upton Sinclair, from The Jungle (1905), p. 552*

5. **How did Washington and DuBois differ?**

   Watch the **Video** *Video Lecture: The Conflict Between Booker T. Washington and W.E.B. DuBois, p. 556*

Other Resources from This Chapter

Read the **Document**

- *Eugene V. Debs, "The Outlook for Socialism in America" (1900), p. 533*
- *Louis Brandeis, from Other People's Money and How Bankers Use It (1913), p. 536*
- *Profiles: Samuel Gompers, p. 543*
- *Report of the Vice Commission, Louisville, Kentucky (1915), p. 547*

View the **Closer Look**

- *Images as History: Exposing the Evils of Child Labor, p. 550*
- *Envisioning Evidence: The Family Economy, p. 554*
- *Competing Visions: Seeking Racial Uplift, p. 557*

View the **Image**

- *Teddy Roosevelt as "Jack the Giant Killer" (1904), p. 535*
- *John D. Rockefeller Cartoon (1901), p. 537*
- *Logo for the Industrial Workers of the World, p. 544*

View the **Map** *Interactive Map: Resources and Conflict in the West, p. 539*

Watch the **Video** *Video Lecture: What was the Progressive Education Movement?, p. 549*

Source: Destruction of the battleship *Maine* in Havana harbor in the Spanish-American war; Havana (Cuba) 1898 Feb. 15; Creator-Kurz & Allison

(((•┤**Hear** the **Audio File** on **myhistorylab.com**

◉┤**Watch** the **Video** *Critical Visions, Chapter 19*

CHAPTER 19

Imperial America
The United States in the World, 1890–1914

On February 15, 1898, a naval officer awoke President William McKinley in the middle of the night with the stunning news that the American battleship the *Maine* had exploded in Havana, Cuba, killing 266 of the 354 crew members. The explosion turned the battleship into a hunk of molten steel. This illustration depicted the blast propelling bodies and debris sky-high in Havana Harbor. Americans also read moving, first-hand accounts in the press, including one from survivor James R. Young. "I was feeling a bit glum," Young recalled, "and in fact was so quiet that Lieutenant J. Hood came up and asked laughingly if I was asleep. I said, 'No, I am on watch.' Scarcely had I spoken when there came a dull, sullen roar. Would to God that I could blot out the sounds and the scenes that followed."

The United States and Spain had long been at odds over the question of independence for Cuba, then a Spanish colony. McKinley had sent the *Maine* to Havana to stop Spanish-instigated attacks on American-held property in Cuba. Many Americans suspected that Spanish saboteurs had blown up the ship to protest the U.S. incursion into Spanish territorial waters. The shocking images and accounts of the *Maine* explosion fueled public anger against Spain for its supposed attack on the U.S. Navy, creating a crisis between the two nations. An official investigation confirmed these widely held views, blaming the *Maine* explosion on a Spanish mine in the harbor. The exact cause of the blast, however, remained a mystery. Some experts now cite a spontaneous combustion from the coal stored alongside ammunition as the most likely culprit, a misfortune thirteen American naval vessels shared between 1895 and 1898. Others suggest that Cuban revolutionaries may have planted the explosives, expecting the United States to blame Spain and declare war.

The *Maine* explosion ignited a four-month war between the United States and Spain in 1898. This "splendid little war," as one official called it, ended with an overwhelming American victory. The overseas possessions that the United States gained from Spain, including Puerto Rico, Guam, and the Philippines, gave the nation a new formal colonial empire. The United States simultaneously constructed an informal economic empire throughout the Caribbean and East Asia. As the United States established itself as a budding world power, Americans offered conflicting visions of how the United States should behave outside its borders.

“Remember the *Maine* and to hell with Spain!”

Newspaper slogan urging war with Spain in the wake of the *Maine* explosion

Becoming a World Power

Throughout the nineteenth century the Atlantic and Pacific oceans provided Americans with a sense of security and detachment from world affairs. By the 1880s, however, advancements in transportation and communication suddenly made the world seem smaller and more dangerous to Americans. Fear alone, though, did not explain Americans' growing interest in venturing overseas. Americans looked outside their borders to find markets for U.S. goods and the raw materials needed to fuel a growing industrial economy. International recognition as a world power and spreading American values also appealed to the country's growing sense of national greatness.

European Imperialism

In the seventeenth and eighteenth centuries, Britain, France, and Spain had based their world prominence on far-flung colonial empires, places that they populated with settlers and soldiers to exploit economic resources and protect ocean trade routes. In the eighteenth and nineteenth centuries, these settler communities launched a slew of successful revolutions that liberated colonies in North and South America from European rule. With the "old" colonial empires now defunct, European nations and Japan sought new ones. As Britain, France, Belgium, Germany, Italy, Portugal, Spain, Russia, the Netherlands, and Japan discovered vulnerable areas around the globe to colonize, they developed a new style of empire building. **Imperialism**, the late nineteenth-century term for colonizing foreign nations and lands, relied primarily on business, political, and military structures rather than settlers to rule colonized peoples and exploit their resources. Europe's drive to create colonial empires in Africa and Asia in the late nineteenth century provided a model to either emulate or reject as the United States embarked on its campaign to become a world power.

Besides exploiting colonies for economic gain, Europeans also drew satisfaction from fulfilling a self-imposed "civilizing" mission to spread Western culture and values to nonwhite and non-Christian populations throughout Africa and Asia. The drawbacks to empires, however, included the need to defend widely dispersed territories and suppress popular uprisings against colonial rule. Americans, therefore, developed conflicting visions from the lessons that they drew from the European experience. Some saw it as an inspiration; others, a cautionary tale.

Ottomon Empire
Britain and possessions
France and possessions
Denmark and possessions
Spain and possessions
Portugal and possessions
Netherlands and possessions
German Empire and possessions
Russian Empire and possessions
Japan and possessions
Italy and possessions
US and territories

As the map (**19.1**) indicates, the world situation in 1898 affected where the United States could hope to expand its influence. By the time the United States began exploring opportunities for expansion beyond the North American continent, Britain, France, Germany, and the Netherlands had already established colonial empires throughout Africa, East Asia, and South Asia. Great Britain exerted the greatest reach, making it the world's preeminent imperial power. This left the Western Hemisphere and China as possibilities for U.S. colonial expansion.

The Impulse for Expansion

Throughout American history territorial expansion played an important role in defining national identity and providing economic opportunity to Americans. In the early nineteenth century, Manifest Destiny, or the belief that Americans had a divine right to expand across North America, fueled expansion. Imbued with a sense of cultural and racial superiority over the indigenous peoples who inhabited these lands, Americans felt justified in taking away land from Indians. In their

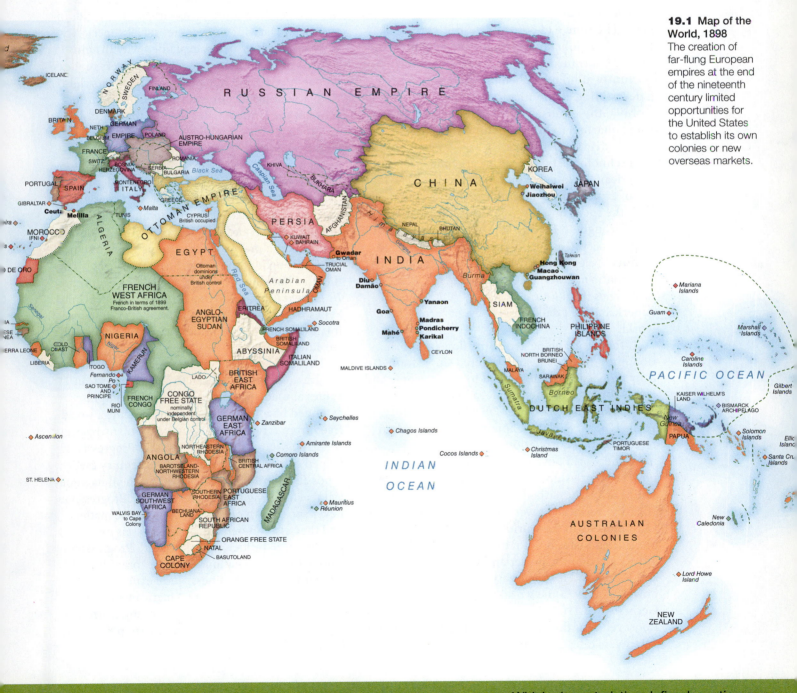

19.1 Map of the World, 1898
The creation of far-flung European empires at the end of the nineteenth century limited opportunities for the United States to establish its own colonies or new overseas markets.

Which characteristics defined a nation as a world power in the late nineteenth century?

view, Native Americans had failed to make the land productive. The government relocated many Indian tribes onto reservations, where officials and missionaries embraced the goal of "civilizing" Indians by teaching them Western capitalist and Christian values (see Chapter 15). The same belief in Manifest Destiny, quest for economic opportunity, and ideas of racial superiority spurred interest in expanding American influence and trade overseas.

Prominent businessmen, commercial farmers, and politicians urged the country to seek territory and markets outside the United States. In the 1890s, American companies and farmers sold 90 percent of their goods to other Americans. The time had come, these critics argued, to develop global markets and even colonies to ensure continued prosperity and economic opportunity at home. When the country suffered a devastating economic depression from 1893 to 1897, these calls crystallized into a resolve in some quarters to build a commercial and colonial empire overseas.

Technological innovations also encouraged Americans to look beyond their borders. The laying of transatlantic telegraph cables increased both the speed and the volume of information sent throughout the world. The telegraph in many respects served as the Internet of the nineteenth century. Telegrams accelerated the exchange of diplomatic notes between governments, while dispatches from journalists overseas connected Americans on a daily basis to events around the world.

If the telegraph hastened the flow of information, the advent of steam-powered ships dramatically reduced the time needed to move people and goods throughout the world. In his seminal 1890 work, *The Influence of Sea Power Upon History, 1660–1783*, U.S. Navy Captain Alfred T. Mahan traced a direct correlation between a strong navy and world power. In the new age of steam-powered battleships, the navy's outdated wooden sailing ships, described by one congressman as "floating washtubs," were ill-suited for advancing U.S. interests in the world. From 1890 onward, the United States built battleships to match its growing economic power and its expansionist ambitions, and it soon boasted the third most powerful navy in the world after Great Britain and Germany. In 1907, President Theodore "Teddy" Roosevelt sent the nation's 16 battleships and four destroyers on a global tour to show off America's world-class steam-powered navy, a trip that took two years to complete.

Americans' growing pride in their nation's economic might and technological prowess encouraged the United States to seek international recognition as a world power. So did the ideological vision encapsulated by social Darwinism, an ideology that applied nineteenth-century naturalist Charles Darwin's theory of biological evolution to human society through the notion of "survival of the fittest." At home Americans often used social Darwinism to justify the dominance of the wealthy and powerful, considered "the fit," over the poor and weak, or "the unfit." These ideas also shaped how Americans viewed the world. In the social Darwinist view, the "racial superiority" of Northern Europeans explained why Britain, France, and Germany were world powers that easily colonized nonwhite peoples. To take its rightful place alongside, or even above, these world powers, the United States needed to demonstrate its fitness by entering the global competition for colonies.

In making a case for expansion, the Congregational minister Josiah Strong linked older ideas of Manifest Destiny with this newer emphasis on survival of the fittest. "It seems to me that God, with infinite wisdom and skill, is training the Anglo-Saxon race to prevail" in the competition to control lands throughout the world, Strong wrote in his influential book, *Our Country: Its Possible Future and Its Present Crisis* (1885). In Strong's view the United States risked losing its chance for global eminence if it failed to join the scramble for colonies underway worldwide.

Driven to perfect democracy at home, many Progressives found the call to spread American values abroad appealing. Their reform impulse extended beyond U.S. borders to imagine a world freed from tyranny and injustice. In many respects the strong, activist government that Progressives helped construct at the turn of the century made it possible for the United States to extend its imperial reach during the Progressive Era. Progressives never spoke with one voice on domestic matters, and they also offered competing visions on expanding U.S. influence in the world. Progressives who opposed the nation's overseas forays feared strengthening big business at the expense of exploited foreign peoples and American workers. They also believed that imperial ventures drew attention away from Progressive reform projects at home.

The Spanish-American War

The first significant opportunity to expand U.S. influence overseas came when Cuba rose in revolt against Spanish rule. Extensive press coverage of Spanish atrocities and U.S. economic interests in Cuba prompted the nation to take note of this colonial struggle for independence. After a mysterious explosion sank the *Maine* and killed hundreds of American sailors, many Americans accused Spain of deliberately attacking the ship. Fearing that Congress might declare war on its own, a reluctant President William McKinley finally agreed to an armed intervention. The war with Spain was short, but the outcome was dramatic. The peace treaty with Spain granted the U.S. island possessions in the Caribbean and Pacific that became the territorial foundation for the new U.S. colonial empire.

The Growing Conflict with Spain

In the early nineteenth century, when Spain's other Western Hemisphere colonies successfully fought for independence, Cuba (and Puerto Rico) remained loyal to Spain. By 1868, however, oppressive Spanish rule provoked a rebellion in Cuba that ended ten years later with Spain's pledge to grant the island increased autonomy. Failure to fulfill this promise, economic hardships inflicted by the 1890s depression, and continued agitation by exiled Cuban rebels living in the United States fanned the flames of rebellion again in 1895. By the time the second revolt began, the United States and Cuba had established strong commercial ties. Cuba sent over 90 percent of its exports to the United States, and American investment totaled nearly $50 million in Cuban sugar, cattle, mining, and tobacco industries.

Spain paid a heavy price to maintain this symbol of its imperial past. Of the 278,000 Spanish troops sent to Cuba to suppress the revolt, nearly 50,000 had died of yellow fever or malaria by 1898, and an equal number lay too sick to fight. A much smaller force of 20,000–30,000 Cuban rebels drew on their knowledge of the terrain and support from civilians to fight a guerrilla war that ravaged tobacco and sugar plantations to deprive the Spanish government of revenue. Rebels purposefully steered clear of American-owned plantations to avoid antagonizing the United States.

Cuban exiles in the United States drew appealing analogies between their struggle for independence and the American Revolution, highlighting the similar desire of Cuban and American colonists to free themselves from an exploitive ruler and establish democratic self-rule. If any uncertainty existed among the American public over which side they supported, Spanish General Valeriano Weyler's infamous reconcentration policy ended those doubts. Through reconcentration Spanish soldiers tried to crush the Cuban rebellion by herding peasants off their farms into heavily fortified camps and then systematically destroying the crops that fed the rebel armies. This policy created a humanitarian crisis in Cuba, as famine and disease ravaged the civilian population, killing nearly 100,000 civilians. Outraged Americans denounced reconcentration as uncivilized and illegal warfare.

The yellow press, tabloid journalists and newspapers that reported sensationalist stories with a strong emotional component, fueled public anger against the Spanish. This unique name for nineteenth-century tabloid journalism derived from competing "Yellow Kid" comic strips in leading New York newspapers that portrayed the antics of a precocious boy living in the city's tenements. Yellow journalism emerged in the 1880s when Joseph Pulitzer began using melodramatic, partly fictionalized stories to bolster sales of his newspaper, the *New York World*. After William Randolph Hearst took over the *New York Journal* in 1895, the two newspapers waged daily battles over who could print the most lurid tales.

In the Cuban crisis both papers saw a chance to report the kinds of scandal-driven stories guaranteed to sell newspapers. Exiled Cuban rebels living in the United States provided a steady supply of atrocity stories (some fabricated, some true) to the yellow press, and the vivid illustrations accompanying these accounts helped the public visualize Spanish brutality.

Why did Americans take an interest in the Cuban rebellion against Spain?

The importance of illustrations to the yellow press became clear in a fabled exchange between Hearst and the artist Frederic Remington. Remington, already famous for his portraits of the American West, went to Cuba to draw illustrations for the *New York Journal*. Tiring of the rebellion's slow pace, Remington told Hearst he was leaving Cuba. Hearst supposedly replied, "Please remain. You furnish the pictures, and I'll furnish the war." This exchange passed quickly into American folklore as proof of Hearst's determination to use shocking images, real or staged, to provoke a war with Spain. No evidence exists, however, that Hearst ever wrote or sent this reply. *Images as History: Atrocity Stories and Public Opinion* examines how yellow press illustrations shaped American public opinion.

The Decision to Intervene in Cuba

With the yellow press clamoring for military action, President McKinley turned to diplomacy to end the impasse over Cuba peacefully and repeatedly asked Spain to grant Cuba more autonomy. In 1897, the Spanish government ended reconcentration by recalling Weyler and allowing displaced Cuban peasants to return to their homes. Spain also announced a plan for limited Cuban self-government, inviting protests from all sides. Cuban rebels urged Americans to help them attain complete independence. Meanwhile Cubans still loyal to Spain reacted angrily to the limited autonomy plan and rioted in Havana. An alarmed McKinley decided to send the *Maine* battleship to Havana to deter loyalists from attacking Americans or their property. Acting within the boundaries of acceptable international practice, McKinley expected the battleship's presence (with the implied threat of bombardments) to restore calm to Havana. Events in February, 1898, however, conspired against McKinley's effort to resolve the crisis peacefully. First Hearst's *Journal* published a private letter written by the Spanish ambassador, which described McKinley as "weak and a bidder for the admiration of the crowd." Although tame compared with the vicious statements American newspapers routinely made about the president, the letter outraged the public.

> ## "Worst Insult to the United States in Its History."
> ### Yellow press headline regarding Spanish ambassador's disparaging comments about McKinley

Next the *Maine* exploded in Havana Harbor. After a month of press speculation about the cause of the explosion, an official naval investigation erroneously blamed a Spanish harbor mine for the disaster, rather than the real culprit: faulty ship design that caused an internal explosion, or perhaps sabotage by Cuban rebels who wanted the United States to declare war on Spain. In the weeks immediately following the sinking of the *Maine*, McKinley tried unsuccessfully to convince Spain to grant Cuba independence and to calm calls for war from Congress. "I have been through one war," McKinley told a friend, referring to his service in the Civil War. "I have seen the dead piled up, and I do not want to see another." For many other Americans, however, memories of brutal Civil War battles had faded. They enthusiastically viewed war as a manly adventure that would instill discipline and vigor in American men. The assistant secretary of the navy, Theodore Roosevelt, championed this competing view, writing to a friend in 1897, "I should welcome almost any war, for I think this country needs one."

With the Democrats championing war, Republicans feared that McKinley's resistance to fighting might hurt the party at the polls. Some senators even suggested that Congress declare war whether McKinley agreed or not. The pressure for war increased when Senator Redfield Proctor, several days before the navy released its findings on the *Maine* attack, gave the Senate a grim accounting of the appalling effects of Spain's reconcentration policy on the Cuban people. "I went to Cuba with a strong conviction that the situation had been overdrawn," Proctor noted, then went on to detail the starvation, squalor, and sickness he had seen. This sober address from a conservative Republican and stalwart friend of McKinley's convinced many wavering congressmen and Americans that the country had a humanitarian duty to save Cuba.

To head off a war, Spain made one last offer to grant Cuba increased autonomy, rejecting McKinley's call for total independence. "Mr. President, I can no longer hold back the Senate," Vice President Garrett Hobart told McKinley. "They will act without you if you do not act at once." Accepting that he had failed to settle the crisis, McKinley asked Congress to authorize an armed intervention to end the civil war in Cuba without declaring war on Spain.

Images as History
ATROCITY STORIES AND PUBLIC OPINION

Ever since the yellow press helped raise American ire against Spain in the years leading up to the Spanish-American War, Americans have pondered the power of the press in the United States. How much power do atrocity stories and pictures have to shape public opinion? Can the press convince the public to fight a war?

On February 12, 1897, the *New York Journal* published a story by Richard Harding Davis about a young Cuban woman whom Spanish authorities had expelled for carrying secret messages between Cuban rebels. Davis reported that "Spanish officers" followed Clemencia Arango and her companions onto an American ship. The Spanish officers "demanded that a cabin should be furnished to them to which the girls might be taken, and they were then undressed and searched" for messages to exiled Cuban rebels living in the United States. Frederic Remington's illustration "Spaniards Search Women on American Steamers" accompanied Davis's story.

The paper next took up the cause of Evangelina Cisneros. Sentenced to 20 years in prison for trying to lure a Spanish officer into a rebel death trap, Cisneros was awaiting deportation to an African penal colony. According to the *New York Journal*, her only crime was calling for help from nearby Cuban rebels to stop a Spanish officer, "a beast in uniform," from raping her. On October 10, 1897, the paper triumphantly announced that a *New York Journal* reporter had helped Cisneros break out of jail and sail to the United States. The yellow press presented Clemencia and Evangelina as symbols for the virtuous and victimized Cuban people, fueling public sympathy for the Cuban rebellion.

Frederic Remington (who was in the United States when this incident occurred) drew a beautiful naked white woman standing defiantly before the three overly curious and swarthy-looking Spanish officers who had undressed her. In fact, female prison matrons performed the search.

"There are things more dreadful than even war and one of them is dishonor," the *New York Journal* editorialized about the Clemencia Arango incident.

This 1897 illustration of dark-skinned men viewing and touching the body of a white woman resonated powerfully with many white Americans because it aroused their racial prejudices.

"Spaniards Search Women on American Steamers." *New York Journal*, February 12, 1897.

Press coverage of Cisneros's escapades generated so much interest that huge crowds gathered to hear of her adventures when she appeared in New York and Washington, D.C., where President McKinley received her in the White House.

The headline criticized diplomatic inaction and suggested that only military-style action could save Cuban rebels.

New York Journal accounts exaggerated Cisneros's light-skinned beauty, noble birth, and prison sufferings.

Nearly 15,000 women, including President McKinley's wife, signed the newspaper's petition to Spain's Queen María Cristina demanding Cisneros's release.

"Evangelina Cisneros Rescued by the Journal." *New York Journal*, October 10, 1897.

View the **Closer Look** *Images as History: Atrocity Stories and Public Opinion*

Why did popular media accounts depict the Cubans as light-skinned and the Spanish as dark-skinned?

Congress complied. On April 24, 1898, however, Spain declared war on the United States. The next day Congress responded with its own declaration of war, dating it retroactively to April 21, 1898.

To underscore the nation's altruistic motives, Colorado Senator Henry M. Teller added an amendment to the war resolutions that disavowed any intention of annexing Cuba. The **Teller Amendment (1898)** promised "to leave the government and control of the [Cuban] Island to its people" at the end of the Spanish-American War. Congress made no such promise to other colonized peoples under Spanish control in the Caribbean and Pacific.

Fighting the War against Spain

America's victory in the Spanish-American War, which lasted from April to August 1898, paved the way for U.S. territorial expansion in the Caribbean and Pacific. One week after the war began, Commodore George Dewey sailed into Manila Harbor, in the Spanish colony of the Philippines, (**19.2**) and destroyed the Spanish Pacific fleet. Why, Americans wondered, did the navy fight the first battle to liberate Cuba halfway around the world in the Philippines, an archipelago of 7,000 islands in the Pacific Ocean? By eliminating the Spanish Pacific fleet, Dewey prevented it from sailing to Cuba. The defeat also put added pressure on Spain to sue for peace. Dewey's stunning victory catapulted the Philippines into the spotlight, and Americans learned that the Filipinos were in the midst of their own

19.2 The Spanish-American War, 1898
The U.S. Navy first attacked the Spanish in the Philippines, and then blockaded Cuba as U.S. forces invaded.

"I could not have told where those darned islands were within two thousand miles."
President McKINLEY on the location of the Philippines before the Spanish-American War

rebellion against Spain. At first the Filipino rebels, who controlled much of the interior, welcomed the Americans as liberators. "I have studied the Constitution of the United States, and I find in it no authority for colonies and I have no fear," rebel leader Emilio Aguinaldo told one American general. Time would prove him wrong.

Besides securing a foothold in the Philippines, the McKinley administration also used the war against Spain as a pretext for settling the festering question of annexing Hawaii that had divided Americans for the past six years. Americans had a long history of involvement in Hawaiian affairs.

CHINA

FORMOSA
(TAIWAN)
(Japanese)

PACIFIC OCEAN

● Hong Kong
(British)

Gulf of Tonkin

HAINAN

PHILIPPINE ISLANDS

Dewey

Manila

Manila Bay

South China Sea

SIAM

Sulu Sea

FRENCH INDOCHINA

BRITISH NORTH BORNEO

Pacific Theater
▢ Spanish Territory ceded to United States
✴ Major battle, May 1, 1898
➡ US forces

By the 1880s, American-owned sugar plantations dominated the Hawaiian economy, American missionaries had waged a successful campaign to eradicate native religions, and the U.S. Navy had established a permanent base at Pearl Harbor on the island of Oahu. Responding to popular discontent over the erosion of native Hawaiians' economic standing and cultural traditions, Queen Liliuokalani promised to curtail U.S. dominance, when she assumed the throne in 1891. In 1893, however, American businessmen and missionaries working on the islands (representing 5 percent of the islands' population) overthrew Queen Liliuokalani. U.S. Marines sent ashore from a nearby warship, ostensibly to protect American property, ensured the revolution's success. Thousands of Hawaiians took to the streets to protest the coup, to no avail.

The new Hawaiian republic's immediate request for annexation by the United States proved controversial, however. Disavowing the role that U.S. officials had played in the coup, President Grover Cleveland apologized to the Queen and demanded her restoration to the throne. The new Hawaiian government ignored Cleveland's request, choosing instead to renew its appeal when the pro-annexation McKinley became president five years later. McKinley believed that acquiring Hawaii would foster U.S. commercial interests in the Pacific. This time the Hawaiian Patriotic League blocked a formal U.S. takeover by presenting the Senate with a 556-page anti-annexation petition signed by over half of native-born Hawaiians. Faced with Hawaiians' overwhelming opposition to annexation, the Senate voted the measure down in 1897. A year later, however, with the Spanish-American War underway, Congress reversed course. Supporters of annexation argued that U.S. ships headed to the Philippines needed guaranteed access to the naval base in Pearl Harbor. Putting its own strategic and economic needs ahead of Hawaiians' desire to remain independent, the United States assumed sovereignty over Hawaii on July 7, 1898. Without enough votes in the Senate to approve a formal annexation treaty, McKinley settled for a congressional joint resolution that authorizied annexation with a majority vote. The president appointed a territorial governor to head the Hawaiian government, and in 1900, Congress granted Hawaiians the right to elect a territorial legislature.

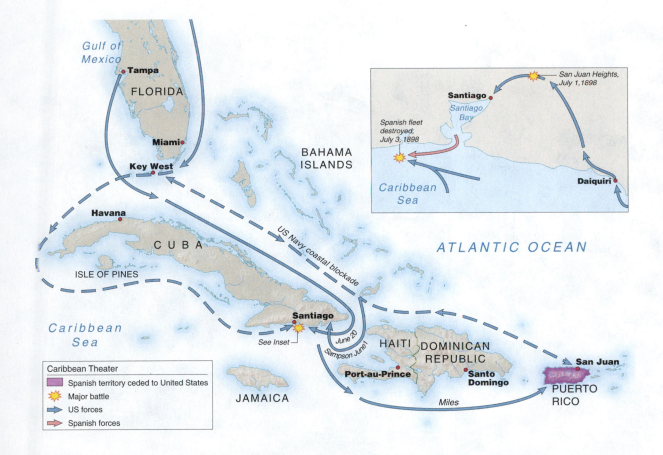

Meanwhile military planners focused on defeating the Spanish in Cuba. The accompanying map, "Spanish-American War, 1898" (19.2) illustrates how the navy immediately blockaded Cuba, trapping the Spanish Atlantic Fleet in Santiago. America's small peacetime army, however, was woefully unprepared to train and equip the thousands of volunteers enlisting throughout the country. Theodore Roosevelt resigned as assistant secretary of the navy and formed the First U.S. Volunteer Calvary by recruiting Americans from wildly diverse backgrounds. Many of the recruits had personal connections to Colonel Roosevelt, a result of his eclectic lifestyle that included attending Harvard, hunting expeditions in the West, and a stint as police commissioner in New York City. Dubbed the Rough Riders, this collection of cowboys, Ivy League athletes, policemen, and Pawnee scouts was one of the few volunteer units that actually fought in the war. Although American forces swelled from 28,000 to 275,000, most never left the United States.

On June 22, 17,000 U.S. troops landed in Cuba to join Cuban rebels on a slow march through heavy jungle to the port of Santiago, which sheltered the bulk of the Spanish navy and army. Hidden Spanish sharpshooters harassed U.S. soldiers as they made their way to the San Juan Heights, the hills that encircled Santiago. On July 1, the Americans, under the command of General William Shafter, attacked 750 Spanish soldiers along the San Juan Heights.

"I have seen many illustrations and pictures of this charge on the San Juan hills, but none of them seem to show it just as I remember it," recalled journalist Richard Harding Davis, who watched the battle from the sidelines as the Americans walked up the hill. Like most illustrations of the battle seen in newspapers at the time, this painting (19.3) erroneously shows waves of eager American soldiers advancing on horseback with the flag flying, suggesting "an invincible overpowering weight of numbers," Davis noted. Yet, he continued, "I think the thing which impressed one the most, when our men started [walking] from cover, was that they were so few. It almost seemed as if someone had made an awful and terrible mistake. One's instinct was to call to them to come back." Roosevelt led the Rough Riders to the top of the San Juan Heights, a feat that garnered him and the unit acclaim. They stood alongside African American

19.3 Charge up the San Juan Heights, 1898 This painting depicted a horseback charge up the San Juan Heights that was glorious and heroic, with flags flying and no casualties. In reality, the soldiers advanced slowly on foot to reach the crest.

How accurate were the legends that surrounded the charge up the San Juan Heights?

Watch the **Video** *Roosevelt's Rough Riders*

troops from the Ninth and Tenth Calvary who had actually reached the top first, which Roosevelt and the mainstream media failed to mention when celebrating the victory.

The battle provided another opportunity for the yellow press to whip up war fervor on the home front. Responding to (false) rumors that Spanish soldiers had mutilated the corpses of American servicemen killed during the clash, a *Judge* magazine cover (**19.4**) pictured a Spaniard drenched in the blood of American soldiers who lay at his feet. In one hand the ape-like figure holds the bloody knife responsible for the atrocity. His other hand rests on the gravestone of U.S. sailors whom he allegedly killed by exploding the *Maine*. This image of a brute that trampled on the American flag reinforced yellow press portrayals of Spain as a beast that the United States needed to subdue. The caricature also fed into racist notions of white supremacy—just like African Americans at home, and soon the Filipinos abroad, the dark-skinned Spanish posed a threat to the civilized world. In future conflicts American propaganda used strikingly similar images to arouse passionate hatred of the nation's German and Japanese enemies.

Legendary accounts attributed the American success in charging up the San Juan Heights to heroic frontal charges; in fact, the Americans' three Gatling machine guns made the decisive difference. Believing his exhausted troops could go no farther after reaching the top, General Shafter decided to lay siege to Santiago instead of attacking the city directly. While American troops encircled the city atop the surrounding hills, U.S. ships blocked the port, thus trapping the bulk of the Spanish navy and army in Santiago. When the Spanish fleet made a dash to leave on July 3, American ships sank or beached every Spanish vessel. In both Manila and Santiago, the newly modernized U.S. navy outclassed the decrepit Spanish fleet, scoring easy, one-sided victories. On July 17, the Spanish surrendered the city and Cuba to the Americans. After defeating the Spanish in Cuba, U.S. forces landed in Puerto Rico, also a Caribbean Spanish colony, where they encountered only token opposition. American troops fought one more battle to take Manila on August 13, having not yet received word that the war between the United States and Spain had ended the day before.

The war concluded on a sour note, however. With limited understanding of how malaria, yellow fever, and typhoid spread, Army physicians could not stop these diseases from ravaging

19.4 *The Spanish Brute,* 1898 This wartime caricature portrayed the Spanish as bloodthirsty beasts who murdered and mutilated American servicemen.

the troops that occupied Cuba during the summer of 1898. Victory celebrations among U.S. troops soon gave way to panic, when hundreds of soldiers fell ill and healthy young men became hollow-eyed, walking skeletons. It was "a heartbreaking sight" to see her husband, a yellow fever victim whose weight had dropped from 165 pounds to 89 pounds, Grace Paulding recalled. He needed a year's nursing before he could work again.

Despairing over the lack of qualified hospital attendants, the surgeon general turned in desperation to the female nurses offering their services to the military. Eventually, 1,500 professional and Red Cross female nurses worked side by side with army doctors at home and overseas. Overall the Americans counted 385 officers and soldiers killed in combat (excluding those killed on the *Maine*), and nearly 2,000 deaths from disease.

The peace treaty, signed on December 10, 1898, set the terms of the U.S. victory. In the **Treaty of Paris**, Spain relinquished its claim to Cuba, and the United States received Puerto Rico

View the Image *Our Victorious Fleet in Cuban Waters*

Were Americans right to characterize the Spanish-American War as "the splendid little war"?

in the Caribbean and Guam, the largest of the Mariana Islands, in the Pacific. In return for $20 million, Spain also ceded the Philippines to the United States. How this land transfer would affect the political future of the Philippines remained in doubt. Did the United States intend to grant the Philippines independence or keep it as a colony? Americans soon offered competing visions on how to resolve this question.

Despite the idealistic guarantees given in the Teller Amendment, Cuba became an independent nation in name only. The United States linked the withdrawal of American occupation troops to concessions from Cuba. The **Platt Amendment (1901)** required Cuba to give the United States the right to maintain a naval base at Guantánamo Bay and to intervene militarily to protect "life, property, and individual liberty." Besides granting the United States a privileged trading relationship, the Cuban government also needed permission from the United States before entering into treaties with other nations. The former Spanish colony essentially became a U.S. protectorate, a relationship in which a superior power assumes authority over a weaker country or territory to protect it from invasion and dominate its affairs. The United States took advantage

of these rights and occupied Cuba numerous times until Congress repealed the Platt Amendment in 1934. The United States continues to maintain a naval base at Guantánamo Bay, using it to jail and interrogate prisoners captured during the wars in Afghanistan and Iraq that began in 2001 and 2003, respectively.

In his successful 1900 reelection bid against Democrat William Jennings Bryan, McKinley made a strong connection between events at home and abroad. One campaign poster (**19.5**) featured portraits of the president and his war hero running mate, Theodore Roosevelt. The individual images reminded Americans of Cuban suffering under Spanish rule and blamed the devastating depression of the 1890s on the Democrats. The poster then noted that domestic prosperity returned and social justice prevailed overseas, once the United States led by the Republicans stepped out into the world. The claim that American intervention improved life for both U.S. and world citizens became a powerful argument in favor of constructing an American empire. Bryan focused his campaign on the evils of imperialism, but McKinley carried the election with a "full dinner pail" slogan that emphasized restored prosperity.

19.5 McKinley Campaign Poster, 1900
This poster helped voters visualize how expanding the nation's global influence created trading opportunities that made the whole country more prosperous. Emphasizing the American humanitarian mission abroad resonated with Progressive reformers and religious groups dedicated to spreading American values and institutions.

What steps did the United States take to construct a formal and informal empire after its victory over Spain?

📖 **Read** the **Document** *The Platt Amendment (1901)*

Creating an American Empire

The Senate's razor-thin ratification of the Treaty of Paris, with just two votes to spare, ignited a strident internal debate over whether the United States should annex or free the Philippines. In the wake of ratification, both imperialists and anti-imperialists offered competing economic, political, and racial arguments about the wisdom of colonizing the Philippines. Unwilling to leave their fate in the hands of American politicians, Filipinos revolted against U.S. forces. The rebellion soon evolved into a vicious all-out war with high casualties on both sides.

The Debate over Colonies

In a risky strategic move that divided Democrats, party leader William Jennings Bryan had urged anti-imperialist Democratic senators to support ratification of the Treaty of Paris, so that the United States could grant the Philippines independence, once Spain relinquished control. But after the Senate had ratified the treaty, the majority of Republicans fought to keep the Philippines as a colony. Maps in the popular press helped Americans visualize the strategic and commercial importance of the nation's new island possessions. The "Map of the China Seas … Under the National Flags, 1898" (**19.6**), published in *Harper's Weekly*, portrayed key parts of the imperialist argument for building an American empire in East Asia. By showing the proximity of the Philippines to European colonial possessions in East Asia, the map reinforced McKinley's claim that another European power would colonize the islands if the United States withdrew. The map also illustrated the imperialist slogan, "trade follows the flag." The closeness of the Philippines to China, for example, underscored the usefulness of the colony for developing a strong trading relationship between the United States and China.

A competing economic argument came from the Anti-Imperialist League, an organization that attracted a broad cross-section of politicians, Progressive reformers, writers, industrialists, and labor activists who opposed overseas colonial expansion. How would markets for American industrialized goods suddenly materialize in undeveloped Asian countries, the league asked? Instead of economic gains anti-imperialists foresaw decades of expenses to maintain colonial outposts.

Debate also centered on the ability of the Filipinos to govern themselves. On the imperialist side, McKinley adopted a strong paternalistic stance, arguing that "We could not leave them to themselves—they were unfit for self-government, and they would soon have anarchy and misrule worse then Spain's was." Caricatures helped imperialists

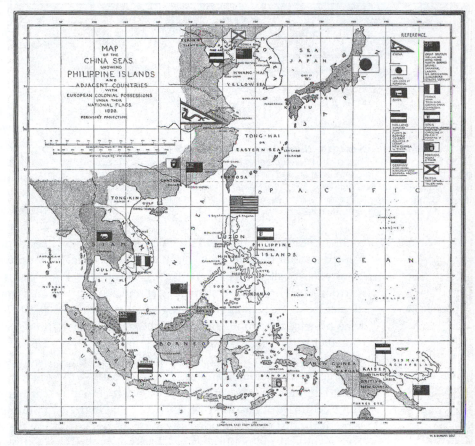

19.6 "Map of the China Seas … Under the National Flags, 1898"
This *Harper's Weekly* map depicted the United States taking its rightful place alongside other world powers with colonial empires in East Asia.

What competing economic arguments did imperialists and anti-imperialists offer about colonies?

19.7 *Give the Child Over to the Nurse, Uncle, and It Will Stop Crying*
Uncle Sam protects a Filipino child from ignorance and crime, portrayed as a savage black nurse, by feeding him education and civilization. This 1899 pro-expansionist political cartoon accused anti-imperialists like Senator Hoar of Massachusetts of failing to realize that the racially inferior Filipinos were too immature to rule themselves, no matter how much the Filipinos protested.

Anti-imperialists viewed the question of governing the Filipinos differently. They claimed that subjugating the Philippines to imperial rule violated the principles of representative government outlined in the Constitution. Their slogan, "the Constitution follows the flag," conveyed their belief that Congress could not withhold constitutional rights, including the right to self-government, from colonial subjects.

In the 1900–1904 Insular Cases, the Supreme Court affirmed Congress's authority to govern the Philippines, Hawaii, and Puerto Rico as colonies. The Court upheld the acquisition of colonies as constitutional and ruled that colonial populations did not become American citizens until the United States incorporated the colonies as territories. The justices offered a more mixed response on the question of extending constitutional rights to colonial subjects. In these cases the Court denied colonial subjects some constitutional protections, such as procedural rights that guaranteed a fair trial, but held that Congress could not abridge the "natural rights" of free speech and religion. Recognition of these limited rights did not appease anti-imperialists, however. "Yes, as near as I can make out the Constitution follows the flag—but doesn't quite catch up with it," quipped Secretary of War Elihu Root. In 1900, Congress granted inhabitants of Hawaii and Alaska American citizenship, making them eligible for full protection under the Bill of Rights. Puerto Ricans had to wait until 1917 and residents of Guam until 1952. Filipinos never held American citizenship.

This 1899 editorial cartoon (**19.8**) by Louis Dalrymple, *School Begins. Uncle Sam (to his new class in Civilization)* encapsulated the debate between imperialists and anti-imperialists over whether the United States needed the consent of colonized peoples to govern them. Appearing in *Puck*, a magazine that specialized in political satire, the cartoon portrays Uncle Sam as an annoyed teacher pointing sternly at frightened black pupils representing the Philippines, Hawaii, Puerto Rico, and Cuba. Getting ready to teach from a book entitled *U.S.— First Lessons in Self Government*, the teacher tells the students that they have to "learn these lessons

publicize their case, incorporating popularly accepted notions of Americans' racial and moral superiority to so-called uncivilized peoples. This political cartoon (**19.7**) contained strong racial undertones, depicting Uncle Sam as a nurturing white father who protects the wailing savage Filipino child from Independence (pictured as a depraved mammy-like figure) and from anti-imperialists like Senator George Hoar, a Republican from Massachusetts. Most Filipinos had converted to Catholicism under three centuries of Spanish rule, a religion that many Americans distrusted. Besides spreading Anglo-Saxon cultural and political values, McKinley called upon Americans to take control of Filipinos' spiritual lives by turning them into Protestants.

19.8 *School Begins.* **Uncle Sam (to his new class in Civilization)** Before the Spanish-American War, images in the popular press depicted Cuba as a virginal white woman (see *Images as History: Atrocity Stories and Public Opinion*, p. 567) to arouse Americans' sympathies. Afterward, editorial cartoons consistently portrayed Cuba as a black child in need of instruction to justify ruling Cuba as a protectorate.

whether you want to or not!" He then urges them to "take a look at the class ahead of you, and remember that, in a little while, you will feel as glad to be here as they are!" Does he mean the studious white students studying from books bearing the names of recently added states like California and Nevada? Or is he referring to the African American boy washing windows, the Indian sitting in the corner reading a book upside down, or the Chinese child refused entry into the classroom—all previous subjects of missionary zeal? The satirical signs on the wall trumpet the imperialist emphasis on precedents—in this case the willingness of Britain and the Union to govern colonies and the former Confederacy, respectively, without their consent. The debate between imperialists and anti-imperialists is explored further in *Competing Visions: Annexing the Philippines* (page 576).

In 1899, the British poet Rudyard Kipling entered the American debate over colonizing the Philippines when the popular magazine *McClure's* published his poem, "The White Man's Burden—The United States and the Philippine Islands." Kipling pictured Americans embracing "**the white man's burden**," the Anglo-Saxon quest to better the lives of so-called racially inferior peoples by spreading Western economic, cultural, and spiritual values and institutions. Black newspapers offered a competing vision, publishing an array of poems and editorials that detailed "the black man's burden" of living in a country that accepted Jim Crow practices in the South.

The Philippine-American War

On June 12, 1898, the Filipino leader Emilio Aguinaldo declared the Philippines independent of Spain. In January, 1899, he formed a provisional government that concentrated power in the hands of elites from the main island of Luzon to rule the ethnically and religiously diverse societies that inhabited the archipelago. Fighting began

> "[T]here was nothing left for us to do but to take them all, and to educate the Filipinos, and uplift and civilize and Christianize them."
>
> President McKINLEY explaining the imperialist vision
> for annexing the Philippines as a colony

View the **Closer Look** *Competing Visions: The White Man's Burden*

How did imperialists define the nation's civilizing mission?

Competing Visions

ANNEXING THE PHILIPPINES

Debate over annexing the Philippines did not follow party lines, as revealed in the differing views of two leading Republicans, Carl Schurz, a former secretary of the interior and senator from Missouri and Senator Henry Cabot Lodge of Massachusetts. Schurz and Lodge both evoked the nation's previous expansionist drives to strengthen their arguments, offering historical analogies between the nation's prior success acquiring and absorbing new territories and the present dilemma over the Philippines. Did annexing the Philippines represent a continuation or break with past expansionist methods and policies?

In this 1899 anti-annexation speech, Carl Schurz argued that the past offered no guide to the present crisis.

Has not the career of the Republic almost from its very beginning been one of territorial expansion? Has it not acquired Louisiana, Florida, Texas, the vast countries that came to us through the Mexican war and Alaska, and has it not digested them well?... If the Republic could digest the old, why not the new? What is the difference?...

1. All the former acquisitions were on this continent and, excepting Alaska, contiguous to our borders.
2. They were situated, not in tropical, but in the temperate zone, where democratic institutions thrive and where our people could migrate in mass.
3. They were but very thinly peopled in fact, without any population that would have been in the way of new settlements.
4. They could be organized as territories in the usual manner, with the expectation that they would presently come into the Union as self-governing States with populations substantially homogeneous to our own.
5. They did not require a material increase of our Army and Navy, either for their subjection to our rule or for their defense against any probable foreign attack provoked by their being in our possession.

In 1900, Senator Henry Cabot Lodge saw strong continuities between the past and present in urging for annexation of the Philippines.

It has been stated over and over again that we have done great wrong in taking these islands without the consent of the governed, from which, according to American principles, all just government derives its powers. The consent of the governed! It is a fair phrase and runs trippingly upon the tongue, but I have observed a great lack of definite meaning in those who use it most … What do we mean by the "consent of the governed?" We quote it from the Declaration of Independence. What did Jefferson mean by the phrase? … The Declaration of Independence was the announcement of the existence of a new revolutionary government upon American soil. Upon whose consent did it rest? Was it upon that of all the people of the colonies duly expressed. Most assuredly not. In the first place we must throw out all negroes and persons of African descent, who formed about one quarter of the population, and who were not consulted at all as to the proposed change of government …. Were women included in the word "governed?" They certainly were not permitted by voice or vote to express an opinion on this momentous question. They must, therefore, be excluded…. Did the revolutionary government rest on the consent of all the white males in the colonies? Most assuredly not. There was the usual age limitation … Everywhere the suffrage was limited, generally by property qualifications, sometimes by other restrictions…

… Under the guidance of Thomas Jefferson … we took Louisiana without the consent of the governed, and ruled it without their consent so long as we saw fit. Who is there to-day who will stand up and say that Thomas Jefferson did not do well and rightly when he bought Louisiana?

… Then came the Mexican war, and by the treaty of Guadalupe Hidalgo we received a great cession of territory from Mexico, including all the California coast … There were many Mexicans living within the ceded territory. We never asked their consent….

Did Schurz and Lodge interpret history correctly in their arguments?   **View** the **Closer Look** *Competing Visions: Annexing the Philippines* on February 4, 1899, when U.S. and Filipino patrols clashed in the darkness, igniting a full-scale battle on the outskirts of Manila. The U.S. government called the conflict the Philippine Insurrection, using *insurrection*, a term used to describe an illegitimate revolt against an established government, to underscore that the Philippines was now a U.S. colony, not an independent nation with the right to wage war. The conflict nonetheless soon became a full-fledged war. In the Philippine-American War, fought from 1899 to 1902, the United States eventually defeated Filipino rebel forces. The cost of the two-and-a-half-year war in human lives differentiated it immediately from the quick American victory in Cuba. Between 1899 and 1902, 70,000 U.S. soldiers (nearly 70 percent of the army) fought a grueling war against the insurrectionists, and 4,196 U.S. troops lost their lives. Estimates place the number of Filipino soldiers and civilians killed as high as 220,000.

The rebels used conventional warfare tactics at first, but eventually turned to ambushes, sniping, and sabotage to drive out U.S. occupying forces. American soldiers called the Filipino way of war "amigo warfare" (amigo being the Spanish word for friend) because the guerilla fighters posed as friendly peasants during the day, then fought for the rebel army at night. The difficulties of supplying troops with food and medical care as they marched through the jungle in search of insurgents contributed to American soldiers' miseries. To uproot the guerillas, the U.S. Army adopted a mix of persuasive and coercive tactics. In many villages the army built roads, improved sanitation, vaccinated civilians, and created schools. Tens of thousands of Filipinos aided the U.S. Army during the rebellion by providing information and supplies, a sign of their gratitude for American-engineered improvements in their daily life and of their own religious, class, or ethnic disagreements with the Aguinaldo-led independence movement. Rebel soldiers dealt harshly with civilians who refused to supply them with food or told the Americans where to find insurgent hideouts.

Benevolent policies won over only half of the archipelago, however. In provinces where these reforms failed to curtail guerilla attacks, U.S. troops lashed out with increasing brutality. "With an enemy like this to fight, it is not surprising that the boys should soon adopt 'no quarter'

as a motto, and fill the blacks [Filipinos] full of lead before finding out whether or not they are friends or enemies," a soldier from Utah wrote home. American soldiers burned villages and crops to deprive rebels of shelter and food, tactics that created a starving civilian refugee population and encouraged resentful peasants to join Aguinaldo's force. Critics were quick to point out that these tactics resembled those used by Spain in Cuba. Exposés in the American press and Senate investigations revealed the inventive tortures the army used to extract information from captured Filipino rebels, fueling the ongoing debate over whether the United States was civilizing or conquering the Philippines. In the "water cure," for example, interrogators shoved a bamboo shoot down a victim's throat to keep his mouth open while they poured water into his throat and nose until his stomach swelled and he could not breathe, and then pushed on the stomach to expel the water. The victim had a few minutes to release the desired information before his interrogators repeated the entire process.

"Every tree seemed to shoot at us!"

An American soldier confronting Filipino rebel guerilla tactics

---

Justifying annexation of the Philippines as part of the "white man's burden" posed a particularly thorny dilemma for the 6,000 African American soldiers fighting in their own segregated regiments to subdue the Filipino rebels. White soldiers constantly referred to Filipinos as "niggers," the same derogatory term they used when speaking about their African American comrades. Knowing that many African American civilians opposed the war as "an unholy war of conquest," a term coined by Methodist minister Henry McNeal Turner, black soldiers nevertheless hoped that their honorable military record would advance civil rights and economic opportunities for African Americans. Filipino rebels posted signs on trees that chastised African Americans for fighting "against people who are struggling for recognition and freedom, [while] your people in America are being lynched and disfranchised by the same who are trying to compel us to believe that their government will deal justly and fairly by us." Yet these Filipino appeals to lay down their arms had little effect on most African American troops, who focused instead on avenging the lives of comrades killed by Filipino rebels. One exception was Corporal David Fagan, a black soldier who had fought in Cuba and defected to the Filipino army shortly after arriving in the Philippines. He was one of five black soldiers who deserted to the other side. Fagan's reputation grew to mythic proportions as he eluded capture and organized guerilla raids on his former comrades-in-arms.

Emilio Aguinaldo was not so fortunate. In March 1901, a prisoner revealed the location of Aguinaldo's hideaway 50 miles into the jungle. To capture Aguinaldo, General Frederick Funston assembled a group of Macabebe scouts, a Philippine ethnic group that had traditionally served Spain and now aided the United States. Posing as reinforcements, the Macabebe soldiers entered Aguinaldo's camp accompanied by five American soldiers pretending to be prisoners. The group arrived as a birthday celebration for Aguinaldo was underway, and when the infiltrators reached for their weapons, Aguinaldo's guards assumed they were preparing to fire an honor salute. Instead the Macabebe scouts began shooting, the signal for the rest of Funston's men, who were waiting on the perimeter, to invade the camp. Aguinaldo's guards fled in panic, leaving him in the hands of the Americans.

A chastened Aguinaldo called on his followers to lay down their arms and accept U.S. rule. One by one his generals surrendered, and the war ground to a halt. Theodore Roosevelt, who became president after McKinley's 1901 assassination (see Chapter 18), declared the war over on July 4, 1902. American troops nonetheless remained in the Philippines for another 11 years to subdue separate revolts by Muslim Moro tribal leaders in remote islands.

In 1900, William Howard Taft became the first civilian governor general of the Philippines. When the war ended, he expanded efforts to build roads and schools and improve sanitation. Taft also convinced Congress to purchase church-held land from the Vatican, which the colonial administration then helped peasants buy with low-cost mortgages. To put the debate over annexing the Philippines to rest, the government sponsored exhibits at the 1904 St. Louis World's Fair that championed the imperialist vision of colonization. In the Philippine Reservation display, visitors walked through six reconstructed Filipino villages and watched partially clothed members of remote Filipino tribes demonstrate native practices that included feasts of dog and headhunting. By inviting tribes with the most exotic customs to participate, organizers intended to juxtapose the primitiveness of Filipino culture with the civilizing influence of U.S. rule. Photographs captured the U.S.-sponsored effort to provide illiterate, nearly naked Filipinos with a Western education. In this image (**19.9**) an educated Filipina instructor wearing a traditional butterfly dress (representing the positive aspects of modernization) teaches her "uncivilized" pupils before a gallery of onlookers who appear unconcerned about putting these people on display as a tourist attraction. Instead Americans who talked with villagers at the exhibit quickly "disabused themselves of any impression that the natives could take care of themselves," one newspaper reported. Other displays at the World's Fair championed America's scientific, economic, and cultural achievements. Collectively these exhibits suggested that as a leading nation in the civilized world, the United States had the duty and right to become a colonial power.

19.9 American Rule in the Philippines
The 1904 St. Louis World's Fair included exhibits on American efforts to school native tribes in the Philippines, turning these exotically dressed people into tourist attractions.

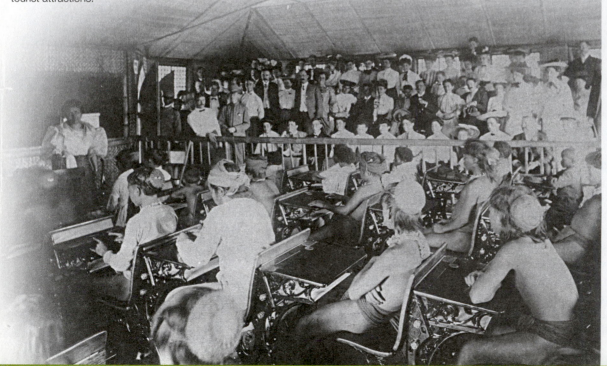

How does this image of a Philippine classroom compare to the schoolroom setting satirized in *School Begins. Uncle Sam (to his new class in Civilization)* (Figure 19.8 on page 575)?

America and East Asia

The United States fought a war of conquest in the Philippines to secure an independent trade route to East Asia only to discover that the coveted China market was in danger of disappearing. To prevent the world's leading powers from carving China up into formal colonies, the United States turned to diplomacy, convincing these nations to keep Chinese trade open to all. Americans also viewed their nation's role in negotiating an end to the Russo-Japanese War in 1905 as a sign of America's growing world stature. Not all international conflicts in this period originated outside the United States, however. In 1907, President Roosevelt used diplomacy to smooth over the crisis that arose in Japanese-American relations when California initiated a campaign to segregate and ban Japanese immigrants.

The Open Door in China

Throughout the nineteenth century China granted most-favored trading status (commercial privileges) to every world power that asked. This strategy prevented any one foreign nation from gaining too much influence over the Chinese economy and helped China remain independent in an age when Europe and Japan colonized most other Asian lands. Any nation contemplating a campaign to colonize China risked provoking the wrath of angry competitors eager to protect their own access to Chinese trade.

In the 1880s and 1890s, American Protestant missionaries began venturing into the interior of China, away from the ports where foreign businessmen concentrated their commercial activity. In their letters to American churches, missionaries exaggerated Chinese interest in Western agricultural crops such as wheat and cotton. By whetting public curiosity about a vast Chinese market, some missionaries hoped to bolster domestic support for their religious work in China. In his book *Chinese Characteristics* (1900), missionary Arthur Smith offered a competing vision. Chinese clothing, he pointed out, had no pockets. The Chinese placed little emphasis on acquiring personal possessions like "a cork-screw, a boot-buttoner, a pair of tweezers, a minute compass, a folding pair of scissors … a fountain pen" that most Americans deemed essential to their daily lives.

> ## "What is the process of civilizing but the creating of more and higher wants?"
>
> Expansionist JOSIAH STRONG, linking the civilizing mission to capitalist consumption, 1886.

American access to these potential customers, however, appeared in danger of evaporating at the turn of the century. The world's leading nations descended on China to each claim a **sphere of influence**, the term used to describe the exclusive political and trading rights that a foreign nation enjoyed within another nation's territory. American missionaries continued their religious activities in these new spheres of influence, areas that American businessmen also coveted as future markets for U.S. goods. At this point the involved nations only demanded a monopoly over trade in a specific region, but the U.S. government feared that an outright division of China into formal colonies would soon follow. "All Europe is seizing on China and if we do not establish ourselves in the East that vast trade, from which we must draw our future prosperity" would close to the United States forever, Senator Henry Cabot Lodge warned.

Already stretched to the limit in the Caribbean and Philippines, and facing strong anti-imperialist sentiments at home, McKinley never considered sending troops to China to seize a port or territory. Instead Secretary of State John Hay circulated a carefully worded set of notes that laid the foundation for the **Open Door Policy**, a U.S.-sponsored nonbinding international agreement that kept the Chinese market open to all foreign nations. The first set of Open Door Notes asked Britain, France, Germany, Italy, Japan, and Russia to allow other nations to trade freely within their respective spheres of influence, refrain from imposing arbitrary

Why did Americans develop a strong interest in China at the turn of the century?

duties on foreign goods, and let Chinese officials collect customs fees (thereby recognizing China's continued political control). By January 1900, Hay reported that all nations with a sphere of influence in China had agreed to abide by these terms. For the time being the allure of trading opportunities in the spheres of others outweighed the desire for full-fledged colonies in China. Hay neglected to consult China in his diplomatic negotiations.

Angry over the humiliating foreign domination, Chinese militants vowed to restore Chinese sovereignty over its land and economy. In 1900, a secret society called the Righteous and Harmonious Fists initiated a terrorist campaign to drive the "foreign devils" out of China, a crusade that members of the Chinese imperial government secretly funded. Westerners called this group the Boxers because of the clenched fist they adopted as their emblem and

the militants' martial arts training. When thousands of Boxers began roaming the countryside, attacking foreigners, an international force of ground troops and battleships assembled to crush the insurgency. Tensions escalated dramatically when the Boxers besieged foreign diplomats and businessmen in Beijing (called Peking by Westerners).

Throughout the crisis Secretary Hay worked frantically to prevent the involved nations from using the Boxer Rebellion as an excuse to colonize China. In a second round of Open Door Notes, Hay asked the same nations that had accepted the first Open Door Notes to respect the "territorial and administrative integrity" of China. To avoid negative responses, Hay did not ask for a formal reply to his request. To further protect American missionary and economic interests in China (pictured in **19.10**), McKinley sent 2,500 U.S. soldiers to join a

19.10 Foreign Activity in China, 1901 American missionaries and businessmen established a presence in China that the U.S. government tried to protect by negotiating with nations that had spheres of influence there.

What does this map reveal about relations between China and the world's leading powers, including the United States?

[ ] **Read the Document** *Katherine Mullikin Lowry on the Boxer Rebellion (1900)*

multinational force in rescuing the foreigners and ending the Boxer Rebellion. As punishment for the imperial government's support of the Boxers, the international coalition demanded $333 million in indemnities from China. The United States used its share to provide scholarships for Chinese students studying at American universities.

Relations with Japan

Despite the Open Door Policy, the competition for rights to control railroads, mines, and ports in China continued, and within a few years, Japan and Russia fought to control China's resource-rich Manchurian province and the Korean peninsula. The Russo-Japanese War of 1904–1905 threatened to topple the balance of power that the United States was trying to maintain in China. Concerned that an overwhelming Japanese victory "may possibly mean a struggle between them and us in the future," President Roosevelt offered to negotiate a peace settlement. In August 1905, a financially exhausted Japan and a militarily defeated Russia came to the peace table in Portsmouth, New Hampshire. Many Americans delighted at the sight of their president mediating a conflict between two world powers. In 1906, Roosevelt received the Nobel Peace Prize for his role in encing the Russo-Japanese War.

But Roosevelt soon faced the possibility of losing the Japanese friendship he had worked so hard to protect. In 1905, California legislators, newspapers, and labor leaders mounted a strident campaign to halt Japanese immigration. Japanese and Korean exclusion leagues urged Congress to follow the precedent of the 1882 Chinese Exclusion Act and prohibit Asians from entering the nation. These groups denounced Asians as a degenerative element that threatened American culture and unfairly competed for jobs that rightfully belonged to native-born white workers.

California legislators lumped all Asians together when they spoke about defending the nation from the "Yellow Peril," but Roosevelt understood the vast difference between a weak, humiliated China and a powerful, proud Japan. "If we show that we regard the Japanese as an inferior and alien race, and try to treat them as we have treated the Chinese; and if at the same time we fail to keep our navy at the highest point of efficiency and size—then we shall invite disaster," Roosevelt wrote privately. In 1906, the San Francisco Board of Education decided to send Japanese, Chinese, and Korean children to one set of segregated schools. With Japan bristling at the insult of Americans lumping Japanese together with Asian peoples whom they viewed as inferior to themselves, Roosevelt intervened to control the damage to U.S.-Japanese relations. California agreed to revoke the segregation order in return for an end to Japanese immigration, but Hawaiian sugar planters protested that they needed Japanese workers. As a compromise Roosevelt issued an executive order that allowed Japanese workers into Hawaii. The president then negotiated a reduction in Japanese immigration to the mainland. In the **Gentlemen's Agreement (1907–1908)**, Japan agreed to deny passports to Japanese workers intending to immigrate to the United States. This informal agreement helped Japan escape the indignity of joining China as the only other nation legally banned from sending immigrant workers to the United States.

Angel Island

In the Gentlemen's Agreement Japan reserved the right to issue passports to professionals and the relatives of Japanese migrants or citizens already living in the United States. Until the United States closed this loophole in 1921, Japan gave passports to Japanese wives so they could join their husbands in the United States. Americans called these women "picture brides" because couples often exchanged photos of each other through a matchmaker who arranged long-distance marriages for Japanese men residing in the United States. The 300–500 Japanese "picture brides" who immigrated annually to the United States met their new husbands for the first time when they arrived.

Chinese immigration also surged during this period. The 1906 earthquake in San Francisco destroyed the city's birth records and without any way to prove otherwise, hundreds of Chinese men successfully claimed that they were American-born. As citizens they asserted their right to bring their families to the United States. Many brought in "paper sons," boys whose families paid a fee to Chinese men already in the United States to fraudulently claim to be their fathers.

In 1910, U.S. authorities opened up an immigration processing station on Angel Island in San Francisco Bay to verify the identities of Japanese and Chinese immigrants claiming the right to enter the United States. Chinese "paper sons" endured long periods of detention on Angel Island while authorities investigated their background. Before leaving China "paper sons" memorized details about their "fathers," including descriptions of relatives, houses, and key events in a family's history. Once these men arrived at Angel Island, inspectors quizzed sons and fathers separately and refused entry to those whose answers failed to match. Chinese men detained on Angel Island sometimes passed the time by etching poetry onto the barrack walls, including one anonymous poet who expressed his angst by writing, "who was to know two streams of tears would flow upon arriving here?"

In 1919, California politicians reignited their campaign against the Japanese, making it illegal for Japanese immigrants to own property. Naturalization laws allowed only people of white or African ancestry to become citizens, preventing Japanese immigrants from seeking U.S. citizenship to circumvent these restrictions. In *Takao Ozawa v. United States* (1922), the Supreme Court held that Japanese immigrants were indeed ineligible for citizenship because they were not white. *Choices and Consequences: The Legal Construction of "Whiteness"* explores this decision. The fact that Japanese picture

brides bore children who were U.S. citizens, and therefore eligible to own property, did not escape the notice of those campaigning for a ban on Japanese property ownership. Senator James D. Phelan, a California Democrat, led the campaign to stop admitting picture brides to the United States, ominously predicting that a booming birthrate among Japanese immigrants would lead to Japanese dominance of California agriculture. To garner publicity for their anti-Japanese crusade, a congressional delegation traveled to Angel Island in 1920. The legislators invited news photographers to take photos (**19.11**) as they sternly lectured a group of bewildered, frightened young women, dressed in their best clothes to meet their new husbands. Fearful that rising anti-Japanese prejudice might lead to a Japanese exclusion law, Japan agreed to stop issuing passports to picture brides in 1921. Congress banned all immigration from Asia in 1924 (see Chapter 21).

19.11 Japanese Picture Brides, 1920 To rally public support for cutting off the flow of Japanese women coming to the United States, a delegation of congressmen posed for the cameras as they confronted these shy, pretty Japanese picture brides, whose ethnicity made them unwelcome.

What insights does this photo offer into issues of ethnicity and gender in the early twentieth century?

Choices and Consequences

THE LEGAL CONSTRUCTION OF "WHITENESS"

Takao Ozawa was a Japanese immigrant who lived in California and Hawaii for 28 years before he applied to become a citizen of the United States. Aware that naturalization laws allowed only Caucasians and people of African ancestry to become citizens, Ozawa argued that he was white. He emphasized his complete assimilation into American society and the lightness of his skin. When the Supreme Court heard his case in 1922, the justices faced four options about how to define "whiteness."

Choices

1 Differing physical features divided the human species into white, black, and yellow races.

2 Skin color established racial identity.

3 Whiteness was a socially constructed notion with no scientific basis.

4 Assimilating into American culture made one "white."

Decision

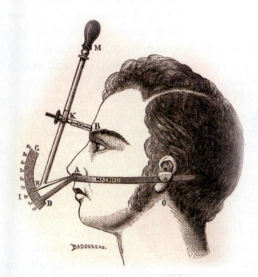

Measurement of the Head and Face, 1883

The Court rejected Ozawa's contention that skin pigmentation signified whiteness and his claim of complete assimilation. In a unanimous decision the justices ruled that "the words 'white person' are synonymous with the words 'a person of Caucasian race.'" This decision accepted contemporary anthropologists' assertions that measurements of facial features provided scientific evidence to classify the Japanese as members of the "Mongolian race."

Consequences

Within three months the court unanimously reversed its reasoning, deciding instead that whiteness was a socially, not scientifically, constructed category. When Indian immigrant Bhagat Singh Thind applied for citizenship, he argued that anthropologists categorized Asian Indians as Caucasians. In rejecting Thind's claim of whiteness, the Supreme Court now ruled that "the words 'free white persons' are words of common speech, to be interpreted in accordance with the understanding of the common man." Deciding who was legally white now depended on the whims of the larger culture, not the claims of scientists.

Continuing Controversies

What determines racial identity?

Well into the twentieth century, many Americans continued to believe that biologically based racial differences existed, even within the Caucasian race. In the 1920s, the United States severely curtailed immigration from eastern and southern Europe, viewing northern Europeans as racially superior (see Chapter 21). The fear that light-skinned blacks were "passing" as whites caused many Southern states to bar individuals with any African ancestry, the so-called "one-drop" of blood rule, from using "whites-only" facilities. The view of racial identity as a social construct also drew adherents. Radical black civil rights leaders tried to cultivate a racial identity based on African Americans' cultural distinctiveness, while others sought a color-blind society that did away with racial identities completely.

What different methods have Americans used to define racial identity?

In America's Backyard

Establishing a U.S. presence and maintaining favorable relations in East Asia became key aims of American foreign policy at the turn of the century. Americans also, however, explored opportunities to expand closer to home. The government focused on constructing a canal through Central America to facilitate U.S. trade with China and better protect the nation's coastlines. Earlier transportation breakthroughs such as the Erie Canal, National Road, and transcontinental railroad quickened the movement of people and goods and helped the United States expand across the continent. The Panama Canal secured U.S. dominance of the Caribbean, and the government resolved to keep foreign powers out of the region.

The Panama Canal

At the end of the nineteenth century, American canal advocates emphasized increased trade and better defense as reasons for building the **Panama Canal**, a manmade waterway through Panama completed in 1914 to link the Pacific and Atlantic oceans. The canal project received a boost when one of its strongest supporters, Theodore Roosevelt, became president in 1901. Roosevelt took up the canal project immediately. "No single great material work which remains to be undertaken on this continent is of such consequence to the American people," he told Congress the first time he addressed the legislators.

Roosevelt intended to take up where Ferdinand de Lesseps, the French mastermind who built the 1869 Suez Canal in Egypt that linked the Mediterranean and Red Seas, had left off. In the 1880s, de Lesseps had begun building a canal through Panama (then part of Colombia). Battling mudslides, earthquakes, and disease, de Lesseps eventually abandoned the project and sold his concession from the Colombian government to the New Panama Canal Company, a French company headed by Philippe Bunau-Varilla, a longtime engineer on the project.

In 1902, the United States offered the New Panama Canal Company $40 million for its concession and assets, a sum that Bunau-Varilla eagerly accepted. Colombia, however, rejected Roosevelt's offer of $10 million to secure the rights to maintain a U.S.-controlled canal in Panama indefinitely. The New Panama Canal Company's concession expired in 1904, and by stalling, Colombia expected to pocket the $40 million earmarked for the company. "Those contemptible little creatures in Bogotá [the capital of Colombia] ought to understand how much they are jeopardizing things and imperiling their

own future," Roosevelt wrote in frustration to Secretary of State John Hay.

In 1903, Panama revolted against Colombia. The timing was not coincidental. Fearing it would lose everything, the New Panama Canal Company encouraged and financed the rebellion by Panamanian business and political elites who did not want to share revenue from the projected canal with the rest of Colombia. Bunau-Varilla not only set the date for the revolution but also provided its leader, Manuel Guerrero Amador, with money, defense plans, a declaration of independence, and even a flag. Roosevelt never gave Bunau-Varilla a direct promise of U.S. support but, the president later recalled, it was Bunau-Varilla's "business to find out what he thought our Government would do … in fact, he would have been a very dull man had he been unable to make such a guess."

Once the Panamanian revolt began, Roosevelt ensured that events favored the United States. The mountainous terrain separating the rest of Colombia from Panama forced Colombian troops to move by sea. When they arrived, U.S. naval ships patrolling both coasts prevented them from landing in Panama. Roosevelt claimed that an 1846 agreement with Colombia gave the United States the authority to control transit across Panama. The nineteenth-century pact, however, envisioned using U.S. forces to protect, not destroy, Colombian sovereignty in Panama. In the 1920s, Congress apologetically sent Colombia $25 million for Roosevelt's transgression.

With America's help the revolution in Panama succeeded. The United States immediately received its reward from Bunau-Varilla, the new minister to the United States for the Republic of Panama. The Hay–Bunau-Varilla Treaty (1903) gave the United States perpetual control over a strip of land ten miles wide that included the Panama Canal for $10 million and

How did U.S. intervention in Panama compare with its colonization of the Philippines?

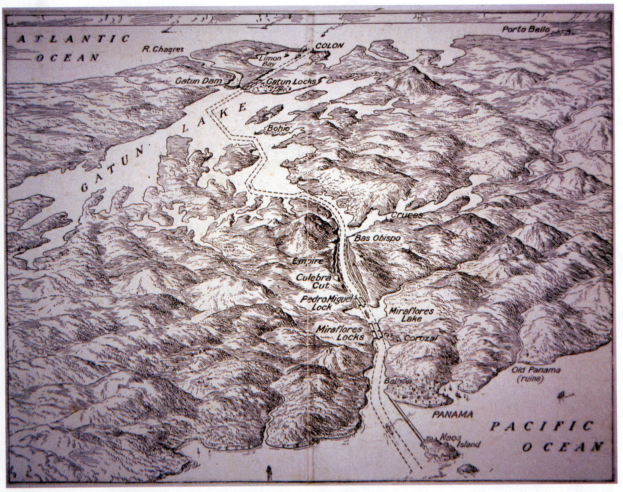

19.12 Building the Panama Canal The Americans used a system of locks and dams to construct the waterway through a mountainous terrain subject to flooding and mudslides.

an annual rent of $250,000. These terms remained in effect until December 31, 1999, when the United States turned control of the canal over to Panama.

When American engineers took over building the Panama Canal in 1904, they confronted a host of geological challenges. The Chagres River crisscrossed the route selected for the canal. Tropical rains regularly poured down the mountains into the Chagres, which, if not diverted, would dump floodwaters and silt into the planned canal. By damming the Chagres, U.S. engineers created the artificial Gatun Lake that ships reached through a stairway of locks on either side. This approach used water rather than shovels to create much of the waterway. The accompanying map (**19.12**) shows the 164 square miles of rain forest that construction crews flooded to create Gatun Lake. The 5,000 American engineers, skilled workers, and foremen at the construction site relied on thousands of foreign workers, mostly blacks from the British West Indies, to dig the rest of the canal.

President Roosevelt shared the public's fascination with the feat of building the canal, and visited the site in 1906. His two-week trip made Roosevelt the first American president to leave the country while in office. Not content merely to watch the huge steam shovels through the window of the train bringing him to the Culebra Cut, the project's largest excavation site, Roosevelt tramped through the mud to reach a steam shovel and climbed into the driver's seat. As photographers snapped away, Roosevelt learned that the Bucyrus steam shovel picked up eight tons of dirt in a single scoop, required a crew of ten, and dug five times more than older machines.

> **"It is an epic feat, and one of immense significance."**
> President ROOSEVELT, after visiting the Panama Canal construction site

How did U.S. engineers overcome the geological obstacles to building the Panama Canal?

"You had to pray everyday for God to carry you safe, and bring you back."

A black worker on felling giant trees and surviving mudslides while building the Panama Canal

This photo of Roosevelt sitting at the controls of a Bucyrus steam shovel (**19.13**) captured the adventurous spirit of an era dedicated to overseas economic expansion, technological innovation, and world prominence. "The real builder of the Panama Canal was Theodore Roosevelt," wrote Major George W. Goethals, chief engineer on the project. Americans usually saw photos of their formally dressed presidents standing on podiums, sitting at desks, or posing with dignitaries. In this photograph Roosevelt appears as the larger-than-life personality he was, literally building the canal he played such a large part in securing for the United States.

Americans solved more than the engineering riddle of constructing the canal. They also conquered the disease-carrying mosquito. Guided by the recent discovery that mosquitoes transmitted malaria and yellow fever, Dr. William C. Gorgas undertook a relentless fumigation campaign that saved thousands

19.13 Theodore Roosevelt Visits the Canal Zone Instead of observing construction of the Panama Canal from a safe distance, Roosevelt climbed into the seat of a steam shovel to work its controls.

What does this photograph convey about Roosevelt and the feat of building the Panama Canal?

of lives. Nonetheless, poor sanitation in the black workers' camps (which Roosevelt criticized during his visit) and the dangers posed by mudslides and working with dynamite exacted a toll. Nearly 4,500 foreign black workers and 500 white Americans died during the American phase of construction.

The Roosevelt Corollary

The Panama Canal was a symbol of U.S. technological achievement, naval power, and economic strength. The canal also increased the importance of the Caribbean to U.S. national security. "America's interests in this hemisphere are greater than those of any European power," Roosevelt stated. Therefore the United States intended to "police and protect" the canal alone. Roosevelt had reason to worry about European naval incursions into the region. Anxious about overdue debts, Britain, Italy, and Germany blockaded Venezuela in 1902, and two years later European nations threatened to intervene in the Dominican Republic for the same reason. To head off a European invasion, the Dominicans asked Roosevelt to accept the nation as a protectorate. Roosevelt privately remarked he had "about the same desire to annex it as a gorged boa constrictor might have to swallow a porcupine wrong-end-to." He nonetheless agreed to help, but only after deciding to use the incident to establish a new principle in U.S. foreign policy.

To prevent European military incursions into the Western Hemisphere, Roosevelt announced a corollary to the 1823 Monroe Doctrine (see Chapter 7), which had declared the Western Hemisphere off-limits to further European colonization. The **Roosevelt Corollary** of 1904 stated that when confronted with "flagrant cases" of wrongdoing by Latin American nations, such as not paying their debts to Western nations, the United States intended to act as an "international police power" in the region.

19.14 Theodore Roosevelt's Big Stick
In this cartoon illustrating the impact of the Roosevelt Corollary, the president pulls a line of naval vessels around the Caribbean to keep nearby nations in line and prevent the creation of European colonies too close to U.S. shores.

In this political cartoon (**19.14**), a gigantic Roosevelt, dressed as a Rough Rider, holds a big stick as he pulls U.S. ships labeled "sheriff" and "debt collector" around the Caribbean. Americans dubbed the Roosevelt Corollary the "big stick" policy in reference to a West African proverb that Roosevelt favored: "Speak softly and carry a big stick, and you will go far." The corollary exempted Argentina, Brazil, and Chile because Roosevelt considered them civilized nations capable of meeting their international commitments and running their own domestic affairs. Satisfied that the United States would help Europe recoup its loans to Central and South American nations, European governments reacted positively to the Roosevelt Corollary.

View the Image *His Foresight* (1901)   How did the Roosevelt Corollary bolster U.S. stature as a world power?

Roosevelt's successor in the White House, William Howard Taft, expanded U.S. influence over Latin America. Not content with ensuring that Caribbean nations paid their debts, Taft initiated a policy of Dollar Diplomacy that encouraged U.S. investment in Latin America to maintain U.S. economic dominance over the region. Hoping to substitute "dollars for bullets," Taft shared Roosevelt's desire to turn the Caribbean into an American lake. In Taft's formulation enlarging America's commercial presence required the establishment of American banks, English-language news bureaus, and trained foreign service personnel in Latin American countries. These would provide U.S. businesses with the credit, information, and active government support that they needed to penetrate the region.

When Democrat Woodrow Wilson became president in 1912, he followed in Roosevelt and Taft's footsteps by aggressively protecting U.S. business interests and curtailing European access to the Western Hemisphere. The map, "American Involvement in Latin America, 1898–1939," (**19.15**) lists the many U.S. military incursions that occurred in areas where American businessmen had invested heavily in fruit and sugar industries. Like his predecessors Wilson denied any intention of seeking "one additional foot of territory by conquest." He acknowledged that U.S. intervention protected America's national security and commercial interests, but also asserted that the nation's main goal was to spread democracy and law and order. Even Wilson's secretary of war William Jennings

19.15 American Involvement in Latin America, 1898–1939
The United States intervened continually in the domestic affairs of its southern neighbors to protect the area as a U.S. sphere of influence.

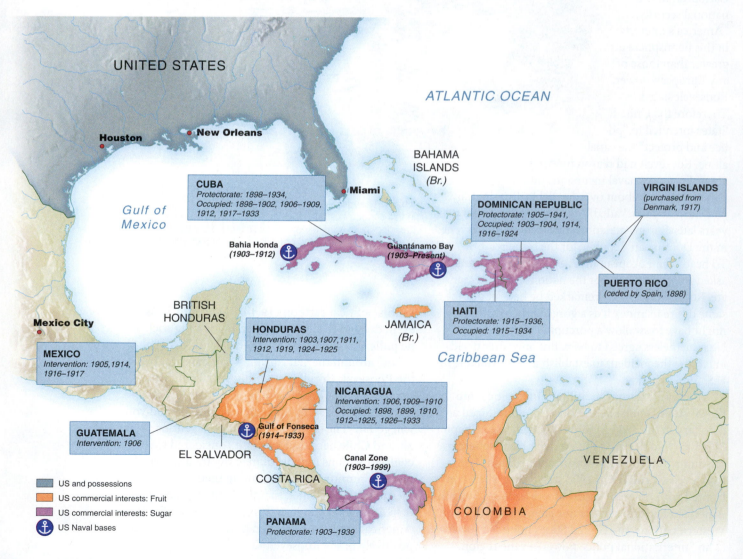

What steps did Taft and Wilson take to protect the Caribbean as a U.S. sphere of influence?

View the **Map** *Activities of the United States in the Caribbean 1898–1930s*

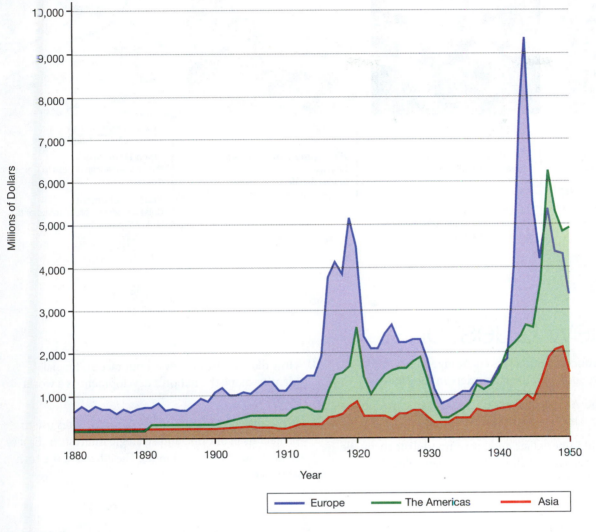

19.16. Exports to the Americas, Europe, and Asia, 1880–1950. Despite intense interest in cultivating the China market, the majority of U.S. exports went to neighboring nations in the Americas and with Europe, especially Great Britain.

Legend: Europe — The Americas — Asia

Bryan, who had vehemently opposed annexation of the Philippines, supported an active U.S. presence in Latin America. During this period U.S. troops invaded Mexico, Guatemala, Honduras, Nicaragua, Haiti, the Dominican Republic, and Cuba for strategic, commercial, and humanitarian reasons. American armies often stayed for years, and in 1915 Haiti joined Cuba, the Dominican Republic, and Panama as a U.S. protectorate.

By creating protectorates, rather than colonies, the government avoided re-igniting the divisive arguments between imperialists and anti-imperialists that had surrounded the decision to annex the Philippines. Military intervention also allowed the United States to control all direct approaches to the Panama Canal and to protect access to raw materials and markets for U.S. exports (**19.16**). Exerting influence over its Caribbean neighbors, through military invasions and protectorates, became a mainstay of twentieth-century U.S. foreign policy.

On August 15, 1914, the Panama Canal officially opened. Newspapers buried this news about America's crowning achievement of the imperial age in their back pages, instead devoting their headlines to the 11-day-old war in Europe. The beginning of World War I ushered in a new era in world history, one of global warfare made possible by the powerful empires constructed in the late nineteenth century. Now actively engaged in the world, the United States would find it difficult to stay out of this spreading conflict, especially as its trade with Great Britain and France in war-related goods exploded.

"Those Latin republics are our political children, so to speak."

Secretary of State WILLIAM JENNINGS BRYAN justifying U.S. intervention in Nicaragua.

Why were protectorates less controversial than colonies?

1893

Four-year depression begins
Intensifies interest in finding foreign markets for American goods

1898

The *Maine* explodes in Havana Harbor
Major cause of Spanish-American War

Treaty of Paris signed
Ends war with Spain; United States gains Caribbean and Pacific islands

1899

Philippine-American war begins
Ignites debate within United States over keeping Philippines as a colony

1900–1901

Open Door Notes
Protects American access to China market

Platt Amendment
Cuba becomes a protectorate of the United States

CHAPTER REVIEW

Review Questions

1. What concerns and fears encouraged the United States to look outside its borders in the 1890s?

2. How did Americans picture Spanish rule in Cuba and the American war against Spain?

3. How did imperialists and anti-imperialists reconcile their ideas with traditional American values?

4. How did American views about race and racial identity shape the nation's development as a world power?

5. What different tactics did the United States use to protect its economic and strategic interests in East Asia versus those used in the Caribbean at the turn of the century?

Key Terms

Imperialism The late nineteenth-century term for colonizing foreign nations and lands, relying primarily on business, political, and military structures rather than settlers to rule colonized peoples and exploit their resources.   **562**

Teller Amendment (1898) Congressional promise "to leave the government and control of the [Cuban] Island to its people" at the end of the Spanish-American War.   **568**

Treaty of Paris Agreement that ended the Spanish-American War, with Spain relinquishing its claim to Cuba and the United States receiving Puerto Rico and Guam. In return for $20 million, Spain turned the Philippines over to the United States.   **571**

Platt Amendment Granted the United States the right to maintain a naval base at Guantánamo Bay, to intervene militarily in Cuban domestic affairs, and a privileged trading relationship with Cuba. The Cuban government also needed permission from the United States before entering into treaties with other nations.   **572**

"The white man's burden" The Anglo-Saxon quest to better the lives of so-called racially inferior peoples by spreading Western economic, cultural, and spiritual values and institutions.   **575**

Sphere of influence The term used to describe the exclusive political and trading rights that a foreign nation enjoyed within another nation's territory.   **579**

Open Door Policy A U.S.-sponsored nonbinding international agreement that kept the Chinese market open to all foreign nations.   **579**

Gentlemen's Agreement (1907–1908) Japanese agreement to deny passports to Japanese workers intending to immigrate to the United States.   **581**

Panama Canal A manmade waterway through Panama completed in 1914 to link the Pacific and Atlantic oceans.   **584**

Roosevelt Corollary (1904) Corollary to the 1823 Monroe Doctrine that announced the U.S. intention to act as an "international police power" in Latin America.   **587**

1904

Roosevelt Corollary
Establishes United States as international police presence in the Caribbean

St. Louis World's Fair
Exhibits highlight industrial progress and "civilizing" mission in Colonies

1906

Roosevelt wins Nobel Peace Prize and visits canal zone
Signals new U.S. international presence

San Francisco Earthquake
Destruction of public records results in Chinese "paper son" phenomenon

1907–1908

Gentlemen's Agreement
Limits Japanese immigration

1914

Panama Canal opens
Symbol of U.S. technological, military, and economic might

World War I begins
Global war engulfs Europe and its empires

MyHistoryLab Connections

Visit www.myhistorylab.com for a customized Study Plan that will help you build your knowledge of *Imperial America*.

Questions for Analysis

1. Who were the world's leading imperial powers in 1900?

View the **Map** *World Colonial Empires (1900), p. 562*

2. How did social Darwinism fuel expansionism?

Read the **Document** *Josiah Strong, from Our Country (1885), p. 564*

3. How does this image announce the emergence of the United States as a world power?

View the **Image** *Our Victorious Fleet in Cuban Waters, p. 571*

4 What views do these poems offer on the benefits and drawbacks of colonization?

View the **Closer Look** *Competing Visions: The White Man's Burden, p. 575*

5. What does this cartoon reveal about American dominance in the Western Hemisphere?

View the **Image** *His Foresight (1901), p. 587*

Other Resources from This Chapter

Read the **Document**
- *The Teller Amendment (1898), p. 568*
- *The Platt Amendment (1901), p. 572*
- *Platform for the American Anti-Imperialist League (1899), p. 574*
- *Katherine Mullikin Lowry on the Boxer Rebellion (1900), p. 580*

View the **Closer Look**
- *Images as History: Atrocity Stories and Public Opinion, p. 567*
- *Competing Visions: Annexing the Philippines, p. 576*

View the **Image** *African American Troops in the Spanish American War, p. 577*

View the **Map** *Activities of the United States in the Caribbean 1898–1930s, p. 588*

Watch the **Video**
- *Burial of the Maine Victims, p. 566*
- *Roosevelt's Rough Riders, p. 570*

CHAPTER

20

((•—|Hear the Audio File on myhistorylab.com

• •—|Watch the Video *Critical Visions, Chapter 20*

The Great War
World War I, 1914–1918

On May 7, 1915, Ernest Cowper was chatting with a friend aboard the *Lusitania*, a British passenger ship traveling from New York to the British Isles, as it passed the lush, green coast of Ireland. Looking into the water, Cowper suddenly felt a stab of terror when he spotted a German torpedo just seconds before it hit the ship. Peering through the periscope the German submarine captain watched hundreds of people jumping into the water in a desperate attempt to reach empty lifeboats. The ship sank within 18 minutes, killing 1,198 passengers, including 128 Americans. Cowper, a Toronto newsman whose vivid recollections soon appeared in American newspapers, was one of the lucky survivors.

The sinking of the *Lusitania* was a defining moment for the United States during World War I, often also called the Great War. The nation had remained neutral when the war began nine months earlier in August 1914, refusing to chose sides among the European powers involved, led by Great Britain, France, and Russia (the Allies) on one side and Germany and Austria-Hungary (the Central Powers) on the other. When, however, the war spread to the high seas and American business initiated a lucrative arms trade with Britain and France, Americans increasingly found themselves in the line of fire.

American newspapers highlighted the tragic deaths of innocent women and children on the *Lusitania*, stirring outrage against Germany. One U.S. news report described the corpse of a mother embracing her three-month old baby, noting that "her face wears a half smile. Her baby's head rests against her breast. No one has tried to separate them." This description inspired the first American war-era propaganda poster, pictured here. The image, by Fred Spear, showed a mother and her baby sinking into the depths of the sea accompanied by one word—"Enlist."

Not all Americans, however, blamed Germany for the attack. German Americans claimed that the *Lusitania* was secretly transporting munitions from New York to Britain. Rural Americans castigated Northeast business interests for trading primarily with the Allies, fearful that favoring Britain and its allies would draw America into the war. President Woodrow Wilson offered a competing vision of the *Lusitania's* importance. Through increasingly strident diplomacy Wilson decided to defend the rights of neutrals to travel wherever they liked. This stance put the United States on a collision course with Germany that resulted in America entering the war two years later. Once America declared war, Wilson gave the country a larger purpose than defeating Germany. Introducing a new, and controversial, vision of American global leadership, he promised to achieve a lasting peace by spreading democracy worldwide.

To mobilize the nation's resources to fight the grim trench warfare underway along the Western Front, the government unfurled a far-reaching propaganda campaign, offered unprecedented support to labor unions, and raised a mass army through conscription. Americans suffered severe casualties in a short time, and their war effort helped the Allies defeat Germany by November 1918. The nation expected a peace treaty that embodied Wilson's promise to make this conflict "the war to end all wars." Americans held conflicting visions, however, over how to achieve this goal.

"The world must be made safe for democracy."
President WOODROW WILSON, 1917 War Address

ENLIST

The Decision for War

NOTICE!
TRAVELLERS intending to embark on the Atlantic voyage are reminded that a state of war exists between Germany and her allies and Great Britain and her allies; that the zone of war includes the waters adjacent to the British Isles; that in accordance with formal no...

In the summer of 1914, Europe ignited as war swept across the continent (**20.1**). Instead of the easy victory that many Europeans expected, the war turned into a prolonged global struggle that took the lives of millions of men. World War I pitted the Allies, initially composed of Britain, France, Belgium, Serbia, and Russia, and eventually totaling 18 nations including Japan, Italy, and the United States, against the Central Powers of Germany and Austria-Hungary, who were joined by the Ottoman Empire and Bulgaria.

Most Europeans rushed into battle without considering what a general war would mean. Americans, however, followed a completely different road to war, openly debating whether this was their war to fight. It took two and a half years for the United States to enter the war. By then few illusions remained about the horror of modern warfare. Unlike Europeans in 1914 Americans knew they were committing to total war—and that winning would require the complete economic and psychological mobilization of the home front.

The War in Europe

On June 28, 1914, a 19-year-old Bosnian Serb named Gavrilo Princip arrived in Sarajevo, the capital of Bosnia, as part of a terrorist band that intended to assassinate the heir to the Austro-Hungarian throne, Archduke Franz Ferdinand, who was also visiting the city. Princip belonged to the Black Hand, a Slavic nationalist group based in the neighboring Kingdom of Serbia that longed to unite Bosnia, then part of the Austro-Hungarian Empire, with Serbia. The group's first attempt to assassinate the archduke failed when the bomb that one of Princip's coconspirators threw at the archduke's motorcade bounced off the side of his car, injuring two Austrian officers instead. Eluding the police Princip disappeared into the crowd. Later in the day the archduke made a fateful decision to visit his injured staff members. On the way to the hospital, the driver made a wrong turn down a narrow street and slowed down to put the car in reverse. Standing at the end of the street was Princip, who could barely believe his good fortune as he saw the archduke and his wife coming toward him. Seizing the opportunity he stepped forward, pulled a pistol from his pocket, and fired, killing them both.

World War I began with these two deaths and ended four years later with over nine million more. In responding to the assassination, Austria-Hungary, Russia, and Germany tried to leverage the crisis to fulfill longstanding territorial ambitions. These events are summarized on the timeline, "Countdown to War, 1914" (**20.2**).

> ## "Mr. Mayor, it is perfectly outrageous! We have come to Sarajevo on a visit and have had a bomb thrown at us."
>
> ARCHDUKE FRANZ FERDINAND
> after surviving the Black Hand's
> first assassination attempt

Austria-Hungary and Russia vied for control of the Balkans, which offered ready access to the Mediterranean and the Middle East. Germany hoped to become the dominant power in Europe and had recently challenged the world dominance of France and Britain by building a strong navy, acquiring colonies, and defeating France in the 1870–1871 Franco-Prussian War.

Austria-Hungary held Serbia responsible for the assassination and demanded that the Serbian government make amends. In response Serbia chose appeasement over confrontation. Serbia accepted all of Austria-Hungary's demands except the one insisting that Austro-Hungarian judges and police participate in the investigation and trials of any Black Hand terrorists captured in Serbia. In early July, German Kaiser Wilhelm II encouraged Austria-Hungary to quickly invade and punish Serbia. But on July 28, when the Kaiser finally read the Serbian response, he jotted in the margins: "a great moral victory for Vienna; but with it every reason for war

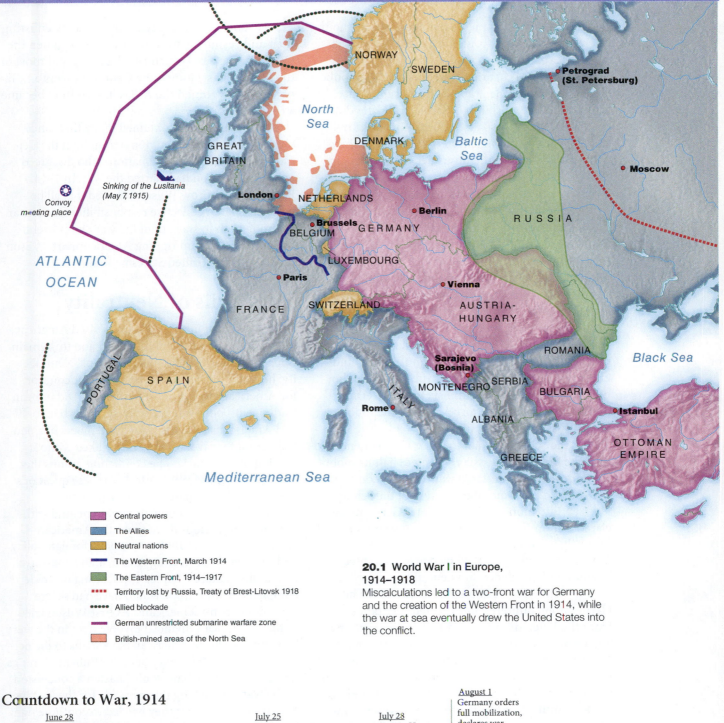

20.1 World War I in Europe, 1914–1918

Miscalculations led to a two-front war for Germany and the creation of the Western Front in 1914, while the war at sea eventually drew the United States into the conflict.

Legend:
- Central powers
- The Allies
- Neutral nations
- The Western Front, March 1914
- The Eastern Front, 1914–1917
- Territory lost by Russia, Treaty of Brest-Litovsk 1918
- Allied blockade
- German unrestricted submarine warfare zone
- British-mined areas of the North Sea

Countdown to War, 1914

June 28
Gavrilo Princip assassinates the Archduke Franz Ferdinand in Sarajevo

July 23
Austria-Hungary sends ultimatums to Serbia

July 25
Serbia accepts all but one ultimatum

July 27
Germany urges Austria-Hungary to invade Serbia

July 28
Austria-Hungary declares war on Serbia

July 30
Russia orders a full mobilization

August 1
Germany orders full mobilization, declares war on Russia

August 3
Germany declares war on France

August 4
German soldiers invade Beligium, implementing Schlieffen Plan. Britain declares war on Germany. President Wilson announces U.S. neutrality

20.2 Timeline, 1914

After the assassination of the Archduke Franz Ferdinand, nations made momentous choices that led to World War I.

Why did the assassination of Archduke Franz Ferdinand spark a global world war?

is removed." His comments came too late. An hour later, on July 28, 1914, Austria-Hungary declared war on Serbia.

As Austro-Hungarian warships on the Danube River bombarded Belgrade, Serbia's capital city, Russia resolved to stand by Serbia and defend its own interests in the Balkans. Tsar Nicolas II ordered a general mobilization of his army on July 30, 1914. It was a momentous decision. Germany viewed Russia's mobilization as a direct threat. Ever since the 1894 alliance between Russia and France, Germany had worried about fighting a two-front war. In 1905, the German Chief of Staff Alfred von Schlieffen developed a plan that called for Germany, in the event of war, to attack and quickly defeat France in the west, while the cumbersome Russian army mobilized in the east. The **Schlieffen Plan** avoided the well-defended border between France and Germany and instead sent German troops on a northward arc. Passing quickly through Belgium, German troops would enter France through its unfortified northern border and capture Paris within six weeks. Germany could then turn its full forces against the much larger Russian army.

For the Schlieffen Plan to work, Germany needed to strike first. With Russia refusing to halt its mobilization, Germany declared war on Russia on August 1, 1914, and put a modified version of the Schlieffen Plan into motion. Two days later Germany declared war on France. When German troops crossed into Belgium on August 4, Britain declared war on Germany, fulfilling its 1839 pledge to guarantee Belgium independence and neutrality.

The Schlieffen Plan quickly unraveled. The Germans encountered unexpected resistance from the Belgians and had difficulty resupplying a mass army on the move, giving the French and British time to mobilize. In the east Russia attacked with its partly mobilized army sooner than Germany expected, prompting German Chief of Staff Helmuth von Moltke to divert troops from France to defend East Prussia. At the Marne River, 35 miles northeast of Paris, the French and British successfully stopped the German drive toward Paris. Instead of defeating France quickly, Germany's attack ignited a general European war. As each army dug defensive trenches in France and Belgium, the trench deadlock of the **Western Front** took shape. For nearly four years men would live and die in the complex system of earthworks that ran for 460 miles from the North Sea to Switzerland. To bolster their forces, Britain,

France, and Germany began immediately enlisting men and resources from their colonies. When the Ottoman Empire (which ruled Turkey and most of the Middle East) joined the Central Powers and Japan and Italy joined the Allies, the conflict became a true world war.

American society contained many first- and second-generation immigrants from both the Central Powers and the Allied nations who disagreed over which nation had started the war. In 1914, President Woodrow Wilson believed that all belligerents shared collective responsibility for the war. Wanting both to stay out of the war and prevent bitter divisions from ripping America apart, Wilson proclaimed the United States neutral.

The Perils of Neutrality

As war engulfed Europe Wilson advised Americans to avoid "passionately taking sides" and to "remain impartial in thought, as well as action." Neutrality, however, turned out to be a difficult concept for Americans to define and maintain. Did it mean trading with both sides selectively, or with no one? Did Americans have the right as members of a neutral nation to travel wherever they liked without coming under attack? The conflicting visions that emerged as Americans confronted these questions created strident debate as the war wore on.

The dilemma was how to remain neutral without inflicting serious damage on the American economy. Since the 1890s, American foreign policy had focused on protecting American business interests abroad (see Chapter 19). Cutting off trade completely with Europe would have had severe consequences for Americans. At first Wilson tried to limit America's financial involvement in the war by banning private American bank loans to the belligerent nations. Secretary of State William Jennings Bryan believed the ban would "hasten a conclusion to the war" by making it impossible for the warring countries to buy what they needed to continue fighting. Wilson, however, lifted the ban in 1915. The Allies were running short of cash, and Wilson feared a widespread U.S. recession if these nations stopped buying American goods.

Trading with or loaning money to both sides was another possible way to stay neutral. In theory American manufacturers and banks were free to do business with both the Allies and Germany. In practice, however, the chart of U.S. Exports to Europe, 1914–1917 (**20.3**) reveals that they chose primarily to help the Allies. By 1917, American banks were loaning

What miscalculations stymied German expectations of a short war?

U.S. Trade with Nations at War

	1914	1915	1916	1916 Figure as a Percentage of 1914 Figure
Britain	$594,271,863	$911,794,954	$1,526,685,102	257%
France	$159,818,924	$369,397,170	$628,851,988	393%
Italy*	$74,235,012	$184,819,688	$269,246,105	364%
Germany	$344,794,276	$28,863,354	$288,899	0.08%

*Italy joined the Allies in April 1915.

20.3 U.S. Exports to Europe, 1914–1917 The nation's robust trade with Britain, France, and Italy—allied nations fighting Germany—provoked debate among Americans holding conflicting visions of neutrality.

Britain an average of $10 million a day. In contrast American trade with Germany had dropped to less than one percent of what it had been in 1914. Even if American manufacturers and banks had wanted to help Germany, trade became nearly impossible when Britain used its navy to blockade Germany and cut the international cable between the United States and Germany. America's financial elite, however, had no desire to trade with both sides. Many upper-class Americans revered British culture and had warm feelings toward the French. Widespread publicity of German atrocities against Belgian civilians also fanned anti-German sentiment. Newspapers published vivid accounts of German soldiers burning homes, ransacking museums, and executing Belgian civilians in retaliation for guerilla attacks against the German army. The press embellished these stories with fabricated tales of German soldiers cutting off women's breasts and children's hands.

Some Americans saw such reports as little more than British propaganda. America's disproportionate aid to the Allies alarmed the sizable German American and Irish American communities (the latter hated British rule of Ireland). Midwesterners and Southerners accused Eastern banks of violating the principle of neutrality, thereby pulling the nation slowly into a war most Americans did not want to fight. These critics embraced a strict vision of neutrality and wanted the government to announce an arms embargo that would prevent American companies from trading with nations at war.

When the war spread to the high seas, these conflicting visions provoked heated debate over America's role in the war. Facing a trench stalemate on the Western Front, Britain used its superior navy to establish a blockade around the Central Powers that included mining the North Sea. The blockade immediately affected American trade. American ships could not sail through the North Sea to Germany without first allowing the British to search their cargo for contraband, merchandise such as guns or ammunition that Britain wanted to stop from entering Germany. Britain soon violated international law by adding cotton and food to the contraband list. In March 1915, Wilson formally protested British blockading practices. The British eventually agreed to buy enough American cotton to offset the loss of the German market.

The president proved less accommodating when Germany declared the waters around Britain a war zone and threatened to attack any ship that entered the area. To combat the British blockade, Germany turned to a new weapon, its U-boat, or submarine, to launch surprise torpedo attacks against Allied merchant and naval ships. International law recognized a naval blockade as a legal weapon of war, but required that the attacking ship give the merchant vessel's crew time to evacuate, and if necessary, take them aboard before sinking the ship and cargo. These prewar rules rendered the U-boat useless, removing the element of surprise that made it so effective. Once spotted, armed merchant vessels did not hesitate to attack fragile U-boats.

On May 7, 1915, a German U-boat sunk the *Lusitania*, a British passenger ship sailing off the coast of Ireland. Calls for war swept through the press. "Germany must surely have gone mad," surmised one Richmond newspaper. Wilson sent a

What competing visions did Americans offer on the question of trading with warring European nations?

> **"The American people do not want to go to war to vindicate the right of a few people to travel or work on armed vessels."**
>
> Missouri Senator WILLIAM J. STONE
> to President Wilson, 1916

> **"I cannot consent to any abridgement of the rights of American citizens in any respect. The honor and self-respect of the nation is involved."**
>
> WILSON'S reply

20.4 German Warning to Travelers in the War Zone When Wilson criticized Germany for sinking the *Lusitania*, German Americans pointed out that the German government had published warnings like this ahead of time urging Americans to stay off ships headed to the war zone.

series of notes demanding that Germany pay reparations and accept the right of Americans to travel on any ship they wished. The Germans defended the sinking, pointing out that they had published warnings to passengers in American newspapers (**20.4**) and claiming that the *Lusitania* was carrying munitions as part of its cargo.

The *Lusitania* sinking was an ideological turning point for the United States. In reaction to the crisis, Wilson redefined the meaning of neutrality, thus putting the United States on a collision course with Germany. The president moved away from his initial definition of neutrality as remaining "impartial in thought, as well as action." He now embraced neutrality as a concept that first and foremost gave neutral nations the indisputable right to trade and travel wherever they liked. Secretary of State Bryan urged Wilson to ban Americans from traveling on ships headed to the U-boat–patrolled waters around Great Britain. Wilson refused. Convinced that the president's preoccupation with the rights of neutrals would lead to war, Bryan resigned in protest.

NOTICE!

TRAVELLERS intending to embark on the Atlantic voyage are reminded that a state of war exists between Germany and her allies and Great Britain and her allies; that the zone of war includes the waters adjacent to the British Isles; that, in accordance with formal notice given by the Imperial German Government, vessels flying the flag of Great Britain, or of any of her allies, are liable to destruction in those waters and that travellers sailing in the war zone on ships of Great Britain or her allies do so at their own risk.

IMPERIAL GERMAN EMBASSY
WASHINGTON, D. C., APRIL 22, 1915.

As the United States and Germany argued over the *Lusitania*, a German U-boat sunk another British passenger ship, the *Arabic*, in August 1915, leaving two Americans among the dead. Worried about further provoking the United States, on September 1, 1915, Germany issued the *Arabic* Pledge, promising not to sink passenger ships without warning. Germany renounced surprise attacks on merchant ships in May 1916 following another controversial torpedoing. For the moment these pledges averted war with the United States.

The debate deepened when prominent pro-Ally political, business, and financial leaders formed the National Security League and began lobbying for universal military training to instruct all men of fighting age in drilling and marksmanship. In response Progressive reformers formed the American Union Against Militarism to denounce preparations for war. The appeal of the pacifist vision made the 1916 song "I Didn't Raise My Son to be a Soldier" a hit. Taking stock of the preparedness versus peace debate, Congress authorized only a modest, but still controversial, expansion of the peacetime army.

Recognizing the potency of antiwar sentiment, Wilson ran for reelection in 1916 on the slogan "He Kept Us Out of War." The banners covering a Wilson reelection campaign truck (**20.5**) revealed the strong connections that he drew between domestic and foreign issues. Wilson reminded voters of his Progressive reform agenda, which included a Federal Reserve System that "broke the money trust" and passage of an eight-hour day for railroad workers (see Chapter 18). The slogan "Peace with Honor" referred to his success in securing pledges from Germany that respected America's right to trade with the Allies. This overseas commerce created the prosperity that Democrats boasted about on the same sign. During the campaign Wilson noted that twice he had sent his trusted advisor

Colonel Edward House to Europe to negotiate a peace settlement, lamenting that House had returned empty-handed each time. Wilson also campaigned on the slogan of preparedness to underscore his commitment to defending the country if necessary.

In contrast Wilson's Republican challenger, former Supreme Court Justice Charles Evan Hughes, never developed an effective slogan or theme. The Hughes campaign believed that Woodrow Wilson had won the presidency in 1912 because progressive Republicans had supported Theodore Roosevelt's run as a third-party Progressive candidate over the incumbent Republican President William Howard Taft (see Chapter 18). With the conservative and progressive factions of the Republican Party now reunited, Hughes tried to avoid controversy with vague calls "for law and liberty" and "undiluted Americanism." On election night, with returns from California still uncounted, Wilson went to bed certain that he had lost. He awoke to discover that he had carried California and won reelection by only 23 electoral votes, 277–254.

Foreign affairs now dominated Wilson's thoughts. Throughout 1914–1917, German spies spent nearly $12 million to support rebel factions in Mexico, who resented the U.S. government's intervention in Mexican domestic politics. In 1916, Francisco "Pancho" Villa raided American border towns, hoping to draw U.S. troops into Mexico and destabilize the new U.S.-backed constitutional government headed by Venustiano Carranza. Much as Villa anticipated, Wilson sent a 12,000-troop punitive expedition under the command of Brigadier General John J. Pershing into Mexico to arrest Villa. Carranza denounced the American expedition as an invasion of Mexico. Tensions between the two countries escalated dramatically after a deadly clash in Carrizal on June 21, 1916. Wilson began planning for war with Mexico until he learned that American

20.5 Wilson Campaign Slogans
In a tight race for reelection in 1916, Woodrow Wilson emphasized his progressive legislative agenda and championed his success at keeping the nation out of the war without sacrificing national honor or economic prosperity.

troops had attacked first at Carrizal. After months of talks between U.S. and Mexican negotiators, American troops left Mexico in January 1917.

That same month Wilson tried again to negotiate a European peace settlement. On January 22, 1917, he outlined a plan for "peace without victory" based on "American principles, American policies." Democracy, freedom of the seas, no entangling alliances, and equality of rights among nations were, Wilson asserted, "the principles and policies of forward-looking men and women everywhere, of every modern nation, of every enlightened community." Wilson's desire to export democracy overseas while simultaneously protecting American access to foreign markets promised to greatly expand America's imperial reach. No longer limiting American intervention to its Pacific colonies or nearby Latin American countries (see Chapter 19), Wilson proposed remaking Europe in the image of America.

His words had little effect on European leaders. Unbeknownst to the president, Germany had

◉━ **Watch** the **Video** *Video Lecture: American Entry into World War I*

How did Wilson link domestic and foreign issues during the 1916 presidential campaign?

already decided to resume unrestricted submarine warfare. Having staked everything on Germany's willingness to let Americans travel unmolested in the war zone, Wilson's neutrality policy collapsed.

America Enters the War

Germany expected the Allies to capitulate quickly once German submarines cut off their lifeline to the United States. Even if the resumption of unrestricted submarine warfare brought the United States into the war, it would take at least a year for the American government to raise, train, and equip a force to send overseas. By then Germany expected to have won the war.

In early February 1917, Wilson pondered whether German violations of American neutrality were grounds for declaring war. This cartoon, *Lincoln's Birthday* (**20.6**), compares Wilson's dilemma to the one that Abraham Lincoln had faced on the eve of the Civil War. Wilson stares at the date of Lincoln's birth, while Lincoln's ghost stands stoically holding a sheet of paper that reads: "Let us have faith that right makes might and in that faith let us to the end dare to do our duty as we understand it. Lincoln." Unbeknownst to Wilson, Germany had already taken steps to defend itself against a potential American attack.

20.6 *Lincoln's Birthday*
This cartoon suggests that Wilson, like Lincoln, faced a difficult decision of leading the country into war to defend higher principles.

> ## "It is a fearful thing to lead this great peaceful people into war."
> President WILSON, 1917 war address before Congress

In mid-February Wilson learned that the German foreign minister Arthur Zimmermann had sent the **Zimmermann Telegram** to Mexico stating that in the event of war with the United States, Germany would help Mexico recover Texas, New Mexico, and Arizona (territory lost in the nineteenth century) if Mexico started a border war with the United States. Zimmermann also asked Mexico to mediate between Germany and Japan, hoping to entice Japan into attacking America's Pacific colonial possessions. Carranza had no interest in fighting the United States after the American withdrawal from Mexico, and Germany had no men or munitions to offer. In one of the war's greatest intelligence coups, British intelligence agents intercepted and deciphered the secret telegram. When the State Department released the Zimmermann Telegram to the press on March 1, many Americans viewed it as evidence that Germany had hostile intentions against the United States. Antiwar activists denounced the telegram as a forgery, but Zimmermann confessed to sending the note. With war between Germany and the United States growing more likely, Zimmermann wanted the United States to believe the threat was real, so it would keep troops at home to protect the border.

Despite the outcry over the Zimmermann Telegram, Wilson hesitated. The president broke off diplomatic ties with Germany, but still did not ask for a declaration of war. German submarines began sinking over 500,000 tons of Allied shipping per month, and the Allies warned Wilson that without these supplies they were doomed. As German submarines began attacking American merchant ships, Wilson agreed to arm these vessels. Finally, on April 2, 1917, Wilson went before Congress to ask for a declaration of war, laying out war goals that went far beyond simply defeating Germany. "We are glad, now that we see the facts," he proclaimed "… to fight thus for the ultimate peace of the world and for the liberation of its peoples … for the rights of nations great and small and the privilege of men everywhere to chose their way of life and of obedience."

Congress declared war with a vote of 90 to 6 in the Senate and 373 to 50 in the House, but a vocal minority opposed going to war. Republican Senator George W. Norris from Nebraska expressed the "rich man's war, poor man's fight" sentiment that ran deep in rural America. Only four days into her term as the first female member of Congress, Jeannette Rankin (R-Montana) caste her maiden vote against the war. She lost her seat in 1918, but returned to Congress in 1940. Sticking to her pacifist principles, she was the only legislator who voted against entering World War II after the Japanese attacked Pearl Harbor. Critics expressed their opposition freely during the debate over declaring war, but once the nation was officially fighting Germany, most Americans rallied behind the flag.

Why did the United States finally decide to fight Germany?   **Read the Document** *The Zimmermann Telegram*

Conflicting Views among the Allies on the War's Purpose

Wilson claimed that the United States "had no selfish ends to serve" by going to war. Skeptical voices from revolutionary Russia soon prompted Wilson to defend this claim. Tsarist Russia had collapsed in February 1917. A weak parliamentary regime replaced it, but on November 7, 1917, seven months after the United States entered the war, the Bolshevik revolutionary Vladimir Lenin seized power in Russia with promises of peace, land, and bread. Lenin's Communist government immediately published secret Allied treaties, revealing that Tsarist Russia, Britain, Italy, and France had agreed to enlarge their empires at the expense of Germany, Austria-Hungary, and the Ottoman Empire if they won the war. This disclosure exposed competing visions on the Allied side: Wilson's vague promises that the war was about democracy and the now-revealed territorial ambitions of the Allies. (The United States never formally joined the Allies. Instead it fought on their side as an "associated power.")

Trying to bridge this gap, Wilson outlined a broad statement of war goals in his **Fourteen Points** speech to Congress on January 8, 1918. The Fourteen Points envisioned a world dominated by democracy, free trade, disarmament, self-determination, resolved territorial disputes in Europe, and a league of nations to mediate international crises. Wilson explicitly linked the spread of democracy with the expansion of capitalism, a position that gained new urgency as Russian Communists began confiscating private property and promised to redistribute wealth to peasants and workers. Whether spreading democracy meant increasing political rights and free trade or reallocating wealth became a cornerstone of the ideological debate between the United States and the new Soviet Union throughout the twentieth century.

Free trade and freedom of the seas offered more than an antidote to communism, however. These principles also advanced American economic interests at the expense of imperialist powers like Britain and France. The Fourteen Points speech revealed contradictions in Wilsonian idealism. Like other world leaders Wilson advanced principles that protected the interests of his own country. Yet he also demanded sacrifices from Americans to make this "the war to end all wars." Once they joined the global association of nations that Wilson proposed, Americans would have to modify their traditional desire to act unilaterally in the Western Hemisphere.

Wilson's Fourteen Points further declared that all peoples should enjoy self-determination, or a voice in selecting their own government. Using this principle Wilson proposed redrawing the map of Eastern and Central Europe along ethnic lines and even proposed extending this right to colonial populations. Robert Lansing, who replaced Bryan as secretary of state, remained dubious. The principle of self-determination "is simply loaded with dynamite," Lansing noted. "It will raise hopes which can never be realized."

> ## "God gave us his Ten Commandments and we broke them. Wilson gave us his 14 points—well, we shall see."
>
> **French Prime Minister**
> **GEORGE CLEMENCEAU, 1918**

Shortly after Wilson issued his Fourteen Points, another model emerged for how the war might end when Lenin negotiated a separate peace. The Treaty of Brest-Litovsk officially ended the war between Russia and the Central Powers on March 3, 1918. This treaty reflected Germany's complete victory over Russia and exposed the imperialist thrust of German war goals in the east. Ukraine, parts of Poland, Finland, Lithuania, Estonia, and Latvia became German satellite states (see 20.1). With these gains Germany intended to eliminate Russia as a rival and expand its empire into resource-rich lands in Eastern Europe.

The Brest-Litovsk Treaty gave the Allies an idea of the terms that a victorious Germany might impose on them. This knowledge hardened the British and French resolve to achieve total victory and inflict punitive terms of their own. The treaty even convinced Wilson that maintaining peace in Europe would require weakening Germany militarily and economically.

With Russia out of the war, Germany finally had the opportunity to fight the one-front war it had sought in 1914. Now holding a clear numerical advantage, Germany prepared to strike along the Western Front. As the American government raced to mobilize the nation's men and industry for total war, many in Europe feared that the United States had entered the war too late to save the Allied side.

▶ ◼ **Read** the **Document** *Woodrow Wilson's Fourteen Points*

How did the Fourteen Points lay the foundation for future domestic and international debates?

The War at Home

America could not mobilize, supply, and feed an army without granting new powers to the federal government. The federal government used a mix of incentives, threats, and patriotic appeals to negotiate the preexisting class, gender, and racial conflicts that threatened to make wartime cooperation difficult. Official propaganda urged unity, but Americans retained conflicting visions about regulating big business, unionizing, female suffrage, and racial equality.

Gearing Up for War

Wilson's democratic rhetoric convinced many Progressive reformers that they could count on the president to use his wartime powers to rein in big business (see Chapter 18). The president, however, feared that the war would make corporations more powerful than ever. "We shall be dependent upon the steel, oil, and financial magnates," Wilson privately worried. "They will run the nation." His concerns were well-founded. Increased wages and federal protections for unions improved the lives of many workers, but the resurgent power of big business prevented Progressives from making these wartime reforms permanent.

In the winter of 1917, gridlock paralyzed the railroad system. Blizzards, fuel shortages, and poor coordination among private railway companies prevented trains from delivering tons of war-related freight. Labor unrest also created havoc as skilled railway workers left in droves for better-paying factory jobs, and railway unions prepared to strike. To sort out this mess, the federal government took over management of the railroads for the duration of the war. The Railroad Administration met union demands for high wages, standardized equipment, and coordinated the use of tracks. To improve the flow of needed materials, the new War Industries Board (WIB) ranked industries, so that those most critical to the war effort received raw materials ahead of nonessential wartime businesses. Steel, for example, went first to manufacturers producing guns and ships, while factories making civilian cars, freezers, and corsets (they needed steel for the inner stays) had to wait. The government paid railroad companies handsomely for wartime use of their trains and track to mute their objections to government management of the railroads. When private companies regained control of railroad lines in 1920, the nation's railroad network lay in shambles, a victim of heavy wartime traffic and the government's failure to maintain the lines.

Food Administration Director Herbert Hoover chose a different path to ensure that the country produced enough to feed civilians at home, soldiers, and refugees overseas. Congress had given the president near dictatorial powers to regulate the food and fuel industries in the 1917 Lever Food and Fuel Act. Hoover, however, opted to use high prices and patriotic appeals to control the nation's food supply rather than rationing. To stimulate production, he had the American and Allied governments pay high prices for agricultural goods. To curb civilian demand, Hoover organized a massive propaganda campaign around the slogan "food will win the war." Citizens signed pledge cards vowing to observe wheatless Mondays, meatless Tuesdays, and porkless Saturdays. Urging Americans to conserve wheat for shipment overseas, the Food Administration plastered the country with posters that tried to popularize cornmeal, which did not transport well, as a tasty substitute for wheat flour. The agency offered housewives cornmeal recipes and cooking classes, and even tried to enlist the cooperation of finicky toddlers (**20.7**) by urging them to eat cornmeal instead of oatmeal.

20.7 "Little Americans Do Your Bit!" This propaganda poster showing a three-year-old saluting a bowl of corn-based porridge underscored the total mobilization of American society.

Little
AMERICANS
Do your bit

Eat Oatmeal-Corn meal mush-
Hominy - other corn cereals-
and Rice with milk.
Save the wheat for our soldiers.

Leave nothing on your plate

What varying strategies did the government use to mobilize economic resources?

Americans responded well to Hoover's patriotic appeals to conserve food, but whether the government could quell labor unrest for the duration of the war remained questionable. Wilson quieted industrial class conflict by throwing money at the problem. The steel, copper, petroleum, and meatpacking industries enjoyed a healthy increase in profits, once they began selling their products to the government. Wilson also offered industrialists, still bristling over Progressive-era laws that curtailed monopolies and regulated working conditions (see Chapter 18), an olive branch by giving them a role in setting the government's wartime price, wage, and production codes.

Labor also benefited during the war. The government built high wages and union protection into its wartime contracts in exchange for a no-strike pledge from labor. The National War Labor Board (made up of representatives from government, business, and labor) required industries that accepted government contracts to honor the eight-hour day and forty-hour week. These companies also had to pay a living wage, maintain high safety standards, and recognize a union's right to recruit members at work. Not all labor groups benefited equally from the sudden government attention. Official support for collective bargaining helped the more moderate unions that formed the American Federation of Labor. Radical labor groups that continued to oppose the war suffered when the government arrested their leaders and members for sedition.

Even the gains for moderate labor unions proved fleeting, however. Workers received higher wages, but after adjusting for wartime inflation, real wages only increased four percent. When the war ended and the government canceled its contracts, workers lost federal protection for organizing unions. Without the government stopping them, many manufacturers quickly returned to their old union-busting ways (see Chapter 21).

20.8 The First Wave of the Great Migration (1916–1919)
"Around the time of WWI, many African Americans from the South left home and traveled to cities in the North in search of a better life," wrote artist Jacob Lawrence to explain this 1940 painting.

Black Migration

Immigrants had long provided American industry with inexpensive labor. The war disrupted the flow of immigrants to the United States just when the demand for industrial goods exploded. In 1914, 1.2 million immigrants entered the country. In 1917, only 110,618 arrived. Labor-recruiting agents soon turned to white and black Southerners to fill the void. During the war over 500,000 African Americans migrated from southern farms and cities to the North, lured by high-paying industrial jobs. The African American painter Jacob Lawrence celebrated this mass exodus in a series of paintings he completed in the 1940s. His first painting showed brightly dressed streams of families preparing to board trains through doors marked "Chicago," "New York," and "St. Louis" (**20.8**). Many migrants exalted at their newfound freedom in the North. "I can quit any time I want," one noted, without forfeiting a year's pay as in the sharecropping system. Another man realized that in Chicago he was no longer afraid "to rub up against a white person" accidentally on the street or sit down next to one on a streetcar. In the South he had constantly feared the consequences of an unintended breach of Southern racial etiquette. Migrants also discovered, however, that despite the absence of overt segregation or intimidation, racial prejudice existed in the North.

The migration of Southern blacks northward also unveiled regional and class tensions within the black community. Working through organizations like the Urban League and the Young Men's Christian Association, paternalistic Northern middle-class blacks tried to help Southern migrants adjust to the rhythms of industrial jobs and urban life. Besides wanting to genuinely assist recent arrivals, middle-class blacks worried that migrants' rural customs might harm the reputation of the entire Northern black community. A list of dos and don'ts published by the *Chicago Defender*, a newspaper serving the African American community, entreated migrants to watch their language, mind their manners, respect the law, keep their houses clean, and send their children to school.

The Urban League had reason to fear that racial rioting might accompany the arrival of black workers from the South. The explosive combination of economic competition, housing shortages, and latent racial hostility triggered racial riots in Northern cities during the war. The most deadly one occurred in East St. Louis, Illinois, in July 1917. In East St. Louis companies recruited immigrants and Southern blacks to undermine union activism. Company owners knew that racial and ethnic prejudices would prevent native-born whites from allowing these new workers to join their unions, which in turn undermined the union's ability to mount a strike. Viewing black migrants as potential strikebreakers, white workers initiated minor attacks on black workers that escalated into a full-fledged racial riot on July 2, 1917. The antilynching black crusader Ida B. Wells-Barnett interviewed over 50 black eyewitnesses for a report that she submitted to Congress. One witness recalled seeing black men exit homes with their hands raised. As they pled for their lives, mobs stoned them to death. Overall the riot left nine whites and 39 blacks dead and hundreds wounded on both sides. The subsequent Congressional investigation held white employers, labor leaders, and politicians responsible, but 6,000 African Americans left the city anyway.

Female Suffrage

The war inadvertently provided an opportunity for women to gain suffrage and for the temperance reform movement (see Chapter 21), where women held leading roles, to build momentum. Mobilizing the home front meant securing the active cooperation of women. During the war, savvy female leaders successfully parlayed their newly recognized economic clout into a demand for political power.

Women did the shopping and cooking in most homes, so the Food Administration needed their full support for its food conservation efforts to succeed. "Will you have a part in Victory?" queried one propaganda poster above the image of a young woman in a stars and stripes gown scattering seeds in a "victory garden" to provide vegetables for her family. Over eight million women volunteered for Red Cross work, producing surgical dressings, sweaters, socks, and mittens for soldiers and refugees. With workers in short supply, companies increasingly recruited women to fill positions in factories, and the government hired many as clerks. In desperate need of laborers, companies in Bridgeport, Connecticut, even hired airplanes to scatter leaflets throughout residential neighborhoods that urged housewives to apply for jobs in munitions factories. Overall, however, few homemakers entered the workforce. Instead, the eight million women already at work shifted positions, taking advantage of new, albeit temporary, opportunities to work at better paying and higher skilled jobs.

Suffragists wanted the nation to thank women for their war work by giving them the right to vote. The vision of an engaged female citizenry working to defend the nation reduced the appeal of longstanding arguments against votes for women. In the past the close ties between female suffragists and the temperance movement had led some urban and midwestern males to resist enfranchising women, because so many women supported prohibition. The South feared that female suffrage meant extending the right to vote to black women. Other opponents argued that the male head of the household adequately represented his family's interests in the public domain, holding fast to a vision of women as primarily domestic, not public, figures.

In the 1910s, the middle- and upper-class women leading the suffragist movement had divided into radical and conservative factions (see Chapter 18), and each offered a competing vision of how to obtain the vote for women. For months members of the militant National Woman's Party stood outside the White House with banners asking "how long must women wait for liberty?" Once the United States entered the war, militant suffragists turned Wilson's democratic rhetoric against him. They erected a sign (**20.9**) intended to embarrass Wilson as he greeted a delegation from the parliamentary government that ruled Russia for a short time in 1917, before Lenin seized power. Wilson hoped to convince the delegates to keep Russia in the war so democracy could triumph over autocracy in Europe. The suffragists instead focused on the recent introduction of female suffrage in Russia, urging the envoys to "help us make this nation really free" by convincing Wilson to support female suffrage.

Daily scuffles broke out between outraged war supporters and the picketing suffragists, whom the press vilified as unpatriotic. After the police arrested the suffragists, the women initiated a hunger strike to protest their poor treatment in prison. When accounts of prison guards forcing feeding tubes down the throats of suffragists leaked out, Wilson pardoned them. Unbowed the female militants burned him in effigy at the White House gates.

The more moderate National American Woman Suffrage Association (NAWSA) followed a different tack. It presented the vote, not as a question of equality or democracy, but as a way to reinforce the traditional desire of women to protect their families (see Chapter 18). The NAWSA also seized on wartime prejudices against German Americans, whose loyalty many Americans increasingly questioned. "It is a risk, a danger to a country like ours to send 1,000,000 men out of the country who are loyal and not replace those men by the loyal votes of the women they have left at home," NAWSA president Carrie Chapman Catt proclaimed. All these arguments eventually swayed Wilson. In September 1918, he became the first president to endorse national female suffrage, convinced that women's supposedly pacifist nature could help secure his postwar goals for a lasting peace. Congress sent the **Nineteenth Amendment**, which granted women the right to vote, to the states on June 4, 1919, seven months after the war ended. Final ratification came on August 26, 1920.

TO THE ENVOYS OF RUSSIA.
President Wilson and Envoy Root are deceiving Russia. They say, "we are a democracy. Help us win a world war so that democracies may survive."

We, the Women of America, tell you that America is not a democracy. Twenty million American Women are denied the right to vote. President Wilson is the chief opponent of their national enfranchisement.

Help us make this nation really free. Tell our government that it must liberate its people before it can claim free Russia as an ally.

20.9 Suffragists Picket the White House
The radical wing of the suffragist movement criticized Wilson, who claimed that an Allied victory would spread democracy, for refusing to support female suffrage.

Rallying the Public

To control the flow of information and shape public opinion about the war, Wilson formed the **Committee on Public Information** (CPI). Headed by George Creel, a Progressive muckraking journalist, the CPI disseminated propaganda posters, press releases, and films. It translated its pamphlets into multiple languages to reach the nation's huge immigrant population. The agency also recruited so-called Four-Minute Men to speak before audiences in movie halls, markets, fairs, and churches. The CPI limited each speech to four minutes to fill the time that it took to change the reels for silent films in movie theatres. Creel estimated that 75,000 Four-Minute Men gave nearly seven million impassioned speeches during the war on topics such as German submarine warfare and German espionage. Hollywood helped the propaganda effort by making movies like *To Hell With the Kaiser*, which depicted the German leader as a depraved lunatic who receives a much-deserved punch in the mouth from the American soldier who captures him.

The government also used war bond campaigns to win over hearts and minds. Rather than angering the public with higher taxes to pay for the war, the government financed two-thirds of the war's costs with war bonds, short-term loans that individual citizens made to the government. Secretary of the Treasury William G. McAdoo believed that Americans who bought a $50 liberty bond, a $5 war savings certificate, or a 25 cent thrift stamp felt personally connected to the war. "Any great war must necessarily be a popular movement," McAdoo noted. Financing the war through war bonds, however, made it more expensive, because the government had to pay interest to each bondholder.

With the government reaching out to immigrants from Russia, Poland, and Italy through war bond campaigns and military recruitment, many immigrants felt American for the first time. Recent arrivals often lived in ethnic neighborhoods and worked alongside their compatriots, circumstances that had made assimilation difficult. Rather than having to choose between their homelands and their new country, these immigrants could openly support both during the war. "By Helping the American Red Cross You are Helping Italy," read an ad in one Italian-American newspaper.

Immigrants from the Allied nations thrived during the war, but for German Americans the war years were bleak. Wartime propaganda accentuated Americans' sense of duty, concern for troops in the field, and fears of a German invasion. *Images as History: Propaganda Posters* discusses the impact of this anti-German imagery more fully. Propaganda posters whipped up patriotic fervor and hate for the enemy to justify the war and motivate young Americans to fight. To their dismay, Progressive reformers soon realized that the same publicity techniques they had perfected to expose corrupt business practices and spur interest in reform during the Progressive Era (see Chapter 18) could also incite war hysteria. Wartime propaganda ultimately served its purpose. Americans bought nearly $21.4 billion worth of war bonds.

> "When the nation is at war many things that might be said in time of peace … will not be endured so long as men fight."
>
> Supreme Court Justice OLIVER WENDELL HOLMES Jr., upholding the constitutionality of the Espionage Act

German Spies and Civil Liberties

Throughout the period of U.S. neutrality, German spies and saboteurs in the United States tried to disrupt the munitions trade with Britain and France. Spies planted tiny egg-shaped bombs on ships carrying munitions and detonated dynamite in munitions factories. The most spectacular prewar strike by German saboteurs occurred at Black Tom, a munitions depot in Jersey City, New Jersey, along the Hudson River. Citizens as far away as Philadelphia heard the huge explosions on the morning of July 30, 1916. Shrapnel from the blast left holes in the Statue of Liberty, and shock waves shattered thousands of windows in lower Manhattan. Anxious to keep the country neutral, the government labeled each incident an accident despite evidence of sabotage.

Once the country entered the war, government propaganda urged the public to stay alert for "spies and lies" and report "the man who spreads pessimistic stories, divulges—or seeks—confidential military information, cries for peace, or belittles our efforts to win the war." The 1917 **Espionage Act** made it a crime to obstruct military recruitment, to encourage mutiny, or to aid the enemy by spreading lies. These prohibitions had a chilling effect on speech. The **Sedition Act**, passed in 1918, prohibited anyone from uttering, writing, or publishing "any abusive or disloyal language" concerning the flag, constitution, government, or armed forces. Civil liberties and antiwar advocates challenged both laws, but the Supreme Court upheld the acts as constitutional. Upholding the Espionage Act in 1919, the Court established a "clear and present danger" test that limited the right of free speech during wartime. Words used "to create a clear and present danger that…will bring about the substantive evils that Congress has a right to prevent" were not protected under the First Amendment, according to the majority opinion by Justice Oliver Wendell Holmes, Jr.

What limitations did the government put on free speech during the war?

▶ **Read** the **Document** Newton D. Baker, "The Treatment of German Americans" (1918)

Images as History
PROPAGANDA POSTERS

In his war address Wilson told the American people that "we have no quarrel with the German people." But he also privately predicted that "a nation couldn't put its strength into a war and keep its head level; it had never been done." The government soon plastered the country with propaganda posters that relied on negative images of Germany and Germans to rally support for the war.

Teaching Americans to despise anything German had negative consequences on the home front, where German Americans went from being one of the most respected immigrant groups to one of the most hated. Wartime propaganda also questioned the patriotism and masculinity of men who refused to serve. What made these wartime posters effective propaganda?

This 1917 army recruiting poster depicts the Germans as savage beasts who raped, pillaged, and killed.

The gorilla carries the club of culture, alerting Americans to reject the contamination of German culture. Nearly half of the states banned or restricted teaching German, and Americans renamed the hamburger a "liberty sandwich."

The image of Germany threatening the American coastline reminded viewers that German U-boats patrolled the Atlantic coast looking for troop and merchant ships to sink.

In 1939, Adolf Hitler rallied German opinion against the former Allied nations by reprinting this poster with the caption: "When they assaulted us 25 years ago, they wrote on their rotten slanderous poster: 'Destroy this mad beast'—they meant the German people!"

Europe lies in ruins behind the gorilla-like German soldier who carries his limp female victim, a ravaged Lady Liberty, as he makes his way to American soil.

The poster shows a fearful man hiding shamefully in the dark with his back turned against the bright, vibrant scene of virile men marching proudly under a large flag.

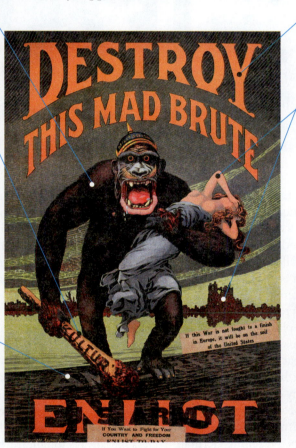

"Destroy this Mad Brute"

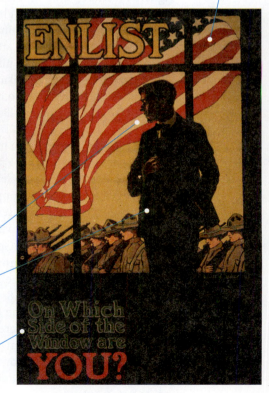

"On Which Side of the Window Are You?"

This man's wistful look implies that he will regret his decision to stand apart from his countrymen.

This loner is a man of privilege, reflecting concerns about the emasculating effect of urban life on middle- and upper-class American men.

Cities held "slacker raids" where policemen stormed into movie theaters and arrested those who could not produce a draft registration card.

View the **Closer Look** *Images as History: Propaganda Posters*

How did visual depictions of the Germans compare to images of the Spanish during the Spanish-American War?

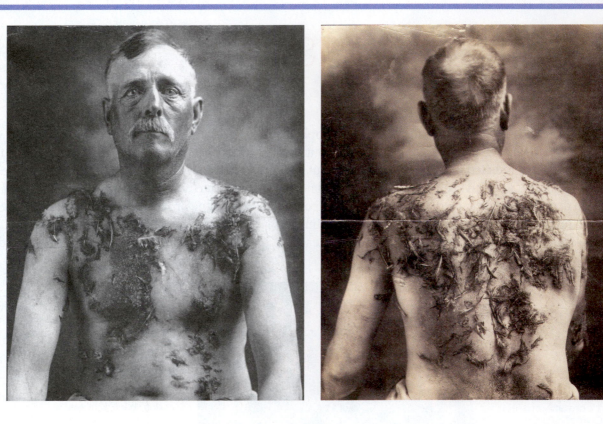

20.10 Tarring and Feathering a German American, 1918 German-American farmer John Meints from Luverne, Minnesota sued the members of the mob that tarred and feathered him, and they eventually paid him $6,000 in 1922 to settle the case.

Some Americans took matters into their own hands, attacking German Americans and their businesses. In the war's most infamous incident of vigilante justice, a mob murdered Robert Prager in Collinsville, Illinois, after he challenged the local mining union for expelling him because of his German descent. When the first attempt to hang Prager failed, the assailants granted his request to write a letter, expecting him to detail a plot to dynamite a mine. Instead Prager wrote to his mother and father who still lived in Germany. "Dear parents," he wrote in German, "I must on this fourth day of April, 1918, die. Please pray for me, my dear parents." The murder went unpunished. To protect themselves from similar assaults, many German American families changed their names, stopped teaching German to their children, and purchased war bonds.

Germans Americans occasionally fought back. Responding to rumors that German-American farmer John Meints would not buy war bonds, 75 of his Luverne, Minnesota neighbors abducted him one summer evening in 1918. Driving Meints to the South Dakota border, the mob beat, whipped, and finally tarred and feathered him. Ignoring warnings to leave the state forever, a defiant Meints sued his assailants for $100,000 in 1919. He used these photos as evidence of the assault (**20.10**). After the presiding judge told the jury

"that the evidence was overwhelming in support of the contention that Meintz [sic] was disloyal," the jury acquitted the defendants (even though they admitted taking part in the attack). Meints appealed, and won a new trial in 1921. Rather than risk public censure now that the war was over, his assailants paid him an out-of-court settlement of $6,000 in 1922.

Besides routing out suspected spies, the Espionage and Sedition Acts also helped the federal government suppress pacifists who refused to give up opposing the war and radical political groups like the Socialist Party and Industrial Workers of the World that had long opposed capitalism. "The master class has always declared the wars; the subject class has always fought the battles," declared Eugene Debs, the leader of the Socialist Party. During the debate over declaring war, before passage of the Espionage Act, members of Congress had uttered similar denunciations of the rich and powerful. But as punishment for uttering these words in 1918, a federal judge sentenced Debs to ten years in prison. Debs became a hero in some quarters for his steadfast opposition to the war. In 1920, two years after the war ended, Debs made his fifth and final bid for the presidency from his jail cell and received one million votes. President Warren Harding pardoned him in 1921.

Fighting the War

Germany had good reason to assume that it would take time for the United States to pose a threat on the Western Front. The country confronted significant challenges raising and training an army quickly. In 1917, the American armed forces numbered just over 300,000. Over the next 19 months, however, the military grew to more than four million and arrived overseas in time to prevent a German victory.

Raising an Army

When the nation entered the war, the government faced the choice of raising its armed forces with volunteers, instituting conscription immediately, or waiting until enlistments began to flag before turning to a draft. In previous wars the government had selected the third option. Wilson, however, chose to implement conscription immediately. He knew that the United States needed to supply the Allies with troops, munitions, and food. The draft gave the government the power to decide who worked in essential wartime industries and who went into the army. Letting individuals decide might deprive industry of its best workers or leave the military understrength once the initial enthusiasm for enlisting subsided. To combat the impression that conscription forced reluctant men to fight, the government renamed the draft "selective service." Selective service, the government repeatedly told the American public, placed men where they could best serve the war effort.

To offer the public a visible demonstration of male patriotism, all men registered publicly for selective service on the same day. On June 5, 1917, ship horns, church bells, and factory whistles rang out, and crowds gathered to cheer for men filling out their draft registration cards. Three million men, or 11 percent of the draft-eligible population, refused either to register or serve. Some went to jail; others eluded authorities by changing jobs often. The Selective Service Act allowed conscientious objectors from recognized pacifist religious sects like the Quakers to apply for noncombatant duty. Those who opposed fighting for philosophical or political reasons had no legal way to stay out of fighting units. The most famous conscientious objector of the war was Sergeant Alvin C. York who, like 80 percent of drafted conscientious objectors, eventually agreed to fight. *Choices and Consequences: Alvin C. York, Deciding to Serve* (page 610) explores York's decision to serve in the army. Conscripts ultimately accounted for 72 percent of the four million men in the wartime army. Overall, 20 percent of draft-eligible males (ages 18–45) served in the wartime military, 15 percent of the total adult male population.

"You're in the Army Now"

In makeshift training camps across the country, soldiers trained (sometimes with wooden rifles) and spoke eagerly of getting to France before the "big show" ended. The army reflected the diversity of the American population. Approximately 18 percent of the entire force, or one in five, were foreign-born. Nearly 12,000 Native Americans served, composing only a small fraction of the total military force, but representing nearly 25 percent of the Native American male population. Sixteen thousand women went overseas as nurses, telephone operators, or welfare workers working in army canteens.

African Americans made up 13 percent of the military, though they were only 10 percent of the country's population. The army remained strictly segregated. Black soldiers received few chances to demonstrate bravery or leadership, since 89 percent served as labor troops under mostly white officers. Although they received little recognition from white authorities, these troops built the roads and bridges required to keep a modern army in the field. In France many black troops discovered a more racially tolerant environment where white French had no qualms socializing with African American soldiers. "You now know that the mean contemptible spirit of race prejudice that curses this land is not the spirit of other lands," noted the African American minister Francis J. Grimké to a group of returning black soldiers. The fear that black servicemen intended to bring the fight for democracy home provoked postwar riots and lynchings that often targeted black veterans in uniform. Determined to fight back against white supremacists, black veterans helped forge a more militant postwar civil rights movement (see Chapter 21).

Choices and Consequences

ALVIN C. YORK, DECIDING TO SERVE

Alvin C. York grew up poor in the Tennessee Appalachian Mountains, where he became an expert marksman hunting wild turkeys in the forests. He spent his youth carousing, gambling, and drinking. As an adult he underwent a religious conversion and joined the Church of Christ in Christian Union, a pacifist Christian sect. Drafted six months before his thirtieth birthday, York faced an agonizing decision on whether to fight. "I believed in my Bible," he said. "And it distinctly said, 'THOU SHALT NOT KILL.'" But, York acknowledged, "I wanted to be a good Christian and a good American too."

Choices

| 1 Request noncombatant duty as a conscientious objector. | 2 Refuse to perform any military duty. | 3 Agree to serve and fight. |

Decision

Like many men claiming conscientious objector status, York faced intense pressure to fight once he entered a training camp. After conversations about the Bible with his commanding officers, York decided that the biblical injunction "Blessed are the peacemakers" overrode the Sixth Commandment prohibiting killing because the war promised to be "the war to end all wars." York agreed to fight.

Consequences

York became the most celebrated American hero of the war for his feats on the battlefield in France. On October 8, 1918, York was credited with killing 24 Germans, silencing 35 machine guns, and capturing 132 enemy soldiers during the Meuse-Argonne offensive. Surviving combat without a scratch reaffirmed York's faith in God, but on his deathbed he still wondered whether God would punish him for killing men in battle.

Continuing Controversies

What is the ultimate meaning of York's experience? Some historians note that York's transformation from pacifist to warrior demonstrated that Wilsonian ideals inspired many Americans to fight in World War I. With Americans divided in 1941 (before the Japanese attacked the American naval base at Pearl Harbor, Hawaii) over the merits of entering World War II, the Hollywood film *Sergeant York* sent the message that fighting to defend the country was a citizen's Christian and patriotic duty. Others note that York personified the poorly educated and underprivileged conscript who did the bulk of the fighting along the Western Front. Some believe that the army exaggerated York's feats to boost morale. Rather than a cause for celebration, his experience reveals the difficulty of becoming a conscientious objector during the war—an experience repeated in future conflicts, especially the Vietnam War.

Sergeant Alvin C. York, with his mother in front of his home in Tennessee

To help the army turn this polyglot force into a functioning military force, civilian psychologists administered intelligence tests to soldiers in the training camps. Quickly assessing a recruit's intelligence could help the army immediately identify whether a man was officer material or better suited for unloading boxes of supplies off ships in France. To the psychologists' surprise, 25 percent of the soldiers had to take the test designed for illiterates. Most native-born white soldiers had completed only seven years of school. Foreign-born men averaged 4.7 years and Southern black men 2.6 years of schooling.

Psychologists claimed their exams measured native intelligence, but the questions suggest the tests primarily assessed level of education, economic background, and familiarity with mainstream American culture (**20.11**). Tabulated results claimed that the white American soldiers had a mental age of 13, while the average for Russians was 11.34, for Italians 11.01, for Poles 10.74, and for American-born blacks 10.41. Critics argued that the tests only showed that immigrants and blacks needed more comprehensive schooling. Social Darwinists, who used Charles Darwin's ideas of survival of the fittest to establish a hierarchy of superior and inferior human races, believed these figures validated their ideas about white northern European superiority. After the war public schools began administering intelligence tests to determine the aptitude of their pupils, a trend that continues today.

On the Western Front

The United States entered the war at a critical moment. The peace with Russia gave Germany a clear numerical advantage on the battlefield. As U-boats began sinking Allied shipping indiscriminately, the Germans transferred over one million men from the Eastern Front with Russia to the Western Front in France. In March 1918, the Germans accomplished what many had thought impossible: They broke through the trench stalemate and began marching once again toward Paris.

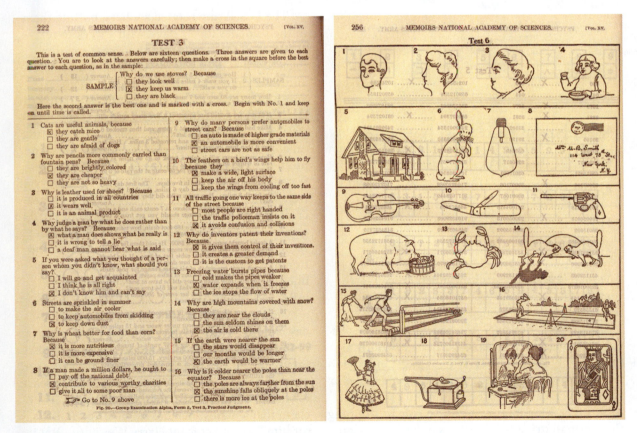

20.11 Intelligence Tests for Soldiers
These questions come from an intelligence test on logic given to literate soldiers in training camps. The pictorial exam for illiterates and non-English speakers required that soldiers draw in the missing item.

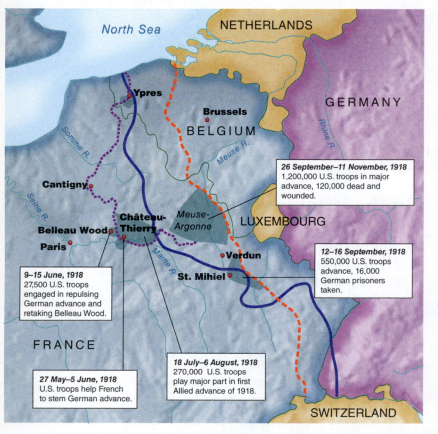

20.12 **American Expeditionary Forces, 1918**
U.S. troops fought hard for six months along the Western Front, winning key victories at Château-Thierry, St. Mihiel, and during the Meuse-Argonne campaign.

Map labels:
- North Sea
- NETHERLANDS
- GERMANY
- Brussels
- BELGIUM
- Ypres
- Somme R.
- Meuse R.
- Rhine R.
- Cantigny
- Seine R.
- Château-Thierry
- Belleau Wood
- Paris
- Meuse-Argonne
- LUXEMBOURG
- Marne R.
- Verdun
- St. Mihiel
- FRANCE
- SWITZERLAND

Boxes on map:
- **26 September–11 November, 1918** 1,200,000 U.S. troops in major advance, 120,000 dead and wounded.
- **12–16 September, 1918** 550,000 U.S. troops advance, 16,000 German prisoners taken.
- **9–15 June, 1918** 27,500 U.S. troops engaged in repulsing German advance and retaking Belleau Wood.
- **27 May–5 June, 1918** U.S. troops help French to stem German advance.
- **18 July–6 August, 1918** 270,000 U.S. troops play major part in first Allied advance of 1918.

Legend:
- Western Front, March 1918
- German offensive, spring 1918
- Armistice line, November 11, 1918
- U.S. military activity

> ## "I hope that you have not arrived too late."
>
> The American ambassador to General JOHN J. PERSHING upon his arrival in France

The map (**20.12**) reveals how much French territory the Germans captured during their spring offensives against the British and French.

As in 1914, however, the pace of the offensive exhausted German troops, who quickly outran their supply lines. The arriving American Expeditionary Forces (AEF), the American soldiers who fought overseas under the command of General John J. Pershing, played a critical role in stopping the German drive toward Paris in battles at Cantigny, Belleau Wood, and Château-Thierry. In July American soldiers fought with the French in a six-week counteroffensive that pushed the German army back to where it had begun the spring offensives. These campaigns initiated American soldiers to the reality of fighting along the Western Front. Men collapsed from the strain of continuous artillery bombardments and the sight of bodies blown to bits. Soldiers diagnosed with shell shock suffered from panic attacks, and some could not sleep or speak. Private Duncan Kemerer arrived at a military hospital in such poor condition that the sound of a spoon dropping sent him frantically searching for cover under his bed.

American soldiers soon settled into the predictable routine of trench warfare. The three-dimensional trench shown in the feature *Envisioning Evidence: Understanding the Battle-field* portrays the components of a working trench. A strip of territory known as No-Man's Land separated the Allied and German trench systems. The actual distance between the two lines averaged 250 yards. Scores of barbed wire entanglements covered this barren area, which was filled with huge craters formed by artillery shells.

The U.S. Army rotated soldiers, putting them in the trenches for 21 days, with a week to recuperate in the rear before their next rotation. Each day just before sunrise, the men assembled and went on alert. If dawn passed with no enemy attack, then the men spent the day trying to stay out of sight from snipers and airplanes that strafed troops with machine gun fire. By feasting on corpses rats grew to gigantic proportions and multiplied by the thousands. Troops became infested with lice and fleas. Adding to the misery of trench life, the constant rain in northern France created a thick, gooey mud in which troops had to stand and often sleep. At night, No-Man's Land came alive as small patrols scrambled out of the trenches to repair damaged wire or raid enemy lines for prisoners who might reveal valuable information.

German artillery bombarded the Allied lines, day and night. "To be shelled is the worst thing in the world," noted one American soldier. "It is impossible to adequately imagine it." Troops developed an array of superstitions to try to make sense of who lived and who died in the trenches. "They claim that a man's shell has his name on it, if it's for him," joked Sergeant Harry Weisburg. "But it is the part of a wise man to keep his nose out of the way of another man's shell." By 1918, one of

Envisioning Evidence

UNDERSTANDING THE BATTLEFIELD

The trenches along the Western Front were intricate defense systems that both protected soldiers and added to their misery in the front lines. As a straight line, the trenches ran for 460 miles from the North Sea to Switzerland. The network of trenches, however, encompassed nearly 35,000 miles, disfiguring the Belgian and French countryside. To survive, soldiers had to learn how to negotiate the complex trench network.

WWI airplane.
Aerial photography of enemy trench lines helped commanders plan attacks. By 1918 plane crews also dropped bombs and strafed enemy lines with mounted machine guns.

No Man's Land.
The desolate strip of land that divided opposing trench lines was covered with huge shell craters, corpes, and barbed wire.

Listening post.
Men in this trench sent up warning flares if the enemy attacked.

Support and reserve trenches.
The bulk of troops remained here unless attacking.

Front-line trench.
Men climbed "over the top" when making an attack.

Machine gun pillbox.
Concrete pillboxes protected machine gunners.

Communication trenches.
Messages, supplies, wounded men and replacement troops funneled through these passages.

Sandbags.
Absorbed enemy bullets.

Wooden planks.
Covering the trench floor, these kept soldiers from sinking into the mud.

L-shaped pattern.
This prevented enemy troops from breaking through and firing machine guns straight down the trench.

Long-range artillery.
Placed about 6 miles behind the lines, long-range artillery weakened front-line enemy forces before an assault and also hampered advancing enemy troops. Exploding artillery shells caused 70 percent of all U.S. casualties.

Dug-outs.
Underground quarters protected troops from artillery shells.

View the **Closer Look** *Envisioning Evidence: Understanding the Battlefield*

What perspective does this diagram offer on the reality of trench warfare?

20.13 Masked Mailman during the 1918 Influenza Epidemic. Wearing protective masks did little to stem the spread of the microscopic influenza virus. Quarantining the sick at home or in hospitals proved more effective.

20.14 Anti-Spitting Campaign, 1918. Trying to stem the influenza epidemic, employers cooperated with public health officials by posting reminders that spitting spread germs.

every four shells fired on the Western Front contained poison gas. Troops especially feared mustard gas, which caused painful burns on exposed skin and was deadly if inhaled. Slow-moving tanks also made their first appearance on the battlefield, but the war ended before either side could exploit their full offensive potential.

Flu Epidemic

In 1918, in the midst of mounting battlefield casualties, the world suddenly encountered a new vicious killer. Without warning, a lethal strain of influenza traversed the globe. The virus became known as **Spanish Influenza** because the Spanish press first reported its outbreak. Biologists speculate that the influenza germ began as a mutated version of avian (bird) flu in the American Midwest in March 1918. American soldiers carried the germ to France, and the virus spread rapidly from Europe to Africa, Asia, and Central America. Nearly 25 million Americans fell ill, a quarter of the entire population, and 675,000 died. The virus also sickened over one million American soldiers, hampering the overseas military campaign. General Pershing, Assistant Secretary of the Navy Franklin D. Roosevelt, and

President Wilson all suffered from the flu, but survived.

Anecdotes of people who went to work healthy in the morning, only to die before dinnertime, illustrated how suddenly the lethal virus could strike. Influenza was usually most severe for children and the elderly, segments of the population with weak immune systems. This flu virus, however, attacked young adults especially hard—making it particularly terrifying.

When the flu struck, victims first felt pain in their muscles. Within hours high fevers made them delirious. Most victims recovered after weeks of bed rest, but 25 percent developed influenza-related pneumonia. Already weakened, half of these patients suffocated to death when their lungs filled with fluid, turning healthy pink tissue into blue sodden masses almost overnight.

Influenza was an airborne virus that could easily penetrate masks or screens, but scientists did not identify disease-causing viruses until the 1940s. Instead, medical experts incorrectly believed that droplets spread the disease, reasoning that sneezes, coughs, or touching contaminated objects transmitted flu germs from person to person. Physicians consequently devised useless precautionary measures to prevent transmission, such as spraying public areas with a topical disinfectant. Public officials closed movie houses, schools, churches, and office buildings in an effort to contain the epidemic. Masked mailmen (**20.13**) and police became familiar sights on city streets, and masked conductors refused to let unmasked passengers board streetcars. Posters, like this one in a naval aircraft factory in Philadelphia alerted people to the dangers of spitting (**20.14**).

In mid-1919, as suddenly as it had come, the virus disappeared, having run out of susceptible human beings to infect. The Spanish Influenza pandemic had a catastrophic effect worldwide. From 1918 to 1919, the disease killed 30 million people. Nine million men died in battle from 1914–1918. The bloodiest war to date thus coincided with the deadliest influenza epidemic yet recorded.

Spanish Influenza has endangered the prosecution of the WAR in Europe. There are 1500 cases in the Navy Yard 30 deaths have already resulted SPITTING SPREADS SPANISH INFLUENZA DONT SPIT

What impact did the flu epidemic have at home and worldwide?

View the **Image** *Warning of Influenza Epidemic (1918)*

The Final Campaigns

In September 1918, the AEF attacked at St. Mihiel (see 20.12). The battle reduced a bulge in the lines (called a "salient"), thereby weakening German defenses. Two weeks later, the Allies began a massive coordinated assault along the entire Western Front. The Americans hit the Germans hard in the Meuse-Argonne region, while the British and French struck farther north and west. Advancing in heavily wooded and hilly terrain against dense German fortifications, the American effort stalled. Regrouping, the Americans began pushing the Germans back in October. Battle casualties averaged 2,550 a day, with 6,000 Americans dying each week of the 47-day Meuse-Argonne offensive, making it the most costly battle in U.S. history. "It was most assuredly the Americans who bore the heaviest brunt of the fighting on the whole battle front during the last few months of the war," the German General Erich Ludendorff later recalled.

Besides making headway on the battlefield, Allied convoys also stymied the German unrestricted submarine warfare campaign. Instead of letting individual ships take their chances at sea, British and American naval vessels began escorting groups of Allied merchant vessels through U-boat infested waters in convoys. In November, the German government requested an armistice. On the eleventh hour of the eleventh day of the eleventh month of 1918, the Armistice went into effect and guns fell silent along the Western Front.

What overall contribution did American troops make to the final victory? During the victory celebrations, American enthusiasts wildly claimed that the United States had single-handedly won the war. Allied critics contended that the British and French had dealt the final devastating blow on the battlefield. The truth lay somewhere in-between. The Americans may not have won the war for the Allies, but they certainly kept them from losing it. At key moments in the German spring offensives in 1918, American soldiers helped stop the Germans from taking Paris. American divisions provided key strength for the French-led counteroffensives over the summer, and in the Meuse-Argonne campaign, American soldiers leveled a devastating blow to the German army that helped make British and French advances to the north possible. Also important, the prospect of fighting a million more fresh American recruits in 1919 convinced Germany to seek a negotiated peace.

The Allies bore a heavy cost for their victory. The numbers of war dead: France (1.3 million), Britain (722,000), and Germany (1.8 million). By comparison, the 116,516 American deaths seem slight. Other figures tell a different story. In the last six months of the war, the American death rate jumped to 820 a day as U.S. troops experienced their share of brutal fighting, fewer than the 900 Frenchmen, but more than the 457 British, who died each day. The "America at War" chart (**20.15**) suggests yet another way to assess the impact of the war on the United States revealing that more Americans died on the battlefield in World War I than in Korea or Vietnam, both much longer wars.

America at War

Conflict	Total Serving	Battle Deaths	Other Deaths	Wounded
Civil War (1861–1865)				
Union	2,213,363	140,414	224,097	281,881
Confederate	600,000 – 1,500,000	74,524	59,297	—
World War I (1917–1918)	4,734,991	53,402	63,114	204,002
World War II (1941–1945)	16,112,566	291,557	113,842	670,846
Korean War (1950–1953)	5,720,000	33,741	2,833	103,284
Vietnam War (1964–1973)	8,744,000	47,355	10,796	153,303

20.15 Battlefield Deaths, Deaths by Disease, and Wounded
World War I was the shortest major American war in the twentieth century, but the second deadliest.

What role did the United States play in the Allied victory?

Peace

The Armistice ended active fighting in Western Europe, but the peace settlement took months to negotiate. Twenty-seven nations and four British dominions sent delegates to the Paris Peace Conference. Germany expected to join the negotiations, but instead the terms of peace were determined in secret by the Big Four: Wilson, French Premier Georges Clemenceau, the British Prime Minister Lloyd George, and the Italian Premier Vittorio Orlando. The Versailles Peace Treaty (named after the palace outside Paris where the treaty was signed) required Germany to pay reparations and disarm. Germany signed the treaty under protest on June 28, 1919, the fifth anniversary of Archduke Franz Ferdinand's assassination. In the end the flawed and controversial **Versailles Peace Treaty** laid the groundwork for future conflict in Europe and raised questions at home about the role America wanted to play in the world.

The Paris Peace Conference

Woodrow Wilson enjoyed worldwide popularity on Armistice Day. Throughout the United States and Europe, his idealistic pronouncements had raised hopes that the slaughter might pave the way for a lasting peace. Wilson broke with tradition and decided to travel overseas to negotiate the peace treaty himself, rather than sending representatives to hash out the details. As he toured Paris, London, Rome, and Milan, newspapers greeted him as "The Savior of Humanity." British and French leaders, however, knew that four years of suffering had created a deep-seated desire for revenge against Germany within their nations. The war had also hardened Wilson's view of Germany, and he agreed to weaken postwar Germany by eliminating its navy and colonies. He disagreed, however, with the French insistence on eviscerating the German economy and military permanently.

Certain that America had played a vital role in winning the war, Wilson felt confident asserting his right, along with Britain and France, to shape the terms of peace. British and French leaders, however, publicly downplayed America's contribution to defeating Germany, hoping to limit Wilson's say in the peace treaty. At the request of Allied leaders, the British and French press began printing disparaging reports about the American army's inexperience and leadership. Resentful over the Allies' apparent ingratitude for their wartime sacrifices, Americans' postwar disillusionment grew as the treaty-making process got underway.

Wilson's domestic political problems weakened his negotiating position. In November 1918, the Republicans won control of Congress despite Wilson's plea to voters to return a Democratic majority as a vote of confidence for his peace proposals. The reasons for the Republican victory were complex, a result of unease with conditions at home and concern about Wilson's ideals. The Democrats' loss energized opponents of the **League of Nations**, a Wilson-supported collective security organization whose member nations agreed to mediate future international disputes to prevent wars and work together to improve global conditions.

Domestic opponents of the League worried that by joining the international organization America would lose control over its own foreign policy and invite international meddling in the Western Hemisphere. They also doubted that the League could maintain world peace. League critics divided into two camps, each offering conflicting visions of America's role in the postwar world. Isolationists, led by Republican Senator William E. Borah from Idaho, preferred adopting an official policy of neutrality. The isolationists believed that if the United States kept out of all foreign disagreements, the country could avoid going to war in the future. By contrast the faction headed by Massachusetts Senator Henry Cabot Lodge, the Republican majority leader and chairman of the Senate Foreign Affairs Committee, favored a return to the former balance of power system in Europe. Lodge wanted the United States to help rebuild, and perhaps join, a strong alliance among democratic European nations that could contain Germany indefinitely.

Eager to shore up support for the League of Nations at home, Wilson briefly sailed home to confer with Republican leaders who were still upset that he had not invited any leading Republicans to join his negotiating team. The possibility of compromise appeared slim. Lodge detested Wilson, whom he regarded as sanctimonious. Wilson returned the distain, viewing Lodge as narrow-minded. Discussion soon stalled. On the day before Wilson returned to Paris, Lodge handed the president a pledge signed by 39 senators who vowed to reject the League covenant in its present form.

Hoping to appease his Republican critics, Wilson managed to incorporate key Republican demands in the final League covenant. The covenant now stated that the League of Nations would respect the Monroe Doctrine, the 1823 American pronouncement that the Western Hemisphere was off-limits to other world powers, and allow nations to withdraw from the League. Wilson also tried outmaneuvering his domestic critics. He opted against creating two international agreements, a peace treaty and a covenant creating the League of Nations that would each require a separate Senate ratification. Instead Wilson decided to incorporate the League covenant into the peace treaty. The Senate he gambled, would never refuse to ratify the peace treaty, even one that contained a controversial League of Nations.

> ## "With his mouth open and his eyes shut, I predict that he will make a Senator when he grows up."
> WILSON'S joke about his infant grandson touched upon his political troubles with Republican Senators

Allied leaders also pressured Wilson to compromise. To get them to accept the League, Wilson gave up his idea of peace without victory. When Supreme Commander of Allied Armies Marshal Ferdinand Foch read the harsh demands of the Peace Treaty, he accurately predicted, "this isn't a peace, it's a twenty year truce." The treaty required that Germany pay reparations to French and Belgian civilians for the mines, factories, and fields its troops had destroyed during "the war imposed upon them by the aggression of Germany." This war guilt clause held Germany alone responsible for starting World War I. The treaty also forced Germany to

disarm. The Reparations Committee set Germany's initial bill at $33 billion in gold, although commissions in the 1920s significantly reduced this amount. The United States accepted no reparation payments and in the 1920s even loaned Germany money to help it pay this debt. The war guilt clause and the reparations bill created tremendous resentment in Germany. In the 1930s, Adolf Hitler cultivated this anger to fuel a resurgent national fervor dedicated to restoring German economic and military strength.

Other nations also left the conference feeling slighted. Italy resented the Allies for denying it more Austrian territory along the Adriatic Sea, a humiliation that the fascist leader Benito Mussolini vowed to avenge when he took power in 1922. Japan protested the failure to incorporate into the League covenant a statement protecting the rights of nonwhite nations, helping breed Japanese resentment against the West. In the Middle East, Africa, and Asia, the peace treaty transferred colonial possessions from the losers (the Ottoman and German empires) to the victors—Britain, France, Belgium, and Japan—under a mandate system.

In theory the mandate system named a Western nation as a League of Nation trustee for territories in need of political instruction before they assumed the responsibilities of self-government. In reality the mandate system simply cloaked old-style imperialism in the new rhetoric of self-determination. By redrawing the map of the Middle East to expand their global influence, Britain and France set in motion political, religious, and cultural conflicts in the region that created tremendous strife throughout the twentieth century and beyond. Denying Arab nationalist demands for independence, France took control of Lebanon and Syria. Britain ruled Transjordan (present-day Jordan) and brought together three distinct groups—the Kurds and Sunni and Shiite Arabs—who had previously lived in semi-autonomous regions under the Ottomans to form the Kingdom of Iraq under a puppet monarch. When the British took over Palestine, they kept wartime promises to open up part of it to Jewish immigration, angering its Arab inhabitants. Competing claims to this territory continue to this day.

The Versailles Treaty settled old territorial disputes in Europe, but the dismemberment of the Russian, German, and Austro-Hungarian empires created new sources of tension. The map of Eastern Europe was redrawn to reflect

Areas lost by Russian Empire to Germany 1918, granted independence after World War I

Areas lost by Austro-Hungarian Empire

Areas lost by German Empire

New Nations after World War I
French mandate
British mandate
Areas lost by Ottoman Empire, under League of Nations mandate after 1920

Wilson's principle of self-determination, fulfilling the ambitions of ethnic groups in Czechoslovakia, Poland, Yugoslavia, Finland, Latvia, Lithuania, and Estonia to create their own nations (**20.16**). But the Allies disregarded the desires of German-speaking peoples in Poland, Czechoslovakia, and the new republic of Austria to unite with Germany. These three weak independent states remained vulnerable to German and Soviet expansionist schemes. Twenty years later, Hitler justified his annexations of Austria (1938), and Czechoslovakia (1938–1939), and his joint invasion of Poland with Soviet leader Josef Stalin (1939) as a drive to unite parts of the German-speaking world separated by the terms of the Versailles Treaty (see Chapter 23).

The Treaty Fight at Home

Wilson saw the flaws in the final treaty, but he hoped that over time the League of Nations could modify the treaty's worst excesses. To counter the initial burst of enthusiasm for joining the League, Republicans challenged Wilson's idealistic pronouncements promising world peace. "Are you ready to put your soldiers and your sailors at the disposition of other nations?" Senator Lodge asked the American people. The political cartoon *Looking*

20.16 Europe and the Middle East after the War.
The victorious Allies dismantled the German, Austro-Hungarian, and Ottoman empires to create independent nations in Central Europe and colonies for themselves in the Middle East.

What significance did the re-drawn maps of Europe and the Middle East have?

View the Image *Blowing Bubbles (1919)*

a Gift Horse in the Mouth (**20.17**) captured the public's mounting concern about the League. While Wilson tries to assure Uncle Sam that the League is better than nothing, the Senate carefully examines the mule. Wary of going against public opinion too strongly, Lodge did not urge outright rejection of the Versailles Treaty. He instead proposed adding 14 American reservations. The most important one required explicit Congressional approval before American troops went overseas. Wilson refused to accept modifications. Instead he tried to create a groundswell of support for the League that would force the Republicans to accept the treaty as written.

To reignite public enthusiasm for the League of Nations, the president traveled 10,000 miles in three weeks by train and made 40 speeches to hundreds of thousands of people. The political cartoon *Ratification Rapids* (**20.18**) offered a sympathetic portrayal of Wilson, shown here using all his strength to steer the treaty and League

Covenant to safety. In the cartoon a young woman clutches both documents to her breast, symbolizing both the besieged nation and innocent victims of war. Wilson dismissed Republican concerns about sending American troops throughout the world as impractical. "If you want to put out a fire in Utah, you don't send to Oklahoma for the fire engine. If you want to put out a fire in the Balkans, if you want to stamp out the smoldering flames in some part of Central Europe, you don't send to the United States for troops," Wilson told an audience in Salt Lake City. *Competing Visions: Joining the League of Nations* (page 620) explores the debate between Wilson and Lodge.

Pushing himself to the limit, an exhausted Wilson paid the price. On September 25, 1919, hours after he reminded a Pueblo, Colorado, audience that American soldiers had died to protect "the liberty of the world," the president fell ill. His physician rushed a twitching and nauseous Wilson

20.17 *Looking a Gift Horse in the Mouth*
This political cartoon expresses skepticism about the League of Nations. By taking a closer look, the Senate realizes that the League (represented here as a broken-down mule) is not strong enough to handle the hard work of keeping the peace.

20.18 *Ratification Rapids*
This sympathetic portrait of Woodrow Wilson trying to steer the Versailles Treaty through the ratification process illustrates how contentious the treaty debate became.

What competing views do these political cartoons offer on the question of ratifying the Versailles Treaty?

Competing Visions
JOINING THE LEAGUE OF NATIONS

In 1919, President Woodrow Wilson and Republican Senator Henry Cabot Lodge debated the wisdom and value of joining the League of Nations. Consider the exact wording of Article X, and then the differing interpretations of it offered by Lodge and Wilson. What changes in American foreign policy does each foresee arising from the League? Are there any points of agreement between the two about the future world role of the United States?

Article X of the League Covenant ignited tremendous controversy over whether the United States should join the League of Nations.

The Members of the League undertake to respect and preserve as against external aggression the territorial integrity and existing political independence of all the members of the League. In case of any such aggression or in case of any threat or danger of such aggression the Council shall advise upon the means by which this obligation shall be fulfilled.

Lodge contended that the League Covenant stripped Congress of its power to declare war in this August 12, 1919, congressional address.

We should never permit the United States to be involved in the internal conflict in another country, except by the will of her people expressed through the Congress which represents them.

With regard to wars of external aggression on a member of the league, the case is perfectly clear. There can be no genuine dispute whatever about the meaning of the first clause of article 10. In the first place, it differs from every other obligation in being individual and placed upon each nation without the intervention of the league. Each nation for itself promises to respect and preserve as against external aggression the boundaries and the political independence of every member of the league. … It is, I repeat, an individual obligation. It requires no action on the part of the league, except that in the second sentence the authorities of the league are to have the power to advise as to the means to be employed in order to fulfill the purpose of the first sentence. …

We may set aside all this empty talk about isolation. Nobody expects to isolate the United States or to make it a hermit Nation, which is a sheer absurdity. But there is a wide difference between taking a suitable part and bearing a due responsibility in world affairs and plunging the United States into every controversy and conflict on the face of the globe.

Wilson defended the League in a speech on September 25, 1919, in Pueblo, Colorado, that recalled the sacrifices of soldiers during the war, bringing many in the audience to tears.

But you will say, "what is the second sentence of article 10? That is what gives very disturbing thoughts." The second sentence is that the Council of the League shall advise what steps, if any, are necessary to carry out the guaranty of the first sentence, namely, that the members will respect and preserve the territorial integrity and political independence of the other members. I do not know of any other meaning for the word "advise" except "advise." The Council advises, and it can not advise without the vote of the United States [as a member of the Council]. … Whether we use it wisely or unwisely, we can use the vote of the United States to make impossible drawing the United States into any enterprise that she does not care to be drawn into…

My friends, on last Decoration Day I went to a beautiful hillside near Paris, where was located the cemetery of Suresnes, a cemetery given over to the burial of the American dead. … I wish some men in public life who are now opposing the settlement for which these men died could visit such a spot as that. I wish that the thought that comes out of those graves could penetrate their consciousness. I wish that they could feel the moral obligation that rests upon us not to go back on those boys, but to see the thing through, to see it through to the end and make good their redemption of the world. For nothing less depends upon this decision, nothing less than the liberation and salvation of the world.

Who has the more compelling argument regarding the League of Nations, Wilson or Lodge?

View the **Closer Look** *Competing Visions: Joining the League of Nations*

back to Washington, D.C., where two days later he suffered a stroke. Permanently paralyzed on his left side, he spent the rest of his presidency hidden in the White House. Wilson, the British Prime Minister Lloyd George remarked, was "as much a victim of the war as any soldier who died in the trenches."

The White House kept the president's illness a secret, issuing a vague statement that he was recovering from exhaustion. For weeks, however, Wilson only spent three hours a day out of bed and saw no one except his physician and his family. His wife, Edith Wilson, controlled all correspondence reaching the president and helped compose his replies. Critics later accused her of serving as a shadow president during Wilson's convalescence, but she maintained that the president made every decision himself. Wilson rejected all private suggestions that he resign and still refused to accept any reservations to the Versailles Treaty.

With Wilson absent from the public stage, opposition to the League of Nations spread. His refusal to compromise doomed the treaty. The Senate rejected both the original treaty and one with Lodge's reservations attached. The Senate therefore never ratified the Versailles Treaty. It also refused to accept Armenia as a mandate, despite Wilson's plea to become the "friends and advisors" of a people ravaged by wartime Turkish massacres and deportations. It took two more years for the war to end officially for the United States. In October, 1921, the Senate finally ratified separate peace treaties with Germany, Austria, and Hungary (the United States had never been at war with the Ottoman Empire or Bulgaria).

Nations that ratified the Versailles Peace Treaty also agreed to join the League, with the exception of Germany, which was not allowed to join until 1926. The League remained headquartered in Geneva, Switzerland, from 1920 until 1946, when the United Nations took its place. Wilson won the Nobel Peace Prize in 1919 for his efforts to establish the League of Nations, but without American membership the League became little more than a place to air grievances. Wilson never regained his health, and he died in February 1924. (Senator Lodge, his unyielding opponent, died just eight months later.)

John Steuart Curry's 1938 painting *Parade to War, Allegory* (**20.19**) captures the growing feeling by the 1930s that U.S. participation in World War I had been a mistake. In the painting uniformed men march off to war, slowly turning into corpses before the cheering crowds. The young boy running alongside them fails to notice this transformation, and instead remains mesmerized by the pageantry and excitement of war. Only the two mothers in the scene (one to the left weeping quietly and the other on the right whom a policeman stops from interfering with the parade) understand the true sorrow that war brings to families and the nation.

20.19 *Parade to War, Allegory*
John Steuart Curry's 1938 painting rejected the Wilsonian idea that war could bring about positive political change, dwelling instead on the lives lost and ruined.

Why did Americans feel disillusioned at the end of World War I?

1914

Archduke Franz Ferdinand assassinated in Sarajevo, Bosnia
Triggers breakdown of European balance of power system

Germany invades Belgium and France
World War I begins; Wilson declares United States neutral

1915

Britain mines the North Sea; German U-Boats patrol British waters
Incites domestic debate over how to stay neutral

German U-Boat sinks *Lusitania*
Wilson asserts rights of neutrals to travel unmolested

1916

Villa raids American bordertowns
U.S. troops sent to Mexico; war narrowly avoided

Germany renounces unrestricted submarine warfare
Wilson wins reelection, promising "peace with honor"

1917

Germany resumes unrestricted submarine warfare; Zimmermann Telegram sent to Mexico
Congress declares war against Germany

Conscription Begins
Creation of nation's first mass, drafted army

CHAPTER REVIEW

Review Questions

1. Was any one nation primarily responsible for starting World War I or did Europe share collective responsibility?

2. How well did the government balance the need to uncover German espionage with protecting civil liberties during the war?

3. How did women and African Americans fare during the war? Which changes were temporary? Which were more permanent?

4. What challenges did soldiers face in the trenches? How was fighting this war different from previous American wars such as the Civil War or Spanish-American War?

5. What concerns did Americans raise about the League of Nations?

Key Terms

Schlieffen Plan A military plan that called for Germany to attack and quickly defeat France while the cumbersome Russian army mobilized.   **596**

Western Front Complex system of trenches and earthworks that ran for 460 miles from the North Sea to Switzerland that pitted Germany against Belgium, France, Britain, and the United States.   **596**

Lusitania British passenger ship sunk by a German U-boat on May 7, 1915, an attack that killed 1,198 passengers, including 128 Americans.   **597**

Zimmermann Telegram German foreign minister Arthur Zimmermann offered to help Mexico recover Texas, New Mexico, and Arizona if Mexico would start a borderland war with the United States and ask Japan to join them.   **600**

Fourteen Points Speech by Woodrow Wilson to Congress on January 8, 1918, that outlined a postwar world dominated by democracy, free trade, disarmament, self-determination, resolved territorial disputes in Europe, and a league of nations to mediate future international crises.   **601**

Nineteenth Amendment Constitutional amendment that granted women the right to vote; it was ratified August 26, 1920.   **605**

Committee on Public Information Government agency that controlled the flow of information and shaped public opinion about the war with posters, Four-Minute Men, pamphlets, and films.   **605**

Espionage Act (1917) Legislation that made it a crime to obstruct military recruitment, to encourage mutiny, or to aid the enemy by spreading lies.   **606**

Sedition Act (1918) Legislation that went even further than the Espionage Act by prohibiting anyone from uttering, writing, or publishing "any abusive or disloyal language" concerning the flag, constitution, government, or armed forces.   **606**

Spanish Influenza A lethal flu virus that killed millions worldwide in 1918.   **614**

Versailles Peace Treaty The controversial treaty that ended World War I by requiring Germany to pay reparations and disarm.   **616**

League of Nations An international collective security organization composed of member nations where member nations agreed to mediate future international disputes to prevent wars and work together to improve global human conditions.   **616**

1917

Congress passes Espionage Act
Dilutes civil liberties and freedom of speech

Race riot in East St. Louis, Illinois
Racial animosities intensify as Southern blacks migrate north

1918

Wilson gives Fourteen Points speech
Establishes democracy, free trade, and collective security as key postwar goals

Peak of influenza pandemic
Deadly flu virus kills 675,000 Americans; 30 million worldwide

1918

Wilson supports female suffrage
Ends picketing outside White House by suffragists

Armistice between Allies and Germany
Germany capitulates before Allies cross into Germany

1919

Germany signs the Versailles Treaty
Punitive terms create resentments Hitler will later exploit to rise to power

Senate rejects the Versailles Treaty
Ends strident debate on the merits of joining the League of Nations

MyHistoryLab Connections

Visit www.myhistorylab.com for a customized Study Plan that will help you build your knowledge of *The Great War.*

Questions for Analysis

1. How did the *Lusitania* crisis shape U.S. foreign policy?

View the **Closer Look** *Choices and Consequences: Defining Neutrality: America's Path into World War I, p. 598*

2. Did the United States overreact to the Zimmermann Telegram?

Read the **Document** *The Zimmermann Telegram, p. 600*

3. What vision of peace did Wilson outline in the Fourteen Points?

Read the **Document** *Woodrow Wilson's Fourteen Points, p. 601*

4. What does this poster reveal about America's reaction to the influenza epidemic?

View the **Image** *Warning of Influenza Epidemic (1918), p. 614*

5. What critique does this cartoon offer of the League of Nations?

View the **Image** *Blowing Bubbles (1919), p. 618*

Other Resources from This Chapter

Hear the **Audio**
- *"The Speech That Sent Debs to Jail", p. 608*
- *Over There, p. 609*

Read the **Document**
- *The Struggle for Women's Suffrage, p. 605*
- *Newton D. Baker, "The Treatment of German Americans" (1918), p. 606*

View the **Closer Look**
- *Images as History: Propaganda Posters, p. 607*
- *Envisioning Evidence: Understanding the Battlefield, p. 613*
- *Competing Visions: Joining the League of Nations, p. 620*

View the **Image** *Soldiers Taking an IQ Test during WWI, p. 611*

View the **Map** *Atlas Map: African American Migration, p. 603*

Watch the **Video**
- *Video Lecture: The Outbreak of World War I, p. 594*
- *Video Lecture: American Entry into World War I, p. 599*

A Turbulent Decade

The Twenties

On a cold December afternoon in 1926, two young women posed for the camera as they danced on the ledge of a Chicago hotel. With their short skirts, bobbed hair, and heel-kicking dance steps, they displayed a carefree lifestyle that defied the stricter morals embraced by their mothers' generation. The pair embodied the high spirits of a generation ready to put the tragedy of World War I behind them and move forward into the modern era. Novelists and journalists referred to these women as flappers, an old slang term for young girls. Now it was used to describe independent young women who smoked, drank, danced to jazz, and flaunted their sexual liberation by wearing revealing clothes. Rebellious postwar writers made flappers a cultural icon. Their youthful exuberance and daring behavior excited some Americans and created a sense of moral outrage in others.

The flapper controversy was one of many cultural conflicts that turned political in the turbulent twenties. Flappers and the equally controversial birth control movement championed the right of women to take control of their bodies. Other Americans preferred using the government to control behavior. Prohibition of the manufacture and sale of alcoholic liquors became the law of the land in 1920, promising to rid the nation of poverty, crime, and disease. To prevent the communist-inspired Russian Revolution of 1917 from spreading to the United States, the government arrested suspected political radicals and drastically reduced the flow of European immigration. Meanwhile religious fundamentalists argued that the country was morally adrift and launched a well-publicized crusade against teaching evolution in public schools. African Americans, too, played an important role in changing America's cultural landscape, creating new artistic centers and political movements that challenged the methods of established civil rights leaders.

Putting the Progressive Era faith in trust-busting aside, the government allowed large industrial conglomerates to dominate key industrial sectors, such as steel and automobiles. Still staunchly antiunion, some factory owners nonetheless became more responsive to workers' grievances to reduce labor strife. Mass production, accompanied by mass consumption, spurred the decade's economic prosperity. Cars, suburbs, and asphalt highways soon dotted the American horizon, changing the living habits of millions.

In the twenties domestic cultural conflict dominated political discourse, yet a distinct foreign policy also took shape. Despite its refusal to join the League of Nations, the country remained active in world affairs. By exerting rising international influence through diplomacy and foreign aid, Republican presidential administrations offered an alternative way to maintain world peace.

How much of the old order would America jettison or protect as it entered the postwar age? Throughout the twenties Americans held competing visions of what modernity had to offer.

"Was every decent standard being overthrown?" Journalist FREDERICK LEWIS ALLEN, commenting on youthful rebellion in the twenties

Cars and Planes:
The Promise of the Twenties

During the twenties America became a car culture. Car registration jumped from 9.2 million in 1920 to 26.5 million ten years later. By 1927, 80 percent of the world's cars were in the United States. Conflicting ideas soon emerged, however, over how much car-based commerce should transform the American landscape and whether all Americans could be trusted with the new freedom their cars bestowed. The push to produce cars and other consumer goods more efficiently caused industrialists to change how they treated their workforce. Competing visions of industrial work culture between industrialists and workers emerged alongside ongoing clashes over wages and hours. Could man and machine coexist harmoniously?

The Car Culture

At the turn of the century, cities were smelly, dirty places. In New York City alone, horses dumped 2.5 million tons of manure and 60,000 gallons of urine on streets yearly. The car seemed to offer a clean, flexible solution to city transportation problems. Paving the streets with asphalt would remove the dust that often forced dwellers to keep their windows shut. No one foresaw that a fleet of privately owned cars would soon clog city streets, or that their exhaust would become a public health hazard.

Although initial expectations focused on the improvements that cars would make in cities, farmers also benefited from the new technology. Tractors made plowing easier, while trucks transported produce more quickly to market. Whole families piled into cars on Saturday morning to head into town, ending the isolation that had characterized farm life.

21.1 Cottage Gas Station
Many businessmen built gas stations that looked like country cottages to assure passing motorists that their establishments were safe and clean.

A car represented a significant purchase for a family. Cars cost between 20 and 45 percent of a non-farm family's annual income, and between 50 and 100 percent of a farm household's yearly earnings. Credit plans required that purchasers pay one-third in cash as a down payment and spread the remaining payments over one year. Most plans also came with hefty interest rates averaging around 16 percent.

Besides enriching automobile manufacturers, the explosion in car ownership meant boom times for numerous other industries. To satisfy the unquenchable thirst for gasoline, the petroleum industry underwent a major expansion with new oil wells appearing daily in Texas and California. The building trades saw their business take off, when millions took advantage of the mobility that cars afforded and moved to the suburbs. An acute need soon developed for tunnels and bridges to link cities by car to ever-dispersed commuter suburbs. In 1927, the Holland Tunnel, the nation's first underwater motor vehicle tunnel, opened between New York City and New Jersey. On its first day of operation, nearly 50,000 people paid 50 cents to drive through the tunnel that ran under the Hudson River.

On the Road

The ease of car travel encouraged many Americans to take vacations away from home for the first time, and to satisfy their wanderlust, the public demanded good roads through rural areas. The government responded with a massive

How did cars transform urban and rural lifestyles?

Watch the **Video** *Video Lecture: The Rise and Fall of the Automotive Industry*

road-building and paving program. Following the precedents set in the nineteenth century when the federal government had funded canal construction and given railroad companies huge land grants to build railroads (see Chapter 15), the federal government now helped states build a new national highway system.

Car travelers also needed food, lodging, and gas. To entice tourists to stop at their establishments, rural businessmen erected eye-catching signs and buildings. A revolution in commercial roadside architecture was soon underway. Small clusters of cottages where tourists could spend the night on long road trips, forerunners of today's motels, appeared in remote areas. The miniature house (**21.1**) emerged as the most popular type of commercial roadside building in the twenties, a way to assure the passersby that the restaurant, store, or gas station was a safe and respectable establishment.

Other retailers used surreal images to entice motorists to stop. An array of giant milk bottles, toads, and hot dogs soon lined the highways of America. The Teapot Dome Service Station (**21.2**), built in 1922 along a highway in Zillah, Washington, humorously reminded patrons of the Teapot Dome political scandal that rocked the Harding

White House in the early twenties. The Republicans had selected Warren Harding, an unassuming senator from Ohio, as their 1920 presidential candidate because his easygoing nature and call for "a return to normalcy" presented the electorate with a welcome respite from Democrat Woodrow Wilson's stern wartime leadership. Winning 60 percent of the popular vote, Harding easily defeated Democrat James Cox, who suffered when he stood by Wilson and his failed League of Nations crusade (see Chapter 20). Harding's two years in office (he died of a heart attack in 1923, making his vice president Calvin Coolidge president) were, however, tarnished by scandal. The largest scandal involved Secretary of the Interior Albert B. Fall, who went to jail for accepting bribes from two wealthy businessmen to lease government-controlled oil reserves in Teapot Dome, Wyoming. The enterprising owner of this service station gave his customers a laugh at the president's expense by selling oil and gasoline in a teapot-shaped gas station.

Cars also transformed recreational habits. Ministers complained that instead of spending Sundays in church,

21.2 Teapot Dome Gas Station, Zillah, Washington Roadside architecture in the twenties often included whimsical structures designed to entice passing motorists to stop. This gas station shaped like a teapot made a joke of the Teapot Dome scandal.

What messages did the architecture of roadside gas stations convey?

many families chose to take all-day drives. Cars let teenagers take their courting out of the family parlor and into the backseat of the family automobile, to the dismay of parents everywhere. "The best way to keep children home is to make the home atmosphere pleasant—and let air out of the tires," quipped author Dorothy Parker. Automobiles also made it harder for town officials to regulate red-light districts, causing one judge to declare that "the automobile has become a house of prostitution on wheels."

Welfare Capitalism and Consumer Culture

During World War I the government had mandated that industrialists with wartime contracts pay high wages, provide clean and safe working conditions, and allow unions to organize within their factories (see Chapter 20). In return for this official protection, the government demanded a no-strike pledge from unions. When the war ended in 1918, the government abruptly canceled its orders and withdrew from managing worker-industrial relations. The government's hands-off attitude emboldened many industrialists to reinstate low wages, long hours, and blacklists for union members. To protect their war-time gains, unions orchestrated the greatest wave of strikes in American history in 1919. Although they rallied millions of workers to the picket lines, out-matched unions lost this battle.

Industrialists accused unions of following in the footsteps of the recent Russian Revolution and trying to spread communism in the United States. These accusations won industrialists the support of local governments, who again forcefully broke up many picket lines. Defeated steel, coal, and garment unions, however, did not give up organizing and continued to attract members. In the early 1920s, union ranks grew to five million, the largest to date. When faced with the dismal vision of unending labor strife, Progressives had crafted government regulation to rein in business and improve working conditions (see Chapter 18). In the 1920s, industrialists used the guarantee of government noninterference to pursue a different vision.

Throughout the decade the Harding and Coolidge administrations left industrialists free to fashion their own solutions to such labor troubles, adopting an openly pro-business stance. *The Wall Street Journal* exulted that "never before, here or anywhere else, has a government been so completely fused with business," referring to Commerce Department workshops that helped businesses eliminate wasteful practices, a Justice Department that largely stopped enforcing anti-trust laws, and a high protective tariff that made imported goods more expensive than American industrial products.

The Progressive Era effort to improve industrial efficiency, however, remained popular. *Envisioning Evidence: Scientific Management in Action* shows how industrialists tried to standardize hiring practices by relying on the "scientific" insights of Social Darwinism. Innovative industrialists also tried to put aside the prevailing idea that the interests of capitalists and workers inevitably clashed. Rather than driving their workers relentlessly to secure a profit, advocates of welfare capitalism suggested that industrialists offer a wide range of benefits such as medical insurance, pensions, and stock ownership plans to create a loyal workforce.

As the vogue for welfare capitalism spread, many industrialists began to change their management practices. To develop a stable, well-trained workforce, industrialists introduced fringe benefits (including paid vacations and sick pay), created industrial committees where workers could air grievances, and offered bonuses for workers who exceeded production quotas. A worker usually needed at least 25 years with one company to qualify for a pension, so this policy alone could potentially keep workers from leaving to pursue other job opportunities. Industrialists also experimented with offering employees stock options, hoping to dilute class antagonism by making each worker an investor who would share in the company's profits.

Despite workers' enthusiasm for welfare capitalism, the reality rarely matched the rhetoric. Seasonal layoffs continued, wage rates fluctuated constantly, and long hours in unhealthy factories persisted. As one worker complained, "we had to wait five years for one week's vacation. And I've seen men work four and one-half years and then get laid off." Industrialists' promises ended up simply whetting workers' appetites for stable well-paid jobs with benefits. During the Great Depression in the 1930s (see Chapter 22), the labor movement would demand that the government fulfill the hopes that industrialists had raised in the twenties.

Increased industrial productivity and efficiency created an unprecedented abundance of affordable goods in the twenties. Blue-collar workers toiling in dead-end jobs in factories staffed with salaried white-collar employees performing unsatisfying clerical tasks produced these items. Frustrated at work, many working- and middle-class Americans used their growing leisure time and access to material goods to create more fulfilling lives. A modern consumer culture arose

How did welfare capitalism promise to help industrialists run their factories more efficiently?

Envisioning Evidence
SCIENTIFIC MANAGEMENT IN ACTION

Scientific management, the effort to use scientific knowledge to maximize output and profit, took many forms in the 1920s. Mirroring how army psychologists had used intelligence tests to rank the aptitudes of different racial and ethnic groups in World War I (see Chapter 20), the Central Tube Company in Pittsburgh devised a chart to assess the abilities of various nationalities to perform skilled and unskilled jobs. The new profession of psychology accepted pseudoscientific social Darwinian ideas that "race" determined aptitude and the factory owner devised his own "scientific" chart to organize and run his business more efficiently. Rather than assessing the experience or capabilities of an individual, an employment agent only had to consult this chart to match the right man with the right job.

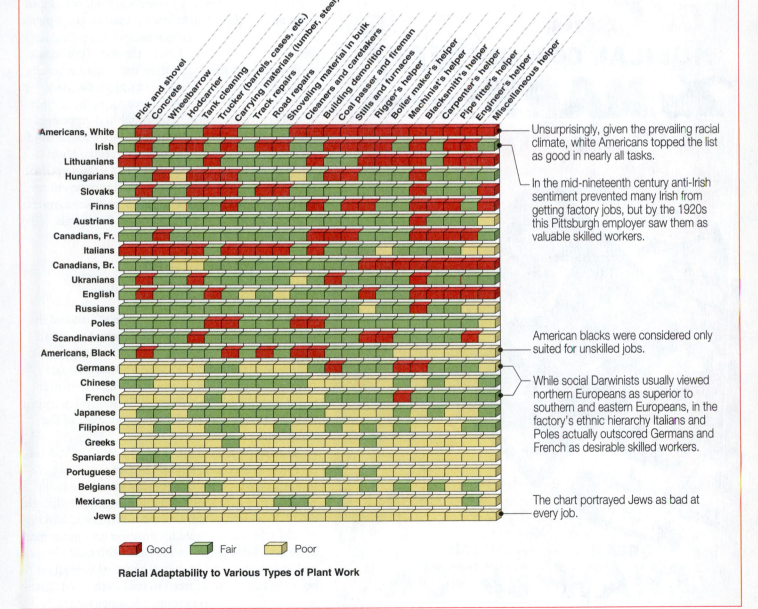

Unsurprisingly, given the prevailing racial climate, white Americans topped the list as good in nearly all tasks.

In the mid-nineteenth century anti-Irish sentiment prevented many Irish from getting factory jobs, but by the 1920s this Pittsburgh employer saw them as valuable skilled workers.

American blacks were considered only suited for unskilled jobs.

While social Darwinists usually viewed northern Europeans as superior to southern and eastern Europeans, in the factory's ethnic hierarchy Italians and Poles actually outscored Germans and French as desirable skilled workers.

The chart portrayed Jews as bad at every job.

Racial Adaptability to Various Types of Plant Work

View the **Closer Look** *Envisioning Evidence: Scientific Management in Action*

What kind of job could you have gotten in this factory?

that deemphasized traditional Victorian values of thrift and restraint. Americans instead increasingly relied on credit to buy cars, radios, and household appliances.

Radio played a key role in forging a national mass culture. Over 60 percent of American homes acquired radios in the twenties, which until 1924 required headphones. Americans from all walks of life now simultaneously gathered around their radios to learn election results. Baseball fans throughout the nation listened to the play-by-play of the World Series, radio broadcasts that made New York Yankee player Babe Ruth a national hero. Farmers closely followed weather reports, and bankers digested the day's financial news. "There is radio music in the air, every night, everywhere," one newspaper observed. Big companies like Walgreen Drugs and Palmolive Soap started sponsoring nationally syndicated radio shows to boost sales of their products. These weekly comedies and dramas, filled with plugs for the sponsor's merchandise, cultivated shared tastes in entertainment and products. Americans increasingly bought the same brand-name toothpaste at a chain store like Woolworths. Big business was not alone in recognizing the power of radio, however. Local radio shows designed specifically for union members, religious groups, immigrant communities, or African Americans helped strengthen bonds within these subcultures as well.

Movie stars and athletes enjoyed nationwide adulation in the twenties. Silent-film actors like the comedian Charlie Chaplin, the sex symbol Rudolph Valentino, and "America's Sweetheart" Mary Pickford became household names among a movie-going public that avidly purchased fan magazines filled with glossy photos of their favorite stars. By the end of the decade, Hollywood was producing films with sound, a novelty highlighted in this 1929 poster (**21.3**) for the Marx Brothers' first film. The verbal repartee of the comedy trio delighted audiences. As silent films disappeared, so did the careers of many silent-film stars whose artistic talents lay in physical, not vocal, expression. Meanwhile professional sports gave rise to a slew of national sports heroes, such as the boxer Jack Dempsey. In an era dominated by cultural heroes, none rose to greater prominence than the pilot Charles A. Lindbergh.

21.3 The End of Silent Films By the end of the decade, Hollywood began advertising "all talking-singing" movies like "Cocoanuts."

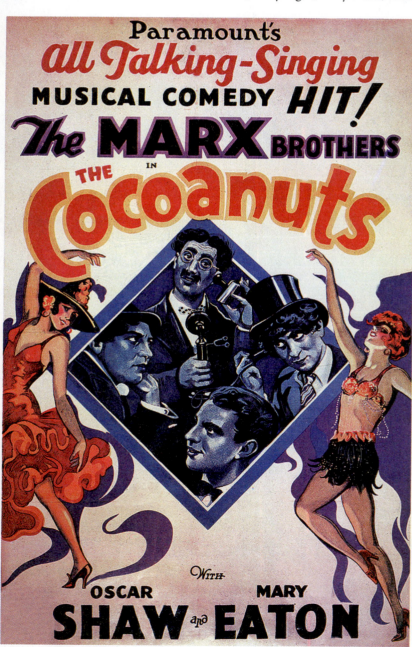

The Age of Flight: Charles A. Lindbergh

The feats of pilot Charles A. Lindbergh ushered the nation into the age of flight. Commentators called the sky the new frontier, a label loaded with potent historical significance for Americans. By the late twenties, a time when machines seemed to matter more than people, the image of the lone pilot against the vast blue sky recalled the pioneer spirit of the nineteenth century.

Lindbergh piloted his plane, the *Spirit of St. Louis*, on the first-ever nonstop solo flight from New York to Paris on May 21, 1927. Flying without the radio or radar that help modern pilots navigate, Lindbergh relied on a few navigational instruments and looking out the window to locate his position on a paper map as he flew. Sitting in a wicker chair with sandwiches and water under it, Lindbergh had a rubber raft on board in case he was forced to land in the cold Atlantic and a flashlight to examine his wings for ice.

> # "The *Spirit of St. Louis* is a wonderful plane. It's like a living creature, gliding along smoothly, happily, as though a successful flight means as much to it as to me."
>
> CHARLES A. LINDBERGH, evoking the perfect symmetry between man and machine

Lindbergh's flight lasted 33.5 hours, enough time to make him the hero of the decade. This photomontage (a composite photo made by pasting together separate images) of the *Spirit of St. Louis* passing the Eiffel Tower combined the symbol of Paris with the image of Lindbergh's iconic plane (**21.4**). "Had we searched all America we could not have found a better type than young Lindbergh to represent the spirit and high purpose of our people," the jubilant American ambassador wired President Coolidge amid the celebrations that followed Lindbergh's landing in Paris. Lindbergh's triumph assured Americans that individual initiative still mattered and that technological advancement benefited humankind at a time when the recent industrialized slaughter on the Western Front (see Chapter 20) suggested otherwise. The vision of planes serving a peaceful purpose by transporting mail and tourists replaced wartime images of aerial dogfights. Lindbergh toured the nation tirelessly to promote commercial air travel, and in 1931 also flew flood relief missions in China with his wife, the author Anne Morrow Lindbergh, to demonstrate the humanitarian good that planes made possible.

In exalting Lindbergh's achievement Americans channeled their own conflicting visions of the modern age. Some praised Lindbergh for exhibiting the same adventurous spirit that had propelled American pioneers across the West in the nineteenth century, values that seemed increasingly at risk in a machine-dominated age. "Charles Lindbergh is the heir of all that we like to think is best in America," opined *Outlook* magazine. Others, including Lindbergh, rejected the idea that his flight epitomized a return to the past. Lindbergh asserted that his flight illustrated the nation's industrial march forward, "the culmination," he said, "… of all that was practicable and best in American aviation." Although differing on whether the flight represented the revival of traditional values or the modern ethos of industrial might, Americans agreed that his flight renewed faith in the benefits of technology.

Lindbergh suffered, however, in the public spotlight. The 1933 kidnapping and murder of his firstborn son became the most reported tabloid story of the day. Later in the decade Lindbergh tarnished his image by expressing anti-Semitism and admiration for Nazi Germany and joining with those who argued against American intervention in World War II. After Japan's bombing of Pearl Harbor in 1941, Lindbergh changed his position. He flew combat missions against the Japanese, and his reputation recovered among many, when he took a strong anti-communist stand during the Cold War in the 1950s.

21.4 Photo Montage of the *Spirit of St. Louis* Flying Near the Eiffel Tower In this imagined scene an unnamed photographer celebrated the moment that pilot Charles Lindbergh arrived in Paris by pasting an image of his famous plane flying past Paris's most recognized monument.

View the **Image** *Charles Lindbergh and Spirit of St. Louis*   Why did Americans celebrate Lindbergh's solo flight to Paris?

Cultural Unrest

Celebrating Lindbergh's achievement was a unique moment of national unity in a decade dominated by cultural turbulence and strife. During the 1920s, societal-wide debates reflected competing visions over what values the nation should embrace as it entered the modern age. Cultural conflict turned political in the twenties as Americans debated the need for legislation to protect the nation's morals, ethnic purity, and capitalist economy.

The Lost Generation

"I've kissed dozens of men. I suppose I'll kiss dozens more," declared the flapper heroine of F. Scott Fitzgerald's novel *This Side of Paradise* (1920), announcing a new attitude of living for the moment that defined the era's youth culture. With his wife Zelda by his side, Fitzgerald put this philosophy into practice, moving from party to party in his fast-paced life as an expatriate in Europe. The Paris-based American writer Gertrude Stein coined the term "the Lost Generation" to describe white intellectuals and artists like Fitzgerald who rebelled against Victorian values in the twenties and lived primarily overseas.

Lost Generation writers used Austrian psychologist Sigmund Freud's theories to justify their revolt against "repressive" codes of conduct. Freud believed that subconscious sexual impulses drove human behavior and that repressed desires sometimes found expression in dreams. Fitzgerald was one of a host of writers including Ernest Hemingway, e. e. cummings, and John Dos Passos who championed sexual liberation as one way to escape the sterile and deadly confines of modern life. Men and women "spend their lives going in and out of doors and factories … they live their lives and find themselves at last facing death and the end of life without having lived at all," asserts a character in Sherwood Anderson's *Many Marriages* (1923) who, in the throes of a passionate extramarital affair, is preparing to end his marriage and leave his job.

The hedonistic lifestyles depicted in many Lost Generation novels, while rarely bestowing lasting happiness on the protagonists, still rankled more traditionally minded Americans. Agreeing that modern culture was flawed, these Americans wanted to bolster, rather than reject, traditional values. These clashing cultural visions had strong political overtones. Alcohol remained central to the Lost Generation ethos of pleasure-seeking, an indulgence that became illegal in the twenties, thanks to temperance reformers who felt that drinking threatened the moral fabric of American society.

Prohibition

Temperance, one of the nation's longest lasting reform movements (see Chapters 17 and 18), took on a new life during World War I. Wartime temperance propaganda claimed that "German brewers in this country have rendered thousands of men inefficient." Organized "wet" opposition to the "dry" campaign materialized slowly, partly because critics of the temperance movement could not easily counter its emphasis on health, thrift, and morals. Some wets focused on personal freedom. Senator James Wadsworth contended that it seemed unfair to tell exhausted workers at the end of the day "you shall not have a glass of beer." Other critics felt uneasy about increasing the power of the federal government so it could enforce prohibition. They argued that a proposed constitutional amendment prohibiting alcohol would violate states' rights. The middle-class Anti-Saloon League's highly structured propaganda and lobbying campaign, however, easily overpowered this disjointed wet response on the local, state, and national level.

Evangelical preacher Billy Sunday converted many churchgoers to the temperance cause, delivering impassioned sermons on the evils of alcohol. Sunday, a former professional baseball player, littered his sermons with slang, winning a large following among the rural poor and urban working class, who flocked to his revival meetings throughout the Midwest. The political elite also embraced the preacher. Sunday often dined at the White House and considered the oil tycoon John D. Rockefeller a friend. In his most famous

What critique did the Lost Generation offer of American society?

Watch the Video *Video Lecture: Post-War Disillusionment in the 1920s*

temperance speech, Sunday urged his listeners in 1908 to "get on the water wagon; get on for the sake of your wife and babies, and hit the booze a blow."

On December 18, 1917, Congress approved the **Eighteenth Amendment**, which banned the sale, manufacture, and transportation of intoxicating liquors. By January 16, 1919, the required 36 states had ratified it. By the time every state had voted, only Rhode Island and Connecticut had rejected it. When prohibition went into effect in 1920, Congress clarified what constituted an intoxicating beverage in the Volstead Act (1919), which defined any beverage with more than 0.5 percent alcohol as intoxicating liquor and established criminal penalties for manufacturing, transporting, or possessing alcohol.

Congress never appropriated enough money for wide-scale enforcement, hampering Justice Department efforts to curb illegal drinking. The police raided working-class neighborhoods to shut down illegal distilleries, but the well-to-do drank their bathtub gin or homebrewed beer without interference. Many reform goals of the temperance movement remained unmet. Belying the expectation that it would create a more virtuous, law-abiding society, prohibition gave birth to a much more insidious form of crime. Organized crime syndicates ran profitable bootlegging operations that financed beer breweries and liquor distilleries, bribed cops, and stocked the shelves of illegal bars throughout major metropolitan areas. Trafficking in forbidden alcohol, the publicity-crazed gangster Al Capone became a powerful figure in the Chicago underworld, a position he maintained with unprecedented violence. In the 1929 St. Valentine's Day Massacre, Capone's men, posing as cops, pretended to arrest rival gang members and then lined them up against a wall and mowed them down with machine guns. Tabloid papers vividly recounted every detail of Capone's "new technique of wholesale murder" to a shocked public. Suffering from syphilis that he contracted from a prostitute in one of his own brothels, Capone became increasingly unstable and violent before he went to prison for tax evasion in 1931.

Secret bars called speakeasies proliferated. To demonstrate Americans' widespread disrespect for prohibition, federal agent Izzy Einstein timed how long it took him to find alcohol in most major cities. It took him 21 minutes in Chicago, and only 31 seconds in New Orleans, when he asked a taxi driver where he could get a drink and the man replied, "right here," as he pulled out a bottle. Einstein

personally shut down over 4,000 speak easies nationwide, prompting bartenders to post his picture with the caption "watch for this man."

Illicit drinking became fashionable among the young urban elite, whose escapades Lost Generation writers helped glamorize. This image of a well-dressed woman barhopping with her male companions (**21.5**) revealed new social acceptance for public drinking by respectable middle- and upper-class women. Americans had previously viewed saloons as male establishments that only women of low moral character, like prostitutes, dared to enter.

The competing visions of whether illegal drinking was harmless fun or a vice that destroyed families kept the political debate over prohibition alive throughout the 1920s. Drys credited prohibition for the prosperous economy. By putting alcohol aside, they claimed, workers had become more productive, could afford to buy cars and furniture, and had more savings. Wets argued that the amendment generated

21.5 Well-Dressed Trio Entering a Speakeasy
Frequenting speakeasies, which patrons entered by giving a secret password to the doorman, became fashionable for women during prohibition. Gone was the stigma that had stopped respectable women from drinking in public.

disrespect for the law as it became socially acceptable for Americans to commit a crime by purchasing alcohol. States' rights advocates increasingly resented the arrival of federal officials trying to track down bootleggers. Picking up the Anti-Saloon League's longstanding emphasis on protecting women and children, the wet lobby emphasized the dangers of teenagers drinking contaminated "moonshine" (a slang term for illicitly manufactured alcohol) in speakeasies run by the mob. Better to have them drink safely in public cafes, they argued.

The beginning of the Great Depression in 1929, which thrust the nation into an unprecedented financial crisis, undermined the dry claim that prohibition brought prosperity. Wets made headway with the argument that enforcing the law drained the federal treasury. When Democrat Franklin D. Roosevelt entered the White House in 1933, he immediately asked Congress to repeal prohibition. With lightening speed the states ratified the **Twenty-First Amendment (1933)**, which repealed the Eighteenth Amendment. The temperance vision remained regionally popular, however, especially in the rural South and Midwest which continued to enforce local prohibition statutes. A few states also passed minimum-age drinking laws in the 1930s, but most states did not enact such laws until the 1980s.

The First Red Scare and Immigration Restrictions

The vision of America as the land of opportunity for peoples worldwide came under attack in the 1920s. Debates over immigration were not new, but for the first time the nativist vision prevailed. In the early twenties the United States underwent a historic shift, changing from a nation that admitted over one million immigrants a year in the decade leading up to World War I to one that grudgingly allowed fewer than 200,000 to enter the country annually.

World War I was the catalyst that turned longstanding nativist attacks against immigrants into a mandate for dramatic change. Alarm over German Americans' continued ties to Germany linked concerns about assimilation to the more potent political question of national security. The 1921 Emergency Immigration Act temporarily allowed 350,000 European immigrants to enter the country each year and set limits on how many immigrants could come from each European nation. Three years

later Congress made these quotas permanent. The **Immigration Act of 1924** allowed unrestricted immigration from the Western Hemisphere, curtailed all Asian immigration, and used quotas to control how many immigrants emigrated from individual European nations. The law authorized a total of 165,000 immigrants from Europe, a figure that Congress reduced to 150,000 in 1929 at the start of the Great Depression.

Assumptions about the racial superiority of northern Europeans strongly influenced the new national quotas portrayed in the "Immigration Act of 1924" chart (**21.6**). In this new quota system, Germany received the highest quota. If Americans no longer feared German immigrants, then why did the country feel compelled to adopt immigration restrictions? The answer: the communist-inspired Russian Revolution of 1917, a critical event that some Americans envisioned immigrants from Russia and Eastern Europe recreating in the United States. To meet this threat, the Justice Department arrested and deported alien anarchists and Communists suspected of trying to destroy American democracy and capitalism during the **First Red Scare (1919–1920)**.

Like Communists, anarchists believed that capitalist exploitation of the working class created widespread social suffering. While Communists wanted to create a workers' government that controlled property, anarchists viewed all governments as corrupt. The anarchist movement's most famous spokesperson was Emma Goldman, an eloquent speaker who had emigrated from Russia as a young girl. Anarchism, she wrote, "stands for the liberation of the human mind from the dominion of religion; the liberation of the human body from the dominion of property; liberation from the shackles and restraint of government." Some anarchists felt justified using violence to advance their cause (one had assassinated President William McKinley in 1901). Goldman, however, disavowed armed conflict and instead tried to popularize the anarchist philosophy through lectures and the magazine that she founded, *Mother Earth*.

In 1919, post office clerk Charles Kaplan helped avert disaster. Reading a newspaper account, as he rode the subway home, of two anarchist mail-bomb attacks, one against the mayor of Seattle and another against a senator from Georgia. Kaplan realized that the description of the booby-trapped

Why did the nation enact strict immigration restrictions in the twenties?

■◖┤**Read** the **Document** *A. Mitchell Palmer on the Menace of Communism*

packages matched that of 16 parcels he had recently set aside for insufficient postage, including one addressed to oil tycoon John D. Rockefeller. Kaplan's discovery triggered a nationwide investigation that netted 18 more mail bombs.

As anxiety mounted, terrorists exploded dynamite outside the home of Attorney General A. Mitchell Palmer, the man heading the Justice Department's hunt for Bolshevik and anarchist terrorists. Palmer warned that "on a certain day which we have been advised of," radicals were planning "to rise up and destroy the Government at one fell swoop." To head off this revolutionary uprising, Palmer raided the homes and offices of suspected radicals and deported hundreds of immigrants with ties to radical organizations, including Emma Goldman.

While the government focused on the need to ensure public safety, radicals asserted their rights to freedom of speech and peaceful assembly. Without concrete evidence of their participation in any criminal activity, they argued, the government was prosecuting them merely for their beliefs. Coming on the heels of wartime arrests under the Espionage and Sedition acts, the government's harassment of radical activists during 1919–1920 made it practically impossible for radical groups to organize, distribute literature, or give public speeches championing their political ideals.

Radicals tried to fight back by taking up the cause of anarchists Nicola Sacco and Bartolomeo Vanzetti, two Italian immigrants arrested in Massachusetts for the robbery and murder of a payroll guard in 1920. Poor Italian immigrants and left-leaning union members made numerous small donations to the Sacco-Vanzetti Defense Committee, which sponsored picnics and wrestling matches to raise funds for their defense. Many intellectuals also supported the pair, including Roger Baldwin, who had recently founded the American Civil Liberties Union (ACLU), to protect constitutional liberties. The portrait that prosecutors painted of Sacco and Vanzetti—foreign-born, openly radical, and in possession of guns and anarchist pamphlets when arrested—epitomized the terrorist threat many Americans feared. Sacco and Vanzetti's radical and liberal supporters embraced a competing vision, blaming growing xenophobia for the pair's conviction and 1927 electrocution.

Northwest Europe and Scandinavia		Eastern and Southern Europe		Other Countries	
Country	Quota	Country	Quota	Country	Quota
Germany	51,227	Poland	5,982	Africa (other than Egypt)	1,100
Great Britain and Northern Ireland	34,007	Italy	3,845	Armenia	124
Irish Free State (Ireland)	28,567	Czechoslovakia	3,073	Australia	121
Sweden	9,561	Russia	2,248	Palestine	100
Norway	6,453	Yugoslavia	671	Syria	100
France	3,954	Romania	603	Turkey	100
Denmark	2,789	Portugal	503	Egypt	100
Switzerland	2,081	Hungary	473	New Zealand & Pacific Islands	100
Netherlands	1,648	Lithuania	344	All others	1,900
Austria	785	Latvia	142		
Belgium	512	Spain	131		
Finland	471	Estonia	124		
Free City of Danzig	228	Albania	100		
Iceland	100	Bulgaria	100		
Luxembourg	100	Greece	100		
Total (Number)	142,483	Total (Number)	18,439	Total (Number)	3,745
Total (%)	86.5	Total (%)	11.2	Total (%)	2.3

Recent findings suggest that Sacco and Vanzetti were indeed dedicated anarchists with close connections to those who planned the spate of 1919 bombings, but no conclusive evidence ties them to the 1920 murder.

The First Red Scare ended quickly. As the anarchist attacks ceased, the press began to poke fun at Palmer's "hallucinations" of a mass uprising and accused him of exaggerating the "revolutionary menace" as part of a failed campaign to win the Democratic presidential nomination in 1920. Although the arrests and deportations stopped, the First Red Scare gave credence to the anti-immigration argument that the country needed protection from foreigners who might import dangerous radical political theories.

Other arguments also helped tip the balance in favor of immigration restriction. Urban elites and rural folk worried about protecting the "racial purity" of American stock, while unions and African Americans feared competition from immigrant laborers. By the early twenties industrialists had dropped their complaint that immigration restrictions would deprive business of a traditionally inexpensive labor source. Many now believed that machines would increasingly replace unskilled immigrant workers in factories and felt confident that there were enough African American or Mexican workers to alleviate any labor shortage. With the consensus moving toward immigration restrictions, immigrant associations sought to

21.6 Immigration Act of 1924
The United States enacted a quota system in the 1920s that allotted most slots to immigrants from northern Europe.

ensure that their nationality received the highest quota possible.

Official quotas, however, do not reveal the exact numbers of immigrants who entered the country. If denied entry under the quota system, which remained intact from 1924 through 1965, determined immigrants exploited loopholes. The 1924 law contained two key provisions that have remained staples of American immigration legislation: the principle of family reunification, which let resident immigrants bring in members of their immediate families, and the desirability of certain skills. The law, for example, established exemptions for trades facing worker shortages in the United States, such as domestic service. Other savvy European immigrants simply entered the country illegally, often by way of Mexico or Canada, two nations that still enjoyed unrestricted immigration to the United States.

Fundamentalism

The cultural debates surrounding prohibition and immigration restrictions assumed a decidedly political edge in the 1920s. Christian Fundamentalists added to the decade's cultural turbulence when they initiated a campaign to stop the teaching of biologist Charles Darwin's views on evolution. Religious conservatives felt that Darwin's theories contradicted the Bible's depiction of God creating the world and humankind in seven days. They instead subscribed to the tenets of **fundamentalism**, an evangelical Christian theology that viewed the Bible as an authentic, literal recounting of historical events and the absolute moral word of God. By critiquing Darwin, Fundamentalists offered a conservative alternative to **modernism**, a liberal Christian theology embraced in many urban areas that emphasized the ongoing revelation of divine truth. Offering competing religious visions Fundamentalists accepted the Bible as errorless, while Modernists reinterpreted the Bible when confronted with new scientific knowledge (such as fossil evidence of evolution).

Believing that "monkey men mean monkey morals," the World Christian Fundamentals Association lobbied for state laws that prohibited teaching evolution in public schools. In 1925, Tennessee made it a crime to teach "any theory that denies the story of the Divine Creation as taught in the Bible, and to teach instead that man has descended from a lower order of animals." Passed

mostly to make sweeping school reforms more palatable to Fundamentalist voters, the state made no effort to enforce the law and even adopted a biology textbook that included an extended discussion of Darwin's ideas.

The ACLU viewed the law as a violation of the First Amendment's guarantee of free speech. Hoping to test its constitutionality, the ACLU offered to help any teacher in Tennessee who wanted to challenge the law in court. Civic boosters in Dayton, Tennessee, responded to the offer. A trial highlighting the clash between science and religion was bound to attract huge crowds, they reasoned, and by hosting this national extravaganza, Dayton expected to draw an influx of visitors with cash to spend. John Scopes, a 24-year-old science teacher and part-time football coach, agreed to step forward, so officials in Dayton could arrest him. The infamous Scopes trial was underway.

Interest in Scopes, the ACLU, and Dayton faded once William Jennings Bryan agreed to prosecute the case and Clarence Darrow arrived to defend Scopes. Bryan was the former leader of the Democratic Party, who had unsuccessfully run for president three times and resigned as secretary of state when President Woodrow Wilson abandoned complete neutrality during World War I. The devout Bryan blamed Germany's embrace of evolutionary notions like "survival of the fittest" for causing the brutal global war. Darrow was an agnostic, famous for defending both radical labor leaders, such as the socialist Eugene Debs, and wealthy murderers.

Hundreds of journalists descended on the town to observe the courtroom confrontation between Bryan and Darrow. Their dispatches helped build publicity for the "monkey trial," a reference to evolutionists' claim that humans had descended from apes. Urban-based reporters billed the case as a conclusive struggle between modern America and the ignorant rural masses (few of whom shared in the general prosperity of the 1920s) whose alleged backward thinking threatened to impede the country's progress. In his widely read reports, nationally syndicated columnist H. L. Mencken regularly referred to Fundamentalists as hillbillies and yokels. Fundamentalists fought back. The carnival-like atmosphere outside the courtroom soon included Fundamentalist revival meetings and performances by trained chimpanzees that mocked evolutionists. Vendors did a brisk business selling

Why did Fundamentalists object to teaching evolution in public schools?

View the **Closer Look** *Immigration Quotas*

Dueling newspaper headlines during the Scopes Trial:
"'They Call Us Bigots When We Refuse to
Throw Away Our Bibles,' Bryan says."

"We say 'Keep Your Bible,' but keep it where it belongs,
in the world of your conscience."

monkey dolls, like the one held by Lena Ruffner (**21.7**), who announced her support of Bryan by pinning a sign "they can't make a monkey out of me" to her dress.

Both Bryan and Darrow argued that they were protecting American democratic institutions. Bryan maintained that the Tennessee legislature had the right to pass any law that the majority wanted; Darrow contended the state had violated the constitution by establishing Christianity as an official religion and limiting freedom of expression. The mainstream press viewed the trial as a showdown between science and religion, with science winning a decisive victory. In their account, the climactic moment came when Darrow called Bryan to the witness stand and trapped him into confessing he did not accept the entire Bible as the literal truth. "We have the purpose of preventing bigots and ignoramuses from controlling the education of the United States," Darrow declared in court, expressing Modernists' view of fundamentalism. The national press labeled Bryan a broken man when he died in his sleep five days after Scopes was found guilty and fined. The courtroom, however, had burst into applause when during his cross-examination Bryan had thundered, "I am simply trying to protect the word of God against the greatest atheist or agnostic in the United States." Southern folk songs popularized this competing heroic image of Bryan as someone who "fought for what was righteous and the battle it was won / Then the Lord called him to heaven for his work on earth was done."

After Scopes's conviction the ACLU appealed to the Tennessee Supreme Court, which upheld the law's constitutionality and then overturned the verdict because the judge rather than the jury had imposed the fine. Scopes's acquittal meant that the ACLU had to find a new case to take before the U.S. Supreme Court. After the ridicule heaped on Dayton, however, no town or teacher was willing to help the ACLU try again. Tennessee did not repeal the law until 1967. A year later the U.S. Supreme Court declared anti-evolution laws unconstitutional.

Although soon forgotten by mainstream America, throughout the twentieth century Fundamentalists created a thriving minority subculture of churches, schools, universities, publishers, radio ministries, and missionary societies. Fundamentalists rejoined the cultural and political mainstream in the 1970s and are generating headlines again with their challenges to teaching evolution in public schools. In one striking break from the past, Fundamentalists now use Darrow's line of reasoning to argue that keeping the biblical theory of creation out of high school biology classes violates the constitutional guarantee to freedom of expression.

21.7 Young Woman Holds Monkey Doll during the Scopes Trial A supporter of prosecutor William Jennings Bryan wears a sign ridiculing the theory of evolution and displays the monkey doll she bought from a vender outside the courthouse.

What cultural and religious tensions were exposed during the Scopes trial?

Racial Violence and Civil Rights

 Advocates of prohibition, immigration restrictions, and fundamentalism had varying degrees of success reshaping American society after the war. African Americans were also active, employing new strategies to advance racial equality. A new generation of black political activists emerged, determined to fight back when whites attacked. The **Harlem Renaissance**, an outpouring of African American artistic expression in the 1920s and 1930s, also stirred debate within the African American community over the best way to improve the lives of African Americans.

Lynching, Racial Rioting, and the Ku Klux Klan

Lynch mobs tortured and killed nearly 5,000 victims between 1880 and 1930, roughly two per week. The souvenir postcard (**21.8**) by studio photographer Lawrence Beitler depicted the lynching of Thomas Shipp and Abram Smith, a disturbing relic from this grisly past. Professional photographers often attended lynchings and sold hundreds of picture postcards to perpetrators and witnesses, who put them in family scrapbooks or sent them to friends and relatives. Besides buying souvenir postcards, whites sometimes took other relics from the victim, including hair, clothing, fingers, and ears. Both the existence of this postcard and the scene it depicts raise chilling questions about the ritual of lynching. Rather than viewing their murderous act as shameful or believing that they needed to conceal their identities to avoid prosecution, these participants smile openly for the camera. Police rarely arrested anyone for a lynching, preferring to claim that the victims died "at the hands of persons unknown." Trumped-up accusations that the victim had raped or murdered a white person usually fueled a lynching frenzy. Police had arrested Shipp and Abram for robbery, murder, and rape. The purpose of lynching, however, went beyond administering extralegal justice. Lynching also created a climate of terror that helped whites maintain social control over all blacks, not just those killed. James Weldon Johnson, a well-regarded poet who served as director of the National Association for the Advancement of Colored People (NAACP) in the twenties,

21.8 Souvenir Postcard, Thomas Shipp and Abram Smith Lynching, Marion, Indiana After witnessing the lynching of two black men, smiling men and women had their pictures taken as a memento. The two girls to the left clutch pieces of the victims' hair. The photographer sold thousands of copies for 50 cents each.

What does this souvenir postcard reveal about the ritual of lynching?

coined the term "The Red Summer of 1919" to describe the wave of vicious assaults against black communities that left at least 43 African Americans dead. Some whites also used organized violence to prevent blacks from competing with whites economically. Mobs attacked thriving black business centers and middle-class homes in Tulsa, Oklahoma, in 1921, and in Rosewood, Florida, in 1923. A headline in a Tulsa newspaper even helped mobilize whites by issuing the call "To Lynch A Negro Tonight."

In both the Tulsa and Rosewood race riots, African Americans fought back, but enraged white crowds still burned both communities to the ground. Officials in Tulsa declared martial law and imprisoned one-half of the city's black population in internment camps. After gaining their freedom a few weeks later, 1,000 families spent the winter in tents before beginning the huge task of rebuilding their community. In 1994, Florida awarded survivors of the Rosewood race riot $150,000 each in reparations. For the first time African Americans received compensation for past racial injustices, raising the question of whether victims of other racially motivated attacks deserved financial settlements.

With the states unwilling to prosecute the members of lynch mobs, the NAACP lobbied to make lynching a federal crime. Hoping to shock the nation into supporting an anti-lynching law, the NAACP used graphic images of lynchings in their pamphlets, parades, and posters. Southern congressmen, however, blocked passage of a federal anti-lynching bill by claiming that it violated the constitutional right of states to police themselves.

This photograph of Shipp and Smith "haunted me for days," recalled Abel Meeropol, a Jewish schoolteacher from New York active in leftist politics. It inspired him to compose "Strange Fruit," a song denouncing lynching that Billie Holiday recorded in 1939. Meeropol's stanzas painted a gruesome picture: "Southern trees bear strange fruit/Blood on the leaves and blood at the root/Black body swinging in the Southern breeze/Strange fruit hanging from the poplar trees." The lyrics also partly misinterpreted the image. Although most lynchings took place in the South, the attack pictured here occurred in Marion, Indiana. Indiana was home to the largest chapter of the Ku Klux Klan in the 1920s, enrolling nearly one-half of the

21.9 Ku Klux Klan in Washington, D.C., 1925
Klan members unfurl a giant American flag on the steps of the Capitol, equating patriotism with white supremacy.

state's white male population even though only three percent of the state's population was black. The federal government had suppressed the original Ku Klux Klan during Reconstruction (see Chapter 15). The Klan revived in the 1910s and became a national organization that drew members from all parts of the country with membership fluctuating between three and six million throughout the twenties.

The new Klan organized their call for white Protestant supremacy under the banner of 100 percent Americanism, and their list of enemies included any group that threatened the traditional order. Anxieties aroused by blacks' wartime migration to northern and midwestern industrial centers, the Red Scare, women's suffrage, mass immigration, prohibition, and postwar strikes caused many conservative whites to listen sympathetically to Klan outbursts against blacks, Jews, Catholics, immigrants, radicals, feminists, and bootleggers. The 1925 Klan march in Washington, D.C. (**21.9**), exposed the group's national appeal. City officials required the 40,000 assembled Klan members to march from the White House to the Capitol without their masks. Like lynch mobs these Klan members were unafraid to reveal their identities as they proudly unfurled an American flag that championed the Klan's "patriotic" slogan of "Native, white, Protestant supremacy." The march represented the high tide of Klan power in the twenties. As fears of social upheaval diminished, Klan membership also decreased.

Read the **Document** *The "Creed of Klanswomen" (1924)*   Why did membership in the Ku Klux Klan surge in the twenties?

Marcus Garvey

The African American community had long debated how to end racial attacks and segregation. In the 1890s, Booker T. Washington squared off against W. E. B. Du Bois over whether blacks should focus first on improving their economic position or demanding political rights (see Chapter 18). Washington died in 1915, and in the 1920s, Jamaican immigrant Marcus Garvey took up his idea of empowering blacks economically. Garvey founded the **Universal Negro Improvement Association (UNIA)** to encourage economic self-sufficiency by creating black-owned businesses. The UNIA organized the Black Star Line, a short-lived capitalist venture that sold $5 stock certificates to finance the world's only black-owned and staffed fleet of steamships. Garvey's working-class followers, native-born African Americans and recently arrived immigrants from the West Indies, purchased stock enthusiastically. Poor management, however, forced the Black Star Line to dissolve in 1922.

Despite their shared message of economic empowerment, the black nationalist Garvey was much more militant than Washington. There was nothing shameful in being black, Garvey told his audiences, criticizing African Americans who used skin lighteners and hair straighteners to make themselves appear more white. "God," Garvey said, "made no mistake when he made us black with kinky hair. We have outgrown slavery, but our minds are still enslaved to the thinking of the Master Race. Now take these kinks out of your mind, instead of out of your hair." Like Washington, Garvey rejected the political goal of dismantling Jim Crow that dominated other civil rights organizations. But unlike Washington, who wanted to improve life for blacks within the United States, Garvey spoke often of acquiring enough economic power to establish an independent African nation that could reunite the world's dispersed black peoples.

Pageantry was a hallmark of the UNIA. Its meetings often included a uniformed male African Legion dressed in blue, and female Black Cross Nurses in white. To give these gatherings an official air, participants waved tri-color flags that Garvey described as, "Black for our race, red for our blood, and green for our hope." Black middle-class detractors ridiculed Garvey's tendency to appear, as pictured here (**21.10**), wearing a plumed hat and military regalia. These critics called him "a clown" in a "gaudy uniform" who led "big parades of ignorant people down the street selling pie in the sky." Garvey, however, believed that seeing a black man dressed as an aristocrat inspired confidence among his followers and challenged the stereotype of black subservience perpetuated by white America. The Justice Department took note of Garvey's theatrics. Worried that his movement was sowing the seeds of a violent black rebellion, government spies monitored his activities.

Competing Visions: Debating Garveyism explores Garvey's vision for black America and the criticism of W. E. B. Du Bois, a leader in the NAACP who supported immediate integration. Some of Garvey's black critics organized a "Garvey Must Go" campaign and helped the government convict him of fraudulent use of the mails in 1923. He served four years in prison and was then deported. Without Garvey the UNIA collapsed. Garveyism, however, offered African Americans an alternative to the integrationist vision of the NAACP and introduced separatist ideas that Black Power advocates would resurrect in the 1960s (see Chapter 27).

21.10 Marcus Garvey
The leader of the UNIA often appeared in full military dress to project an image of strength and racial pride. He challenged prevailing racial stereotypes of black subservience by adopting regalia usually worn by kings.

Why did Garvey elicit such strong emotions among both followers and critics?

Competing Visions

DEBATING GARVEYISM

Many of the traditional civil rights elite despised Marcus Garvey, whom they accused of swindling the poor of their hard-earned money and stirring up racial animosity within the United States. Garvey in turn accused light-skinned African American leaders of racial prejudice, arguing that they could not accept the dark-skinned Garvey as their equal. In the following excerpts Garvey lays out his reasons for urging black Americans to go "Back to Africa," while W. E. B. Du Bois, one of the light-skinned elites Garvey attacked, criticizes Garvey's vision. How does Garvey propose to stop "crimes against the race"? What portrait does Du Bois offer of Garvey?

In "The True Solution of the Negro Problem" (1922) Marcus Garvey argued that creating a homeland in Africa could solve the problem of racial violence in the United States.

We cannot allow a continuation of these crimes [lynching and disenfranchisement] against our race. As four hundred million men, women and children, worthy of the existence given us by the Divine Creator, we are determined to solve our own problem, by redeeming our Motherland Africa from the hands of alien exploiters and found there a government, a nation of our own, strong enough to lend protection to the members of our race scattered all over the world, and to compel the respect of the nations and races of the earth.

Do they lynch Englishmen, Frenchmen, Germans or Japanese? No. And Why? Because these people are represented by great governments, mighty nations and empires … ever ready to shed the last drop of blood and spend the last penny in the national treasury to protect the honor and integrity of a citizen outraged anywhere. Until the Negro reaches this point of national independence, all he does as a race will count for naught, because the prejudice that will stand out against him even with his ballot in his hand, with his industrial progress to show, will be of such an overwhelming nature as to perpetuate mob violence and mob rule.…

If the Negro were to live in this Western Hemisphere for another five hundred years he would still be outnumbered by other races who are prejudiced against him. He cannot resort to the government for protection for government will be in the hands of the majority of the people who are prejudiced against him, hence for the Negro to depend on the ballot and his industrial progress alone, will be hopeless as it does not help him when he is lynched, burned, jim-crowed and segregated. The future of the Negro therefore, outside of Africa, spells ruin and disaster.

In this 1923 biographical sketch, "Marcus Garvey," W. E. B. Du Bois views Garvey as misguided and inept.

Garvey soon developed in America a definite and in many respects original and alluring program. He proposed to establish the "Black Star Line" of steamships under Negro ownership and with Negro money, to trade between the United States, the West Indies, and Africa. He proposed to establish a factories corporation which was going to build factories and manufacture goods both for local consumption of Negroes and for export.… When Mr. Garvey brought his cohorts to Madison Square Garden, and when, ducking his dark head at the audience, he yelled, "We are going to Africa to tell England, France and Belgium to get out of there," America sat up, listened, laughed, and said here at least is something new.… Thus the Black Star Line arose and disappeared, and with it went some $800,000 of the savings of West Indians and a few American Negroes.…

Button won by Marcus Garvey supporters

His African program was made impossible by his own pigheadedness. He proposed to make a start in Liberia with industrial enterprises. From this center he would penetrate all Africa and gradually subdue it. Instead of keeping this plan hidden and working cautiously and intelligently toward it, he yelled and shouted and telegraphed it all over the world. Without consulting the Liberians, he apparently was ready to assume partial charge of their state.… [H]is talk about conquest and "driving Europe out," aroused European governments.…

The present generation of Negroes has survived two grave temptations, the greater one, fathered by Booker T. Washington, which said, "Let politics alone, keep in your place, work hard, and do not complain," and which meant perpetual color caste for colored folk by their own cooperation and consent … and the lesser, fathered by Marcus Garvey, which said, "Give up! Surrender! The struggle is useless; back to Africa and fight the white world."

Claude McKay

"If We Must Die"

(1919)

If we must die, let it not be like hogs
Hunted and penned in an inglorious spot,
While round us bark the mad and hungry dogs,
Making their mock at our accursed lot.
If we must die, O let us nobly die,
So that our precious blood may not be shed
In vain; then even the monsters we defy
Shall be constrained to honor us though dead!
O kinsmen we must meet the common foe!
Though far outnumbered let us show us brave,
And for their thousand blows deal one deathblow!
What though before us lies the open grave?
Like men we'll face the murderous, cowardly pack,
Pressed to the wall, dying, but fighting back!

Countee Cullen

"Incident"

(1924)

Once riding in old Baltimore,
Heart-filled, head-filled with glee,
I saw a Baltimorean
Keep looking straight at me.

Now I was eight and very small,
And he was no whit bigger,
And so I smiled, but he poked out
His tongue, and called me, "Nigger."

I saw the whole of Baltimore
From May until December;
Of all the things that happened there
That's all that I remember.

The Harlem Renaissance

Garvey based the UNIA in Harlem, a thriving African American neighborhood in New York City that became the hub of black politics and culture in the 1920s. African American artists, photographers, musicians, and writers celebrated the distinctiveness of black culture. Many writers published their works in black magazines such as *The Crisis* and *The Messenger*. White literary figures like Carl Van Vechten also helped black writers publish their works with commercial presses, exposing white America to black artistic endeavors. The African American philosopher Alain Locke captured the creative impulse of the Harlem Renaissance in 1925, when he published *The New Negro*, an anthology of essays and poems by emerging literary voices. According to Locke the New Negro embodied a spirit of black racial pride and militancy that set a younger generation of African American artists and civil rights leaders apart from their predecessors, who had emphasized assimilating into white culture.

Harlem Renaissance writers took up themes previously absent from serious works of literature. Poet Langston Hughes discussed black Americans' aspirations; Jean Toomer's novel *Cane* explored the rhythms of working-class life in the countryside and city; Zora Neale Huston exposed the power of female sexuality in her novel *Their Eyes Were Watching God*; poet Countee Cullen confronted the psychological impact of racism; and Claude McKay celebrated manly violence in his poems and novels. The poems displayed here show how McKay, Cullen, and Hughes protested racial discrimination.

The Harlem Renaissance also included the jazz music innovations of trumpeter Louis Armstrong, pianist and arranger Fletcher Henderson, and pianist and composer Ferdinand "Jelly Roll" Morton. Jazz was an original American musical style that melded African American and European musical traditions. White and black patrons flocked to Harlem to listen to black bands at venues like the Cotton Club and the Savoy, while white musicians nationwide formed jazz bands of their own. Thanks to new commercial radio stations and the growing record industry, jazz became so popular that Americans began calling the twenties "The Jazz Age." Jazz music, the white conductor Leopold Stokowski rejoiced, was "an expression of the times, of the breathless, energetic, superactive times in which we are living." James Weldon Johnson's poem "The Prodigal Son" highlighted the dangers awaiting recent southern migrants, unschooled in big-city ways,

In these poems how do responses to racism vary?

((• Hear the Audio *"If We Must Die," poem and reading by Claude McKay*

who flocked to Harlem's jazz clubs. In the two-dimensional drawing by African American artist Aaron Douglas that accompanied the poem (**21.11**), female dancers surround a young man and gyrate to the music provided by a hovering jazz trombone. The fragments of a dollar, playing card, and gin label evoke the temptations confronting this young man. Johnson's poem echoed the rhythms of sermons that folk preachers delivered to their rural southern congregations about the evils of city life: "With the sweet-sinning women of Babylon / And they stripped him of his money / And they stripped him of his clothes / And they left him broke and ragged / In the streets of Babylon."

As Johnson's poem suggested, African Americans expressed conflicting views about jazz. Many artists celebrated the music's originality and exuberance. Like Southern preachers, however, the urban black middle class viewed jazz as "the devil's music," believing that its syncopated rhythms aroused sexual impulses and encouraged lewd behavior. Jazz clubs often served illegal alcohol purchased from organized crime rings, linking jazz music to the immoral lifestyle that many black middle-class prohibition

Langston Hughes

"I, Too, Sing America"

(1925)

I, too, sing America.

I am the darker brother.
They send me to eat in the kitchen
When company comes,
But I laugh,
And eat well,
And grow strong.
Tomorrow,
I'll be at the table
When company comes.
Nobody'll dare
Say to me,
"Eat in the kitchen,"
Then.

Besides,
They'll see how beautiful I am
And be ashamed—

I, too, am America.

advocates wanted to eradicate. The middle class preferred religious spirituals, a distinctive African American musical tradition that they felt projected a more respectable image of black culture to mainstream America.

The literature of the Harlem Renaissance also drew fire. Du Bois criticized Claude McKay for depicting black working-class culture as a collection of pimps, criminals, drunks, and whores in his 1928 novel *Home to Harlem*. Du Bois lambasted McKay for reinforcing the negative stereotypes that white America held of African American culture, thereby undermining the possibility of using art to challenge the racial status quo. Defending New Negro aesthetics and the principle of artistic freedom, Langston Hughes countered, "We younger Negro artists who create now intend to express our dark-skinned selves without fear or shame. If white people are pleased we are glad. If they are not, it doesn't matter. We know we are beautiful."

21.11 *Prodigal Son*, 1927
Aaron Douglas's innovative angular style evoked the fast pace of modern life in an illustration that both portrayed and epitomized the artistic innovations of the Harlem Renaissance.

((•— **Hear** the **Audio** *"I Too,"* poem and reading by Langston Hughes

What competing views arose over the purpose of art during the Harlem Renaissance?

The New Woman

Women began the decade with a significant political victory when the Nineteenth Amendment gave them to right to vote in 1920. Female reformers expected newly enfranchised women to care deeply about issues affecting their gender, but the much-anticipated "women's vote" never materialized. Throughout the twenties Americans offered competing visions of women's proper place in American society. Former suffragists envisioned modern women playing an active role in politics. Popular culture, however, consistently defined the "new woman" as someone who kept herself thin, pretty, and lively for her husband.

Women in the Twenties

When women got the right to vote nationwide, an aging generation of feminists tried immediately to organize the female vote behind causes that particularly affected women. Black women had supported suffrage as a step toward politically empowering the African American community. Southern authorities, however, used poll taxes, literacy tests, and intimidation to stop black women from registering to vote. The League of Women Voters, created by the National American Women Suffrage Association in 1920, drew up a list of issues that it expected to resonate among female voters including child labor, protective legislation for female workers, and cleaning up city politics. This list did not include demanding that the Nineteenth Amendment be enforced for black and white women alike.

Responding to studies that revealed high rates of infant and mother mortality in childbirth, the League of Women Voters lobbied Congress for the nation's first major social welfare measure to help impoverished women and children. The Sheppard-Towner Act (1921) offered eight years of matching funds to states for classes that taught poor mothers about nutrition, hygiene, and prenatal care. It also provided visiting nurses for low-income pregnant women and new mothers.

By 1929, however, it became clear that women did not vote as a bloc. Therefore despite the law's success, Congress did not renew the program. Rather than rallying to gender-specific causes, the best predictor of how a woman would vote was how her husband voted.

Feminists also failed to amend the constitution by adding an Equal Rights Amendment (ERA), which stated that "equality of rights under the law shall not be denied or abridged by the United States or by any State on account of sex." The radical National Women's Party, chaired by Alice Paul, argued that such an amendment would eradicate in one fell swoop all the legal barriers that a dizzying array of archaic state legislation created for women. These laws, Elsie Hill noted, denied a woman "control of her children equal to the father's; they deny her, if married, the right to control her earnings; they punish her for offenses for which men go unpunished," such as adultery. Moderate Progressive reformers, who dominated the League of Women Voters, like future first lady Eleanor Roosevelt, worried that the ERA might endanger the protective legislation for women that they had so carefully crafted in recent years, such as the maximum hour laws designed to shield mothers from overwork (see Chapter 18). They opposed the amendment, arguing that it was better to remove troubling laws individually, like those that prevented women from serving on juries or inheriting property.

In the twenties, younger women displayed little interest in the social movements championed by their elders. Instead many women in their twenties and thirties focused on their economic prospects. Women made up 23.6 percent of the work-force by 1920, although they remained restricted to professions considered appropriate for their gender. During the decade women were primarily employed as secretaries and telephone operators. Rapid expansion of corporate bureaucracies created a new need for office workers, a demand that the growing numbers of white female high school graduates filled. Women earned less than men, but companies were certain that married women made most of the purchasing decisions in American households. Product advertising in the 1920s, therefore, targeted female consumers. *Images as History: Advertising the New Woman* explores how advertisements in the popular media also helped define the feminine ideal in the twenties.

View the **Image** *Feminine Tippler's Ankle Flask (1922)*

Images as History

ADVERTISING THE NEW WOMAN

Popular advertising characterized the "new woman" as an efficient homemaker, devoted mother, high fashion sophisticate, and engaging spouse with the time and energy for a dizzying circle of friends and club activities. Manufacturing discontent about a woman's lifestyle and insecurity about her looks was another advertising strategy designed to get women to purchase products.

Advertisements that featured attractive women to entice potential customers, as in the Fisher car ad pictured here, reflected changing ideas about the ideal female body type. In the nineteenth century upper-class women proudly displayed their corpulence as evidence of their wealth and health. In the twenties, the popular media depicted the vigorous, alert modern woman as thin and tall. But according to a 1928 study, only 17 percent of American women were both slender and over 5 feet 3 inches tall. How does this Fisher car ad both celebrate the new freedoms that women enjoyed in the twenties and perpetuate traditional stereotypes about women?

The slim Fisher girl appeared liberated from the confines of the home and the physical incapacity caused by too much weight. She seemed to be a modern woman on the move.

These tall, elongated figurines depicted an ideal female body that was slim and youthful with legs that formed a straight line from toe to thigh, pointed toes, and a giraffe-like neck. These proportions suggested the women were nearly 9 feet tall!

This female silhouette more closely resembled the body of an adolescent girl than a mature woman, encouraging a female preoccupation with dieting and self-denial that continues today.

The presence of the maid behind the Fisher girl indicates that she is rich as well as thin—an enviable combination to many women.

Most ads of the time displayed men with both feet firmly on the ground. This woman's off-balance pose with one knee bent suggested tentativeness and instability, putting limits on her independence and strength.

Her sleek body, like that of the car being advertised, served mostly as a commodity or decorative object suitable for a modern man.

"Body by Fisher"

Margaret Sanger and the Fight for Birth Control

Advertisers promised that modern electrical appliances would give women more time to spend with their children, and women's popular magazines offered a plethora of articles on how to use this

"No woman can call herself free who does not own and control her own body."

Birth control advocate MARGARET SANGER

21.12 Margaret Sanger Protests When officials in Boston refused to let Sanger speak publicly about birth control, she appeared before a crowd with her mouth bandaged to protest their censorship. Her ploy garnered headlines across the nation, giving the birth control cause a boost.

additional time to raise children properly. Birth control advocate and trained nurse Margaret Sanger viewed the mother's plight differently. Too many children, Sanger argued, ruined women's health and relegated them to the ranks of the poor. In her view providing women with information on safe and reliable contraception was more important than dispensing advice on how to raise children.

In 1916, Sanger opened the nation's first birth control clinic in Brooklyn, New York, where she passed out flyers to advertise the benefits of contraception over illegal and dangerous back-alley abortions. For nine days Sanger dispensed information on diaphragms, condoms, douches, and withdrawal to women who waited in long lines to enter the clinic. The police then shut the clinic down and arrested Sanger for distributing information about birth control. Since 1873, the Comstock Act had prohibited sending information about contraception, abortion, or pornography through the mails, and by 1878, every state except New Mexico banned all means of circulating material about contraception. Sanger served 30 days in jail, one of many unsuccessful attempts to silence her. In 1929, after she spoke on birth control before the Harvard Liberal Club in Boston, the mayor threatened to revoke the license of any hall that allowed her

to speak again. In response Sanger appeared with her mouth bandaged before an audience in Boston's Ford Hall Forum (**21.12**). Her silent protest won headlines across the nation, helping Sanger publicize her cause even more widely.

By openly discussing birth control, Sanger made public the private contraception practices of middle-class couples. Poor mothers, she said, pleaded for her to share "the secret the rich have." Studies suggested that at least twice in their lifetimes, women living in poverty pulled their shawls over their heads to visit the five-dollar abortionist down the street. Sanger often told the story of Sadie Sachs (whose authenticity was never verified), a woman whom Sanger, as a young nurse, met when she accompanied a physician into the tenements to care for Sadie after she fell ill from a botched self-induced abortion. When Sadie begged the middle-class doctor to give her the information she needed to avoid another pregnancy, he replied, "Tell Jake to sleep on the roof." The next time Sanger saw Sadie, she lay in a coma dying from another abortion. Sanger used the story to personalize the extent of the abortion problem (nearly one million abortions that resulted in 50,000 female deaths each year) and to dispel the misguided belief that no "decent" woman needed information about contraception.

Rather than counseling women to avoid sex, Sanger asserted that women had as much right as men to enjoy sexual intercourse without fearing for their lives. Contraception would not make women more promiscuous, she predicted. Once freed from the constant strain of childbearing, women would become more interesting spouses by developing their intellectual, political, and cultural interests much as popular advertising encouraged them to do.

Through her arrests, clinics, and public lectures, Sanger gradually helped change attitudes toward birth control. Although laws censoring information about birth control remained part of the legal code until the 1970s, enforcement became rarer and rarer. By the late 1920s, 30 birth control clinics operated nationwide. Eugenicists, who wanted to improve the human race by controlling its hereditary qualities, also developed an interest in birth control. For eugenicists, contraception could prevent those they viewed as "unfit" from reproducing. Under their influence many states authorized compulsory sterilization of the institutionalized mentally handicapped, criminals, and epileptics until the 1960s.

What arguments did Sanger make to support her campaign for legal contraception?

View the **Closer Look** *Competing Visions: Marriage and Birth Control*

Ensuring Peace: Diplomacy in the Twenties

 Leaders in the birth control movement developed close ties with women's right groups in other countries, just one example of the global presence that Americans maintained throughout the twenties. Although the nation focused mostly on domestic concerns, international issues sometimes dominated the headlines. In 1920, the Senate refused to ratify the Versailles Treaty, which officially ended the war with Germany, or to join the League of Nations, which President Woodrow Wilson had championed to protect world peace. Rejection of Wilson's vision of collective security through the league did not signal a withdrawal from world affairs. Presidents Warren Harding and Calvin Coolidge tried instead to use disarmament and dollars to prevent armed conflict.

Disarmament

The high point of the disarmament movement came when Republican President Warren Harding convened the **Washington Conference (1921–1922)** in Washington, D.C., to negotiate agreements that would limit warships. The conference also reaffirmed America's Open Door Policy (see Chapter 19) that kept Chinese trade open to all and secured pledges of cooperation among the world's leading military powers, including Britain, Japan, Italy and France.

The White House and press referred to the meetings in Washington as a "peace conference" to cultivate the image that the negotiations would correct Wilson's blundering in Paris during the Versailles Treaty proceedings. The opening ceremonies underscored the symbolic comparisons that the Harding administration wanted to draw between the two international conferences by inviting delegates to the solemn burial of an unidentified American soldier who had fallen on the battlefields of France.

The Tomb of the Unknown Soldier (**21.13**) memorialized all deceased soldiers who went missing or unidentified during the war. On the morning of November 11, 1921 (the third anniversary of the Armistice that ended the war), thousands of Americans lined the streets as a horse-drawn carriage carried a flag-draped coffin from the U.S. Capitol to Arlington National Cemetery. Harding, the entire Congress and Supreme Court, along with foreign dignitaries, followed the procession. After the Unknown Soldier was laid to rest, millions of Americans across the nation observed two minutes of silence to honor the fallen warrior and pray for a peaceful future. The nation subsequently buried unknown soldiers in the same tomb after World War II, and the Korean and Vietnam Wars. In 1999, DNA genetic testing determined the identity of the Vietnam serviceman, and it is unlikely that the nation will ever have another "unknown" soldier.

21.13 The Tomb of the Unknown Soldier The allegorical figures of Peace, Valor, and Victory on the Tomb of the Unknown Soldier encapsulated the Harding and Coolidge administration's diplomatic goals in the early 1920s.

How did Harding's foreign policy vision differ from Wilson's?

21.14 *Looking into the Black Hole of Ruin* This 1927 political cartoon forecast disaster if the world powers failed to reach a second naval disarmament agreement. In the cartoon the world is in disarray after a naval gun had showered it with gun powder.

Through the Washington Conference, Harding reshaped the political vision of his Democratic predecessor, Woodrow Wilson. Harding rejected Wilson's idea of using an open-ended commitment to the League of Nations to ensure world peace. He agreed with other Republicans who felt membership in this world body would restrict America's ability to set its own foreign policy. Harding instead sought to prevent another war by convincing all major powers to disarm and agree to mediation when disputes arose. Harding knew that Congress's pennypinching mood meant certain rejection of any administration proposal to maintain a large military or embark on a major shipbuilding campaign. What better way to balance this domestic reality with the need to protect American shores from heavily armed naval competitors than by negotiating multinational disarmament treaties?

To contain Japan in the Pacific and Britain, which still controlled the world's largest navy, Secretary of State Charles Evans Hughes proposed scrapping 30 American, 23 British, and 17 Japanese battleships. One thrilled observer noted that Hughes had single-handedly sunk more British battleships "than all the admirals of the world had destroyed in a cycle of centuries." Japan's 1905 victory in the Russo-Japanese War had signaled its emergence as the premier military power in East Asia. The Japanese, who unlike the British and Americans had only one ocean to patrol, accepted a naval tonnage ratio of 5:5:3 among the United States, Britain, and Japan. This meant that for every five tons of naval shipping that America and Britain maintained, Japan retained three. Besides arms limitation, negotiations focused on settling potentially explosive issues in the Pacific.

There American objectives included curtailing Japanese expansion in East Asia and preserving the Open Door in China. The American delegation met these goals, but at some cost. Japan accepted a smaller navy in return for a pledge that the others would refrain from improving their naval bases or fortifications in the western Pacific. Experts warned that this concession would leave American Pacific possessions vulnerable to a Japanese attack. Hughes, who doubted that Congress would approve funds to improve naval defenses, accepted the deal. The resulting Five Power Treaty (which included smaller tonnage limits for France and Italy) set a ten-year moratorium on battleship construction and limited the guns that ships could carry. The treaty, however, did not set limits for submarines, light cruisers, aircraft, or land forces.

In an accompanying Four Power Treaty, France, the United States, Britain, and Japan agreed to respect one another's Pacific possessions and consult if any dispute arose. The Nine Power Treaty was the conference's final achievement. In this agreement the above five nations and Portugal, the Netherlands, Belgium, and China all agreed to respect the Open Door in China, a policy advocated by the United States since the turn of the century (see Chapter 19).

The resulting agreements essentially protected the United States, Britain, and Japan from an aggressive naval attack. They left Britain in control of the European seas, gave the United States charge of the Americas, and recognized Japanese predominance in East Asia. For the time being, avoiding an arms race and maintaining the status quo served the interests of the world's major powers.

Calvin Coolidge, Harding's successor in the White House, continued the Republican effort to find alternative ways to maintain world peace. Leading powers met again in Geneva in 1927 to broker another disarmament pact. This 1927 political cartoon (**21.14**) offered support for the proceedings by showing a disheveled world covered with gunpowder from a naval gun. This time, however, the leading powers failed to reach an agreement. Secretary of State Frank Kellogg had more success negotiating the **Kellogg-Briand Pact (1928)**, whose signatories renounced aggressive war as an instrument of national policy and agreed to resolve their disagreements through peaceful means. *Choices and Consequences: Preventing War*

What benefits and drawbacks did the Washington Conference agreements offer the United States?

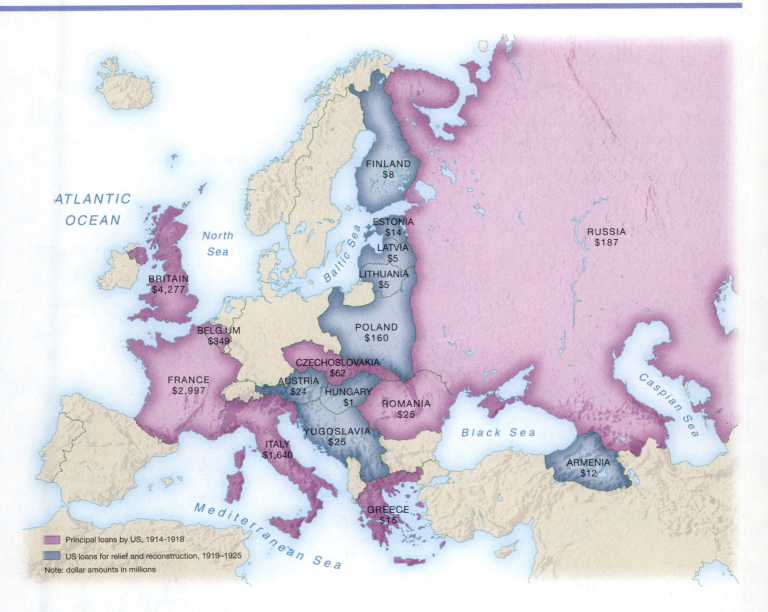

21 15 American Loans to Europe, 1914–1925
The United States demanded that Europe repay loans given to help nations defeat Germany and rebuild after World War I.

in Europe (page 650) examines why Coolidge chose to support a multinational treaty that outlawed war.

Wartime Debts

World War I revealed the importance of European trade to American prosperity, but in the twenties the politically sensitive question of securing repayment from Allied nations for American wartime loans threatened to undermine Europe's economic recovery. From 1914 to 1925, the United States had loaned the Allies nearly $10 billion to finance war-time purchases of American goods and rebuild war-torn Europe (**21.15**). In the 1920s, the Allied governments urged the United States to cancel the loans. How, they asked, could America insist on repayment when the Allies had sacrificed a whole generation of men to the joint cause of defeating Germany? Americans had supplied money while the Allies gave their blood, they argued. The United States, the Allies claimed, could easily afford to cancel the loans as the country had profited enormously from the war.

Which nations received the greatest financial aid from the United States during and after World War I?

Choices and Consequences

PREVENTING WAR IN EUROPE

In 1928, France invited the United States to sign a treaty renouncing war between the two nations, hoping to coax the American government into playing a more active peacekeeping role in Europe. President Coolidge faced four choices on how to respond. Americans had conflicting visions of the best way to avoid another war, and vocal supporters backed each option.

Choices

1 Adopt a non-interventionist policy that kept the United States out of European affairs.

2 Sign a nonaggression pact with France as the first step toward creating a formal defensive alliance that would recreate the pre-World War I balance of power system in Europe.

3 Reject bilateral agreements and join the League of Nations.

4 Negotiate a multinational nonaggression pact.

Decision

Coolidge refused to join the League of Nations but knew that outlawing war had strong appeal at home. Consequently he agreed to let Secretary of State Frank Kellogg meet with French Foreign Minister Aristide Briand to fashion a multinational nonaggression pact. By opening the treaty up to other nations, Coolidge avoided the impression that the United States was allying itself with France. The resulting Kellogg-Briand Pact was eventually signed by 62 nations, including Germany and Japan.

Consequences

The Kellogg-Briand Pact proved popular with Americans because its vagueness allowed it to be all things to all people. Non-interventionists saw the pact as insulating the country from ever fighting another war overseas. They liked the U.S. resolution to stay peaceful yet make no binding commitments to defend other nations. Internationalists, who wanted the United States to play a more active role in maintaining world peace, saw the treaty as the first step toward creating an American presence in international arbitration bodies like the World Court and the League of Nations.

"A Christmas Carol: Peace on Earth, Good Will Towards Man"

Continuing Controversies

What value did the Kellogg-Briand Pact have?
Critics dismissed the treaty as a "letter to Santa Claus," and "not worth a postage stamp," pointing out that the major powers signed the agreement but continued to arm for war. The Kellogg-Briand agreement allowed for wars of "self-defense," a slippery term that nations could easily manipulate. As if to prove the point, when the Senate ratified the treaty with only one dissenting vote, it added a reservation stating that preserving the Monroe Doctrine constituted self-defense. Others acknowledge that the treaty did not prevent World War II but point out that it allowed the victors to convict Nazi officials of violating the Kellogg-Briand Pact in postwar war crimes trials.

Did the Kellogg-Briand Pact represent a new path in American foreign policy?

Americans vehemently opposed canceling the debt. "They hired the money, didn't they," retorted President Coolidge in the mid-twenties, expressing a common American view that Europe had a moral obligation to repay its debts. Coolidge did, however, agree to lower the interest rate on the loans, which reduced the total amount due by 43 percent. Further complicating the debate, the high American tariff enacted in 1922 made it difficult for Allied nations to sell manufactured goods in the United States, depriving them of revenue that they needed to repay their war loans. Using a high tariff to protect American industries from foreign competition had tremendous domestic appeal, and the United States refused to lower it.

The Allies consequently relied on reparation payments from Germany (authorized in the Versailles Treaty) to repay their U.S. war loans. This punitive aspect of the Versailles Treaty troubled many Americans, who viewed the $33 billion reparation bill imposed on Germany as excessive. The United States denied any connection between war loans and reparation payments, seeing the first as an honest debt and the latter as blood money. The Allies, however, refused to reduce the reparation bill as long as the United States insisted on collecting Allied war loans.

In 1923, skyrocketing inflation caused Germany to miss a reparation payment, and in retaliation France and Belgium occupied the Ruhr Valley, a German industrial center. This crisis threatened to undermine American economic interests by thrusting Europe into recession. Having ruled out lowering the tariff or canceling Allied war loans to foster Europe's economic recovery, the United States resolved to help Germany make its reparation payments. Twice in the decade international committees of experts discussed reparations. In 1924, Secretary of State Hughes sent Chicago banker General Charles G. Dawes and General Electric Company head Owen D. Young to Europe. The resulting Dawes Plan (1924) loaned Germany $200 million in gold to pay a reduced reparation bill and gave it more time to meet its debt.

Certain that a German recovery was imminent, American bankers eagerly provided half the funds for the Dawes Plan and made private loans and investments that helped Germany even more. Dawes became Coolidge's vice president in 1925 and won the Nobel Peace Prize. In 1929, the Young Plan further reduced Germany's final bill to $8 billion and restructured the payment schedule.

American money kept the whole system afloat. Between 1923 and 1930, American banks loaned $2.6 billion to Germany; Germany made $2 billion in reparation payments; and the Allies repaid $2.6 billion of their American war loans (one-fifth of the amount owed). The "Global Flow of Reparation Payments" (**21.16**) details the journey that American money took through Germany, France, and Britain until it landed back in American coffers. When the stock market crashed in 1929, American bankers drastically reduced their overseas loans, and the whole arrangement collapsed. First Germany, then the Allied governments defaulted on their payments. In 1931, President Herbert Hoover successfully called for a one-year moratorium on all international debts. With the connection between reparation payments and war loans now formally acknowledged by the United States, the Allied governments canceled most of Germany's remaining reparation payments. By 1934, all governments except Finland had defaulted on their wartime American loans. Finland was the only nation that finally repaid its entire debt of $8 million to the United States by 1969.

21.16 The Global Flow of Reparation Payments American capital kept the reparation system created by the Versailles Treaty afloat in the twenties.

GREAT BRITAIN

WALL STREET BANKERS

Allied War Debt Payments

Reparations

Debt Payments

U.S. INVESTORS

GERMANY

U.S. TREASURY

FRANCE

Allied War Debt Payments

Reparations

"I do not approve in any remote sense of the cancellation of the debts to us."

President HERBERT HOOVER, 1931

How did lingering financial issues from World War I shape relations between the United States and Europe?

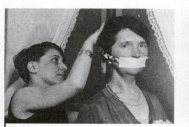

1916
Margaret Sanger opens first birth control clinic
Sanger champions birth control to improve female health and eliminate poverty

1919
First Red Scare
Anti-communist campaign destroys radical political organizations

Eighteenth Amendment ratified
Initiates era of national Prohibition

1920
F. Scott Fitzgerald publishes *This Side of Paradise*
Popularizes flapper revolt against traditional codes of conduct

1921–1922
Washington Conference held
Disarmament becomes a major goal of American foreign policy

UNIA Black Star Line founded
Short-lived black-run steamship operation line embodies Marcus Garvey's ideal of economic self-help

Review Questions

1. What features and controversies characterized America's transformation into a car culture in the 1920s? How did lifestyles and labor relations also change during the decade?

2. Compare the various manifestations of cultural conflict in the twenties. What similar impulses motivated Americans to enact prohibition, immigration restrictions, and laws prohibiting the teaching of Darwin's theory of evolution? How did these various reforms affect American society?

3. Why were the Harlem Renaissance and Marcus Garvey controversial?

4. Were the 1920s a time of political, economic, and social liberation for women? What traditional concerns or ideas remained intact?

5. How did the United States fashion a new role for itself in world affairs in the twenties?

Key Terms

Eighteenth Amendment (1919) Constitutional amendment that banned the sale, manufacture, and transportation of intoxicating liquors.   **633**

Twenty-First Amendment (1933) Constitutional amendment that repealed the Eighteenth Amendment.   **634**

Immigration Act of 1924 Law that allowed unrestricted immigration from the Western Hemisphere, curtailed all Asian immigration, and used quotas to control how many immigrants emigrated from individual European nations.   **634**

First Red Scare (1919–1920) Period when the Justice Department arrested and deported alien anarchists and Communists suspected of trying to destroy American democracy and capitalism.   **634**

Fundamentalism An evangelical Christian theology that viewed the Bible as an authentic, literal recounting of historical events and the absolute moral word of God.   **636**

Modernism A liberal Christian theology embraced in many urban areas that emphasized the ongoing revelation of divine truth.   **636**

Harlem Renaissance An outpouring of African American artistic expression in the 1920s and 1930s.   **638**

Universal Negro Improvement Association (UNIA) Organization founded by Marcus Garvey to spread his message of racial pride, economic self-sufficiency, and returning to Africa.   **640**

Washington Conference (1921–1922) Meeting of world powers that resulted in agreements that limited naval arms, reaffirmed America's Open Door policy that kept Chinese trade open to all, and secured pledges of cooperation among the world's leading military powers.   **647**

Kellogg-Briand Pact (1928) Treaty that renounced aggressive war as an instrument of national policy.   **648**

CHAPTER REVIEW

1924

Immigration Act of 1924
Severely reduces immigration and establishes nationality-based quota system

Dawes Plan
United States uses financial aid to stabilize postwar European economies

1925

Scopes Trial
Highlights cultural conflict between religion and science

Ku Klux Klan marches in Washington, D.C.
White-instigated racial violence surges as the Klan becomes a national organization

1927

Charles A. Lindbergh flies nonstop from New York to Paris
Reassures Americans that man and machine can coexist harmoniously

First feature film with sound
Hastens the creation of mass, celebrity culture

1928

Kellogg-Briand Pact
America uses world influence to secure global pledges of peace

MyHistoryLab Connections

Visit www.myhistorylab.com for a customized Study Plan to build your knowledge of *A Turbulent Decade*.

Questions for Analysis

1. What economic and cultural impact did the auto industry have?

👁 **Watch** the **Video** Video Lecture: The Rise and Fall of the Automotive Industry, p. 626

2. What did it mean to be part of the "lost generation"?

👁 **Watch** the **Video** Video Lecture: Post-War Disillusionment in the 1920s, p. 632

3. How did the Klan define "Americanism"?

📖 **Read** the **Document** The "Creed of Klanswomen" (1924), p. 639

4. What attributes of the "New Woman" are portrayed in this image?

🔍 **View** the **Image** Feminine Tippler's Ankle Flask (1922), p. 644

5. What disagreements arose over the compatibility of birth control and marriage?

🔍 **View** the **Closer Look** Competing Visions: Marriage and Birth Control, p. 646

Other Resources from This Chapter

((•)) **Hear** the **Audio**

- *Prohibition is a Failure, p. 633*
- *"If We Must Die," poem and reading by Claude McKay, p. 642*
- *"I Too," poem and reading by Langston Hughes, p. 643*

📖 **Read** the **Document** *A. Mitchell Palmer on the Menace of Communism, p. 634*

🔍 **View** the **Closer Look**

- *Envisioning Evidence: Scientific Management in Action, p. 629*
- *Immigration to the United States 1870–1915, p. 635*
- *Immigration Quotas, p. 636*
- *Competing Visions: Debating Garveyism, p. 641*
- *Images as History: Advertising the New Woman, p. 645*

🔍 **View** the **Image** *Charles Lindbergh and Spirit of St. Louis, p. 631*

👁 **Watch** the **Video** *Video Lecture: 1920s Media, p. 630*

22

A New Deal for America

The Great Depression, 1929–1940

When Franklin D. Roosevelt (FDR) accepted the Democratic nomination for president in 1932, he promised to remember "the forgotten man at the bottom of the economic pyramid." FDR won the election and took office in the throes of the Great Depression, the most devastating and longest economic crisis in American history. Four years later the photographer Walker Evans traveled to Alabama to document the hardships of three struggling sharecropping families. While there he photographed Floyd Burroughs, who spent his days toiling in the cotton fields alongside his wife and children. For seven years, through the worst of the Depression crisis, Burroughs had struggled to provide the minimal basic needs for his family without government help.

To gain public support for new government programs designed to help sharecroppers, the Farm Security Administration had commissioned this and photos like it to show Americans the faces of poverty-stricken farmers. Evans's portrait of the "forgotten man" aroused more than sympathy, however.

Americans had different visions of how the government should respond to the crisis, and throughout the 1930s, political debate centered on whether and how much the government should intervene. Presidents Herbert Hoover and Franklin D. Roosevelt both championed initiative, freedom, and opportunity. They disagreed, however, over what government action preserved or destroyed these values. In the early thirties Hoover, who preferred minimal government intervention in the economy, took a few historic steps by lending money to banks and businesses and helping farmers. More attuned to the public mood, Roosevelt initiated a broad array of public works programs and social reforms to satisfy the demand for direct government intervention in the economy.

Taken together, policy initiatives by Hoover and Roosevelt paved the way for a complete transformation of the federal government's role in American society. The New Deal did not end the Depression; that honor belonged to World War II. It was, however, one of the most important periods of legislative activity in American history.

Farmers, migrants, and industrial workers did not just passively wait for help during these hard times. They demanded a "new deal" from the federal government that alleviated the sufferings of common people. Organized labor and charismatic populist politicians on the left helped create a groundswell of support for active government intervention in the economy. The Great Depression, therefore, was not just the story of unrelenting hardship. The era also had moments of triumph for ordinary Americans, like Burroughs, who found their political voice.

"I pledge you, I pledge myself, to a new deal for the American people"

FRANKLIN D. ROOSEVELT, 1932

The Early Days of the Depression

 In 1928, the future looked rosy to most Americans, and even President Herbert Hoover believed that permanent prosperity was at hand. Americans venerated Hoover as the "Great Humanitarian" when he began his term. He left four years later amid bitter denunciations that he cared more for banks than for people, earning him the new nickname of the "Great Scrooge." The causes of the Depression were complex, giving rise to competing visions over what action, if any, the government should take and how far it should go to engineer an economic recovery. Hoover went further than any other president to date in offering federal assistance to businesses and farmers, but by 1932 his awkward manner along with his refusal to approve direct governmental relief made him appear uncaring to most Americans.

Herbert Hoover

Herbert Hoover's personal story was a classic rags-to-riches tale that reaffirmed faith in the American Dream. Orphaned at the age of nine, he later recalled that "my boyhood ambition was to be able to earn my own living, without the help of anybody, anywhere." This personal ethos shaped his lifelong political views.

Starting as a mine laborer working for $2.50 a day, by the age of 40 Hoover was a respected engineer with millions in the bank. During World War I he became the country's most famous humanitarian, when he served as food administrator and organized relief missions to help feed hungry Belgians under German occupation during the war and more starving Europeans after it. Hoover's organizational talents and dedication to good works inspired such awe that the first time his name ever appeared on a ballot in 1928, he won by a landslide, becoming president of the United States. Hoover was a poor public speaker, lacked charisma, and closely guarded his private life. But when he became president, he enjoyed immense popularity. After all, Hoover was a success in business, he had fed starving people, he had been a dynamic secretary of commerce under presidents Harding and Coolidge, and he believed that people would do the right thing once the government showed them the way.

Like most Americans, Hoover believed that able-bodied individuals should make their own way in the world. He maintained that if the government

> ## "Just making money isn't enough."
>
> **HERBERT HOOVER, explaining his decision to leave a lucrative engineering career for public service**

stepped in too often to manage the economy, individuals and businesses lost their initiative. For Hoover individualism meant more than individuals selfishly pursuing their own well-being. He felt that Americans and American business also had a responsibility to serve the community; like Progressive reformers he believed that self-interest often caused great harm to others (see Chapter 18). Hoover, however, did not share the Progressive desire to use government regulation to solve economic problems. He envisioned a more cooperative, voluntary approach. Instead of passing more laws, Hoover wanted the government to organize meetings, so industrialists, labor, and farmers could craft their own agreements to address issues such as overproduction, price wars, low wages, and strikes. The beginning of the Depression gave the country a chance to see if Hoover's voluntary and cooperative approach to economic problems could stem the crisis.

Economic Weaknesses in a Time of Prosperity

The economic downturn in 1929 took the country by surprise. However, a hard look at the twenties reveals that problems in the nation's economy existed even during the boom years, both in large-scale industries and on family farms.

Some industries, especially textiles and mining, suffered throughout the twenties from overproduction and falling demand. By 1929, even the

What qualities made Hoover a popular president when he was first elected?

Watch the Video *Prosperity of the 1920s and the Great Depression*

automobile, construction, and appliance industries found it difficult to turn a profit. Cooling demand for automobiles soon rippled outward to industries such as steel and rubber. Some of the reasons for the slump lay in the unequal distribution of income in American society. From 1923 to 1929, corporate profits rose 62 percent, while workers' hourly wages increased by only eight percent. With economic growth now linked to consumer spending, the limited purchasing power of working-class Americans contributed to the growing financial crisis.

High tariffs (taxes levied against imported products) kept foreign-made goods expensive, protecting American companies from overseas competition. Foreign countries responded by levying high tariffs against American goods, reducing overseas markets for U.S. companies. When demand for American-made goods declined at home, American companies were slow to lower prices. By the time they did, demand had fallen so dramatically that massive layoffs were inevitable. As the chances for making money in manufacturing lessened, investors stopped buying industrial stocks. This loss of capital further dampened manufacturers' efforts to recover their earlier momentum. Together, these problems revealed an ailing industrial sector.

More evident problems existed in agriculture. Farmers' boom times had come during World War I, when high demand, generous prices, and easy access to credit induced many to expand their crop production. When the war ended and demand fell, farmers were left with debts, larger farms, and falling crop prices. The long-term trend toward mechanized farming also contributed to the country's looming agricultural crisis. With tractors, farmers could plow and harvest more land on a daily basis. The ability to grow more crops, more easily, paradoxically hurt farmers because overproduction drove prices down even further.

Even before the Depression officially began, Hoover had devised a plan to help farmers escape the vicious cycle of over-production and low prices that kept them from sharing in the prosperity of the twenties. The Agricultural Marketing Act (1929) created a Farm Board with the power to buy and store crops to reduce the harvest-time market glut, which lowered crop prices. In keeping with his ethos of self-help, Hoover expected farmers to do their part to keep agricultural prices high by growing less. These measures, however, were too little, too late. Unsure about what his neighbors would do, no farmer wanted to be the only one to reduce his crop and then suffer both low prices *and* a small harvest. The nation's farmers continued to plant crops in record numbers.

> "In the 93 years of my life, depressions have come and gone. Prosperity has always returned and will again."
>
> Oil Magnate J. D. ROCKEFELLER, doubting the need for government action

The Stock Market Crash of 1929

These underlying problems all laid the foundation for an economic downturn, but by themselves did not predict a worldwide depression. Any chances for a mild recession disappeared in the **stock market crash of 1929**, a ten-day period beginning on October 20, 1929, when the value of stocks plummeted as panicked investors sold off their stock in droves. This is usually considered the official start of the Depression.

Before the crash the stock market promised investors easy profits. When investors buy stock, they own pieces of the company and receive dividends (their share of the profits). Normally the price of a share fluctuates in relation to the expected profitability of the company. By the late 1920s, however, speculators, who did not care about holding on to their share purchases to earn dividends, had taken over the stock market. Instead, they sold their shares as soon as the share price rose.

The epidemic of speculation created three key financial problems:

1. The influx of money into the stock market inflated share prices to such an extent that a stock's price soon bore little relation to the actual worth of a company.

2. Many speculators bought on margin, the name given to the short-term loans used to purchase stock, and planned to cover these loans by quickly reselling their shares at a higher price. When stock prices began to fall, too many investors could not pay these debts.

3. Many investors were speculating with other people's money, funds from ordinary Americans' savings accounts that banks used to finance speculative stock market purchases. That explains why, although only 10 percent of Americans actually owned stock, the life savings of millions disappeared in October 1929.

Why did farmers not prosper in the 1920s?

On Monday, October 20, 1929, the downward spiral began. Stock prices plummeted three days later on Black Thursday when a record 12.9 million shares changed hands. On Black Tuesday the following week, October 29, 1929, 16 million shares were traded and losses totaled $14 billion. That evening James Rosenberg, a Wall Street bankruptcy lawyer who was also an artist, etched an expressionist portrait of the chaotic scenes he had witnessed.

Rosenberg's Oct. 29 *Dies Irae (Day of Wrath) 1929* (**22.1**) captured the panic that swept Wall Street as investors raced to the New York Stock Exchange. In the lithograph the nation's financial institutions teeter on the verge of collapse, frightened crowds gather in the streets, and dark clouds hover over a sky filled with stockbrokers jumping to their deaths. Throughout the crisis rumors circulated about ruined investors committing suicide by leaping from the city's skyscrapers, and ambulance sirens wailed continually as crews responded to false alarms.

22.1 *Oct. 29 Dies Irae (Day of Wrath) 1929*
To convey the panic that swept Wall Street after the stock market crashed, James Rosenberg employed apocalyptic biblical imagery traditionally used to depict God's wrath as the world comes to an end. The photo shows investors racing to the New York Stock Exchange.

What factors led to the stock market crash in 1929?

Hoover's Response to the Depression

When the stock market crashed, no one knew that this was the beginning of a ten-year ordeal. The Great Depression lasted from 1929 to 1939, the most devastating and longest economic crisis in American history. In the 1920s, the federal government played a relatively minor role in the economy, and conservative businessmen urged Hoover to keep it that way. Do nothing, the laissez-faire capitalists told the president, setting in motion a political debate over government intervention that would dominate the Depression era.

Rejecting the laissez-faire suggestion, Hoover envisioned the government fostering a spirit of teamwork that encouraged Americans to work together as the nation weathered the

economic downturn. In keeping with his ideas of service-minded individualism, he brought the leaders of banking, industry, and labor to the White House and urged them to do their bit to keep the economy afloat. Responding to Hoover's plea, industry agreed not to lay off workers or cut wages, and labor leaders accepted a shorter workday to create more jobs. Hoover asked state governments to accelerate their road and public building projects to add jobs in their communities.

Hoover also stepped up hiring for long-planned federal construction projects including the Hoover Dam in the West and asked Congress to extend the tariff on manufactured goods to agricultural imports. Congress complied in 1930, raising tariffs to their highest level ever. When other nations retaliated with their own high tariffs, American companies and farmers lost overseas markets. As a result the world and the United States plunged deeper into economic depression.

In orchestrating this unprecedented federal response to an economic depression, Hoover stayed within limits acceptable to conservatives. Most fiscal conservatives wanted government-built roads and a high protective tariff and preferred non-governmental solutions to economic problems. When it came to helping needy citizens directly, Hoover went no further than asking local governments and charities to assume their traditional role of distributing food and clothing to the poor. This stance surprised Hoover's Progressive supporters, given his previous triumph organizing massive international relief efforts to feed hungry Europeans during and after World War I. It was not a question of helping people, Hoover asserted. "It is solely a question of the best method by which hunger and cold shall be prevented," he explained. To Hoover the American tradition of self-help made relief the responsibility of local governments and charities.

When the crisis entered its second year, U.S. Steel announced a ten percent wage cut. Other companies followed suit, and within ten days American business had slashed millions of workers' wages and begun massive layoffs. The nation's deepening financial woes convinced Hoover to lend federal money to businesses and states. This decision was a dramatic break from past practice. In previous financial panics and depressions, private bankers had put up the money needed for recovery, and presidents had cut federal spending to ensure a balanced budget. In 1932, by proposing a direct economic role for the government in ending the Depression, Herbert Hoover—the man who wanted to decrease

How did Hoover respond to the initial economic crisis?

22.2 *Bread Line—No One Has Starved* (1932) Breadlines became an iconic symbol of Depression-era suffering when private charities began providing free meals to the unemployed. Rather than forming bonds with one another over their shared plight, the men in this drawing remain isolated islands of desperation.

Americans' reliance on the government to solve their problems—went further than any previous peacetime president in similar circumstances.

By providing money to banks, insurance companies, farm mortgage associations, and railroads through the Reconstruction Finance Corporation (RFC) Act of 1932, Hoover helped institutions that were vital to the prosperity of any community. In its first year the government loaned more than $1.5 billion to these businesses, but little relief trickled down to workers. When critics pressured the president to provide direct help to those without work or food, Hoover responded with the Emergency Relief Act (1932), which lent money to the states for public works programs. Although his farm program, the RFC, and state loans failed to bring about recovery, Hoover had unknowingly set a precedent for direct governmental management of the economy that Franklin D. Roosevelt would expand. "We didn't admit it at the time, but practically the whole New Deal was extrapolated from programs that Hoover started," Rexford Tugwell, a key advisor to FDR, later acknowledged.

Reginald Marsh's *Bread Line—No One Has Starved* (**22.2**) depicts a group of downtrodden men waiting for a free meal, visual evidence of the growing crisis. The hunched posture of these former wage-earners symbolizes the shame associated with accepting charity. The men stand close together to keep their place in line, but do not converse or even look at each other. Keeping their hands in their pockets, they have been paralyzed by poverty. Marsh based his title on Hoover's remark that "no one is actually starving." The president had hoped to boost morale, but Marsh's satire portrayed Hoover as out of touch with reality.

With unemployment hovering around 20 percent in 1932, Hoover's popularity declined steadily. Shantytowns constructed by the homeless became known as "Hoovervilles," and people waved "Hooverflags" (empty pockets turned inside out) in street protests. A well-circulated joke began with Hoover asking an aide for a nickel to call a friend from a public telephone. "Here," said the man, tossing him a dime, "call them both."

In the 1932 presidential campaign, Hoover faced off against FDR, a fifth cousin of Theodore Roosevelt. In sharp contrast to how he would govern, Franklin D. Roosevelt ran a fairly conservative campaign and let Hoover's missteps win him the election. One of those mistakes was the violent eviction of war veterans from the nation's capital. Throughout the summer of 1932, the **Bonus March**, a two-month-long demonstration by 40,000 impoverished World War I veterans and their families in Washington, D.C. transfixed the nation. The veterans demanded early payment of a bonus promised them by Congress. The Bonus March ended violently when the army expelled the protesters using tanks, cavalry, and troops with fixed bayonets, further damaging Hoover's popularity at a key moment during the presidential campaign. *Choices and Consequences: Evicting the Bonus Marchers* explores how Hoover lost control of the decision to evict the Bonus Marchers from the city and paid the consequences.

What innovative solutions did Hoover propose as the economic crisis continued?

View the Image *Children with "Hoover's Poor Farm" Sign*

Choices and Consequences

EVICTING THE BONUS MARCHERS

In 1924, World War I veterans had received a federal bond certificate (worth an average of $1,500) set to mature in 1945. In May, 1932, veterans and their families arrived en masse in the nation's capital to demand immediate payment of this bonus. They set up a huge "Hooverville" of makeshift shacks and tents and staged continuous demonstrations on the Capitol steps. Hoover faced three choices about how to deal with the demonstration, depending on what interpretation of the protest he embraced.

Choices

1 Accept the veterans' argument that the government should pay the bonus immediately to alleviate their Depression-caused suffering.

2 Accept his advisers' view that the Bonus March was a communist-inspired plot to incite revolution, and use force to suppress it.

3 Reject their claim but treat the veterans as essentially harmless, if misguided, citizens in desperate financial straits.

Decision

While many in the general public and press viewed the Bonus Marchers as down-on-their-luck citizens, Hoover grew convinced that they were a dangerous, radical force. After a skirmish between veterans and the police in August, Hoover opted to send in troops with instructions to restore order.

Consequences

Once the troops were deployed, Chief of Staff General Douglas MacArthur exceeded Hoover's orders and decided to drive the veterans out of the city using tear gas, tanks, and bayonets. Hoover never publicly revealed MacArthur's insubordination. When Franklin D. Roosevelt heard of the violent eviction, he reportedly told an adviser, "Well, Felix, this will elect me."

Continuing Controversies

Was the government right to use force to evict the Bonus Marchers?

To justify the eviction, the White House mounted a furious public relations campaign that included false accusations of discovering dynamite in the main veterans' encampment. Some upper-class Americans applauded the government's actions, hoping to dampen any revolutionary impulse among the poor. But many working- and middle-class Americans saw their own destroyed lives in the smoldering ruins of the veterans' shantytown and turned against Hoover for refusing to aid men who had served the nation loyally.

The Ruins of a Bonus Army Encampment (1932)

Why was Hoover's choice to evict the bonus marchers significant?

A New President and a New Deal

FDR became president in 1933 during the lowest moment of the Depression with 25 percent of the workforce unemployed. Half of those with home mortgages had defaulted on their loans, and the entire banking system appeared ready to collapse. Empathy for the common people encouraged FDR to act, but so did fear that a social revolution might result if Washington did nothing for them. "I pledge you, I pledge myself, to a new deal for the American people," FDR had proclaimed during his campaign. He entered office dedicated to protecting America as a capitalist society, and his vision of government activism came under severe scrutiny from both sides of the political spectrum.

FDR: The Politician

"Only a foolish optimist can deny the dark realities of the moment," noted FDR upon taking office in 1933. If Roosevelt had a mandate for anything, it was for bold action. He met that expectation with the **New Deal**, an avalanche of legislation from 1933 to 1938 intended to promote economic recovery, reform American capitalism, and offer security to ordinary Americans. The chart "Key New Deal Legislation" (**22.3**) shows the most significant laws passed under Roosevelt's watch.

Having campaigned as a fiscal conservative who would balance the budget, FDR did not have a blueprint for ending the Depression when he came into office. He did, however, have a fairly well-shaped social philosophy. "He had a profound feeling for the underdog, …a very keen awareness that political democracy could not exist side by side with economic plutocracy," according to a key adviser. "We are going to make a country," the president told a Cabinet member, "in which no one is left out." FDR sought advice for specific programs and regulations from the Brain Trust, leading academics who served as presidential advisers in the early years of the New Deal. The Brain Trust wanted to revive the Progressive-era practice of using government regulation to solve economic problems and protect the common good (see Chapter 18). Brain Trust members Raymond Moley, Rexford Tugwell, and Adolf Berle diagnosed under-consumption as the main cause of the Depression, blaming the unequal distribution of income, the farm crisis, rigid prices, and low wages as the key culprits. This cartoon (**22.4**) depicts the conservative complaint that the Brain Trust hurt the country with New Deal programs intended to correct these economic problems. Posing as doctors, these professors have anesthetized the country with propaganda. Now the patient lies on an operating table oblivious to the knives and drills about to destroy his body. Besides attacking the New Deal as a set of unwise experiments, the cartoon touches on conservatives' concern that too much government involvement in the economy

22.3 Key New Deal Legislation

1933	**Reconstruction Finance Corporation** Businesses and banks receive federal loans
1933	**National Industrial Recovery Act** Allows business to set price, wage, and production codes
1933	**Agricultural Adjustment Act** Pays farmers to plant less to raise crop prices
1933	**Civilian Conservation Corps** Employs young men in reforestation and construction
1933	**Public Works Administration** Construction projects provide work relief to poor
1933	**Glass-Steagall Act of 1933** Insures bank deposits; separates commercial and investment banking
1933	**Tennessee Valley Authority** Brings electricity to rural areas; stops devastating floods
1935	**Social Security Act** Guarantees eligible workers a pension and unemployment insurance; aid to disabled and married women with dependent children
1935	**Wagner Act** Offers government protection to unions
1935	**Works Progress Administration** Extensive public works program employs 8 million ranging from artists to construction workers
1938	**Fair Labor Standards Act** Establishes federal minimum wage and maximum working hours per week

How did the competing social philosophies of Hoover and FDR differ?

View the **Image** John Baer, "We Demand a New Deal!" (1931)

22.4 Conservatives Attack the New Deal
This 1934 cartoon mocks the Brain Trust for experimenting with the nation's well-being, implying that New Deal policy initiatives did more harm than good.

"If it fails, admit it frankly and try another. But above all, try something."

FDR's approach to shaping the New Deal

Americans differed in their reactions to Eleanor Roosevelt's left-leaning political activities. Conservative detractors advised her to "stay at home and make a home for your husband." Her civil rights activism particularly upset southern Democrats in Congress. She had equally ardent supporters and consistently won a two-thirds approval rating in Gallup polls—often bettering her husband. Thousands of Americans wrote to her each week, to ask for financial help, or to praise her work.

Like his wife, FDR connected well with the public. Throughout his presidency FDR used weekly radio addresses that he called "fireside chats" to speak directly to the nation. After the president's death in 1945, people stopped Eleanor on the street to tell her how much "they missed the way the President used to talk to them. They'd say, 'He used to talk to me about my government,'" she recalled. FDR was often photographed smiling and smoking from an elegant-looking cigarette holder (**22.5**), and the public found his visible cheerfulness refreshing.

FDR infused hope into a time of trouble and confusion. Yet little in his background suggested that he would understand the plight of common people. The only son of doting, wealthy parents who imbued him with tremendous self-confidence, the athletic, charming, and brilliant FDR attended Harvard and passed the New York State bar exam after just one year at Columbia Law School. In 1929, he became governor of New York. A personal tragedy in his life, however, convinced the public that FDR understood what it meant to overcome adversity. In 1921, at the age of 39, polio left him partially paralyzed for the rest of his life, and in pain much of the time. His disability "made it possible for the common people to trust him to understand what it is to be handicapped by poverty and ignorance, as well as by physical misfortune," Secretary of Labor Frances Perkins noted.

22.5 FDR's Trademark Cigarette Holder and Smile
Most Americans found FDR's cheerfulness reassuring, and he inspired confidence in America's security and future prosperity.

(like too many pointless operations) would do more harm than good.

In formulating his policies FDR leaned on another critical adviser: his wife. Eleanor Roosevelt served as the president's "eyes and ears" by traveling around the country and reporting to him what she observed. In 1933 First Lady Eleanor Roosevelt traveled 30,000 miles visiting Americans where they worked and lived. Two years later, the Washington *Star* felt it newsworthy to print the headline "Mrs. Roosevelt Spends the Night at the White House."

Over time Eleanor Roosevelt became more outspoken in advancing causes dear to her heart concerning racial injustice and poverty. She invited prominent African Americans to the White House to talk directly to the president about civil rights. Eleanor Roosevelt's visible participation in political affairs set her apart from former First Ladies, who had mainly served as official hostesses at White House functions. Her activism opened up political opportunities for other women. There were many firsts for women in the thirties: first ambassador, first judge on the Court of Appeals, and first cabinet secretary, Secretary of Labor Frances Perkins.

((•— **Hear** the **Audio File** *FDR's First Inaugural Address*

What role did Eleanor Roosevelt play during her husband's administrations?

Managing Appearances

Although FDR benefited from people knowing that he had overcome a misfortune, he also believed that visual images of his handicap would convey the impression that he was weak and physically unfit for his responsibilities. He made a personal and political decision to conceal his paralysis. To hide his heavy leg braces, FDR wore extra long pants and had the visible portion of the braces painted black to blend with his shoes. He learned to stand upright by holding onto a cane with one hand and the arm of an aide, usually his son, with the other (**22.6**). He would then use his hips to swing his legs forward in a semi-arch to give the illusion of walking. All of this required tremendous physical exertion. James Roosevelt later noted that he often had bruises on his arms from the force of his father's grip. Father and son disguised their physical effort by smiling and joking as they "walked" together before audiences.

Away from the crowds, aides carried FDR up stairs or from the car to a wheelchair. In public he often used his automobile as a prop to hide his disability, and by holding a bar installed in the backseat of an open touring car, he could pull himself up to address crowds. At one stadium rally a ramp was constructed so that the president's car could be driven onto the stage in the center of the field. FDR gave his speech without leaving the car.

The press obeyed White House rules that prohibited taking photos of the president in a wheelchair or being carried. As a result there are only two known photographs of FDR in a wheelchair. This

22.7 FDR Running
Political cartoons never showed the president's physical disabilities.

self-censorship even extended to political cartoons, which never once depicted the president as incapacitated. Instead, these caricatures usually portrayed an energetic FDR running or jumping like this 1936 caricature from the *Kansas City Star* (**22.7**), in which a sprinting FDR replicates Benjamin Franklin's kite-flying experiment to bring electricity to the rural poor.

The Temper of the Poor: Passivity and Anger

Hoover kept his distance from common people and paid the price. FDR was a more astute politician. But what was the temper of the people he needed

22.6 FDR Walking
Shunning his wheelchair, candidate FDR holds onto his son's arm as the two greet supporters during his first presidential campaign in 1932.

> "There is something about the first anniversary of your layoff which makes you feel more hopeless."
>
> A worker during the Great Depression

to help? Two competing images of the poor soon emerged. One emphasized their helplessness and suffering; the other saw them as teetering on the brink of revolt.

Countless government investigators detailed the plight of hardworking family men suddenly without jobs. "I find them all in the same shape—fear, fear driving them into a state of semi-collapse; cracking nerves; and an overpowering terror of the future," reported one social worker. Many Americans chose to suffer silently, making their own decisions about how to cope, sometimes blaming themselves rather than the Depression for their troubles. This portrait by Dorothea Lange (**22.8**) conveys this "quiet desperation" of the poor. In Lange's image an unemployed man grasps his empty tin cup and leans over the rail as if he is kneeling at a church altar praying for salvation. The man's plight is moving, but his passivity is also vaguely reassuring to those who feared angry demonstrations or social revolution.

As the Bonus March revealed, however, not all Americans were waiting patiently for conditions to improve. Federal investigator Lorena Hickok feared that a social revolution was brewing: "I still feel that vast numbers of unemployed in Pennsylvania are 'right on the edge,' so to speak—that it wouldn't take much to make Communists out of them." The Communist Party hoped that she was right. Unlike Roosevelt and his conservative critics, Communists had no interest in saving capitalism. They hoped that the crisis would provoke a social revolt that abolished private property. The 1930s were the "heyday of American Communism," as the party grew from 7,000 members in 1930 to 100,000 in 1939. Across the country Communists organized unemployed councils that blocked evictions from city apartments, mounted hunger marches, and reconnected gas and electricity lines for workers who could not pay their bills.

Grocery store robberies were also common, although newspapers rarely reported these crimes. When the manager of a grocery store in Detroit denied a group of men credit, they ransacked his store. Witnessing the food riot, the novelist John Dos Passos wondered why the manager did not call the police. "If more people heard about affairs like this, there would be more trouble," the manager replied.

While the urban poor stole food, farmers demonstrated to demand higher prices for their crops. Across the Midwest farmers disrupted food shipments by blocking highways with logs and pouring milk onto roads. When banks seized land, cattle, or farm machinery from farmers who defaulted on their loans, they needed help from the police to ensure that public sales of the confiscated property went smoothly. At some farm auctions farmers devised an effective strategy to help their neighbors by offering only a penny for the property on sale. Nooses hung on barn doors at penny auctions warned prospective buyers that bidding on a farm family's possessions would not be wise. "If anyone in the farmyard might be so ignorant of what was going on as to put in a serious bid, a suitably burly man would be likely to step up and put a hand on his shoulder with the words, 'That bid's a little high, ain't it?'" one farmer recalled.

22.8 "Breadline" San Francisco, 1933
The man's empty cup symbolized his pervasive hunger. His unthreatening pose created sympathy for his plight, while the militant poor provoked fears of social revolution.

Recovering from the Depression

 "First of all," FDR stated in his first inaugural address, "let me assert my firm belief that the only thing we have to fear is fear itself." These courageous words inspired confidence in the country's new leader at a time when financial institutions were on the brink of collapse. Jump-starting the economy involved restoring confidence in the banking system, putting people to work, and keeping businesses afloat. Following Hoover's lead, FDR established a cooperative relationship between the government and business and provided federal money for banks and businesses. But unlike Hoover, he was willing to provide jobs through extensive public works programs and to fund temporary direct relief for average citizens.

Revamping Banking and Financial Institutions

By the time FDR took office, Americans had lost nearly $2.5 billion in 9,000 bank failures. The new president declared an immediate bank holiday on March 6, 1933, that closed the nation's banks for a week. An obedient Congress quickly passed emergency banking legislation that allowed only banks with the Federal Reserve's stamp of approval to reopen. "I can assure you that it is safer to keep your money in a reopened bank than under the mattress," FDR told the public in his first fireside address. When the "holiday" ended, millions of Americans demonstrated their faith in the president by depositing more money than they withdrew in the weeks that followed. "Capitalism," a FDR adviser said later, "was saved in [those] eight days."

"It was the Government's job to straighten out this situation," FDR told radio listeners. His administration soon proposed more reform measures to inspire public confidence in the nation's banks. The Glass-Steagall Act of 1933 created the Federal Deposit Insurance Corporation (FDIC), insuring the accounts of small depositors in member banks. The FDIC still exists. The same legislation protected the deposits of ordinary Americans by separating investment and commercial banking, so bank officials could no longer make speculative loans or stock purchases with depositors' money. This provision was repealed in 1999.

Finally, the New Deal tackled the problems caused by an unregulated stock market that had contributed to the crash of 1929. Laws established the Securities and Exchange Commission (SEC) and reformed the practices of buying and selling stock. The SEC required companies to disclose financial details to potential investors, so they could make an informed stock purchase. The SEC also regulated the practice of buying stocks on margin.

Reforms in home mortgage lending practices probably had a more immediate impact on the lives of ordinary Americans than stock market reform. In 1933, 40 percent of homeowners were on the brink of losing their homes to bank foreclosures. In response FDR created a program that refinanced one out of every ten home mortgages and spread the payments over 20 years instead of the usual five. Designed to encourage Americans to purchase homes (and thereby boost the construction industry), the Federal Housing Authority (FHA), founded in 1934, offered insurance to private lenders who financed home mortgages for new homes. FHA backing allowed creditors to reduce the down payment required, lower interest rates, and lengthen the life of the loan. These government-supported initiatives helped form the modern mortgage-lending practices that enabled the percentage of Americans who owned their own homes to increase by one-third over the next 40 years.

Father Charles Coughlin

Many businessmen and bankers supported these reforms because they renewed public faith in the basic structures of capitalism. With internal squabbles dividing its members, the Communist Party never effectively challenged the New Deal. Instead, the most influential challenger on the left to New Deal banking reforms was Father Charles Coughlin.

A popular "radio priest" from Detroit who spoke with an Irish brogue, Father Coughlin gave sermons on a weekly radio program that drew audiences of 30 to 40 million. In 1934, he received more mail

How did FDR reform the nation's banking and financial institutions?

Read the Document *Franklin D. Roosevelt—Radio Address (1933)*

than anyone in the United States, including Roosevelt, most of it from adoring fans making donations to Coughlin's cause. Coughlin singled out financiers and international bankers as the culprits who caused the Depression. The popularity of his relentless attacks on the elite helped push FDR increasingly to the left during his first administration.

Following the lead of the Populists of the nineteenth century (see Chapter 17), Coughlin focused on how existing currency and banking arrangements helped bankers but hurt the common people. With currency in short supply, average citizens had to work harder to pay off their debts. Putting more money into circulation made sense in the midst of a depression. Bankers, however, held firm to their orthodoxy that all sound economies were based on the gold standard, which required that money be redeemable in gold, thereby limiting the amount of money that the government could print or coin. Coughlin proposed a revaluation of the price of gold and the monetization of silver (letting people also redeem paper money in silver, which was cheaper and more plentiful than gold) to allow the government to put more dollars into circulation. Finally he wanted to nationalize the banks to take money lending out of the hands of private bankers.

Coughlin initially supported the New Deal in sermons like "The New Deal Is Christ's Deal" and praised the president when he took the country off the gold standard in 1933. FDR welcomed Coughlin's support at first but eventually grew tired of the priest's impromptu visits to the White House. As their relationship soured, Coughlin began criticizing the administration for doing too little to rein in powerful banking and capitalist interests. Many of his followers begged him to reconsider his break with FDR, before they withdrew from the short-lived third party that he headed. By 1938, Coughlin's star was in decline. His broadcasts became increasingly strident, filled for the first time with anti-Semitic diatribes against an imagined international Jewish banking conspiracy. He stayed on the air until 1942, when his bishop ordered him to cease all political activities.

Helping Industry and People

Besides shoring up banks, FDR also immediately sought to get people back to work. As the graph (**22.9**) reveals, FDR faced the most severe jobs crisis in American history. At first he followed in Hoover's footsteps. The Reconstruction Finance Corporation continued to make loans and began buying bank stocks to help banks acquire the liquid capital

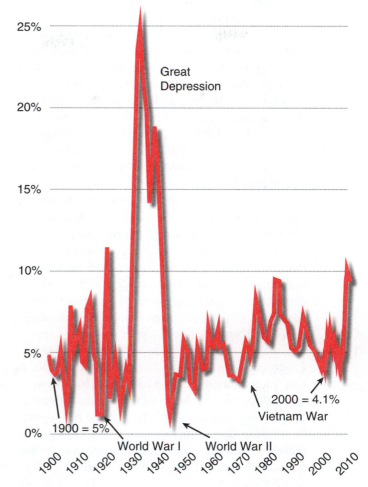

Unemployed Persons as a Percentage of the Civilian Labor Force

Great Depression

1900 = 5%
World War I
World War II
2000 = 4.1%
Vietnam War

22.9 Soaring Unemployment This graph reveals the historically high unemployment rate during the Great Depression. In the 2008–2011 recession, unemployment figures also climbed dramatically amid fears of another depression.

needed to stay open. The National Recovery Administration (NRA), established by the 1933 National Industrial Recovery Act, was the cornerstone of FDR's efforts to devise a Hoover-like cooperative solution to the crisis. Suspending antitrust laws, the NRA established industrial boards for each sector of the economy that brought competitors together to set prices, production quotas, and wages. Architects of the NRA believed these industrial codes would stop manufacturers from cutting wages to subsidize lower prices, a practice that reduced the purchasing power of workers, contributing to overproduction and under-consumption.

When prices rose without a corresponding increase in wages, however, many Americans became unhappy with the NRA. Even the larger corporations that benefited from the price codes remained leery of it, fearful that the agency might force them to negotiate with labor unions. To everyone's relief the Supreme Court declared the NRA unconstitutional in 1935, ruling that it delegated too much

Read the Document *Father Charles E. Coughlin, "A Third Party" (1936)*

Why did New Deal banking reforms and relief programs generate criticism?

power from the legislative to the executive branch and regulated more than interstate commerce.

FDR's reading of the public mood encouraged him to depart from Hoover's policies and offer direct financial relief to individuals out of work. FDR encouraged Americans to write to him, and in their correspondence destitute Americans bared painful details of their poverty and often asked for specific items, such as a coat or shoes. Attuned to the widespread misery, FDR created the Federal Emergency Relief Administration (FERA), which worked with state governments to distribute direct relief to the unemployed.

Although many Americans were grateful for this help, applying for relief or a "dole" was humiliating for previously self-sufficient working people. Even at the height of the Depression, accepting relief carried the stigma of personal failure. Although they envisioned the roots of poverty differently, both conservatives and Progressives viewed relief with suspicion. Conservatives felt that laziness, alcoholism, lack of ambition, and a poor work ethic created a class of indigent poor undeserving of help. Progressives thought that dismal living and working conditions caused the poor to turn to drink or succumb to apathy, but believed that handouts would further discourage workers from trying to support themselves. One could feel sympathy for the poor, therefore, and still worry about the negative consequences of distributing charity or relief.

Like many of his contemporaries, FDR disliked using federal monies to fund direct relief. He always preferred federal programs that employed the poor to those that simply handed out food or money. In 1935, he decided to stop providing direct cash grants to the needy. "To dole out relief in this way is to administer a narcotic, a subtle destroyer of the human spirit," FDR told Congress. From this point on the states handled relief, while the federal government tackled the problem of putting "employable" persons to work.

Putting People to Work

To the dismay of conservatives and the gratitude of the unemployed, the New Deal created a variety of programs, each administered by a different agency, that provided 15 million jobs during the Depression. The Civil Works Administration (CWA), Civilian Conservation Corps (CCC), and Public Works Administration (PWA) were all founded in 1933. During its four-month existence, the CWA provided jobs that helped more than four million workers survive the winter of 1933–1934 and stemmed growing unrest among the unemployed. The CCC (which lasted until World War II) focused on giving economically disadvantaged young men a chance to gain work experience. It undertook major reforestation projects, constructed campgrounds, restored historic battlefields, and stocked rivers and lakes with fish. The PWA, run by Harold Ickes, funded public works projects, especially roads and buildings, to help revive the construction industry.

After deciding in 1935 to fund only work relief programs, Roosevelt created the Works Progress Administration. The WPA, managed by Harry Hopkins, was a major public works program that from 1935 to 1943 employed more than eight million workers, one-fifth of the workforce. During its existence, the WPA constructed 200,000 buildings and bridges along with 600,000 miles of roads. It also funded the arts, subsidizing painters and writers. Thanks to massive New Deal government spending on work-relief, and the subsequent strengthening of consumer spending power, the economy began gradually recovering in the mid-thirties.

> "I gave the best part of my life to the American country, and I spent every cent I made here. They owe it to me to take care of me."
>
> A worker, happily accepting a WPA job

> "I wouldn't plow nobody's mule from sunrise to sunset for 50 cents per day when I could get $1.30 for pretending to work on a DITCH."
>
> A Georgia farmer, criticizing the WPA work ethic

Who benefited from the wide range of New Deal work-relief programs?

View the Image CCC worker (1938)

22.10 *Turning a Corner*
Like most Depression-era post office murals, this one celebrated workers as the backbone of the nation.
"My interest," artist Joe Jones noted, "was in portraying man at work—his job before him—and how he goes
about it with his tools—man creating."

Even permanent government agencies put Americans to work during the Depression. The Treasury Department, for instance, hired artists to decorate post offices throughout the nation. Edward Bruce, who directed the program, wanted to "enrich the lives of all our people" by making "beauty part of their daily lives" when they visited the post office. Post office murals celebrated working Americans and their communities, but eschewed controversial themes like class conflict. In rural areas these murals projected images of prosperous farmers running family farms. Joe Jones painted *Turning a Corner* (**22.10**) for the Anthony, Kansas, post office, a mural that showed a farmer using a tractor to harvest a field of golden wheat before an approaching storm damaged his crops. The mural made no reference to the drought or dust storms that ravaged farms during the thirties, nor criticized farmers for overproducing and causing crop prices to fall. Instead, Jones celebrated farmers for growing the food that fed the nation and romanticized their relationship with the land.

Americans disagreed over whether work relief was ruining or saving the country. For critics of work relief, the sight of WPA construction crew workers standing around talking instead of working led to jokes that WPA stood for "We Piddle Around." Farmers looking for day laborers also complained bitterly that federal work relief often paid more than working in the fields. Many WPA employees, however, saw government-provided jobs as a right that they had earned.

In a 1935 *Fortune* magazine survey, nearly 90 percent of lower-middle-class and working-class respondents answered yes when asked, "Do you believe that the government should see to it that every man who wants to work has a job?" Roosevelt agreed to a point. He consistently tried to terminate these programs at the slightest sign of recovery to rein in deficit spending, remaining true to his conservative fiscal values. The government reduced funds to the WPA when unemployment dropped in 1937 to 7.7 million from a high of 12.8 million in 1933. However, the sharp reduction in government spending, combined with new taxes and higher interest rates, caused the fledgling recovery to grind to a halt. During the subsequent 1937 recession, automobile production declined by 50 percent, steel by 70 percent, rubber by 40 percent, and the unemployment rate rose to 9.5 million (17 percent of the working population). With no federal funds for new relief projects available, New Jersey issued licenses to beg on the streets. The next year FDR restored public works funding.

A New Deal for Farmers

New Deal public works programs dotted the American landscape with new roads, bridges, murals, and dams, a lasting legacy of Depression-era recovery efforts. Reforms in the agricultural sector also outlived the immediate crisis, part of FDR's commitment to save American capitalism and create "greater security for the average man than he has ever known before in the history of America." Americans from all walks of life, however, questioned the government's desire to help displaced farm workers.

Handling the Farm Crisis

Assisting farmers protected an American way of life that had strong mythic connections to the nation's beginnings as a land of opportunity. Farmers received more direct aid than any other group during the Depression. The Agricultural Adjustment Act (AAA) of 1933 tried to ensure that farmers earned an adequate income by paying them to take land out of cultivation, which the administration hoped would cause crop prices to rise. When reducing acreage failed to sufficiently lower output, FDR approved laws that established marketing quotas for each commodity. If farmers tried to sell more than their allotted quota, they were hit with a heavy fine.

The administration departed temporarily from this approach when the Supreme Court ruled the AAA unconstitutional in 1936. The Court decided that the tax on food-processing plants used to finance the acreage-reduction program violated the Tenth Amendment by usurping regulatory rights reserved for the states. Congress passed a second AAA in 1938, but by the mid-1930s the problems facing farmers in parts of the country had changed.

In the **Dust Bowl** drought and soil erosion caused massive dust storms across southern and plains states throughout the thirties. During one storm in May 1934, experts estimated that the winds transported 350 million tons of soil from the West to the East. Dust fell like snow on Chicago, the sun was obscured in Washington, D.C., and ships 300 miles out to sea reported dirt settling on their decks. This photo (**22.11**) captures an approaching dust storm carrying deadly amounts of dirt. Each storm left piles of dead cattle and wildlife

22.11 "Approaching Dust Storm" Ominous clouds of dirt descend on a small town in Colorado during one of the dust storms that plagued the plains states and the southwest in the thirties. The storms killed livestock and kept people inside for days.

in its wake as residents barricaded themselves inside their houses with damp towels over their mouths to avoid suffocation or wore Red Cross-provided gas masks. But even these precautions did not completely prevent deaths from occurring when a duster hit.

To encourage better farming practices, the government began paying farmers in the Dust Bowl to plant soil-improving crops like legumes instead of traditional cash crops such as wheat, cotton, and tobacco that exhausted the soil. In one innovative program the government planted 220 million trees in a 100-mile-wide swath from Childress, Texas, to the Canadian border. These trees stopped western dust from traveling east by cooling the air and reducing the wind velocity of dust storms.

Bringing electricity to rural areas was another way the New Deal improved daily life for the rural poor. Most of the urban population had electricity to ease the daily tasks of pumping water and washing clothes, advantages available to only one in ten rural families in 1930. Begun in 1933, the Tennessee Valley Authority (TVA) was a government-owned utility company that provided thousands of jobs as it built dams that generated power, provided flood relief, and created recreational lakes throughout the seven states (Tennessee, Alabama, Mississippi, Kentucky, Virginia, North Carolina, and Georgia) serviced by the Tennessee River. These areas soon enjoyed good fishing, cheap electricity, and relief from debilitating floods

Government-sponsored low-interest loans enabled rural cooperatives to string electrical lines and manufacture power. "The women went around turning the switches on and off," noted an observer after one home received its hookup. "The light and wonder in their eyes was brighter than that from the lamps." By 1941, almost half of all American farms had access to electricity, a figure that rose to 90 percent by 1950.

Native Americans were another rural population aided by New Deal policies. Commissioner for Indian Affairs John Collier pressed successfully for passage of the 1934 Indian Reorganization Act that ended the land allotment policies sanctioned under the 1887 Dawes Act (see Chapter 15) and returned some self-government to Indian reservations. The stage was set for a gradual rebirth of Native American cultures in the twentieth century.

Overall, New Deal subsidies improved farm owners' lives. Farm income doubled from $2 billion in 1929 to $4.6 billion in 1939. Although farmers still made only 37.5 percent of what nonfarm workers earned, farming had become a much more profitable business. These agricultural policies created unexpected problems, however, by helping landowners at the expense of tenant farmers and farm laborers whose services were no longer needed once the government began paying farm owners to take land out of cultivation. The Farm Security Administration helped a few tenants purchase land, offering share–croppers a way to break out of the traditional cycle of debt that bound them to landowners. But millions of tenant farmers and farm laborers, white and black, had to find their own way out of the crisis.

Hitting the Road

Over 2.5 million farmers hit the road in search of work in the thirties. Besides families traveling together in cars, nearly 250,000 teenagers, usually young men, "rode the rails" by hopping into empty freight cars. Constantly on the move, these youths found companionship in "hobo jungles" (homeless encampments) as they looked for jobs, lived off handouts, and sometimes stole to get by. Nearly 400,000 Americans left farming areas in the middle of the country and headed to California. Old trucks piled high with personal belongings flooded western highways, demonstrating how completely the United States had become a car culture. The United States was "the only Nation in the history of the world that ever went to the poorhouse in an automobile," quipped the cowboy humorist Will Rogers.

California state officials tried to discourage migrants. Near Tulsa, Oklahoma a billboard on Route 66, the main highway that migrants took west, proclaimed: "NO JOBS in California, If YOU are looking for work—KEEP OUT, 6 men for Every Job, No State Relief Available for Non-Residents." The signs did little to discourage families from heading to California.

Most new California arrivals settled into the nomadic life of the migrant worker, traveling an average of 516 miles during the six-month harvest season. Despite their dependence on migrant workers to pick the crops, native Californians did not welcome "Okies," the pejorative term for Dust Bowl refugees, with open arms. "Okies" were now subject to the same kinds of discrimination that migrant workers of Mexican, Chinese, Japanese, and Filipino descent had suffered for years in California. Migrant workers often lived in makeshift roadside camps

[■◀] Read the Document *Carey McWilliams, Okies in California (1939)*

How did displaced farmers act to improve their own lives?

22.12 Migrants Hit the Road Rickety trucks piled high with possessions and children filled western highways as families fled the Dust Bowl in search of employment elsewhere.

children followed the crops in Oklahoma and Texas. "We'll be in California yet," he proclaimed. Lange was renowned for her ability to take photographs that revealed her subjects' true feelings. Left lame by polio, she believed that her own disability made strangers trust her. Her photographs, discussed more fully in *Images as History: "Migrant Mother"—An American Icon*, had a distinct political purpose: to cement public support for migrant worker aid programs.

Repatriating Mexican Immigrants

Reducing competition from immigrants seeking work was another way the government tried to help native-born farm workers. In 1929, the government effectively ended legal immigration from Mexico for the duration of the Depression to protect jobs for American citizens. Foreshadowing today's debate over the benefits and drawbacks of immigration, California officials argued that alien workers held jobs that should go to native-born Americans. Owners of large farms disagreed, predicting that they would face a serious labor shortage if they lost their traditional workforce since few Americans wanted these jobs.

near disease-ridden water ditches. When the government tried to create camps that offered migrants better and cleaner facilities, some Californians objected. Growers worried that concentrating migrant workers in government-run camps would make it easier for them to organize unions and strikes. Other Californians believed that improving living conditions would draw even more displaced farmers to their state.

In 1935, California-based photographer Dorothea Lange began taking photographs for the Resettlement Administration to document migrant workers' suffering and arouse the public's sympathy. This photo (**22.12**) shows a father from Arkansas changing the tire on his truck as he and his seven

Anti-immigration forces prevailed. Faced with the offer of a free trip back to their original homes (financed by the United States and Mexico) or the option of staying in a country where employment options had dwindled, thousands of Mexican workers accepted repatriation. Local and federal officials arrested and then deported others who had entered the country illegally. With the advent of the New Deal, immigrants' interest in voluntary repatriation dwindled. New Deal regulations made legal aliens eligible for food relief, although most public works programs gave jobs only to citizens. Overall approximately 415,000 Mexicans left the United States during the 1930s, both voluntarily and involuntarily.

> "Social change is a difficult thing in our civilization unless you have sentiment."
>
> President FRANKLIN D. ROOSEVELT

What happened to Mexican immigrants during the Depression?   Watch the Video Video Lecture: Dorothea Lange and Migrant Mother

Images as History

"MIGRANT MOTHER"—AN AMERICAN ICON

In March 1936, the photographer Dorothea Lange entered a makeshift migrants' camp and saw a 32-year-old woman sitting with four of her seven children and all the family's possessions. Taking six quick pictures, Lange jotted down notes about the family: "Destitute in pea pickers' camp, Nipomo, California, because of the failure of the early pea crop. These people had just sold their tires in order to buy food. Of the 2,500 people in this camp most of them were destitute."

Lange's final portrait, "**Migrant Mother**," was a masterpiece. The viewer has the sense of intruding on an intensely personal moment, but Lange made no apologies for invading this woman's privacy. "She asked me no questions," the photographer later recalled. Instead, the woman "seemed to know that my pictures might help her, and so she helped me." When these photographs appeared in the *San Francisco News*, relief authorities immediately sent food to the entire camp of starving pea pickers. "Migrant Mother" and her family, however, had already left the camp. In later years, Florence Thompson, the subject of "Migrant Mother," tried to suppress the diffusion of this photograph because she felt that it stigmatized her as poor. As she lay dying of cancer in 1983, however, her children used the image to raise funds for their mother's medical expenses.

This initial photograph did not send the clear message that Lange wanted. In subsequent photos she focused on the despair of the mother and her small children rather than their general poverty.

The father was nowhere in sight, conveying either the comforting possibility that he was out looking for work or the discomforting suggestion that he had abandoned the family.

"Migrant Mother series, no. 2"

The presence of an older daughter raised potentially troublesome questions about when the woman began having children, why she continued to have so many, or why the teenager was not working to help the family.

In her next shots, Lange carefully framed out the open luggage and trash to erase any suggestion that the family lacked discipline.

"Migrant Mother series, no. 6"

Because they wanted their photographs to arouse public sympathy and support for federal aid, government photographers always depicted the migrants as heroic victims. They were never shown smiling, angry, or as responsible for their misery.

As adults Thompson's daughters believed that this image underscored the importance of individual initiative, not the need for federal aid. To make sure that they "never lived like that again, we all worked hard and we all had good jobs and we all stayed with it," one explained.

Lange's composition suggests "a sort of anti-Madonna and Child," wrote one critic.

View the **Closer Look** *Images as History: "Migrant Mother"— An American Icon*   What was the purpose and impact of Dorothea Lange's migrant farmer photographs?

Reforms to Ensure Social Justice

 In 1935, the New Deal moved beyond measures intended to help the nation recover from the Depression to policies designed to correct basic inequities in American society and provide security to ordinary Americans. Reforms protected unions, guaranteed many elderly a government pension, established a minimum wage for factory workers, and abolished child labor. The momentum for these New Deal reforms came from the growing strength of left-leaning politicians, unions, and senior citizens who were unafraid to press FDR to adopt their vision of a more just society.

The Challenge from Huey Long: "Share Our Wealth"

Roosevelt's move to the left toward the end of his first administration was partially a response to the popularity of Father Coughlin and Senator Huey Long of Louisiana. Before he became a senator, Long was an adored, although corrupt, governor of Louisiana who provided free school textbooks, built roads and hospitals, and curbed the power of the state's oil industry. "They do not merely vote for him," a reporter wrote of Louisianans in 1935, "they worship the ground he walks on."

Long supported the New Deal at first, but his dissatisfaction with the pace of change and his own political ambitions caused a break with FDR. As an alternative to the New Deal, Long proposed his **Share Our Wealth** plan to redistribute money from the rich to the poor. Long wanted to limit every person to $1 million in income and $8 million in capital investments each year. The government would confiscate all other personal income and corporate profits and redistribute $2,000 annually to every American family. Besides offering Americans a guaranteed income, Long also championed old-age pensions, expanded veterans' benefits, a shorter working day, and government support for education. He created a Share Our Wealth Society and claimed a membership of five million, promising to make "every man a King."

Long argued that under his plan the rich would still enjoy a life of luxury, and even published a budget for a family of four on $1 million a year to show that they could easily afford $10,000 of jewelry each season and a new $100 suit a day. Yet even the great fortunes amassed by the richest Americans were too small to support the kind of program Long proposed. Despite the flaws in his plan, Long tapped into public anger at the rich, whom many blamed for causing the Depression, and long-standing resentments about the concentration of wealth in the hands of a few. Long never had a chance to challenge FDR as a third-party candidate, however, because a disgruntled man who detested Long assassinated him on the steps of the Louisiana state capitol in the fall of 1935. "I wonder why he shot me," Long asked before he died, a question the assassin, killed on the spot by Long's bodyguards, could never answer. *Competing Visions: Sharing the Wealth* explores the Depression-era debate over redistributing income.

Social Security

Alongside the larger-than-life personas of Huey Long and Father Coughlin stood Dr. Francis Townsend, an unassuming sixty-six-year-old physician who organized a campaign for old-age pensions in 1933 after seeing three old women outside his house in Long Beach, California, rummaging through the trash. The combined activism of these three men, and the support each enjoyed, convinced FDR in 1935 to create a comprehensive social-welfare system that protected the aged, the unemployed, and those unable to care for themselves.

Townsend's call for government pensions for the elderly set in motion a powerful grassroots

> ## "It is hard to be old and not have anything."
> ### A woman from North Dakota, writing to Roosevelt

Competing Visions

SHARING THE WEALTH

Should money be redistributed from the haves to the have-nots? During the Depression, many Americans answered a resounding "yes." Below are two views, reflecting different visions of how income redistribution might affect American capitalism and democracy. What justification or objection does each give for redistributing wealth throughout the population?

In this 1935 radio address, Senator Huey Long outlines his proposal to redistribute wealth from the rich to the poor.

We find not only the people going further into debt, but that the United States is going further into debt…. And with it all, there stalks a slimy specter of want, hunger, destitution, and pestilence, all because of the fact that in the land of too much and of too much to wear, our president has failed in his promise to have these necessities of life distributed into the hands of the people who have need of them….

But we have been about our work to correct this situation. That is why the Share Our Wealth societies are forming in every nook and corner of America …

Here is what we stand for in a nutshell:

Number one, we propose that every family in America should … have a home and the comforts of a home up to a value of not less than around $5,000 or a little more than that.

Number two, we propose that no family shall own more than three hundred times the average family wealth, which means that no family shall possess more than a wealth of approximately $5 million—none to own less than $5,000, none to own more than $5 million.

Number three,… We propose that no family will have an earning of less than around $2,000 to $2,500 and that none will have more than three hundred times the average less the ordinary income taxes, which means that a million dollars would be the limit on the highest income.

We also propose to give the old-age pensions to the old people, not by taxing them or their children, but by levying the taxes upon the excess fortunes to whittle them down, and on the excess incomes and excess inheritances, so that the people who reach the age of sixty can be retired from the active labor of life … We also propose the care for the veterans, including the cash payment of the soldiers' bonus. We likewise propose that there should be an education for every youth in this land and that no youth would be dependent upon the financial means of his parents in order to have a college education.

In the following letter to Eleanor Roosevelt, a woman from Columbus, Indiana, protests that government-distributed relief robbed hardworking honest men to help "good-for-nothing loafers."

Dec. 14, 1937

Mrs. Roosevelt: … We have always had a shiftless, never-do-well class of people whose one and only aim in life is to live without work. I have been rubbing elbows with this class for nearly sixty years and have tried to help some of the most promising and have seen others try to help them, but it can't be done. We cannot help those who will not try to help themselves and if they do try a square deal is all they need and by the way that is all this country needs or ever has needed: a square deal for all and then, let each one paddle their own canoe, or sink …. As for the old people on beggars' allowances: the taxpayers have provided homes for all the old people who never liked to work, where they will be neither cold nor hungry: much better homes than most of them have ever tried to provide for themselves. They have lived many years through the most prosperous times of our country and had an opportunity to prepare for old age, but they spent their lives in idleness or worse and now they expect those who have worked like slaves, to provide a living for them and all their worthless descendants…. There is many a little child doing without butter on its bread, so that some old sot can have his booze and tobacco: some old sot who spent his working years loafing around pool rooms and saloons, boasting that the world owed him a living….. During the worst of the depression many of the farmers had to deny their families butter, eggs, meat, etc. and sell it to pay their taxes and then had to stand by and see the dead-beats [who qualified for relief] carry it home to their families by the arm load, and they knew their tax money was helping pay for it…. Is it any wonder the taxpayers are discouraged by all this penalizing of thrift and industry to reward shiftlessness, or that the whole country is on the brink of chaos?

View the **Closer Look** *Competing Visions: Sharing the Wealth*

What competing images of the poor do Long and this Indiana woman offer?

22.13 Three Steps to Security
This 1936 poster deliberately emphasized the monthly check workers would receive during retirement, not the payroll deductions that would reduce their take-home pay to help finance immediate pensions for the elderly.

movement. For many working-class Americans, their final years had always been a steady decline into poverty. Unable to work due to age, illness, or the unwillingness of employers to hire them, most relied on family members or charities to survive. The plight of the aged assumed crisis proportions when Depression-era bank failures swept away much of their savings. Townsend clubs, formed to promote government pensions for the elderly, barraged Congress with petitions signed by ten million supporters, sending a clear message to the president and legislators in Washington, D.C.

Sensing an opportunity to enact other reforms long-championed by the left, Roosevelt attached some controversial measures to the bill that provided pensions for the elderly. Unwilling to risk voting against the extremely popular pension proposal, conservative congressmen grudgingly voted for a law that also provided unemployment benefits, assistance to the disabled, and aid for dependent children.

FDR wanted to help the "deserving poor," needy Americans legitimately entitled to public support, a category open to differing interpretations. What made someone deserving of aid in the new social security system? This poster (**22.13**) urging Americans to apply for their old-age benefits clearly noted that only industrial workers working for a salary or wage were eligible for the new pension program. The system did not cover agricultural and domestic workers until 1950, a concession to southern and agricultural business interests, who claimed they could not afford the mandatory employers' contribution to their employees' Social Security accounts (employers paid half). The Social Security Act of 1935 also set the following criteria for its other categories of aid: being laid off (not fired for cause) from an industrial job, being physically disabled or a widow (not an unwed mother) with children to raise.

The Social Security pension system operated along the same lines as private insurance by collecting premiums from individual subscribers in the form of payroll taxes. The public embraced Social Security as a system that simply returned these earlier deposits to retirees. Retired workers, however, began receiving checks in 1940, clearly too soon for them to have paid enough to cover the costs of their pension benefits. Ida May Fuller, a retired legal secretary, received the nation's first Social Security check for $22.54 after paying a total of $24.75 in payroll taxes. She collected more than $22,000 in Social Security checks before she died at age 100 in 1975.

Supporting Unions

Political pressures from the left and empathy for the poor had encouraged Roosevelt to create the Social Security system. These same forces influenced the president as he faced a different set of choices concerning the standoff between business and labor. His desire to curtail political challenges from the left and solidify his voter base by building a new coalition that included unions encouraged Roosevelt to choose the side of labor in this simmering industrial dispute. Business leaders' open hostility to New Deal

Who was considered part of the "deserving poor" in the new Social Security system?

relief and public works programs also prompted FDR to ally himself with labor in 1935. When he proposed a heavy tax on the rich (again inspired by Long), the business elite denounced the wealthy president as "a traitor to his class."

FDR openly mocked his opponents when running for reelection in 1936. "I should like to have it said of my first Administration that in it the forces of selfishness and of lust for power met their match. I should like to have it said of my second Administration that in it these forces met their master," declared Roosevelt in his last campaign speech before defeating the Republican candidate, Kansas Governor Alf Landon. The general public's antipathy to the rich was captured perfectly in this photo (**22.14**) by Dorothea Lange of a gas station in Kern County, California, which displayed a sign declaring "This is your country, don't let the big men take it away from you" next to the free air pump.

Roosevelt's actions matched his rhetoric. Throughout the great strikes of the nineteenth century, the federal government had usually sided openly with industrialists to break workers' movements. Thanks to legislation passed during the New Deal, the federal government suddenly became labor's friend. The National Industrial Recovery Act (1933), the same law that created the NRA, provided the first hint of things to come by declaring that workers had the right to organize and bargain collectively. Labor officials often referred to this section of the law, 7(a), as the "Magna Carta" of organized labor because it recognized a right that many industrialists still refused to acknowledge. (Issued in 1215, the real Magna Carta established the basic liberties of Englishmen.) When the Supreme Court declared the National Industrial Recovery Act unconstitutional, FDR signed the Wagner Act (1935), a law sponsored by Senator Robert Wagner (D-NY) to increase the purchasing power of workers by giving them the power to negotiate for higher wages. The Wagner Act created the National Labor Relations Board (NLRB) to supervise unions' elections for their collective bargaining agents. The law prevented employers from firing or blacklisting workers who joined a union, or from infiltrating unions with spies. With this government protection, the union movement exploded. Between 1933 and 1941, union membership rose from 2.9 million to 8.7 million workers.

In 1938, FDR went even further with the Fair Labor Standards Act, which established a national minimum hourly wage (set initially at 25 cents, rising gradually to 40 cents), set maximum hours for the workweek (44 hours), and outlawed labor by children under 16 (with some exemptions, such as newspaper carriers). Aimed at industrial workers, the act excluded agricultural and domestic workers. FDR again demonstrated political savvy in maneuvering the bill through Congress. He attached the controversial wage and hours measures to a bill prohibiting child labor, knowing that few congressmen would vote against such a popular measure.

22.14 This Is Your Country
This sign reflected the general resentment toward the rich that encouraged Roosevelt to attack business and support unions in 1935.

How did government support of unions change during the 1930s?

The Resurgence of Labor

Government regulation gave crucial support to unions, but the task of building a successful labor movement lay with workers. Overcoming workers' fears that they would lose their jobs if they joined a union posed a significant hurdle for all organizers. When the United Auto Workers (UAW) took on Henry Ford, a strident opponent of unions, organizers passed out handbills assuring workers that "the Wagner Bill is behind you! Now get behind yourselves!" Ford had offered the best terms of employment with his $5-a-day wages and eight-hour workdays in the 1910s and revolutionized American industry with his introduction of the assembly line (see Chapter 18). By the thirties, however, workers in unionized auto plants had much higher wages and guaranteed benefits.

Ford ruled his plants with an iron fist, and in 1937 when five labor organizers tried to pass out handbills to workers entering the Ford motor plant in Dearborn, Michigan, 40 members of the company's private security force attacked them. As seen in this photo (**22.15**), the guards unleashed a flurry of punches and kicks, throwing each man face first onto the pavement before tossing him down a set of stairs. One man's back was broken, and another recounted how two men held his legs apart while the security guards kicked him repeatedly in the groin.

A few news photographers managed to smuggle out photographs of the attacks, thwarting the attempt by Ford's security force to confiscate their film. The shocking images caused a public outcry. The NLRB ordered Ford to stop interfering with union organizing, but securing industry-wide recognition of the UAW required more dramatic action at Ford Motor Company and elsewhere. Ford's antiunion intimidation had worked in the past, but by the mid-1930s, many workers were ready to fight back. In 1934 alone, 1.5 million workers participated in 1,800 strikes.

Support from the government helped the labor movement grow, but so did a new vision of who could join a union. The **American Federation of Labor (AFL)** was a craft-based union that accepted only skilled workers, like carpenters or cigar makers, who practiced a trade. Excluding unskilled workers from the labor movement made little sense once assembly-line mass production began to dominate the manufacturing process. John L. Lewis, head of the United Mine Workers, argued that to become truly powerful unions needed to find room for unskilled workers, no matter their race or ethnicity. When the AFL expelled Lewis for trying to organize these groups, he formed the **Congress of Industrial Organizations (CIO)**, a new type of labor union that organized workers within an entire industry rather than by their trade orientation.

Within two years of its founding, the CIO boasted 3.7 million members as compared to

22.15 Ford Security Guards Attack Labor Organizers
Ford's guards pull a labor organizer's jacket over his head to immobilize his arms as they pummel him. Signaling new support for the labor movement, the federal government intervened after this photo was published.

Why were the CIO's innovative organizing and strike tactics effective?

Read the **Document** *Investigation of Strikebreaking (1939)*

the 3.4 million workers who belonged to the AFL. CIO organizers warned the diverse ranks of unskilled workers not to fall for their employers' old tricks. "The man working beside you, be he Negro, Jew or Pollock [Polish] is a working man like yourself … You work together—FIGHT TOGETHER," one CIO labor organizer told steelworkers. "We were making a *religion* of racial unity," noted another CIO official. In sharp contrast to its enlightened racial views, the CIO joined with the AFL in urging women to voluntarily leave their jobs so men could have them. The CIO did, however, reverse the labor movement's indifference to electoral politics. Now that the government was actively supporting unions, keeping sympathetic officials in public office became a major CIO goal.

Recruiting members became easier when the CIO devised new methods of collective action that bore results. Automobile workers seized the spotlight when they pioneered a new and effective tactic: the sit-down strike. During a **sit-down strike** workers occupied a factory to paralyze production lines and prevent strikebreakers or management from entering the building. Because sit-down strikes caused the employer, as well as his striking employees, to lose money, this tactic brought employers to the negotiating table more quickly than traditional picket lines. Nearly 400,000 workers participated in sit-down strikes in 1937 alone, causing *Time* magazine to comment that "sitting down has replaced baseball as the national pastime."

When the UAW took over the main General Motors plant in Flint, Michigan, in 1937, the governor of Michigan and FDR (who had just received 84 percent of the votes cast by organized labor and 81 percent from low-income voters in the 1936 presidential election) refused to authorize the use of troops to retake the plant. By standing with the strikers, FDR solidified his support among the working class. Within six weeks General Motors capitulated and recognized the union. Ford finally recognized the UAW in 1941. Having lost the battle on the ground, the automobile companies fought back through the courts. In 1939, the Supreme Court ruled that sit-down strikes were illegal seizures of property.

The union movement's successes in the automobile, steel, and textile industries markedly improved the daily lives of workers, but even with these gains, workers had few material comforts compared to laborers today. By 1941, factory workers earned an average of $1,449 a year, enough for a married father with two children to buy two dresses for his wife every year, shoes for his children every other year, and a coat for himself every six years while living in a five-room apartment and driving a used car.

A New Deal for African Americans

As late as 1932, most black northern voters (few African Americans could vote in the South) remained loyal to the Republican Party and Herbert Hoover. Four years later Gallup polls estimated that 76 percent of northern blacks had voted for FDR. What had FDR done to deserve this newfound loyalty among black voters? Little, it seemed at first glance.

During his first administration, powerful Southern Democrats in Congress prevented FDR from proposing any civil rights legislation or guaranteeing equal treatment by New Deal agencies. Still, New Deal programs offered African Americans more federal and state aid than they had ever received before. Southern blacks usually received smaller relief payments than whites, but before 1933, most state agencies had given them nothing. In the 1936 presidential election, Democrats emphasized the benefits that the New Deal had brought to the African American community, proclaiming on billboards: "Do not bite the hand that feeds you." Eleanor Roosevelt's well-known interest in civil rights also helped draw black voters to FDR.

When black voters abandoned the Republicans for the Democratic Party, they joined the **New Deal coalition**, a political partnership formed in the mid-1930s among liberals, trade unionists, Catholics, and northern blacks that redrew the nation's political map. The strength of the New Deal coalition increased FDR's freedom to pursue his legislative agenda. In the newly elected 75th Congress, he did not need a single Southern or Republican vote to pass New Deal legislation.

As the black vote gained new importance to the Democratic Party, the administration became more responsive to African American demands. During FDR's second term, public works projects hired more black workers. FDR also appointed the first black federal judge and convened an unofficial Black Cabinet to investigate civil rights abuses and advise him on racial matters. Nonetheless, racial discrimination continued to plague the lives of African Americans in

Why did many African Americans switch from the Republican to the Democratic Party in the 1930s?

22.16 "There's No Way Like the American Way" In 1937 this photo captured the irony of trumpeting America as the land of opportunity for whites, while needy black citizens stood in line at a soup kitchen.

the thirties. In Margaret Bourke-White's 1937 photo (**22.16**), black residents wait for emergency relief during the Louisville, Kentucky flood, while above them, a billboard poster shows a carefree well-dressed white family driving a car. The image symbolically showcased the racial divide that remained intact throughout the decade. The fate of the Scottsboro Nine, nine black teenagers accused of rape by two young white women while riding on a freight train through Alabama in 1931, underscored the persistence of racial prejudice. The NAACP and the Communist Party took up their defense in well-publicized court cases, while the nine struggled to survive inmate violence, chain gangs, and guard abuse. The last of the Scottsboro Nine was not freed until 1950.

The Supreme Court Weighs In

In 1936, FDR won reelection with 61 percent of the popular vote, carrying every state except Maine and Vermont. By the late 1930s, Gallup public opinion polls offered another way besides elections to measure support for the president and his policies. *Envisioning Evidence: Interpreting Public Opinion Polls* indicates strong faith in FDR among the working class. The same could not be said of the Supreme Court. Of the nine justices, four consistently opposed New Deal

legislation, and two remained unpredictable. By 1937, the Court had declared two major pieces of early New Deal legislation, the NRA and AAA, unconstitutional. With lawsuits against the Wagner Act and Social Security Act on the Court's docket, Roosevelt decided to act.

Suggesting that advanced age (rather than conservative ideology) was hampering the work of the Court, FDR proposed increasing the number of justices to a maximum of 15 by adding one new justice for every one over age 70 who had served more than ten years on the Court. With the conservative bloc all over age 70, Roosevelt's plan would either increase the size of the court or force the older justices to retire. Either way he would have a chance to appoint judges who were sympathetic to the New Deal.

Dubbed the "Court-packing scheme" by detractors, the clash consumed a whole session of Congress and ended with a resounding defeat for FDR. He always maintained that though he lost the battle, he won the larger war with the Court. As Congress debated his proposal to add more justices, the Supreme Court surprised everyone by upholding the constitutionality of the Wagner Act and the Social Security Act. Over the next few years, death and retirement gave FDR the chance to appoint seven justices.

The fallout from the Court struggle had negative repercussions for the president, however. Although the Court began upholding New Deal legislation, the battle alienated progressive Republicans who had previously supported the president and pushed conservative Democrats into an alliance with like-minded Republicans. In 1938, Republicans narrowed the Democratic majority in Congress. The bipartisan conservative coalition was now strong enough to thwart new reform initiatives and begin cutting expenditures for New Deal recovery programs. The New Deal thus ground to a halt in 1938, after five years of public policy initiatives, experiments, and reforms. The federal government was now an active presence in the lives of millions, provoking a debate that continues into the twenty-first century over the proper role of the government in the economy and who is deserving of help.

What role did the Supreme Court play during the New Deal?

Read the **Document** *Mrs. Henry Weddington, Letter to President Roosevelt (1938)*

Envisioning Evidence

INTERPRETING PUBLIC OPINION POLLS

Claiming to offer insight into the mindset of the common man, George Gallup's American Institute of Public Opinion began publishing its well-received public opinion polls in 1935. Previous polls had based their accuracy on collecting as many responses as possible. Relying on new statistical sampling theories, Gallup instead interviewed small (3,000–4,000) demographically representative groups in person and through mail questionnaires. Gallup viewed popular opinion polls as a way for "the plain people of the United States" to communicate directly to their elected representatives, but Gallup played a critical role in that conversation. The wording of questions affected responses and Gallup freely interpreted the meaning of his surveys through regular newspaper columns. "What are the main cleavages that exist today in American public opinion?" he asked. According to Gallup polls, "the split between the 'haves' and the 'have nots.'"

Relief and Roosevelt, August 24, 1938
Both questions asked together of all income levels, except farm owners.

1. If you (or your husband) lost your (or his) job and couldn't find other work, about how long could you hold out before you had to apply for relief?

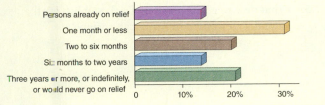

2. Are you for or against Roosevelt today?

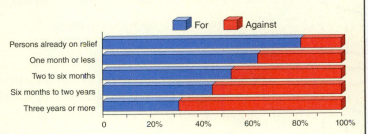

Gallup Interprets His Data

"In view of the relatively high feeling of insecurity among large sections of the population it is not difficult to understand the popularity of old age pensions and other provisions of the Social Security Act."

"It seems clear from this evidence that political attitudes today are determined not so much by theories of government [strong federal government, states rights, communism] as by bread-and-butter economics, that support from the financially insecure continues to be the backbone of New Deal strength."

Source: The New York Times, August 24, 1938, p. 10.

Married Women Working, December 25, 1938

Do you approve of a married woman earning money in business or industry if she has a husband capable of supporting her?

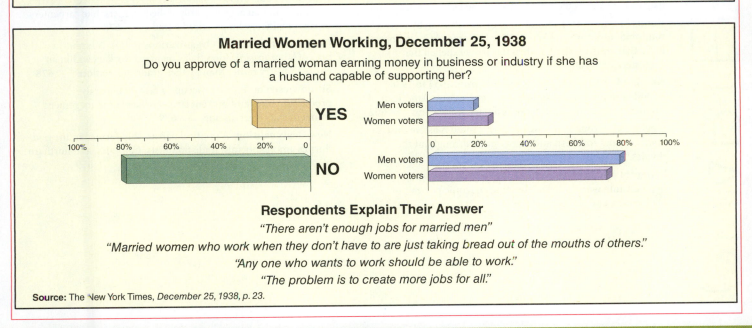

Respondents Explain Their Answer

"There aren't enough jobs for married men"

"Married women who work when they don't have to are just taking bread out of the mouths of others."

"Any one who wants to work should be able to work."

"The problem is to create more jobs for all."

Source: The New York Times, December 25, 1938, p. 23.

View the **Closer Look** Envisioning Evidence: Interpreting Public Opinion Polls

How did economic insecurity shape political views during the Depression?

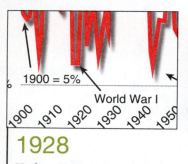

1928

Herbert Hoover elected president
Predicts permanent prosperity

1929

Stock market crashes
Signals beginning of Depression

1932

Reconstruction Finance Corporation established
Hoover's effort to help businesses and banks with federal loans

Bonus March
Public outrage over army's eviction of protesting veterans from Washington, D.C.

1933

FDR inaugurated president
Restores faith and confidence in government and capitalism

New Deal begun
Five year creation of federal agencies, laws, and reforms that restructure American capitalism and provide economic security to citizens

Review Questions

1. What groups of people did the New Deal help and why?

2. Why did images of breadlines and migrant farmers become enduring symbols of Depression-era suffering?

3. Why were there labor protests in the thirties, a time when one might expect workers simply to be grateful for any job on any terms?

4. What conflicting visions prompted the right and left to criticize the New Deal?

5. What new roles did the New Deal establish for the federal government in American society?

Key Terms

Stock market crash of 1929 A ten-day period beginning on October 20, 1929, when the value of stocks plummeted as panicked investors sold off their stock in droves. This moment is usually considered the official start of the Depression.   **657**

Bonus March A two-month-long demonstration by forty thousand impoverished World War I veterans in Washington, D.C., that ended violently when the army expelled the protesters.   **660**

New Deal An avalanche of legislation from 1933 to 1938 intended to promote economic recovery, reform American capitalism, and offer security to ordinary Americans.   **662**

Dust Bowl Drought and soil erosion caused massive dust storms across southern and plains states throughout the thirties.   **670**

"Migrant Mother" Dorothea Lange's 1936 photograph of a destitute woman, which became an iconic portrait of Depression-era suffering.   **673**

Share our wealth Louisiana Senator Huey Long's plan to redistribute money from the rich to the poor.   **674**

American Federation of Labor (AFL) A craft-based organization that accepted only skilled workers, like carpenters or cigar makers, who practiced a trade.   **678**

Congress of Industrial Organizations (CIO) A brand-new type of labor organization that organized workers within an entire industry rather than by their trade orientation.   **678**

Sit-down strike Workers occupy a factory to paralyze production lines and prevent strikebreakers or management from entering the building.   **679**

New Deal coalition A political partnership formed in the mid-thirties among liberals, trade unionists, Catholics, and northern blacks that redrew the nation's political map.   **679**

CHAPTER REVIEW

1935

Works Progress Administration
Public works program employs
one-fifth of the workforce from 1935
to 1943

Wagner Act
Offers government protection to
unions

1935

Share Our Wealth Movement
Senator Huey Long's proposal to
redistribute wealth pushes FDR to
the left

CIO founded
Organizes workers by industry rather
than by trade

1936

Dust Bowl crisis worsens
Drought, soil erosion result in major
ecological disaster

FDR wins reelection
New Deal coalition forms

1937

**FDR tries to reform
Supreme Court**
Proposal's failure exposes limits of
FDR's power

**Social Security payroll
taxes begin**
Establishes funding mechanism
for federal pensions

MyHistoryLab Connections

Visit www.myhistorylab.com for a customized Study Plan that will help you build your knowledge of *A New Deal for America*.

Questions for Analysis

1. Why would the sentiments expressed in this political cartoon lead to dissatisfaction with Hoover?

View the **Image** *John Baer, "We Demand a New Deal!" (1931), p. 662*

2. How did FDR reassure the public about his plan for alleviating their financial hardships?

Read the **Document** *Franklin D. Roosevelt — Radio Address (1933), p. 666*

3. What values did post office murals celebrate?

View the **Closer Look** *Images as History: Post Office Murals, p. 669*

4. Why did interpretations of "Migrant Mother" differ?

Watch the **Video** *Video Lecture: Dorothea Lange and Migrant Mother, p. 672*

5. How did employers try to break strikes in the 1930s?

Read the **Document** *Investigation of Strikebreaking (1939), p. 678*

Other Resources from This Chapter

Hear the **Audio File** *FDR's First Inaugural Address, p. 663*

Read the **Document**
- *Father Charles E. Coughlin, "A Third Party" (1936), p. 667*
- *Carey McWilliams, Okies in California (1939), p. 671*
- *Mrs. Henry Weddington, Letter to President Roosevelt (1938), p. 680*

View the **Closer Look**
- *Images as History: "Migrant Mother" — An American Icon, p. 673*
- *Competing Visions: Sharing the Wealth, p. 675*
- *Envisioning Evidence: Interpreting Public Opinion Polls, p. 681*

View the **Image**
- *Children with "Hoover's Poor Farm" Sign, p. 660*
- *CCC worker (1938), p. 668*

View the **Map** *Interactive Map: The Great Depression, p. 670*

Watch the **Video**
- *Prosperity of the 1920s and the Great Depression, p. 656*
- *Video Lecture: Responding to the Great Depression, Whose New Deal?, p. 679*

((•⊶Hear the Audio File on myhistorylab.com

⊙—Watch the Video *Critical Visions, Chapter 23*

World War II
Fighting the Good War, 1939–1945

In early December 1941, a Japanese fleet secretly steamed toward Hawaii, stopping within 250 miles of the Hawaiian island of Oahu. At 6:00 a.m. on December 7, Admiral Chuichi Nagumo launched two consecutive waves of bombers, torpedo planes, and dive-bombers. As Japanese pilots approached Pearl Harbor, a naval station on Oahu, they saw American warships parked in a neat row. Moments later those battleships, cruisers, and destroyers were engulfed in flames. It took the government nearly a year to release photos, like the one here, of American ships under attack.

Before Pearl Harbor debate raged in the United States over how to respond to the growing threat of war in the Pacific and Germany's conquest of Europe. Non-interventionists and interventionists offered competing visions of how to protect America's vital interests in a world torn apart by war. The Japanese assault on Pearl Harbor ended this debate. Questions instead arose over why the United States had given the Japanese such an inviting target. Hoping to pressure Japan into withdrawing from China, President Franklin D. Roosevelt had sent the U.S. Pacific Fleet to Hawaii. There, he believed, the battleships were far enough away from Japan to escape attack but close enough to convince Japan to end its expansionist drive into East Asia. Roosevelt erred on both counts. Instead, Japan resolved to drive the Western powers—the United States, Britain, the Netherlands, and France—out of East Asia.

In their attack on Pearl Harbor, the Japanese sank or damaged 18 ships and killed 2,405 Americans. Congress declared war on Japan the day after the attack. On December 11, Germany and Italy declared war on the United States, and Germany's allies Romania, Bulgaria, and Hungary quickly followed suit. The United States now faced the challenge of fighting resolute and capable enemies in Europe and the Pacific against whom victory was not certain.

The attack on Pearl Harbor silenced debate about whether America needed to fight, but were all the changes the war caused in American society positive ones? World War II thrust the United States into a new position of global leadership. Mobilizing the nation's resources to fight also created vast economic and social changes at home. The United States eventually prevailed against its enemies, but the cost of victory was high on the battlefield and on the home front.

The Approaching War

From 1939 to 1945, war engulfed nearly the entire globe, as shown on the map (**23.1**). Huge areas fell under German and Japanese control, naval battles occurred on vast stretches of sea, and colonies provided key materials needed by warring nations. Until 1941, however, the United States remained on the sidelines as Germany attacked continuously in Europe, and Japan launched steady invasions in East Asia. As long as the fighting remained far from their shores, Americans disagreed over whether these wars were theirs to fight. Still coping with the social and financial problems created by the Great Depression, **non-interventionists** urged the nation to put "America First" and stay out of overseas conflicts. By the late 1930s, however, **interventionists** increasingly challenged this view, arguing that only direct engagement could prevent the world conflagration from reaching American shores.

Fascism and Appeasement

In the midst of the Depression, the United States had to formulate responses to Adolf Hitler's rise to power in Germany in 1933, Italy's invasion of Ethiopia in 1935, and the Spanish Civil War in 1936–1939. Appointed chancellor in 1933, Hitler immediately began turning Germany into a fascist state under Nazi control, a dictatorial form of government that glorified the state over the individual. Widespread economic suffering, lingering resentments against the harsh terms of the Versailles Treaty (see Chapter 20), and virulent anti-Semitism created fertile ground for Nazism to flourish. Stripped of their German citizenship, Jews could not practice medicine or law, attend public school after the age of 14, marry non-Jews, or enter public parks, zoos, and libraries. Promising to restore Germany's economic and military prowess and protect the presumed "racial superiority" of the German people, Hitler rearmed the country and sought allies.

In formulating their response to the rise of fascism in Europe, non-interventionists in Congress sought to avoid repeating the mistakes that had led to involvement in the bloodbath of World

23.1 The World at War
German and Japanese wars of conquest set the world aflame.

NEW ZEALAND

PACIFIC OCEAN

PACIFIC OCEAN

Hawaii   **Pearl Harbor**

Midway

Guam

AUSTRALIA

USA

CANADA

ARCTIC OCEAN

JAPAN
Tokyo

SOUTH AMERICA

CHINA

USSR

BRITAIN
GERMANY
FRANCE
ITALY

INDIA

ATLANTIC OCEAN

AFRICA

INDIAN OCEAN

- Allied powers
- Axis powers
- Occupied countries
- Neutrals
- Principal areas of submarine warfare

What does this map convey about the scope of World War II?

War I. Senator Gerald P. Nye, a Republican from North Dakota, chaired a series of Senate investigations in the mid-1930s into the role that American arms manufacturers had played in the nation's decision to enter World War I. Although the investigations unearthed little hard evidence of a conspiracy, they did reinforce the consensus that the United States had entered that war to continue profitable arms sales and to guarantee that the Allies, the powers who had fought Germany, repaid their war loans to private banks. When these European countries defaulted on their loans during the Depression, public sentiment hardened against helping foreign nations.

To ensure that trading with belligerent nations did not drag the country into another war, Congress passed the **Neutrality Acts** from 1935 to 1939, which restricted arms sales, loans, and transport of goods with nations at war (see U.S. Countdown to War timeline, **23.2**). These popular laws encapsulated the widespread non-interventionist vision of avoiding involvement in overseas conflicts that did not directly threaten U.S. territory. Depending on the official policy pursued, the Atlantic and Pacific Oceans could serve as buffers protecting the nation or as pathways to war. Trying to ensure the former, the 1935 Neutrality Act prohibited the sales of arms and ammunition to nations at war. In 1936, Congress barred all loans to warring nations. The 1937 Neutrality Act allowed belligerent nations to purchase non-war-related goods if they paid cash for them and transported them on their own ships, a policy known as "**cash and carry**."

FDR challenged the non-interventionist vision with his 1937 Quarantine Speech which urged peace-loving countries to isolate aggressor nations and seek peace. Outraged non-interventionists accused him of trying to turn the United States into the world's policeman. "It's a terrible thing to look over your shoulder when you are trying to lead—and find no one there," the president remarked to an aide before he publicly reaffirmed his support for the Neutrality Acts. Non-interventionist sentiment peaked in 1938, when Congress debated but did not approve a constitutional amendment that required a national referendum for any declaration of war, except in response to an enemy invasion.

The United States was not alone in its desire to remain at peace. Eager to avoid war with Germany, Britain and France recalled how a relatively minor incident (the assassination of Archduke Franz Ferdinand) had become the catalyst for war in 1914 (see Chapter 20). Instead of mobilizing their armies when Germany violated the Versailles Treaty by rearming and threatening its neighbors, France and Britain tried to negotiate. In 1938, Germany annexed Austria and then demanded the Sudetenland, a German-speaking province made part of Czechoslovakia against its will by the Allies, when the Austro-Hungarian Empire collapsed at the end of World War I. By the 1930s many Europeans felt that the Versailles Peace Treaty had punished Germany too severely, creating the widespread impression that Hitler's actions and demands were reasonable. Taking Hitler at his word that he was interested only in reuniting German-speaking peoples into one nation, Britain and France agreed at the **Munich Conference** in 1938 to let Germany occupy the Sudetenland.

Instead of dampening Hitler's ambitions, the Munich Conference convinced him that the Western democracies were too weak to oppose him militarily. Arguing that Germany needed "living space" in the East for its people, Hitler initiated his master plan to displace what he demeaningly called the "inferior" Slavic "races," the peoples living in Eastern Europe, and to exterminate the Jews. Intent on avoiding the mistakes of World War I, when Germany had fought a two-front war, Hitler resolved to fight one war at a time. To accomplish this, in August 1939, he signed a non-aggression pact with Josef Stalin, the dictator of the Soviet Union (USSR). Germany and the USSR

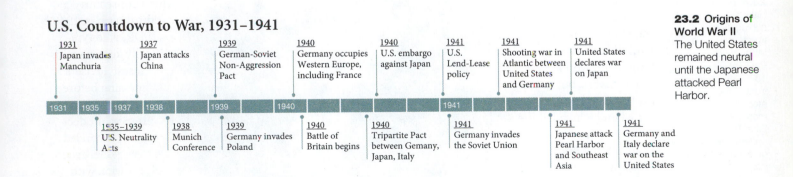

U.S. Countdown to War, 1931–1941

1931 Japan invades Manchuria	1937 Japan attacks China	1939 German-Soviet Non-Aggression Pact	1940 Germany occupies Western Europe, including France	1940 U.S. embargo against Japan	1941 U.S. Lend-Lease policy	1941 Shooting war in Atlantic between United States and Germany	1941 United States declares war on Japan

1931	1935	1937	1938	1939	1940	1941

| | 1935–1939 U.S. Neutrality Acts | 1938 Munich Conference | 1939 Germany invades Poland | 1940 Battle of Britain begins | 1940 Tripartite Pact between Germany, Japan, Italy | 1941 Germany invades the Soviet Union | 1941 Japanese attack Pearl Harbor and Southeast Asia | 1941 Germany and Italy declare war on the United States |

23.2 Origins of World War II The United States remained neutral until the Japanese attacked Pearl Harbor.

Watch the Video *Video Lecture: Hitler and Roosevelt*

What different lessons did America and other world powers draw from World War I?

secretly agreed to partition Poland and other parts of Eastern Europe, and the USSR offered Hitler supplies for his pending attack on France and Britain. The non-aggression pact ensured that Germany's eastern border remained peaceful when it attacked Western Europe and the Balkans. Only days after signing the pact, Hitler invaded Poland on September 1, bringing a declaration of war from Britain and France. World War II had officially begun.

In April 1940, Hitler began his massive assault on Western Europe by invading Norway and Denmark. He then marched through Luxembourg, Holland, and Belgium to invade France in May. Unlike in 1914, when Germany's broad attack against French lines ended in a trench stalemate, in 1940, Germany's Blitzkrieg (lightning war) punched holes in the French defense system and then sent tanks, infantry, artillery, and aircraft through these openings to disrupt communications and threaten the French army from the rear. When German troops entered Paris on June 14, Hitler underscored his triumph by visiting the Eiffel Tower. In this photograph (**23.3**) Hitler is posing before the landmark, transforming a banal tourist excursion into an act that, by symbolizing his control of Western Europe, carried sinister and tragic overtones. With France under Nazi domination, Italy entered the war on the side of Germany. Through a combination of alliances and force, the **Axis**, those nations fighting on the German side, quickly took control of the rest of Eastern Europe and the Balkans.

As German troops were rolling toward Paris, the British army had escaped capture by evacuating its forces from the French port of Dunkirk. For a full year Britain fought Germany alone, surviving a massive bombing campaign known as the Battle of Britain. That changed in June 1941, however, when Hitler invaded the USSR. Frustrated in his efforts to subdue Britain, Hitler decided that with British forces off the continent, it was time to conquer Russia. Until this point Hitler had fought and won a series of isolated wars, but he made his first major strategic error when he invaded the Soviet Union. Instead of advancing quickly to Moscow, German troops

23.3 Hitler in Paris Hitler's quick subjugation of Western Europe brought him to Paris by June 1940. He posed in front of the city's most recognizable monument, the Eiffel Tower, to underscore France's defeat and his own power.

found themselves bogged down by the late autumn in a massive campaign along an Eastern Front that stretched for thousands of miles from the Baltic to the Black Seas.

The Arsenal of Democracy

As these events developed in Europe, both President Franklin D. Roosevelt and most of the American people opposed entering the war. Publicly embracing non-interventionist measures during his first two terms, Roosevelt adopted an officially neutral stance as the war spread.

Unlike Wilson in World War I, however, FDR did not ask Americans to remain impartial in thought. Immigration restrictions had limited the number of first-generation immigrants from Europe, and Roosevelt had few concerns that well-assimilated Americans of German ancestry might retain strong loyalties to Germany. Indeed, public opinion polls in 1939 revealed that nearly 84 percent of Americans supported the **Allies**, the powers fighting Germany, with only two percent expressing pro-German views.

Despite FDR's public declaration of neutrality, in private the interventionist argument that inaction would invite catastrophe increasingly influenced his thinking. For the time being Roosevelt tried to satisfy both non-interventionists and interventionists by finding a way to defeat Hitler without actually declaring war. "Our national policy is not directed toward war," Roosevelt assured Americans. "Its sole purpose is to keep war away from our country and our people." To help Britain and France without risking the direct involvement that non-interventionists opposed, the Neutrality Act of 1939 revised the "cash and carry" policy to include munitions as well as non-war-related goods.

Breaking with the self-imposed two-term limit set by George Washington and respected by every other subsequent president, Roosevelt made the unprecedented decision to run for a consecutive third term in 1940. FDR, who typically kept even his closest advisers guessing before he reached an important decision, surprised everyone, even his wife, with his

"[I]t is a matter of most vital concern to us that European and Asiatic war-makers should not gain control of the oceans which lead to this hemisphere."

President FRANKLIN D. ROOSEVELT, radio "Fireside Chat," December 29, 1940

announcement. He never explained his decision, but the shock of France falling to Nazi control undoubtedly influenced him to run again. FDR's candidacy and his selection of a liberal New Dealer, Henry Wallace, as his vice president caused grumbling among conservative Democrats, who nonetheless rallied around him in the general election. The Republican challenger Wendell Willkie and Roosevelt each argued that the nation should offer all the help it could to the Allies short of entering the war. Willkie tried to paint Roosevelt as bent on direct intervention, but this charge and Willkie's anti-New Deal rhetoric resonated poorly with voters. Roosevelt easily won a third term.

FDR saw his task as satisfying "the wish of 70% of Americans to keep out of the war" and "the wish of 70% of Americans to do everything to break Hitler, even if it means war." To accommodate the public's conflicting emotions, Roosevelt proposed turning the nation into a "great arsenal of democracy." By telephone and telegraph, British Prime Minister Winston Churchill pressed FDR continually for aid. Stressing America's vulnerability, Churchill warned that "overwhelming sea power would be in Hitler's hands" if Germany defeated Britain, threatening America's well-being. FDR responded as Churchill hoped. Besides selling Britain arms, FDR agreed to trade 50 old American destroyers for 99-year leases on seven British air and naval bases in the Western Hemisphere. Britain needed these ships to transport weapons overseas. FDR also supported a peacetime draft and invited a leading interventionist, Republican Henry Stimson, to become secretary of war.

By 1941, Britain had run out of cash, and neutrality laws still prohibited the United States from loaning the British the money they needed to buy munitions. FDR circumvented these restrictions with a policy called **Lend-Lease** that loaned rather than sold arms to Britain. The United States would "say to England, we will give the guns and ships that you need, provided that when the war is over you will return to us in kind the guns and ships that we have loaned you," Roosevelt told Secretary of the Treasury Henry Morgenthau. Lend-Lease, FDR explained to the nation, was simply one neighbor helping another to put out a fire. No one would say, FDR noted, "Neighbor, my garden hose cost me $15; you have to pay me $15 for it … I don't want $15—I want my garden hose back after the fire is over." Congress, however, prohibited the U.S. Navy from escorting British convoys carrying American goods across the Atlantic. Fittingly, given the analogy that FDR used to explain Lend-Lease, one of the first shipments to Britain contained boxes of fire hoses.

When Hitler attacked the USSR in 1941, the United States extended Lend-Lease aid to the Soviets. FDR had formally recognized the Soviet Union in 1933, hoping to find another overseas market for American goods. Trade with the Soviets remained minimal during the Depression, but exploded during the war. By 1945, the United States had provided $50 billion of materiel to the Allies under this program. No one, however, expected Britain and the Soviet Union to return "loaned" ammunition or arms to the United States. Instead, the law left it up to the president to decide what form repayment would take. After the war President Harry S. Truman accepted favorable postwar trade relations as repayment from Britain and demanded $2.6 billion from the Soviet Union for nonmilitary lend-lease goods. Russia did not pay its debt until after the fall of communism in 1991.

The debate between non-interventionists and interventionists intensified throughout 1941. Non-interventionists embraced the slogan "America First" and urged Americans to remember the debt and death wrought by the last war. As part of this heated exchange, Dr. Seuss (the alias used by Theodore Geisel, who was to gain fame in the 1950s as the author-illustrator of *The Cat in the Hat* and other children's books) drew editorial cartoons for *PM,* a short-lived left-wing New York magazine that denounced non-intervention as folly. Dr. Seuss depicted non-interventionists as ostriches with their heads in the ground, anti-Semites, and appeasers.

Read the Document *Charles Lindbergh, Radio Address (1941)*   How did the competing visions of non-interventionists and interventionists influence FDR's rhetoric and actions?

This Seuss cartoon (**23.4**) shows a non-interventionist wearing an "America First" hat in a bathtub that is jumping with predatory sea creatures adorned with swastikas, the symbol of the Nazi Party. His eyes closed tight, the man ignores the danger, saying with a satisfied smile, "The old Family bath tub is plenty safe for me." As he moved closer to the interventionist position, FDR voiced similar concerns about the vulnerability of the American coastline.

Non-interventionists challenged this assertion. "Water Hazards" (**23.5**) appeared in the *Chicago Tribune*, a staunchly Republican newspaper that criticized both the New Deal and intervention. The cartoon ridicules the notion that Germany posed a danger to the United States, arguing that since Hitler (the inept golfer) had yet to land his forces (the golf ball) 22 miles across the English Channel in Britain, the United States had nothing to fear. The false alarms spread by interventionists (the hysterical golf caddy) hurt the nation by drawing Uncle Sam's attention away from addressing the nation's domestic problems (in this case, playing his own golf game).

As non-interventionists feared and interventionists hoped, Lend-Lease opened the door to further U.S. involvement in the European war. Securing American guns and ammunition solved only half the problem for Britain. Because of the number of German submarines patrolling the Atlantic, Secretary of War Henry Stimson warned, sending arms to Britain was like pouring water into a leaky bathtub. When the American destroyer *Greer* exchanged fire with a German submarine, FDR used the incident to invoke his authority as commander in chief by ordering U.S. naval ships to escort all ships headed to Britain as far as Iceland, which the United States also occupied, and "shoot on sight" any German submarine or ship. Although it remained unclear whether the Germans knew that the *Greer* was an American ship, FDR denounced the skirmish as a deliberate attack in American waters. "We have sought no shooting war with Hitler. We do not seek it now," FDR declared in September 1941. "But when you see a rattlesnake poised to strike, you do not wait until he has struck before you crush him. These Nazi submarines and raiders are the rattlesnakes of the Atlantic." Three months before Japan's attack on Pearl Harbor, the United States was fighting an undeclared naval war with Germany.

23.4 Dr. Seuss Lampoons Non-Interventionists in 1941
Dr. Seuss lampooned non-interventionists for closing their eyes to the threat that Hitler's navy (depicted here as swastika-marked monsters) posed to American shores.

23.5 "Water Hazards," 1941
This *Chicago Tribune* editorial cartoon accuses interventionists of unduly alarming the country about the possibility of a Nazi attack.

What competing visions did these two cartoons offer on the threat that Hitler posed to the United States?

War with Japan

The catalyst for America's formal entry into the war did not come in the Atlantic, however, but on the other side of the globe when Japanese pilots attacked **Pearl Harbor**, a large naval base in Hawaii, on December 7, 1941. The attackers discovered a neat line of battleships, reproduced in this miniature version of Pearl Harbor (**23.6**) that Japanese filmmakers constructed for a wartime propaganda film that reminded Japanese audiences of their nation's great victory against the United States.

The attack on Pearl Harbor was the culmination of two decades of tension and mistrust between the two nations. Japan's desire to establish itself as the major power in the Pacific alarmed the United States, which maintained an array of island possessions and a strong naval presence in the Pacific to support its trade with China. Access to Chinese markets had been a cornerstone of American foreign policy since the Spanish-American War. For the Japanese, claiming East Asia as their proper sphere of influence was no different from the United States declaring the Western Hemisphere off-limits to foreign powers through the 1823 Monroe Doctrine and 1904 Roosevelt Corollary. Japan aimed to build the Greater East Asia Co-Prosperity Sphere, creating satellite states throughout Asia that would free Japan from dependence on Western-controlled resources like oil, tin, and rubber. In the 1920s the United States and Japan mediated their differences, with Japan agreeing to reduce the size of its navy and renouncing war as an instrument of foreign policy (see Chapter 21). The Japanese army's 1931 invasion of Chinese-held Manchuria (land long disputed by China, Russia, and Japan), however, signaled the beginning of a direct confrontation between Japan and the United States. Claiming that Manchuria rightfully belonged to Japan, the Japanese army assumed control of all raw materials and industry to support Japan's military endeavors.

In July 1937, Japan attacked China, unleashing a brutal war of conquest. During the infamous Rape of Nanking, a Chinese city, over 250,000 Chinese perished, including 20,000 women, who were raped, tortured, and then executed. "Soldiers impaled babies on bayonets and tossed them still alive into pots of boiling water," a Japanese soldier later admitted. The Japanese killed more than six million Chinese over the next eight years.

American sympathy for Chinese victims and concern over protecting American economic interests in Asia coincided with rising tensions in Europe. By 1940, aiding Britain had become FDR's foreign policy priority. Containing Japan through escalating economic sanctions and warnings, FDR reasoned, was the best way to defuse the situation in the Pacific,

23.6 Japanese Model of Pearl Harbor
This mock-up of Pearl Harbor, constructed for a Japanese wartime film of the attack, showed American battleships lined up in a row, making them easy targets for aerial bombs.

so the nation could focus on the war in the Atlantic and Europe. Hoping that a show of force would convince Japan to abandon its imperialist ambitions, the United States began building ships and stationed the Pacific Fleet in Pearl Harbor, 2,500 miles from California (see 23.1). Roosevelt also sent aid to China and in July 1940 imposed a limited embargo on scrap iron and high-octane aviation fuel to Japan.

Japan was not deterred. Instead of withdrawing from China, Japan seized parts of French Indochina, in present-day Vietnam. In response, on September 26, 1940, the United States announced a total embargo on scrap metal shipments to Japan. The following day Tokyo signed the Tripartite Pact with Germany and Italy, an agreement dedicated to "the establishment of a new order" in East Asia and Europe. Aimed at offering mutual aid if the United States attacked, the pact did not lead to strategic coordination between the European and Asian theaters of war. Japan and Germany shared mutual enemies during the war, but little else.

When Japan strengthened its occupation of French Indochina in the summer of 1941, the American government froze Japanese assets in the United States and stopped oil shipments (which accounted for four-fifths of Japan's oil supply). Diplomatic exchanges continued until the eve of the attack on Pearl Harbor, even though Japan decided in September to launch an expansionist war into resource-rich Southeast Asia to push the United States, the Netherlands, and Britain out of the region.

The Japanese calculation that the United States would withdraw from East Asia after a devastating attack on Pearl Harbor proved as faulty as the American belief that sanctions would prevent a war with Japan. The assault on Pearl Harbor ended all debate over entering the war. Having agonized over how far to pull the country toward war, Roosevelt reportedly told an aide that the attack took the matter "entirely out of his hands, because the Japanese had made the decision for him."

Despite catching the Americans by surprise, the Japanese victory at Pearl Harbor was far from complete. Although the attack prevented the United States from interfering with Japan's subsequent invasion of Southeast Asia, Japan failed to destroy America's Pacific Fleet. Fearing a counterattack Nagumo, on the day of the attack, called off a third air strike on storage tanks containing millions of gallons of fuel oil and on repair facilities. Most American sailors in Hawaii survived the attack, and the navy eventually repaired six of the eight damaged battleships. In another stroke of luck, the Pacific Fleet's two aircraft carriers were at sea and escaped the attack. The navy also had eleven battleships and two aircraft carriers stationed elsewhere to defend the nation from further attack. Nonetheless, the short-term damage was severe. Over the next 24 hours, Japan attacked American, British, and Dutch territories throughout Southeast Asia. While the attack on Pearl Harbor horrified Americans, it brought hope to the British. Churchill knew immediately that the United States would soon be in the war against Germany.

After Pearl Harbor die-hard non-interventionists questioned whether the Japanese attack could have been prevented. Charges of dereliction of duty against the commanders of Pearl Harbor and suspicions that Roosevelt had allowed the attack to take place to enter the war against Hitler (through the back door) surfaced. By early December, American commanders expected a Japanese attack against American Pacific possessions. Most intelligence data, however, indicated that the Japanese would invade the Philippines and mainland Southeast Asia, as they subsequently did. American officials simply overlooked the few bits of information indicating that Hawaii was both a possible and a probable first target.

> ## "The United States was in the war, up to the neck and in to the death…. I went to bed and slept the sleep of the saved and thankful."
>
> British Prime Minister WINSTON CHURCHILL, upon learning of the 1941 Japanese attack on Pearl Harbor

How significant was the attack on Pearl Harbor in the short and long run?

Read the Document *Franklin D. Roosevelt, "The Four Freedoms" (1941)*

On the Home Front

The U.S. government made the formal declaration of war, but winning it required the active participation of the American people. Americans remember World War II as the "good war" not only because it ended the Depression, but also because it united the nation against its enemies. While unified in the desire to prevail on the battlefield, Americans embraced conflicting visions that kept ethnic, gender, race, and class divisions intact.

Images of the Enemy

Americans had long exhibited disdain for Asian immigrants and Americans of Asian descent. Before the war discriminatory laws targeted Asian immigrants and their American-born children. These laws segregated swimming pools and dance halls, denied Asians the right to own land, prohibited intermarriage with whites, and prevented Asian immigrants from becoming citizens. The attack on Pearl Harbor provoked more virulent expressions of hatred for the Japanese, leading to even greater discrimination.

In the opening days of the war, *Life* and *Time* magazines offered the nation a crash course in "how to tell a Chinese from a Jap." Understanding the difference was crucial, *Life* magazine asserted, to protect the Chinese Americans, "whose homeland is our staunch ally," from unwarranted attacks. As the Chinese embassy prepared to hand out identification buttons for Chinese immigrants and Chinese Americans to wear, *Life* and *Time* instructed the nation in distinguishing pseudoscientific, stereotypical "racial" characteristics. *Life* used photos (**23.7**) to compare the facial features and expressions of a Chinese civil servant with those of General Hideki Tojo, the prime minister who ruled Japan until 1944. The magazine called on readers to note Tojo's heavy beard and cheekbones and humorless expression, all supposedly key traits of Japanese physiognomy. *Time* and *Life* were not alone in feeling a sudden need to distinguish members of the "yellow race." Congress lifted the ban on Chinese naturalization and granted China an annual quota of 105 immigrants a year. This act symbolically differentiated the Chinese from the Japanese (banned as immigrants in 1924 and prohibited from becoming naturalized citizens, see Chapters 19 and 21), but protected the nation from any substantial increase in Chinese immigration.

Renewed outrage against Japan greeted news of atrocities in the Pacific war, such as the April 1942

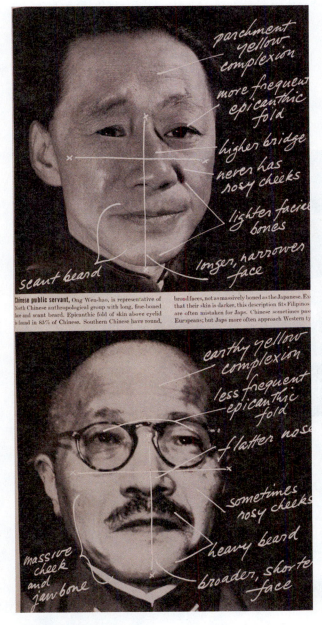

23.7 "How to Tell Japs from the Chinese"
Lamenting the American tendency to lump all Asians together, *Life* magazine analyzed the facial features of Chinese and Japanese men to instruct readers in the difference between the two groups—one an ally, the other the enemy.

What distinctions did Americans now make between the Japanese and Chinese?

Bataan Death March. When American and Filipino soldiers finally surrendered their position on the Bataan Peninsula in the Philippines, their Japanese captors forced the sick, starving troops to walk almost 90 miles through the intense heat and jungle to a prisoner of war camp. Out of 70,000 men who began the trek, between 5,000 and 11,000 succumbed to illness, starvation, and beatings from Japanese soldiers.

Still these horrors were not enough to explain Americans' deep-seated hatred for the Japanese. "In Europe we felt that our enemies, horrible and deadly as they were, were still people," Ernie Pyle wrote in one of his newspaper columns toward the end of the war. "But out here I soon gathered that the Japanese were looked upon as something subhuman and repulsive; the way some people feel about cockroaches or mice." As Pyle noted, general views toward the Germans were decidedly different. Remembering the vigilante attacks against German Americans in World War I (see Chapter 20), government propaganda focused on Hitler and Nazism as the enemy, not the German people.

Internment Camps

In the immediate wake of the attack on Pearl Harbor, Americans were eager for explanations. Rumors circulated that Japanese-American farmers on Hawaii had plowed arrows in their fields to show Japanese pilots the way to military installations. Yet no evidence of internal spying ever surfaced, and suggestions that the government round up and quarantine these Hawaiian residents went nowhere. Composing one-third of Hawaii's population, people of Japanese descent were too important to the local economy to deport, and there were no ships available to transport replacement workers to the islands.

The 110,000 Japanese and Japanese Americans who lived in California, Oregon, and Washington, where they were less vital to the economy, met a different fate. The day after the attack on Pearl Harbor, air raid sirens wailed in San Francisco. Then, when a Japanese submarine torpedoed an American ship off the California coast, Americans feared that the West Coast would soon be under attack. Frenzied officials instituted blackouts; Coast Guard units patrolled the seas. Throughout the war West Coast defense factories camouflaged their plants, as illustrated in these "Plant Camouflage, Before and After" photos (**23.8**). This aircraft factory in Burbank, California, stretched a tarp over its facilities to make it look like suburban housing from the air. The camouflagers hoped to fool an attacking Japanese pilot seeking a more recognizable military target.

Within this atmosphere of heightened anxiety, many viewed Japanese immigrants and Japanese Americans on the West Coast as potential enemy agents. Increasingly the larger public and the government believed that their presence near vital ports and military bases posed a threat to national security. On February 19, 1942, President Roosevelt signed Executive Order 9066, permitting the military to declare certain areas off-limits to any or all persons. General John L. DeWitt, head of the Western Defense Command, immediately declared the entire West Coast a military zone closed to "all persons of Japanese ancestry, both alien and non-alien." His order called for the evacuation of anyone of Japanese descent; even orphanages had to relocate Japanese-American babies.

In mid-March 1942, Roosevelt created the War Relocation Authority to oversee the forced removal

23.8 Plant Camouflage, Before and After
This aircraft factory in Burbank, California, camouflaged its facility with a painted tarp and cardboard houses to create the facade of a suburban housing development to deceive Japanese pilots on the lookout for military targets.

What do these photos reveal about American fears of a Japanese attack?

Read the Document *Japanese Relocation Order, February 19, 1942*

of 38,000 Japanese immigrants and 72,000 Japanese-American citizens to **internment camps**, where they were held under armed guard. Posted "Instructions to All Persons of Japanese Ancestry" informed Japanese inhabitants that they had only a few days to sell their belongings and settle their affairs. "It is difficult to describe the feeling of despair and humiliation experienced by all of us," one internee later said, "as we watched the Caucasians coming to look over our possessions and offering such nominal amounts knowing we had no recourse but to accept whatever they were offering." Evacuees could take only what they could carry. With numbers pinned on their coats, they rode trains to recently abandoned stables or stockyards to await transport to one of ten internment camps in remote areas of the interior West.

Offering a conflicting vision that emphasized their loyalty to the United States, most Japanese and Japanese Americans complied quietly with the evacuation order. A few, however, registered their protest against this wholesale violation of their civil rights. For propaganda purposes the Office of War Information hired photographer Dorothea Lange to document that the government was treating evacuees humanely as it contained this suspect population. Sympathetic to the plight of Japanese Americans, Lange managed to capture this scene (**23.9**) of a Japanese-American veteran reporting to a Santa Anita assembly center in his old military uniform, a silent demonstration of his long-standing loyalty to the country.

In January 1943, the army decided to recruit Nisei men, the American-born children of Japanese immigrants. While their parents remained in the camps, these men joined with Japanese Americans from Hawaii to form the 442nd Regimental Combat Team, which became the most decorated American unit in the nation's history. These men opted to prove their loyalty by fighting for their country in Europe. Other Japanese Americans sought redress in the courts, but the Supreme Court upheld the government's evacuation policy in 1944. *Competing Visions: Civil Liberties and National Security Clash* (page 696) examines this civil liberties controversy in more detail.

As the tide of the war began to turn in America's favor, the justification for interning people of Japanese descent weakened. In 1945, the government let inmates return to the West Coast. In 1948, the government offered some restitution to those who had lost homes or businesses. It took until 1988, however, for Congress to offer an apology and a reparation payment of $20,000 to each of the 60,000 surviving internees.

Prosperity, Scarcity, and Opportunities for Women

Japanese Americans were among the few to suffer financially from the war. For most Americans jobs were plentiful and wages high. During the war the nation's gross national product rose 60 percent, and 17 million new jobs were created. To mobilize the economy, the government quickly established a slew of agencies to allocate scarce resources, help businesses convert factories to a wartime footing, and enlist the public's support for the war. After the difficult years of the Depression, the war-fueled boom was a welcome relief. "People are crazy with money," one store owner exclaimed. "They don't care what they buy. They purchase things … just for the fun of spending." Madison Avenue advertising firms assured the public that consumerism was essential to the American way of life. "Will you ever own another car?" asked one ad. "Another radio? Another gleaming new refrigerator? Those who live under dictators merely dream of such possessions."

Concerns over unemployment gave way to worries about inflation as the money flowing into the economy sent prices soaring. The government tried to curb inflation by instituting price and wage controls. Because the nation's resources were now being poured into producing military equipment and supplying the troops, consumers faced shortages of all kinds. To deal with the scarcity of resources, the government rationed many goods, including gas, butter, and sugar, by distributing coupon books that allotted families a set amount of each item.

23.9 A Japanese American Protests Internment Government officials censored this photograph of a Japanese-American veteran who reported to the evacuation center in his old uniform. He gave his name to a Japanese-American staff member who decided instead to affirm his loyalty by cooperating openly with the authorities.

What competing responses did Japanese Americans have to internment?

Competing Visions

CIVIL LIBERTIES AND NATIONAL SECURITY CLASH

In *Korematsu v. United States* (1944), the Supreme Court upheld the constitutionality of relocating and interning Japanese Americans as a justifiable military measure. Three justices dissented from the majority opinion, concluding that internment violated the constitutional rights of Japanese-American citizens. Which side made the stronger argument? How has America resolved a similar dilemma over national security versus civil rights in the aftermath of the 9/11 attacks (see Chapter 29)?

Justice Hugo Black wrote the majority opinion that upheld the constitutionality of interning Japanese Americans.

Exclusion of those of Japanese origin was deemed necessary because of the presence of an unascertained number of disloyal members of the group, most of whom we have no doubt were loyal to this country…. We are not unmindful of the hardships imposed by it upon a large group of American citizens…. But hardships are part of war, and war is an aggregation of hardships. All citizens alike, both in and out of uniform, feel the impact of war in greater or lesser measure. Citizenship has its responsibilities as well as its privileges, and in time of war the burden is always heavier. Compulsory exclusion of large groups of citizens from their homes, except under circumstances of direct emergency and peril, is inconsistent with our basic governmental institutions. But when under conditions of modern warfare our shores are threatened by hostile forces, the power to protect must be commensurate with the threatened danger….

Regardless of the true nature of the assembly and relocation centers—and we deem it unjustifiable to call them concentration camps with all the ugly connotations that term implies…. Korematsu was not excluded from the Military Area because of hostility to him or his race. He was excluded because we are at war with the Japanese Empire, because the properly constituted military authorities feared an invasion of our West Coast and felt constrained to take proper security measures, because they decided that the military urgency of the situation demanded that all citizens of Japanese ancestry be segregated from the West Coast temporarily, and finally, because Congress, reposing its confidence in this time of war in our military leaders—as inevitably it must—determined that they should have the power to do just this. There was evidence of disloyalty on the part of some, the military authorities considered that the need for action was great, and time was short. We cannot—by availing ourselves of the calm perspective of hindsight—now say that at that time these actions were unjustified.

Justice Frank Murphy dissented, arguing that internment was racially motivated.

This exclusion of "all persons of Japanese ancestry, both alien and non-alien," from the Pacific Coast area on a plea of military necessity in the absence of martial law ought not to be approved. Such exclusion goes over "the very brink of constitutional power" and falls into the ugly abyss of racism … it is essential that there be definite limits to military discretion, especially where martial law has not been declared. Individuals must not be left impoverished of their constitutional rights on plea of military necessity that has neither substance nor support….

No one denies, of course, that there were some disloyal persons of Japanese descent on the Pacific Coast who did all in their power to aid their ancestral land. Similar disloyal activities have been engaged in by many persons of German, Italian and even more pioneer stock in our country. But to infer that examples of individual disloyalty prove group disloyalty and justify discriminatory action against the entire group is to deny that under our system of law individual guilt is the sole basis for deprivation of rights…. To give constitutional sanction to that inference in this case, however well-intentioned may have been the military command on the Pacific Coast, is to adopt one of the cruelest of the rationales used by our enemies to destroy the dignity of the individual and to encourage and open the door to discriminatory actions against other minority groups in the passions of tomorrow….

I dissent, therefore, from this legalization of racism. Racial discrimination in any form and in any degree has no justifiable part whatever in our democratic way of life.

Japanese-American girl saying the Pledge of Allegiance

Did a legitimate military reason exist to place Japanese Americans in internment camps?

🔍 ▶ **View** the **Closer Look** *Competing Visions: Civil Liberties and National Security Clash*

23.10 Norman Rockwell, "Rosie," *Saturday Evening Post*, 1943.
The lyrics to a popular 1942 song, "There's something true about/Red, white, and blue about/Rosie the Riveter," inspired Rockwell to set his Rosie against the backdrop of an American flag and place her foot on Hitler's *Mein Kampf*. Rockwell thus assured Americans that patriotism, rather than money or career ambitions, encouraged women to take factory jobs.

Nearly 19 million women held jobs during the war, for the moment a record high. Many of these women would have worked anyway. Only three million new female workers entered the wartime workforce. Norman Rockwell's cover illustration for the *Saturday Evening Post*'s 1943 Memorial Day edition (**23.10**) introduced the public to "Rosie the Riveter," an iconic figure representing all female defense workers. Rosie is strong and confident, containing both masculine and feminine attributes. Her bulging biceps offer assurance that she has mastered the skill of shooting rivets through sheets of metal to fasten them together, traditionally a job for men. But she also wears lipstick and rouge as she munches her home-made sandwich, demonstrating her feminine interest in cosmetics and cooking. Rockwell's Rosie wears no wedding ring, and most working women were single. The War Manpower Commission, a wartime agency charged with keeping American workers on the job, tried with mixed success to lure "Mrs. Stay-at-Home" into the wartime workforce. Many mothers, however, expressed mixed feelings about leaving their children in day care.

Once victory seemed ensured in 1944, government-sponsored propaganda reversed course, emphasizing women's domestic responsibilities instead of their public duties. Toward the end of the war, the *Saturday Evening Post* carried this "Mothers at Work" ad (**23.11**) that urged women to consider the toll that working outside the home had on their children. The ad also emphasized this woman's imminent postwar need for new appliances.

To save wool, cotton, and nylon, the War Production Board (WPB) dictated fashion trends by forbidding tailors to make cuffs, vests, or double-breasted jackets for men. The WPB's demand that bathing suit manufacturers use ten percent less material meant that skintight one-piece bathing suits replaced billowing bathing costumes on beaches. Skirt hemlines also rose to save fabric.

The government spent as never before, expanding the federal budget from $9 billion in 1939 to $106 billion by 1945. As in World War I, the nation used conscription to fill the ranks and enlisted the help of big business to provide the guns, tanks, ships, airplanes, and bullets that a modern army needed. Numbers help convey the immensity of the American war effort. The military grew from 227,000 to 16 million, of whom 10 million were conscripted. American industry produced 77,000 ships, 300,000 airplanes, 2.5 million trucks, and 20 million small arms for the American and Allied armed forces. Nearly 15 million civilians relocated during the war to take advantage of opportunities in cities with booming wartime industries such as Los Angeles, New Orleans, Seattle, Detroit, and Philadelphia. The sudden growth of many cities forced hundreds of thousands of recent migrants to live in "the backs of stores, in public buildings, warehouses, and garages," the Bureau of Labor reported.

23.11 "Mothers at Work"
As the war drew to a close, official posters and private advertisements encouraged women to revert to their traditional roles as homemakers.

View the **Closer Look** *Images as History: "We Can Do It!" Visual Myths about Women's Roles During World War II*

What competing visions of working women emerged during the war?

As expected the overall percentage of women working fell to 28 percent (from a wartime high of 36 percent) in 1947 as women quit their jobs to raise families or employers fired them to free up positions for returning veterans.

Over 350,000 women served in the armed forces, including 150,000 in the Women's Army Corps (WAC). Most women in uniform served as nurses and clerks, fulfilling vital communication and record-keeping services. Many men and the media mocked these clerical roles. The press nick-named the WACs the "Petticoat Army" and their quarters "Fort Lipstick." The recruiting slogan for the WACs—"Release a man for combat"—under-scored the different risks faced by women and men in the military.

Female soldiers also performed more tradition-ally "male" tasks, serving as gunnery instructors, mechanics, and truck drivers, and 1,000 women even flew combat aircraft from domestic manufactur-ers to overseas bases. General Douglas MacArthur called female troops "my best soldiers." At least one congressman, however, offered a competing vision, wondering "what has become of the manhood of America?" now that women had a formal place in the armed forces.

After the war only a few thousand women re-mained in uniform as the military cut slots reserved for female troops. Their position within the armed forces rebounded a bit, however, in 1948, when Congress gave women a permanent, though segre-gated, place in the army, navy, and air force. The debate over whether to limit female soldiers to sup-port tasks or use them in active operations was only beginning.

Even children pitched in to help the war effort. To encourage children's active participation, the government released photographs of small girls and boys doing their bit (**23.12**). This young boy takes care of the family shopping while his parents work in war-related jobs, handing the family's ration card to the merchant. At home this little girl carefully saves tin and foil in separate jars for the local scrap drive. Millions participated in these morale-building ac-tivities, but weapons manufacturers discarded most of the poor-quality aluminum and rubber collected. Money, however, was always in short supply. Class-rooms across the nation collected pennies and nick-els for war bonds, which the federal government sold to Americans to help finance the war. The remoteness of the war often made it seem like a great adventure to children. War games gained popularity on the nation's playgrounds, and children joined the Junior Commandos, which trained young uniformed recruits, only a few years away from qualifying to fight in the army, on a rugged obstacle course.

23.12 Children and War
Children helped in the war effort by collecting metal for neighborhood scrap drives and by shopping with a ration card while their parents worked.

How did World War II affect childhood?   **View** the **Image** *"Get in the Scrap" Poster*

With the economy booming, many Americans concluded that wars, by nature, were good for the economy. However, several unique factors made World War II particularly beneficial for the American economy:

- The war effort withdrew 16 million servicemen and women from the workforce just as millions of new positions were created, absorbing all surplus labor and creating a labor shortage.

- Massive government spending on the war, not the war per se, ended the Depression. If the government had been willing to spend $323 billion (the total cost of the war) on New Deal programs, the economy would likely have rebounded earlier.

- The wartime boom years came at the expense of future generations. Taxation paid for less than half of the war's cost. The government did not pay off its war debts until 1970.

Prosperity and unity of purpose failed to guarantee tranquility in labor relations on the home front. Competing visions on the meaning of wartime sacrifice emerged immediately. The chairman of the National War Labor Board dramatized the difficulty of asking unions for wage concessions by noting, "If you say to the boys, 'Why don't you make a sacrifice for your country?' they are going to say, 'That is fine. I am making a sacrifice for my country, but I am not going to make it to increase the profits of General Motors.'" Big business profited tremendously from the war. Government contracts with generous profit margins, federal loans for factory conversion or expansion, and tax write-offs went overwhelmingly to the nation's 100 largest companies. Even companies that appeared peripheral to the war effort prospered. Both Coca-Cola and Wrigley's Gum, for instance, got their products declared essential war commodities, thus gaining access to carefully rationed sugar and shipping space. By following American servicemen around the globe, Coca-Cola cultivated a worldwide taste for its beverage. Wrigley's Gum convinced the War Department that chewing gum reduced stress in workers and troops. The company provided a free stick for every soldier's combat rations.

During the war, labor's clout, like that of big companies, also expanded. Union rolls swelled from 8.7 to 14.7 million thanks in part to supportive War Labor Board policies. Industrialists tried to use the wartime rhetoric of sacrifice to rein in these growing unions. In one advertisement, for example, the Jenkins Valve firm linked work slowdowns (used to pressure a company to agree to labor's demands) to the unnecessary deaths of American sailors. The ad showed a small child staring at a sailor's cap that had washed up along the shore; the caption asked "Is a Plant Slow Down Worth It?" Unions did not abandon strikes, but the war ushered in a less militant era of collective bargaining.

Racial Discord

The war provided many opportunities for racial minorities to assert their claims for equal rights in American social and political life. These groups offered a strikingly different view of the war's ultimate purpose. Unlike most white Americans who confined their thoughts to the struggle against fascism abroad, many civil rights leaders championed a competing vision that sought to eradicate discrimination at home. Using the war to promote a double-victory campaign against both fascism overseas and racial prejudice at home, these activists promoted a vision of an egalitarian and color-blind society.

> **"If you are going to … go to war … in a capitalist country, you have to let business make money out of the process or business won't work."**
>
> Secretary of War HENRY L. STIMSON

At first the wartime boom threatened to leave African Americans behind, because many essential wartime industries refused to hire blacks. In 1941, the African American labor leader A. Philip Randolph threatened to assemble 10,000 blacks in front of the Lincoln Memorial in Washington, D.C., to "demand the right to work and fight for our country." Nationally known for organizing a union for black railroad porters, Randolph realized that FDR's lock on the black vote gave him little reason to offer more than sympathy in private meetings with black leaders about rampant racial discrimination. To pressure FDR to act on blacks' behalf, a step certain to anger the president's white southern supporters, Randolph resolved to publicly protest employment discrimination.

Randolph's idea for a march on Washington immediately attracted the support of civil rights groups and the ire of the White House. When FDR tried to convince Randolph to call off the march, Randolph told him, "We feel as you have wisely said: 'No people will lose their freedom fighting for it.'" To avoid an embarrassing demonstration that highlighted racial problems at home, FDR agreed to issue an executive order that forbade discrimination in the defense industries and government if Randolph canceled the march. Roosevelt's order also established the Fair Employment Practices Committee to handle complaints of discrimination. For the first time since Reconstruction, the period following the Civil War, the federal government was intervening directly to protect the civil rights of African Americans. Randolph's aborted demonstration later inspired the 1963 march on Washington, where black civil rights leader Martin Luther King Jr. delivered his "I Have a Dream" speech standing before the Lincoln Memorial (see Chapter 27).

Interest in direct action grew throughout the war. The Fellowship of Reconciliation's Committee on Racial Justice initiated a wave of sit-ins, where blacks and whites entered segregated restaurants together and refused to leave when denied service. In Washington, D.C., Howard University students picketed segregated restaurants with signs that read "We Die Together. Let's Eat Together" and "Are You for Hitler's Way or the American Way? Make Up Your Mind."

Nearly one million blacks served in the armed forces during the war, including Brigadier General Benjamin O. Davis, the first African American general in the U.S. Army. The War Department finally agreed to train African American pilots, and the Tuskegee Airmen (who received their stateside training at Alabama's Tuskegee Institute) amassed an admirable war record in Europe. The military remained segregated, however, and most black soldiers served in noncombatant units where they cleared beaches in France of mines, manned supply lines transporting food and ammunition to front-line troops, and built roads and railroads for the advancing army.

Within the U.S. black servicemen received daily reminders of their second-class status. When black soldiers entered a whites-only restaurant in Salina, Kansas, the owner stopped them. We "just stood there inside the door, staring at what we had come to see—the German prisoners of war who were having lunch at the counter.... This was really happening. It was no jive talk. The people of Salina would serve these enemy soldiers and turn away black American G.I.'s," one soldier recalled. The proper epitaph to mark each black soldier's grave in the Pacific, African Americans

sarcastically said, would be "here lies a black man killed fighting a yellow man for the protection of a white man."

The double-victory campaign laid the groundwork for the postwar civil rights movement by pioneering new strategies that would later prove extraordinarily successful. The accelerated migration northward also created new bases of political power that would aid the civil rights movement in the 1950s and 1960s. Throughout the war hundreds of thousands of African American civilians hit the road in search of job opportunities in midwestern and western cities. In 1943, Los Angeles welcomed 10,000 black migrants a month, most from Texas and Louisiana. Overcrowding and changing demographics created explosive racial situations in many urban areas. The most serious wartime race riot took place in 1943 in Detroit. Home to the nation's largest automobile manufacturers, Detroit became the leading producer of military goods when these companies began manufacturing jeeps and tanks for the military. Plentiful jobs drew thousands of migrants to the city, including African Americans, who had trouble finding adequate lodging in the strictly (albeit unofficially) segregated city housing market. White workers, resentful of working next to blacks, staged slowdowns in the city's wartime defense plants. To protest racial discrimination, some black residents initiated a "bumping campaign," nudging whites off sidewalks. The anticipated confrontation finally came on a warm spring afternoon when black and white teenagers tussled at a crowded amusement park on Belle Isle. As the violence escalated, a mob of 5,000 whites formed to attack blacks as they crossed the bridge back to the mainland. Racial rampaging soon engulfed the city. Hundreds of African Americans were injured and 25 were killed, before state and federal troops restored order. Nine whites also died in the rioting.

Horace Pippin, a self-taught African American painter who rocketed to fame in the late 1930s, took note of the racial discord on the home front in his 1943 painting *Mr. Prejudice* (**23.13**). Pippin's composition expressed doubt that the double-V campaign would succeed. In the painting a racist white worker, backed by a Klansman, hammers a chisel down the center of a V, the symbol of victory. A fellow worker to his left holds a noose—a reference to lynching. The Statue of Liberty, portrayed as an African American woman, is toppling down as the dream of racial unity unravels. The fractured

How did African Americans challenge racial discrimination during the war?

Read the **Document** *Jim Crow in the Army Camps*

V threatens to crack into two, permanently dividing the friendly white servicemen reaching out to their black comrades in arms—a doctor, sailor, aviator, and soldier, who are all serving loyally during the war.

African Americans were not the only targets of racial violence, however. The same summer that racial rioting rocked Detroit, white sailors and soldiers on leave in Los Angeles began a ten-day rampage against Mexican-American zoot-suiters, youths who wore baggy pants, long oversize coats, and broad-brimmed hats. The zoot-suit was a fashion trend established by African American men in the 1930s. By the war years white Americans viewed zoot-suiters at best as juvenile delinquents, who refused to dress and act properly, and at worst as criminal gangs bent on robbery and rape. Some *pachucos*, as zoot-suiters called themselves, engaged in criminal activity, but most limited their adolescent rebellion to wearing different clothes from adults.

The explosive growth in the Mexican-American community, coupled with a general intolerance for nonconformity during war, set the stage for the conflict in Los Angeles. Street fights between sailors and Mexican-American men escalated into full-scale rioting, when organized groups of servicemen began attacking boys as young as 12 and Mexican-American businesses. White civilians joined in the rioting, and when a mob came upon a zoot-suiter, they often beat and stripped him and even burned his clothes. The casualties included more than 100 seriously injured Mexican Americans, and at least 100 more who refused hospital care. Newspapers in Los Angeles egged on the white crowds by praising their efforts to rid the city of "hoodlums" and "gangsters." Federal investigators cited racial prejudice as the cause of the riots, but Los Angeles nonetheless prohibited wearing zoot-suits on city streets. The image of Mexican Americans as disaffected youths belied the reality that 500,000 Latinos served alongside whites in the armed forces during the war, playing a significant role in the doomed defense of the Philippines and winning many Medals of Honor.

Perceived as natural warriors, Native Americans encountered less hostility within the armed forces than blacks or Latinos. More than 25,000 Native Americans served, including the famed Navajo code talkers who transmitted secret messages between units in their native language,

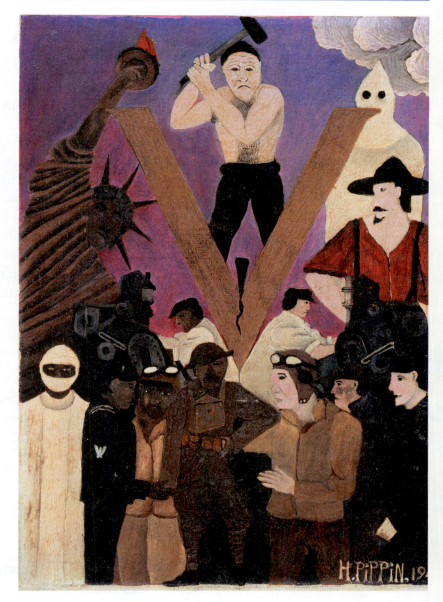

baffling the Japanese, who never deciphered it. Military service offered many young Native Americans their first decent wages and a chance to leave the reservation. Government officials expected military service to hasten assimilation, since Native-American soldiers lived among whites. Yet sending men into combat also gave some tribes a reason to resurrect rituals surrounding battle, such as requiring returning soldiers to spend time in a sweat lodge to cleanse themselves of the evils associated with war. Serving in the military, therefore, both expanded veterans' knowledge of the wider world and reinforced their own cultural traditions, helping them to see themselves and mainstream society in a different light.

23.13 Horace Pippin, *Mr. Prejudice* (1943) The fractured V in Pippin's painting suggested that the African American vision of using the war to secure democracy at home and abroad was in jeopardy.

How did the wartime experiences of African Americans compare to those of Latinos?

On the Front Lines

No bombs fell on mainland American cities and no occupying armies marched through the streets, but with 16 million men in the armed forces, nearly everyone knew someone who might not make it home. The United States essentially fought two separate wars in World War II: one against Germany and its allies in Europe; the other against Japan in the Pacific. The initial news from the battlefront was not good, as the American armed forces encountered one setback after another. Defeating Japan and Germany required time and patience. Victories finally came, but the closer the Allies got to Japan and Germany, the harder their enemies fought. Initially leery of exposing Americans to blood and gore, over time magazines and newspapers began to publish photographs that registered the rising death toll at the front. The public welcomed photographs of enemy destruction as evidence that the nation was nearing victory, but reacted strongly to any sign of suffering by American soldiers. Nothing prepared the public, however, for the shocking details that emerged from liberated Nazi concentration camps in 1945.

23.14 War in the Pacific Allied victories at Guadalcanal, the Coral Sea, and Midway halted Japanese expansion, preparing the way for the American island-hopping campaign in 1944–1945.

Defeat, Then Victory

Until mid-1942, the American military reeled from one defeat to another in the Pacific. The attack on Pearl Harbor prevented the United States from interfering with Japan's sweeping conquest of Southeast Asia and the western Pacific islands, as shown in this map (**23.14**). American and Filipino soldiers fought courageously in the Philippines; but lacking supplies these troops finally surrendered in early 1942.

To solidify its control of East Asia, Japan planned to attack Australia through Port Moresby, on New Guinea, and then fight a decisive battle with the American navy in the western Pacific that would force the United States to sue for a negotiated peace. The Americans thwarted these plans in the Battle of the Coral Sea (May 3–8, 1942) and the Battle of Midway (June 4–6, 1942). In the former a duel of naval aircraft ended with Japan calling off its invasion of Australia. In the latter

What does this map reveal about the military challenges facing the United States in the Pacific?

🔍—**View** the **Map** Interactive Map: World War II, Pacific Theater

American dive-bombers surprised Japanese aircraft carriers in the midst of refueling their planes. Japan's heavy losses at Midway prevented it from launching any major naval offensives for the rest of the war. Midway was a crucial turning point that put Japan permanently on the defensive.

America adopted a "Europe First" strategy, but the war in the European theater began equally poorly for the Allies. Initially the United States wanted to get supplies across the Atlantic and open up a second front against Germany in Western Europe. Meeting the first goal required winning the Battle of the Atlantic. For 18 months the Allied cause looked grim, as German submarines controlled the seas, sinking an average of 100 ships a month. The extensive submarine activity on Map 23.1 illustrates the ferocity of the struggle to control the Atlantic. Finally, in summer 1943, the tide turned in the Allies' favor. Better air surveillance, improved radar, the discovery that the Germans had broken the convoy-routing code, and breaking the German naval code all contributed to Allied success in the Atlantic.

The issue of opening a second front in Europe remained. Roosevelt was reluctant to commit American land forces until the army was better equipped and supplied than its adversaries. But he recognized that committing American ground troops to the war in Europe would build morale at home; it would also prevent the Russians from seeking a separate peace with Germany.

Soviet leader Joseph Stalin urged Britain and the United States to invade Nazi-occupied France in 1943. Churchill and FDR refused. Britain worried about repeating the trench stalemate of World War I, while the Americans

doubted that their inexperienced army could prevail against the first-rate German troops stationed in France. As an alternative FDR and Churchill decided to attack "the soft underbelly of Europe" by first establishing supply and air bases in North Africa and then invading Italy. Despite American blunders on the battlefield, by summer 1943, the Allies had gained control of North Africa and invaded Sicily, as shown in the map "The European Theater" (**23.15**).

Italy's surrender on September 8, 1943, meant little, however. German forces invaded the Italian peninsula, saving Mussolini's regime and bogging Allied troops down in a bloody campaign that lasted until May 1945. When Mussolini tried to escape in 1945 with the retreating Germans, Italian resistance fighters captured him and his mistress, shot them, and strung them upside down in a

23.15 The European Theater The Soviet army fought alone in Europe until the Western Allies invaded Italy in 1943 and launched the D-Day invasion of France in 1944.

Why did the Western Allies attack the Axis powers first in Italy, rather than France?

public square in Milan, where resistance fighters had been executed.

In 1943, the Western Allies launched the first major incendiary attack of the war. The bombing raids on Hamburg, a major industrial German city and port, ignited a firestorm in the hot, dry conditions that killed 45,000 people and wounded nearly 40,000. Germany's aerial attacks during the Battle of Britain in 1940–1941 had hardened British views about bombing German civilians, while the Americans preferred trying to hit actual military and industrial installations. Dresden, home to key railroad lines, was the site of another devastating incendiary bombing raid in February 1945, which killed approximately 35,000 Germans. Although many American bombs failed to hit their precisely designated industrial or military targets, in fighting Germany, the United States never formally adopted terror bombing, the strategy of dropping high concentrations of bombs on civilian populations to create panic and misery.

In November 1943, FDR and Churchill met with Stalin for the first time in Tehran, the capital of Iran, to discuss Allied strategy for the coming year. During the conference FDR privately described Stalin as "altogether quite impressive," and the president stayed in the Soviet Embassy to build a good rapport with the Soviet leader. Churchill remained leery of Soviet intentions to expand its influence into Eastern Europe after the war. The Soviet victory at Stalingrad (January–February 1943), a pivotal battle that put the Allies on the path to victory, buoyed optimism that the tide had turned in Russia's favor on the Eastern Front. Within a few months, the Soviets would

23.16 General MacArthur's Return to the Philippines MacArthur used the press to publicize his return to the Philippines in 1944. Military photographers captured his purposeful stride ashore, and that evening MacArthur proclaimed in a radio address, "People of the Philippines: I have returned … Rally to me."

also end a 900-day German siege of Leningrad that lasted from September 1941–January 1944.

Churchill wanted to forestall a Soviet takeover of Eastern Europe by launching an Anglo-American invasion of the Balkans through the Adriatic Sea. FDR doubted that Americans would support such a campaign, when the nation's traditional interest lay in defending Britain and France. He was also reluctant to send American troops into a region that the USSR clearly intended to dominate after the war. The president was wary of antagonizing the Soviet Union, when he still hoped to convince Stalin to declare war against Japan once the European war ended. Instead, the United States persuaded Britain to join it in an invasion of France in 1944.

The campaign in the Pacific followed a similar strategy of attacking Japan in the "soft underbelly" of its empire in the South Pacific. The Americans opened this campaign with successful, but difficult attacks on Guadalcanal in the Solomon Islands and on New Guinea. In early 1943, Japan accepted its defeat in the South Pacific by withdrawing its fleet and aircraft to a new defensive line that extended through Southeast Asia, the Philippines, and the Mariana Islands.

To keep up the pressure on Japan, the Americans launched a two-pronged attack on Japanese forces in the Central and South Pacific. From the Central Pacific the Americans hoped to establish a naval blockade that cut Japan off from supplies in the south. The United States quickly took the Gilbert and Marshall Islands. During the subsequent invasion of the island of Saipan in the Marianas, the Americans destroyed so many Japanese naval aircraft in the Battle of the Philippine Sea (June 19–20, 1944) that the battle became known as "the Great Marianas Turkey Shoot."

The final capture of the Marianas in August 1944 put the United States, armed with massive and heavily-loaded B-29s that could travel up to 2,000 miles, within striking distance of Japan.

"I shall return," General Douglas MacArthur had proclaimed when FDR ordered him to head to Australia and leave his troops on the Philippines in 1942. On October 20, 1944, he fulfilled this promise by wading ashore in the Leyte Gulf four hours after the first American force landed in a carefully choreographed act

How did the tide gradually turn in favor of the Allies in Europe and the Pacific?

the first kamikaze pilots plowed their planes into six American ships, setting off a cascade of explosions from the ships' gasoline and ordnance that damaged five and sank one.

A month later seaman James Fahey was on a ship under attack. The sailors battled for hours, shooting down a steady stream of incoming aircraft. "The explosions were terrific as the suicide planes exploded in the water … the water looked like it was on fire," Fahey wrote in his diary. Parts of the destroyed planes fell onto his ship, and during a lull in the action, the sailors sifted through the debris for souvenirs. "The deck near my mount was covered with blood, guts, brains, tongues, scalps, hearts, arms etc. from the Jap pilots," Fahey recalled. He watched men select body parts to preserve in alcohol and send home to relatives. Soldiers involved in the Pacific island–hopping campaigns exhibited a similar macabre interest in collecting Japanese soldiers' body parts. In May 1944, *Life* magazine published "A Wartime Souvenir," showing an attractive young woman writing a thank-you note to her fiancé for sending her a souvenir Japanese skull (**23.17**). "The armed forces disapprove strongly of this sort of thing," *Life* noted. Yet the image of this woman calmly contemplating her war trophy elicited no controversy. Instead, many Americans exorcised their own desire for revenge against Japan through such images. The press had to handle photographs of American war dead more carefully (see *Images as History: Combat Photography*, page 706).

23.17 "A Wartime Souvenir" In 1944, *Life* magazine chose this photo as its picture of the week. The young woman's fiancé sent her a Japanese skull with an inscription that read: "This is a good Jap—a dead one picked up on the New Guinea beach." Collecting enemy body parts as war trophies was common among American troops fighting Japan, but not in the European theater.

that MacArthur insisted on filming several times to get just right. To build morale and enhance his reputation as a fearless leader, MacArthur presented himself as part of the invasion force, a general who was willing to get his boots wet and resolutely press forward, as seen in this photo (**23.16**). The Battle of Leyte Gulf (October 23–25, 1944), the largest naval battle in history, ended with an American victory. It took until July 1945, however, to completely liberate the Philippines from isolated infantry garrisons.

With the war advancing well in the Pacific, Americans began to feel optimistic about achieving a swift victory. These hopes faded, however, when Japan switched from fighting a strategic war to waging a war of attrition. Mounting losses, Japan's leaders reasoned, would force the United States to the negotiating table. With conventional weapons like ships, guns, and planes in short supply, Japan introduced suicidal battlefield tactics on land and sea in the fall of 1944, intensifying the struggle. In the western Caroline Islands, Japanese soldiers fought to the last man. Forcing the Americans to rout out every enemy soldier from an interlocking system of caves and bunkers prolonged the battle and raised American casualties. During the Battle of Leyte Gulf,

The Final Push in Europe

On June 6, 1944, the Allies launched D-Day (for "debarkation day"), their long-anticipated invasion of Normandy, in northern France, under the command of General Dwight D. Eisenhower. "The eyes of the world are upon you," the popular leader told his troops. Eisenhower, raised in a poor Jehovah Witness family in Kansas, became a national hero for his successful planning and execution of the D-Day invasions and subsequent offensives through France and Germany. His achievements and sunny personality would make him an appealing postwar presidential candidate in 1952 (see Chapter 24).

Although stormy weather made traversing the English Channel treacherous, and the Americans

Images as History
COMBAT PHOTOGRAPHY

War photography brings the realities of combat into the homes of ordinary citizens. How do pictures of combat force viewers to think about the overall meaning and worthiness of the conflict?

For the first year and a half of American involvement, when there was little good news to report, the military believed that photographs of dead American soldiers would weaken morale on the home front. In 1943, Allied victories in the South Pacific and North Africa raised spirits at home—perhaps a bit too much for some officials. Aware of the long road ahead and the need for continued civilian sacrifice, the War Department approved the dissemination of bloody battlefield photographs.

In September 1943, *Life* published a photograph of three American soldiers lying partially buried in the sand in New Guinea. In the accompanying editorial *Life* anticipated the public's shock at seeing the first photograph of American war dead. "Why print this picture, anyway, of three American boys dead upon an alien shore? Is it to hurt people? To be morbid?" *Life* editors wrote. "Those are not the answers. The reason is that words are never enough."

Magazine editors chose their images from an ever-increasing supply of casualty pictures. Two-thirds of the 291,557 American troops killed in battle during the war died in 1944–1945. Photographer Joe Rosenthal's "Old Glory Goes Up on Mt. Suribachi, Iwo Jima," a candid shot of five marines and one navy corpsman raising a flag on the Pacific Island of Iwo Jima on February 23, 1945, remains the most famous image from World War II. Rosenthal's Pulitzer Prize–winning photograph would inspire a Marine Corps statue, erected in Washington, D.C., in 1954.

Military censors forbade publication of photographs containing identifiable war dead or badly mutilated corpses, worried that such pictures might depress morale on the home front.

"Publication of photos showing some of our boys killed in action had a sobering effect on people and brought the realities of war closer to home," a satisfied War Department official noted.

Here Lie Three Americans," 1943.

The image of six men working together to push the flag upright conveyed the teamwork necessary to defeat Japan, and that the uphill struggle to victory was not over.

Critics later accused Rosenthal of staging this photo, a charge he denied.

Three of the marines in Rosenthal's photograph died in the ensuing battle. The others returned home and toured the country in an overwhelmingly successful war bond campaign.

"Old Glory Goes Up on Mount Suribachi, Iwo Jima," 1945.

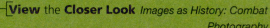

How did the political and military situation influence the way Americans viewed these photographs?

View the **Closer Look** *Images as History: Combat Photography*

faced fierce German resistance on Omaha Beach, one of five landing points, the D-Day invasion was an overwhelming success. The heavy buildup for the attack, involving 175,000 troops, 6,000 aircraft, and 6,000 naval vessels, made complete surprise impossible. But the Allies had increased the invasion's chances of success by deceiving the Germans into expecting the attack to come elsewhere. Diversionary bombing, false agent reports, and misleading radio communications convinced the Germans to station most of their first-rate infantry divisions farther north. Hitler continued to hold these units and his crack tank formations in reserve even after the D-Day invasion began, certain that the Normandy landings were just a diversion. The German delay in responding gave the Allies the time they needed to establish a beachhead that stretched for 55 miles by the end of the first day.

Life photographer Robert Capa hit the beaches with the troops, living up to his famous statement, "If your pictures aren't good enough, you aren't close enough." Anxious to see Capa's photographs, a rushing darkroom technician used too much heat to dry the film and inadvertently melted nearly all his images. The excessive heat blurred the remaining few, creating a surreal aura to this instantly iconic image (**23.18**) of an American soldier struggling through the turbulent surf to reach the shore. Capa put down his camera long enough to pull this soldier to safety after a bullet struck him in the right shoulder.

It was still a long way from Normandy to Berlin, however. After two more months of hard fighting, the Allies finally began to push forward. On August 15, 1944, the Americans launched a second invasion through the south of France. Within a month these troops had joined with the Normandy invasion forces to establish a continuous Allied front from the English Channel to the German frontier. But Hitler had no intention of going down without a fight. In December 1944, the Germans launched a massive counter-offensive. The Battle of the Bulge, so named for the Germans' pocket of penetration into Allied lines, was the most massive battle fought by the American Army in Europe. Fighting in the snow and bitter cold, the Allies suffered 77,000 casualties before halting the German counter-attack a month later.

> ## "Two kinds of people are staying on this beach, the dead and those who are going to die."
>
> Colonel GEORGE TAYLOR, urging his dazed troops forward on Omaha Beach during the 1944 D-Day invasions

When Roosevelt, Churchill, and Stalin met again in February 1945 at Yalta, a town in the Crimea on Russia's Black Sea coast, to discuss their next step, Roosevelt was fresh off an unprecedented fourth-term victory in the 1944 presidential election. The Republican candidate Thomas Dewey, a popular New York State governor, had attacked Roosevelt as a "tired old man" no longer up to the challenge of running the war. Roosevelt solidified support within the Democratic Party by replacing the controversial liberal Henry Wallace with Harry S. Truman, a straight-talking moderate senator from Missouri, as his vice-presidential candidate. The selection of an acceptable vice-presidential candidate was important to Democratic Party bosses who feared that the ill Roosevelt might not live to complete a fourth term in office. Suffering from advancing heart disease and the strain of war, Roosevelt nevertheless displayed renewed energy during the campaign, convincing Americans not to "change horses in mid-stream." He won 432 to 99 votes in the Electoral College, receiving 54 percent of the popular vote.

23.18 D-Day Invasion, 1944 Robert Capa's grainy photograph conveyed the chaos and danger American soldiers faced when they hit the beaches in Normandy, France.

At Yalta the larger question of how to defeat Germany was behind the Allies. The issues now on the table included governing postwar Germany, ensuring victory over Japan, and maintaining peace in the postwar world. At the conference FDR secured a Soviet promise to enter the war against Japan three months after Germany capitulated. In return Stalin wanted the United States and Britain to grant the Soviet Union territorial concessions in Japan, China, and eastern Poland. For the moment FDR acceded to Soviet control of Eastern Europe, but secured a pledge from Stalin, never honored, to hold free elections in a liberated Poland.

The decision at Yalta to name the United States, Britain, France, China, and the USSR as permanent members of the proposed United Nations Security Council, each with the power to veto any resolution, cleared the way to officially create a United Nations (UN) to replace the defunct League of Nations. Delegates from 50 nations met in San Francisco between April 25 and June 26, 1945, to found the UN, an international organization that offered nations a place to discuss their differences and collectively promote economic development and peace throughout the world. To ensure that the United States joined the UN, its creators made participation in UN-peacekeeping missions voluntary. The Security Council veto also gave the United States (and the other major powers) a way to control UN activities. In contrast to World War I, when it failed to join the League of Nations, the United States was one of the first countries to join the UN, which built its headquarters in New York City.

Now unstoppable in Europe, the Allies crossed the Rhine River into Germany in March. On April 30, 1945, Hitler committed suicide in a bunker 55 feet underground in Berlin. After dictating his will and marrying his longtime companion Eva Braun, Hitler bit into a cyanide capsule and shot himself in the head. Two days later Russian soldiers entered the bunker and took Hitler's burned remains, so an autopsy could confirm he was dead. Germany surrendered unconditionally on May 7, 1945.

America's Response to the Holocaust

In spring 1945, Allied troops began liberating the concentration camps holding Jews, Poles, prisoners of war, and other groups that the Nazis considered enemies or racially inferior. News of the Final Solution, Hitler's plan to systematically murder the Jews and other "lesser" peoples, first reached the West in August 1942. Along with ten other nations, the United States condemned "in the strongest possible terms this bestial policy of cold-blooded extermination." During the war mainstream American newspapers, fearful of reporting falsified atrocity stories amid a glut of war news, had published little about the Holocaust, the term used to describe this Nazi-engineered extermination. The United States did little initially to aid European Jews. In January 1944, however, Secretary of the Treasury Henry Morgenthau, who was Jewish, protested to FDR that anti-Semitism within the State Department had thwarted a plan to ransom 70,000 Romanian Jews with private funds, leaving the United States open to charges that it was acquiescing in the "murder of the Jews." FDR immediately issued an executive order establishing the War Refugee Board (WRB). Over the next year the WRB saved approximately 200,000 lives by convincing Romania and Hungary to stop deporting Jews and by helping Jews and other victims of Nazi persecution escape or survive in hiding. *Envisioning Evidence: Deciphering the Holocaust* depicts both the response of the United States to the Holocaust and the scope of German atrocities.

Pressed by Jewish groups to undertake a dramatic rescue of Europe's Jews by bombing either the concentration camps or the railroads leading to them, Roosevelt demurred. He argued that any diversion of military resources from the ultimate goal of winning the war would only prolong the Jews' suffering. In February 1944 the War Department decided not to send armed forces to rescue "victims of enemy oppression unless such rescues are the direct result of military operations conducted with the objective of defeating the armed forces of the enemy." Bombing Auschwitz, the main Nazi extermination camp in Poland, became a real possibility only in the summer of 1944. In August Allied planes dropped more than 1,000 bombs on synthetic-oil plants less than 5 miles from Auschwitz.

Whether the Allies should have also bombed the gas chambers has provoked heated debate since the war. Advocates argue that destroying the railroad lines leading to Auschwitz or its gas chambers would have slowed down the killing as liberating Allied troops approached the camps, perhaps saving as many as 100,000 Jews. These would have included Anne Frank, a 13-year-old German refugee who was sent to Auschwitz after her family's capture in Amsterdam and whose journal of her experience in hiding, *The Diary of Anne Frank*, became a postwar literary classic. Detractors note the Nazi

What significant decisions were reached at the 1945 Yalta Conference?

Envisioning Evidence
DECIPHERING THE HOLOCAUST

Over-simplifications about the Holocaust depict German Jews as the main victims of Hitler's Final Solution and the United States primarily as liberators. As the graph shows, most of the six million Jews who died in the Holocaust were Poles. The Germans also killed over three million Soviet prisoners of war, two million non-Jewish Poles, nearly 200,000 disabled individuals, 10,000 Jehovah Witnesses, and an undetermined number of homosexuals and Roma or Gypsies. The timeline reveals that during the Depression-plagued 1930s the United States reacted cautiously to Hitler's persecution of the Jews. Nonetheless, of all nations, the United States still accepted the largest number of Jewish refugees fleeing Nazi persecution. The map marks the major concentration camps that American ground troops liberated in Western Europe, including Buchenwald, Dachau, and Mauthausen, forced labor camps and detention centers where thousands were "worked to death," starved, executed, and subjected to medical experiments. The Soviet army liberated the extermination camps, including Auschwitz, all located in Eastern Europe.

Liberation of Major Nazi Camps, 1944-1945

- Camps liberated by the United States
- Camps liberated by Great Britain/Canada
- Camps liberated by the Soviet Union
- May 1945 Date of liberation

"I have gotten rid of the Jews." Adolf Hitler, 1944

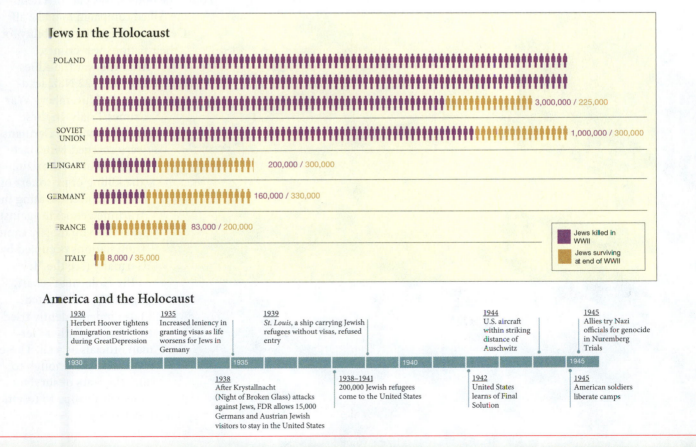

Jews in the Holocaust

POLAND — 3,000,000 / 225,000

SOVIET UNION — 1,000,000 / 300,000

HUNGARY — 200,000 / 300,000

GERMANY — 160,000 / 330,000

FRANCE — 83,000 / 200,000

ITALY — 8,000 / 35,000

Jews killed in WWII
Jews surviving at end of WWII

America and the Holocaust

1930 — Herbert Hoover tightens immigration restrictions during Great Depression

1935 — Increased leniency in granting visas as life worsens for Jews in Germany

1939 — *St. Louis*, a ship carrying Jewish refugees without visas, refused entry

1944 — U.S. aircraft within striking distance of Auschwitz

1945 — Allies try Nazi officials for genocide in Nuremberg Trials

1938 — After Krystallnacht (Night of Broken Glass) attacks against Jews, FDR allows 15,000 Germans and Austrian Jewish visitors to stay in the United States

1938–1941 — 200,000 Jewish refugees come to the United States

1942 — United States learns of Final Solution

1945 — American soldiers liberate camps

🔍 **View** the **Closer Look** *Envisioning Evidence: Deciphering the Holocaust*

What insights do this data offer on the scope of the Holocaust and the American response?

> "The wrongs which we seek to condemn and punish have been so calculated, so malignant, and so devastating, that civilization cannot tolerate their being ignored, because it cannot survive their being repeated."
>
> American prosecutor, Supreme Court Justice ROBERT JACKSON, in opening the Nuremberg War Crimes Trials

23.19 German Civilians Viewing Corpses in a Concentration Camp Photographs from liberated concentration camps, like this one from Buchenwald, Germany, shocked the world. American military commanders forced German civilians, who professed ignorance about the atrocities, to view and bury the dead.

determination to use any means possible to slaughter the Jews, including mass executions by firing squads and forced marches, until the very end of the war.

As the camps were liberated, reporters tried through words and pictures to convey how six million Jews had met their deaths. Even though Americans had grown accustomed to seeing photos of war dead, nothing prepared them for images from the concentration camps. American commanders invited the press into the camps to head off denials over the scope of the Holocaust and Nazi atrocities. Photographs of concentration camps were, one reporter wrote, "so horrible that no newspaper normally would use them, but they were less horrible than the reality." Soldiers set themselves up as witnesses (a term used to describe both survivors

and liberators) who could personally vouch for the extent of the horrors by posing in photographs before piles of corpses and skeletal survivors. "You can photograph results of suffering but never suffering itself," observed one British politician.

By documenting the act of discovering Nazi atrocities, witness photographs helped Americans share the horror that soldiers felt. The American military also posted photographs of concentration camp atrocities in German towns and villages for civilians to see, but many American commanders went further. In the photo shown here (**23.19**), American soldiers assembled German civilians before a truckload of corpses to listen to a lecture on the barbarity. Forcing German civilians to view the carnage with their own eyes, and in some cases to bury the bodies, was part of a deliberate Allied campaign to make all Germans accept responsibility for their nation's war crimes.

After the war the Allies jointly tried 22 Nazi leaders in the Nuremberg War Crimes Trials. In these trials individual Germans were charged with starting the war, authorizing the killing of prisoners of war, and orchestrating the wartime genocide against victims, who mostly came from nations occupied by Germany (see the "Jews in the Holocaust" chart, page 709). The United States independently tried thousands of other German officials as well. These trials were not enough to calm the fears of survivors. Many left Europe to resettle elsewhere.

How did images instruct Americans about the meaning of the Holocaust and their role as liberators?

Watch the Video *Nazi Murder Mills*

Ending the Pacific War

 Germany was now under Allied control, but in the Pacific the war raged on. There the fighting took a desperate turn in 1945, and each victory cost the United States dearly. Despite a mounting death toll, American troops edged closer to Japan, and officials began planning an invasion of the Japanese mainland. News of a successful atomic bomb test in the New Mexico desert dramatically altered political and military calculations on how to achieve victory. Employing this new, terrible weapon eventually generated conflicting views within the United States over the ethics of atomic warfare.

Edging Closer to Japan

American pilots brought the war home to the Japanese people from new air bases in the Marianas. When the bombing campaign began in earnest in the Pacific theater in 1945, the United States quickly abandoned efforts to differentiate between civilian and military targets as it had in Germany. "There are no civilians in Japan," declared one air force official. "We are making War and making it in the all-out fashion which saves American lives, shortens the agony which War is, and seeks to bring about an enduring peace." The United States targeted 67 Japanese cities for incendiary bombing in 1945, resulting in the destruction of 187 square miles and approximately 300,000 deaths (**23.20**). During one night raid the entire city of Toyama burned to the ground. The most destructive air attack of the war came on March 9–10, 1945, when incendiary bombs ignited fires in Tokyo that American bombers kept going by spreading gasoline and chemicals over the city. This attack destroyed 16 square miles and killed nearly 90,000 Japanese—more than would perish from the atomic bomb blast over Hiroshima five months later.

Japan's use of "cave and bunker" tactics on land and kamikazes at sea dramatically raised the cost of capturing Iwo Jima (February 19–March 26, 1945) and Okinawa (April 1–June 21, 1945), the last two islands left to be taken before the United States could invade the Japanese homeland. Battles on Iwo Jima and Okinawa produced some of the toughest fighting of the war.

The Americans coveted the seven-mile porkchop-shaped island of Iwo Jima for its airstrips, both to stop Japanese fighter planes from harassing B-29s headed to Japan and to provide emergency landing fields for crippled planes returning from mainland bombing raids. In their conquest of Iwo Jima, the Americans took only 216 prisoners out of 21,000 enemy troops, the rest perishing in the fighting. As the marines shot flamethrowers into caves to flush out enemy soldiers, "the scene became wild and terrible," one correspondent recalled. "More Japs rushed screaming from the caves. They tumbled over the rocks, their clothes and bodies burning fiercely." The capture of Okinawa, needed as a staging area for the invasion of Japan, was equally bloody. Weeks of

23.20 Attacking Japan
In 1945, American firebomb attacks destroyed 67 Japanese cities, while extensive mining of major waterways severely reduced trade. Millions of Japanese civilians were homeless and starving by the time the United States dropped two atomic bombs in August.

kamikaze attacks alone killed 5,000 sailors, while ground troops squared off against an entrenched enemy determined to fight to the last man.

As on Iwo Jima vast numbers of Japanese soldiers (70,000) perished on Okinawa. In this battle, however, an equal number of Japanese civilians either killed themselves (they had been told of mass rape and torture if taken prisoner) or were killed by Japanese soldiers if they tried to surrender. The Americans suffered 75,000 casualties in capturing Okinawa. With the actual invasion of the Japanese homeland targeted next, the Americans feared facing, in the words of Harry Truman, "an Okinawa from one end of Japan to the other."

Dropping the Atomic Bomb

Franklin D. Roosevelt died at the age of 65 of a cerebral hemorrhage on April 12, 1945, while at his cottage in Warm Springs, Georgia. Throngs of mourners lined railroad tracks and streets as the casket holding his remains traveled first to Washington, D.C., for funeral services in the White House and then to his final resting spot at his home in Hyde Park, New York. Many Americans could barely remember a time when FDR had not been president.

Roosevelt's firm grip on power had kept Vice President Harry Truman in the dark about the four-year, $20 billion **Manhattan Project**, the code-named secret government research program to produce the atomic bomb. Thrust into the presidency, Truman faced critical strategic decisions in Europe and the Pacific, none more important than what to do with the new atomic bomb. In mid-July 1945, the United States exploded its first atomic bomb in the New Mexico desert. *Choices and Consequences: How to Use the Atomic Bomb* traces Truman's options and the consequences of his decision to use the bomb against Japan.

On August 6, 1945, a B-29 bomber christened the *Enola Gay* dropped an atomic bomb on the Japanese city of Hiroshima. As pilot Captain Paul Tibbets turned the *Enola Gay* away from Hiroshima, Sergeant George Caron snapped seven photographs, giving Americans their first look at the telltale mushroom cloud that came to signify nuclear annihilation. Three days later, acting on a standing order to use the atomic bomb "as made ready," a second atomic bomb was dropped on Nagasaki.

Saved from firebomb attacks because of their minimal military value, Hiroshima and Nagasaki presented virgin ground for a clear demonstration of the bomb's force. The United States wanted to make a profound impression on the Japanese. Secretary of War Stimson believed "the atomic bomb was more than a weapon of terrible destruction; it was a psychological weapon." The firebombed ruins of cities like Tokyo, therefore, presented a much less appealing target for demonstrating the full power of a nuclear bomb.

American soldiers scheduled to take part in the planned invasion gave little thought to civilian victims. "When we learned to our astonishment that we would not be obliged in a few months to rush up the beaches near Tokyo assault-firing while being machine-gunned, mortared, and shelled, for all the practiced phlegm of our tough facades we broke down and cried with relief and joy. We were going to live. We were going to grow to adulthood after all," recalled literary critic Paul Fussell in a 1988 essay, "Thank God for the Atom Bomb."

The Final Surrender

Truman and his advisers recognized that American possession of the atomic bomb would reshape postwar relations between the United States and the Soviet Union. To key presidential advisers, America's nuclear monopoly increased the chances of limiting Soviet influence over Eastern Europe and ending the Pacific war without Soviet help. Spies in the Manhattan Project had already alerted Moscow of the bomb's existence, before Truman finally told Stalin in July 1945 at the Potsdam Conference, held near Berlin, that the United States had developed a potent new weapon. When the first bomb destroyed Hiroshima, the Soviets quickly invaded Manchuria on August 8 to seize their planned territorial objectives before the war ended.

By August 10, the combination of two atomic bomb blasts and the Soviet entry into the war caused Japanese Emperor Hirohito to take the unprecedented step of imposing his own views on official policy. Traditionally the emperor simply approved decisions taken by his cabinet. With the peace and militarist factions within his government still divided over whether to make a last stand against the Allies, Hirohito decided for peace. After key military leaders accepted the emperor's wishes, Japan sued for peace with the condition that the Imperial Institution remain

Choices and Consequences

HOW TO USE THE ATOMIC BOMB

President Harry Truman considered the bomb a legitimate weapon to use alongside the more conventional tactics of terror bombing, an economic blockade, and a planned invasion of Japan. He did, however, face four choices over how to exploit this new weapon to meet his goals of securing an unconditional surrender from Japan, saving American lives, and establishing American postwar supremacy over the Soviet Union.

Choices

1 Demonstrate the bomb's destructive power in a trial blast on an uninhabited area to convince Japan to surrender.

2 Drop one atomic bomb and give Japan time to react.

3 Drop the two atomic bombs America had developed.

4 Inform the Soviet Union about the bomb before dropping it.

Decision

Truman chose to drop both atomic bombs on virgin sites in Japan to magnify the psychological shock of one bomb causing so much destruction. Senior advisers rejected a test demonstration of the bomb as impractical. Truman vaguely informed Stalin of "a new weapon of unusual destructive force," unaware that spies in the Manhattan Project had already alerted Stalin of the bomb's existence.

Consequences

On August 6, 1945, "Little Boy," the atomic bomb dropped on Hiroshima, destroyed three-fourths of the city and killed 80,000 people instantly. "Fat Man" destroyed two-fifths of Nagasaki and killed 35,000 people on August 9. The Emperor announced Japan's surrender on August 14. Truman's attempted secrecy increased Soviet distrust of the United States and unleashed a nuclear arms race between the two nations.

Continuing Controversies

Should the United States have dropped the bomb?
Supporters of Truman's decision claim that dropping the bomb ended the war. It saved one million American lives by making an invasion of Japan unnecessary and convinced the Japanese government to end the war. Not all supporters, however, agree that the second bomb on Nagasaki was militarily necessary. Critics counter that the bomb was not needed to end the war. Traditional bombing, the blockade, and the Soviet invasion of Manchuria would have ended the war without the planned invasion, they claim. Because the United States accepted a modified surrender that allowed Japan to retain the Emperor, abandoning the demand for unconditional surrender earlier may have convinced Japan to surrender sooner. Finally, some detractors accuse Truman of using the bomb mainly to curtail Soviet territorial ambitions in postwar Europe and Asia.

Bomb over Nagasaki, 1945

Watch the Video *Atomic Bomb at Hiroshima*

Why does so much controversy surround the dropping the atomic bomb and not conventional weapons?

intact. Truman agreed, thereby modifying the original goal of unconditional surrender. Could a Japanese surrender have come sooner if the United States had guaranteed the emperor's office earlier? Before August 6, Truman likened keeping Hirohito to allowing Hitler to remain in power, and he believed that the American people would never accept these terms for peace. In mid-August, however, Truman concluded that letting Hirohito tell the Japanese people to lay down their arms would facilitate the occupation of Japan. Hirohito paved the way for a peaceful surrender, when he addressed the Japanese people on the radio for the first time ever, calling on them to accept his decision. Many of his subjects did not understand Hirohito's formal Court language, illustrating the social distance

maintained between the emperor and his subjects. The formal surrender took place on September 2 aboard the battleship *Missouri* in Tokyo Bay, attended by delegates from Japan and the Allied nations. The deadliest war in human history, whose death toll is charted in "The Human Cost of Global War" (**23.21**), had finally ended.

When news of the Japanese surrender hit the United States, Americans swarmed into the streets to celebrate the good news. "Every female was grabbed and kissed by men in uniform," recalled one woman who joined the crowd in Times Square, New York City. The celebrants included a sailor whose impromptu kiss with a passing nurse was captured by *Life* photographer Alfred Eisenstaedt. The candid shot, "Kiss in Times Square," became known as "the smack seen round

23.21 The Human Cost of Global War Worldwide wartime casualties, those killed and wounded, numbered in the millions.

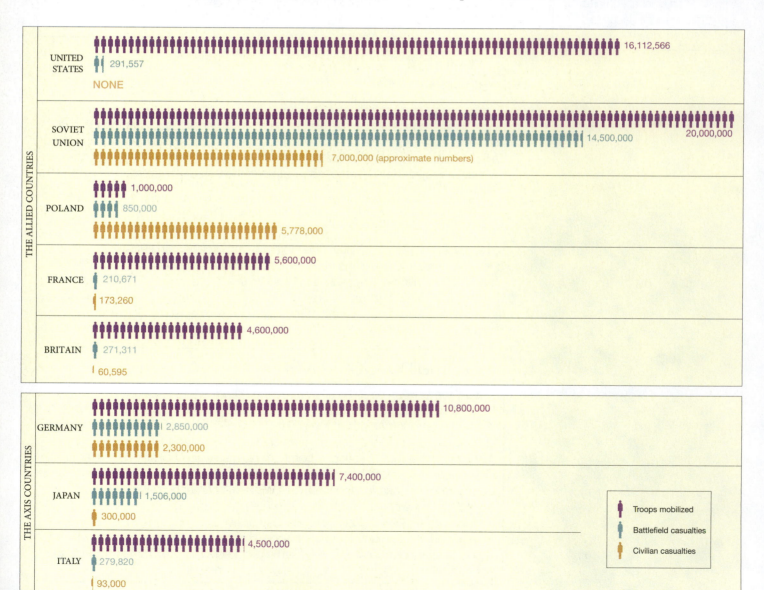

THE ALLIED COUNTRIES

UNITED STATES — 16,112,566 — 291,557 — NONE

SOVIET UNION — 20,000,000 — 14,500,000 — 7,000,000 (approximate numbers)

POLAND — 1,000,000 — 850,000 — 5,778,000

FRANCE — 5,600,000 — 210,671 — 173,260

BRITAIN — 4,600,000 — 271,311 — 60,595

THE AXIS COUNTRIES

GERMANY — 10,800,000 — 2,850,000 — 2,300,000

JAPAN — 7,400,000 — 1,506,000 — 300,000

ITALY — 4,500,000 — 279,820 — 93,000

Troops mobilized
Battlefield casualties
Civilian casualties

How might this distribution of wartime casualties have shaped the postwar world?

23.22 Kiss in Times Square, 1945
Jubilation greeted the news that Japan had surrendered. Two strangers shared a passionate kiss in Times Square, conveying the life-affirming energy that filled the air.

the world" (**23.22**). Eisenstaedt never revealed the identity of the kissing couple, preferring to let their shielded faces symbolize the exuberance of young men and women who had survived the war. Three nurses and eleven sailors later claimed that they were the individuals in the photograph.

Hirohito was not tried as a war criminal, but the Allies intended to punish other Japanese leaders. In the few weeks between the Japanese surrender and the Allied occupation of Japan, more than 1,000 officials and officers committed suicide and others destroyed thousands of documents concerning Japanese mistreatment of prisoners

of war and massacres of civilians in occupied countries. Nonetheless, the Allies convicted thousands of Japanese in war crimes trials throughout East Asia, including 28 major Japanese leaders in Tokyo.

Combat, genocide, and terror bombing took millions of lives during World War II. Americans could rightly see themselves as having both suffered and caused the war's deadly violence. The United States emerged from World War II as a military superpower, with new moral and strategic reasons to stay engaged in world affairs after its victories against Germany and Japan.

Why did this photo become an iconic image of World War II?

1937

Japan attacks China
Initiates Japan's expansionist drive in East Asia

1939

Germany invades Poland
Beginning of World War II

Neutrality Acts completed
Restrictions on arms sales reflects strong non-interventionist sentiments

1940

France falls to Germany
Completes Hitler's conquest of continental Western Europe

Economic sanctions against Japan
FDR attempts to halt Japanese aggression

1941

Lend-Lease begins
Interventionist vision prevails as America offers economic aid to Allied side

Japanese attack Pearl Harbor
United States officially enters World War II

CHAPTER REVIEW

Review Questions

1. What conflicting visions did Americans offer in response to the expansionist drives of Germany and Japan? How did these visions influence the American path to war?

2. How did visual images shape Americans' views of the war and their enemies?

3. How did the war affect racial, labor, and gender relations on the home front? What conflicting visions emerged?

4. What strategic challenges and battlefield conditions did the United States face in the Pacific and European theaters? How did the United States prevail against Japan and Germany?

5. Why did the United States drop the atomic bomb?

Key Terms

Non-interventionists Those urging the nation to stay out of overseas conflicts. **686**

Interventionists Those advocating direct engagement in overseas conflicts. **686**

Neutrality Acts A series of laws from 1935 to 1939 which restricted arms sales, loans, and transport of goods with nations at war. **687**

"Cash and carry" A policy that required belligerent nations to pay cash for goods and transport them on their own ships. **687**

Munich Conference (1938) Hoping to avoid war, Britain and France agreed to let Germany occupy the Sudetenland, a German-speaking part of Czechoslovakia. **687**

Axis Name for nations fighting the Allies, including Germany, Italy, and Japan. **688**

Allies (World War II) Name for powers fighting Germany, eventually including the United States, Britain, France, and the Soviet Union. **688**

Lend-Lease A policy that circumvented "cash and carry" by loaning rather than selling arms to the Allies. **689**

Pearl Harbor A U.S. naval base in Hawaii that the Japanese attacked on December 7, 1941. **691**

Internment camps Camps in the United States that held people of Japanese descent under armed guard in isolated areas. **695**

Manhattan Project Code-named secret U.S. government research program to produce the atomic bomb. **712**

1942

FDR issues Executive Order 9066
Creation of Japanese American internment camps

U.S. government learns of Final Solution
Limited exposure of Hitler's plan to exterminate the Jews

1944

D-Day landings
Beginning of Anglo-American march to Berlin

Supreme Court upholds constitutionality of internment camps
Rules that national security outweighs civil rights

1945

American troops enter concentration camps
Published images confirm German atrocities

FDR dies
Harry Truman assumes presidency

1945

Germany surrenders
End of European war

United States drops atomic bombs on Hiroshima and Nagasaki
Ends war in Pacific, initiates nuclear arms race

MyHistoryLab Connections

Visit www.myhistorylab.com for a customized Study Plan that will help you build your knowledge of *World War II*.

Questions for Analysis

1. **What arguments did non-interventionists offer against entering World War II before Pearl Harbor?**

   Read the **Document** *Charles Lindbergh, Radio Address (1941), p. 689*

2. **What values influenced the portrayal of female war workers?**

   View the **Closer Look** *Images as History: "We Can Do It!" Visual Myths about Women's Roles During World War II, p. 697*

3. **How was childhood militarized during World War I?**

   View the **Image** *"Get in the Scrap" Poster, p. 698*

4. **Why did U.S. generals and German civilians visit the liberated concentration camps?**

   Watch the **Video** *Nazi Murder Mills, p. 710*

5. **What message does this film convey about the atomic bomb?**

   Watch the **Video** *Atomic Bomb at Hiroshima, p. 713*

Other Resources from This Chapter

Read the **Document**

- *Franklin D. Roosevelt, "The Four Freedoms" (1941), p. 692*
- *Japanese Relocation Order, February 19, 1942, p. 694*
- *A. Philip Randolph, "Why Should We March" (1942), p. 699*
- *Jim Crow in the Army Camps, p. 700*

View the **Closer Look**

- *Competing Visions: Civil Liberties and National Security Clash, p. 696*
- *Images as History: Combat Photography, p. 706*
- *Envisioning Evidence: Deciphering the Holocaust, p. 709*

View the **Image** *Operation Overlord, Normandy (1944), p. 707*

View the **Map**

- *Interactive Map: World War II, Pacific Theater, p. 702*
- *Interactive Map: World War II in Europe, p. 703*

Watch the **Video** *Video Lecture: Hitler and Roosevelt, p. 687*

A Divided World
The Early Cold War, 1945–1963

As World War II ended, Soviet and American troops, converging from different directions, met and shook hands on a bridge spanning the Elbe River in Germany. Each side was pleasantly surprised by this first encounter with their wartime ally. "They looked like ordinary people. We had imagined something different," recalled one Soviet soldier of American troops. "I guess we didn't know what to expect from the Russians," an American soldier said after the meeting. "If you put an American uniform on them, they could have been American!" Within two years the lost promise of this friendly encounter was obvious to all. A 1947 U.S. propaganda film replayed footage of this historic meeting and struck a lightning bolt across the frozen image of Soviet and American soldiers shaking hands. "Here two worlds actually met," the narrator thundered, "but this coalition was to be torn asunder" by Soviet postwar incursions in Eastern Europe that the United States viewed as part of a Soviet plan for global conquest. In the decade after the Allies' victory against Hitler, relations between the United States and the Soviet Union soured dramatically. As the contours of the Cold War between the United States and the Soviet Union took shape, two competing ideological visions, an escalating nuclear arms race, and confrontations in Europe and Asia, including a war in Korea, heightened fears that another world war was in the making.

From 1946 to 1965, most Americans viewed the world as sharply divided into free and totalitarian societies. American leaders proclaimed that the United States was engaged in an epic struggle with the Soviet Union over the future of humankind. Protecting the world from the menace of Soviet-led communism became a key American foreign policy goal. Americans also fought the Cold War at home, where citizens expressed differing views on whether government tactics in rooting out Soviet spies undermined American democracy or saved it. On the other side of the ideological divide, Soviet leaders developed an abiding distrust of Western motives as they sought to counter the American nuclear advantage with territorial and technological gains. As each nation struggled to extend its world influence, Americans again confronted the crucial question of defining their nation's role in the world.

"Communism is on the march on a worldwide scale, which only America can stop."

Senator ARTHUR VANDENBERG, April 26, 1946

Origins of the Cold War

The United States and the Soviet Union worked effectively together in World War II to defeat Adolf Hitler, but each nation had dramatically different visions of the postwar world. The United States remained dedicated to free markets and democracy, while the Soviet Union embraced a Marxist vision that eschewed private property and celebrated concentrated state authority. Each nation also drew different lessons from the war. For the Soviet leader Josef Stalin, Hitler's invasion of the Soviet Union underscored the need to secure its borders by controlling vast territories in Eastern Europe. The United States feared that Stalin was a Hitler-like dictator, intent on controlling all of Europe. American political leaders believed that peace in Europe hinged on spreading capitalism and democracy. These differing, often conflicting, visions triggered an immediate postwar clash between the former allies.

Differing Goals in the Postwar World

The origins of the Cold War hark back to World War II. The victory against Hitler came at a huge cost for the Soviet Union. An estimated 25 million Soviet soldiers and civilians died, almost 90 times the 291,551 Americans who perished in combat.

Germany had attacked Russia twice in the 30 years, a fact that contributed to Stalin's obsession with protecting his nation from future attack. Stalin also suspected that the Americans and British had delayed opening up a second front in Europe (see Chapter 23) to further weaken the Soviet Union, causing him to distrust the United States. This photo (**24.1**) of a soldier waving the Soviet flag from the

24.1 Soviet Soldier Raises Flag over Reichstag, 1945
The Soviet triumph over Germany in World War II came at a high cost for both nations. Stalin sought future security for his nation by keeping war-destroyed Germany weak and installing puppet regimes throughout Eastern Europe.

How does this photograph symbolize the Soviet victory over Germany?

"I have never been talked to like that in my life,"
Soviet foreign minister VYACHESLAV MOLOTOV to Truman

"Carry out your agreements and you won't get talked to like that."
TRUMAN'S retort, angered over the Soviet's refusal to hold democratic elections in postwar Poland

roof of the Reichstag, the German parliament building, above the ruins of Berlin, illustrated Germany's complete defeat at the end of World War II. It also represented a past that the Soviet Union had no intention of repeating. To protect his borders, Stalin installed puppet Communist governments throughout Eastern Europe to create a buffer zone between Germany and the Soviet Union. He also tried to keep Germany as weak as possible by carting off German heavy machinery to the Soviet Union, disarming the German military, and requiring large reparation payments.

In the postwar era Stalin fully expected to retain his firm grip on power within the Soviet Union. Standing only five feet four inches tall with a bushy mustache, yellowed teeth from smoking, and a pock-marked face, Stalin was not physically imposing. In this case, however, images were deceiving. "An unforewarned visitor would never have guessed what depths of calculation, ambition, love of power, jealously, cruelty and sly vindictiveness lurked behind this unpretentious façade," an American diplomat noted. Stalin had been responsible for the deaths of nearly ten million Soviet citizens before World War II, a result of failed agricultural policies that created widespread famine and relentless executions of all suspected opponents. The Soviet dictator was willing to sacrifice countless more lives to achieve his new territorial objectives.

The postwar goals on the American side reflected lingering dismay over the nation's failure to prevent the rise of expansionist regimes in Japan and Germany during the 1930s. Before his death in April 1945, President Franklin D. Roosevelt had argued that American leadership in the new United Nations (UN) could promote a peaceful future by deterring and punishing aggression before it spun out of control. Roosevelt also stressed the importance of preventing another global depression like the one that had helped bring Hitler to power and had fueled non-interventionist sentiment in the United States.

By themselves these differing ideas on how to maintain peace in Europe did not necessarily guarantee a future clash between the United States and the Soviet Union. During the war the United States and Britain had accepted that the Soviet Union would exert considerable postwar political influence over Eastern Europe. FDR and British Prime Minister Winston Churchill, however, had exacted a promise from Stalin to hold free elections in the region. Stalin had offered some backing for Western postwar schemes, agreeing to support the UN and a joint occupation of a defeated Germany. When Harry Truman became president after Roosevelt's death, even the first signs of Soviet intransigence on fulfilling its wartime agreements failed to produce a permanent rift. To put pressure on Stalin to hold free elections in Soviet-occupied Poland, Truman abruptly canceled Lend-Lease payments, thereby denying much needed aid to the war-torn Soviet Union. When the Soviet foreign minister Vyacheslav Molotov called on the new president in the White House, Truman went even further, berating Molotov for Stalin's failure to schedule the promised elections. The long-term impact of this heated exchange was minimal, however. Truman quickly sent an emissary to Moscow to patch things up with Stalin. As a gesture of goodwill, he also reversed his decision to suspend Lend-Lease shipments to the Soviet Union.

The American Vision Takes Shape: Kennan's Long Telegram

Over time, however, these initial skirmishes developed into the Cold War. This intense ideological conflict between the United States and the Soviet Union and their allies led to hot wars around the globe, although the Americans and Soviets never fought each other directly. In the opening phases of the Cold War, each side focused on defining

How did differing memories of the recent past shape U.S. and Soviet goals in postwar Europe?

the exact threat that the other posed. At the heart of this clash lay both conflicting visions of the future and a mutual distrust that only deepened whenever the balance of power threatened to shift dramatically in favor of one nation or the other. To Stalin the American monopoly on nuclear weapons placed the Soviet Union at a strategic disadvantage that he intended to remedy as quickly as possible. For the United States Stalin's attempt in 1946 to use military force to extend his reach into the Middle East and Mediterranean raised concerns that the Soviet leader sought world domination.

Tensions mounted in 1946 when Stalin gave a belligerent speech predicting the inevitable triumph of communism over capitalism. Concerned State Department officials asked the American embassy in Moscow for more information about Stalin's intentions. The response was the "**long telegram**," an influential 5,000-word missive in which diplomat George F. Kennan outlined why America needed to develop an aggressive foreign policy aimed at containing Soviet expansionist impulses. Kennan concluded that Stalin needed an outside enemy to keep himself in power, because an external threat kept the Soviet public from focusing on his ruthless dictatorship. Stalin, Kennan also explained, believed that conflicts between capitalist societies would lead to their demise, allowing communism to triumph when capitalist societies collapsed. Given this Soviet mind-set, negotiations to resolve differences between the two nations would be fruitless, Kennan advised. He suggested strengthening Western-style capitalist and democratic structures to foil communist efforts to woo impoverished peoples. He predicted that Stalin would moderate his ambitions only if he encountered strong and steady resistance from the West each time he tried to expand beyond the Western-accepted Soviet sphere of influence in Eastern Europe. "It is clear that the main element of any U.S. policy toward the Soviet Union must be that of a long-term, patient but firm and vigilant *containment* of Russian expansive tendencies," Kennan wrote in a version of the telegram that he published in 1947 under the pseudonym Mr. X in *Foreign Affairs* magazine. With this one statement Kennan articulated the philosophical foundation for **containment**, the label affixed to multiple American foreign policy initiatives meant to prevent the Soviet Union from increasing its influence around the globe. Kennan had

economic and political policies in mind when he penned these words, but hard-liners in the Truman administration seized on his analysis to craft a new vision of U.S. military engagement in the world.

A month after Kennan sent his long telegram, the former British prime minister Winston Churchill visited Westminster College in Fulton, Missouri, where he used Kennan's words to underscore that a military, not just ideological, standoff lay ahead. In his speech Churchill declared that there was nothing the Soviets "admire so much as strength, and there is nothing for which they have less respect than for military weakness." Stalin accused Churchill of trying to provoke a war with his comment that an "**iron curtain**," Churchill's characterization of the military and ideological barrier erected by the Soviet Union, separated Western and Eastern Europe into free and dominated halves. Many American newspapers agreed, denouncing Churchill's speech as too belligerent.

The Truman Doctrine and the Marshall Plan

Turning the principles of containment into concrete action that had public approval took another year. By the end of 1947, the Truman Doctrine and the Marshall Plan established containment as the new course of American foreign policy, a direction strengthened even further in 1949 with the creation of a post-World War II military alliance between the U.S. and Western European powers through the **North Atlantic Treaty Organization (NATO)**. These initiatives evolved in response to a series of crises in Europe, portrayed in **24.2**.

> ## "From Stettin in the Baltic to Trieste in the Adriatic, an iron curtain has descended across the continent."
>
> Former British Prime Minister
> WINSTON CHURCHILL in Fulton,
> Missouri, March 1946

What analysis did Kennan's Long Telegram offer of Stalin's beliefs and behavior?

Read the **Document** *George F. Kennan, "The Long Telegram" (1946)*

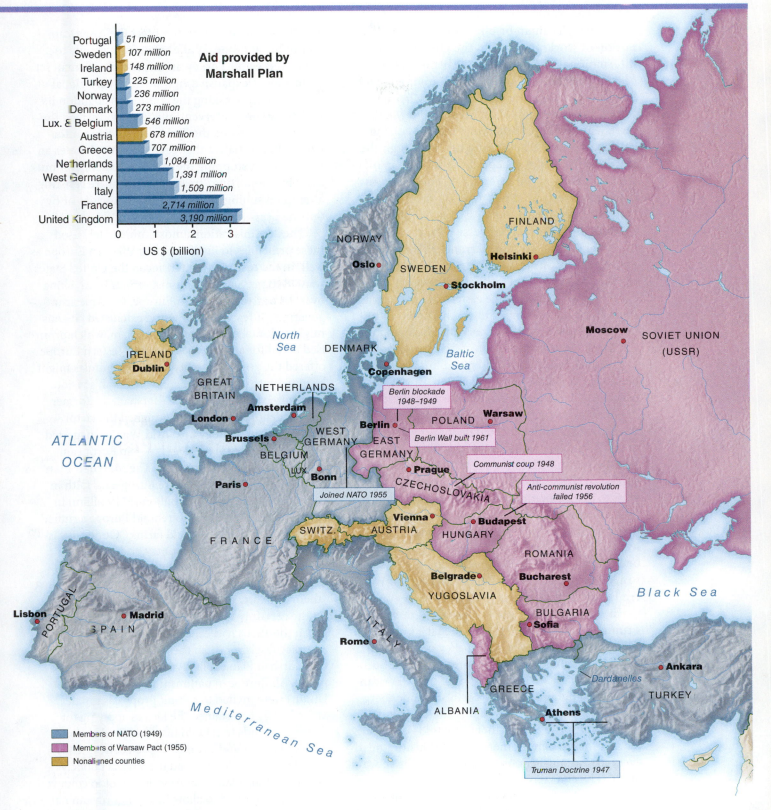

Aid provided by Marshall Plan

Country	Aid
Portugal	51 million
Sweden	107 million
Ireland	148 million
Turkey	225 million
Norway	236 million
Denmark	273 million
Lux. & Belgium	546 million
Austria	678 million
Greece	707 million
Netherlands	1,084 million
West Germany	1,391 million
Italy	1,509 million
France	2,714 million
United Kingdom	3,190 million

US $ (billion)

■ Members of NATO (1949)
■ Members of Warsaw Pact (1955)
■ Nonaligned counties

Berlin blockade 1948–1949
Berlin Wall built 1961
Communist coup 1948
Anti-communist revolution failed 1956
Joined NATO 1955
Truman Doctrine 1947

24.2 The Cold War in Europe
Europe divided into two competing alliance systems after World War II. The United States used the NATO alliance and Marshall Plan aid to strengthen ties with Western Europe.

Read the Document *Winston Churchill, "'Iron Curtain' Speech" (March 5, 1946)*

What new role did the United States play in Western Europe after World War II?

In 1947, Truman briefly returned to FDR's notion of working through the UN to resolve international disputes. That year the UN successfully pressured Stalin into removing Soviet troops from northern Iran. Truman also stationed the American Sixth Fleet in the Mediterranean to prevent the Soviets from seizing Turkish-controlled shipping lanes through the Dardanelles. Stalin accepted the setback in oil-rich Iran without fanfare, but he continued to demand unrestricted naval access through the Dardanelles passage, the only way for Soviet military and commercial vessels to travel from the Black Sea to the Mediterranean. In 1947, Stalin sent troops to the Turkish-Soviet border to force Turkey to keep the passage open.

The sense of crisis in the eastern Mediterranean soon deepened, encompassing both Turkey and Greece. Throughout 1946, the British had supported the Greek monarchy in its efforts to subdue Greek Communist rebels and had sent aid to Turkey to help it stand firm against the Soviet Union. In 1947, as part of a general decision to renounce its worldwide imperial role, a financially strapped Britain informed the United States that it could no longer give economic or military aid to Greece and Turkey. Fearing that the British withdrawal meant certain Communist success in Greece and Turkey, Truman asked Congress to grant American assistance to these countries. Under Secretary of State Dean Acheson outlined the threat to America in a meeting with congressional leaders. "Like apples in a barrel infected by one rotten one," Acheson explained, "the corruption of Greece" would "carry the infection" of communism to Western Europe, Africa, and the Middle East.

In preparing his speech before Congress in 1947, Truman pondered how to convince the public that events in far-off Greece and Turkey necessitated an unprecedented peacetime interference in European affairs. "Scare [the] hell out of the American people," Republican Senator Arthur Vandenberg suggested. Truman followed this advice. Dividing the world into "us" and "them," he told Americans that "at the present moment in world history nearly every nation must choose between alternative ways of life. The choice is too often not a free one." The Western side of the divide championed democracy and freedom. On the other were Communist states where "terror and oppression, a controlled press and radio, fixed elections, and the suppression of personal freedom" were parts of daily life. Drawing a line in the sand to stop the spread of communism was the nation's responsibility to the world and the only way to protect the American way of life at home. While asking specifically to help Greece and Turkey, in this speech Truman set forth a more expansive view of America's global responsibilities, asking the country to abandon its traditional non-interventionist stance. Instead the president proposed the **Truman Doctrine**, a foreign policy initiative that gave the United States an active role in stopping the global spread of communism by supporting "free peoples who are resisting attempted subjugation by armed minorities or by outside pressures."

The administration almost immediately used these principles to justify helping Western Europe as well. In the eastern Mediterranean the United States wanted to prevent Communist armies from taking over. In war-torn Western Europe, the American government feared that hungry, exhausted citizens might voluntarily turn to communism, which promised bread for all. Free elections in Western Europe offered the grim possibility that Communists might be voted into power. Embracing Kennan's vision, Secretary of State George C. Marshall, the former army chief of staff who had designed the victorious American strategy in World War II, suggested offering massive financial aid to help European capitalistic economies recover. The **Marshall Plan (1948–1952)** aimed to restore Europeans' faith in capitalism by sending $13 billion ($119 billion in today's dollars) overseas to rebuild Europe's ruined roads, bridges, factories, and farms. "Our policy is directed not against any country or doctrine but against hunger, poverty, desperation, and chaos," Marshall claimed, avoiding the dualistic "us" against "them" rhetoric of the Truman Doctrine. Based on the certainty that widespread economic suffering in the 1930s had caused desperate people to embrace fascism, which then led to World War II, the Marshall Plan explicitly linked peace with prosperity. All European nations (including the Soviet Union) were invited to submit proposals for aid. Stalin briefly entertained the idea of applying for American funds to rebuild his devastated nation, but as Marshall and Truman expected, he quickly abandoned this idea. Instead the Soviets publicly denounced the plan as an American plot to colonize Europe and refused to allow Eastern European nations to participate. Besides cash, the Marshall Plan offered European nations technical and management advice that helped spread American farming techniques, labor policies, and manufacturing practices.

The economic recovery of Western Europe under the Marshall Plan furthered the ideological

How did the Truman Administration convince the public to accept a new direction in U.S. foreign policy?

Watch the **Video** *President Truman and the Threat of Communism*

24.3 American View of the Marshall Plan
The Marshall Plan is portrayed as a lifeline offered by the United States to help a desperate Western Europe pull itself out of war-inflicted misery and away from the influence of the Soviet Union, seen in the distance.

raw materials, food, machines, and fuel, creating a taste for American goods that continued even after the Plan ended.

The Berlin Airlift and NATO

Containment quickly evolved into more than a vision of American financial assistance for struggling governments and economies overseas. By 1949, it also meant a firm military commitment to defend Western European nations that allied themselves with America. Almost overnight the United States shed its traditional reluctance to intervene militarily in European affairs, as Americans became convinced that only they could stop Stalin from controlling Europe.

In 1948, Stalin supported a coup by Czech Communists that overthrew the only democratic government in Eastern Europe. The quick demise of democracy in Czechoslovakia caused the West to fear that Germany, with its wrecked economy and nonexistent military, might be the next target for a Soviet-inspired communist revolution. With the country still divided into four occupied zones (American, British, French, and Soviet), the German economy was in shambles. Keeping Germany weak to punish it for World War II, initially a shared American and Soviet objective, made little strategic sense as the Soviet menace grew. By 1948, the United States saw strengthening Germany as a way to halt the Soviet expansionist drive across Europe. With this goal

divide between the United States and the Soviet Union. These political cartoons (**24.3** and **24.4**) show the conflicting views of the United States and the Soviet Union. The American cartoonist Daniel R. Fitzpatrick (24.3) portrays the Marshall Plan as a lifeline to Western Europe pulling people out of war-inflicted misery and away from the looming Soviet menace (represented by the distant towers of the Kremlin in Moscow, a recognizable symbol of the Soviet Union to Americans). Americans took pride in the wave of Western European prosperity that resulted from the Marshall Plan, making it one of the great economic success stories of the Cold War. The contrasting Soviet view critiques capitalism as an exploitive, class-based system that enriched a few at the expense of many. Published in the Soviet magazine *Krokodil*, the Soviet cartoon (24.4) shows European leaders groveling at the feet of their American lord, depicted as a paunchy Uncle Sam relaxing with his feet on their backs. This cartoon implied that the Marshall Plan, rather than fostering recovery, enslaved Western Europe to the United States, which grew richer by the day. There was some truth to the Soviet claim that the Marshall Plan, which ran from 1948 to 1952, strengthened the American economy. Western European nations spent most of their funds in the United States on

24.4 Soviet View of the Marshall Plan
In this Soviet cartoon, European leaders grovel at the feet of their American capitalist master, who has used the Marshall Plan to conquer Europe.

What conflicting views of the Marshall Plan do these two cartoons present?

24.5 A Divided Berlin
Key showdowns during the Cold War took place in Berlin, including the Berlin airlift in 1948–1949 and the construction of the Berlin Wall in 1961.

military confrontation of the Cold War between the United States and the Soviet Union.

The United States faced difficult choices. One option was to try to breach the blockade by sending an armed convoy down the autobahn (the German name for freeway) with permission to fire back if attacked by Soviet forces. In the midst of a difficult election campaign, Truman doubted Americans' willingness to fight the Soviet Union to help a recent enemy. The other option was to try to circumvent the blockade by supplying the Western-occupied sectors of Berlin from the air. The chances of an airlift working appeared slim, since each plane could carry only three tons of supplies, and the West normally sent an average of 12,000 tons of supplies a day to sustain a combined population of 2.3 million in their three zones. Faced with two unappealing choices, Truman gambled on the airlift and won.

> ## "The situation was dark and full of danger."
> **State Department official GEORGE F. KENNAN on the Soviet blockade of Berlin in 1948**

in mind, the United States, Britain, and France began discussing consolidating their separate occupation zones of Germany to form a new democratic German government and offering it Marshall Plan funds to bolster its economy. The Soviet Union firmly opposed any plan for rebuilding Germany and protested that its former allies were violating the 1945 Yalta agreement, which had stated that all four nations had to agree before any restructuring of Germany could occur.

As the West and the Soviet Union argued, the stakes rose precipitously. To pressure the United States, Britain, and France to abandon either their plan to reunify Germany or their stake in Berlin, Stalin ordered his army to stop all overland traffic between the Western and Soviet zones of Germany. Berlin lay in the heart of the Soviet-occupied sector, but at the end of World War II, the Allies had agreed to divide the German capital into four zones of occupation, as portrayed on the map (**24.5**). To supply and reach their respective zones in Berlin, the Americans, British, and French needed to travel on roads, rail lines, and waterways that ran through the Soviet sector of Germany. Stalin now barred them from using these facilities, setting in motion the first direct

In the **Berlin airlift (1948–1949)**, American and British planes resupplied West Berlin for nearly a year to stymie the Soviet blockade of the city. It was a brilliant success, both a spectacular logistical feat and a propaganda coup for the United States worldwide. In sharp contrast to dour Soviet soldiers turning away convoys carrying needed food and medicine, the world saw photographs of German children cheering the arrival of American and British planes. This photo (**24.6**) underscored how much the world had changed in just three years. The children stood on the rubble of a building destroyed by Allied bombers during the war. Instead of fleeing for their lives as American planes approached, they now welcomed the Americans as saviors for a city where strict rationing meant most children received only gruel (hot milk and flour) for their noontime meal. Lieutenant Gail Halvorsen was so touched by the sight of children scanning the skies for food planes that he attached candy bars and gum to

Which international disputes led to the 1948–1949 Soviet blockade of Berlin?

miniature parachutes (with a return address) and dropped them as he flew by. Hundreds of German children sent the original parachutes (and some homemade ones) back to Halverson, along with directions to their homes. "I live in the bombed out house on the corner. I'll be in the backyard every day at 2 pm, drop it there," Peter Zimmerman wrote in a letter than included a hand-drawn map. Halverson tried without success to find Peter's home, resulting in a flurry of increasingly frantic letters. The pilot eventually just mailed him a package of candy after landing in West Berlin. The two later met and became lifelong friends.

Images and stories like these convinced Americans of the stark contrast between Western humanitarian impulses and Soviet oppression. They also boosted Truman in the 1948 presidential campaign, as he squared off against the Republican challenger, Thomas Dewey, who led in the polls, and two other third party candidates. Faced with public dissatisfaction over rampant inflation at home and a badly divided Democratic Party, the Berlin airlift bolstered Truman's image as a resolute leader.

Truman could not correct all his political problems with photographs, however. The 1948 presidential campaign presented voters with sharply competing visions of what direction the country should take. Angry over Truman's proposal that the federal government investigate racial discrimination in voting and employment, many conservative southern Democrats supported Governor Strom Thurmond of South Carolina in his presidential bid as a segregationist candidate for the States' Rights Party. Meanwhile liberal Democrats, upset with Truman's tepid reform agenda (see Chapter 25), formed the Progressive Party and nominated Henry A. Wallace, who championed national health insurance. The former vice president's downplaying of the Soviet threat brought charges that Wallace had communist sympathies. Dewey, who had run against FDR in 1944, was a moderate Republican and, like Truman, supported civil rights and containing communism. Many believed that the president's unpopularity and the three-way split within the Democratic Party assured Dewey's election. Determined to "give them hell," Truman traveled nearly 22,000 miles during the campaign, appealing to the New Deal coalition of farmers, northern blacks, Catholics, unions, and liberals, who had secured FDR's victory in 1936. Dewey's unwillingness to attack the president's foreign policies during this time of international crisis also helped Truman. In summer 1948, Truman issued an executive order desegregating the military to prevent the defection of black voters to

24.6 The Berlin Airlift, 1948–1949 Photographs of German children welcoming American food planes convinced Americans that their help was both needed and welcomed overseas.

View the Image *Truman Ends Military Jim Crow*   What political impact did this photo have?

24.7 Truman's Triumph
Truman celebrated his 1948 election by holding the *Chicago Daily Tribune,* with its mistaken headline, from his campaign train before supporters in St. Louis, as he traveled back to the White House.

Wallace, who called for an immediate end to Jim Crow. Thanks to votes from African Americans and labor, Truman won a second term, with 303 electoral votes and 49.5 percent of the popular vote, defeating Dewey who received 189 electoral votes and 45.1 percent of the popular vote,

Thurmond (39 electoral votes; 2.4 percent of the popular vote), and Wallace (no electoral votes; 2.4 percent of the popular vote). This victory surprised many, including the *Chicago Daily Tribune,* which tried to get a jump on the competition by declaring Dewey the victor on election night before all the votes were counted. In a photo (**24.7**) that became an instant classic, a jubilant Truman held the paper and its erroneous headline "Dewey Defeats Truman" above his head the next morning when his victory was confirmed.

Besides helping Truman win the election, the sight of wave after wave of planes arriving 24 hours a day in Berlin also demonstrated America's strength and resolve to the Soviet Union. Stalin finally admitted defeat and revoked the

blockade on May 12, 1949. The capitalist enclave in the heart of the Soviet sector of Germany had survived. By that time the Americans, British, and French had created the Federal Republic of Germany, or West Germany, out of their three occupied zones. In response the Soviets organized a Communist-led German government in their sector, the German Democratic Republic, or East Germany. Germany was now formally divided into two separate states.

After the Soviet-backed coup in Czechoslovakia and the blockade of Berlin, the United States refined its policy of containment. These events had shattered any chance of creating consensus within the Truman administration around Kennan's vision that economic aid through the Marshall Plan could safeguard democracy and prosperity in Western Europe. If peace were to prevail, it would be an armed peace. Western European nations took the first step by allying themselves in the Brussels Pact in 1948. This alliance blossomed into the American-led NATO alliance in April 1949. The Soviet Union responded with their own alliance, the Warsaw Pact, among Eastern European nations. The map of the Cold War in Europe portrays the two alliance systems that divided Europe into capitalist and communist camps (see 24.2).

By joining NATO the United States created its first formal military alliance since the Revolutionary War. There would be no repeat of World War I or World War II, when the United States had waited over two years each time before declaring war. As a member of NATO, it was obligated to come immediately to Western Europe's defense in the event of a Soviet attack. Besides putting American bases and soldiers permanently in Europe, NATO extended the protection of America's atomic shield to its NATO partners.

Like the Marshall Plan NATO was designed to do many things at once. Besides creating a permanent role for the United States overseas and containing communism, NATO also helped keep peace among European nations that had clashed repeatedly in the last hundred years. A popular saying claimed that NATO kept "the Soviets out, the Americans in, and the Germans down" by ensuring that West Germany remained friends with western democracies even after the nation regained its economic vigor.

Why was NATO an important development in the Cold War?

Fighting Communism: Cold and Hot War

 As the Cold War took shape, the United States did not gain any noticeable advantage from its atomic monopoly in dealing with Stalin. Losing it, nonetheless, caused angst in the United States. In 1949, the Soviet Union successfully tested its own atomic bomb, challenging Americans' view of their own nation as the world's dominant military power. Suddenly the chances of an international crisis escalating into nuclear war appeared greater. As Americans digested this news, the epicenter of the Cold War shifted to Asia. By 1950, a Communist government controlled China, and the Korean War had begun. In the Korean War (1950–1953), the United States and its allies fought Communist North Koreans and Chinese to a stalemate, frustrating Americans.

Communism Rising: 1949

The United States did not have long to celebrate its achievements during the Berlin airlift. Three months after Stalin admitted defeat in Berlin, an American spy plane detected radioactive fallout in the desert of Kazakhstan, a Soviet republic. This could mean only one thing: the Soviet Union had successfully tested its own atomic bomb. The news shattered the American certainty that it would retain a nuclear monopoly for at least ten years. Waiting impatiently for a formal announcement from the Kremlin, Truman finally broke the news to the world in September 1949. The Soviet Union confirmed the American report, but gave no other information about Stalin's plans for his nuclear program.

Fearful that Stalin might use nuclear weapons to expand beyond the iron curtain, the Truman administration broadened the scope of America's containment strategy beyond NATO and the Marshall Plan. Truman decided to station American troops in Western Europe permanently to both deter and, if necessary, respond to a nuclear attack. The United States also began stockpiling atomic bombs to gain a numerical advantage over the Soviet Union. Finally Truman authorized the development of a "superbomb," a thermonuclear hydrogen bomb that was 1,000 times more powerful than the uranium-enriched atomic bomb dropped on Hiroshima and the plutonium bomb that destroyed Nagasaki.

Americans were still recovering from the shock of the Soviet bomb, when they received more bad news. The 25-year-old Chinese Civil War had finally ended with the Communist Mao Zedong victorious over the Nationalist leader Jiang Jieshi (Chiang Kaishek), who fled with his government to Taiwan, an island off the southeast coast of mainland China. Mao was an avid swimmer who refused even as an old man to be deterred by the human waste floating in China's polluted rivers. A master of staying afloat in water and politics, Mao adopted Stalin and Soviet-style policies as his model, inflicting similarly painful waves of famine and political oppression on the Chinese people that killed more than 20 million. Fearful that the United States intended to attack China and restore Jiang to power, Mao immediately reached out to Stalin. "There should be some division of labor between us," Stalin suggested, with the

> ## "There is only one thing worse than one nation having the atomic bomb— that's two nations having it."
>
> American physical chemist
> HAROLD ULREY, September 1949

Soviet Union furthering the communist cause in Europe, and Mao doing the same in Asia. Accepting Stalin's offer Mao spent two months in Moscow devising a joint strategy that resulted in the 1950 Sino-Soviet Treaty, which pledged mutual assistance in the event of an enemy attack. This alliance created a second front in the Cold War that forced the United States to divide its attention between Europe and Asia.

In light of these new threats, Truman ordered a full review of American foreign policy. The State Department responded with a document known as

How did the USSR acquiring nuclear weapons and the rise of communist China change the contours of the Cold War?

National Security Council Report 68, or NSC-68. Not mincing words NSC-68 declared that "the issues that face us are momentous, involving the fulfillment or destruction not only of this Republic but of civilization itself." Secretary of State Acheson later admitted that NSC-68's cataclysmic vision of a Soviet enemy "animated by a new fanatic faith" and bent on worldwide domination was meant to convince the president to use all means "short of war" to halt the apparent Soviet drive for world conquest. NSC-68 crystallized the piecemeal developments of the last four years into one clear vision: The United States must build up "the political, economic, and military strength of the free world to frustrate the Kremlin design of a world dominated by its will." This message was transmitted to the public through political speeches, films, and novels. Perhaps no writer better encapsulated the public's fears of worldwide communist domination than George Orwell in his classic novel *1984,* which hit bookstores in 1949. Orwell envisioned a future where totalitarianism has triumphed and the people's loyalty to a Stalin-like dictator "Big Brother," who watches over everyone and censors their behavior, is ensured by a cycle of endless wars and torture. As the main character Winston Smith undergoes another round of torture, his tormentor tells him, "Imagine a boot stamping on a human face—forever." This image neatly expressed the American public's view of communism in the Cold War.

The Korean War

At the end of World War II, the United States and the Soviet Union had agreed to divide the former Japanese colony of Korea, a peninsula along the north Asian Pacific Coast, into two zones of occupation. The country was split along the 38th parallel, with the USSR occupying the north and the United States the south. In 1945, partitioning the country seemed like a good way to deprive Japan of Korean resources and prevent the Soviet Union from completely taking over the peninsula. When the Soviet Union organized a Communist government under Kim Il-sung in North Korea and the United States selected Syngman Rhee to head a capitalist government in the south, the previously unified nation appeared permanently divided.

By 1949, however, the United States had begun to reevaluate its military commitment in South Korea. The occupation was expensive, and

Pentagon officials doubted the strategic importance of the peninsula. The State Department agreed, believing that economic aid and political reforms could strengthen South Korea enough to discourage a North Korean attack. In January 1950, Secretary of State Acheson openly questioned the importance of South Korea to the overall defense of American interests in East Asia. In a speech before the National Press Club, Acheson outlined a defensive perimeter in the Pacific that the United States would defend against communist incursions. It included Japan, Okinawa, Taiwan, and the Philippines, but not South Korea. Accordingly Truman began withdrawing American soldiers from South Korea. To deter North Korea from attacking, the United States left a stockpile of conventional weapons and promised continued financial aid.

Yet when North Korea launched a surprise invasion of South Korea in June 1950, Truman immediately reversed course. The speed and success of the North Korean attack alarmed him. Within two days North Korean troops had entered Seoul, the capital of South Korea (**24.8**), and by the end of one week North Korea had pushed the bulk of the South Korean army and its American advisors into the toe of the Korean peninsula around Pusan. Viewing this overpowering offensive as confirmation of NSC-68, Truman believed the USSR was behind the attack. He was partly right. Kim Il-sung had secured reluctant support from Stalin and Mao Zedong for the invasion by promising an easy victory. If the United States intervened in Korea, Stalin saw advantages to diverting American attention away from Europe.

By June 1950, many Americans felt that the West was losing the Cold War. China had fallen to communism, and the Soviets had exploded an atomic bomb. At home sensational spy trials fueled continued doubts about Truman's leadership. In this political climate doing nothing was hardly an option for him.

Truman's intimate understanding of World War I (he had served as an artillery captain in France) and World War II encouraged him to break with the precedent set by these recent conflicts. In each of these wars, Americans had debated the merits of fighting for more than two years before declaring war. "I remembered how each time the democracies failed to act it had encouraged the aggressors to keep going ahead," Truman noted. Determined to respond quickly this time, he committed American troops to combat within days. Although Truman

Why did the United States decide to fight in Korea?

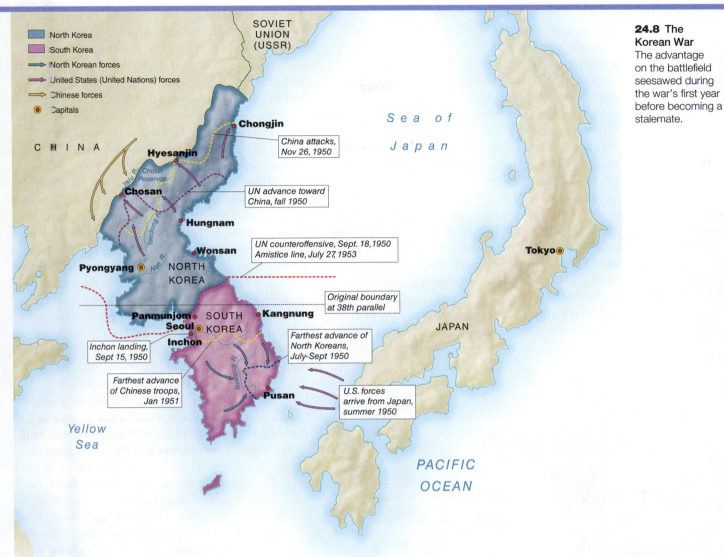

24.8 The Korean War
The advantage on the battlefield seesawed during the war's first year before becoming a stalemate.

Map labels:
- North Korea
- South Korea
- North Korean forces
- United States (United Nations) forces
- Chinese forces
- Capitals

- SOVIET UNION (USSR)
- CHINA
- Sea of Japan
- Chongjin — China attacks, Nov 26, 1950
- Hyesanjin
- Chosin Reservoir
- Chosan — UN advance toward China, fall 1950
- Yalu R.
- Hungnam
- Taedong R.
- Nan R.
- Wonsan — UN counteroffensive, Sept. 18, 1950 / Amistice line, July 27, 1953
- Pyongyang
- NORTH KOREA
- Original boundary at 38th parallel
- Tokyo
- Panmunjom
- Seoul
- SOUTH KOREA
- Kangnung
- Inchon — Inchon landing, Sept 15, 1950
- Farthest advance of North Koreans, July-Sept 1950
- JAPAN
- Naktong R.
- Farthest advance of Chinese troops, Jan 1951
- Pusan — U.S. forces arrive from Japan, summer 1950
- Yellow Sea
- PACIFIC OCEAN

consulted Congress, he never asked for a declaration of war against North Korea. Instead he decided to work through the UN, which authorized the use of force to restore the original 38th-parallel boundary between North and South Korea. Sixteen nations sent troops to Korea to serve in the UN police force, but the United States provided the bulk of troops and commanded military operations. When polled, three-quarters of Americans approved of Truman's decision to send military aid to South Korea. Americans, for the time being anyway, subscribed to his vision that "the future of civilization depends on what we do."

The situation on the battlefield, however, was grim, with South Korean soldiers holding on precariously around Pusan. To reverse the situation, General Douglas MacArthur, commander-in-chief of the United Nations forces, devised a dramatic and risky strategy. Rather than simply confronting the North Koreans head-on, he staged an amphibious landing at Inchon, a port near Seoul. This attack on the North Koreans' rear would cut their supply lines and force them to fight on two fronts. The tides at Inchon, however, were the second highest in the world, varying 29 feet between high and low tides. Within minutes, the receding tide could mire a boat in mud. Inchon, MacArthur reasoned, was the right place to attack precisely because it was so uninviting and would take the enemy by surprise. As he predicted, the North Koreans had stationed only 6,500 troops there, and the UN force of 40,000 encountered little resistance in taking the city. This operation turned MacArthur, already famous for his feats in World War II, into a national hero. Following the Inchon invasion UN forces quickly drove North Korean troops out of South Korea.

After this victory, Truman pondered giving the war a new purpose. Instead of simply restoring the

View the Map Interactive Map: The Korean War, 1950–1953

What accounted for America's initial successes on the battlefield?

status quo of a divided Korea, he decided to try to reunify Korea under an anti-Communist government. Rolling back communism, rather than containing it, became the new goal sanctioned by the UN in October 1950. At that same moment, however, China was preparing to aid North Korea. When American troops crossed the 38th parallel into North Korea, they did not know that Mao was massing Chinese troops and guns along the North Korean-Chinese border.

Still unaware of Mao's intentions, American troops moved swiftly up the peninsula to celebrate Thanksgiving by the Yalu River. Victory seemed assured: MacArthur promised Truman that the troops would be home by Christmas. Then in late November waves of Chinese troops began pouring across the border, shrieking and blowing bugles. Terrified UN forces suffered heavy casualties as they withdrew in the harsh winter. *Life* photographer David

24.9 "The Price of Victory: A Soldier Grieves for His Lost Buddy" An American soldier comforts a comrade distraught over the death of a friend during the Korean War in 1950.

Douglas Duncan, warming his camera in his coat pocket to keep the film from breaking, chronicled the bitter retreat of 10,000 Marines who fought their way to safety. Nearly every soldier suffered frostbite; half the men were wounded or killed. "If I were God and could give you anything you wanted, what would you ask for?" Duncan asked one Marine. After several minutes the Marine replied, "Give me tomorrow."

Military leaders disagreed over how to respond as the Chinese continued their advance, which UN forces eventually contained around the 38th parallel. The Joint Chiefs of Staff urged Truman to seek a negotiated peace, advice he followed. MacArthur, however, publicly endorsed all-out war utilizing nuclear weapons. The president and theater commander now began to pursue two competing visions. As Truman made diplomatic overtures to the Chinese for a ceasefire along the 38th parallel, MacArthur warned the Chinese to surrender or face destruction.

"There is no substitute for victory," MacArthur wrote to Republican Congressman Joseph Martin of Massachusetts, echoing the feelings of countless Americans. This was not, however, Truman's vision of how to end the war; when Martin read these words on the House floor, he sealed MacArthur's fate. Truman fired MacArthur the next week, triggering, as Secretary of State Acheson had predicted, "the biggest fight of your administration."

MacArthur came home, not in disgrace, but to great acclaim. Many Americans shared his frustrations with the stalemate on the battlefield. Six years after defeating two great military powers in World War II, the United States found itself unable to reunify Korea under an anti-Communist government. Responding to MacArthur's vision of total victory, huge crowds greeted the general when his ship docked in San Francisco, and he reveled in a ticker-tape parade held in his honor in New York City. Congress debated impeaching Truman but then opted instead to hold hearings into MacArthur's removal. During the hearings MacArthur's critics interrogated the

How did the entry of the Chinese into the Korean War affect political and military debates within the United States?

general about the possibility that using nuclear weapons in Korea might lead to a global nuclear war. MacArthur's response, "that doesn't happen to be my responsibility," caused the general's popularity to plummet. The cooling enthusiasm for MacArthur's vision of all-out war did little to bolster public confidence in Truman. In public opinion polls only 24 percent of Americans approved of how he was handling the presidency, reflecting public disappointment over Korea, anger at "losing China," and well-publicized Soviet spy scandals that together revived the image of Truman as an ineffectual leader. His aggressive support for civil rights and his domestic reform agenda (see Chapter 25), too much for conservatives and too little for liberals, also contributed to his poor rating.

Korea was the last American war that the public viewed primarily through photographs. Only 34 percent of American homes had television sets in 1952, rising to 86 percent by 1960. In 1950, *Newsweek* published the photograph "The Price of Victory: A Soldier Grieves for His Lost Buddy" (**24.9**). One reader's suggestion that this image should serve as the iconic photo of the Korean War, just as "Old Glory Goes Up on Mt. Suribachi, Iwo Jima" had served to represent World War II, revealed a significant shift in the public's attitudes over the last five years (see *Images as History: Combat Photography,* Chapter 23, page 706). The World War II image of five marines and one navy corpsman raising the flag suggested teamwork, victory, and the triumph of democracy. In sharp contrast "The Price of Victory" looked at the personal cost of war—the sorrow and compassion that drew men together on the battlefield—even as the photograph reaffirmed the willingness of soldiers to die for their country. Photographers and the public were beginning to probe the impact of fighting on soldiers, stoking the ambivalence that the country increasingly felt about the war.

With MacArthur gone, General Matthew Ridgway took over command of UN operations in 1951, and armistice negotiations began. Talks were still underway two years later when a new president, Dwight D. Eisenhower, took office. His sunny demeanor offered a sharp contrast to Truman's more combative and coarse personality. Whereas Truman cussed, told off-color jokes, and picked fights with reporters, Eisenhower was gregarious and friendly to all. Some Democrats had tried to draft Eisenhower as a presidential candidate in 1948. Four years later the Republican "We Like Ike" campaign finally convinced Eisenhower to seek office. The young women adorned here (**24.10**), with "Ike" dresses and umbrellas, illustrate Republicans' gusto for Eisenhower on the eve of the nominating convention where delegates enthusiastically selected him as their candidate.

Admired by Americans for his command of the D-Day invasion in World War II, Eisenhower's military experience convinced Americans that he would be a capable leader in wartime. The negotiations remained deadlocked, however, until Eisenhower threatened to reconsider employing nuclear weapons. Finally the two sides agreed to a permanent ceasefire in July 1953.

The war was costly on all sides. More than 400,000 Chinese soldiers and nearly two million North and South Koreans (soldiers and civilians) perished. For the first time since the War of 1812, the United States could not claim outright victory over its opponent despite nearly 33,000 men killed in combat and 103,000 men wounded. "What the hell is there to celebrate?" remarked one soldier when news of the armistice reached the front. The silence at home offered a marked contrast to the jubilant demonstrations that had filled the streets eight years earlier, when Japan surrendered. China embraced a competing vision of the stalemate,

24.10
"We Like Ike"
The enthusiasm displayed by Republicans in 1952 convinced Eisenhower to run for president.

reveling in the ability to hold its own against the United States.

The Korean War had major geopolitical consequences by turning the Cold War into a global conflict. The war tied South Korea and Japan, economically resurgent thanks to American aid, even more closely to the United States, and both became staunch allies in creating a defensive perimeter against communism in East Asia. Holding the line against communism in Korea increased America's interest in other regional civil wars, including one underway in Vietnam. The war poisoned relations with China, and the two nations did not reestablish diplomatic relations until 1979. Pledged to defend South Korea, the United States still maintains a large military presence along what continues to be the world's most heavily armed border.

Nuclear Fallout and Fear

While soldiers fought and died on the battlefield, Americans at home waged their own defensive war against nuclear weapons. The government sponsored atmospheric and underwater tests of nuclear bombs in the 1940s and 1950s both in the United States and on the Bikini Atoll in the Marshall Islands in the Pacific. Even when the United States had a secure monopoly on nuclear weapons, many Americans expressed concern about nuclear fallout, the deadly pollution that descends through the air after a nuclear explosion.

In the 1950s, popular science fiction writers and filmmakers tapped into this preoccupation. In the Japanese film classic *Godzilla*, for example, a nuclear explosion awakens a fire-breathing monster who, as the film's promotional poster (**24.11**) illustrated, terrorizes Tokyo. Like the atomic bombs that ravaged Hiroshima and Nagasaki, Godzilla is an unstoppable nuclear force that obliterates everything in his path. Americans, however, saw only an edited version of the film, with all critical commentary on America's ongoing nuclear testing program in the Pacific excised. Two popular Marvel comic book characters, the Incredible Hulk and Spider-Man, were also spawned by contact with radioactive material. In the *Incredible Hulk*, a scientist exposed to gamma rays is transformed into a green, 300-pound giant, while a bite from an irradiated spider turns nerdish lab assistant Peter Parker into Spider-Man.

Teaching Americans how to live with the constant threat of nuclear war meant convincing citizens to remain vigilant and calm. To combat both indifference and panic, governmental propaganda underscored the seriousness of the threat, while also reassuring the public that they could survive an atomic blast, if they took precautionary measures such as building fortified fallout shelters or remembering to "duck and cover." *Images as History: Surviving an Atomic Bomb Blast* explores how government-generated images presented competing visions that both reassured and frightened Americans about the likely effect of a nuclear attack.

24.11 Godzilla
A 1954 Japanese horror film used the ravages of a nuclear-spawned dinosaur named Godzilla to criticize American use and testing of its nuclear arsenal. This political message was edited out of the version shown in the United States.

Images as History
SURVIVING AN ATOMIC BOMB BLAST

How people will react to advice or propaganda can be difficult to predict. Why did the government disseminate images of a possible nuclear attack? What unintended effects could these images have on the Americans viewing them?

By 1950, schoolchildren throughout the nation had learned to jump out of their seats and under their desks with their hands clasped firmly over their heads when their teachers shouted "Drop!" during civil defense drills. In government-produced civil defense films and comic books distributed to schools, Bert the

Turtle instructed children to "duck and cover" during a nuclear attack. Advocates of this approach argued that flying debris and shattered windows had killed many victims in Hiroshima and Nagasaki; therefore, teaching children to "duck and cover" was practical advice.

To ensure that Americans remained vigilant in preparing for a nuclear attack, the government also released "before" and "after" photographs from a test explosion in the Nevada desert on March 17, 1953. *Time* magazine estimated that nearly three-quarters of the nation saw these pictures.

The stick of dynamite dangling from a string symbolized a nuclear attack, exactly the kind of danger children needed to learn to recognize.

A catchy jingle accompanied this lesson in civil defense: "There was a turtle by the name of Bert, and Bert the Turtle was very alert / When danger threatened him he never got hurt / He knew just what to do / He'd Duck and Cover / Duck and Cover."

The intact shell implies that one could safely survive a nuclear attack by hiding under something.

Authorities advised children— who did not carry their shelters on their backs like Bert—to seek protection beside walls and trees or under tables if an atomic bomb hit.

The "before" blast images portrayed a normal middle-class suburban home and yard.

The "after" blast photographs showed this suburban house engulfed in flames and blown to bits within two seconds of being hit with a nuclear bomb.

This image directly contradicted the vision that one could survive a nuclear attack by seeking shelter under a bed as "Bert the Turtle" advised.

View the **Closer Look** *Images as History: Surviving an Atomic Bomb Blast*

What conflicting messages did these images send about surviving a nuclear blast?

Fallout Shelters

With the successful test explosion of the hydrogen bomb in 1954, the Eisenhower administration embraced mass evacuation from city centers as the best civil defense against nuclear attack. The president's decision to construct an interstate highway system changed official policy "from 'Duck and Cover' to 'Run Like Hell,'" the *Bulletin of the Atomic Scientists* concluded. Multilane highways served peacetime needs by linking cities to suburbs and military needs by making the evacuation of civilians and the mobilization of the military easier if the United States was attacked. Practice evacuation runs were not encouraging, however. "Operation Kids," for example, an effort to move 37,300 schoolchildren in Mobile, Alabama, out of the city without warning, resulted in heavy traffic jams.

Eisenhower also urged Americans to build family shelters at their own expense. The government distributed pamphlets with suggested floor plans and advised women to store enough food and medical supplies to sustain their families if a nuclear attack contaminated water supplies or destroyed grocery stores. "Grandma's pantry was ready" whenever guests unexpectedly arrived; "is your 'pantry' ready in event of emergency?" one government pamphlet asked.

Given their high cost (even a barebones shelter cost $1,000, about one-fifth an average family's annual income), few Americans could afford to construct their own fallout shelters. During another moment of crisis in 1961 when the United States and the Soviet Union clashed again over the fate of Berlin, Eisenhower's successor, John F. Kennedy, dedicated public funds to preparing mass underground shelters in schools and public buildings. Signs with three yellow triangles superimposed on a black circle (**24.12**) that pointed toward underground public fallout shelters became ubiquitous in schools and government buildings.

In 1956, the government began constructing secret centers throughout the nation to house officials in the event of a nuclear attack. The government did not make these preparations public, avoiding uncomfortable questions about what would happen to the rest of the country. These secret plans sought to ensure the continued functioning of Congress by transporting legislators and some staff members (without their families) to an underground shelter in White Sulphur Springs, West Virginia. As part of its preparations, the Treasury Department put an eight-month supply of $1 bills and a two-year supply of $5, $10, and $20 bills in bombproof shelters. The military scattered mini-Pentagons throughout the country, including underground facilities for the president and his cabinet near Gettysburg, Pennsylvania. Plans to whisk the government to safety during a nuclear attack remained in place until 1995.

24.12 Fallout Shelter Sign
In the early 1960s, fallout shelter signs posted in neighborhoods, schools, and public buildings were daily reminders of the nuclear threat that hung over the nation.

What defensive measures did Americans take against a possible nuclear attack?

View the **Closer Look** *Images as History: Fallout Shelters*

Spies in Our Midst

Recently released documents from the former Soviet Union suggest that as many as 300 Americans spied for the USSR during the 1930s and 1940s. Does this justify the attack on civil liberties that occurred during the anti-communist crusade that swept across the country during the 1940s and 1950s? During the Cold War many Americans believed that this anti-communist campaign made the country safer and freer; a minority voiced the competing vision that the government was using spy investigations to limit legitimate political discourse by eliminating the radical left. The government's crusade against communism in the First Red Scare (1919) after World War I lasted only a few months. The effort to root out Communist spies after World War II lasted for nearly a decade.

The Second Red Scare

To a country reeling from the loss of China to communism and the detonation of a Soviet bomb, the suggestion that the government was rife with communist spies offered a simple explanation for these complex events. The House Un-American Activities Committee (HUAC), which had investigated fascist activities in the United States during World War II, now probed the communist threat. Other measures from World War II also took on new life during the Second Red Scare, including the Smith Act (1940), which outlawed advocating the forceful destruction of the government. Acting on a precedent set by Franklin D. Roosevelt in World War II, Truman created a federal employee loyalty program in 1947 that gave the Federal Bureau of Investigation (FBI), the police arm of the Justice Department, the right to investigate the backgrounds of federal workers. Congress tightened restrictions on radical political activity even further with the McCarran Acts in 1950 and 1952, which stopped communists from entering the country and required communist or communist-front organizations to register with the attorney general.

Most of the people investigated by HUAC and the FBI had once belonged to the Communist Party, which had attracted many new members during the labor unrest of the 1930s (see Chapter 22). Whether past or even present membership in the Communist Party made one a traitor was another question. When David Wellman was a young boy, his family was under constant police surveillance. Two unmarked cars sat outside their Detroit home and followed him and his sister to school, ball games, and the store. "Trying to turn fear into fun, we made shaking them a game," he later recalled. Wellman

maintained that his father, a wounded World War II veteran and leader in the Michigan Communist Party, and his mother, a communist active in trade unions, were not traitors but people who believed that revolution was an American ideal.

The constant surveillance took a toll on the family. "It felt as if the government penetrated the deepest recesses of our lives every minute of the day," Wellman recalled. Paranoia caused the family to censor speech within the home and on the telephone, certain that the police were always listening. As an adult Wellman got access to his family's police file and was stunned to learn that the reports contained almost no information about his parents' political activism. The police had discovered little through this constant surveillance, succeeding mostly in terrorizing the family, which, Wellman suspected, was their true intent.

> ## "They were trying to put the fear of police power in the minds of the people they spied on. To a large degree, it worked."
>
> DAVID WELLMAN, whose family was under police surveillance during the Second Red Scare

The two biggest spy cases of the era involved Alger Hiss and Ethel and Julius Rosenberg. In 1948, Whittaker Chambers, a *Time* magazine editor and former member of the Communist Party, accused Alger Hiss, a high-ranking official during the

What insights does Wellman's story offer into the Second Red Scare?

Roosevelt administration, of being a communist. Hiss denied the charge before HUAC, announcing under oath that "I am not and never have been a member of any Communist front organization." Chambers responded by charging that Hiss spied for the Soviet Union in the 1930s and as proof produced rolls of microfilm that Chambers had hidden in a hollow pumpkin in his garden. The microfilm contained copies of secret State Department papers from 1938 regarding the Soviet Union, Nazi Germany, and the Spanish Civil War that had been typed on Hiss's typewriter. The "pumpkin patch" papers corroborated Chambers's account and recently declassified intelligence documents have confirmed that Hiss worked as a Soviet spy through at least 1945. Because the statute of limitations on espionage had expired, a federal court convicted Hiss of perjury for lying to HUAC about his communist ties. Hiss served four years in jail. Congressman Richard Nixon, a member of HUAC, believed that the "Hiss case, for the first time, forcibly demonstrated to the American people that domestic communism was a real and present danger to the security of the nation." Nixon's leading role in the Hiss investigation catapulted him into the national spotlight. His prominence increased when he was elected vice president on the Republican ticket with Eisenhower in 1952.

24.13 The Rosenbergs Spy Case, 1953
Protesters urge the government to execute convicted spies Julius and Ethel Rosenberg, reflecting the fury many Americans felt toward anyone believed to have betrayed the United States.

In 1953, another spy case involving Ethel and Julius Rosenberg, the Jewish parents of two young boys, captivated the nation. The federal government charged Julius with passing atomic secrets to the Soviet Union during World War II, information he had supposedly gathered from his brother-in-law, a Soviet spy working for the Manhattan Project, who later testified against the couple. Although Julius's wife Ethel was never personally implicated in the spy ring, the government charged her with knowing of her husband's involvement. Arrested to spur her husband into confessing, Ethel went on trial for espionage along with her husband. They each maintained their innocence even when convicted and sentenced to death by electric chair.

As the execution date neared, demonstrators from the right and the left took to the streets, offering the public two competing visions of the Rosenbergs and the government's anti-communist investigations. Men carrying signs that read "Burn All Reds" and "No Mercy for Spies" picketed before the White House (**24.13**). Supporters who believed that the Rosenbergs were being persecuted for their radical beliefs organized marches for clemency. Radio and television reporters witnessing the execution shared intimate details with a nation riveted on the couple's final moments, including Ethel's botched electrocution on June 19, 1953, when it took three tries to kill her. Their two young sons, aged ten and six, also endured intense media scrutiny. Relatives put them in an orphanage, and New Jersey revoked their right to attend public school. Rosenberg supporters Abe Meeropol (the author of the anti-lynching ballad "Strange Fruit," see Chapter 21) and his wife eventually adopted the boys and changed their names. As adults they were active in leftist causes and until recently steadfastly maintained their parents' innocence. For decades the right and the left embraced two competing visions of the Rosenbergs case. The right viewed the couple as traitors whose cooperation with the Soviet Union demonstrated the internal threat that the nation faced from Soviet spies. The left, believing the Rosenbergs innocent, felt that mainstream politicians exaggerated the communist menace to gain public support for eradicating all left-leaning political groups from American society. In some respects both portraits were accurate. Newly released Soviet documents reveal that Julius did indeed pass valuable atomic data to the Soviet Union, but it appears that Ethel knew nothing of her husband's espionage activities, making her, along with countless others in the 1950s, a victim of overzealous investigators, who equated leftist politics with treason.

What competing visions arose over the Hiss and Rosenbergs spy cases?

HUAC against Hollywood

The effort to expose the evildoings of communists went far beyond punishing government officials who spied for the Soviet Union. In 1947, HUAC began an investigation into alleged communist activities in Hollywood. Hundreds of screenwriters, producers, directors, and actors were called to testify. Initial hearings focused on the supposedly subversive plotlines and imagery of selected motion pictures, such as *Mission to Moscow,* a World War II–era film that presented the Soviet Union as paradise on earth. Jack Warner, the head of Warner Studios, had produced *Mission to Moscow* after the Roosevelt administration requested a film that would improve the public's impression of the nation's wartime ally. This episode in producing left-wing political propaganda was the exception rather than the rule in Hollywood. Most studio heads subscribed to Sam Goldwyn's view that "if you want to send a message, use Western Union." The iron grip of the Hollywood studio system allowed directors little independence to include political content in their films that was not approved by the studio bosses. As a result HUAC could find little evidence of "subversive" content in Hollywood films. Rather than abandoning its investigation of Hollywood, however, HUAC shifted focus to the political affiliations and beliefs of the people involved in making movies.

After ten screenwriters, dubbed the "Hollywood Ten," were convicted of contempt of Congress for refusing to cooperate with HUAC investigations and sentenced to a year in prison, studio executives created a Hollywood blacklist of individuals with suspected past or present communist ties, whom film studios refused to hire. The FBI had already infiltrated the Communist Party and provided HUAC with the names of all those in Hollywood with present or past communist affiliations. HUAC nonetheless pressured subpoenaed witnesses to publicly name names, not to gain information, but to test witnesses' loyalty. Many cooperated with HUAC to salvage their careers. Most of those who refused to testify or to name names never worked in films again. Others, like future president Ronald Reagan, then the president of the Screen Actors Guild, joined the anti-communist crusade by privately providing the FBI with the names of individuals in Hollywood with potential communist connections. Reagan testified before HUAC as a liberal Democrat (his shift to the right came later), where he denied that communists "have ever at any time been able to use the motion-picture screen as a sounding board for their philosophy."

Director Elia Kazan and playwright Arthur Miller used their artistic work to explain the different choices they made when asked to testify by HUAC. Kazan's film *On the Waterfront* (1954) starred Marlon Brando as an ex-prizefighter turned longshoreman, who overcomes his aversion to "ratting on your friends" and testifies against his corrupt union bosses. Kazan, who had been a member of the Communist Party in the 1930s, made the film to justify his own decision in 1952 to provide HUAC with the names of eight former Communist Party colleagues (see *Competing Visions: Naming Names in Hollywood,* page 740). *On the Waterfront* won Academy Awards for Best Picture, Best Director, and Best Actor. Conversely Miller refused to testify when called before HUAC in 1956 and criticized the hysteria created by the Second Red Scare in his play *The Crucible,* which likened the HUAC investigations to the Salem witch trials in colonial Massachusetts.

> ## "We will not knowingly employ a Communist nor a member of any party or groups which advocates the overthrow of the Government of the United States by force or by illegal or unconstitutional methods."
>
> Studio executives' statement announcing the creation of a Hollywood blacklist, 1947

McCarthyism

The government's anti-communist crusade during the Second Red Scare also became known as **McCarthyism,** named for the media-savvy Republican Senator Joseph McCarthy from Wisconsin, who, along with HUAC, spearheaded numerous investigations into communist activities, many of them spurious. Anti-communist spy investigations predated McCarthy, but his flair for the dramatic made the senator an instant media sensation. McCarthy burst onto the scene after waving around a piece of paper during a speech before the Women's Republican Club in Wheeling, West Virginia, on February 9, 1950, thundering that he

Read the Document *Joseph McCarthy, "Wheeling, West Virginia Speech" (1950)*

What was the purpose and impact of HUAC's Hollywood investigations?

Competing Visions

NAMING NAMES IN HOLLYWOOD

The following opinions, one from former First Lady Eleanor Roosevelt who wrote a syndicated magazine column, "My Day," and the other from film director Elia Kazan, offer opposing views on aiding the HUAC investigations. Consider how Roosevelt and Kazan defined the threat to American democracy in this period. What risks were involved in following the different suggestions each made? Could their two views be reconciled?

In a 1947 "My Day" column, Eleanor Roosevelt expressed concerns that HUAC was creating a police state atmosphere that would squash artistic creativity and freedom of expression.

I have waited a while before saying anything about the Un-American Activities Committee's current investigation of the Hollywood film industry. I would not be very much surprised if some writers or actors or stagehands, or what not, were found to have Communist leanings, but I was surprised to find that, at the start of the inquiry, some of the big producers were so chicken-hearted about speaking up for the freedom of their industry.

One thing is sure—none of the arts flourishes on censorship and repression. And by this time it should be evident that the American public is capable of doing its own censoring…. The film industry is a great industry with infinite possibilities for good and bad. Its primary purpose is to entertain people. On the side, it can do many other things. It can popularize certain ideals, it can make education palatable. However, in the long run, the judge who decides whether what it does is good or bad is the man or woman who attends the movies. In a democratic country I do not think the public will tolerate a removal of its right to decide what it thinks of the ideas and performances of those who make the movie industry work…. What is going on in the Un-American Activities Committee worries me primarily because little people have become frightened and we find ourselves living in the atmosphere of a police state, where people close doors before they state what they think or look over their shoulders apprehensively before they express an opinion…. If you curtail what the other fellow says and does, you curtail what you yourself may say and do. In our country we must trust the people to hear and see both the good and the bad and to choose the good. The Un-American Activities Committee seems to me to be better for a police state than for the USA.

Many people in Hollywood never forgave Elia Kazan for cooperating with HUAC. In his 1988 autobiography Kazan refused to apologize. Instead he asserted his right to protect his career and the need to defend the country.

I believed it was the duty of the government to investigate the Communist movement in our country. I couldn't behave as if my old "comrades" didn't exist and didn't have an active political program. There was no way I could go along with their crap that the CP [Communist Party] was nothing but another political party, like the Republicans and the Democrats. I knew very well what it was, a thoroughly organized, worldwide conspiracy. This conviction separated me from many of my old friends …

Did I really want to change the social system I was living under? Apparently that was what I'd stood for at one time. But what s**t. Everything I had of value I'd gained under that system …

Why had I taken so long to even consider telling the country—that's what it amounted to—everything I knew? Was it because of the moral injunction against "informing," which was respected only depending on which side you were on? … If the situation were reversed, wouldn't the "comrades" protect themselves without hesitation and by any means? Including naming me…. I began to measure the weight and the worth of what I was giving up, my career in films, which I was surrendering for a cause I didn't believe in. It seemed insane. What was I if not a filmmaker? … If you expect an apology now because I would later name names to the House Committee, you've misjudged my character…. The people who owe you an explanation (no apology expected) are those who, year after year, held the Soviets blameless for all their crimes.

Hearings before the House Committee on Un-American Activities during the Second Red Scare

---

How do Roosevelt and Kazan differ on the best way to protect the right to freedom of expression?

View the **Closer Look** *Competing Visions: Naming Names in Hollywood*

had a list of 205 known communists who worked in the State Department. (The paper turned out to be just a prop.) When pressed for the names of the people on his list, McCarthy stalled and announced that he would only show their names to Truman, which he never did. In each subsequent speech the number cited by McCarthy dropped until he finally settled on 57.

> ## "When a great democracy is destroyed, it will not be from enemies from without, but rather because of enemies from within."
>
> Senator JOSEPH R. McCARTHY, Wheeling, West Virginia, 1950.

As a Republican attacking a Democratic administration, McCarthy's accusations had a partisan ring. Taking advantage of the media spotlight, he issued new charges against State Department officials, ruining the careers of many who could not mount an effective defense against his bullying. Reveling in the press attention that every new allegation brought, McCarthy sought bigger targets, even attacking Secretary of Defense George C. Marshall, who had authored the Marshall Plan while secretary of state, for having joined "a conspiracy so immense and an infamy so black as to dwarf any previous such venture in the history of man."

In 1954, a year after the Rosenbergs were executed, the career of Joseph McCarthy as an anti-communist crusader ended, when the senator began investigating the army for subversion. National television broadcast the hearings, and Americans watched aghast for 36 days as McCarthy intimidated witnesses, ignored facts, and made ludicrous charges. The climactic moment in the hearing came when the army's attorney Joseph Welch rebuked McCarthy, telling him, "You have done enough. Have you no sense of decency, sir, at long last?" Approval ratings for McCarthy plummeted from 50 percent to 35 percent in Gallup polls.

The public unraveling of support for McCarthy mirrored growing concerns among his fellow Republicans in Congress. Eisenhower and former HUAC member Richard Nixon were now in the White House. Attacking a Republican-controlled administration yielded fewer political benefits, and fellow Republicans privately urged Eisenhower to rein in McCarthy. Leery of having his own anti-communist credentials challenged, Eisenhower refused to confront McCarthy directly. Instead the president tried to take the high road. "I will not get down in the gutter with that guy," Eisenhower vowed, reasoning that if he gave McCarthy enough rope, he would eventually hang himself. This hands-off approach allowed McCarthy to run wild until 1954, when, as Eisenhower predicted, he went too far. Eventually it was the mainstream press, not the president, who denounced McCarthy. After the Army-McCarthy hearings, the esteemed journalist Edward R. Murrow exposed McCarthy's slander and lies in a television documentary. McCarthy, Murrow pointedly told his audience, "didn't create this situation of fear; he merely exploited it." However, when the Senate censured McCarthy on December 2, 1954, for violating Senate rules, the legislators chose to depict McCarthy as solely responsible for the excesses of anti-communism. A disgraced McCarthy died from liver failure caused by alcoholism three years later at age 49.

> ## "No one man can terrorize a whole nation unless we are all his accomplices."
>
> Journalist EDWARD R. MURROW during a 1954 television exposé on McCarthy

---

As Murrow suggested, the end of McCarthy's career as a red-baiter did not stop the government's anti-communist crusade. Republicans and Democrats alike took their cue from McCarthy and freely attacked any suspected radical working in local or state governments, public schools, or universities. The Smith Act remained in place, as did loyalty oaths, Hollywood blacklists, and police surveillance of suspected radicals. By the 1950s, using the charge of communism to discredit political opponents or liberal activists (such as Martin Luther King Jr.) was commonplace in American politics.

⊙ ▶Watch the Video on *Video Lecture: McCarthyism and the Politics of Fear*

Is the term McCarthyism a useful or misleading way to characterize the Second Red Scare?

Averting Nuclear War

The worldwide ideological, political, and military struggle between the United States and the Soviet Union fueled Americans' fear of communism, both at home and throughout the world. The vision of fighting a nuclear war continued to haunt Americans even after the ceasefire in Korea. Technological advances in long-range ballistic missiles and satellites provoked a new threat in the Cold War standoff between the United States and the Soviet Union. A missile fitted with a nuclear warhead could now reach the United States within half an hour from the Soviet Union. Armed uprisings in Eastern Europe, renewed Soviet demands that the West abandon Berlin, and the Cuban Missile Crisis created a climactic moment when the world teetered on the edge of all-out nuclear war.

Sputnik

On October 4, 1957, the Soviet Union sent the world's first satellite, nicknamed Sputnik ("fellow traveler"), into outer space. The size of a basketball and weighing just 183 pounds, Sputnik (**24.14**) nonetheless became a symbol of Soviet technological superiority, a satellite that could orbit the earth in 98 minutes. Today satellites serve a host of peaceful functions, transmitting television images and telephone calls around the globe. In 1957, however, Americans focused primarily on the new strategic advantage that satellite technology gave the Soviets. The Soviets could easily fit a missile that sent Sputnik into orbit with a nuclear warhead and launch it at the United States. To help Americans picture another danger, *Life* magazine traced the hypothetical path of Sputnik over a 24-hour period (**24.15**), warning "The Orbit Weaves a Web as Whole World Watches." Several orbits each day (marked in red as a reminder of the communist control of Sputnik) passed directly over the United States, bringing the Soviets ever closer to America's doorstep as they gradually ensnared the world. Fearing that the United States was losing the "space race," the government created the National Aeronautics and Space Administration (NASA) to launch America's own investigation of space, and the Defense Department scrambled to develop American satellite technology.

Predicting how the Soviet Union's volatile new leader might use this

technological breakthrough kept Americans on edge. In the power struggle that followed Stalin's death from a brain hemorrhage in March 1953, Nikita Khrushchev emerged as the new Soviet premier. A poorly educated peasant, who rose through the ranks to become a Stalin protégé, Khrushchev reveled in rhetorical excess. He proclaimed that the USSR was producing missiles "like sausages," and enjoyed keeping his American visitors off-balance. During a visit by Minnesota Senator Hubert

24.15
Life magazine illustrated the Sputnik threat by showing how its orbits gave the Soviets control of space, including areas over the United States.

24.14 Sputnik, 1957
For Americans this small satellite symbolized Soviet technological superiority over the United States, fueling the arms race between the two nations.

Humphrey to Moscow, Khrushchev stopped his threatening tirade long enough to ask Humphrey where he was from. "That's so I don't forget to order them to spare the city when the rockets fly," he said good naturedly.

Eager to catch up with the Soviet Union in missile technology and cut the defense budget (conventional military forces cost more than building nuclear weapons), Eisenhower oversaw a tremendous increase in American nuclear weaponry, which grew from 800 to nearly 8,000 warheads between 1953 and 1960. This build-up was part of a strategic vision called the "New Look." In 1954, Eisenhower's tough-talking secretary of state, John Foster Dulles, announced that the United States would focus on developing "massive retaliatory power" to deter Soviet aggression. The National Security Council agreed with Dulles that the country would go bankrupt trying to develop adequate defenses against Soviet nuclear weapons and policing the world with ground troops. Dulles maintained that a strong arsenal of intercontinental missiles (ICBMs) armed with nuclear warheads would allow the United States to "retaliate, instantly, by means and at places of our choosing" when the Soviets stepped out of line. Eisenhower liked the New Look because it offered a way to counter the Soviet manpower advantage while maintaining a small peacetime army. The appeal of "massive retaliation" was simple—it provided "more bang for the buck," some commentators noted.

Getting accurate data on the Soviet arsenal became critical once the United States embraced the doctrine of massive retaliation. The year before the Soviets launched Sputnik, the Americans began using a new U-2 spy plane to photograph Soviet military installations. Soviet radar could detect the U-2, but the plane flew at altitudes out of range for Soviet fighter pilots or antiaircraft missiles. For four years the United States used U-2 missions to collect intelligence about Soviet long-range missiles before turning to spy satellites. The photographs were reassuring. At the end of 1959, the United States learned, the Soviet Union had only six ICBM sites able to launch a missile carrying a nuclear warhead. Because it took 20 hours to fuel each missile, which could travel through space to reach targets 5,000 to 6,000 miles away in half an hour, the United States would have ample time to respond if the Soviet Union launched a first strike with six missiles. Despite Khrushchev's claims that the Soviets possessed a huge nuclear arsenal, American had far more nuclear warheads and ICBMs.

INNOVATION	USA	USSR
Nuclear-powered submarine launched	1954	1958
First Trial of ICBM	1958	1957
ICBM operational	1960	1959
Submarine-launched ICBM operational	1960	1957

24.16 Nuclear Arms Race, 1950s The United States and Soviet Union tried to best each other by developing increasingly sophisticated nuclear weapons.

Having made much of the claim that the Soviet Union possessed more ICBMs than the United States in his successful 1960 presidential campaign against Richard Nixon, President John F. Kennedy waited a few months before revealing the truth in 1961. Calling Khrushchev's bluff Kennedy announced that the United States had a "second strike capability which is at least as extensive as what the Soviets can deliver by striking first. Therefore, we are confident that the Soviets will not provoke a major nuclear conflict." The gap only kept growing in America's favor. Continuing the policy of massive retaliation, Kennedy oversaw an increase in the American ICBM stockpile from 63 to 424 from 1961 to 1963.

The attention given to the missile gap during the 1960 presidential campaign revealed the constant pressure that Americans felt to retain the upper hand in the ever-evolving nuclear arms race. The chart (**24.16**) lists the key developments in early Cold War nuclear weaponry, illustrating the intense competition between the United States and Soviet Union to develop nuclear weapons, including nuclear-powered submarines that could stay submerged for two months and fire nuclear-fitted missiles.

The Berlin Wall

Americans weighed Kennedy's reassuring words about the missile gap against recent events that again demonstrated the heavy hand of Soviet authority in Eastern Europe. In 1956, Khrushchev denounced Stalin's crimes against the Soviet people at a Communist Party Congress. His speech, taken as a cue that the new Soviet regime would be more open and tolerant, set off rebellions in Poland and Hungary. The Polish communists reasserted control themselves, but Soviet troops crushed the rebellion in Hungary, revealing that Khrushchev intended to retain Soviet control over Eastern Europe.

Khrushchev also moved to consolidate Soviet power over Berlin, twice issuing ultimatums to the West to vacate the divided city. The stark differences between life in East and West Berlin had become a public embarrassment to the Soviet Union. Lavishly rebuilt by West Germany and the Marshall Plan, West Berlin teemed with new housing, industry, and commerce. Moving freely between the more prosperous western half and the areas under Communist control, hundreds of thousands of East Germans voted with their feet. After defecting they traveled easily from West Berlin into West Germany to start new lives.

Khrushchev viewed the 44-year-old Kennedy as an inept, inexperienced leader, whom he could intimidate. A botched U.S.-sponsored invasion of Cuba in 1961 (discussed more fully below) only reaffirmed Khrushchev's low opinion of Kennedy. Believing that Kennedy would crumble under pressure, Khrushchev demanded that the West leave Berlin when the two met in Vienna. To Khrushchev's surprise the president stood firm. Kennedy left the summit "shaken and angry," one reporter claimed. He never met with Khrushchev again. Instead he returned home and requested funds for additional nuclear and conventional forces. The public fully supported their president. More than 82 percent favored maintaining American, French, and British forces in Berlin, even if it meant war with the Soviet Union.

With Kennedy unwilling to abandon the city, Khrushchev resisted the temptation to erect another blockade. Instead of revoking permission for the West to use roads through East Germany to supply the city, as Stalin had in 1948, he decided to build a wall between West Berlin and East Germany (see 24.5 on page 726). In the twilight hours of August 13, 1961, construction of a barbed wire fence began. East German tanks and troops rolled up to the monumental Brandenburg Gate, the original entry point to Berlin which lay in the Soviet sector of the city, to prevent a popular protest from breaking out in front of this symbol of German nationhood. East German workers quickly laid a thin line of barbed wire in front of the Brandenburg Gate, turning the popular square into a desolate no-man's land.

> ## "Freedom has many difficulties and democracy is not perfect, but we have never had to put a wall up to keep our people in, to prevent them from leaving us."
>
> President JOHN F. KENNEDY, in a speech before the Berlin Wall, 1963

West Germans flocked to the construction site in shock. Some East Germans made desperate last-minute escapes, jumping from the windows of buildings that straddled the boundary into nets held by West German firefighters. Twelve-foot-high concrete barriers with rounded piping on top (to make scaling the wall more difficult) soon replaced the barbed wire. *Envisioning Evidence: The Berlin Wall* depicts the complex defensive system that stood until 1989.

The wall stopped the flow of people from East to West Berlin without provoking a major confrontation with the United States. As the wall went up in 1961, Kennedy remarked to his aides that "a wall is a hell of a lot better than a war." When he finally visited the wall in June 1963, he expressed solidarity with the people on both sides of the divided city by announcing, "Ich bin ein Berliner" (which Kennedy thought meant "I am a Berliner," not realizing that *ein Berliner* was the name for a popular doughnut).

Bay of Pigs and the Cuban Missile Crisis

Americans viewed communist activities in Germany with dismay, but the prospect of a communist Cuba alarmed the government more: Cuba lay just 90 miles south of Florida. In 1959, Fidel Castro had overthrown the dictator Fulgencio Bastista y Zaldívar. Castro quickly consolidated his power. He declared himself a communist, confiscated a billion dollars in American property, and accepted aid from the Soviet Union. In response an alarmed Eisenhower broke off diplomatic relations and imposed economic sanctions, including an embargo that banned the export of American goods to the island. The Central Intelligence Agency (CIA) urged more forceful action and began planning the covert

Envisioning Evidence

THE BERLIN WALL

During the Cold War, the 96-mile long Berlin Wall around West Berlin became an iconic symbol of Soviet oppression to the western world. Initially nothing more than a barbed wire fence, the Berlin Wall quickly evolved into a complex network of 12-foot-high concrete walls, electrified fences, bunkers, land mines, observation towers, spotlights, guard dogs, and sirens. Fugitives' footprints in the soft sand spread on the eastern side of the wall (raked each day) alerted guards to breaches in the wall's defenses. Guards had strict orders to shoot anyone they saw attempting to escape. Nearly 5,000 people succeeded in circumventing the wall (some by digging tunnels under it) but over 175 people died trying.

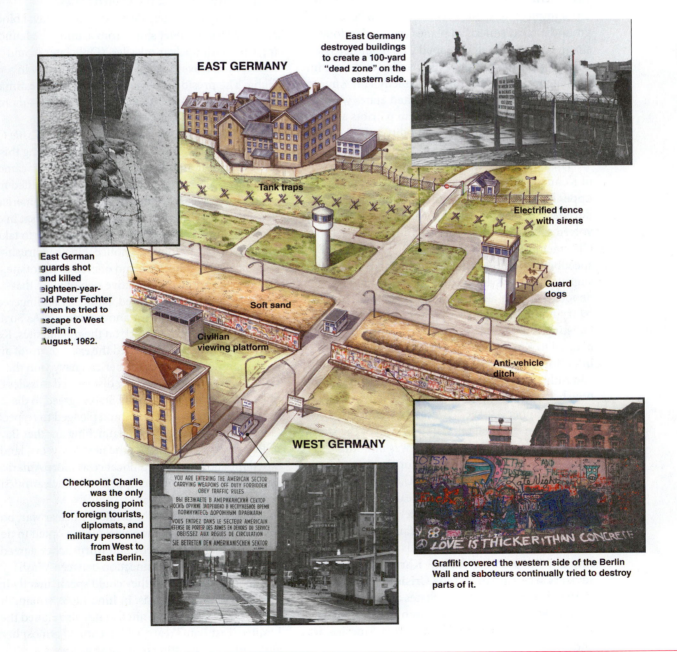

East Germany destroyed buildings to create a 100-yard "dead zone" on the eastern side.

EAST GERMANY

Tank traps

Electrified fence with sirens

Guard dogs

Soft sand

Anti-vehicle ditch

Civilian viewing platform

East German guards shot and killed eighteen-year-old Peter Fechter when he tried to escape to West Berlin in August, 1962.

WEST GERMANY

Checkpoint Charlie was the only crossing point for foreign tourists, diplomats, and military personnel from West to East Berlin.

YOU ARE ENTERING THE AMERICAN SECTOR
CARRYING WEAPONS OFF DUTY FORBIDDEN
OBEY TRAFFIC RULES

LOVE IS THICKER THAN CONCRETE

Graffiti covered the western side of the Berlin Wall and saboteurs continually tried to destroy parts of it.

View the **Closer Look** *Envisioning Evidence: The Berlin Wall*

How did the Berlin Wall serve as the front lines of the Cold War?

"We're eyeball to eyeball, and I think the other fellow just blinked."

Secretary of State DEAN RUSK, upon receiving word that Soviet ships had turned back during the Cuban Missile Crisis in 1962

Bay of Pigs operation, a failed amphibious invasion by Cuban exiles in 1961 to overthrow Castro.

Eisenhower left office before the scheduled invasion, but Kennedy endorsed the plan. Problems arose immediately, however. Two days before the ground attack, American planes (painted to look like stolen Cuban aircraft) bombed Cuban air defenses. On April 17, 1961, 1,400 exiles landed and were immediately killed or captured. Kennedy's unconvincing public statement that the United States was not involved in this "struggle of Cuban patriots against a Cuban dictator" hurt his credibility at home and overseas.

The Bay of Pigs fiasco hardened the resolve of Kennedy, Khrushchev, and Castro to gain the upper hand in this new Cold War hotspot. The CIA devised schemes for overthrowing Castro that involved sabotage and terrorism. In November 1961, CIA agents and Cuban exiles covertly traveled in speedboats from Florida to Cuba, where they burned sugar plantations and blew up factories and oil depots. The CIA also plotted to assassinate Castro by trying to poison his ice cream and cigars and enlisting Mafia crime bosses to kill him. Castro complained to Khrushchev about America's murderous intentions, and in return received Soviet economic and military aid. Protecting communism in Cuba now became a major goal for the Soviet Union.

On October 22, 1962, President Kennedy appeared on national television to deliver the stunning news that the Soviet Union was building missile launching pads in Cuba for short- and intermediate-range nuclear missiles. U.S. bases in Italy, Britain, and Turkey housed nuclear missiles aimed at the Soviet Union. Putting Soviet missiles in Cuba, a mere 90 miles from the American coast, would teach Americans "just what it feels like to have enemy missiles pointing at you," Khrushchev told his advisors. The **Cuban Missile Crisis**, a showdown in 1962 between the United States and the Soviet Union over Khrushchev's decision to place Soviet missiles in Communist Cuba aimed at America, was underway.

Instead of accepting the Soviet view that missiles in Cuba simply leveled the playing field, Kennedy responded with a competing vision that the Soviet actions represented "a provocative change in the delicate status quo both countries have maintained." Short- and intermediate-range Soviet missiles in Cuba threatened to reduce the strategic advantage that America held with its larger long-range nuclear arsenal. This was unacceptable to Kennedy. Intelligence officials estimated that the missile sites would become operational in two weeks, giving Kennedy only a small window of time before the Soviets would double their ability to launch a devastating nuclear strike against the United States.

Kennedy ultimately decided to use a naval blockade to prevent Soviet ships from arming the launching sites with nuclear missiles. (Only later would Kennedy discover that missiles were already in Cuba. The president never learned that the estimate of 10,000 Soviet troops in Cuba was wrong—there were actually 42,000).

Choices and Consequences: The Cuban Missile Crisis, outlines the options facing Kennedy during this tense fortnight, the closest that the world ever came to fighting an all-out nuclear war. The world waited for 13 days as Soviet ships steamed toward the American fleet guarding Cuban ports. American pilots sat in planes loaded with nuclear weapons, waiting to take off for Cuba at a moment's notice. Finally Khrushchev called the ships back and offered to negotiate. The public breathed a collective sigh of relief that nuclear war had been averted, but the crisis lingered on behind closed doors for another month. As Soviet engineers continued to work on the missile sites, Kennedy and Khrushchev debated the exact terms of an agreement. In the end the American navy won the right to inspect ships carrying dismantled missiles out of Cuba. In return the United States agreed to dismantle its missiles in Turkey and pledged to respect Cuban independence by not launching another Bay of Pigs–type invasion. Over the next few years, land-based missile sites lost significance as more American and Soviet submarines equipped with nuclear missiles began patrolling the oceans.

Having teetered on the brink of nuclear war, both the United States and the Soviet Union opted to de-escalate tensions. Kennedy and Khrushchev agreed to establish a hotline connection between Washington and Moscow, so they could speak directly in the event of another crisis. In June 1963, Britain, the Soviet Union, and the United States also signed the Limited Test Ban Treaty, which banned atmospheric and underwater testing of nuclear weapons.

What was the ultimate significance of the Cuban Missile crisis?

 View the **Image** *JFK and Krushchev*

Choices and Consequences

THE CUBAN MISSILE CRISIS

Long-range missiles (4,000–5,000 miles) launched from the USSR could already reach America, but short-range (1,100 miles) and intermediate-range (2,200 miles) nuclear-armed missiles in Cuba would help close the missile gap by giving the Soviets more weapons to use against the United States. Determined to get Soviet missiles out of Cuba, Kennedy and his advisors debated how to respond on October 16, 1962.

Choices

1 Use air and ground forces to attack Cuba and destroy the missile sites.

2 Follow up an attack on Cuba with a full-scale invasion to depose Castro.

3 Negotiate with the Soviet Union and Cuba.

4 Use a naval quarantine to prevent Soviet-supplied missiles from reaching Cuba.

Decision

Kennedy opted for the quarantine. He sent the American navy 500 miles from Cuban shores to intercept Soviet vessels carrying missiles, and threatened a nuclear attack on the Soviet Union if missiles were launched from Cuba.

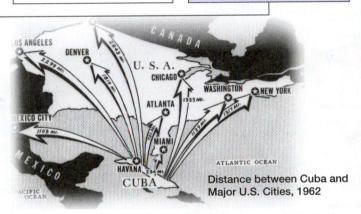

Distance between Cuba and Major U.S. Cities, 1962

Consequences

For two tense days Soviet ships steamed toward American naval vessels. At the last minute Khrushchev called the ships back and offered to negotiate by removing the missiles if Kennedy pledged not to attack Cuba and the United States dismantled its missiles in Turkey. Kennedy privately agreed to these terms. By deciding against an air strike, Kennedy may have averted a nuclear war. Unbeknownst to the president, nuclear warheads were already in Cuba. Soviet commanders on the ground had permission to use them if the United States attacked and considered using them against the blockade.

Continuing Controversies

Did Kennedy react correctly during the Cuban Missile Crisis?

Supporters argue that Kennedy effectively used the threat of an American nuclear attack, traditional naval tactics, and old-fashioned diplomacy to end the crisis without resorting to war. By doing so he maintained America's strategic advantage against the Soviet Union and improved the nation's image worldwide after the Bay of Pigs fiasco. Detractors claim that Kennedy provoked a crisis where there was none. Short- and medium-range missiles in Cuba did not alter the Soviets' ability to attack with long-range missiles or of the United States to launch a devastating second-strike. Supporters counter that the improved accuracy of shorter-range missiles fired from Cuba posed a real threat. Critics also point out that because Kennedy made concessions privately to Khrushchev, the crisis gave rise to the myth that "brinkmanship," or threatening nuclear war, rather than diplomatic negotiations, caused the Soviets to back down. Overconfidence after the Cuban Missile Crisis would lead to missteps in America's growing military involvement in the Vietnam War and elsewhere.

Watch the **Video** *President John F. Kennedy and the Cuban Missile Crisis*

What political and military considerations influenced Kennedy during the Cuban Missile Crisis?

1946
Kennan's Long Telegram
Makes containing communism a key American goal

1947
Truman Doctrine
Gives United States a role in helping other nations resist communism

HUAC begins investigating Hollywood
Leads to establishment of blacklist

1948
Marshall Plan
Grants U.S. aid to rebuild war-torn Europe and prevent spread of communism

Berlin airlift
Highly visible Cold War victory for the United States

1949
NATO formed
First formal American military alliance since the Revolutionary War

China falls to communism
Provokes fears that communists are winning the Cold War

CHAPTER REVIEW

Review Questions

1. What key contributions did Truman, Eisenhower, and Kennedy make to the strategy of containment?

2. How did international crises influence domestic politics from 1945 to 1963?

3. How did images and popular culture shape Americans' ideas about the Soviet Union and the atomic bomb?

4. Why did Americans consider West Berlin so important? What key decisions and risks did Truman and Kennedy take in resolving Berlin-related crises?

5. What competing visions did policymakers offer on how the United States should contain the Soviet threat?

Key Terms

"Long telegram" An influential 5,000-word missive by diplomat George F. Kennan that outlined why America needed to develop an aggressive foreign policy aimed at containing Soviet expansionist impulses.   **722**

Containment The label affixed to multiple American foreign policy initiatives meant to prevent the Soviet Union from expanding its influence around the globe.   **722**

Iron curtain Winston Churchill's characterization of the military and ideological barrier erected by the Soviet Union that separated Western and Eastern Europe into free and dominated halves.   **722**

North Atlantic Treaty Organization (NATO) A post-World War II military alliance between the U.S. and Western European powers.   **722**

Truman Doctrine A foreign policy initiative that gave the United States an active role in stopping the global spread of communism by supporting "free peoples who are resisting attempted subjugation by armed minorities or by outside pressures."   **724**

Marshall Plan (1948–1952) Aimed to restore Europeans' faith in capitalism by sending $13 billion ($119 billion in today's dollars) overseas to rebuild Europe's ruined roads, bridges, factories, and farms.   **724**

Berlin airlift (1948–1949) Americans and British used planes to resupply West Berlin to stymie the Soviet blockade of the city.   **726**

McCarthyism The government's anti-communist crusade named for Senator Joseph McCarthy from Wisconsin, who, along with the House Committee on Un-American Activities (HUAC), spearheaded numerous governmental investigations into communist activities, many of them spurious.   **739**

Bay of Pigs operation (1961) Failed attempt to use an amphibious invasion by Cuban exiles to overthrow the Cuban dictator Fidel Castro.   **746**

Cuban Missile Crisis (1962) A showdown between the United States and the Soviet Union over Khrushchev's decision to place Soviet missiles aimed at America in Communist Cuba.   **746**

1950

Joseph McCarthy gives Wheeling, West Virginia, speech
Begins career as major figure in Second Red Scare

Korean War begins
United States enters fighting; Cold War extends into East Asia

1953

Stalin dies; Khrushchev assumes power
Ruthless dictator replaced by brash and unpredictable one

Julius and Ethel Rosenberg executed
Spy case fuels Second Red Scare

1961

Bay of Pigs invasion
Failed attempt to oust Castro in Cuba embarrasses the United States

Berlin Wall built
Becomes symbol of communist oppression

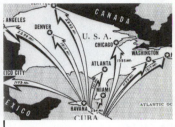

1962

Cuban Missile Crisis
Showdown between the United States and the USSR prompts fears of nuclear war

MyHistoryLab Connections

Visit www.myhistorylab.com for a customized Study Plan that will help you build your knowledge of *A Divided World*.

Questions for Analysis

1. What advice did Kennan give on dealing with the Soviet Union?

📖 **Read** the **Document** *George F. Kennan, "The Long Telegram" (1946), p. 722*

2. How did the Truman Doctrine speech set a new direction for U.S. foreign policy?

👁 **Watch** the **Video** *President Truman and the Threat of Communism, p. 724*

3. Why did the *Chicago Defender* urge readers to "save this paper, it marks history?"

🔍 **View** the **Image** *Truman Ends Military Jim Crow, p. 727*

4. What advice did Americans receive on constructing their own fallout shelters?

🔍 **View** the **Closer Look** *Images as History: Fallout Shelters, p. 736*

5. How does this cartoon depict Kennedy's actions during the Cuban Missile Crisis?

🔍 **View** the **Image** *JFK and Krushchev, p. 746*

Other Resources from This Chapter

📖 **Read** the **Document**
- *Winston Churchill, "'Iron Curtain' Speech" (March 5, 1946), p. 723*
- *Joseph McCarthy, "Wheeling, West Virginia Speech" (1950), p. 739*
- *Kennedy's Address to the People of Berlin (June 28, 1963), p. 744*

🔍 **View** the **Closer Look**
- *Images as History: Surviving an Atomic Bomb Blast, p. 735*
- *Competing Visions: Naming Names in Hollywood, p. 740*
- *Envisioning Evidence: The Berlin Wall, p. 745*

🔍 **View** the **Image**
- *U.S. Hydrogen Bomb Test Over Uninhabited Pacific Island (1952), p. 729*
- *Sputnik I, p. 742*

🔍 **View** the **Map** *Interactive Map: The Korean War, 1950–1953, p. 731*

👁 **Watch** the **Video**
- *Ike for President: Eisenhower Campaign Ad (1952), p. 733*
- *Duck and Cover, p. 734*
- *Video Lecture: McCarthyism and the Politics of Fear, p. 741*
- *President John F. Kennedy and the Cuban Missile Crisis, p. 747*

In a Land of Plenty
Contentment and Discord, 1945–1960

On September 3, 1957, a young black teenager, Elizabeth Eckford, walked past an angry mob after state troopers refused to let her enter the all-white Central High School in Little Rock, Arkansas. This photo captures her harrowing ordeal as a young white woman, Hazel Bryan, her face contorted with rage, screamed at Eckford. In the days that followed, a sympathetic white man put an ad in the local newspaper featuring this photograph. "Study this picture and know shame," he told his neighbors. Instead, for years Bryan received congratulatory letters from diehard segregationists for her verbal assault on Eckford that day. Five years later Bryan tracked down Eckford in Little Rock to apologize. Eckford went on to graduate from college, served in the army, and then became a probation officer.

This photograph challenges the traditional image of the 1950s as a tranquil period of material contentment and ideological consensus. Americans enjoyed unprecedented prosperity during the decade but also experienced domestic discord along racial, generational, and political lines. New energy surged into the Civil Rights Movement in the 1950s. Acts of extraordinary bravery by Elizabeth Eckford and others like her took on new significance in an era when Supreme Court rulings pushed the federal government to take an active role in protecting the civil rights of African Americans. Leadership from black churches and black students infused the movement with an ethos of nonviolent direct action that forced white America to see the injustice of Jim Crow, the Southern legal structure that relegated African Americans to second-class citizenship.

A different type of discord permeated American home-life throughout the 1950s. In many respects families were the focus of American society from 1945 to1960. Enjoying a rising standard of living in generally prosperous times, American families grew at an unprecedented rate. Lured to fast-growing suburbs by low-cost loans and affordable housing, an exploding middle class filled their homes with possessions previously out of reach for most Americans. The **baby boom generation**, those 76.4 million Americans born between 1946 and 1964, who were now coming into adolescence, embraced new standards in dress, music, and movies that distinguished the "teen" generation from their parents. Some teenagers rebelled against authority in more overtly political ways. High school and college students, for instance, were the ground troops in many civil rights demonstrations. Others joined the counterculture Beat movement to express their rebellion against social norms through poetry, novels, and art.

From 1945 to 1960, Americans debated the divergent political paths that the country could take domestically during the Cold War era. They pondered the effects of New Deal programs, unions, suburbs, civil rights, and consumption on American society. The changing American way of life created a sense of both contentment and crisis for the nation.

"It was the longest block I ever walked
in my whole life."

ELIZABETH ECKFORD, confronting a mob as she walked from
the bus stop to school in Little Rock, Arkansas

Securing the New Deal Legacy

Once prosperity returned after World War II, Republicans tried to undo the New Deal, arguing that these Depression-era programs hampered the free market and deprived industrialists of the freedom to run their companies as they saw fit. Moderate Democrats, like President Harry Truman, focused on preserving past reforms. When labor unions launched unpopular postwar strikes, Republicans joined with conservative southern Democrats to roll back New Deal legislation that had benefited the labor movement. The victory over labor, however, did not provide enough momentum for conservatives to achieve their ultimate goal: dismantling the entire New Deal.

25.1 Striking Steel Workers, 1946 Picketing steel workers carried signs with slogans meant to win sympathy from ordinary Americans, but widespread strikes caused a public backlash against labor unions.

The Labor Movement Curtailed

In 1945, the labor movement enjoyed unparalleled strength. Government support for union organizing during the New Deal and World War II, combined with a wave of successful sit-down strikes in the 1930s, had made labor a powerful force in American society. This was the high point of the labor movement in American history. Over 14 million workers belonged to unions, nearly 35 percent of the industrial workforce. Labor flexed its muscle in 1946, when the lifting of wartime price controls sent prices skyrocketing.

What arguments do these signs make for labor's demands?

Nearly 4.6 million workers participated in 5,000 strikes nationwide in 1945–1946, demanding not just higher wages and benefits but also the right to participate in management decisions regarding investments, product lines, production methods, and plant locations. The signs held by striking steelworkers in this photo (**25.1**) outside a Bethlehem Steel Plant were intended to mobilize public support. The slogans demanded fairness to returning veterans, gave assurances that higher wages would not lead to higher prices, and proposed a living wage for workers who made such a valuable commodity. Black and white steelworkers manned this picket line together, reflecting the success of the Congress of Industrial Organizations (CIO) in mending racial divisions that had previously weakened the labor movement (see Chapter 22).

As the labor unrest widened, popular support for strikes diminished. The public had little sympathy for threats to shut down the steel and car industries, which formed the core of the national economy. Strikes in the coal and meatpacking industries also made it more expensive for Americans to heat their homes and eat meat. When railroad workers went on strike, Truman intervened. The railroad strike "threatens to paralyze all our industrial, agricultural, commercial, and social life," leading to potential starvation at home and abroad, the president proclaimed. Although supportive of New Deal labor legislation, Truman announced he would use the army to run the railroads and draft striking workers into the military if they did not return to work. Moments before he was scheduled to ask Congress to authorize this legislation, the strikers returned to work.

Workers in other industries fared a bit better. Negotiated settlements in the steel and auto industries set the benchmark for wages, benefits, and shop floor practices that other companies, even nonunionized ones like the general merchandiser Sears Roebuck, adopted to maintain peaceful labor relations. Industrialists also gained in these agreements. Longer contracts ensured an extended period of tranquility with no strikes, and in all settlements company owners maintained control over management decisions.

The Republicans' successful mid-term campaign slogan, "Had Enough? Vote Republican," capitalized on voters' dismay over labor conflicts and higher prices. In 1946, for the first time since 1933, the Republican Party won majorities in both the House and the Senate. Republicans hoped to use this victory as a springboard for unseating Truman in 1948. The Eightieth Congress immediately passed strong anti-labor legislation over Truman's veto. Although dismayed with the strikes of 1946, Truman knew that he would need labor's vote in the upcoming presidential contest. The **Taft-Hartley Act (1947)** abolished the closed shop, a practice that required all workers who benefited from a union-negotiated contract to join the union. The law also banned so-called sympathy boycotts, strikes by workers who wanted to support another union's protest. Finally the requirement that all union officers sign affidavits certifying that they were not members of the Communist Party encouraged unions to purge their most radical members, often those who had pioneered new tactics, like the sit-down strike in the 1930s. The Taft-Hartley Act was a serious blow to the labor movement. The merger in 1955 between the CIO and the more conservative American Federation of Labor (AFL) ushered in a more cautious era of labor organizing that mostly ignored unskilled and Southern workers.

Presidential Agendas: Truman and Eisenhower

Conservative Republicans hoped that the Taft-Hartley Act would spearhead a drive to dismantle the New Deal. Instead the curtailment of labor removed the most visible symbol of what was supposedly "wrong" with the New Deal just as the 1948 presidential campaign got underway. To win, Truman decided that the votes of labor and Northern African Americans were more important than retaining the solid South. The Democratic Party adopted the slogan "Don't let them take it away," referring to the minimum wage, unemployment insurance, and Social Security that the New Deal had granted to industrial workers. Liberal Democrats successfully pushed Truman to take a stronger stand on civil rights. In July 1948, for both principled and pragmatic reasons, Truman ordered the desegregation of the armed forces, an important civil rights milestone.

Truman's embrace of civil rights caused Southern conservatives to bolt from the Democratic Party; his earlier confrontations with labor also convinced social progressives to leave the party. Vowing to preserve segregation, conservative Southern Democrats formed the States Rights Party and nominated South Carolina Governor Strom Thurmond to run against Truman and the Republican candidate,

Thomas Dewey. On the political left former Vice President Henry Wallace ran on the Progressive Citizens of America ticket, representing a coalition of liberals and radicals upset about the assault on civil liberties at home and the nation's aggressive foreign policy as the Cold War took shape. Truman's campaign assault on big business as "gluttons of privilege," strong support from labor and blacks, and the success of the Berlin airlift propelled him to a clear victory in the Electoral College (303 to 189), but he led Dewey by just two million in the popular vote (see Chapter 24).

> ## "The time has come to walk out of the shadow of states' rights and into the sunlight of human rights."
>
> Minneapolis Mayor HUBERT HUMPHREY, urging Democrats to adopt a strong civil rights stance in the 1948 presidential election

For much of his second term, Truman focused on managing foreign affairs and fending off assaults on his administration from Senator Joseph McCarthy (see Chapter 24). Abandoning his earlier stance of merely sustaining the New Deal, Truman put forth the **Fair Deal**, proposals for national health care, public housing, education, and public works projects. The Democratic majority that controlled the Eighty-First Congress funded state school systems and urban public housing, increased the minimum wage, and continued bringing electricity and telephones into rural areas. Proposals for national health insurance stalled, but Congress did vote to build more hospitals and expanded public health facilities for the poor.

In June, 1950, North Korea invaded South Korea and political debate shifted to the Korean War (see Chapter 24). Truman, wary of undermining bipartisan support for his Cold War policies and the Korean War, did not push hard for controversial Fair Deal initiatives such as repealing the Taft-Hartley Act, price and wage controls, or universal health care. Only a fraction of Truman's

Fair Deal proposals became law, but his program foreshadowed the more successful and extensive liberal agendas of Presidents John F. Kennedy and Lyndon B. Johnson, both Democrats.

By the end of the Truman administration, most Americans could not imagine a society without Social Security or a minimum wage, expectations that shaped the political vision of the nation's next president. In 1952 and again in 1956, the Republican candidate Dwight Eisenhower won in landslide elections, both times defeating Democrat Adlai E. Stevenson of Illinois. The virtually unknown Stevenson faced the daunting challenge of overcoming Southern anger at Truman's civil rights reforms (which Stevenson supported) and America's affection for Eisenhower, a World War II hero. A gifted orator, Stevenson stuck to traditional stump speeches, while Eisenhower became the first presidential candidate to use televised political ads. He honed his folksy image in short ads that aired during the commercial breaks of popular nighttime TV programs. America voted overwhelmingly for the man they knew and liked, with Eisenhower defeating Stevenson by 422 to 89 electoral votes. In 1956, running on a slogan of "peace and prosperity" that noted his success in ending the Korean War, Eisenhower polled even higher numbers, receiving 457 electoral votes to Stevenson's 73.

Republican critics like Senator Robert Taft of Ohio attacked the Fair Deal as "creeping socialism" because these expensive programs required high taxes and, in Republicans' view, gave the government too much power. The 1953 editorial cartoon *Who Said 'Creeping Socialism'* (**25.2**) reflected the conservatives' fear that Eisenhower would have trouble taming New Deal and Fair Deal programs. The congressman in the cartoon, a symbol of runaway big government, holds a briefcase labeled "Govt. in Business, Housing, Power, Transport," and his running head start makes it impossible for Eisenhower to catch up. The cartoon actually misrepresented Eisenhower's intentions. The president liked to say that he was "conservative when it comes to money and liberal when it comes to human beings." To appeal to the moderates in each party, Eisenhower announced that he had no intention of dismantling popular New Deal programs. "Should any political party attempt to abolish social security and eliminate labor laws and farm programs,

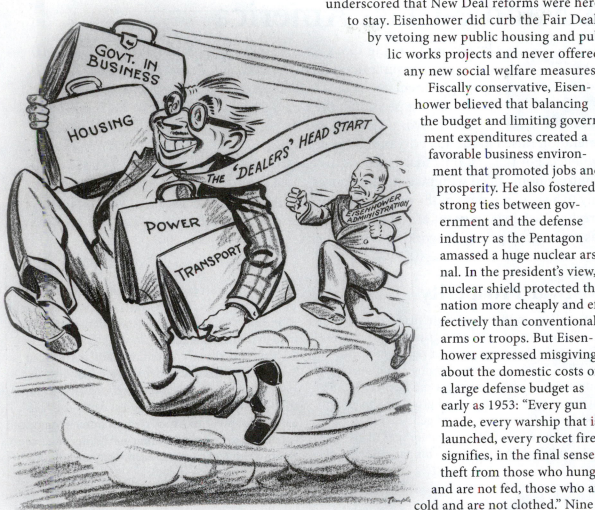

25.2 *Who Said 'Creeping Socialism,'* 1953
During the 1952 presidential election, conservative Republicans criticized the New Deal and Fair Deal as "creeping socialism." This caricature portrays the newly elected Republican President Dwight Eisenhower struggling to catch a sprinting congressman who clutches programs enacted during previous Democratic administrations.

underscored that New Deal reforms were here to stay. Eisenhower did curb the Fair Deal by vetoing new public housing and public works projects and never offered any new social welfare measures. Fiscally conservative, Eisenhower believed that balancing the budget and limiting government expenditures created a favorable business environment that promoted jobs and prosperity. He also fostered strong ties between government and the defense industry as the Pentagon amassed a huge nuclear arsenal. In the president's view, a nuclear shield protected the nation more cheaply and effectively than conventional arms or troops. But Eisenhower expressed misgivings about the domestic costs of a large defense budget as early as 1953: "Every gun made, every warship that is launched, every rocket fired, signifies, in the final sense, a theft from those who hunger and are not fed, those who are cold and are not clothed." Nine years later, as he prepared to vacate the White House, Eisenhower suggested that he had gone too far in promoting the convergence of military and industrial interests. In a well-remembered speech, he urged Americans to keep an eye on the **"military-industrial complex,"** his term for the close ties between the defense industry and the Pentagon that might unduly influence government policy. "We must never let the weight of this combination endanger our liberties or democratic processes," Eisenhower warned.

you would not hear of that party again in our political history," Eisenhower concluded, to the dismay of Republican conservatives. His "victory of the moderates," as commentators termed it,

> "I have always assumed that what was good for the United States was good for General Motors, and vice versa."
>
> Secretary of Defense CHARLES E. WILSON, when asked about a possible conflict of interest between his government position and his former job as the head of General Motors, 1953

Read the Document *Dwight D. Eisenhower, Farewell Address (1961)*   Why was Eisenhower's "victory of the moderates" significant?

A Middle-Class America

By any measure the 1950s were a prosperous decade. From 1945 to 1960, per capita consumption rose 50 percent, wages grew by one-third, and unemployment averaged 4.6 percent. American productivity also boomed. With only six percent of the world population, the United States produced half of the world's manufactured goods in the 1950s. The 1950s gave the generation raised in the austerity of the Great Depression something they had never known: affluence. For the first time many Americans enjoyed the trappings of middle-class life—a suburban home filled with modern appliances and a car in the garage—previously available only to a small segment of the population. By 1960, the nation crossed a significant historic threshold, when 60 percent of Americans were classified as middle class. The United States was no longer a primarily working-class society.

Postwar Prosperity

In 1948, Vernon Presley brought his family to Memphis, Tennessee, to escape the grinding poverty of Mississippi. Gladys Presley later recalled that her son, Elvis, "would hear us worrying about our debts, being out of work and sickness and he'd say, 'Don't you worry none, Baby. When I grow up, I'm going to buy you a fine house . . . and get two Cadillacs—one for you and Daddy, and one for me.'" Elvis Presley fulfilled this promise to his parents when he

became the most famous rock-and-roll star of the era. For the rest of his life, Elvis, an extreme example of the era's conspicuous consumption, gave away cars to friends and family.

Few Americans enjoyed this level of financial success, but the kind of deprivation that Elvis experienced as a child became a relic of the past for millions in the 1950s. The typical American "has access to amenities—foods, entertainment, personal transportation, and plumbing—in which not even the rich rejoiced a century ago," economist John

25.3 and 25.4 Buying on Credit "What They Have" vs. "What They Own." The before and after photos of this *Life* magazine spread demonstrated Americans' reliance on credit to accumulate the trappings of middle-class life in the fifties.

Kenneth Galbraith noted. Having discretionary income for a television, vacations, or sending a child to college transformed the lives of American workers. "If what we lived through in the 1950s was not liberation," Jack Metzgar, the son of Pennsylvania steelworkers, noted, "then liberation never happens in real human lives."

An aggressive union movement seeking higher wages and benefits and the New Deal safety net of guaranteed pensions and unemployment insurance helped fuel this leap into the middle class for many industrial workers. Other government initiatives also helped transform the way Americans lived. In 1944, just 44 percent of Americans owned their homes. By 1960, this figure had risen to 60 percent thanks to the 1944 GI Bill of Rights that offered returning veterans low-interest loans and to a tax code that provided incentives for homeowners. In addition state and federal governments constructed the roads, schools, bridges, and sewers that new suburban developments required.

During World War II production of consumer goods was scant, and many Americans had accumulated savings that they were now eager to spend. In 1950 alone, Americans snatched up 6.2 million refrigerators, 14.6 million radios, and 6.2 million automobiles. This represented three-quarters of the appliances purchased worldwide. Installment plans helped millions of Americans purchase these key consumer items. Consumer debt rose from $8.3 billion in 1946 to $56.1 billion in 1960, a trend that caught *Life*'s attention in 1955. To illustrate the newly affluent lifestyle of middle-class Americans, *Life* photographer Loomis Dean put a couple with their two children in front of their Los Angeles suburban home alongside all their furnishings and car. The first picture (**25.3**) showed "what they have": an oven, refrigerator, two television sets, car, and furniture. The second photograph (**25.4**), "what they own," put the family in front of the foundations of a house and automobile tires to reflect how far along they were in their mortgage and car payments. The refrigerator, couch, stove, and one television set—all bought on credit—were missing. By purchasing so heavily with credit, this family risked losing nearly everything if a recession hit, and the father lost his job.

American leaders felt that their nation's material abundance demonstrated the superiority of capitalist societies over communist ones, where basic consumer items were often in short supply. Others condemned American materialism. In his biting social commentary *The Status Seekers*, Vance Packard criticized Americans for jettisoning the frugality of the past in favor of status-seeking conspicuous consumption. Manufacturers helped create this

Compare this family's possessions and home life to those of previous generations.

new consumerist orientation. One executive conceded that it was the advertisers' job to "see to it that Americans are never satisfied." A middle-class family now considered their car or refrigerator "obsolete after two or three years even though it works well," financial columnist Sylvia Porter noted.

The Move to the Suburbs

Suburbs built in the 1920s ringed major cities and remained connected to the metropolitan core by streetcars or rail lines. In the 1950s, suburbs moved farther away from cities, becoming insular communities that depended increasingly on cars to transport people. The roads Eisenhower built to help evacuate urban areas if the nation came under nuclear attack (see Chapter 24) were now filled with suburbanites running errands and commuting to work. Of the 13 million new houses constructed between 1948 and 1958, 85 percent were built in suburban neighborhoods. By 1960, 37 million Americans lived in suburbs out of a total population of 189 million.

When developer William Levitt erected thousands of mass-produced houses on the former potato fields of Long Island, in New York State, he pioneered building techniques that transformed the housing market. Applying Henry Ford's automobile assembly line–style innovations to the housing industry, Levitt built "**Levittowns**,"—planned suburban communities where developers standardized every part of the construction process. Levitt claimed that his crews could assemble a house in 15 minutes, while it took only three minutes to complete the paperwork to purchase one. Levitt passed these savings onto home-buyers, dropping the prices of new houses from $14,000 to $8,000. When other developers copied his techniques nationwide, the low price of suburban houses, coupled with readily available government-backed financing, brought home ownership within reach of millions of Americans.

These new suburban houses typically contained living-room picture windows that developers installed to make their 1,000-square-feet houses feel more spacious. When the curtains were open, these large windows also displayed a family's possessions and prosperity to the neighborhood. Suburban houses had "living kitchens" where families both prepared and ate their meals and "family rooms" to accommodate the television, toys, and games that brought the family together at the end of the day. A garage sheltered the automobile that every suburban family needed.

Americans offered competing visions on whether suburban living improved daily life or encouraged mindless conformity. Conflicting interpretations greeted images of idealized suburban life. "For literally nothing down" Americans could purchase a "box" in a suburban development "inhabited by people whose age, income, number of children, problems, habits, conversation, dress, possessions and perhaps even blood type are also precisely like [theirs]," wrote John Keats in *The Crack in the Picture Window* (1957). Abraham Levitt, the son of developer William Levitt, fought back against these charges: "Houses are for people, not critics . . . — and the people for whom we do it think it's pretty good." This debate is explored in *Competing Visions: Suburbs—American Dream or Nightmare?*

The move to the suburbs converged with an explosion of childbearing among couples who had put off having children during the Depression and World War II and younger couples encouraged by boom times to start their families immediately. Between 1935 and 1955, the birth rate jumped nearly 40 percent. Levittown's nickname, "Fertility Valley," underscored this link between the suburbs and the baby boom generation.

The baby boom generation shaped American society for decades. As babies and children they helped stimulate a huge industry devoted to diapers, baby formulas, and toys. Teenagers, a new term to describe adolescents, formed the backbone of 1950s popular culture and the antiwar movement and cultural upheavals of the 1960s. In the twenty-first century, as the baby boomers begin to retire, the imperative to care for a large aging population poses significant challenges for American society.

The 1950s ushered in other key lifestyle changes besides suburban living and an emphasis on family life. As more Americans entered the middle class, they increasingly worked at white-collar jobs ranging from clerks to professionals to corporate executives. The effect of corporate culture on American society was as hotly debated as the impact of suburban life. In an era when McCarthyism eliminated radical discourse as a legitimate form of political expression, social critics worried that suburbs and corporations were bleaching individuality and innovation out of the national character. "When white-collar people get jobs, they sell not only their time and energy but their personalities as well," sociologist C. Wright Mills contended. Others, including *Fortune* magazine, regularly defended corporations for extending job security and prosperity to millions.

Why did suburbs boom in the 1950s?

Hear the **Audio** *Little Boxes*

Competing Visions

SUBURBS—AMERICAN DREAM OR NIGHTMARE?

As the suburbs grew social critics debated whether suburban life represented the epitome of the American dream or a nightmarish existence that isolated Americans from one another. To challenge historian Lewis Mumford's assertion that the suburbs were cultural wastelands, sociologist Herbert J. Gans moved his family into a Levittown to study its residents. As you read the following excerpts from Mumford and Gans, consider how each links the suburbs to changing lifestyles. What positive and negative changes do these writers attribute to suburban life? What different futures do they envision for a suburban-based American culture?

Lewis Mumford in *The City in History* (1961) contended that suburban life bred conformity, loneliness, and alienation.

In the mass movement into suburban areas a new kind of community was produced … a multitude of uniform, unidentifiable houses, lined up inflexibly, at uniform distances, on uniform roads, in a treeless communal waste, inhabited by people of the same class, the same income, the same age group, witnessing the same television performances, eating the same tasteless pre-fabricated foods, from the same freezers, conforming in every outward and inward respect to a common mold …

The town housewife, who half a century ago knew her butcher, her grocer, her dairyman, her various other local tradesmen, as individual persons, with histories and biographies that impinged on her own, in a daily exchange, now has the benefit of a single weekly expedition to an impersonal supermarket, where only by accident is she likely to encounter a neighbor.…

The cost of this detachment in space from other men is out of all proportion to its supposed benefits. The end product is an encapsulated life, spent more and more either in a motor car or within the cabin of darkness before a television set.

Levittown Street Scene

Herbert J. Gans defended suburbanites in *The Levittowners: Ways of Life and Politics in a New Suburban Community* (1967).

[Levittowners] are not apathetic conformists ripe for takeover by a totalitarian elite or corporate merchandiser; they are not conspicuous consumers and slaves to sudden whims of cultural and political fashion.… even though Levittowners and other lower middle class Americans continue to be home-centered, they are much more "in the world" than their parents and grandparents were. Those coming out of ethnic working class backgrounds have rejected the … ethnocentrism which made other cultures and even other neighborhoods bitter enemies. This generation trusts its neighbors, participates with them in social and civic activities, and no longer sees government as inevitably corrupt. Even working class Levittowners have begun to give up the suspicion that isolated their ancestors from all but family and childhood friends. Similarly, the descendants of rural Protestant America have given up the xenophobia that turned previous generations against the Catholic and Jewish immigrant, they have almost forgotten the intolerant Puritanism which triggered attacks against pleasure and enjoyment, and they no longer fully accept the doctrine of laissez-faire that justifies the defense of all individual rights and privileges against others' needs.

These and other changes have come about not because people are now better or more tolerant human beings, but because they are affluent. For the Levittowners, life is not a fight for survival any more; they have been able to move into a community in which income and status are equitably enough distributed so that neighbors are no longer treated as enemies, even if they are still criticized for social and cultural defiance. By any yardstick one chooses, Levittowners treat their fellow residents more ethically and more democratically than did their parents and grandparents. They also live a "fuller" and "richer" life.… superior to what prevailed among the working and lower middle classes of past generations."

View the **Closer Look** *Competing Visions: Suburbs— American Dream or Nightmare?*

What competing visions emerged over suburban living and corporate jobs?

Popular Culture in the Fifties

Television transformed the home life of millions of Americans. So did the emergence of an autonomous youth culture, with its own slang, rock-and-roll music, and dress. Were these harmless expressions of adolescent rebellion or signs of the disintegration of American culture? These stirrings of generational conflict in the 1950s exploded a decade later into full-fledged revolt.

The Television Age Arrives

The first commercial television transmission in the United States occurred in 1939 when President Franklin D. Roosevelt visited the New York World's Fair. The war slowed the introduction of televisions into the consumer market, but by the 1950s, the television age had arrived. In 1948, just 178,000 homes had televisions. Seven years later three-quarters of American households owned one.

Eisenhower set the tone for the decade with the widely publicized image of the president and his wife, Mamie, eating dinner each night off tray-tables in front of a television in their private White House parlor. Whereas in the forties Americans had flocked to movie theaters for entertainment, now they stayed home. "Don't be a Living Room Captive—Step Out and See a Great Movie," film studios urged. Many Americans, however, appeared to agree with Eisenhower, who wrote in his diary, "If a citizen has to be bored to death it is cheaper and more comfortable to sit at home and look at television than it is to go outside and pay a dollar for a ticket." Many movie theaters closed, and the studios made fewer films. Only drive-in theaters in suburban towns, where customers sat in their cars next to individual speakers to watch a movie on a giant outdoor screen, thrived. Drive-in theaters appealed to young parents who could pile their children into the car for a night out and teenagers who could escape the watchful eyes of adults for a few hours.

What were Americans watching at home? Many early television shows dealt with the social conditions and cultural values of the day, paying particular attention to family and consumerism. In *The Honeymooners*, the working-class Kramdens lived in a sparsely furnished apartment and often clashed, particularly when one of the get-rich-quick schemes devised by bus driver Ralph (played by comedian Jackie Gleason) started to unravel. His wife Alice always stood her ground, even when Ralph threatened her with one of the show's trademark lines: "One of these days, Alice … one of these days … POW, right in the kisser." By the end of each episode, the couple had reconciled, with Ralph often telling his wife, "Baby, you're the greatest."

I Love Lucy began in a small Manhattan apartment, but eventually Lucy Ricardo (played by Lucille Ball) and her Cuban husband Ricky (Ball's real-life husband Desi Arnaz) relocated to suburban Connecticut to raise their son. Lucy's farcical adventures trying to enter show business or best her husband always ended with her realizing that being a caring wife and mother was fulfilling enough. Situation comedies like *Father Knows Best* and *Leave It to Beaver* focused on the roles that each member of an ideal white suburban family played: Father worked hard and came home in time to resolve the minor crises of the day; mother kept a spotless home, volunteered, and supported her husband's career; and children learned to tell the truth, work hard, and obey their parents.

Sitcoms in the 1950s provided plenty of escapist fare. Nightly news broadcasts, however, brought glimpses of the wider world into American homes and played an increasing role in politics. Politicians quickly learned to use the new medium to their advantage. Republican vice presidential candidate Richard M. Nixon was the first politician to give a televised speech to defuse a political scandal. During the 1952 presidential election, the press revealed that Nixon had a secret fund financed by California businessmen. Hoping to stem the damage, Nixon appeared on television to refute charges that the money was for his personal use or that these businessmen were buying "secret favors" from him with their donations. Laying out the details of his personal finances, Nixon defiantly told viewers that without campaign donations only the rich could run for office. In the speech's most famous passage, Nixon mentioned one personal gift that he would not return: "A man down in Texas heard Pat [his wife] on the radio mention the fact

What insights do 1950s television shows offer into American culture?

View the **Closer Look** *Choices and Consequences: Does Father Know Best?*

that our two youngsters would like to have a dog" and surprised the family with the gift of a black-and-white cocker spaniel. "And our little girl Tricia, the six year old, named it 'Checkers.' And you know, the kids, like all kids, love the dog, and I just want to say this, right now, that regardless of what they say about it, we're gonna keep it."

After the speech, Nixon posed with his family and Checkers (**25.5**). The Checkers speech saved Nixon's place on the Republican ticket alongside Eisenhower. Like Nixon, John F. Kennedy also astutely used posed photographs, like this one with his attractive young family (**25.6**). By creating such images Kennedy hoped to distract attention from his inherited wealth and Catholicism, long considered an undesirable religious affiliation for a national politician.

On September 26, 1960, Kennedy and Nixon faced off in the first televised presidential election debate. Nearly 77 million Americans, or 60 percent of the adult population, watched this historic event. Nixon, still pale and underweight from a two-week stint in the hospital, squared off against a tan and fit Kennedy, who impressed viewers with his comfortable presence before the cameras. By contrast Nixon refused to wear make-up, looked as if he needed a shave, wore a poorly fitted shirt, and was visibly sweating throughout the exchange. Most Americans who watched the debate felt that Kennedy had won, while the majority who listened on the radio gave the edge to Nixon. Kennedy went on to narrowly win the election, revealing the power of images to sway political judgments.

Teen Culture and Rock-and-Roll

Teenagers came into their own in the 1950s. Their parents remained haunted by memories of Depression-era deprivation and the life-and-death struggle of World War II. By contrast in the 1950s, many middle-class teenagers grew up with an abundance of material possessions. Most teenagers agreed with their parents when it came to politics, sharing their concern about communist expansion and the growing Soviet nuclear threat. Many, however, adopted an ethos of pleasure-seeking that often put them at odds with their parents who emphasized thrift and self-discipline. Unlike their parents' generation teenagers were no longer expected to earn money to help support their families. Millions of young people experienced unprecedented leisure time and longer schooling, and were free to spend money earned from after-school jobs as they liked.

25.5 and 25.6
Two candidates, one family portrait
Throughout their political careers, Richard M. Nixon and John F. Kennedy used portraits of their family life to connect with voters. These images fit with the era's idealized image of the perfect American family, which included a supportive wife, two children, and at least one dog.

▶ **Watch** the **Video** *Kennedy-Nixon Debate*

How did politicians use television and photographs to shape their public image?

Teenagers flocked to buy record players and radios to play music marketed specifically to them. In 1958, the Coasters scored a number-one record with their song, "Yakety Yak," which depicts a teenager rebelling against household chores. In one refrain, the parent orders the teenager to "Take out the papers and the trash / Or you don't get no spendin' cash," to which the teenager replies "yakety yak," with the parent then retorting: "don't talk back."

"Teenagers are my life and triumph. I'd be nowhere without them."

ELVIS PRESLEY, whose stardom demonstrated the strength of teen culture in the 1950s

Teens' freedom to create their own social world filled with slang and fads that adults did not understand disturbed critics. By the end of the decade, sociologist Edgar Friedenberg noted that "the 'teenager' seems to have replaced the Communist as the appropriate target for public controversy and foreboding." In this cultural clash traditionalists lambasted horror comic books and teen films for encouraging teenagers to revolt against their parents and social norms. But rock-and-roll music and musicians provoked the most outrage.

Rock-and-roll burst onto the national scene when Bill Haley and his Comets recorded "Rock Around the Clock" in 1955, the first rock-and-roll tune. The following year Chuck Berry thundered "Roll over, Beethoven, and tell Tchaikovsky the news!" proclaiming rock-and-roll the music of choice for this teenage generation. It took Elvis Presley, however, to make rock-and-roll (which got its name from a rhythm and blues slang term for sexual intercourse) a phenomenon. Exposed to the raw sexuality and powerful rhythms of African American rhythm and blues music as a boy in Mississippi, Presley also sang gospel and country music in church. Melding the sounds and explosive delivery of these musical traditions with catchy pop lyrics, he developed his own eroticized dancing style. "If I could find a white man who had the black sound and the black feel, I could make a billion dollars," predicted record producer Sam Phillips, the owner of Sun Records, a small recording company in Memphis, Tennessee. Philips found his man when Presley walked into Sun Records to record a song as a gift for his mother.

Americans embraced competing visions over whether the growing popularity of rock-and-roll meant the triumph of consumer tastes or the downfall of American civilization. Nicknamed "Elvis the Pelvis" for his suggestive hip thrusts while dancing, partially captured in this photograph (25.7), Presley became a lightening rod for critics who denounced rock-and-roll from the pulpit, in the press, and even in congressional hearings. When teenager Ron Kovic's family watched Presley on TV's *Ed Sullivan Show*, his sister went "crazy in the living room jumping up and down," his mother sat "on the couch with her hands folded in her lap like she was praying" and his dad shouted from the other room that "watching Elvis Presley could lead to sin." In introducing Presley the affable Sullivan assured parents that the 22-year-old Presley was "a real decent, fine boy." To avoid controversy, however, Sullivan ordered camera crews to frame out Presley's legendary pelvic thrusts and gyrations, showing only his head and chest. It took the draft to tame Elvis. "Presley wiggled off to military service," one newspaper columnist wrote, "but comes marching home … shorn of his sideburns and behaving the way a sedate, serious-minded youngster should." The new "clean-cut" Presley kept his original fan base but had limited appeal to the teenage generation coming of age in 1960.

Ed Sullivan showcased a range of music, skits, and comedy acts to keep the whole family watching together during the hour-long show. Dick Clark, however, helped pioneer television programming exclusively for teenagers with his daily afternoon show *American Bandstand,* which featured Philadelphia high-school students dancing to the latest hits. The advent of pocketsize transistor radios meant that teenagers could listen to radio stations broadcasting the top 40 best-selling records or independent rhythm and blues stations in the privacy of their bedrooms, away from critical adult ears.

Hollywood also catered to teenage tastes with films like *The Wild One* (1953), which featured Marlon Brando as part of a rebellious motorcycle gang, and *Rebel Without a Cause* (1955). In the latter film James Dean and Natalie Wood played teenagers from upper-middle-class suburban homes; unsure how to handle their racing hormones, the two become defiant. Dean's character tries to prove his masculinity by drag racing, while Wood's character uses promiscuity to rebel against an overprotective father. This view of the suburbs as hotbeds of intergenerational conflict and alienated youth frightened adults but thrilled teenagers. Embracing the persona of an angry youth discontented with mainstream society, Dean (who died at age 24 in a car accident) became an icon of teenage rebellion in the 1950s.

How did larger economic and technological changes make a mass teen culture possible?

Read the Document *The Teenage Consumer (1959)*

identity, while their parents announced their new middle-class status by buying cars and suburban houses. Beats or beatniks, members of the bohemian communities of poets, novelists, and artists that flourished in New York's Greenwich Village and San Francisco's North Beach, offered an alternative vision. The Beats rejected home ownership, career, and marriage in favor of individual freedom and immediate pleasure (including drugs and casual sex).

The national spotlight briefly shined on City Lights Bookstore in San Francisco when it published the controversial poem *Howl* (1955) by then-struggling Beat poet Allen Ginsberg. "I saw the best minds of my generation destroyed by madness, starving hysterical naked, dragging themselves through the negro streets at dawn looking for an angry fix," began the opening stanza. The poem sent readers on a journey into the underground lives of the drug addicts, musicians, artists, radicals, and homosexuals, who lived on the margins of mainstream society. In the 1950s, most states had so-called antisodomy laws that criminalized same-sex intercourse. Ginsberg's open celebration of gay sex in *Howl* offended anti-obscenity crusaders in San Francisco. The police arrested the owner of the City Lights Bookstore for selling the poem, but a judge dismissed the charge, arguing that it was a socially significant artistic work.

In his novel *On the Road* (1955), the Beat writer Jack Kerouac celebrated the spiritual quest for a meaningful life away from the suffocating materialism and conformity of middle-class society. Guilty at times of over-romanticizing working-class life for its "authenticity" without appreciating the deadening effects of poverty, the Beats nonetheless laid the foundation for the youth protests of the sixties (see Chapter 27).

25.7 Elvis Presley Nicknamed "Elvis the Pelvis," Elvis Presley's suggestive dancing enraged parents but earned the singer millions of adoring teenage female fans.

Parental norms often prevailed. Teenagers in the 1950s grew up quickly. Students who dated a lot in high school tended to marry soon after graduation. Once married, they quickly started families, conforming to the standards set by their parents.

The Beats

Teens in the 1950s used their purchases—of music, clothes, fan magazines—to define their generational

What competing visions of youth rebellion did rock-and-roll and the Beat movement embody?

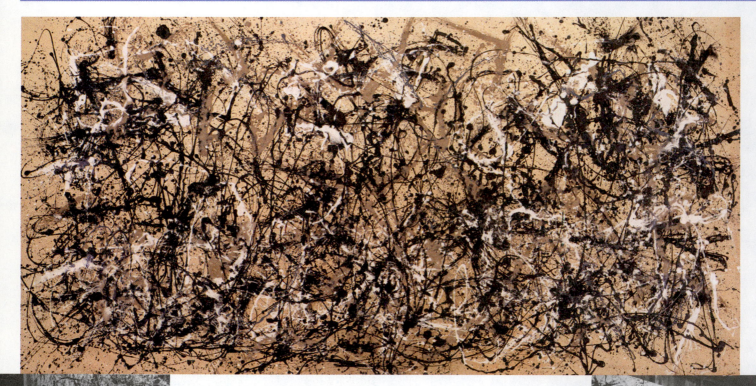

25.8 *Autumn Rhythm* 1950.
Hans Namuth photographed Jackson Pollock in action as he dripped and swirled paint to evoke the sensations of a fall day: light and dark, heavy and buoyant, graceful and chaotic. Pollock painted spontaneously, but also deliberately. "I can control the flow of paint: there is no accident," he stated.

Most Americans never read *Howl* or *On the Road*. They instead formed their impressions of the Beats from watching *The Many Loves of Dobie Gillis*, a TV series that showcased a beatnik best friend, who urged Dobie to reject his father's single-minded drive to make money and instead enjoy life to the fullest. This televised depiction of Beat culture helped interject new expressions, such as "dig it," "cool," and "man" that the Beats took from African American culture, into the vocabulary of white teenagers.

Beat poets and novelists were not the only artists rebelling against received traditions in the 1950s. American modern artists formulated a new mode of visual art called Abstract Expressionism that broke with the predominant painting styles of the previous generation. Before World War II leading artists included the Cubist painter Pablo Picasso, who reordered the physical world in his paintings, and American social realist painters, who captured the lives of ordinary people during the Depression. Politics informed much artistic work in the 1930s and 1940s. In the 1950s a restless generation of new artists chose instead to emphasize personal expression over politics. "The big moment came when it was decided to paint…. Just TO PAINT. The gesture on the canvas was a gesture of liberation, from Value—political, aesthetic, moral," wrote art critic Harold Rosenberg in 1952. Jackson Pollock dripped paint on the canvas to create paintings bursting with energy (**25.8**). German photographer Hans Namuth captured Pollock's rhythmic dance as he obscured painted figures with splats of paint. Mark Rothko painted fields of color to reflect feelings rather than objects, and refused to title or explain his paintings, so that viewers could interpret his work freely. Each created signature styles that epitomized the rebellious nature of Abstract Expression. Young artists idolized these painters for refusing to represent reality or use their art to send a message. More tradition-bound artists denounced their work as trivial. Like James Dean in films and Elvis Presley in music, the painters Pollock and Rothko embodied the rebellious streak of fifties youth culture.

How does Pollock's painting compare to social realist paintings in the 1930s (see Chapter 22)?

Freedom Now:
The Civil Rights Movement

The Civil Rights Movement entered a pivotal phase in the 1950s. Key Supreme Court rulings, new leadership, and innovative strategies emboldened thousands of black and white people to demand the end of racial segregation in the South. The National Association for the Advancement of Colored People (NAACP) successfully challenged the constitutionality of segregated public schools. Martin Luther King Jr. emerged as a major leader, alongside a generation of activist black and white college students who employed new nonviolent strategies to compel white Americans to confront the harsh realities of Jim Crow. Supreme Court decisions pressured the federal government to intervene on behalf of African Americans. Meanwhile television and news magazines transmitted shocking images of racial violence that made it impossible for the nation to ignore the demands of civil rights activists.

Separate and *Unequal*: Challenging Segregated Schools

Black and white southern children, as this photo of a street scene in a small Southern town suggests (**25.9**), grew up in separate worlds. They lived in different parts of town, went to segregated schools, drank from separate water fountains, ate in different restaurants, waited for buses in different waiting rooms, sat in separate sections of movie theatres, and often shopped in different stores. For many black children segregation meant daily humiliation and unanswered questions. "I guess if you are from a small Georgia town, as I am," one black college student recalled, "you can say that your first encounter with prejudice was the day you were born. ... My parents never got to see their infant twins alive because the only incubator in the hospital was on the 'white' side."

After World War II ethnic and racial minorities successfully challenged the legality of segregated schools. In 1947, the Supreme Court ruled that educating children of Mexican ancestry in separate California schools was illegal, because state law only authorized segregated schools for children of Asian decent. After this ruling, California repealed this discriminatory law. Ending legalized racial segregation nationwide came next.

In 1954, the Supreme Court overturned the 1896 *Plessy v. Ferguson* "separate but equal" ruling that had allowed the South to maintain

"Tastes the same to me, Mom."

LEO LILLARD, after secretly sampling water from "white" and "colored" fountains as a boy in Nashville

segregated schools from elementary school to graduate school. In *Plessy v. Ferguson* the Court had concluded that separate facilities (schools, waiting rooms, railroad cars) for whites and blacks were constitutional as long as they offered each race similar amenities. (See *Choices and Consequences,* Chapter 14.) In practice legalized segregation usually resulted in

25.9 A Southern Town
On their visit to town, these white and black children carefully avoided mixing, demonstrating how early children in the South learned to respect their region's racial customs.

Read the Document Brown v. Board of Education of Topeka Kansas (1954)

How did racial discrimination shape Southern children's lives?

25.10 Emmett Till and his mother

"If you have to get on your knees and bow when a white person goes past, do it willingly," Emmett's mother told her Northern-raised son before he left to visit relatives in Mississippi, instructions that the teenager tragically disregarded.

inferior accommodations and schools for black citizens. The Supreme Court ruled in **Brown v. Board of Education** (1954) that segregated schools indeed violated the equal protection clause of the Fourteenth Amendment.

The *Brown* case concerned seven-year-old Linda Brown, whose parents wanted to send her to an all-white school closer to their home. In mounting the case NAACP lawyer Thurgood Marshall (who later became the first African American appointed to the Supreme Court), and his team based their argument on more than the law. To convince the public and the Court that segregation was wrong, they needed to dramatize its effects. "To show damage and a violation of equal protection under the Fourteenth Amendment, you had to show that being segregated actually damaged children," psychologist Kenneth Clark asserted.

To demonstrate the irreversible effects of segregation on African American children, the NAACP cited Clark's controversial research. In a series of studies, Clark asked white and black children whether they liked a white or black doll best. Most children picked a white doll because it was "nice" and rejected the black doll as "bad." Clark next asked the children to identify the doll that was the most like them. The black children now had to pick the doll that many of them had just rejected as "bad." In the North black children often burst into tears rather than respond. In the South, however, reactions like the one from a young boy in Arkansas, who laughed, "pointed to the brown doll, and said, 'That's a nigger. I'm a nigger,'" convinced Clark that segregation taught African American children to accept their inferiority to whites.

Not everyone agreed with Clark's methodology, so the NAACP relied heavily on his findings in preliminary court challenges and then mentioned them only briefly in their Supreme Court filing. The wording of the *Brown* decision, however, revealed that the NAACP had guessed right in emphasizing the impact of segregation on the self-esteem of black children. In reaching its unanimous decision, the Court noted that "to separate [black children] from others of

similar age and qualifications solely because of their race generates a feeling of inferiority as to their status in the community that may affect their hearts and minds in a way unlikely ever to be undone."

Emmett Till

In 1955, Emmett Till was just another 14-year-old posing for the camera with his mother. Their portrait reveals a boy with a beaming smile and a mother's pride in her growing son (**25.10**). That summer Mamie Till-Bradley sent Emmett from his home in Chicago to visit relatives in Mississippi. To prepare her Northern-raised son for the racial customs of Southern society, she warned him to think of his safety when encountering Southern whites. One morning at a country store in Money, Mississippi, Emmett forgot his mother's warning. While playing with black teens on the porch of the store, Till bragged that he had a white girlfriend in Chicago. "Hey, there's a [white] girl in that store there," one of the boys retorted, "I bet you won't go in there and talk to her." Responding to the dare, Till walked into the store, bought candy, then grabbed the arm of Carol Byrant, who ran the store with her husband, and allegedly asked, "How about a date, baby?" Till's aghast cousin ran in and pulled him out of the store.

Three days later a car pulled up to his granduncle's house in the middle of the night. Two white men burst into the house and dragged Till out of bed. The husband of the young woman in the store, Roy Bryant, and her brother, J. W. Milam, threw a terrified Till into their truck and drove away. This was the last time his relatives saw him alive. The white men drove to an abandoned shed on a nearby plantation where they beat Till, then drove to the Tallahatchie River and forced him to strip before they shot him in the head and tossed his body into the river. With his mother's permission, *Jet* magazine and the *Chicago Defender*, stalwarts of the black press, published the grisly photos of the corpse. *Images as History: Inspiring a New Generation to Act* discusses how images of Emmett Till's murder transformed the Civil Rights Movement.

Why did the Supreme Court rule that segregated schools were unconstitutional?

View the Image *Kenneth Clark Testing Children's Choices of Dolls (1924)*

Images as History
INSPIRING A NEW GENERATION TO ACT

The photo of Emmett Till's broken body, printed in African American newspapers and magazines, became the wake-up call for young people destined to play major roles in the future Civil Rights Movement. The Emmett Till case gave the nation more than a clear image of the victim. It also provided a snapshot of the killers and the vigilante justice dealt out in many small towns across the Deep South. At first, some Southern officials and citizens denounced the murder. But when the Northern press castigated the entire South for the crime, Southerners fought back claiming that Till was alive and in hiding or that the NAACP had set up the murder to embarrass the South. Why are these images important for understanding the history of race relations and the Civil Rights Movement?

Deciding that "the world is going to have to look at this," Mamie Till-Bradley took her son's body back to Chicago where she insisted on an open casket funeral that thousands attended.

The black Northern press provoked outrage over the killing by pairing this gruesome image of Till's battered corpse with the photograph of him smiling with his mother (25.10).

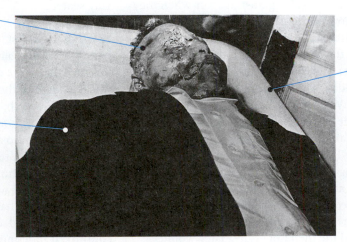

After seeing these photos future civil rights activist Julian Bond "felt vulnerable for the first time in my life—Till was a year younger—and [I] recall believing that this could easily happen to me—for no reason at all."

Emmett Till's corpse

The accused men's nonchalance in the courtroom and the show of support from the white observers sent a warning to the African American witnesses who testified against the pair, illustrating how communities like Money, Mississippi, at that time preserved the racial status quo.

Bringing their children into the courtroom demonstrated that the accused were upstanding family men and helped teach white youth about the importance of maintaining white supremacy.

For many of his neighbors, Roy Bryant's defense of his wife protected her honor and his reputation, and fulfilled his duty to help the white community keep the color bar intact.

Men on trial for Emmett Till's murder, sitting with their families.

View the **Closer Look** *Images as History: Inspiring a New Generation to Act*

How do these photos compare to postcards of lynchings (see Chapter 21)?

What made Emmett Till's murder different from previous racist killings of African Americans in the South was the courageous decision of his family to fight back. Ignoring the kidnappers' warnings to keep quiet (so Till would become yet another black boy who went mysteriously "missing"), Till's cousin called the sheriff and Till's mother the next day. The sheriff found Till's body and three days later arrested Roy Bryant and J. W. Milam. When Mamie Till-Bradley saw her son's tortured body, a sight that would have caused many mothers to fall apart, she instead vowed that "here's a job that I got to do now."

Till's granduncle, Moses Wright, had begged the white men to just whip him, while his wife offered them money to leave the boy alone. Now Moses Wright decided to testify against the pair when they went on trial for murder. The 64-year-old Wright later recalled that as he entered the courtroom, he could "feel the blood boil in hundreds of white people as they sat glaring." When the prosecutor asked him to identify Milam as one of the men who took Emmett, Wright stood up, pointed his finger, and said, "Thar he." His testimony emboldened other black sharecroppers to step forward and testify about hearing Till crying for his mother as he was beaten. Fearing for their lives, all of these sharecroppers left town after appearing in court.

At first it seemed they had risked everything for naught. The all-white male jury took less than an hour to find the men not guilty. They would have returned the verdict sooner, the jury foreman bragged, "If we hadn't stopped to drink pop." A second jury acquitted the men on the charge of kidnapping. Two months after their murder trial, Bryant and Milam sold their story to an Alabama journalist for $4,000 and admitted killing Till. Double jeopardy, a legal concept that prevents authorities from retrying someone for the same crime, protected the pair from prosecution after their confession. Nonetheless, the sight of ordinary black citizens standing up in court to accuse their white oppressors electrified a generation ready to strike back. Four months later, partly because of the Emmett Till case, the Montgomery Bus Boycott began.

Montgomery Bus Boycott, 1955

The *Brown* decision was a milestone in the fight for racial equality, but by the mid-1950s, civil rights activists were no longer content simply to fight for justice through the courts. Many resolved to use economic boycotts, picketing, and mass demonstrations to force white America to take note of the injustice and violence experienced daily by African Americans. Courageous men and women, ordinary people who took extraordinary risks, set this new direction in civil rights protest.

On December 1, 1955, Rosa Parks, a 43-year-old black seamstress, boarded a bus in downtown Montgomery, Alabama, and selected a seat. She was one of 40,000 blacks who paid a dime twice a day to the white driver, then stepped down and entered the bus through the rear door. When a white man demanded her seat, Parks had to decide whether to comply. *Choices and Consequences: Rosa Parks Makes History* explores her decision to stay seated.

As soon as English professor Jo Anne Robinson heard of the arrest, she mimeographed 35,000 handbills urging black citizens to stage a one-day bus boycott on the day of Parks' trial. Robinson was president of the Montgomery Women's Political Council, which had been planning a one-day bus boycott for months. Parks's arrest offered a perfect moment to act. Two of her students helped Robinson distribute the handbills to black schools, businesses, and churches. "Negroes have rights, too, for if Negroes did not ride the buses, they could not operate," the handbill read. When the day-long boycott succeeded, community leaders decided to continue it indefinitely.

The **Montgomery Bus Boycott (1955–1956)** was a year-long boycott that brought a new leader, Martin Luther King Jr., and a new strategy of nonviolent protest to the forefront of the Civil Rights Movement. The boycotters' initial demands were moderate: courteous treatment from bus drivers, first-come-first-served seating so no one would have to give up a seat, and hiring black bus drivers. The city administrators and bus company executives refused. The Montgomery Improvement Association (MIA) now prepared for a lengthy boycott. Mass meetings twice a week kept boycotters' spirits high and helped disseminate accurate information within a black community that had no radio station or newspaper. The MIA also set up an elaborate carpool system to transport black workers to their jobs and back home. Volunteers picked up passengers from one of 42 collection points throughout the city, which became the target of terrorist bombings. Images of black workers waiting peacefully for carpools contrasted with the burnt remains of bombed cars and provided good

Choices and Consequences

ROSA PARKS MAKES HISTORY

Unlike the signs above water fountains or posted in waiting rooms, there was no clear section marked "colored" on Montgomery city buses. Instead as more white passengers boarded a bus, black passengers had to vacate their seats for them. When three other black passengers heeded the white driver's request to move on the afternoon of December 1, 1955, Rosa Parks faced a set of choices over how to respond.

Choices

1 Move to the back of the bus.	2 Refuse to give up her seat.	3 Vacate her seat but express her outrage by participating in a planned one-day bus boycott.

Decision

Rosa Parks refused to give up her seat. When the driver threatened to call the police, Parks quietly replied, "You may do that." She was arrested.

Consequences

On the day of Parks's trial (she was found guilty and fined), the Montgomery Women's Political Council organized a one-day boycott that it had been planning for months and nearly all Montgomery's black citizens stayed off the buses. That evening the city's black male clergy met and formed the Montgomery Improvement Association (MIA), which voted to continue the boycott. The group chose 26-year old Martin Luther King Jr., the minister who headed the Baptist church that Rosa Parks attended, as their president. When the Supreme Court ruled that bus segregation was unconstitutional in 1956, the year-long boycott ended.

Continuing Controversies

Who was the real Rosa Parks?
The folklore is that Parks was simply a tired seamstress who impulsively decided to stay seated. This narrative leaves out key details. Parks was also secretary of the Montgomery chapter of the NAACP and had attended the left-leaning Highlander Folk School in Tennessee, where civil rights and labor leaders trained. She knew that the NAACP wanted to test the bus segregation law in the courts and had recently participated in a mass meeting protesting Emmett Till's murder. Boycott leaders played down Parks's activist past, worried that it would diminish her "everywoman" appeal and that moderates might view her as a radical agitator. Some activists later suggested that this simplified tale sent the wrong message about how to initiate social change. Rosa Parks's bravery mattered, they agreed, but so did careful preparation, organization-building, and ideological dedication.

What is the enduring legacy of Rosa Parks's decision?

footage for the national television networks that covered the boycott extensively. Television interviews with King, a 26-year-old Baptist minister who headed the MIA, turned him into a celebrity overnight and allowed him to appeal directly to moderates throughout the nation. To raise money and garner publicity for the boycott, King also toured the country giving speeches.

> ## "If Martin Luther King had never been born this movement would have taken place. I just happened to be there."
>
> MARTIN LUTHER KING JR., commenting on his role in the Montgomery Bus Boycott.

Instead of discouraging the protesters, white resistance convinced the MIA to broaden its demands to include the complete desegregation of the buses. The violence now threatened to spiral out of control. When King's house was bombed, a crowd of supporters arrived carrying knives and guns. "If you have weapons, take them home," King told them as news cameras rolled. Publicizing the new civil rights ethos of nonviolence, King declared, "'He who lives by the sword will perish by the sword.' … We must meet hate with love."

Over time white opposition fractured. Some whites had been openly sympathetic to the boycott from the beginning, even though their businesses and social life suffered as a result. Others had more pragmatic reasons for helping black workers reach their jobs. When the mayor chastised white women for chauffeuring their black maids to and from work, one defiant white woman wrote to the newspaper: "If the mayor wants to do my wash and wants to cook for me and clean up after my children let him come and do it."

After nearly a year the boycott was victorious. In November 1956, the Supreme Court ruled that segregated buses were unconstitutional. On December 21, 1956, Martin Luther King Jr. boarded the first integrated bus in Montgomery with the African American minister Ralph Abernathy and the white Reverend Glenn Smiley, both key leaders in the boycott. In their carefully choreographed ride, pictured here (**25.11**), all three followed the guidelines that the MIA had established for integrating

buses. An MIA pamphlet advised: "For the first few days try to get on the bus with a friend in whose non-violence you have confidence. You can uphold one another by a glance or a prayer." The MIA cautioned black riders not to respond to curses or shoves. When King entered the bus, the presence of newspaper reporters and cameramen protected him from violence. "We are glad to have you here this morning," the bus driver cordially greeted King as he climbed aboard. The ride was not so smooth for other Montgomery citizens. Over the next few weeks snipers fired into buses, and Abernathy's house was bombed.

Two months later King met with ministers from 11 other Southern states to form the **Southern Christian Leadership Conference (SCLC)**. Black churches, they decided, could help the Civil Rights Movement devise a new nonviolent strategy of direct action that challenged segregation and discrimination throughout the South. At first King saw nonviolence mainly as a way to gain sympathy and prevent authorities from using violence against demonstrators. He employed a bodyguard throughout the boycott and had applied for a permit to carry a gun (which the police refused). "King sees the inconsistency, but not enough. He believes and yet he does not believe … if he can *really* be won over to a faith in non-violence there is no end to what he can do," Smiley noted privately.

Over the next few years, King would develop that faith. His social justice fundamentalism evolved from his reading of Jesus's biblical "Sermon on the Mount" that urged Christians to create "a beloved community" by winning over enemies with love and humility rather than seeking to punish or defeat them. King was also influenced by activists like Reverend James Lawson who had traveled to India to study the Hinduism version of nonviolence pioneered by the Indian activist Mahatma Gandhi in the 1930s to win independence from Britain. Lawson was in India during the Montgomery Bus Boycott but returned to instruct members of the SCLC and university students as they broadened their attack on Jim Crow in the early 1960s.

The Little Rock Nine, 1957

The *Brown v. Board of Education* case launched a decades-long struggle to integrate public schools. Many white Southerners had grown up without ever questioning segregation. *Brown* forced them to either formulate a defense and rationale for segregation or consider changing generations-old

Why was the Montgomery Bus Boycott a turning point in the Civil Rights Movement?

▶ Watch the Video *Video Lecture: African American Women and the Struggle for Civil Rights*

habits. Throughout the South diehard segregationists dug in. "The Negro race, as a race, plainly is not equal to the white race, as a race," asserted James Jackson Kilpatrick, the editor of a Richmond newspaper. Segregationists also advanced a states' right argument, arguing that the federal government had no right to dictate racial policies to the South. Sympathetic to claims that it would be difficult to change ingrained habits overnight, the Supreme Court issued only a vague directive for school systems to desegregate "with all deliberate speed" in 1955. This ruling encouraged entrenched segregationists to try to delay integration indefinitely.

In a few Southern cities, moderate whites accepted the piecemeal dismantlement of Jim Crow. Little Rock, Arkansas, for instance, had desegregated its parks, buses, and libraries with little controversy. After the *Brown* decision, the school board made plans to integrate slowly by inviting nine black

teenagers to attend high school alongside 2,000 white students. Nicknamed the **Little Rock Nine**, the nine teenagers who integrated Central High School in Little Rock, Arkansas, in 1957 became the focus of a national crisis that required the intervention of federal troops to resolve.

Segregationists quickly organized statewide opposition to the planned integration of Central High School. Concern about states' rights and segregationists' claims that integration would lead to white and black students dancing together at school social functions won over some moderates. Two weeks before the school year started, the threats began. One night a rock shattered the living room window of Daisy Bates, secretary of the local NAACP chapter. The note tied around the rock read "Stone this time. Dynamite next."

Influenced by polls showing 85 percent of white Arkansans opposed school integration, Arkansas Governor Orval Faubus, who faced a difficult

25.11 First Ride on an Integrated Montgomery Bus, 1956 Martin Luther King Jr., seated on the left, rides with other activists on the first day that buses were integrated in Montgomery after a year-long bus boycott. Fearing vigilante attacks from angry whites, King urged all black bus riders to exude steely resolve and ride in pairs.

Watch the **Video** *Video Lecture: How did the Civil Rights Movement Change American Schools?*

What messages did this planned scene send to whites and blacks?

reelection campaign, declared he would not "force acceptance of change to which the people are so overwhelmingly opposed." In September 1957, he decided to ring Central High with state troops on the first day of school to stop the black students from entering the high school. Using state troops to defy a federal mandate fit well with the desire of moderate whites and die-hard segregationists to protect the sanctity of states' rights.

To protect the black teenagers, Daisy Bates asked parents to drop the students off at her house so they could go to school together. Elizabeth Eckford, whose family did not have a telephone, never received the message. Instead she took a bus to the school by herself and confronted the angry mob alone. At first she felt reassured when she saw the troops, whom she assumed were there to protect her. She quickly realized her error. When she tried to squeeze past a guard, "He raised his bayonet, and then the other guards moved in." As she stood there confused, the crowd started to chant "Lynch her! Lynch her!" Television cameras, tempering the crowd's enthusiasm for a lynching, likely saved Elizabeth's life. Also a godsend, Grace Lorch, a white woman, came out of the crowd to help Elizabeth flag down a city bus and escape.

Over the next few days, as the crowds in front of the high school grew, attacks against news photographers and cameramen became more common. The television footage coming out of Little Rock, reporter David Halberstam noted, "made it hard for people watching at home not to take sides" as they saw "orderly black children behaving with great dignity" being assaulted by a "vicious mob of poor whites." Outrage outside of the South over such images put pressure on President Eisenhower to act, as did the negative worldwide attention that the Little Rock incident garnered. "Our [Communist] enemies are gloating over this incident and using it everywhere to misrepresent our whole nation," Eisenhower warned the country.

Resistance to Supreme Court–mandated integration created more than a racial crisis. It also led to a showdown between the federal government and the state of Arkansas. Under pressure from the White House, Faubus withdrew state troops. It was the president's responsibility to enforce federal law, Eisenhower told the American people, announcing his decision to send federal troops to Little Rock to ensure that Arkansas obeyed the Supreme Court's ruling. With paratroopers from the 101st Airborne Division ringing the school, the Little Rock Nine walked up the front steps surrounded by armed guards.

This was the first time that the federal government had used troops to protect the civil rights of African Americans since Reconstruction. The troops, Melba Pattillo Beals recalled, meant a "declaration of war" in the hallways of Central High where white teenagers insulted, kicked, shoved, and ostracized the Little Rock Nine, who were each sent to different classrooms. Eight of the nine finished the year. (Minnijean Brown was expelled for dumping chili on a white student's head after he insulted her in the cafeteria.) The following year Faubus defied the order to integrate by keeping the schools closed all year. In 1959, Central High reopened with one black student in attendance; in 1960, there were five; then eight in 1961. The small numbers of black students in Central High signified the long, slow road to complete the process of school integration.

The Sit-Ins

A 1950 survey of segregation statutes across the nation (see *Envisioning Evidence: A National Snapshot of Racial Discrimination*) revealed a staggering array of state laws that prevented races from mixing in their daily lives. By the end of the 1950s, with the nonviolent Civil Rights Movement in full bloom, the movement's attention shifted from schools to segregated lunch counters. In 1958, James Lawson began conducting SCLC workshops to prepare college students in Nashville for a sit-in campaign to desegregate the city's lunch counters. At these meetings students studied Christian pacifist principles, Gandhi's theories of nonviolence, and the nineteenth-century American philosopher Henry David Thoreau's ideas on civil disobedience. During **sit-ins** protesters occupied seats at whites-only lunch counters and remained there even after they were refused service, sometimes for hours. The sit-ins employed the tactic of civil disobedience, breaking the law in a peaceful way to call attention to an unjust law, and replicated a tactic used successfully by the CIO in the 1930s when workers had occupied factories during strikes (see Chapter 22). Sit-ins, like sit-down strikes, disrupted business, making it impossible for white businessmen to ignore the protesters' demands. Highly visible sit-ins in downtown Nashville department stores were also guaranteed to attract press attention.

Lawson warned the students that their anger over Jim Crow was not enough to sustain them through the challenges ahead. Instead they needed to embrace nonviolence as the governing principle of their lives. They were fighting back, he assured them, but in a way that broke the cycle of violence.

Why did Eisenhower send troops to integrate Central High School in Little Rock?

View the Image *Opposition to Integration*

Envisioning Evidence

A NATIONAL SNAPSHOT OF RACIAL DISCRIMINATION

Calling civil rights a "national problem," the 1947 Presidential Commission on Civil Rights urged the federal government to act immediately to stop racial violence and eliminate discriminatory laws. This 1950 survey of state laws (which did not include local ordinances or regional customs) provided a broad overview of how segregation functioned in 33 states. Prohibition against mixed marriage was the most common law; more unusual ones included Oklahoma's requirement for separate phone booths and North Carolina's prohibition against white and black students sharing textbooks. Examples of other segregation laws are listed below.

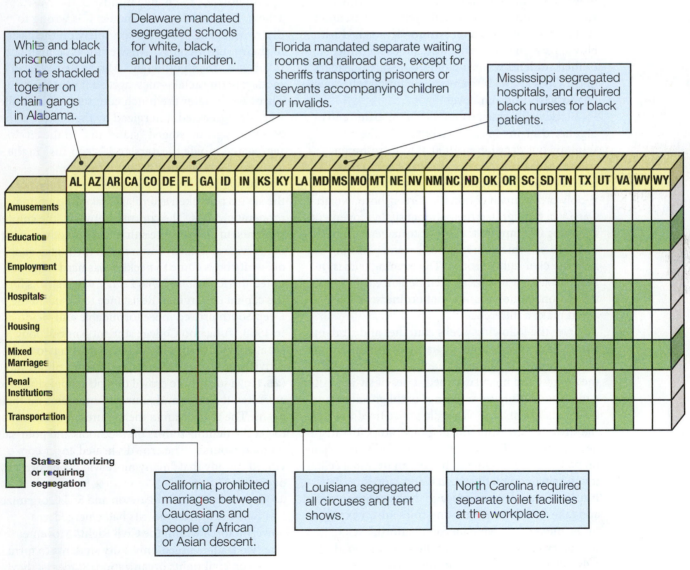

White and black prisoners could not be shackled together on chain gangs in Alabama.

Delaware mandated segregated schools for white, black, and Indian children.

Florida mandated separate waiting rooms and railroad cars, except for sheriffs transporting prisoners or servants accompanying children or invalids.

Mississippi segregated hospitals, and required black nurses for black patients.

California prohibited marriages between Caucasians and people of African or Asian descent.

Louisiana segregated all circuses and tent shows.

North Carolina required separate toilet facilities at the workplace.

States authorizing or requiring segregation

Source: *Pauli Murray,* States' Laws on Race and Color *(1951).*

View the **Closer Look** *Envisioning Evidence: A National Snapshot of Racial Discrimination*

What do these statutes suggest about daily life for African Americans in the South?

> ## "Do show yourself friendly on the counter at all times. Do sit straight and always face the counter. Don't strike back, or curse if attacked. Don't laugh out. Don't hold conversations. Don't block entrances.… Remember the teachings of Jesus, Gandhi, Thoreau, and Martin Luther King, Jr."
>
> Instructions to sit-in demonstrators in Nashville, Tennessee, 1960

Armed resistance was not only morally wrong, Lawson argued, it was also futile to believe that blacks could take on the police and army with guns. Students learned how to ignore the taunts and blows that whites would heap on them during a sit-in, to go limp when pulled from the seats, and to curl into a protective fetal position if attacked with blows. Lawson's Nashville workshops identified and trained students who would become major leaders in the Civil Rights Movement, including John Lewis, Diane Nash, and Jim Bevel.

Black civil rights protesters had intermittently organized sit-ins since 1942, but it was the spontaneous decision in 1960 of four freshmen from the all-black North Carolina Agricultural and Technical College to request service at a Woolworth's lunch counter in Greensboro, North Carolina, that ignited the national sit-in movement. By acting on impulse these four teenagers ignored SCLC rules, which emphasized careful planning before any civil rights protest. The evening television news broadcast images of their defiance throughout the nation, demonstrating that ordinary people could make a difference.

Over the following weeks churches and students worked together to unleash waves of sit-ins throughout the South. In Nashville Lawson's group unfurled the longest and most sustained series of sit-ins. After a month of letting roving gangs of thugs punch and kick the students, the Nashville police tried to end the sit-ins by arresting the demonstrators for "disorderly conduct." The students responded with a "jail-no bail" strategy. "Only so many can fit into a cell; if you remain here, there can be no more arrests! Imprisonment is an expense to the state; it must feed and take care of you. Bails and fines are an expense to the movement, which it can ill afford," SCLC organizer Bayard Rustin told the students. With the jails full and the sit-ins continuing, the SCLC increased the pressure with a successful boycott of the downtown stores.

The standoff came to a head when the home of a prominent black lawyer (who had represented the students in court) was bombed. Marching to city hall the students demonstrated the power of nonviolence to change minds. Diane Nash asked: "Mayor West, do you feel it is wrong to discriminate against a person solely on the basis of their race or color?" Answering as "a man had to answer, not a politician," Mayor Ben West, a moderate on racial issues, agreed it was wrong. Three weeks later the lunch counters in Nashville were desegregated. Energized by their success the Nashville, group staged "stand-ins" in the city's segregated movie theaters and "sleep-ins" in the lobbies of whites-only hotels.

Throughout the upper South photographs of the sit-ins provoked a similar awakening among moderate whites. The contrast between "the colored students, in coats, white shirts, ties" quietly requesting service at a lunch counter and the ragtag gangs of "white boys come to heckle" was hard to ignore, noted the *Richmond News Leader* when sit-ins hit the capital of Virginia. Resistance to sit-ins in the Deep South proved more formidable and vicious. In 1963, Tougaloo College student Anne Moody sat at a Woolworth's lunch counter with two white activists in Jackson, Mississippi. As this photo shows (**25.12**), a lunchtime crowd of high school students assaulted the three and poured condiments on their heads. The older man in the picture urged the mob to get the demonstrators off the stools and pour salt on their wounds. The crowd's heated anger convinced Moody that "many more will die before it is over with."

By spring 1960, Jim Lawson and SCLC organizer Ella Baker saw that students had emerged as a powerful force within the Civil Rights Movement. The two leaders urged university students to form their own civil rights organization. Students, they realized, were willing to take more risks than were many adult activists. Employing the lyrics of a

What principles lay at the heart of nonviolent direct action?

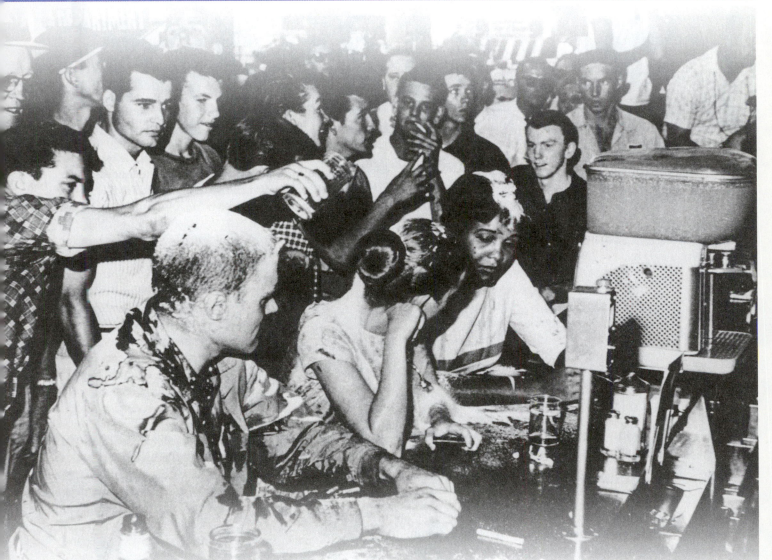

25.12 Mississippi Sit-In, 1963 Assaults on sit-in protesters grew more vicious as the demonstrations moved into the Deep South.

movement song that urged protesters to "keep your eyes on the prize," Baker told the students that their goal needed to be "bigger than a hamburger." The students responded by forming their own civil rights organization, the **Student Nonviolent Coordinating Committee**, or **SNCC** (pronounced Snick) in 1960. SNCC founder Diane Nash noted that "the media and history seem to record it as Martin Luther King's movement, but young people should realize that it was people just like them, their age, that formulated goals and strategies, and actually developed the movement."

In the struggles ahead SNCC and SCLC often forged a crucial partnership between black churches and university students. Idealistic and enthusiastic college students, white and black, eagerly put themselves in the frontlines during civil rights demonstrations. Black churches provided the experienced organizers, meeting spaces, and funds to organize successful protests.

The Civil Rights Movement brought together many critical features of the 1950s. While print media remained important, film footage shown on evening television news broadcasts of confrontations between racist whites and nonviolent protesters forced the rest of the nation to confront the realities of Jim Crow and racial violence in the South. Thanks to television what happened in the South no longer remained news only in the South. The rise of a distinctly teenage culture within the baby boom generation also helped to create a strong generational bond among those young adults who joined the movement. Finally the ideological overtones of the Cold War that pitted democratic capitalism against communism helped civil rights protesters focus attention on the inherent contradictions between America's self-proclaimed goal of spreading democracy throughout the world and visible racial discrimination at home.

Read the Document SNCC Statement of Purpose (1960)

What different strengths did students and churches bring to the Civil Rights Movement?

1945–1946

Five thousand labor strikes sweep the country
Creates public backlash against unions

Baby Boom begins
Generation sets cultural trends from cradle to grave

1947

Taft-Hartley Act
Puts restrictions on labor unions

First Levittown built
Mass migration to suburbs begins

1950

Pollock paints *Autumn Rhythm*.
Abstract Expressionism and Beat writing transform the arts

1952

Nixon's "Checkers" speech
First use of television to diffuse a political crisis

CHAPTER REVIEW

Review Questions

1. How successful were efforts to undo the New Deal and curtail the Fair Deal from 1945 to 1960?

2. What debates arose over suburbanization and teen culture?

3. How did the media in the 1950s affect intergenerational conflicts? What role did the media play during the Civil Rights Movement?

4. What key social conditions and events triggered the modern Civil Rights Movement?

5. What roles did ordinary citizens play in the fight against Jim Crow? How important were Civil Rights Movement leaders?

Key Terms

Baby boom generation The 76.4 million Americans born between 1946 and 1964.   **750**

Taft-Hartley Act (1947) Law that abolished the closed shop, banned so-called sympathy boycotts, and required that all union officers sign affidavits certifying that they were not members of the Communist Party.   **753**

Fair Deal Truman's proposals for national health care, public housing, education, and public works projects.   **754**

Military-industrial complex Eisenhower's term for the close ties between the defense industry and the Pentagon that might unduly influence government policy.   **755**

Levittowns Planned suburban communities where developers standardized every part of the construction process.   **758**

***Brown v. Board of Education* (1954)** Supreme Court decision that segregated schools violated the equal protection clause of the Fourteenth Amendment.   **766**

Montgomery Bus Boycott (1955–1956) A year-long bus boycott that brought a new leader, Martin Luther King Jr.,
and a new strategy of nonviolent protest to the forefront of the Civil Rights Movement.   **768**

Southern Christian Leadership Conference (SCLC) Civil rights organization founded by Martin Luther King Jr. that used black churches to devise a new nonviolent strategy of direct action.   **770**

Little Rock Nine Nine black teenagers who integrated Central High School in Little Rock, Arkansas, in 1957 and became the focus of a national crisis that required the intervention of federal troops to resolve.   **771**

Sit-ins Nonviolent demonstrations where civil rights protesters employed the tactic of civil disobedience to occupy seats at whites-only lunch counters.   **772**

Student Nonviolent Coordinating Committee (SNCC) Student-run civil rights organization founded in 1960.   **775**

1954

Brown v. Board of Education
Supreme Court rules segregation of public schools unconstitutional

1955

Emmett Till murdered
Images of corpse spark civil rights protest

Montgomery Bus Boycott
Martin Luther King Jr. emerges as civil rights leader

1957

Elvis Presley appears on *The Ed Sullivan Show*
Culture clash over rock-and-roll

Little Rock Nine integrate high school in Arkansas
Showdown between federal and state governments over *Brown* ruling

1960

Sit-ins across the South
College students become a major force in the Civil Rights Movement

Nixon-Kennedy debate
Television shapes public opinion of presidential candidates

MyHistoryLab Connections

Visit www.myhistorylab.com for a customized Study Plan that will help you build your knowledge of *In a Land of Plenty.*

Questions for Analysis

1. What image does this song conjure of suburban life?

(●—**Hear** the **Audio** *Little Boxes, p. 758*

2. What do sit-coms reveal about 1950s popular culture?

●—**View** the **Closer Look** *Choices and Consequences: Does Father Know Best?, p. 760*

3. What key roles did women play in the Civil Rights Movement?

◉—**Watch** the **Video** *Video Lecture: African American Women and the Struggle for Civil Rights, p. 770*

4. What challenges did the Little Rock Nine face as high school students?

●—**View** the **Image** *Opposition to Integration, p. 772*

5. How did SNCC define nonviolence?

📖—**Read** the **Document** *SNCC Statement of Purpose (1960), p. 775*

Other Resources from This Chapter

📖—**Read** the **Document**
- *Dwight D. Eisenhower, Farewell Address (1961), p. 755*
- *The Teenage Consumer (1959), p. 762*
- *Brown v. Board of Education of Topeka Kansas (1954), p. 765*
- *Jo Ann Gibson Robinson, Bus Boycott, p. 768*

●—**View** the **Closer Look**
- *Competing Visions: Suburbs—American Dream or Nightmare?, p. 759*
- *Images as History: Inspiring a New Generation to Act, p. 767*
- *Envisioning Evidence: A National Snapshot of Racial Discrimination, p. 773*

●—**View** the **Image** *Kenneth Clark Testing Children's Choices of Dolls (1924), p. 766*

◉—**Watch** the **Video**
- *Kennedy-Nixon Debate, p. 761*
- *Video Lecture: How did the Civil Rights Movement Change American Schools?, p. 771*

A Nation Divided
The Vietnam War, 1945–1975

Vietnam was America's longest war to date, a conflict that divided the nation to an extent not seen since the Civil War. For 30 years the United States invested money and then eventually soldiers in the struggle to prevent the establishment of communism in the small Southeast Asian country of Vietnam. From 1945 to 1964, the United States fought a proxy war by funneling supplies and aid to others willing to fight the Vietnamese Communists. In 1965, the conflict became an American war when President Lyndon Johnson sent U.S. ground forces to fight in Southeast Asia.

By 1967, the antiwar movement had taken to the streets to protest America's involvement in Vietnam. On October 21, 1967, antiwar protesters held a peace rally before the Lincoln Memorial in Washington, D.C., after which thirty thousand demonstrators linked arms and marched to the Pentagon, the headquarters of the Department of Defense. When they arrived, soldiers advanced toward the crowd with their guns drawn. An 18-year-old actor from New York with a flair for the dramatic stepped forward holding a bouquet of pink carnations and carefully placed one into each soldier's rifle. *Washington Star* news photographer Bernie Boston captured this poetic gesture in "Flower Power," an iconic photo of the civil strife that the war triggered. Competing interpretations of this image revealed key divisions of the era. For peace advocates the photograph illustrated the stark contrast between government-sponsored violence in Vietnam and American citizens' demand for peace. Critics of the peace movement, who accused activists of destroying respect for law and order, viewed the gesture as a ploy to distract the soldiers moments before demonstrators stormed the steps of the Pentagon and armed guards beat them back.

The Vietnam War originated as an anticolonial struggle to win independence from France, and then evolved into a civil war between North and South Vietnam. At first the crucial debates about Vietnam took place behind closed doors in the White House. Over the course of the country's 30-year engagement in Vietnam, despite being presented continuously with other viewpoints, five American presidents from Truman to Nixon chose escalation when faced with the option of pulling back or pressing forward. Viewing the Vietnamese conflict through the prism of the global Cold War, each president feared that losing all of Vietnam to communism would set off a chain reaction of communist revolutions throughout Southeast Asia.

World War II had united the nation. Vietnam fractured it. The guerilla war under way in South Vietnam, in which Communist soldiers intermingled with the civilian population to avoid detection, made it particularly difficult for Americans to separate enemy combatants from civilians. When the American military tried using overwhelming force to flush Communist guerillas out of South Vietnamese villages, the civilian death toll turned many Americans against the war. The conflict ultimately tore apart both Vietnam and America before the United States finally withdrew in 1973. The war ended with a Communist victory in 1975.

"We will not be defeated. We will not grow tired. We will not withdraw."
President LYNDON B. JOHNSON in 1965

The Long Road to War

From 1945 to 1965, America gradually shifted its Cold War focus from Europe to Asia. The United States first supported French efforts to recover Vietnam as a colony, and then sustained an independent anti-communist South Vietnam with financial aid. At home some American policymakers envisioned the war as part of the worldwide struggle between democracy and communism. In Vietnam, however, Americans confronted a country torn apart by a civil war that reflected its long-standing religious and political divisions. No American president sought a war in Vietnam, and key advisors offered competing assessments of America's chances for victory. Yet at critical moments when the intractable political and military situation called for a response, each president chose to bolster the American commitment rather than turn back.

The Escalating Importance of Vietnam

America first became involved in Vietnam during World War II, when Japan took over the French colony of Indochina (present-day Laos, Cambodia, and Vietnam). In 1945, U.S. intelligence operatives worked with Ho Chi Minh, the leader of an underground Vietnamese communist resistance movement that launched guerilla attacks against the Japanese occupiers. When the war ended Ho Chi Minh and his rebel force formed a provisional government in Hanoi and declared independence from France. Eager to reestablish its position as a world power after the humiliating occupation by Germany in World War II, France sent in troops to crush the Vietnamese independence movement.

In search of international support for Vietnamese independence, the Western-educated Ho Chi Minh turned to the United States. Ho Chi Minh had previously tried to interest the United States in Vietnamese independence by submitting a petition to the American delegation at the Paris Peace Conference in 1919 after World War I that called for democratic reforms in French Indochina. The American delegation ignored his request, mindful that his proposal would anger the French, whose support President Woodrow Wilson needed to create the League of Nations (see Chapter 20). After the rebuff in Paris, Ho Chi Minh became a communist, attracted by communism's revolutionary promise to free colonized peoples. "It was patriotism, not communism, that inspired me," he later claimed. In 1941, after nearly three decades abroad working as a Soviet spy, Ho

Chi Minh returned to Vietnam to help organize communist resistance to the Japanese occupation. Despite this revolutionary background he hoped that the United States would support Vietnamese independence when Japan withdrew in 1945. His communist credentials, however, tainted him in the eyes of President Harry S. Truman, who remained unmoved by Ho Chi Minh's truthful assurances that the Soviet Union did not control or finance him.

In the 1940s, the Americans saw Ho Chi Minh as a communist puppet doing Moscow's bidding. His Vietnamese followers, however, viewed him as a charismatic leader ignited with a patriotic desire to free his nation from French colonial control. As one disciple recalled, the 55-year-old "Uncle Ho" spoke with an "ardent and idealistic nationalism" that encouraged many Vietnamese to join the Vietminh, the term used initially to describe all Vietnamese communists, and after 1954 solely for North Vietnamese communists. This photograph (26.1) of Ho Chi Minh sitting with children reinforced his reputation in Vietnam as a beloved, wise elder. The image tapped into prevailing Confucian ideals, including filial piety (respect toward living and dead relatives), loyalty, and humane treatment of others. Ho Chi Minh broadened his appeal by eschewing personal luxuries and living simply in a small cottage. By the time American troops arrived in the late 1960s, an ailing Ho Chi Minh played almost no official role in the conflict. He nonetheless remained the face of Vietnamese communism for supporters and opponents throughout the war.

Cold War geopolitics consistently influenced how Americans reacted to the Vietnamese Communist revolt. As the emerging Cold War with the

Who was Ho Chi Minh to his supporters and foes?   ▣ Read the Document *Declaration of Independence for Vietnam (1945)*

Soviet Union in the 1940s made containing communism in Europe a national obsession, Vietnam took on new political significance. The United States needed help from a vigorous and cooperative France to defend Western Europe from Soviet incursion. To rebuild the French economy and establish goodwill, the United States gave France arms and funds beginning in 1947 (see Chapter 24). The French government used some of this aid to finance the war in Vietnam. The United States also agreed to support French efforts to regain control of its Vietnamese colony.

In 1950, the strategic importance of Vietnam for the United States changed dramatically. The fall of China to communism in 1949 and the outbreak of the Korean War in 1950 when Communist-led North Korea invaded the anti-communist South Korea created fears that all of Asia might fall to communism. The "who lost China" debate hurt Truman politically, and no subsequent president wanted to be the one blamed for Vietnam falling to communism. Containing communism in both Europe and Asia became cornerstones of American foreign policy from this point on, requiring the United States to maintain military bases throughout Western Europe and along a string of Pacific islands from Japan to the Philippines.

As the Cold War spread to Asia, key presidential advisors saw the hand of the Soviet Union behind every communist victory. By the early 1950s, National Security Council Report 68, or NSC-68, a document that described a global communist monolith, set the tone for U.S. foreign policy (see Chapter 24). Any more territory "under the domination of the Kremlin," the National Security Council warned, would make the Soviet Union invincible in a future military conflict. The threat would deepen if the Soviets gained control of resource-rich Southeast Asia, whose rubber, rice, tin, and oil were important economically to the United States. These resources were even more vital for Japan, now a key American ally in the struggle against communism, and the United States wanted to ensure Japanese access to these materials by preventing them from falling into unfriendly communist hands.

Hardliners in the Truman and Eisenhower administrations embraced the **domino theory**, the fear that a communist Vietnam would open the door to a complete communist takeover of Southeast Asia, with communists repeating Japan's conquest of the region in World War II. Announcing the domino theory President Dwight D. Eisenhower explained in a 1954 press conference: "You have a row of dominos set up, you knock over the first one, and what will happen to the last one is the certainty that it will go over very quickly. So you could have a beginning of a disintegration that would have the most profound influences." Events in the 1950s gave credence to these fears. Josef Stalin's success in pressuring China and North Korea to accept an armistice to end the Korean War strengthened the American conviction that the Soviet Union could start or stop

26.1 Ho Chi Minh Poses with Children, 1954
Ho Chi Minh's followers revered him as a wise elder who loved his nation.

What political and strategic importance did Vietnam assume in U.S. foreign policy by the mid-1950s?

Taking Over from the French

To hold the line in Vietnam, the American government was willing to foot the bill but wanted the French to do the actual fighting. The United States upheld its end of the bargain. By 1954, the United States was paying for 80 percent of the war's costs, money used to both purchase arms and fund humanitarian projects including free health clinics, food for refugees, and seeds for farmers. Increasingly, however, the United States doubted, in the words of Truman's outgoing secretary of state Dean Acheson, the "French will to carry on." As Acheson anticipated, the incoming Eisenhower administration soon faced a crisis in Vietnam. In 1954, the Vietminh defeated the French at Dien Bien Phu, in the northwest corner of the country, prompting the French to seek an international agreement with the Vietminh. The resulting **Geneva Accords (1954)** called for a temporary partition of Vietnam along the seventeenth parallel, with the Vietminh in the north and the French in the south, and a general election in two years to reunify the country under one government. Refusing to sign the Geneva Accords, the Eisenhower administration instead resolved to use the two-year period to ease the French out of South Vietnam and create a new government capable of raising and training a strong military to resist communist aggression.

To head the new South Vietnamese government, the United States selected Ngo Dinh Diem, a wealthy Catholic who had served as minister of the interior in the French colonial administration before resigning, when the French refused to enact reforms he proposed. A staunch nationalist, Diem moved to the United States, where he became well known to American policymakers. Neither Diem nor the United States intended to let the scheduled election take place, certain that Ho Chi Minh's authoritarian government would use force and fraud to ensure victory in the North and perhaps in the South as well. Instead the United States tried to destabilize Ho Chi Minh's fledgling Communist government by creating political turmoil in North Vietnam. Central Intelligence Agency (CIA) operatives destroyed government printing presses, contaminated the oil used in bus engines, sabotaged railway tracks, and planted rumors of Chinese troops raping North Vietnamese women.

Eisenhower supported the creation of an anti-communist South Vietnam to stem the tide of communism in Southeast Asia. As an additional defense

26.2 *How About the Other Buttons?* This 1953 illustration shows Soviet leader Josef Stalin pressing his finger on a button labeled "Korea" to end the Korean War. This cartoon suggested that Stalin could stop other conflicts that he had initiated, including the war in Indochina.

communist insurgencies around the globe. This political cartoon (**26.2**) by Marcus Edwin showed Stalin pressing the stop button for Korea, and suggested that he could also stop the conflict in Indochina (Vietnam) if he wished. Indeed, Stalin had encouraged the Chinese leader Mao Zedong to take charge of promoting communist revolution throughout Asia. The immediate influx of Communist Chinese advisors to train Vietminh officers, plus mountains of Chinese-manufactured vehicles, arms, and ammunition, seemingly confirmed that the Vietminh were part of an international communist conspiracy masterminded in Moscow.

American policymakers failed to appreciate, however, that a shared belief in communism did not override the nationalistic ambitions of the Soviet Union, China, or Vietnam. Ho Chi Minh accepted help from the Chinese, but remembering China's ancient colonization of Vietnam; he remained suspicious of their ulterior motives and had no intention of turning Vietnam over to them. "It is better to sniff French dung for a while than eat China's all our life," warned Ho Chi Minh. In an American worldview that saw every communist revolution as part of the Soviet Union's master plan, the specific grievances or goals of the Vietminh became irrelevant.

What key choices did Eisenhower make in 1954 that increased U.S. involvement in Vietnam?

Read the **Document** *Dwight D. Eisenhower, Dien Bien Phu (1954)*

against communism, the United States formed the **Southeast Asian Treaty Organization (SEATO)** in 1954. Through SEATO the United States, Britain, France, Australia, New Zealand, Thailand, Pakistan and the Philippines (granted independence by the United States in 1946) pledged to "meet common danger" in Southeast Asia together. A separate agreement identified Vietnam, Laos, and Cambodia as areas that would endanger the "peace and security" of SEATO members, if any of these three nations came under attack. Unlike the North Atlantic Treaty Organization (NATO), which guaranteed the mutual defense of member nations in Europe, the SEATO treaty left each nation's exact commitment vague. Secretary of State John Foster Dulles wanted it that way, reluctant to overextend American military responsibilities around the world by guaranteeing the borders of SEATO members. Even if this loosely worded pact failed to deter communist aggression, Dulles reasoned, it would provide a justification for direct American involvement in Vietnam to protect SEATO members, if the United States decided to escalate its involvement in the future. An important development in America's ever-increasing involvement in Vietnam, SEATO illustrated how completely the United States linked the civil war in Vietnam to the global crusade against communism.

With the United States poised to embark on a major campaign to create an independent South Vietnam, dissenting voices within the government urged the president to pull back. Secretary of Defense Charles E. Wilson warned that he could "see nothing but grief in store for us if we remained." The Joint Chiefs of Staff complained it would be impossible to build a capable South Vietnamese army without a "reasonably strong, stable civil government in control." This "chicken and egg" argument over which needed to come first, a strong South Vietnamese government or a strong military, divided American policymakers for the next 15 years.

With Diem the United States got neither. A short, stocky man who always dressed in white, Diem's stiff and privileged appearance contrasted poorly with the plain dress and manners of Ho Chi Minh. The Eisenhower administration recognized Diem's shortcomings, but Secretary of State Dulles accepted the American ambassador's conclusion "that there is no one to take his place who would serve U.S. interests better." The United States quickly realized that Diem intended to build a dictatorial regime in South Vietnam.

Diem modeled his rule on nineteenth-century Vietnamese emperors, issuing decrees and refusing to abide criticism. "I know what is best for my people," he declared in one interview. The secret police, headed by Diem's brother, Ngo Dinh Nhu, arrested, tortured, and executed thousands of South Vietnamese accused of opposing his rule.

Most Vietminh had relocated to North Vietnam when the country split into two, but remnants of the communist guerilla force still existed in the south. They found ample discontent with Diem among peasants, students, Buddhists, and even South Vietnamese soldiers. To destabilize the Diem regime, the Communists unleashed a wave of assassinations targeting wealthy landlords and rural officials who worked for the regime. Diem tried to cut off guerilla fighters from their supply base. He moved peasants off their ancestral lands and into "strategic hamlets" protected by moats and walls and imprisoned thousands of civilians suspected of aiding the rebels. Enraged over the forced removals, the peasants were like a "mound of straw ready to be ignited," claimed one Vietnamese Communist.

The U.S. government and press revealed none of Diem's internal difficulties to the American people. When Diem visited the United States in 1957, the American press praised him as the "tough little miracle man" who had brought stability to South Vietnam. "We can take pride in our support," *Newsweek* trumpeted.

In the mid-1950s, Ho Chi Minh offered southern Communists little support. He was instead preoccupied with subduing the widespread protests that greeted his forced land redistribution in North Vietnam, a campaign that sent armed posses into the countryside to confiscate land. These "land reforms" left thousands of property owners dead, destroyed communities, and created famine. By 1960, however, the North Vietnamese government was sending soldiers and supplies to southern Communists, unleashing a terror campaign to pave the way for a Communist takeover of South Vietnam. In 1960, the southern Communists formed the National Liberation Front (NLF) to unite the factions in South Vietnamese society opposed to the Diem regime into a fighting coalition. Diem derogatorily called South Vietnamese Communists Vietcong, slang meaning "Vietnamese Commies." The name stuck. From this point on Americans called all Communists from South Vietnam "Vietcong" and Communists from North Vietnam "Vietminh."

Why did the civil war in Vietnam reignite in the late 1950s and early 1960s?

Debates within the Kennedy Administration

John F. Kennedy became president in 1961 having proclaimed Vietnam the "cornerstone of the free world in Southeast Asia." Kennedy understood the negative political consequences of "losing" a nation to communism. As a congressman he had joined the chorus criticizing Truman when China succumbed to communism. In 1961, Kennedy suffered two setbacks of his own in the global war against communism with the botched Cuban Bay of Pigs invasion and his inability to stop the Soviets from constructing the Berlin Wall (see Chapter 24). His leadership during the Cuban Missile Crisis in 1962, however, redeemed his reputation as a Cold War warrior. Kennedy did not intend to let the conflict in Vietnam bring his administration down.

Faced with a worsening political and military situation in Vietnam, Kennedy received conflicting recommendations from his advisors. One group envisioned escalating the American commitment by sending in combat troops. Another wanted to seek a diplomatic resolution to the conflict. Faced with these divided opinions, Kennedy chose a middle path. Instead of infantry troops he sent more financial aid and increased the number of American military "advisors" in South Vietnam from one thousand to sixteen thousand. Officially these advisors helped train the South Vietnamese Army. In actuality many "advisors" were Green Berets, the army's special-force troops who organized South Vietnamese attacks on Vietcong supply lines, flew planes when South Vietnamese pilots were unavailable, and picked up casualties in helicopters after skirmishes. When word of these activities leaked out, Kennedy publicly denied that Americans were participating in active combat operations in Vietnam.

"Supporting the Diem regime while applying pressure for reform appears to be the only practicable alternative at this time," the Joint Chiefs convinced Kennedy, cautioning that "any reversal of U.S. policy could have disastrous effects" throughout Southeast Asia. As South Vietnamese anger against his rule intensified, Diem privately voiced his own mounting frustration with the growing American presence in South Vietnam. "All these soldiers," he fumed, referring to the Green Berets and military advisors. "I never asked them to come here." To rid South Vietnam of Americans, Diem and his police chief brother Nhu decided to seek a negotiated settlement with North Vietnam in 1963. Upset with Diem's overture to North Vietnam,

the turning point for the Kennedy administration came in June, when a Buddhist monk set himself on fire in a busy street in Saigon, the capital of South Vietnam.

The Catholic Diem had long discriminated against Buddhists. Thousands of North Vietnamese Catholics fled to the south when the Communists took over in 1954, and Diem rewarded them with land and governmental positions. In May 1963, Nhu refused to let the Buddhists fly a multicolored flag honoring Buddha on his birthday. Widespread street protests ensued, which Nhu suppressed with soldiers who used water hoses, tear gas, and on one occasion bullets, killing a woman and eight children. On June 10, 1963, a Buddhist monk invited Associated Press photographer Malcolm Browne to witness "something important" the next morning. Browne arrived at the designated street crossing and watched monks take a canister of gasoline out of the white car shown in this picture (**26.3**) and place a brown mat in the middle of the street. Moments later a Buddhist monk, Thich Quang Duc, sat down on the mat in the lotus position. After another monk poured gasoline over him, Duc struck a match. Flames instantaneously engulfed his body. "His eyes were closed, but his features were twisted in apparent pain," Browne recalled. As Browne snapped this memorable photo, a monk shouted into a microphone in Vietnamese and English: "A Buddhist priest burns himself to death. A Buddhist priest becomes a martyr." Monks (seen in the background) lined the streets to prevent anyone from trying to save Duc. Immediately proclaimed a Buddhist saint, Duc's ashes were distributed to pagodas, towering Buddhist temples, throughout South Vietnam.

Duc carefully staged his suicide to gain maximum exposure for the Buddhists' political protest, using the Western press to help rally opposition to Diem within South Vietnam and the United States. The burning monk image shocked but also bewildered Americans. The American government and press had continually praised Diem as a valiant Cold War ally, but this photo suggested strong opposition to his rule at home. Students, Buddhist priests, and soldiers in South Vietnam responded to the suicide as a call to action. Street protests erupted, the military began planning a coup, and six other monks set themselves on fire in front of Western journalists. With a framed copy of Browne's burning monk image on his desk, Kennedy secretly agreed to support a military coup to overthrow the Diem regime.

What conflicting recommendations did Kennedy receive from his advisors about Vietnam?

26.3 Burning Monk
Thich Quang Duc wanted the Western press to photograph his 1963 suicide to publicize the Buddhist protest against the corrupt Diem regime.

> "I must say that during the monk episode, I had no impulse to try to go in and save him. I knew for one thing that he intended it this way."
>
> Photographer MALCOLM BROWNE, on photographing Thich Quang Duc's self-immolation in 1963

The Kennedy Assassination

The military coup supported by President Kennedy led to the murder of Diem and Nhu, but Americans had little time to reflect on these events. Three weeks later, on November 22, 1963, Lee Harvey Oswald shot and killed President Kennedy in Dallas, Texas, as Kennedy waved to onlookers from an open convertible with his wife by his side. In the midst of his presidential reelection bid, Kennedy was visiting Dallas to shore up his fading popularity among Texans angered by his support for the Civil Rights Movement (see Chapter 27). This was the first trip that Jackie Kennedy had taken with her husband since the death of their two-day-old son Patrick three months before. Kennedy decided to ride in an open-air convertible, rejecting the suggestion from his Secret Service guards that he sit within a bulletproof clear glass bubble for the ride past the crowds. An amateur movie by Abraham Zapruder, a Russian immigrant and Kennedy supporter, gave the nation its most enduring images of this killing, film stills that provoked countless controversies over who killed the president. In its investigation of the assassination, the Warren Commission cited the Zapruder film as evidence that Oswald acted alone, claiming that the film footage showed bullets entering the president's body from

What insights does the story behind this 1963 photo offer into the Vietnam War?

only one direction. Counterclaims that the assassination was the result of a wider conspiracy involving other gunmen, the mafia, Cuban dictator Fidel Castro, and the CIA continue to this day.

Vice President Lyndon Baines Johnson (LBJ) was riding two cars behind Kennedy in the Dallas motorcade. When Kennedy died within hours of the shooting, Johnson, who was next in line to assume the presidency, insisted on taking the oath of office before Judge Sarah Hughes with Jackie Kennedy on one side and his wife on the other before the presidential airplane Air Force One left Dallas. The presence of the slain president's widow would, Johnson felt, immediately legitimatize the transfer of power in the eyes of the American people. Already on board the plane, which was carrying her husband's body back to Washington, D.C., Jackie Kennedy complied with Johnson's request, but had no chance to change her clothes. In this portrait (**26.4**) of Johnson's swearing in, photographer Cecil Stoughton carefully framed out Jackie Kennedy's skirt, which was stained with her husband's blood. Her pale and drawn expression nonetheless reflected the day's ordeal.

A wealthy Massachusetts-born Catholic, Kennedy had selected Johnson, a powerful Texan politician, as his vice presidential running mate to help broaden his appeal in the South. Johnson grew up poor and worked as a teacher before entering national politics as an avid supporter of the New Deal in 1937. Johnson relied heavily on his superior political instincts and outgoing personality to rise to prominence. In the Senate, he became the most powerful majority leader in history. A larger-than-life figure, his brashness contrasted sharply with the slain president's debonair manner. Johnson's most legendary gaff came in 1965, when he lifted his shirt during a press conference to show reporters his 12-inch scar from recent gallbladder surgery. Johnson wanted to reassure the nation about his recovery, but critics lampooned the act as crude and undignified.

The Gulf of Tonkin

Lyndon Baines Johnson inherited a rapidly deteriorating situation in Vietnam after the Diem assassination. Like his predecessors he faced the choice of pulling back or escalating the American commitment, which at this point consisted of sixteen thousand military advisors and Green Berets and substantial financial aid to South Vietnam. After the Diem assassination, South Vietnam slipped into perpetual political instability as a succession of rulers failed to gain the support of the people. The shifting geopolitical situation also prompted a reappraisal of the American assumption that the Soviet Union was controlling the movements of communists throughout the world. The previous American conception of a global communist conspiracy became harder to maintain in the face of the open split between the Soviet Union and China in 1964. The Sino-Soviet alliance fell apart, when the Soviets suggested that the two countries scale back their support of worldwide Communist insurgencies to improve relations with the United States. Mao refused.

Once again elected officials and policymakers differed behind closed doors on the best course of action. National Security Advisor McGeorge Bundy told Johnson that "the right course is to continue to strengthen our struggle against the Communist terror (which is exactly what this is)." Senator Richard Russell, a close confidant of the president, disagreed with those who claimed that "we'll lose everything in Southeast Asia if we lose Vietnam." Johnson himself feared that

26.4 Jackie Kennedy
On November 22, 1963, the day President John F. Kennedy was assassinated in Dallas, Texas, the First Lady's personal tragedy became enveloped in political symbolism. Here she stands by as the new president, Lyndon B. Johnson, takes the oath of office to visibly assure the nation that she supported the smooth transition of power.

How did images both provoke and quell controversy surrounding the Kennedy assassination?

Read the **Document** *George Ball's Dissenting Opinion on Vietnam (1965)*

withdrawal would mark him as a weak leader, emboldening conservative challenges to the civil rights laws and expanded social welfare programs for the poor that he wanted to enact. "I was determined to keep the war from shattering that dream," Johnson later admitted, by which time the war had indeed consumed the financial resources and political goodwill that the president needed to fully realize this dream (see Chapter 27).

Events off the coast of North Vietnam soon gave Johnson an excuse to act boldly. On August 2, 1964, North Vietnamese torpedo boats attacked an American destroyer, the USS *Maddox*, in the Gulf of Tonkin. The *Maddox* easily repelled the confirmed attack. Two days later its crew and a second destroyer, the USS *Turner Joy*, both reported coming under attack from North Vietnamese torpedoes. After failing to locate any North Vietnamese boats, U.S. Navy pilot James Stockdale landed on the *Maddox* where officers met him "all with sheepish grins on their faces." Citing improperly working radar, overeager sonar operators, and no visual sightings of the torpedo boats, the ships' joint commander now doubted that a second attack had taken place. Accepting initial reports of a second attack as conclusive, Secretary of Defense Robert McNamara told Johnson that "we cannot sit still as a nation and let them attack us on the high seas and get away with it." A television reporter asked Secretary of State Dean Rusk why North Vietnam would attack an American ship. "I can't come up with a rational explanation for it," Rusk answered. Behind closed doors the president admitted to knowing better, acknowledging in a private conversation that "there have been some covert operations in that area that we have been carrying on—blowing up some bridges … roads and so forth. So I imagine they wanted to put a stop to it."

Besides ordering reprisal bombing against North Vietnam, Johnson used the Gulf of Tonkin incident to win congressional approval for further military action in Vietnam. In August of 1964, rallying behind the president, Congress approved the **Gulf of Tonkin Resolution** with only two dissenting votes in the Senate. The resolution gave Johnson permission "to take all necessary measures to repel any armed attack against the forces of the United States and to prevent further aggression" in Vietnam.

"No one ever won a battle sitting on his ass."
General EARLE WHEELER,
supporting the troop buildup in Vietnam

On March 8, 1965, the first American Marines landed at Da Nang along the northern coast of South Vietnam, where young women put leis around their necks during an official ceremony. In the years that followed, troops received a distinctly less warm welcome. As the American Air Force began a major bombing campaign against North Vietnam called Rolling Thunder, General William Westmoreland requested a dramatic escalation in American ground forces. "You must take the fight to the enemy," General Earle Wheeler, the Joint Chiefs of Staff chairman, agreed.

Choices and Consequences: Making Vietnam America's War (page 788) explores how Johnson decided to intensify America's involvement in the war. By choosing escalation Johnson sealed his legacy as the American president who made winning the war a priority for the United States. In 1966, the political cartoonist David Levine reimagined the 1965 scene of Johnson lifting his shirt to expose his gallbladder incision. In Levine's rendition (**26.5**), the mark now assumed the shape of Vietnam, the conflict destined to scar Johnson's presidency and the nation. Johnson's willingness to expose the minute details of his health to the public contrasted sharply with the ethos of misinformation and secrecy (suggested by the Pinocchio-like nose of the caricature) he embraced as commander-in-chief.

26.5 *Johnson's Scar*
In 1966 the political cartoonist David Levine transformed President Lyndon Johnson's scar from gallbladder surgery into the shape of Vietnam, portraying the conflict as an ugly mark on Johnson's administration.

Read the Document *Johnson's Defense of the U.S. Presence in Vietnam (1965)*

Why was the 1964 Gulf of Tonkin incident a turning point in the Vietnam War?

Choices and Consequences

MAKING VIETNAM AMERICA'S WAR

In early 1965, Johnson initiated a regular bombing campaign against North Vietnam and sent 82,000 ground troops to South Vietnam. The theater commander General William Westmoreland soon requested 150,000 more. In deciding how to respond to Westmoreland's request, the president's advisors gave Johnson the following choices in the summer of 1965.

Choices

1 Avoid a protracted war with little chance for a military or political victory over the Communists and seek a negotiated settlement in Vietnam.

2 Continue at the present level of military aid to South Vietnam and push for political reforms there to create a more democratic anti-Communist government.

3 Send the requested troops, expand the bombing campaign, and work for political reforms in South Vietnam.

Decision

Johnson considered a negotiated settlement as tantamount to losing Vietnam to communism, an outcome he viewed as a threat to both Southeast Asia and his presidency. Certain that South Vietnam would lose the war without additional U.S. aid, he publicly agreed to send fifty thousand troops immediately. He privately guaranteed Westmoreland an additional fifty thousand and promised to send more as needed. He also approved heavy bombing of Vietcong strongholds in South Vietnam and tried to institute political reforms in South Vietnam to erode support for the Vietcong.

Consequences

The United States was no longer simply aiding South Vietnam in its struggle against communism, but now took the lead in fighting the Vietcong and the North Vietnamese. By 1967, there were nearly 500,000 American troops in Vietnam. During the war the United States dropped more bombs there than it had in World War II.

Johnson's Dilemma. He is shown here with Defense Secretary, Robert McNamara.

Continuing Controversies

Should the United States have fought a major war in Vietnam?

Detractors claim that Johnson committed the United States to an unwinnable war by trying to use the military to solve a political problem in South Vietnam. He underestimated the will of the Vietcong and exaggerated the importance of South Vietnam to containing communism in the rest of Southeast Asia. He failed to build strong domestic support for a long war, leading to unrest at home over the draft and rising casualties. Johnson's supporters argue that he honored a commitment to South Vietnam made by his predecessors. This reassured American allies worldwide that they could count on the United States. Retreat would only have invited further Communist aggression in Southeast Asia and Europe. Losing Vietnam would have weakened Johnson politically, putting his controversial domestic reform and civil rights legislative agenda in jeopardy.

Why was Johnson's decision to escalate U.S. troop levels in 1965 important?

Fighting in Vietnam

David Halberstam, reporting for *The New York Times* in 1962, summed up the military dilemma in Vietnam perfectly: "It is often impossible to separate the cruel and dedicated foe you want to kill from the simple and illiterate peasant you want to woo." America and North Vietnam embraced competing strategic visions in fighting the war. While the American military preferred fighting against uniformed soldiers on a clearly defined battlefield, the Communists embraced guerilla warfare, where troops blended into the civilian population or stayed hidden in underground tunnels. The American military tried to defeat Vietnamese guerillas by bombing enemy bases and destroying their village refuges. These tactics created another set of competing visions about the war: the soldiers' view of an unending conflict versus the image of imminent victory that the government championed at home.

The Bombing Campaign

The American military relied heavily on bombing to defeat the Vietcong and North Vietnamese. The American bombing campaign was the largest air war in world history, with American planes dropping nearly five million tons of bombs in eight years. The Americans hoped to pressure North Vietnam into ending the war. The North Vietnamese instead learned to live with bombs. The sighting of American planes over the North Vietnamese capital city of Hanoi sent inhabitants scurrying into bombproof underground shelters. The government built thirty thousand miles of tunnels, which moved the nation's transportation and communication infrastructure underground. The sustained bombing campaign bred anti-American feelings among the civilian population that made it easier for the North Vietnamese government to mobilize the country to "foil the war of aggression of the U.S. imperialists."

Navy Captain James Stockdale led the first American air strike against North Vietnamese oil tanks in the wake of the Gulf of Tonkin incident. A year later during another air raid, he was shot down over a small coastal village in North Vietnam where angry villagers beat him and broke his knee. Stockdale spent the next seven and a half years in a prisoner of war (POW) camp. His jailers brutally tortured him when he taught fellow POWs a wall-tapping code so they could communicate with one another during their years in solitary confinement.

American planes also targeted the **Ho Chi Minh Trail**, a 600-mile North Vietnamese supply route that ran along the western border of Vietnam through the mountainous rain forest of neighboring Laos and Cambodia. Nearly five thousand Communist soldiers and workers completed the arduous three-month journey each month, bringing troops, munitions, and food to the Vietcong. North Vietnamese propaganda glorified the difficult journey with images that emphasized the toughness and determination of its people. This photo (**26.6**) shows a North Vietnamese camera crew filming teenage volunteers from the north as they push bicycles, which the North Vietnamese called "steel horses," through the woods to carry rice and guns to Communist troops in the south. Improvements turned the dirt paths into an open road by the 1970s. Surface-to-air missiles and antiaircraft guns helped protect trucks from bombing.

26.6 Hardships along the Ho Chi Minh Trail
North Vietnamese propaganda relentlessly publicized the arduous journey along the Ho Chi Minh Trail to highlight how Communist ingenuity had stymied the world's greatest military power. Here, a Communist movie crew films teenage volunteers transporting bags of rice and guns strapped to their bicycle handlebars in 1970.

What messages did North Vietnamese propaganda send?

Americans also extensively bombed South Vietnamese "free fire zones," villages that supposedly contained only enemy combatants. The American air campaign included spraying defoliants, usually Agent Orange, that stripped trees of their leaves to expose Vietcong hideouts and killed the crops that might feed enemy troops. "Only you can prevent forests," American pilots quipped, a satirical

"I wanted to be a hero."

Vietnam veteran RON KOVIC, explaining why he joined the Marines

reworking of a popular environmental slogan "only you can prevent forest fires." Defoliants ultimately destroyed half of Vietnam's forests and caused lasting health problems for both American pilots and the Vietnamese that included cancers and birth defects. Responding to negative publicity, the military stopped using defoliants in 1971. American pilots also dropped napalm, a jellylike gasoline that ignited on impact, to destroy South Vietnamese villages hiding enemy troops. Napalm severely burns the body, contributing to the misery of civilians subject to bombing attacks.

Reports of mounting civilian suffering energized the U.S. peace movement, a loose coalition of antiwar activists that included pacifists, students, professors, clergy, hippies (young people who rejected middle-class values and adopted a bohemian lifestyle), civil rights activists, and middle-class liberals. In making his decision to go to war, Johnson had focused on placating his hawkish critics without considering the political fallout of antagonizing the left. By 1967, however, belatedly realizing the price he was paying for waging the war, the president noted, "The major threat we have [politically] is from the doves."

On the Ground

The initial wave of American troops sent to Vietnam consisted mostly of army volunteers. Raised on tales of heroism during World

War II, Phil Caputo viewed joining the Marines as a way to escape suburbia and serve his country. "I saw myself charging up some distant beachhead, like John Wayne in *Sands of Iwo Jima*," noted Caputo, recalling a popular 1949 film that romanticized the battle responsible for the iconic World War II photo of six men raising the flag over Mount Suribachi (see *Images as History*, Chapter 23).

Combat, however, quickly shattered the idealism of men like Caputo. In 1965, *Life* photojournalist Larry Burrows spent a month with helicopter crews, documenting their heroism and the harrowing combat. In this photo (**26.7**) gunner James Farley fires on enemy troops below as the pilot lands to rescue a downed American helicopter crew. Subsequent photos captured the anguish on Farley's face when he realized that the rescued pilot had died.

The drafted men sent to Vietnam in later years had fewer illusions than the initial volunteers. Conscripts were often working-class men who did not qualify for draft deferments, which only college-bound and married men enjoyed. Volunteers and conscripts served one-year tours in Vietnam, and as the time to return home neared, they often became more averse to taking risks in combat. Some soldiers even used their helmets as calendars, openly marking off the days left until their tour of duty ended.

In World War II American soldiers had fought against a clearly distinguishable enemy in the Pacific island jungles. Vietcong forces, however, infiltrated

26.7 American Gunner Rescues Downed Comrades 1965
Life photographer Larry Burrows captured the harrowing nature of combat in a photo that shows a U.S. soldier clearing the ground of enemy fire as his helicopter lands to aid a downed American helicopter crew.

What motivated American men to volunteer to fight in Vietnam?

View the **Closer Look** *Competing Visions: Popular Music and the Vietnam War*

the civilian population. They wore civilian clothes, stored arms in the walls of huts, and sent spies to work on American military bases. Civilians gave the Vietcong crucial support, by choice or out of fear that the Vietcong would torture or murder them. On search-and-destroy missions, American soldiers tried to draw the enemy out of hiding to kill them and destroy their supply base with ground forces and air attacks. To locate the enemy American soldiers marched in darkness through the steamy jungle and tried to stay alert while sweat poured down their faces and saw-edged grass cut into their skin. They walked gingerly, on the lookout for enemy ambushes, land mines, and leaf-covered punji stake traps (holes in the ground lined with sharpened spears that would impale a soldier who fell into one).

Search-and-destroy missions reduced villages that were suspected of aiding Vietcong to mounds of rubble. American troops blew up or contaminated wells, burned straw huts, and salted the ground so no crops would grow. Even in the middle of search-and-destroy missions, however, American soldiers remained capable of compassion. It was "the paradoxical kindness-and-cruelty that made Vietnam such a peculiar war," Phil Caputo remembered. On one search-and-destroy mission, for instance, men in his unit tried to treat and comfort a baby with skin ulcers. A few yards away, other soldiers threatened to kill an old woman for preparing metal stakes that the Vietcong placed in fields to prevent helicopters from landing.

To combat American air superiority, the Vietcong moved many of their command posts, dormitories, and supply depots underground. This drawing (**26.8**) illustrates an elaborate Vietcong tunnel complex. Village huts camouflaged some entrances. Punji stake traps are pictured on one side of the tunnel entrance, and snipers hiding in a hole protect the other side. The Vietcong also laid traps for American "tunnel rats" who entered the complex in search of enemy troops. A wrong turn down the false tunnel could mean overturning baskets of scorpions and poisonous snakes or falling into a punji stake

trap. The twisted tunnel design stymied American attempts to fill the tunnels with water, while poison gas escaped through the airshafts. Heavy bombing demolished many tunnel complexes, but at the high cost of also destroying homes and forests.

American soldiers fought a war of attrition, trying to kill as many Vietcong as possible while also destroying their resources and sapping their morale. When the enemy could no longer replace its fighters in the field, the reasoning went, the Vietcong would surrender. In previous wars, winning meant taking territory away from the enemy. In Vietnam, the United States measured victory by accumulating a high body count of enemy dead. The Communists had the same goal, hoping to inflict so many American casualties that the United States would abandon the war.

Tallying enemy dead accurately proved impossible, however. Soldiers encountered genuine difficulties determining how many Vietcong they had killed. The aftermath of battle often littered the jungle with body parts and trails of blood rather than intact countable bodies. The military also

26.8 Drawing of Vietcong Hideout Intricate tunnel complexes concealed Vietcong guerilla forces beneath villages.

unintentionally created incentives for soldiers to lie. "You guys want a day off, we got to be getting more kills," one commander told his men. In compiling their body counts, troops made little effort to separate friend from foe. The credo, "If it's dead and it's Vietnamese, it's Vietcong," lumped enemy soldiers with innocent civilians. Eventually the inaccuracy of body counts became common knowledge. Gary Trudeau mocked the preoccupation with body counts in this Doonesbury comic strip (**26.9**). His rendition of an American captain using the day's

had killed more enemy soldiers than the Communists could replace in the field. To boost morale at home, Westmoreland publicly assured the nation that "we have reached an important point where the end begins to come into view." Johnson was also upbeat. "The enemy is not beaten," he told the nation before Christmas, "but he knows that he has met his master in the field."

A Vietnamese offensive in 1968 exposed the hollowness of these claims. On January 30, 1968, during the Vietnamese New Year holiday known as Tet,

26.9 Doonesbury Lampoons Body Counts
Cartoonist Gary B. Trudeau underscored the meaninglessness of the official body count figure. Many Americans were becoming skeptical of the government's claim that victory was imminent.

date as his official body count echoed an uncomfortable truth about the value of these officially circulated figures.

The Tet Offensive

In 1967, Americans' support for the war began to flounder. Nearly nineteen thousand American soldiers had died so far, and each month draft boards inducted another thirty thousand into the military. Johnson's call for new taxes to meet rising war expenses further dismayed Americans. Some leading policymakers also changed their minds. Secretary of Defense Robert McNamara underwent the greatest shift in views. He went from strenuously advocating war (some critics called it "McNamara's war") to conceding that "Ho Chi Minh is a tough old S.O.B. And he won't quit no matter how much bombing we do." Rather than making his breach with the president over Vietnam public, however, McNamara quietly left the administration.

In the same year General Westmoreland assured Johnson that the war of attrition had reached a crossover point, meaning that American soldiers

North Vietnamese and Vietcong forces launched the **Tet Offensive**, a massive, coordinated assault against more than 100 cities and towns in South Vietnam. The map of Vietnam (**26.10**) depicts the wide-ranging attacks. "Uncle Ho was already quite old," and the entire army and population were exerted to do "their best to liberate the South before his passing" a North Vietnamese officer recalled. By demonstrating their determination to fight forever, the North Vietnamese wanted to convince Johnson that the cost of an American victory was too high. The Communists also expected their attack on previously calm cities to spark a revolution within South Vietnam.

Before the Tet Offensive the Communists had lured nearly fifty thousand American troops away from the cities by laying siege to a remote Marine garrison in Khe Sanh and attacking a few isolated towns. The weakened American presence left the urban centers vulnerable to enemy attack. A shocked American public watched on television as 19 Vietcong commandos entered the courtyard of the American Embassy complex in Saigon and battled guards there for six hours. It took heavy fighting and more than a month before American troops regained control of South

Vietnamese towns and cities. In the end the Communists paid a heavy price for forsaking the jungles and tunnels that provided such effective cover, suffering forty thousand casualties and military defeat. Nearly twelve thousand civilians died during the battle, along with 3,500 American and South Vietnamese soldiers.

Yet rather than celebrating this victory over the Communists, Americans' support for the war plunged. The daily televised images of the month's fierce fighting undercut the rosy predictions of imminent victory issued by the White House. At a time when 60 percent of Americans got their news from television, Vietnam became the first war in which Americans viewed the fighting in the comfort of their living rooms on a nightly basis. Televised news reports suggested that no matter who won the battle the fighting would go on. These newscasts stoked the shift in public sentiment already well under way before Tet. *Images as History: The Power of the Press in Vietnam* (page 794) considers how viewers' political leanings influenced their interpretation of photographs from the battlefront. The revered CBS-TV news anchor Walter Cronkite spoke for millions when he declared the war a stalemate. "We have been too often disappointed by the optimism of the American leaders, both in Vietnam and Washington, to have faith any longer in the silver linings they find in the darkest clouds," Cronkite told his listeners on February 27, 1968. He urged the government to seek a negotiated peace.

Cronkite's assessment mirrored reports from the new secretary of defense Clark Clifford. As the joint chiefs pressed the president for more troops, "I couldn't get hold of a plan to win the war" [from the military], Clifford later complained. "When I asked how many more men it would take, would 206,000 more men do the job, no one could be certain." Responding to these rising doubts, Johnson made a surprise announcement in a televised address to the nation on March 31, 1968. "I want to speak to you of peace in Vietnam," Johnson told listeners. He would not seek reelection, he said. Instead of campaigning he would halt most bombing of North Vietnam and devote the rest of his time in office to peace negotiations.

26.10 Map of Vietnam
From the French defeat at Dien Bien Phu in 1954 to the final evacuation of U.S. personnel in 1975, the United States tried to defeat Communist forces in Vietnam.

View the **Map** *Interactive Map: The Vietnam War*

Why did the 1968 Tet Offensive have such tremendous political fallout?

Images as History
THE POWER OF THE PRESS IN VIETNAM

Photographers typically convey a point of view through their photos. However, the differing interpretations surrounding some of the most famous photographs from the Vietnam War suggest that each photo took on a life of its own as Americans disregarded the photographer's original reason for taking the photo and imposed a different meaning on the image that reflected their own political views. Rather than creating new ideas or values, these images became iconic visual statements about the war because they reinforced strongly held beliefs within the population. In examining the text and photos in this box, consider what kind of power the press had to mold public opinion about the war.

In the midst of the 1968 Tet Offensive, Associated Press photographer Eddie Adams saw South Vietnamese police apprehend a Vietcong suspect in the streets of Saigon. Adams snapped his prize-winning photo just as South Vietnamese General Nguyen Ngoc Loan aimed his pistol at the man's head and pulled the trigger.

"He killed many of my men and many of your people," Loan told Adams. *The New York Times* caption echoed Loan's justification for his act. "GUERILLA DIES: Brig. Gen. Nguyen Ngoc Loan, national police chief, executes man identified as a Vietcong terrorist in Saigon. Man wore civilian dress and had a pistol."

Instead of justifiable retribution many Americans saw an execution. Prisoners of war have the right to a trial under international law, critics argued.

This striking image of one man's death became a symbol of the failed U.S. effort to establish the rule of law in South Vietnam, prompting fears that American soldiers were also killing prisoners of war.

Adams regretted taking a photo that forever tarnished Loan's reputation, whom he felt had simply acted impetuously in the heat of combat. "Pictures do not always tell the full story, and this is one case where that is true," Adams contended.

Supporters of Loan noted that the Vietcong ruthlessly executed thousands of South Vietnamese officials and police during the Tet Offensive.

Why did this image become the defining one of the Tet Offensive?

View the **Closer Look** *Images as History: The Power of the Press in Vietnam*

In 1966, *Life* photographer Larry Burrows went into the field with a group of marines trying to stop North Vietnamese infiltration through the demilitarized zone along the seventeenth parallel, a supposedly combat-free strip of land that separated North and South Vietnam.

He snapped this image of a wounded black soldier reaching out to a white buddy sprawled on the ground. *Life* published the photo twice, once right after Burrows took it and again in 1971 to eulogize Burrows after he died a helicopter crash in Laos.

In their letters to *Life*, many readers said that Burrows's portrait illustrated how the shared burden of combat inspired men to transcend the "great racial problems" of American society. Burrows's photo gave some viewers hope that whether "purple, polka-dotted or streaked," Americans could also learn to live together as brothers at home.

In his captioning Burrows emphasized soldiers' suffering in the midst of combat, simply noting, "At a first-aid center, during Operation Prairie, a wounded GI reaches out towards a stricken comrade."

The interracial compassion captured by Burrows's photo told only one side of the story. Racial conflict permeated the armed forces in the rear and on ships, suggesting that fighting together did not magically heal the racial divide.

The wounded soldier lies in a crucifix position, establishing a symbolic link between Christ who suffered on the cross to redeem humankind and a soldier sacrificing his life to save his nation.

How does this image compare to combat photographs from World War II and the Korean War (see Chapters 23 and 24)?

Controversy on the Home Front

Advocates for peace have opposed every American war, but their dissent rarely influenced the mainstream political debate. During the Vietnam War these rebellious voices offering an alternative vision of peace moved from the fringes to the center of American political life. Growing in strength as more Americans began to oppose the war, the peace movement made itself visible through mass demonstrations, propaganda posters, and press coverage of celebrities who joined it. The very existence of a vocal peace movement in the midst of a war, however, also invited controversy because Americans held differing views on the legitimacy of wartime dissent. Many peace activists believed they were preserving the American tradition of freedom of speech. Public opinion polls from 1965 to 1973, however, consistently showed that most Americans disliked both the war and the peace movement.

The Antiwar Movement

In announcing his decision not to run for reelection in 1968, Johnson noted that "there is division in the American house right now." In the 1960s the rise of a youth-based counterculture and a powerful civil rights movement roiled the country (see Chapter 27). The night of his announcement, however, Johnson was referring to the domestic debate over the war in Vietnam.

Although many working- and middle-class people opposed the war, overcoming existing cultural and class divisions in American society to create a unified antiwar movement proved difficult. The organized antiwar movement tended to attract mostly white, middle-class, college-educated Americans or individuals already engaged in crusades of social justice. Many working-class women and African Americans with grade-school educations and low-paying jobs, opposed the war, but had little interest in marching alongside middle-class college students in street demonstrations.

> ## "Hey, hey LBJ, how many kids did you kill today?"
>
> A popular chant during antiwar demonstrations

Uniting around one universal vision also posed difficulties for the antiwar movement. All peace activists wanted to end the war in Vietnam, but they offered different arguments for doing so. Some made a primarily moral argument. They claimed that a war involving napalm, search-and-destroy missions, and forced relocation into strategic hamlets hurt the Vietnamese more than living under Communist rule did. Others focused on the futility of fighting an unwinnable civil war. Another group accepted that the nation needed to stop Communist China from expanding its influence. They argued that working with Ho Chi Minh could accomplish this goal more effectively than fighting a war in Vietnam. These critics noted that while Ho accepted Chinese aid to fight the United States, he was leery of Chinese ambitions to control Vietnam. America had worked successfully in Europe with the independently minded communist leader Josip Broz Tito in Yugoslavia to contain Soviet ambitions in the Balkans. Why could it not do the same in Vietnam? Other activists saw a chance to open the nation's eyes to injustice at home, as well as overseas. Student leaders from the nation's top universities founded the Students for a Democratic Society (SDS) at Port Huron, Michigan, in 1962. A leader in the New Left movement, SDS combined staunch opposition to the war with a scathing critique of the inequities of capitalism (see Chapter 27).

Although their reasons for opposing the war differed, peace advocates agreed that the war was destroying American democracy. They noted violations of American democratic values: going to war without a formal declaration of war from Congress, presidential secrets and lies, FBI surveillance of peace protesters, and unjust draft deferments for middle- and upper-class men who could afford to go to college. When civil rights leader Martin Luther King Jr. spoke out against the war in 1967, he denounced both the destruction of Vietnamese culture and the war's negative impact on African Americans. The war's high cost diverted funds from antipoverty programs at home, King rightly

What differing visions did peace activists offer on the war?

View the Image *"Vietnam—I want out"*

contended. The disproportionately high numbers of African American men fighting and dying in Vietnam further illustrated ongoing racial injustice within the United States, he continued. (King's criticism was valid in 1967, but over the entire war, black soldiers did not incur higher casualty rates than the rest of the population.) One antiwar poster (**26.11**) captured this link between racial inequality and the war by picturing two African American soldiers as they advanced into the jungle under the headline, "The only time we're in the front is when it's time to die." The rebuke against King for these statements was swift and severe, including criticism from civil rights activists who worried that his antiwar views would discredit their cause. King died a year later from an assassin's bullet, cutting short his career as a civil rights leader and antiwar activist.

The peace movement brought the debate over the war out of the halls of government and into the streets. In 1965, University of Michigan faculty and students organized the first teach-in, a series of public lectures and debates protesting the war. Over the next eight years, scholars and students on hundreds of other college campuses held teach-ins. Some teach-ins invited counterprotests. At the conclusion of a teach-in at the University of Wisconsin, for example, six thousand students signed a petition supporting President Johnson. Like other Americans, college students held differing views about the war.

The draft made the war more than an abstract humanitarian or foreign policy question for millions of American men. Male college students would lose their draft deferments once they graduated, giving many personal, as well as political and moral, reasons to oppose the war. Peace activists organized ceremonies where men burned the notices from their draft boards ordering them to report for induction. When 1,500 peace activists gathered in New York City in 1965 to watch five men burn their draft cards, an onlooker bolted from the crowd with a fire extinguisher and doused the protesters before the cards caught fire. The activists nonetheless managed to ignite their soggy draft cards while hundreds of New Yorkers stood on the other side of police barricades and chanted "Burn yourselves, not your cards!" a macabre reminder, perhaps unintentional, of the Buddhist suicides in Vietnam in 1963.

Johnson tried to discredit the peace movement by claiming it was communist-run and gave solace to the enemy. Other defenders of the war charged the peace movement with treason. However, some war supporters believed that the general unpopularity of the peace movement helped bolster the resolve

The only time we're in the front is when it's time to die.

We've been dying to be in the front here in the United States. Yet in Vietnam we're dying in the front everyday.

The vast majority of Black troops in Vietnam are placed on the front lines...to fight and die for this war.

Think about it. Why should we be in the Vietnam war, when we haven't won our own war here?

Organize in your community to protest the war, or write to the political representative in your community for information about how to end it. Help Unsell The War, Box 903, FDR Station, New York, N.Y.

Stop the war. It's killing us.
Help Unsell The War, Box 903, F.D.R. Station, N.Y., N.Y. 10022

of Americans in the political center to stay the course.

The presumption that Senator Robert Kennedy, brother of the slain president, would seek the Democratic nomination as a peace candidate had encouraged Johnson to abandon a quest for a second term. On June 4, 1968, Sirhan Sirhan, a Jordanian immigrant upset with Kennedy's pro-Israel stance, shot and killed the senator as he walked through the kitchen of a California hotel moments after finishing his victory speech for winning the state primary. At the Chicago nominating convention, the Democratic Party selected Vice President Hubert Humphrey as its presidential candidate, a man much like Johnson who supported liberal causes at home and the war in Vietnam. Instead of uniting liberal and conservative Democrats, Humphrey's candidacy fractured the party. Outside the convention hall radical antiwar protesters denounced his nomination and clashed violently with police. "The war is destroying our

26.11 Stop the War. It's Killing Us This antiwar poster highlighted the disproportionate numbers of African Americans fighting and dying on the frontlines in the late 1960s, linking that imbalance to continued racial inequity in American society.

Read the Document *Martin Luther King Jr., "Conscience and the Vietnam War" (1967)*

How did the peace movement publicize its cause?

Dueling Bumper Stickers

"Peace Through Victory in Vietnam"

"Join the Army; travel to exotic distant lands; meet exciting, unusual people and kill them."

country as we are destroying Vietnam," the writer I. F. Stone lamented.

The outcome of the 1968 presidential election suggested that the peace movement had helped the conservative cause. Believing that the protesters, rather than the police, had gone too far in Chicago, many working- and middle-class Americans responded positively to Republican candidate Richard Nixon's call for a return to "law and order." During the campaign Nixon suggested that he had a "secret plan" to bring about a "peace with honor" that he could not reveal to the enemy. The election became a three-man race when Alabama Governor George Wallace ran as an independent candidate, attracting conservative Southern whites and white Northern blue-collar workers with his attacks on

integration, elites in Washington, D.C., and antiwar protesters. "If any demonstrator ever lays down in front of my car," Wallace proclaimed, "it'll be the last car he'll ever lay down in front of." As Election Day neared Humphrey picked up liberal support by pledging to end bombing over North Vietnam immediately. Despite losing conservatives' votes to Wallace, Nixon won the Electoral College vote handily but only received 44 percent of the popular vote (**26.12**).

Opposition to the war never resulted in widespread support for the peace movement. Most Americans remained staunchly anti-communist, even as their dissatisfaction with the war in Vietnam grew. Gallup Polls in 1969 revealed that by a margin of 55 percent to 31 percent, Americans labeled themselves as doves not hawks and most described the war as indefensible. Three-fifths, however, also believed that the peace movement helped the enemy and made it more difficult for the president to end the war. Americans, it seemed, wanted an end to the fighting overseas and at home.

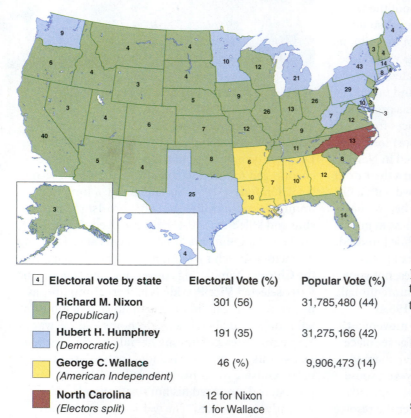

26.12 The Presidential Election of 1968 Republican Richard Nixon won easily in the Electoral College, but he received only about a half million more popular votes than his Democratic opponent, Hubert Humphrey.

[4] Electoral vote by state	Electoral Vote (%)	Popular Vote (%)
■ **Richard M. Nixon** (Republican)	301 (56)	31,785,480 (44)
■ **Hubert H. Humphrey** (Democratic)	191 (35)	31,275,166 (42)
■ **George C. Wallace** (American Independent)	46 (%)	9,906,473 (14)
■ **North Carolina** (Electors split)	12 for Nixon 1 for Wallace	

My Lai

Johnson had calmed the American public in March 1968 by announcing he would open negotiations with the North Vietnamese. Keeping his promise, he began fruitless negotiations with Hanoi. Johnson continued trying, however, to win the war before he left office. Believing that a final push against a weakened enemy could finish the job, American soldiers renewed their attacks on the Vietcong. The largest search-and-destroy missions of the war occurred in March and April, involving more than 100,000 troops. During one of these in the village of **My Lai**, American soldiers massacred hundreds of civilians, an atrocity that fueled the strident domestic debate over the American mission in Vietnam.

On March 16, 1968, 75 American soldiers in two platoons under the command of Lieutenant William Calley entered My Lai. Before the mission, these troops had spent long days wading through the rice paddies and even longer nights battling snipers and insects, looking for Vietcong who had killed a popular sergeant the week before. By the time the men approached My Lai, they were in an ugly mood. By attacking during the morning hours, the company's officers anticipated that their troops would confront 250 enemy troops and few civilians, whom the Americans expected would follow the usual daily ritual of leaving the village to visit a local market. None of these predictions came to pass. In the village the men found only unarmed women, children, and the elderly. The Vietcong had retreated into the western mountains before the Americans arrived.

Rather than leaving, however, the Americans engaged in an orgy of rape, torture, and slaughter that took four hours to complete and left more than 500 villagers dead. Army photographer Ron Haeberle snapped this image (**26.13**) of terrified women and children huddled together moments before American soldiers killed them. "Guys were about to shoot these people, I yelled, 'Hold it' and I shot my pictures. As I walked away, I heard M-16s open up, and from the corner of my eye I saw bodies falling but I did not turn to look," Haeberle recalled. Seeing the carnage from the air, pilot Hugh Thompson landed his helicopter between the soldiers and 11 survivors, whom he flew to safety. Thompson reported the atrocity to his superiors to no avail. Only the perseverance of Ron Ridenhour, a sergeant who was not even at My Lai, finally brought the massacre to light. After hearing stories from men who took part, an outraged Ridenhour wrote to President Nixon, the Pentagon, and members of Congress. When the story broke in 1969, Haeberle sold his photos to *Life*. A military investigation headed by Lieutenant General William Peers resulted in Calley's court martial for premeditated murder.

Calley's conviction in 1971 exposed Americans' conflicting views over the meaning of My Lai. Was the atrocity a unique episode or representative of American conduct in Vietnam? *Competing Visions: Who Was Responsible for the My Lai Massacre?* (page 800) explores this question in more detail.

Responding to the public outcry over Calley's conviction, Secretary of the Army Howard "Bo" Callaway reduced Calley's life sentence to ten years, and President Nixon pardoned Calley after he had served only five months in prison. By this time Calley had been transformed from villain to hero in the American imagination. People on both the left and the right of the political spectrum defended Calley. The left saw him as a scapegoat for failed American policies, while the right argued that civilians were fair targets in a guerilla war.

26.13 My Lai Villagers Moments before their Execution, 1968 Americans expressed more outrage over the publication of photographs from My Lai than over the actual killings.

▶ **Watch the Video** *Video Lecture: Atrocity and Cover Up: My Lai Massacre*

Why did photos of the My Lai massacre provoke conflicting responses from Americans?

Competing Visions

WHO WAS RESPONSIBLE FOR THE MY LAI MASSACRE?

Americans disagreed over who bore responsibility for the massacre at My Lai. Some commentators focused on those directly involved in the killings, others on the orders given by higher-ranking officials to destroy the village. As you read the following excerpts, try to reconstruct the domestic dispute over My Lai. Is one argument stronger than the other? Who was to blame: Calley, the two platoons, the commanding officers, or the American people?

Fellow soldier Dennis Conti told Army investigators that he saw Calley and Private Paul Meadlo kill civilians in My Lai.

They were bringing people out [of their huts], and then we pushed them out into the rice paddy, onto the dike there … Lieutenant Calley came back, and said: "Take care of them." So we said: "Okay." And we sat there and watched them like we usually do. And he came back again, and he said: "I thought I told you to take care of them." I said: "We're taking care of them," and he said: "I mean kill them." So I looked at Meadlo and he looked at me, and I didn't want to do it, and he didn't want to do it … then [Calley] said: "Come on, we'll line them up here, we'll kill them." So I told him: "I'll watch the tree line" … Then they opened up, and started firing. Meadlo fired a while. I don't know how much he fired, a clip, I think. It might have been more. He started to cry, and he gave me his weapon.

This *New York Times* editorial suggested that higher-ranking officials than Calley bore some responsibility for ordering and observing the My Lai massacre.

Who gave the orders? Who knew what was going on? Was any attempt made to stop it? Who is responsible? … [Paul Meadlo] was one of 18 witnesses to describe a briefing the night before the assault at which Captain [Ernest L.] Medina told the men they were going into battle with a hardened Vietcong battalion; that their mission was "search and destroy" and they were to destroy everything in the hamlet—houses, crops and people … Helicopter pilots, radio men and artillery observers said the higher officers had flown over the scene for several hours and had seen bodies on the ground, had conference with the other officers and, as one pilot said, "knew what was going on" all through the day … the Geneva conventions, the Nuremburg doctrines and the Army's own rules of land warfare make plain that obedience to orders is not a blanket defense, that orders that to a "prudent" or "reasonable" man seem patently illegal need not be obeyed. The question here, then, is whether the order, if that is what it was, to kill everything was one that a prudent man should obey when he found that everything included women, children, and infants.

The *National Review* rejected suggestions that the nation bore the blame and should abandon the war in Vietnam.

"That America and Americans must stand in the larger dock of guilt and human conscience for what happened at My Lai seems inescapable." So observed *Time* [magazine], adding: "Men in American uniforms slaughtered the civilians of My Lai, and in so doing humiliated the U.S. and called in question the U.S. mission in Vietnam in a way that all the antiwar protesters could never have done." One's mind staggers: Are "America and Americans" generally guilty, the same America and Americans now preparing to bring the accused to trial? And even if it turns out that atrocities were committed, how does this call in question the U.S. mission in Vietnam? Do the innumerable atrocities committed by both sides in World War II add up to the proposition that resistance to the Nazis ought to have been abandoned? … Irrational and irresponsible comment on [My Lai] has become collective madness.

Lieutenant William Calley

What was the ultimate historic significance of the My Lai massacre?

 View the **Closer Look** *Competing Visions: Who Was Responsible for the My Lai Massacre?*

The Long Road to Peace

When Richard Nixon entered the White House in 1969, he told his advisors, "I'm going to stop that war. Fast." Nixon was also intent, however, on preserving America's international reputation. He had a different vision from his predecessor, he assured the public, pledging to seek "peace with honor." Nixon's promises proved empty, however. The war did not end quickly, but continued for four more years. At home Nixon benefited politically by portraying the peace movement as out of step with the values of law-abiding citizens. When he extended the war into Laos and Cambodia and became embroiled in political scandal, his actions fueled the political debate over whether Americans could trust their government.

Seeking Peace with Honor

For Nixon a peace with honor meant winning the war. He and his national security advisor, Henry Kissinger, pursued four different tactics to achieve this goal. First Nixon implemented **Vietnamization**, which turned the bulk of the ground fighting over to the South Vietnamese Army. By 1971, the American presence in Vietnam had diminished dramatically. In many respects this was a return to the pre-1965 approach when America propped up an independent South Vietnam with financial and military aid. Announcing Vietnamization in November 1969, Nixon asked for support from "the great silent majority of Americans," referring to the many Americans who supported the war quietly in the privacy of their homes. He also rebuked the peace movement. "Let us be united for peace. Let us also be united against defeat. Because let us understand: North Vietnam cannot defeat or humiliate the United States. Only Americans can do that." Polls indicated that the "silent majority" overwhelmingly supported his plan.

Vietnamization promised to give America exactly what it wanted: victory with minimal loss of American lives. The United States quickly transformed the South Vietnamese Army into one of the largest and best-equipped military forces in the world. At the ongoing peace talks, a North Vietnamese negotiator wondered aloud how the United States, when it could not win with its own troops, thought it could "succeed when you let your puppet troops do the fighting." That dilemma, Kissinger admitted, "also torments me."

In implementing Vietnamization Nixon hoped to disarm the peace movement by replacing images of civilian suffering on the evening news with pictures of troops withdrawing and returning home.

In March 1970, he announced the incremental withdrawal of another 150,000 soldiers to "drop a bombshell on the gathering spring storm of antiwar protest." He simultaneously reformed the draft, replacing the controversial deferment system with a lottery that randomly drafted men by date of birth. Nixon hoped these changes would buy his administration enough time to win the war.

The controversial actions of peace activists inadvertently helped Nixon solidify the support of Middle America. In 1972, the actress Jane Fonda accepted an invitation from the North Vietnamese government to visit Hanoi. While in the enemy capital, she made radio broadcasts urging American pilots to mutiny. A photo of Fonda joking with North Vietnamese soldiers as she sat on an anti-aircraft gun used to shoot down American planes created a backlash against the peace movement that Nixon exploited.

Vietnamization was more than a reaction to declining popular support for fighting in Vietnam. It was also part of Nixon's attempt to reshape the role that the United States played in global geopolitics. Nixon and Kissinger viewed the longstanding vision of a bipolar world that pitted the United States against the Soviet Union as obsolete. They embraced a competing strategic vision of multipolarity that focused on negotiating with Europe, China, Japan, and the Soviet Union to construct a new balance of power system to keep the peace. In this foreign policy reformulation, the United States would refrain from direct involvement in regional conflicts, such as Vietnam. The Nixon Doctrine, formulated in 1969 and 1970, announced that the United States expected its friends to take the lead in defending themselves.

Nixon's second tactic linked Vietnamization to the resumption of massive bombing in North

📖 Read the Document *Richard Nixon, Vietnamization (1969)*   Why did Nixon implement Vietnamization?

Vietnam, which Johnson had halted when he initiated peace talks in 1968. As American troops left Vietnam between 1969 and 1972, the number of bombs dropped increased spectacularly (see this shift in *Envisioning Evidence: Vietnam: The War by the Numbers*). America had not used enough military force to achieve victory, the president and Kissinger concluded. They intended to correct this problem. For a while the news of troop withdrawals diverted attention from the intensified bombing of North Vietnam.

Alongside Vietnamization and renewed bombing of North Vietnam, Nixon and Kissinger's third tactic used diplomacy to decrease Soviet and Chinese support for North Vietnam. Exploiting the discord between China and the Soviet Union, Nixon pursued independent negotiations with each nation to strengthen their ties to the United States and deepen their distrust of each other. He reshaped the Cold War by pursuing his vision of multi-polarity through **détente**, using diplomatic, economic, and cultural contacts to improve U.S. relations with China and the Soviet Union. Fearing that the United States might form an alliance with the other, the Soviet Union and China each eagerly accepted these overtures. In return for a more congenial relationship with the United States, Nixon expected China and the Soviet Union to end their support of North Vietnam. Although both countries continued to send aid to North Vietnam, once they decided to normalize trade relations and enter into arms limitations agreements with the United States, the Soviet Union and China began pressuring Hanoi to seek a negotiated peace.

Cambodia: Invasion and Outrage

The fourth tactical component of Nixon's Vietnam policy involved the neutral country of Cambodia, which bordered Vietnam to the west. In 1969, Nixon initiated a secret bombing campaign of Cambodia. He hoped to cut off supplies filtering through the Ho Chi Minh Trail and thus pressure North Vietnam into accepting the American terms for peace that included an independent South Vietnam.

In April 1970, Nixon shattered the public consensus he had carefully created for Vietnamization by ordering an American ground force invasion of Cambodia. Before the invasion Nixon sought inspiration from repeated showings of the movie *Patton* in the White House, a film that portrayed the hard-nosed and belligerent World War II tank commander General George S. Patton leading American forces to victory. Nixon announced in a televised speech that American troops needed to destroy Communist bases in Cambodia to help the South Vietnamese army defeat the Vietcong. But the two-month-long incursion only pushed the North Vietnamese further into the interior of Cambodia, where they began supporting the Khmer Rouge, Communist rebels who seized power in Cambodia in 1975 and unleashed a wave of mass murder so brutal that the country became known as "the killing fields."

Nixon's claim that he was expanding the war to end it sooner persuaded few. Protest erupted on college campuses nationwide and in Congress where the Senate symbolically terminated the Gulf of Tonkin Resolution. Many university demonstrations turned violent as protesters clashed with police and set fire to college buildings. A defiant Nixon stood his ground, assuming that the "silent majority" agreed with his assessment that the protesters were just "bums blowing up the campuses."

In Kent, Ohio, student-organized demonstrations protesting the invasion of Cambodia took a nasty turn, recalled Phil Caputo, who had left the Marines after two tours in Vietnam and was now a reporter for the *Chicago Tribune*. In a May weekend rampage, "store windows had been smashed in town, [and] radicals had burned down the ROTC building," according to Caputo. Calling the protesters "the worst sort of people we harbor in America," Governor James Allen Rhodes promised to "use every weapon possible to eradicate the problem," as he sent National Guardsmen to restore order.

On Monday morning a few hundred students gathered on the campus of Kent State University for a rally, defying a ban on protests. National Guardsmen fired tear gas to disperse the demonstrators, who responded by throwing rocks and shouting obscenities at the troops. Suddenly, as bystanders and students on their way to class watched the mini-battle unfurl, the troops sprayed bullets into the crowd, killing four and wounding nine. The National Guardsmen claimed that they had fired in self-defense when protesters began throwing concrete slabs. Two of the victims were passers-by, however, and all four were too far away from the troops to have hit them with anything more than pebbles.

Envisioning Evidence

VIETNAM: THE WAR BY THE NUMBERS

Americans' opinions about the Vietnam War varied over the course of the war, eventually influencing the strategy pursued there. Even as the war became more unpopular, however, at least 40 percent of the nation continued to believe that the nation had done the right thing by sending troops to fight in Vietnam. The United States also tried to use its air superiority to win the war, dropping more bombs in the Vietnam War than in World War II.

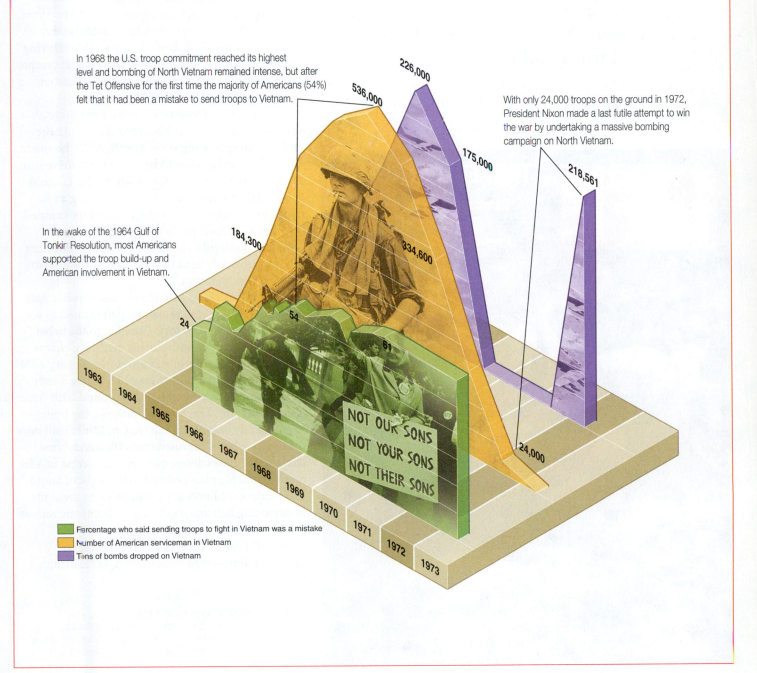

In 1968 the U.S. troop commitment reached its highest level and bombing of North Vietnam remained intense, but after the Tet Offensive for the first time the majority of Americans (54%) felt that it had been a mistake to send troops to Vietnam.

With only 24,000 troops on the ground in 1972, President Nixon made a last futile attempt to win the war by undertaking a massive bombing campaign on North Vietnam.

In the wake of the 1964 Gulf of Tonkin Resolution, most Americans supported the troop build-up and American involvement in Vietnam.

NOT OUR SONS
NOT YOUR SONS
NOT THEIR SONS

536,000
226,000
175,000
218,561
184,300
334,600
24
54
61
24,000

1963 1964 1965 1966 1967 1968 1969 1970 1971 1972 1973

Percentage who said sending troops to fight in Vietnam was a mistake
Number of American serviceman in Vietnam
Tons of bombs dropped on Vietnam

View the **Closer Look** *Envisioning Evidence: Vietnam: The War by the Numbers*

What do these data reveal about the stages of America's involvement in Vietnam?

Responding to Nixon's earlier characterization of the protesters, the father of one of the dead told reporters, "My child was not a bum." The cover of *Life* (**26.14**) showed terrified students trying to save the life of one victim, underscoring that the war's killing had come home to America. This photo, along with the others inside the magazine, inspired musician Neil Young to write the song "Ohio" to protest the shootings, the war, and the Nixon administration.

> **"Tin soldiers and Nixon coming,
> We're finally on our own.
> This summer I hear the drumming,
> Four dead in Ohio."**
>
> Lyrics from Neil Young's song "Ohio,"
> written in response to the Kent State shootings

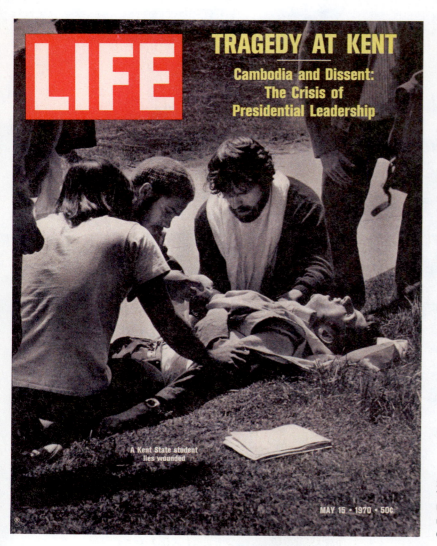

LIFE

TRAGEDY AT KENT

Cambodia and Dissent:
The Crisis of
Presidential Leadership

A Kent State student
lies wounded

MAY 15 · 1970 · 50¢

"A nation driven to use the weapons of war upon its youth is a nation on the edge of chaos," concluded the presidential commission that investigated the Kent State incident.

The Kent State shootings unmasked the growing "town and gown" divide over the war and latent anger at the peace movement. "They should have shot more of them," suggested one Kent resident, still angry over the weekend riot. Radio stations refused to play Young's "anti-Nixon" song. While protests over the shooting engulfed more than half the nation's college campuses, working-class unions staged counter-protests to support the war. In New York City hundreds of longshoremen wearing hard hats attacked students who were protesting the Cambodian invasion. During a subsequent meeting at the White House, sympathetic labor leaders presented the president with a "commander-in-chief" hard hat.

The wave of protests after the Kent State shootings nonetheless bothered Nixon. At the end of a sleepless night on May 9, 1970, he made an impulsive decision to have his valet drive him, without his Secret Service detail, to the Lincoln Memorial at five o'clock in the morning so he could talk to the antiwar demonstrators camped out there. According to the protesters Nixon talked disjointedly about college sports and surfing and assured them that he shared their wish for peace in Vietnam.

Despite his clumsy attempt to talk directly with peace activists, Nixon remained determined to see the war through to victory. Clinging to the belief that success would vindicate his methods, Nixon expanded the theater of war again in February 1971 by ordering an invasion of Laos. This time South Vietnamese troops fought on the ground with American air support. Once again, however, the hopes of permanently disrupting the Ho Chi Minh Trail bore meager results. Administration officials claimed that the Laos invasion illustrated the success of Vietnamization. Skeptics pointed to the sight of South Vietnamese soldiers clinging in panic to the skids of departing helicopters during their chaotic retreat back into South Vietnam.

In 1971, antiwar demonstrators staged 62 demonstrations in Washington, D.C., bringing

26.14 Kent State University, 1970
The images of students wounded and killed at Kent State University by National Guardsmen prompted fears that a war undertaken to protect American democracy was instead destroying it.

What competing visions emerged in response to the Kent State killings?

👁—[Watch the Video] *Video Lecture: Protest, Counterculture, and the Antiwar Movement during the Vietnam Era*

over 100,000 demonstrators to the nation's capital (**26.15**). That summer *The New York Times* published the Pentagon Papers, a secret Department of Defense study that criticized the way Kennedy and Johnson had handled the war, stoking the flames of antiwar sentiment in the wake of the Calley conviction, the failed Cambodian and Laos invasions, and the Kent State killings. The Pentagon Papers, leaked by Pentagon official Daniel Ellsberg, confirmed that presidents Kennedy and Johnson had intentionally lied to the public about the extent of previous American involvement in the war. Many Americans assumed that Nixon was also misleading the country. By now only 34 percent of Americans approved of his handling of the war.

Controversy over the war also seeped into the military. Morale plummeted as soldiers became unwilling to risk their lives for a cause that the nation seemed poised to abandon. In 1970, the military reported nearly 200 incidents of "fragging," which were deadly fraternal attacks by enlisted men on officers, named for the hand grenade fragments that did most of the damage. Escalating use of marijuana, opium, and heroin, all readily available in Vietnam, among servicemen was another sign of disintegrating discipline.

> ## "How do you ask a man to be the last man to die for a mistake?"
>
> Vietnam veteran and antiwar activist
> JOHN KERRY

Withdrawal

Nixon envisioned détente creating a new world order in which the United States used trade agreements and arms limitation treaties to curtail the expansionist ambitions of its enemies. His administration made significant headway with this approach in 1972, beginning with a highly publicized trip to China in February and culminating with a May summit meeting in Moscow. The carefully orchestrated pictures of the staunch anti-communist Nixon toasting China's communist leader Mao during an official banquet and lauding the achievements of Chinese civilization during a trek to the Great Wall signaled an important turning point in

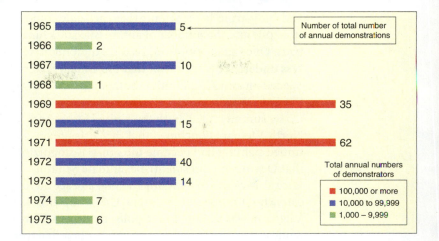

Sino-American relations. Improved relations with China also demolished one of the main arguments used to justify the war in Vietnam. American leaders had always linked the war to the larger American goal of containing communism in Southeast Asia. They considered the region, rather than Vietnam itself, vital to American strategic interests overseas. Nixon now demonstrated that diplomacy could perhaps contain communism in Southeast Asia more effectively than war. Why then, many Americans wondered, was the nation still fighting in Vietnam?

The improving relations between its communist benefactors and the United States alarmed North Vietnam. When the North Vietnamese grumbled about Mao shaking hands with Nixon, Mao advised them to sign a peace treaty, regroup while the Americans withdrew, and then resume the war. North Vietnam eventually followed Mao's advice. They first tried, however, to replicate the political success of the Tet Offensive by launching a major invasion of the South. The North Vietnamese timed the so-called Easter Offensive of March 1972 to coincide with the start of the American presidential campaign. In response Nixon ordered a massive retaliation against North Vietnam that included bombing, a blockade, and mining a key harbor.

Unlike Tet the Easter Offensive did not greatly alter the political equation in the United States or worldwide. At home Nixon's approval ratings rose for defending South Vietnam from attack. Moving from his successful meeting in China to Moscow, the U.S.-Soviet summit proceeded as planned. When Nixon returned with the first disarmament agreement ever signed by the Soviet Union, he bolstered his image as a tough negotiator who got results. The Strategic Arms Limitation Treaty (SALT I) limited the number of intercontinental ballistic missiles

26.15 Antiwar Demonstrations in Washington, D.C., 1965–1975. The overall number of demonstrations and marchers protesting the war peaked in 1969 and 1971.

and submarine-launched missiles each side could stockpile and the number of antimissile launching pads. Once again, however, Nixon's diplomatic success undercut his argument that the United States needed an anti-Communist South Vietnam to win the Cold War.

By summer 1972, both the United States and North Vietnam concluded that the costs of continued fighting had become too great. Recognizing that Democratic presidential candidate Senator George McGovern of South Dakota, a peace advocate who promised to withdraw U.S. troops from Vietnam, was trailing in the polls, the North Vietnamese decided to seek the best terms possible from Nixon. Although Nixon had discredited McGovern by suggesting that he would abandon American POWs in Vietnam, the president was also eager to negotiate. With his reelection assured Nixon wanted to fulfill his campaign promise to end the war, so he could pursue his larger goal of refashioning Cold War relations among the world's superpowers.

Despite this renewed willingness on both sides to negotiate, it still took months to seal the deal. The final 1973 peace treaty called for American withdrawal, allowed North Vietnamese troops to remain in South Vietnam, and left the existing South Vietnamese government in place.

All left the Paris negotiating table knowing that the cease-fire existed only on paper. The war would go on, only now without American advisors, soldiers, or pilots.

Despite the spiral downward in Vietnam, Nixon retained a durable base of domestic support due to the success of détente with China and the Soviet Union and his effective portrayal of the antiwar movement as out of step with mainstream America. This political base, however, eroded quickly when he became embroiled in a major political scandal. The **Watergate scandal (1972)**, a botched Republican-engineered break-in of the Democratic National Committee headquarters in Washington, D.C., forced Nixon to resign in 1974. On June 17, 1972, members of Nixon's campaign staff had broken into the Watergate building office to fix broken wiretaps (listening devices on telephones) that they had installed during a previous burglary in May. Congressional challenges to his Vietnam policies and investigations into potential criminal activity by Nixon and members of his administration (see Chapter 28), weakened Nixon politically as he began his second term.

26.16 The Final Evacuation
Fleeing Vietnamese scramble for a spot aboard an American helicopter as the North Vietnamese Army approaches Saigon in 1975, a final portrait of the failed American mission in Vietnam.

How did the Vietnam War finally end for the United States and the Vietnamese?

In the midst of the Watergate crisis, Congress passed the War Powers Resolution to curtail presidential war-making powers. The 1973 law required congressional approval for any deployment of American troops overseas that lasted for more than 60 days. Critics pressed for even greater restrictions, arguing that the constitutional authority to declare war lay solely with Congress whether a war lasted 60 days or 60 years. Nixon countered that the law interfered with the president's constitutional role as commander in chief of the armed forces. Ignoring Congress's desire to end American involvement in Vietnam, he tried to continue funneling money and arms to South Vietnam. In response Congress sharply reduced funding for South Vietnam in 1974.

When Nixon resigned the presidency on August 9, 1974 to avoid impeachment, Vice-President Gerald Ford assumed office. (Nixon had appointed Ford as his vice president in 1973 when Spiro Agnew resigned following an unrelated corruption scandal.) The political controversy at home and Americans' widespread distrust of executive power in the wake of the failed war in Vietnam and the Watergate scandal weakened President Ford's ability to respond to the imminent collapse of South Vietnam. In March 1975, North Vietnam renewed its offensive. With no American help in the offing, South Vietnam collapsed. Within eight weeks North Vietnamese troops neared Saigon. They walked along highways littered with boots and uniforms discarded by deserting South Vietnamese soldiers who hoped

Total Serving in the American Military (worldwide)	8.7 million men 250,00 women
Total Serving in Vietnam	3.4 million men 6,421 women
Total Killed in Vietnam	47,415 battle deaths 10,785 other causes
Total Wounded	153,303
Total Draft Evaders	600,000 (tens of thousands fled to Canada)
Vietnamese Casualties (North and South)	2 million
Total Cost of War	$173 billion

26.17 The Human and Financial Cost of the Vietnam War, 1964–1973. The numbers of draft evaders fleeing to Canada illustrated the growing unpopularity of the war.

to blend into the civilian population and avoid execution.

Ho Chi Minh did not live to see the end of the war (he died in 1969), but the Communists renamed Saigon "Ho Chi Minh City" in his honor. Victory in the 30-year conflict did not end civilian suffering in Vietnam, however. Famine and prison camps caused thousands to flee in overcrowded boats to refugee camps in Thailand and Malaysia, where they faced an uncertain future waiting for permanent asylum in the United States or Europe.

For America the war concluded with the image of South Vietnamese citizens climbing a ladder on the roof of the American Embassy in Saigon to board one of the American helicopters that flew American citizens and 150,000 South Vietnamese to safety in the final days of the war (**26.16**). The frantic evacuation was a disheartening end to America's longest war to date, one that claimed the lives of 47,415 combatants and cost the nation $173 billion (**26.17**).

How to remember such a divisive and controversial war continued to provoke debate within the United States. The 1982 Vietnam Veterans Memorial in Washington, D.C., listed all the names of American war dead on two black marble slabs that descended into the ground. "Hidden in a hole, as if in shame," complained one veteran. "It is exactly the right memorial for that war," countered another. Festering rumors that Vietnam was still holding American soldiers hostage deepened public bitterness against the nation's former foe. The United States finally normalized diplomatic relations with Vietnam in 1995, 20 years after the fall of Saigon. It was time, one veteran wrote, "to recognize the truth. The war is over."

Why does the Vietnam War continue to provoke controversy among Americans?

1950

Truman offers aid to French in Vietnam
United States begins financing 80 percent of France's war effort

1954

Geneva Accords
Peace settlement between France and Vietminh divides Vietnam at seventeenth parallel

Eisenhower uses domino theory to explain U.S. involvement in Vietnam
Links defeating communism in Vietnam to protecting U.S. interests in Southeast Asia

1963

Buddhist monk sets himself on fire to protest corrupt Diem Regime
Kennedy supports overthrow of Diem

President Kennedy assassinated
Johnson resolves to stay the course in Vietnam

1964

Gulf of Tonkin Resolution
After alleged North Vietnamese attack on U.S. destroyers, Congress gives Johnson permission for military action in Vietnam

CHAPTER REVIEW

Review Questions

1. How important were early decisions (1945–1954) in setting the course of U.S. involvement in the Vietnam War?

2. How did the Cold War influence presidential decision making about Vietnam from 1945 to 1975?

3. What military challenges did American troops face while fighting in Vietnam?

4. How did competing images of the war create turmoil at home?

5. What do the debates surrounding the My Lai massacre and Kent State shootings reveal about Americans' competing visions of the war?

Key Terms

Domino theory The fear that a communist Vietnam would open the door to a complete communist takeover of Southeast Asia.   **781**

Geneva Accords (1954) Called for a temporary partition of Vietnam along the seventeenth parallel, with the Vietminh in the north and the French in the south, and a general election in two years to reunify the country under one government.   **782**

Southeast Asian Treaty Organization (SEATO) 1954 alliance among the United States, Britain, France, Australia, New Zealand, Thailand, the Philippines, and Pakistan who pledged to "meet common danger" in Southeast Asia together.   **783**

Gulf of Tonkin Resolution (1964) Gave Johnson permission "to take all necessary measures to repel any armed attack against the forces of the United States and to prevent further aggression" in Vietnam.   **787**

Ho Chi Minh Trail A 600-mile North Vietnamese supply route that ran along the western border of Vietnam through neighboring Laos and Cambodia.   **789**

Tet Offensive (1968) A massive, coordinated Communist assault against more than 100 cities and towns in South Vietnam.   **792**

My Lai A Vietnamese village where American soldiers massacred 500 civilians in 1968.   **799**

Vietnamization A Nixon administration policy that turned the bulk of the ground fighting over to the South Vietnamese Army.   **801**

Détente Relaxing Cold War tensions by using diplomatic, economic, and cultural contacts to improve U.S. relations with China and the Soviet Union.   **802**

Watergate scandal (1972) A botched Republican-engineered break-in of the Democratic National Committee headquarters in Washington, D.C. that forced Nixon to resign in 1974.   **806**

1965

American ground forces arrive in Vietnam
Vietnam becomes America's war

1968

Tet Offensive
Major North Vietnamese attack convinces majority of Americans that war is futile

My Lai Massacre
Controversy erupts over who was responsible for U.S. troops killing five hundred unarmed villagers

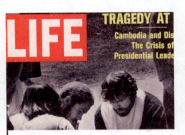

1970

U.S. forces invade Cambodia
National Guardsmen fire on protesters at Kent State University, killing four

1973–1975

Paris Peace Accords
Ends direct American involvement in war

North Vietnamese troops enter Saigon
North Vietnam wins the war

MyHistoryLab Connections

Visit www.myhistorylab.com for a customized Study Plan that will help you build your knowledge of *A Nation Divided*.

Questions for Analysis

1. **What increasing role did Eisenhower envision for the United States in Vietnam?**

   📖 **Read** the **Document** *Dwight D. Eisenhower, Dien Bien Phu (1954), p. 782*

2. **How did Johnson justify fighting in Vietnam?**

   📖 **Read** the **Document** *Johnson's Defense of the U.S. Presence in Vietnam (1965), p. 787*

3. **What differing views do these two songs offer on the war in Vietnam?**

   🔍 **View** the **Closer Look** *Competing Visions: Popular Music and the Vietnam War, p. 790*

4. **What message does this film send to middle America about the peace movement?**

   👁 **Watch** the **Video** *Protests Against the Vietnam War, p. 798*

5. **What is the significance of My Lai?**

   👁 **Watch** the **Video** *Video Lecture: Atrocity and Cover Up: My Lai Massacre, p. 799*

Other Resources from This Chapter

📖 **Read** the **Document**

- *Declaration of Independence for Vietnam (1945), p. 780*
- *George Ball's Dissenting Opinion on Vietnam (1965), p. 786*
- *Martin Luther King Jr., "Conscience and the Vietnam War" (1967), p. 797*
- *Richard Nixon, Vietnamization (1969), p. 801*

🔍 **View** the **Closer Look**

- *Images as History: The Power of the Press in Vietnam, p. 794*
- *Competing Visions: Who Was Responsible for the My Lai Massacre?, p. 800*
- *Envisioning Evidence: Vietnam: The War by the Numbers, p. 803*

🔍 **View** the **Image**

- *"Vietnam —I want out," p. 796*
- *Kent State Demonstrations, p. 802*

🔍 **View** the **Map** *Interactive Map: The Vietnam War, p. 793*

👁 **Watch** the **Video** *Video Lecture: Protest, Counterculture, and the Antiwar Movement during the Vietnam Era, p. 804*

((•─ **Hear** the **Audio File** on **myhistorylab.com**

◉─ **Watch** the **Video** *Critical Visions, Chapter 27*

A Decade of Discord
The Challenge of the 1960s

In April 1968, civil rights leader Martin Luther King Jr. traveled to Memphis, Tennessee, to support a black garbage men's strike. Around 6:00 p.m. on April 4, 1968, as King leaned over a balcony railing outside his second-story room at the Lorraine Motel to chat with two friends in the courtyard below, shots rang out. A wounded King collapsed on the floor of the balcony, and colleagues frantically tried to stem the bleeding with towels while waiting for the ambulance to arrive. Within an hour hospital doctors pronounced the 38-year-old minister dead. As news of King's assassination spread, rioting erupted in black communities throughout the nation, and images of violence saturated the television airwaves. In this photo King's 13-year-old daughter Yolanda sits inside a car peering at mourners, reflected in the car window, while her mother Coretta Scott King sits solemnly behind her as they leave King's funeral in Atlanta, Georgia. This somber photograph, as much as the images of rioters, captured the crushing disappointment of dashed dreams. It was a sentiment shared by many Americans in the 1960s, white and black, who failed to fully realize their goals of either reforming America or ending the cultural turmoil.

America was rife with discord during the 1960s. Much debate centered on liberalism and its willingness to use the government to protect civil rights and expand economic opportunity. Throughout the decade social reformers working within the liberal tradition advanced competing visions of social justice and shared prosperity. Some visions were bold; some, truly radical. King dreamed of using nonviolence to achieve racial equality; more militant activists advocated armed self-defense. Building on the reform legacies of the Progressive Era and the New Deal, Democratic Presidents John F. Kennedy and Lyndon B. Johnson launched their own wars against poverty. Their legislative agendas were too timid for young radical activists, who wanted to revolutionize American capitalism. Feminists, Chicano activists, and Native American protesters also mobilized to demand equal rights.

These visions of reform, especially the more radical revolutionary ones, appeared like nightmares to conservative segments of the population that abhorred liberalism. Southern segregationists organized to prevent government-mandated dismantling of Jim Crow, and white Northerners increasingly resented taxpayer-supported programs for unruly minorities. The rise of a hippie counterculture that emphasized love and pleasure convinced many working- and middle-class whites that liberalism meant the end of law and order and traditional values.

If there was one point of agreement throughout the 1960s, it was that the political and cultural battles that defined the decade, for good or ill, transformed the nation. By 1970, frustration over unfulfilled dreams left Americans divided over whether the nation had changed too much or not enough.

"We know through painful experience that freedom is never voluntarily given by the oppressor; it must be demanded by the oppressed."

MARTIN LUTHER KING JR., 1963

The Liberal Moment

The 1960s was the heyday of American liberalism, thanks in part to presidential reform agendas and to pivotal Supreme Court rulings. Presidents Kennedy and Johnson viewed themselves as heirs to the New Deal legacy, and they intended to follow in Harry Truman's footsteps, who as president had desegregated the American military and secured federal funds for urban public housing, education, and public works projects. Kennedy and Johnson each believed in the power of the federal government to reform American society, but each faced intense resistance from conservatives who were certain that the less the government interfered in the economy or society, the better.

Kennedy and the New Frontier

Nearly 20 percent of Americans, 70 percent of them white, lived in dire poverty during the most prosperous moment in American history. Many middle- and upper-class Americans learned this startling statistic by reading Michael Harrington's *The Other America: Poverty in the United States* (1962). Harrington documented the deteriorating schools, substandard hospitals, and dead-end jobs that created a cycle of poverty that continued unabated for generations. Just like Jacob Riis's nineteenth-century exposé, *How the Other Half Lives* (see Chapter 17), Harrington made the lives of the nation's poor "visible" to the rest of the nation. Harrington claimed that a "culture of poverty" filled with extramarital sex, illegitimate children, and broken families created "a different kind of people" who did not share the values or outlook of middle-class America. Like Riis 70 years earlier, Harrington succeeded in awakening the social consciousness of affluent liberals, including John F. Kennedy.

While campaigning in West Virginia during his 1960 presidential bid, Kennedy came face to face with appalling poverty as he sat and talked with coal miners, pictured here (**27.1**), about their lives. This moment of intimate conversation, one of his speechwriters noted, was "Kennedy at his best" as he gathered details about children who never drank

27.1 Presidential Candidate John F. Kennedy Speaking with Coal Miners, 1960
Kennedy's personal touch and charisma helped him connect with voters, who educated him about the entrenched poverty endemic to many rural and industrial communities.

What social problems associated with poverty became visible in the early 1960s?

 View the **Image** *New Frontier Legislation*

milk and their fathers' dangerous work underground. "I was better off in the war than they are in the coal mines," Kennedy, a World War II veteran, told his campaign staff after this photo was taken. "It's not right."

"Let us begin anew," John F. Kennedy told the nation in his 1961 inaugural address, setting a tone

---

> ## "Ask not what your country can do for you—ask what you can do for your country."
> Kennedy's Inaugural Address, 1961

---

of hope that inspired young people and liberals throughout the nation. After eight years with the moderate Republican Dwight Eisenhower in the White House, Kennedy wanted to reinvigorate the liberal agenda through a legislative program called the New Frontier. Kennedy's proposed reforms included raising the minimum wage, reducing overcrowding in schools, and providing health care for the elderly. Kennedy advocated cutting taxes and increasing government spending to stimulate the economy, reasoning that as incomes rose more tax revenue would flow into federal coffers to pay for these programs.

Kennedy also needed large sums for the ongoing space race with the Soviet Union, begun when the Soviets launched Sputnik in 1957 (see Chapter 24). The Soviets sent the first astronauts into space in 1961, prompting Kennedy to announce that the United States intended to recover its reputation as the world's technological leader by putting a man on the moon.

The youngest elected president in American history, Kennedy's charisma and idealism inspired many baby boomers, who were just reaching adolescence or entering college. Thousands rushed to join the Peace Corps, an agency established by Kennedy that sent recent college graduates to work on humanitarian projects in developing nations. "I really believed that I was going to change the world," recalled one teenager. By 1970, over 10,000 Peace Corps volunteers had traveled abroad to teach, build hospitals, set up water treatment plants, and establish irrigation systems.

Kennedy raised unemployment and Social Security benefits and the minimum wage, but he had trouble implementing other parts of his liberal legislative program. Unskilled in lobbying legislators, just over one-third of his proposals became law. Conservative congressmen balked at using deficit spending to fund the tax cuts and programs Kennedy proposed. Southerners objected to Northerners' insistence that federal education funds go only to racially integrated schools, while Protestants resisted offering public monies to private Catholic parochial schools. It was one of the "great ironies of American politics," a *New York Times* reporter noted, that "JFK, the immensely popular president, could not reach his legislative goals."

A Liberal Court

Under the leadership of Chief Justice Earl Warren from 1953–1969, the Supreme Court became an aggressive champion of individual rights, fostering the liberal agenda more successfully than Kennedy and Democrats in Congress. Warren believed that the Constitution gave the government the power, and the responsibility, to protect the relatively powerless against oppression by the majority. By rendering opinions on a wide range of social justice issues, the Warren Court brought about a legal revolution in the United States that permanently altered American schools, politics, the criminal justice system, and cultural norms. Northern liberals cheered these decisions, but conservatives in both parties viewed the Warren Court as an activist court, rewriting rather than upholding the Constitution.

In 1954, the *Brown v. Board of Education* decision (see Chapter 25) paved the way for school desegregation. Throughout the 1950s and 1960s, the court dismantled Jim Crow piece by piece, striking down segregated interstate and city buses, upholding the rights of civil rights protesters to hold sit-ins, and embracing mid-1960s federal laws that desegregated public places and guaranteed the right to vote as constitutional.

Another innovative judicial premise, the right to privacy, accompanied the Supreme Court's new support for civil rights. The court struck down state laws that outlawed possession of obscene publications, prohibited the use of contraception, and prevented interracial marriages. Individual Americans, the court ruled, had the right to decide what to read, to use birth control, and to marry whom they wanted. Other decisions redefined how the police arrested and interrogated suspected criminals. The police now had to inform individuals of their constitutional rights to have a state-funded

---

Read the Document *John F. Kennedy, Inaugural Address (1961)*

Why did many young people find Kennedy inspiring?

1954   **Brown v. Board of Education** outlawed racial segregation in public schools.

1962   **Baker v. Carr** gave federal courts right to intervene if states created voting districts of unequal size.

1962   **Engel v. Vitale** outlawed official school prayer in public schools.

1963   **Gideon v. Wainwright** gave accused felons the right to free legal counsel.

1965   **Griswold v. Connecticut** established "right to privacy," overturning state laws banning use of contraception.

1966   **Miranda v. Arizona** required that police inform suspect of right to remain silent and have a lawyer present during police questioning.

1967   **Loving v. Virginia** prohibited state laws banning interracial marriages.

27.2 Major Decisions of the Warren Court
The Supreme Court presided over a major "rights revolution" in the 1960s.

attorney present during questioning and to not answer questions that might incriminate them in a crime.

The court also championed freedom of speech, ruling against Red Scare–era laws that required Communist Party members to register with the government and striking down official school prayer. For years children across America had begun their school days by reciting the "Pledge of Allegiance," to which Congress added the words "under God" in 1954 to contrast American religiosity with the godless communism embraced by the Soviet Union. Most schoolchildren then sang a patriotic song like "America," and some concluded this opening ritual with a short reading from the Bible. The court's ruling against official school prayer in *Engel v. Vitale* (1962) is explored in *Choices and Consequences: Is School Prayer Constitutional?* The decision ignited a firestorm of controversy among conservative Protestants and Catholics. President Kennedy, however, endorsed the decision. Having encountered anti-Catholic bigotry during his 1960 presidential campaign, he welcomed the chance to make religion a strictly private matter as he geared up for his reelection campaign. The chart, *Major Decisions of the Warren Court* (**27.2**), summarizes key court decisions.

The 1964 Election

When Lyndon B. Johnson (LBJ) assumed office after Kennedy's assassination on November 22, 1963 (see Chapter 26), he took up the slain president's liberal agenda. "Let us continue," Johnson proclaimed, echoing Kennedy's earlier entreaty, "let us begin." Unlike Kennedy, Johnson excelled at forging the deals needed to move legislation through Congress, and under his stewardship liberalism gained tremendous momentum. Over the next few months, Johnson used the nation's grief to political advantage by cajoling Congress into enacting key pieces of Kennedy's legislative initiatives, including civil rights legislation, a tax cut, and federally funded public housing. Johnson also announced his own War on Poverty, creating an Office of Economic Opportunity that formed the Jobs Corps to teach inner-city youth vocational skills and created Volunteers in Service to America (VISTA), a domestic Peace Corps that sent privileged young adults to work on community projects in impoverished urban and rural areas.

Despite these successes, Johnson knew that "for millions of Americans I was still illegitimate . . . a pretender to the throne," because he had not been elected president. Johnson saw the 1964 election as an opportunity to validate his presidency. His campaign, however, got off to a rocky start. LBJ expected to lose Southern votes for having openly supported federal civil rights legislation. Segregationist Alabama Governor George Wallace's strong showing in a few Northern Democratic primaries was unwelcome evidence that the president's civil rights record might cost him votes in Northern white working-class ethnic neighborhoods and some middle-class suburbs.

Racial controversy also rocked the Democratic Party's presidential nominating convention in Atlantic City when two separate delegations from Mississippi appeared. Disenfranchised blacks could not vote in Mississippi's official Democratic primary, so the Mississippi Freedom Democratic Party (MFDP) had held a shadow primary to elect their own delegates. This delegation challenged the all-white Democratic Party's claim to represent the state.

Choices and Consequences

IS SCHOOL PRAYER CONSTITUTIONAL?

In 1962, parents in New York State challenged the constitutionality of the short nondenominational prayer that the state Board of Regents had adopted in 1951 for use in the public schools. The question was whether government-directed prayer violated the First Amendment clause that "Congress shall make no law respecting an establishment of religion, or prohibiting the free exercise thereof." The Fourteenth Amendment made this clause applicable to state law.

Choices

1 The prayer was constitutional because students were not required to recite it.

2 An official prayer, regardless of its content, violated the First Amendment.

3 School prayer simply recognized the importance of religion in American society without establishing an official religion.

Decision

In *Engel v. Vitale* (1962) the Supreme Court ruled 6 to 1 that state-directed school prayer was unconstitutional. Justice Hugo Black wrote the majority opinion, stating that the First Amendment prohibited "official prayers for any group of American people to recite as part of a religious program carried on by government."

Consequences

The Warren Court received more mail opposing this case than any other. In 1963, the court also banned reciting the Lord's Prayer and Bible-reading in public school, ruling that to remain neutral the government could not support "the tenets of one or all religions." Outrage over school prayer rulings helped forge a new political coalition between Southern fundamentalist Protestants and Northern Catholics, whose grassroots activism against liberalism contributed to the conservative right's resurgence in the late 1960s. Subsequent court decisions in the 1980s and 1990s prohibited moments of silence for private prayer, minister-led prayers at high school graduations, and student-led prayers at high school football games.

First-graders praying

Continuing Controversies

Does school prayer violate the First Amendment? Those who answer "yes" believe that the Founding Fathers included the establishment clause in the Constitution because the union of government and religion often leads to persecution of those not adhering to mainstream religious views. Freedom of religion requires a completely secular government that neither advances nor inhibits religious beliefs. Many conservatives argue that the court's decisions violated their First Amendment right to exercise free speech and destroyed the spiritual heritage of the nation that stretched back to the Pilgrims.

Why did so many Americans object to the Supreme Court's ruling against school prayer?

27.3 Sequence of Stills from the Daisy Girl Campaign Ad, 1964
This Democratic campaign ad implied that Republican candidate Barry Goldwater would start a nuclear war if elected. The ad script included these directions: "Ominous male voice counts down launch sequence, 10, 9, 8, 7, 6, 5, 4, 3, 2, 1. Close up of girl's face as camera progressively zooms in on her eye. Overlay an atomic explosion into the pupil of her eye."

In deciding which delegation to seat, the convention's Credentials Committee heard gripping testimony from MFDP delegate Fannie Lou Hamer. Thanks to the live television feed covering the proceedings, Americans throughout the nation heard her describe being beaten, losing her job, and receiving a $9,000 water bill even though her house had no running water—all retribution for trying to register to vote. "Is this America, the land of the free and the home of the brave, where we are threatened daily because we want to live as decent human beings?" she asked before the cameras. Suddenly the networks broke away for an impromptu presidential news conference that Johnson had called to interrupt coverage of Hamer's moving personal story. Johnson did not want the convention and his subsequent campaign to center on civil rights. To end the matter, he tried to broker a deal off-camera. When the MFDP rejected the offer of two delegate seats, the all-white Mississippi delegation took the floor.

In the election of 1964, the Democrat and Republican parties fielded candidates who offered starkly different visions of the role that government should play in American society. Johnson spoke of creating a **Great Society** with social welfare reforms that would make the amenities of modern life—a decent standard of living, education, health care, clean water—available to all Americans. Like turn-of-the-century Populists and Progressives, and 1930s New Dealers, he wanted to use the power of the federal government to rein in the wealthy and help economically disadvantaged Americans. Having begun his congressional career as an avid New Dealer in the 1930s, Johnson shared Franklin D. Roosevelt's desire to provide the deserving poor with a decent standard of living. Johnson, however, believed even more strongly than previous generations of liberal reformers in the ability of the government to improve the quality of life in America. Under Johnson the federal government began com-

bating pollution, supporting the arts, and planting trees and flowers along the nation's highways—a beautification project strongly endorsed by his wife, Lady Bird Johnson. Johnson aspired to do more than put food in people's bellies; he also wanted to nurture their spirits.

Barry Goldwater, a conservative Republican senator from Arizona, offered a radically different view of what responsibilities the government should assume. Instead of more government Goldwater proposed dismantling most of the New Deal, including Social Security, and opposed federal civil rights laws, because he saw them as the first step toward creating "a police state." "My aim is not to pass laws but to repeal them," he declared. Goldwater spoke for the radical right, staunch conservatives who felt that the government's interference in the economy and society did more harm than good. His extreme conservative views, however, alarmed prominent moderate Republicans who openly supported Johnson.

In the campaign the Democrats astutely used Goldwater's most extreme pronouncements against him, making the liberal Johnson look almost moderate in comparison. Amplifying a remark by Goldwater that NATO commanders should have the authority to use nuclear weapons, a Democratic television campaign ad pictured a little girl counting as she picked the petals off a daisy (**27.3**). When she reached nine the camera froze on the image of her uplifted face before dissolving into a countdown to a nuclear bomb explosion. As the mushroom cloud dissipated, the screen turned dark and these words appeared: "Vote for President Johnson on November 3. The stakes are too high for you to stay home." The ad provoked its own firestorm of controversy and only aired once. It succeeded, however, in planting the image of Goldwater as a dangerous extremist who might lead the nation into nuclear war.

What competing views of government emerged during the 1964 presidential election?

Watch the **Video** *Lyndon Johnson Presidential Campaign Ad: Little Girl vs. Mushroom Cloud*

VOTE FOR PRESIDENT JOHNSON
ON NOVEMBER 3.

"In Your Heart You Know He's Right."
Republican billboards

"In Your Guts You Know He's Nuts."
Democratic bumper stickers

Dueling campaign slogans in the 1964 presidential election centered on
Republican candidate Barry Goldwater

Johnson won the election with over 61 percent of the popular vote, the largest percentage in American history. The Democrats also widened their control of Congress, strengthening Johnson's hand. Johnson knew that he had to strike immediately to enact his legislative agenda. "Hurry, boys, hurry," he told his staff. "Get that legislation up to the hill and out. Eighteen months from now Landslide Lyndon will be Lame-Duck Lyndon."

The Great Society

Admiring the trees and landscaping along a national highway, reading a food label listing nutritional content in the supermarket, buying unleaded gas at a service station, and watching a documentary on the Public Broadcasting System (PBS): these are all experiences of modern life made possible by Johnson's Great Society. Reflecting liberal faith in the power of the government to do good, the adherents of the Great Society hoped to remove the causes of debilitating poverty by improving the nation's educational system, providing health care to the aged, disabled, and indigent, and creating a new cabinet-level position in housing and urban affairs

to oversee housing and economic relief to struggling cities. Johnson's Great Society also included a new Department of Transportation to manage the federal funds pouring into highway construction and landscaping.

Johnson worked hard to create consensus for his liberal ideals. He offered conservative industrialists tax breaks in return for supporting his social welfare programs, arguing that his programs would create highly skilled workers who consumed more. "Doing something about poverty is economical in the long run," he told them. From his long years in Congress, Johnson knew how to lobby legislators. To secure a needed vote, Johnson brought legislators to the White House and subjected them to "The Treatment," a mixture of cajoling, horse-trading, and intimidation. One congressman recalled the 6'3" Johnson grabbing him by the lapels of his coat, pulling him close and holding his face inches away while he "talked and talked. I figured it was either getting drowned or joining." Johnson pushed through over 65 percent of his proposals, a level of success only surpassed by Franklin D. Roosevelt's 80 percent legislative passage rate. Unable to stop the Great Society juggernaut, Republicans complained bitterly of

View the **Closer Look** *Competing Visions: The Federal Government, Friend or Foe?*

Why was Johnson such an effective politician?

1964   **Economic Opportunity Act**—created VISTA, a domestic version of the Peace Corps, and community-based antipoverty programs that residents designed and administered.

Wilderness Act—protected public lands from development to preserve their unspoiled state.

1965   **Social Security Act**—created Medicare, government health insurance for Americans over 65, and Medicaid, government health insurance for the poor.

Department of Housing and Urban Development—established a new Cabinet-level position to administer Great Society legislation intended to clear slums and build new public housing.

Elementary and Secondary Education Act—allocated $1 billion to improve education for impoverished children.

Higher Education Act—created federal scholarships and loans for students in need.

Immigration Act—eliminated national quotas, set new guidelines favoring family unification and desirable occupational skills.

Highway Beautification Act—provided funds for landscaping along nation's highways.

Motor Vehicle Air Pollution Control Act—set first federal standards for motor vehicle emissions.

1966   **The Department of Transportation**—established a new Cabinet-level position to administer federal funds to improve highways and urban mass transit.

Fair Packaging and Labeling Act—required manufacturers to label number of servings and nutritional information on food packages.

1967   **Public Broadcasting Act**—created public television and radio stations dedicated to educational programming.

27.4 Key Great Society Legislative Achievements
The Great Society built on liberal legislation initiated during the Progressive Era and New Deal to expand the federal government's role in society.

"the three-B Congress—bullied, badgered, and brainwashed."

After pushing first for federal aid to schools, Johnson turned to providing health care to senior citizens and the poor. Facing opposition from health insurance companies and medical professionals to government-provided health care, Johnson compromised. Medicare, government-funded health insurance for the elderly, reimbursed doctors and hospitals whatever they charged senior citizens instead of establishing government rates. Johnson also agreed to let the states, not the federal government, run Medicaid, which provided health services to the poor.

In creating the Great Society, Johnson wanted to restore America's identity as the land of opportunity for immigrants. The Immigration Act of 1965 eliminated the quota system established in the 1920s that set stringent caps on immigration from Southern and Eastern Europe and barred all Asian immigration (see Chapter 21). In the first great wave of immigration since the 1910s, unprecedented numbers of Koreans, Chinese, Filipinos, and Vietnamese migrated to the United States over the next 30 years. Whether immigration benefited or hurt the nation again became a topic on which Americans offered competing visions (see Chapter 29).

By detailing the destructive impact of pesticides, Rachel Carson's best-selling book *Silent Spring* (1962) helped create a politically favorable climate for the environmental regulation that Johnson proposed. *Silent Spring* vividly detailed the destructive impact of pesticides on native birds, provoking alarm over the possibility of a future silent spring when no bird songs would be heard. Johnson noted that Americans had always been proud of "America the beautiful," but polluted air, disappearing forests, and filthy rivers had tarnished this image. The air in some cities was so bad that motorists had to use their headlights after noon. The pronouncement that Lake Erie was "dead" and the sight of oil slicks on the Cuyahoga River in Cleveland burning for eight days after a man tossed a lit cigar into the water underscored the environmental deterioration. These ecological catastrophes helped spawn an exploding grassroots environmental movement that included Greenpeace, a radical direct-action group, and a resurgent Sierra Club, a long-standing conservation society. Responding to environmental activism and growing middle-class concerns, Congress enacted bipartisan environmental measures that required pollution controls on cars and established national standards for acceptable air and water pollution. Johnson also created federally protected wilderness areas to safeguard endangered domestic species at risk of extinction, such as the whooping crane. *The Great Society* chart (**27.4**) contains a list of Johnson's most significant legislation.

What social problems did Great Society laws and programs address?

Read the **Document** *Rachael Carson, Silent Spring (1962)*

Nonviolence Triumphant: The Civil Rights Movement, 1960–1965

Kennedy's and Johnson's strong civil rights agendas came in response to carefully planned grassroots protests against segregation and disenfranchisement in Alabama and Mississippi. These highly visible demonstrations imperiled many civil rights workers, and their leaders hoped to win support from white liberals and moderates nationally by showing them the face of Southern segregationists' resistance. Putting increased pressure on the federal government to act, the Civil Rights Movement ended legalized segregation and disenfranchisement by 1965.

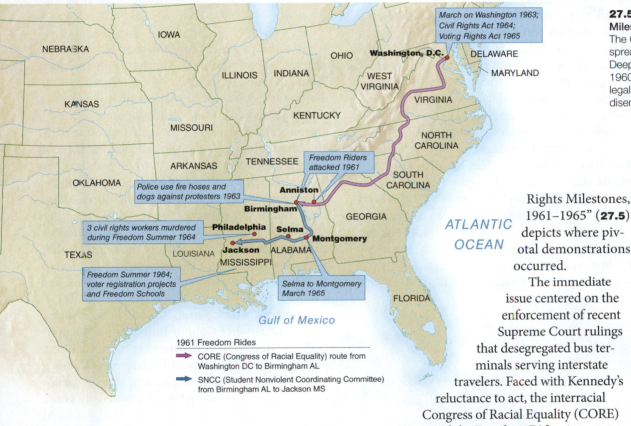

27.5 Civil Rights Milestones, 1961–1965
The Civil Rights Movement spread across the Deep South in the early 1960s, pushing to end legalized segregation and disenfranchisement.

Rights Milestones, 1961–1965" (**27.5**) depicts where pivotal demonstrations occurred.

The immediate issue centered on the enforcement of recent Supreme Court rulings that desegregated bus terminals serving interstate travelers. Faced with Kennedy's reluctance to act, the interracial Congress of Racial Equality (CORE) organized the **Freedom Rides**, interstate bus journeys by black and white activists who entered segregated bus waiting rooms together throughout the South. "We felt we could count on the racists of the South to create a crisis, so that the federal government would be compelled to enforce the law," the African American CORE leader James Farmer recalled.

The Freedom Rides began when 13 whites and blacks (including Farmer and John Lewis, a veteran of the 1960 Nashville sit-ins) boarded an interstate bus on May 4, 1961, in Washington, D.C., headed for the Deep South. Expecting the worst, several riders left sealed letters for their families to open

Kennedy and the Freedom Riders

Inspired by Kennedy's pronouncement during his inaugural address that "the torch has been passed to a new generation of Americans," civil rights leaders expected the new president to aggressively seek an end to Jim Crow. Kennedy, however, adopted a cautious stance, and like his predecessors, remained silent on civil rights. The movement would have to compel the new president to act. The map of "Civil

if they were killed. After a smooth ride through the upper South, in Atlanta the Freedom Riders decided to take two separate buses into the heart of the rigidly segregated Deep South. As the first bus carrying Freedom Riders entered the depot in Anniston, Alabama, a mob pelted the bus with stones and slashed its tires. The driver drove away without stopping, pursued by 50 cars carrying vigilantes. When a flat tire obliged him to stop along a deserted country road, a firebomb forced the Freedom Riders off the bus and into the waiting gauntlet of sticks and crowbars. State troopers arrived in time to save the lives of the traumatized Freedom Riders, two of whom sit stunned on the ground in this photo (**27.6**) of the bus burning. Meanwhile the second bus arrived in Birmingham, where Ku Klux Klansmen beat white Freedom Rider James Peck, a 47-year-old labor and peace activist, when he entered a white-only waiting room with a black colleague. "When you go somewhere looking for trouble, you usually find it," the governor of Alabama remarked unsympathetically.

A photo of Klan members beating Peck accompanied the front-page story in the *New York Times* that informed President Kennedy about the organized attacks on the Freedom Riders. Still dealing with the fallout from the Bay of Pigs invasion that had ended in disaster four weeks earlier and preparing for a summit with Soviet leader Nikita Khrushchev (see Chapter 25), Kennedy urged the Freedom Riders to call off the rest of their scheduled journey. Instead members of the Student

Non-Violent Coordinating Committee (SNCC), the student-run civil rights group founded in 1960 during the sit-ins (see Chapter 25), rushed to Birmingham to ride alongside John Lewis, a founding member of SNCC, taking the place of riders unable or unwilling to continue.

> ## "We can't let them stop us with violence. If we do, the movement is dead,"
> SNCC leader DIANE NASH upon resuming the Freedom Rides, 1961

Avoiding a violent confrontation became the administration's priority. Attorney General Robert Kennedy (the president's brother) secured a promise from the governor of Alabama that state troops would protect the riders. When the state reneged on this promise and another savage attack occurred at the Montgomery, Alabama bus depot, Robert Kennedy sent 600 federal marshals to protect the riders as they traveled to the Mississippi border. Rather than allowing vigilantes to attack the riders, Mississippi authorities took a different tack. As the riders filed off the bus in Jackson, police escorted them into waiting patrol cars. Most of the riders spent four months in jail for violating segregation laws.

The Freedom Rides continued through the summer of 1961, and eventually 300 white and black protesters took part. In the fall the Interstate Commerce Commission required the integration of all interstate travel facilities. The Freedom Rides, however, did not achieve the organizers' broader goals of securing President Kennedy's enthusiastic support for the Civil Rights Movement. Despite his own integrationist views, President Kennedy remained preoccupied with protecting his white Democratic Southern base and feared that open discussion of America's racial problems provided fodder for Soviet propaganda. It would take a shocking visual demonstration of racial violence in Birmingham, Alabama, to make him a champion of civil rights.

27.6 Freedom Riders Attacked in Anniston, Alabama, 1961 Traumatized civil rights activists sit on the ground after a mob firebombed the bus the Freedom Riders were riding to protest the segregation of interstate bus facilities.

Who made key choices that affected the course and outcome of the Freedom Rides?

Birmingham, 1963

In 1963, the Southern Christian Leadership Conference (SCLC), Martin Luther King Jr.'s church-based civil rights organization, unfurled a carefully coordinated campaign to desegregate Birmingham, Alabama, perhaps the most segregated city in the nation. "We were trying to launch a systematic, wholehearted battle against segregation that would set the pace for the nation," explained the Birmingham SCLC leader Fred Shuttlesworth. Volatile Police Chief Bull Connor made the city an especially dangerous place to launch such a protest. SCLC accurately predicted that they would gain the attention of the president once the world saw Connor's police attacking nonviolent demonstrators with high-power water hoses and dogs. Television was vital to this campaign: The images of violence pouring into living rooms would make it impossible for moderate white Americans to ignore the nation's racial problems.

In April 1963, King and the SCLC initiated their **Birmingham campaign** with economic boycotts and sit-ins. Press coverage increased when King and Shuttlesworth led a march in defiance of a state injunction that prohibited public demonstrations. Police immediately arrested and jailed the pair. King timed his arrest to occur on Good Friday, the day that Jesus died on the cross, using religious symbolism to underscore the immorality of racial persecution.

As King sat in solitary confinement, the *Birmingham News* published an open letter to him from white liberal Southern clergymen who criticized the demonstrations as "unwise and untimely" for trying to provoke hardcore segregationists. The opinion of liberal and moderate Southern whites mattered to King. The nonviolent strategy depended on swaying those who may have traditionally supported segregation but were not die-hard racists. Visitors to King smuggled out his response, written on the margins of newspapers and scraps of toilet paper during his eight-day jail stay. King's "Letter from a Birmingham Jail" did not influence events in Birmingham (by the time it was published, the protests had ended), but the text was one of his most eloquent statements on the dehumanizing aspects of racial discrimination. "For years now I have heard the word 'Wait!' It rings in the ear of every Negro

with piercing familiarity. This 'Wait' has almost always meant 'Never,' " King wrote. How would whites feel about sleeping in their cars when traveling because "no motel will accept you," telling their children that they could not go to the segregated amusement parks advertised on television, and "living constantly on tiptoe stance, never quite knowing what to expect next"? These were the reasons, King explained, "why we find it difficult to wait."

Hoping to stop downtown demonstrations that were keeping shoppers away and worried that the federal government might intervene, moderate white business owners initiated secret talks with SCLC leaders without Chief Connor's knowledge. To increase pressure on the businessmen, SCLC went ahead with marches despite lukewarm support from Birmingham churches and adults. To fill the ranks Jim Bevel, another veteran of the Nashville sit-ins, proposed turning Birmingham into a "children's crusade" by recruiting from the city's high schools and, if necessary, middle and elementary schools. "A boy from high school has the same effect in terms of being in jail, in terms of putting pressure on the city, as his father, and yet there's no economic threat to the family, because the father is still on the job," Bevel argued.

On May 3, 1963, the second day of the protests, Carolyn McKinstry, like many others, left her high school without telling her parents that she was joining the demonstrations. When the teenagers arrived downtown, Connor was waiting with water hoses and police dogs. A shocked nation viewed television and newspaper images of firefighters directing torrents of water at McKinstry and her friends and police dogs biting protesters. (See *Images as History: Birmingham, 1963*, page 822.)

As the SCLC had hoped, Northerners reacted with outrage to this blatant display of police brutality, while Southern moderates worried that Connor's heavy-handed tactics would invite more federal scrutiny of Southern politics and racial customs. The Civil Rights Movement scored a major victory in Birmingham. Besides winning a commitment to desegregate lunch counters and schools and the promise of jobs, the protests renewed President Kennedy's interest in civil rights. Concerned about losing momentum in the Cold War, he asked the nation: "Are we to say to the world—and much more importantly to each other—that this is the land of the free, except for the Negroes … ?"

Read the Document *Martin Luther King Jr., "Letter from Birmingham City Jail" (1963)*

Why did the Birmingham campaign succeed?

Images as History
BIRMINGHAM, 1963

In Birmingham civil rights activists developed a strategy that included using television and news photos to their advantage. The Civil Rights Movement got exactly the images the activists wanted in 1963 when the Birmingham Police Chief Bull Connor unleashed extreme violence against protesters in the downtown area. How important was the press to the success of the Birmingham campaign? Why did the public react so strongly to these photos?

As a white child in rural Alabama, *Life* photojournalist Charles Moore had accepted segregation "as the way things were." Birmingham was a turning point in his own evolving social consciousness:

"The water hoses hurt a lot," recalled Carolyn McKinstry, the high school sophomore girl pictured here.

Three teenage protesters clung to a doorway as water whipped their bodies, an ordeal that Moore immortalized in this iconic photograph of the Birmingham protests.

Fire Hoses, Birmingham, 1963

McKinstry remained "proud of what I had done," but afterwards questioned "the tactics that they [SCLC] were using because I think I felt that you could actually be hurt."

Moore avoided taking photos that might send a mixed message to the public. He took no pictures of students, only partly schooled in nonviolent techniques, who threw pieces of concrete at the police—even after a slab hit and injured him.

Does knowing more about McKinstry and Moore alter this photograph's meaning?

Watch the **Video** *Video Lecture: Photographing the Civil Rights Movement, Birmingham, 1963*

"My emotional involvement in the story grew as I saw what was happening." On the afternoon of May 3, 1963, Moore arrived in downtown Birmingham just as firefighters turned their high-pressure hoses and police dogs on teenage demonstrators. When Moore's photos appeared in *Life*, a magazine read by half of American adults in the 1960s, his images, along with television coverage of the mayhem, helped transform Birmingham from a local crisis into an event that prompted national soul-searching about democracy in America. Inspired by these images, civil rights activists initiated 1,000 demonstrations in nearly 100 cities throughout the South.

Movement leaders wanted liberal and moderate Americans to blame the police for escalating the violence in Birmingham, and Moore's pictures left little room for an alternative explanation.

The police arrested Moore when he refused to stop taking pictures. "It was scary to be a victim" of abusive police, Moore recalled, an experience that strengthened his solidarity with the protesters.

"The sight of snarling dogs, and the possibility of dogs ripping flesh, was revolting to me," Moore recollected.

Moore sided with the protesters, but the story that accompanied his photos blamed extremists on both sides for the melee. "[The pictures] are frightening because of the brutal methods being used by white policemen in Birmingham, Ala. against Negro demonstrators. They are frightening because the Negro strategy of 'nonviolent direct action' invites that very brutality—and welcomes it as a way to promote the Negroes' cause, which, under the law, is right," *Life* told readers.

Police Dogs, Birmingham, 1963

View the **Closer Look** *Images as History: Birmingham, 1963*

How did *Life* magazine and Moore differ over the meaning of this photo?

In his televised address to the nation Kennedy proposed a civil rights act that would outlaw racially segregated public facilities nationwide. The white supremacist response came immediately. The next day a Klansman shot and killed Medgar Evers, the head of the National Association for the Advancement of Colored People (NAACP) in Mississippi, as Evers stood in the driveway of his Jackson home. Evers's killing was the first, but not the last, assassination of a major political figure of the 1960s.

March on Washington

Birmingham had given the civil rights cause national and international visibility, and Evers's shocking assassination reinforced Kennedy's determination to enact a sweeping civil rights bill. Southern Democratic senators were equally prepared to filibuster to prevent its passage. Intent on winning this legislative battle, King and other civil rights leaders decided to organize the **March on Washington**, a massive demonstration in the nation's capital that would demand passage of a federal civil rights act. Adopting the slogan, "Jobs and Freedom," organizers underscored the link between greater economic opportunity and civic equality. The organizing committee included African American labor leader A. Philip Randolph, founder of the Brotherhood of Sleeping Car Porters. Randolph had cancelled his own March on Washington in 1941 when President Franklin D. Roosevelt agreed to guarantee fair protection at the workplace during World War II (see Chapter 23).

On August 28, 1963, in the nation's largest political protest to date, more than 200,000 marchers walked from the Washington Monument to the Lincoln Memorial to listen to three hours of music and speeches. This photo (**27.7**) of Martin Luther King Jr. talking to a reporter reveals why organizers put their speakers' platform before the Lincoln Memorial. On the hundredth anniversary of the Emancipation Proclamation, the larger-than-life statue of President Abraham Lincoln in the background offered a potent reminder of how long African Americans had waited for equal rights. "I have a dream that my four little children will one day live in a nation where they will not be judged by the color of their skin, but by the content of their character," declared King in the day's most memorable speech.

The march received the national media's full attention. It was also among the first events that television viewers throughout the world could watch live, thanks to a new communications satellite. From Cairo to Amsterdam people participated in sympathy marches before American embassies and sent petitions to Kennedy. By August nearly 78 percent of white Americans believed that images of racial discrimination in the United States made it harder for the nation to achieve its Cold War foreign policy goals.

Two weeks after the March on Washington, a bomb tossed into Birmingham's Sixteenth Street Baptist Church killed four girls attending Sunday school. Carolyn McKinstry, the young woman that Charles Moore had photographed during the Birmingham protests, was in the church at the time, a friend to the girls. The attack convinced her that she too would one day die at the hands of white supremacists. "I guess this bombing is Birmingham's answer to the march," exclaimed an enraged Anne Moody, who was working on a voter registration campaign in Mississippi. President

27.7 March on Washington, 1963 Martin Luther King Jr. speaks to a reporter while standing inside the Lincoln Memorial to underscore that 100 years after Lincoln issued the Emancipation Proclamation blacks were still second-class citizens in the segregated South.

What symbolism and rhetoric connected the 1963 March on Washington to the past and future?

Watch the **Video** *Martin Luther King Jr.'s Speech at the March on Washington, August, 1963*

Kennedy's assassination two months later only underscored her growing conviction that "nonviolence is through."

Freedom Summer

With SCLC's Birmingham campaign to desegregate public facilities successfully concluded, the spotlight turned to Mississippi. **Freedom Summer**, a multipronged attack on white supremacy in Mississippi during the summer of 1964, was a turning point in the Civil Rights Movement. It forced the federal government to deepen its commitment to equal rights, laid bare the rising tensions within the Civil Rights Movement, and trained a generation of student activists who would soon spearhead new leftist and feminist movements.

In the summer of 1964, the Council of Federated Organizations (COFO) coordinated the efforts of civil rights groups to launch Freedom Summer, including SNCC and CORE. With ambivalence SNCC recruited many Northern whites to work on the voter registration projects. SNCC had reluctantly concluded that the national media, which had started to ignore blacks-only protests, would pay attention to Freedom Summer only if white students

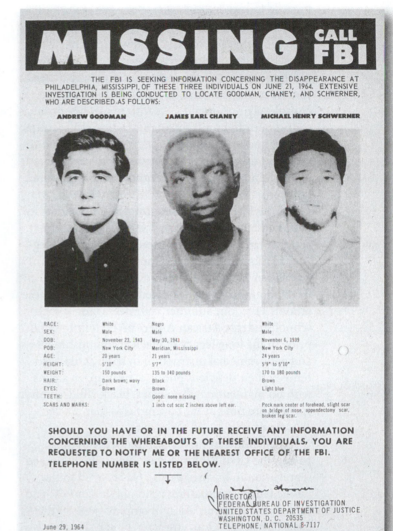

27.8 FBI Poster of Three Slain Freedom Summer Civil Rights Workers, 1964 The murder of these three CORE workers hardened the resolve of many Freedom Summer volunteers to continue registering blacks to vote, but some blacks resented that the nation seemed to care only if white activists disappeared.

> ## "At night, people should not sit in their rooms without drawn shades."
> ### Rule from CORE security handbook meant to protect Freedom Summer workers from sniper attacks

were involved. SNCC, CORE, and COFO hoped that the media spotlight would protect Freedom Summer workers from racial violence, protection that the federal government was unwilling to give. This calculation proved incorrect.

On the first day of Freedom Summer, three CORE workers went missing in Mississippi. Twenty-four-year-old Michael Schwerner was a white Jewish social worker from Manhattan who, one coworker recalled, "had been deeply affected by the photographs of Negroes sprawling under the dogs and fire hoses" in Birmingham. On June 21, 1964, Schwerner went with James Chaney, a 21-year-old Mississippi black activist, and 20-year-old Andrew Goodman, another white Jewish volunteer from New York, to inspect a church that the Ku Klux Klan had burned to stop CORE from opening a school there. On the return home they passed near Philadelphia, Mississippi, where local sheriff (and Klansman) Cecile Price recognized Schwerner's car and license plate from a circular the governor's office had issued concerning "outside agitators." Price arrested them for speeding and then alerted fellow Klansmen to join him for an ambush after he released the three men from jail in the middle of the night.

The trio's disappearance created national headlines, forcing the FBI to launch a manhunt across five states to find them. The FBI posted this circular (**27.8**) seeking information about the men's whereabouts, haunting images that conveyed more than the dangers of vigilante violence.

Read the **Document** *Letters from Mississippi Freedom Summer*

What interracial tensions within the Civil Rights Movement did Freedom Summer expose?

Putting her own grief aside, Schwerner's wife Rita, herself a CORE field worker, publicly voiced her suspicion that "if Mr. Chaney, who is a native Mississippian, had been alone at the time of the disappearance, . . . this case, like so many others that have come before it, . . . would have gone completely unnoticed." As if to prove her point, sailors sent to comb through Mississippi swamps for the bodies of the three men (now assumed to be dead) discovered the corpses of three lynched black men whose disappearances authorities had ignored.

As the FBI investigation unfolded, Freedom Summer continued. Nearly 1,000 black and white activists fanned out throughout Mississippi to register blacks in rural areas. Hoping to recruit and train a new generation of student leaders, SNCC and COFO founded summer Freedom Schools. In these schools Freedom Summer volunteers taught high school students African American history to build pride in the long legacy of black accomplishment and gave remedial instruction in basic subjects to remedy their deficient public education. In a state with no mandatory school laws, black children often spent more time in the cotton fields than in the classroom.

In the midst of Freedom Summer, Congress passed the **Civil Rights Act of 1964**, which banned segregation in businesses and places open to the public (such as restaurants and public schools) and prohibited discrimination in employment on the basis of race, religion, ethnicity, or sex. This landmark legislation, the most sweeping civil rights law since Reconstruction, came about because thousands of individuals risked arrest, murder, or unemployment to participate in boycotts, sit-ins, and street demonstrations in towns and cities throughout the South. Their activism went unnoticed in the national press, which focused mostly on a few dramatic moments such as the disappearance of Schwerner, Chaney, and Goodman.

A month after the Civil Rights Act's passage, after six weeks of searching, the FBI paid $30,000 to an informant who helped officers locate the three men's bodies buried in an earthen dam. All three had been shot in the head, and Chaney's shattered bones attested to the savage beating he had received. No one was ever convicted of the murders, although Price and nine others were found guilty on federal conspiracy charges in 1967 and served a few years in jail.

Like Kennedy, Johnson knew that the world was watching events unfold in Mississippi. Passage of the Civil Rights Act was front-page news overseas, and world leaders rushed to congratulate Johnson. Winning the 1964 Nobel Peace Prize, King was now an international figure who inspired social justice activists worldwide.

Passage of the 1964 Civil Rights Act was a great victory for the Civil Rights Movement, but the combat-like conditions during Freedom Summer took their toll. Fearful SNCC volunteers began to arm themselves for self-defense. Many blacks resented the media attention given to white activists. Meanwhile female civil rights workers, black and white, objected to males' expectations that they would clean and cook for them. The stage was set for a fracturing within the activist community.

Selma and the Voting Rights Act of 1965

The nonviolent Civil Rights Movement registered one more significant victory before that fracturing occurred, using a stand-off in Selma, Alabama, to secure President Johnson's open support for federal legislation guaranteeing blacks the right to vote. On Sunday March 7, 1965, a day soon known as "Bloody Sunday," about 600 marchers left the small town of Selma, Alabama, and began walking across the Edmund Pettis Bridge that spanned the Alabama River. They intended to march 50 miles to Montgomery, the state capitol, to demand voting rights. At the other end of the bridge, county troopers armed with clubs and tear gas waited for them. When the marchers knelt in prayer at the end of the bridge, Sheriff Jim Clark ordered the troopers to attack as white spectators cheered.

Photographers and television crews witnessed the violent attack. That evening ABC interrupted the film *Judgment at Nuremburg*, a dramatized account of trials that convicted Nazi leaders of crimes against humanity, to show news footage of the Bloody Sunday assault. The juxtaposition between the film's portrayal of the Holocaust and events in Selma haunted viewers. Late that evening the door opened to the chapel in Selma that served as the marchers' headquarters. "We have seen on the television screen the violence that took place today, and we're here to share it with you," announced a group of blacks and whites from New Jersey who had chartered a plane to arrive that night.

Read the **Document** *Voting Literacy Test (1965)*

On Monday, March 15, 1965, President Johnson, who had spoken privately with King before Selma about how to win public support for voting rights legislation, announced in a televised address that he was sending a federal voting rights act to Congress. "It's not just Negroes, but really it's all of us, who must overcome the crippling legacy of bigotry and injustice," Johnson told the nation. "And we shall overcome," he concluded, quoting the anthem of the Civil Rights Movement.

A triumphant march from Selma began the following Sunday, March 21, 1965. Along the way a group of men, women, whites, blacks, and veterans stopped to pray in front of a billboard claiming that King was a communist (**27.9**). Erected by the John Birch Society, the sign showed a photo of King attending a workshop at the Highlander Folk School for social activists, labeling it a "Communist Training School." Like the

> ## "I asked my mother and father for my birthday present to become registered voters."
>
> Eight-year-old SHEYANN WEBB, youngest member of the first Selma to Montgomery march.

Republican's 1964 presidential candidate Barry Goldwater, the arch-conservative Birch society opposed federal civil rights legislation as a violation of state and individual rights. The marchers took advantage of every opportunity to enlist the sympathies of mainstream journalists like Haynes Johnson, the white reporter standing and taking notes who won a Pulitzer Prize for his coverage of the Selma march. When the marchers arrived in Montgomery five days later, King addressed the crowd on the steps of the state capitol, looking down at the Dexter Avenue Baptist Church where he had helped initiate the Montgomery Bus Boycott ten years earlier (see Chapter 25): "I know you are asking today, 'How long will it take?' ... How long? Not long, because no lie can live forever." Five months later Johnson signed the **Voting Rights Act of 1965**, which prohibited literacy tests and poll taxes and authorized the use of federal registrars to register voters if states failed to respect the Fifteenth Amendment. Within a year over 9,000 blacks had registered in Dallas County, Alabama, enough to block Jim Clark's reelection as sheriff.

27.9 Prayer Vigil During the March from Selma to Montgomery, March 21, 1965 This image of peaceful protesters praying was meant to counter charges from ultra-conservative groups that the civil rights movement was intentionally provoking violence to pave the way for a communist revolution.

The Fractured Left

Conservative Republicans and Democrats never liked the antipoverty initiatives of Kennedy and Johnson, while die-hard segregationists adamantly opposed the integrationist goals of nonviolent civil rights leaders like King. The most potent attacks on these progressive visions, however, came from the left where competing visions proliferated. By the mid-1960s, disaffected student activists increasingly dismissed the Great Society as too cautious and protested against "Johnson's War" in Vietnam, while others renounced all ties to mainstream culture. Within the Civil Rights Movement, militancy replaced nonviolence as the dominant ethos. Meanwhile many white women left the Civil Rights Movement to pursue women's liberation.

The New Left and the Counterculture

The baby boom generation came of age in the 1960s. By 1968, over half of the American population was under the age of 25. By then a core of white middle-class college students had created the **New Left**, a small, but highly visible, coalition of student-based organizations that attacked racial discrimination, poverty, and the war in Vietnam.

Al Haber formed Students for a Democratic Society (SDS) in 1960 at the University of Michigan, believing "that if any really radical liberal force is going to develop in America, it is going to come from the colleges and the young." In 1962, Tom Hayden, a white activist in the Civil Rights Movement, penned the group's manifesto, "The Port Huron Statement." Hayden urged his peers to act, noting "we are people of this generation, bred in at least modest comfort, housed now in universities, looking uncomfortably to the world we inherit."

Although most college-age Americans did not attend university, their ranks were increasing. By 1965 nearly 6.5 million students attended colleges or universities, compared with 2.2 million in 1950. Strict rules governed student behavior. Students lived in single-sex dormitories, had to obey curfews each evening, and abide by dress codes that prohibited female students from wearing pants. The University of California, Berkeley, even forbade political debate or discussion on campus, a rule in place since the 1930s to prevent communist student groups from recruiting.

For years students had used a small strip just outside the Berkeley campus main gate to hand out political pamphlets or give speeches. In the fall of 1964, the university administration shut this down as well, provoking the Free Speech Movement, a mass student protest that accused the University of California

of denying students the right to freedom of speech. Protest leader Mario Savio, who had just returned from Freedom Summer, pointed out that "the two battlefields [in Mississippi and Berkeley] may seem quite different to some observers, but this is not the case. The same rights are at stake in both places—the right to participate as citizens in a democratic society." Aided by sympathetic television coverage, the Free Speech Movement succeeded after four months of demonstrations and inspired left-leaning students on other university campuses. Most college students never joined any organized protests, but in response to those who did, universities eliminated codes of conduct, introduced more elective courses into curriculums, and established black and women's studies.

After 1964, SDS chapters organized antiwar demonstrations on university campuses that included teach-ins and draft-card burnings (see Chapter 26). SDS at first embraced the liberal vision of using representative government to implement incremental reforms, but in the course of its antiwar protests the group became more radical. By 1968, New Left leaders expressed open admiration for Marxist-inspired communist revolutionaries like the Vietnamese leader Ho Chi Minh and Ernesto "Che" Guevara, a colleague of Cuban dictator Fidel Castro trying to foster revolution in Bolivia and the Congo. When student-led protests roiled Europe and South America in 1968, the American New Left assumed they were part of a global youth rebellion that would reshape the world.

Once the novelty of student demonstrations wore off, getting television reporters to cover their protests required more outlandish theatrics, images that increasingly radicalized student leaders eagerly provided. Press scrutiny sometimes backfired, however. Nightly news reports of demonstrators hurling bricks and expletives frightened moderates, who viewed the New Left as unpatriotic and dangerous.

The challenge to the liberal vision went beyond the New Left. An emerging counterculture, the heir to the Beat cultural ethos of the 1950s (see Chapter 25), emphasized rejecting middle-class lifestyles more than agitating for political change. Hippies, youthful social rebels who renounced material acquisition and used drugs to explore their inner spiritual selves, refused to dedicate their lives to acquiring the same suburban home, car, and corporate job as their parents. The hippie utopian vision embraced peace, pleasure, sexual liberation, and sharing of material resources, an ethos captured in this 1968 photograph (**27.10**) of a hippie gathering by Robert Altman (who became a renowned filmmaker).

Drugs, especially marijuana and lysergic acid diethylamide (LSD), formed an essential part of the counterculture's challenge to the values of middle-class society. Rock music exposed many young people to these counterculture ideals. Bob Dylan, a folk troubadour whose songs had inspired civil rights protesters, transformed himself into a rock musician with poetic lyrics steeped in drug references. The Beatles underwent a similar transformation after taking America by storm. Nearly 60 percent of the nation watched the four mop-headed British musicians sing their masterful pop concoctions during the band's first televised performance on the *Ed Sullivan Show* in 1964. In just three years the group underwent a complete makeover with the release of an album, *Sgt. Pepper's Lonely Hearts Club Band,* that broadcasted the counterculture message, "I'd love to turn you on"—a reference to taking drugs and having sex. The heyday of the marriage between rock music and the counterculture was Woodstock, a free three-day drug-infused music festival held on a farm in upstate New York, in August 1969.

New Left and young civil rights activists adopted a hippie-style of dress and experimented with drugs, but unlike hippies they remained dedicated to political activism. Most black civil rights activists, rather than rejecting white middle-class materialism, were fighting for their fair share of the nation's wealth and prosperity. New Left radicals shared the hippie belief that acquisitive capitalism bred inequality and injustice, but they were committed to social action, not "tuning out."

Out of the spotlight conservative college students were also active, laying the foundation for the coming conservative resurgence within a Republican Party dominated by moderates. College students formed the Young Americans for Freedom (YAF) in 1960 under the guidance of *National Review* founder William F. Buckley. Throughout the 1960s the Radical Right YAF attracted more members than the New Left SDS. Goldwater supporters in 1964, these conservative students championed limited economic regulation, states' rights, respect for law and order, and staunch anticommunism. For the time being, however, the New Left had center stage.

27.10 Holding Together In their quest to define an alternative lifestyle, hippies emphasized love and harmony in their gatherings—sometimes wearing clothes, sometimes not.

Malcolm X: An Alternative to Nonviolence

The New Left and counterculture did not speak with one voice, and by the mid-1960s fractures within the Civil Rights Movement were also apparent. The Nation of Islam, an African American religious sect founded in the 1930s, rejected integration as the path to salvation for the black community and instead wanted to establish a separate black nation within the United States. Followers of Nation of Islam leader Elijah Muhammad prayed to Mecca five times a day, dressed modestly, and avoided pork and alcohol. The Nation of Islam departed from mainstream Islamic practices, however, by viewing whites as "blue-eyed devils" whom Allah would condemn to eternal damnation on a forthcoming Day of Judgment. The celebrated African American writer James Baldwin understood the appeal of Elijah Muhammad's prophecies, even though he rejected them. "The white God has not delivered them, perhaps the black God will," wrote Baldwin in *The Fire Next Time* (1963) to explain the Nation of Islam's growing popularity within Northern urban neighborhoods.

Malcolm X moved armed self-defense and black separatism from the fringes to the center of the civil rights debate. A magnetic speaker, he had converted to Islam while serving a six-year stint in prison. After his release he changed his name from Malcolm Little to Malcolm X, the X signifying the lost name of his African ancestors.

27.11 Malcolm X Snaps a Photo of Muhammad Ali, 1964.
This meeting between two mid-1960s icons of black manhood came just after Ali won the heavyweight boxing title. Both Black Muslims, Malcolm X and Muhammad Ali enjoyed keeping whites on edge with militant rhetoric that emphasized black pride and physical prowess.

"I don't see any American dream; I see an American nightmare."
MALCOLM X, ridiculing King's "I Have a Dream Speech" during the 1963 March on Washington

Even during the heyday of nonviolence in the 1950s and early 1960s, more militant voices within the black community championed a competing vision of self-defense and racial pride that extended back to Marcus Garvey (see Chapter 21). Malcolm X ridiculed the nonviolent strategy of the Christian-led SCLC. "If someone puts his hand on you, send him to the cemetery," he proclaimed in 1963. He received an increasingly sympathetic hearing among Northern blacks who could already vote and sit alongside whites at lunch counters but encountered racial prejudice that relegated them to segregated ghettos, limited their employment opportunities, and subjected them to police harassment.

Malcolm X linked the domestic black struggle for civil rights to the anti-colonial movements underway in Africa and Asia, underscoring that the American Civil Rights Movement was one of many liberation movements being waged worldwide, including a campaign to end apartheid (rigid racial segregation) in South Africa. Malcolm X's rhetorical links with Africa resonated among northern blacks, who adopted African clothing, hairstyles, and music. Many jettisoned the old label "Negro" in favor of "black" to reflect their growing color consciousness and racial pride.

This photo (**27.11**) of Malcolm X smiling as he photographs boxer Muhammad Ali in a Miami restaurant after Ali won the heavyweight championship in 1964 conveys the charisma that each man radiated, and the

strong bonds they maintained to the black urban community. Ali, who called himself "the greatest," gained fame not just for his athletic feats but, like Malcolm X, also for his defiance of authority. The day after this photo was taken, he announced his conversion to the Nation of Islam, changing his name from Cassius Clay to Muhammad Ali. His mentor Malcolm X applauded Ali's announcement, knowing that the magnetic boxer would help attract other converts.

By the time Malcolm X's ideas began to gain widespread currency among disaffected blacks, however, his own philosophies were starting to shift. Viewing the increasingly powerful Malcolm X as a potential rival, Elijah Muhammad had silenced Malcolm X a few months before this photo was taken. Malcolm X's transgression was calling the assassination of President Kennedy "a case of 'the chickens coming home to roost'" because whites were finally experiencing the vigilante violence that had terrorized blacks for decades. Malcolm X left the Nation of Islam soon afterward, and Ali severed all ties with him. In 1964 Malcolm X made a pilgrimage to Mecca, Islam's holiest city, in Saudi Arabia, where he saw pilgrims "of all colors" coming together to worship. This trip gave him new faith in the possibility of interracial cooperation. His more moderate stance did little to mollify his Nation of Islam critics. On February 21, 1965, as he stood to address a gathering in Harlem, three Nation of Islam members shot him dead.

Watts and Chicago

Malcolm X did not live to help heal the fractures that divided the Civil Rights Movement. In the mid-1960s, tensions among activists led to an overt split between those who continued to advocate non-violence and integration and those who assumed a more militant, nationalistic approach. Stalwart civil rights veterans like John Lewis and Martin Luther King Jr. never stopped advocating their vision of nonviolent collective action. But after 1965, the vision of armed self-defense won many adherents. When riots and demonstrations in Northern cities moved the civil rights struggle to their own backyards, the limits of Northern whites' support for the goal of racial equality became evident.

August 6, 1965, the day that President Johnson signed the Voting Rights Act of 1965, represented the high-water mark of the nonviolent Civil Rights Movement. Five days later, with activists

still basking in the afterglow of this achievement, riots erupted in Watts, a Los Angeles black ghetto rife with high unemployment, poor schools, and drug use. The routine arrest of a black man for drunk driving, which residents viewed as yet another example of the police harassment that plagued them daily, sparked the uprising. Watts burned for six days before 16,000 national guardsmen managed to stop the violence. The Watts riot left 34 dead and destroyed $35 million in property, including many businesses and homes owned by blacks.

Watts changed the image of African American protest in the white imagination from a portrait of nonviolent demonstrators kneeling in prayer before their attackers to one of lawless mobs shouting "Burn, baby, burn." The same cameras that helped awaken the liberal and moderate white consciousness now stoked white fears about unchecked black violence. The press ignored residents' complaints about police harassment and instead portrayed Los Angeles police and firemen (**27.12**) as heroes who struggled to prevent black rioters from destroying their own community. Watts was the prelude to four long, hot summers of racial rioting that rocked cities throughout the nation from 1965–1968.

27.12 Watts Riots, 1965. Images of heroic policemen arresting looters and firemen putting out fires set by rebellious blacks reassured anxious whites that authorities were restoring law and order. Only two years earlier, photographs of police and firemen attacking peaceful black demonstrators in Birmingham had encouraged whites to support integration and voting rights.

> "It's much easier to integrate lunch counters than it is to eradicate slums."
>
> MARTIN LUTHER KING JR, 1968

Why did many Northern whites lose sympathy for the Civil Rights Movement?

King rushed to Watts intent on teaching residents to employ nonviolent means to express their grievances. Instead, it was King who came away with a valuable lesson. When he toured the smoldering ruins, a crowd of black youths shouted "We won!" "How can you say you won when 34 Negroes are dead, your community is destroyed and whites are using the riot as an excuse for inaction?" King asked. Their reply taught him the extent of despair among Northern blacks: "We won because we made them pay attention to us."

The Watts riots convinced King to move aggressively to end economic inequality nationwide now that battles against legalized segregation and disenfranchisement were won. But the SCLC's 1966 Chicago campaign dramatically demonstrated the limits of moderate Northern whites' support for racial equality. When protesters marched through all-white neighborhoods to protest racial discrimination in renting and selling houses, white crowds pelted them with bottles and rocks, which some marchers threw back. "I have never seen—even in Mississippi and Alabama—mobs as hostile and hate-filled as I've seen in Chicago," King noted with dismay. After King's death in 1968, President Johnson successfully lobbied Congress to pass the Fair Housing Act that prohibited discrimination in selling, renting, or financing housing as a memorial to the slain leader.

Black Power and the Black Panthers

The "black power" slogan emerged during James Meredith's 1966 "March against Fear" in Mississippi. Meredith had faced down hostile crowds in 1962 when he became the first black student to graduate from the University of Mississippi. Four years later he decided to march 220 miles by himself from Memphis, Tennessee, to Jackson, Mississippi, hoping that his courage would inspire blacks to register to vote. On the second day of his march, a sniper waiting in the bushes wounded Meredith. When activists flocked to continue his march, SNCC leader Stokely Carmichael told participants "we been saying freedom for six years, and we ain't got nothing. What we gonna start saying now is black power." **Black Power**, however, soon became a slippery term that people employed in different ways. *Competing Visions: Defining "Black Power"* explores how black leaders with different ideologies embraced competing definitions of Black Power.

In 1966, Black Power militants came to the forefront of traditionally nonviolent civil rights organizations like SNCC, which expelled whites to foster black community leadership. That same year Bobby Seale and Huey Newton founded the Black Panther Party for Self-Defense in Oakland, California. The Black Panthers were a militant civil rights group dedicated to armed self-defense, racial pride, and inner-city renewal.

To project an image of strength that would appeal to inner-city youth, the Black Panthers wore commando-style attire including black leather jackets, black pants, black berets, and dark sunglasses, items already fashionable among young black men. The 1967 photo (**27.13**) that became the emblem of the Black Panther Movement depicted Newton sitting in a throne-like wicker chair surrounded by a zebra rug and warrior shields, symbols of a racial identity rooted in African culture. Wearing Western military-style clothing and holding a rifle in his right hand and a spear in his left, Newton stared into the camera with the steely resolve of a revolutionary.

The paramilitary group initiated community projects including free breakfasts for school children and health clinics, but the

27.13 Black Panther Leader Huey Newton, 1967 This staged photo showed Newton dressed in guerrilla-style clothing surrounded by symbols of African warrior culture to convey the Black Panthers' militant, nationalistic ideology.

Did the tactics used by the Black Panthers to publicize their militant vision help or hurt them?

Competing Visions

DEFINING "BLACK POWER"

The image of a raised, clenched black fist became the most enduring symbol of "Black Power," but it only represented one view of the slogan's meaning. In the following excerpts civil rights leaders debate the meaning and implications of Black Power. Malcolm X never used the term directly, but his separatist message laid the groundwork for Black Power nationalism later in the decade. In contrast Martin Luther King Jr. advocated using nonviolent methods to empower the black community. Political scientist Charles Hamilton notes the various interpretations given to the "Black Power" slogan and embraces one that emphasizes pride in being black. Is there any agreement among these competing definitions? How does this debate compare to the one between Marcus Garvey and W. E. B. DuBois in the 1920s (see *Competing Visions*, Chapter 21)?

The revolutionary, nationalist rhetoric in Malcolm X's fiery 1963 "Message to the Grassroots" greatly influenced later advocates of Black Power.

There's no such thing as a nonviolent revolution. The only kind of revolution that is nonviolent is the Negro revolution. The only revolution in which the goal is loving your enemy is the Negro revolution. It's the only revolution in which the goal is a desegregated lunch counter, a desegregated theater, a desegregated park, and a desegregated public toilet; you can sit down next to white folks—on the toilet. That's no revolution. Revolution is based on land. Land is the basis of all independence. Land is the basis of freedom, justice, and equality …

Whoever heard of a revolution where they lock arms … singing "We Shall Overcome"? You don't do that in a revolution. You don't do any singing, you're too busy swinging.

In a "Conversation with Martin Luther King," March 25, 1968, King offered a definition of Black Power that supported his strategy of nonviolence.

We have always stood up against injustices. We have done it militantly. Now, so often the word 'militant' is misunderstood because most people think of militancy in military terms. But, to be militant merely means to be demanding and to be persistent, and in this sense I think the non-violent movement has demonstrated great militancy. It is possible to be militantly nonviolent. … I haven't advocated violence, because I do not see it as the answer to the problem. I do not see it as the answer from a moral point of view and I do not see it as the answer from a practical point of view.…

Let me briefly outline the positives [of Black Power]. First, Black Power in the positive sense is a psychological call to manhood. This is desperately needed in the black community, because for all too many years black people have been ashamed of themselves.… Secondly, Black Power is pooling black political resources in order to achieve our legitimate goals.… Thirdly, Black Power in its positive sense is a pooling of black economic resources in order to achieve legitimate power.… Withdrawing economic support from those who will not be just and fair in their dealings is a very potent weapon.

Writing to white America in *The New York Times Magazine* in 1968, Charles Hamilton outlined competing views of Black Power and stressed the importance of maintaining black racial identity.

Black Power has many definitions and connotations in the rhetoric of race relations today. To some people, it is synonymous with premeditated acts of violence to destroy the political and economic institutions of this country. Others equate Black Power with plans to rid the civil rights movements of whites who have been in it for years. The concept is understood by many to mean hatred of and separation from whites; it is associated with calling whites 'honkies' and with shouts of 'Burn, baby, burn!' Some understand it to be the use of pressure-group tactics in the accepted tradition of the American political process. And still others say that Black Power must be seen first of all as an attempt to instill a sense of identity and pride in black people.…

Black Power rejects the lessons of slavery and segregation that caused black people to look upon themselves with hatred and disdain. To be 'integrated' it was necessary to deny one's heritage, one's own culture, to be ashamed of one's black skin, thick lips and kinky hair. … The black man must change his demeaning conception of himself; he must develop a sense of pride and self-respect. Then, if integration comes, it will deal with people who are psychologically and mentally healthy, with people who have a sense of their history and of themselves as whole human beings …

View the Closer Look *Competing Visions: Defining Black Power*

Why do all three writers emphasize racial pride and manhood?

press only saw their rifles. The Black Panthers organized paramilitary patrols that openly carried weapons (then legal under California law) and, Newton explained, "stopped whenever we saw the police questioning a brother or a sister" to ensure that no beatings or abuse occurred. In May, 1967, 30 armed Black Panthers filed onto the floor of the California State Assembly in Sacramento to protest the imminent passage of a law banning the open display of weapons, a bill meant to shut down the Black Panther street patrols. As security forces disarmed them, Bobby Seale called on "black communities of America to rise up as one man."

By October, 1967, Newton was under arrest, wounded by police during a shoot-out and accused of killing a white policeman who died in the melee. FBI chief J. Edgar Hoover viewed the Panthers as "the greatest threat to the internal security of the country" and used spies to plan raids on Panther offices and create rifts within the group to weaken the Panthers internally. When the courts overturned Newton's conviction in 1970, he emerged from jail to find the Black Panthers in shambles.

The Women's Liberation Movement

Another fracture within the Civil Rights Movement, this one between men and women, energized the modern women's movement. When young white female activists began leaving the Civil Rights Movement to join the women's movement, they joined a crusade already well underway. Feminists did not speak with one voice, but instead offered competing visions of how to empower women.

Helen Gurley Brown and Betty Friedan each wrote bestsellers that helped re-ignite the women's movement, which had faltered since the 1920s. Marriage was overrated, Brown asserted in *Sex and the Single Girl*, a 1962 advice book counseling young, single women to explore their sexuality while they

had the chance. By using their sex appeal intelligently, young women could thrive despite earning less than men and having fewer career opportunities. Brown's prescription was: find a job you liked, flirt to get special treatment, have your dates pay for everything, and wait to get married until your looks start to deteriorate.

Friedan also challenged the accepted notion that women should focus solely on homemaking and child-rearing. Men were free to make careers, enjoy hobbies, and engage in politics, Friedan noted in her 1963 treatise *The Feminine Mystique*. By contrast, women "never had a chance to be anything else" than a "housewife-mother." As they shopped for groceries, made beds, and drove their children to afterschool activities, many wondered, "Is this all?" Unlike Brown, Friedan did not believe that sex could fill the void, nor did she urge women to avoid marriage or having children. Instead she believed that women should be able to engage in the full range of meaningful activities available to men. Her analysis resonated strongly among white middle-class women who felt imprisoned within their suburban lives.

Brown continued to promote her philosophy of "empowerment through sexuality" in *Cosmopolitan,* a provocative women's magazine that she launched in 1965. Friedan took a different path, joining the political activists frustrated with the government's failure to fully enforce the Civil Rights Act of 1964, which barred discrimination in employment on the basis of race, religion, ethnicity, or sex. The new Equal Employment Opportunity Commission took complaints of racial discrimination seriously, but ignored charges of sexual discrimination. "Men are entitled to female secretaries," the Commission chairman glibly remarked. In 1966, Friedan helped found the **National Organization for Women (NOW)** to secure equal rights for women in employment, education, and politics—traditionally, male domains. NOW also wanted to give women control over their own bodies through unfettered access to contraception and legal abortions. A relatively small organization with only 5,000 members in the late 1960s, NOW nonetheless convinced President Johnson to issue an executive order that required government agencies and federal contractors to create affirmative action programs to hire and promote women and minority men. NOW also persuaded airlines to stop employing only attractive single women under age 32 as flight attendants.

> ## "I'm a server of food and a putter-on of pants and a bedmaker…But who am I?"
>
> A middle-class housewife quoted in
> *The Feminine Mystique,* 1963

What competing visions did Brown and Friedan offer on empowering women?

Watch the **Video** *Video Lecture: The Birth Control Pill: The Solution to the World's Problems or Sexual Chaos?*

The women's movement grew as younger female activists, unhappy with gender discrimination within the Civil Rights Movement and New Left, took up the cause of female liberation. College-age women had participated enthusiastically in Freedom Summer by teaching in the Freedom Schools and registering blacks to vote. Women, however, also performed virtually all the clerical chores and housework for SNCC, and this gendered allocation of work provoked complaints. At the height of Freedom Summer black female SNCC workers staged a sit-in at a SNCC office in Atlanta to protest gender discrimination within the Civil Rights Movement. The "assumptions of male superiority are as … crippling to the woman as the assumptions of white supremacy are to the Negro," asserted white activists Mary King and Casey Hayden. Few males took these complaints seriously. "What is the position of women in SNCC?" joked Stokely Carmichael while relaxing with staffers one evening. "The position of women in SNCC is prone!" The punch line won Carmichael appreciative laughter from his male colleagues, but this oft-repeated story hastened the departure of white female activists. Women in the New Left experiencing similar problems with gender discrimination within SDS also redirected their energies to the women's movement. Black women were more reluctant to abandon the Civil Rights Movement. In their view racial oppression affected them more severely than sexual discrimination.

The feminists who founded NOW lobbied for legislative solutions to women's problems. In contrast, more radicalized feminists, steeped in New Left ideology and nonviolent tactics, adopted a grassroots approach that used consciousness-raising—heightening awareness of social and political issues—to help women "understand the universality of our oppression." They emphasized changing attitudes rather than lobbying for legislative changes. To combat the ways that sexism pervaded normal social interactions, feminists introduced the word "Ms." into the American lexicon to replace "Miss" or "Mrs.," titles that linked a woman's identity to her marital status. When Robin Morgan brought busloads of women to Atlantic City to protest the annual Miss America pageant in 1968, she sought maximum media coverage. Demonstrators carried the photograph (**27.14**) of an attractive, naked young woman with lines dividing her body like cuts of beef to protest how beauty pageants dehumanized women. "Welcome to the Miss America Cattle Auction," they chanted while filling a trash can with bras, high heeled shoes, fashion magazines, and copies of *Playboy*, items they believed reinforced "the Mindless Sex Object Image" of women. In deference to a local ordinance, the protesters never set the trash can on fire, but from this point onward detractors dismissed feminists as "bra-burners."

Despite their different styles and messages, both moderate and radical feminists had trouble expanding their support beyond the white middle class. "If your husband is a factory worker or a tugboat operator, you don't want his job," noted Democratic Congresswoman Barbara Mikulski to explain why NOW's emphasis on equality in employment failed to resonate among working-class women.

27.14 Feminists Picket the Miss America Pageant, 1968 This satirical portrait of a woman marked up like a side of beef criticizes beauty pageants for reducing a woman's value to the quality of her body parts.

How did activists' competing visions and media coverage shape the women's liberation movement?

The End of an Era

As the Civil Rights Movement unraveled, the Great Society also floundered. Republicans widened their appeal by promising to end the cultural strife that was tearing the nation apart. Although most liberal and radical causes lost energy after 1968, Chicano and Native American activists helped keep the protest tradition alive as the decade ended.

The Faltering Civil Rights Movement

Embittered by years of violent attacks in the South, young activists either left the movement altogether or migrated to more militant organizations. By 1967, King's weakening leadership reflected a movement adrift. When King attacked the Vietnam War, he strained his relationship with President Johnson, losing a valuable ally in the White House. King's call for a complete restructuring of American capitalism to eliminate poverty also cost him the support of moderate blacks and whites. In fall 1967, after a summer of deadly race riots in Detroit and Newark, King proposed setting up a poor people's encampment in front of the White House. When the Poor People's Campaign stalled, King made a quick trip to Memphis to support a garbage men's strike.

On April 4, 1968, a sniper's bullet tore through the knot in King's necktie and fatally wounded him as he leaned over the balcony of his Memphis motel. Within hours *Life* photographer Steve Schapiro entered King's motel room and snapped a haunting photograph of King's open suitcase containing a copy of his book *Strength to Love*, a wrinkled shirt, and the remnants of a meal (**27.15**). "The half-drunk cup of coffee gave me a moment of pause," Schapiro noted. "He had left his room planning to return." King's portrait appeared on the motel television during a newscast reporting his death to complete this eerie scene. The three-week urban rampage in 100 cities across the nation that followed King's murder further alienated the white community, which increasingly supported using troops to restore "law and order." Two months later a white man, James Earl Ray, admitted to killing King, a confession he later retracted.

The Great Society Unravels

Diminishing sympathy for the Civil Rights Movement also meant less support for Great Society programs directed at the urban poor. Congress had written much of the legislation quickly, but the public had no patience to wait for the Great Society to work through its growing pains. Critics from the left and right continued their attacks. The New Left advocated redistributing corporate profits more equitably throughout society. The Radical Right denounced the Great Society as a "hodgepodge" of programs that humiliated the poor and encouraged dependency on government welfare. Ethnic working-class

27.15 King's Room in the Lorraine Motel, April 4, 1968

King stepped out of this motel room to chat briefly with friends over the balcony and never returned. The television above King's suitcase announces his death to an empty room. The former motel is now a civil rights museum, where this room is preserved in its original state.

Why was King's death a serious blow to the Civil Rights Movement?

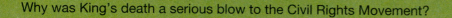

whites and left-leaning suburbanites, groups that had traditionally supported the Democratic liberal agenda, began to resent federal programs that they felt helped primarily blacks and other minorities. The shift among the white working class had political significance. In 1964, nearly 60 percent had voted for the Democratic ticket; four years later only 35 percent did.

The Great Society's troubles reflected more than persistent racism, however. Johnson's unwillingness to raise taxes to pay for an exploding array of domestic programs and the war in Vietnam also contributed to its undoing. As the economy overheated interest rates doubled, the national debt exploded, and inflation caused prices to rise faster than wages. This sudden decline in the standard of living after decades of prosperity dismayed Americans.

This 1967 Herblock political cartoon (**27.16**) illustrated Johnson's dilemma in trying to fund both the Vietnam War and the Great Society. In the drawing Johnson prepares for an evening out with his mistress, a robust and expensively attired woman wearing a mink stole emblazoned with the words "Vietnam War." As they leave he tries to assure the other woman in his life, a thin homemaker wearing a tattered apron labeled "U.S. Urban Needs," that "There's Money Enough to Support Both of You—Now, Doesn't That Make You Feel Better?" As this cartoon suggested, the administration was neglecting its domestic programs and giving the war the bulk of its attention and funds. In 1968, Johnson agreed to raise taxes to finance the expanded war in Vietnam, but Southern conservative congressmen refused to vote for the measure until the president cut funding for his domestic programs.

The Democratic Convention in 1968 pulled together these strands of disenchantment with liberal politics. With Vice President Hubert Humphrey on track to secure the nomination, ten thousand antiwar activists led by New Left leader Tom Hayden protested outside the Chicago Convention Center to support the antiwar candidate Eugene McCarthy. Yippies, a New Left splinter group that stood for blending "pot and politics," joined the protest. As Democratic delegates debated the administration's Vietnam policy inside the convention hall, the police attacked the demonstrators outside. Televised images of long-haired, pot-smoking protesters who waved North Vietnamese flags and threw excrement swayed

"There's Money Enough To Support Both Of You — Now, Doesn't That Make You Feel Better?"

27.16 Torn between Two Mistresses, 1967
This Herblock cartoon illustrated how Johnson's escalation of the war in Vietnam deprived his Great Society programs of funds.

public opinion more than news reports of police brutality. Over 70 percent of adults supported the police crackdown.

Critics of liberalism found the public suddenly much more receptive to their competing political vision. Richard Nixon won the presidency in 1968 promising to restore "law and order," a Republican catch-phrase that fueled the political shift underway in many traditionally Democratic blue-collar and suburban neighborhoods. With grassroots conservatism on the rise, the liberal vision appealed to fewer Americans by 1970.

A rare moment of national celebration occurred on July 20, 1969 when astronaut Neil Armstrong became the first man to walk on the moon. Watching the event on their television sets, Americans heard Armstrong declare "that's one small step for a man, one giant leap for mankind" as he began to stride across the moon's surface. Announcing the U.S. space race victory over the Soviet Union to the world, astronaut Buzz Aldrin

How did presidential choices and public attitudes undermine Johnson's Great Society agenda?

27.17 The First Moon Landing, 1969

National pride surged at the sight of an American flag planted on the moon. For many Americans, beating the Soviets to the moon challenged the radical left's view that American society was faltering.

planted an American flag (**27.17**) near manmade footprints that would permanently mark the moon's surface. This iconic photo of the United States conquering the moon bolstered many citizens' faith in the superiority of the American way of life, giving them another reason to reject the New Left and counterculture critique of American culture.

The Demise of the Counterculture

As with the Civil Rights Movement and the Great Society, the hippie counterculture also unraveled. Media coverage drew large crowds to the 1967 "Summer of Love" in San Francisco's Haight-Ashbury neighborhood, a hippie gathering dedicated to free food, drugs, sex, and music. In the fall hippie stalwarts organized a mock "Death of Hippie: Son of Media" funeral procession, blaming the over-hyped media image of the free-loving hippie for the drug-related violence and epidemic of rapes that now beset Haight-Ashbury. They then departed en masse, moving the foci of hippie culture to rural communes away from the media glare, where some kept the hippie utopian ideal alive.

Ronald Reagan, the Republican Governor of California, echoed the views of mainstream America in 1969 when he characterized a hippie as someone who "dresses like Tarzan, has hair like Jane, and smells like Cheetah," a reference to the counterculture's embrace of public nudity, long hair, and disdain for un-

derarm deodorant. Worried that the counterculture had made addictive drugs such as heroin popular among the young, states passed stringent anti-drug laws. At the federal level, in 1972, President Nixon announced a "war on drugs" to disrupt the illicit drug trade.

The quick commercialization of the counterculture also hastened its demise as a potent alternative social vision. Modes of hippie dress, slang, and values (albeit in diluted form) swept into the mainstream. Granola appeared on supermarket shelves, and middle-aged men grew their hair long. Affluent and educated adults increasingly smoked marijuana and listened to rock music. More sexually explicit movies and highly profitable rock record sales fueled rather than undermined acquisitive capitalism.

Keeping Protest Alive: Mexican Americans and Native Americans

The declining fortunes of the Civil Rights Movement and the counterculture did not mean the end of all campaigns for social justice in the late 1960s. Mexican American and Native American activists drew inspiration from the African American struggle and launched their own highly visible, if short-lived, crusades to end ethnic discrimination. Ultimately, however, factionalism and police harassment also hurt these crusades.

In the 1960s, the life expectancy for Mexican American migrant workers hovered around age 50, while their infant mortality rate was double the national average. The short-handed hoe represented the nearly complete exploitation of California migrant workers. "The short one" forced workers to bend all day (**27.18**) as they worked in the fields, often causing crippling back pain that sidelined workers who could not afford health care. California regulators finally banned the tool in 1975.

Rallying Mexican Americans around the slogan *Si Se Puede* ("Yes, it can be done"), César Chávez, head of the United Farm Workers union, used strikes and marches to secure better working and living conditions. Chávez also appealed directly to consumers, convincing 17 million Americans to stop buying nonunion-picked grapes. These tactics provoked a backlash in some quarters. One Safeway grocery store manager reported antiunion customers loading up "their car with grapes and nothing else." By

1970, however, the economic toll of the boycott forced growers to recognize the United Farm Workers and raise wages.

Latino urban radicals in Texas, California, and Colorado embraced a competing vision called La Raza (The Race) that emphasized racial identity over union organizing. The Brown Berets modeled themselves after the Black Panthers and proudly called themselves "Chicanos," embracing their Mexican American heritage while demanding an end to Anglo-American discrimination. In March 1968, 10,000 high school students in East Los Angeles staged a "blow-out" by walking out of their classrooms to protest the poor education they received in their mostly Hispanic schools. By this point most white Americans had little tolerance for radical political protest and overwhelmingly supported the police for shutting the demonstrations down. Internal divisions within the Mexican American community over the wisdom of mass demonstrations and steady harassment from the police hastened the demise of the Chicano student movement.

Native American activists also drew inspiration from the integrationist vision that championed equality and the competing militant one that emphasized racial identity. After encouraging Indians to move off their reservations in the 1950s, the Bureau of Indian Affairs (BIA) began terminating the rights of some Indian tribes to federal protection. Ending their dependence on the BIA to run schools, manage their lands, and provide health care, the agency argued, would encourage Indians to assimilate into mainstream culture more quickly. Indian activists wanted the federal government to continue its financial assistance, while also allowing more self-government on reservations.

On November 20, 1969, a group calling themselves "Indians of All Tribes" took over the abandoned federal prison on Alcatraz Island in San Francisco Bay. The Indian activists issued the sardonic Alcatraz Proclamation that offered to purchase the island for $24 in glass beads and red cloth, the same amount that the Dutch had paid indigenous people for Manhattan Island in 1626. The proclamation described Alcatraz as the perfect site for an Indian reservation because it lacked running water, sanitation, schools, mineral resources, and productive soil, plus "the population has always been held as prisoner and kept dependent upon others." Eventually the cold and isolation took its toll, and the protest ended in June 1971.

Native Americans staged nearly 70 other occupations throughout the nation, including the American Indian Movement's armed takeover of the village of Wounded Knee, South Dakota, in 1973, the site of the army's massacre of 300 Sioux in 1890. These highly visible protests prompted Nixon to increase funds for social services on Indian reservations and establish the Office of Indian Water Rights. In the early 1970s, the federal government ended the policy of termination, and Congress increased Indian self-rule on the reservations. Indian tribes also began successfully suing the government for past treaty violations. But government harassment, part of a general crackdown on revolutionary political movements in the early seventies, eviscerated radical Indian groups.

27.18 Hispanic Farm Workers Using Short Hoes Workers nicknamed short hoes "the devil's arm" because using them caused intense back pain. Every time union activist César Chávez saw a head of lettuce in the supermarket, he remembered the suffering field workers had endured and felt renewed determination to organize strikes and boycotts to improve their working conditions.

Read the **Document** Cesar Chavez, "He Showed Us the Way" (1978)

What problems did Chicanos and Native Americans face in the 1960s?

1961

Peace Corps established
Program sends U.S. aid volunteers worldwide

Freedom Rides
Kennedy administration begins enforcing Supreme Court ruling against segregated interstate travel

1962

Supreme Court rules school prayer unconstitutional
Furor lays the foundation for religiously based conservative resurgence

Port Huron Statement
Motivates student activists to join SDS

1963

Birmingham
Outrage over fire hose and dog attacks on civil rights protesters prompts Kennedy to support a federal civil rights law

March on Washington
International press coverage turns the peaceful march into a triumphant movement for the nonviolent Civil Rights Movement

1964

Freedom Summer
Murder of three Civil Rights workers in Mississippi prompts Congress to pass the Civil Rights Act of 1964

Great Society begins
Largest legislative liberal reform effort since the New Deal

CHAPTER REVIEW

Review Questions

1. Why were the Freedom Rides, the Birmingham campaign, and the March on Selma effective nonviolent civil rights protests?

2. How did the Great Society compare to the New Deal? What continuities or differences existed between them?

3. Why did black nationalist sentiment increase among African Americans after 1965?

4. How did media coverage affect protest movements in the 1960s?

5. How did the 1960s transform American society?

Key Terms

Great Society President Johnson's wide-ranging social welfare reforms intended to make the amenities of modern life—a decent standard of living, education, health care, and clean water—available to all Americans.   **816**

Freedom Rides Interstate bus journeys by black and white activists who entered segregated bus facilities together throughout the South.   **819**

Birmingham campaign Civil rights effort to desegregate Birmingham, Alabama, where shocking images of police brutality prompted Kennedy to push for a federal civil rights act.   **821**

March on Washington, 1963 Massive demonstration in the nation's capital that demanded passage of a federal civil rights act and more economic opportunities.   **824**

Freedom Summer, 1964 Multipronged attack on white supremacy in Mississippi that included a voter registration drive and the creation of Freedom Schools.   **825**

Civil Rights Act of 1964 Legislation that banned segregation in businesses and places open to the public (such as restaurants and public schools) and prohibited discrimination in employment on the basis of race, religion, ethnicity, or sex.   **826**

Voting Rights Act of 1965 Legislation that prohibited literacy tests and poll taxes and authorized the use of federal registrars to register voters if states failed to respect the Fifteenth Amendment.   **827**

New Left A small, but highly visible, coalition of left-leaning student-based organizations that attacked racial discrimination, poverty, and the war in Vietnam.   **828**

Black Power A call for blacks to unite politically and economically in black-only organizations to protect their racial identity as they fought for equality.   **832**

National Organization for Women (NOW) An organization dedicated to securing equal rights for women in employment, education, and politics.   **834**

1965

March from Selma to Montgomery
Congress responds to vigilante attacks on marchers by passing the Voting Rights Act of 1965

Watts Riot
Violent rampage in Los Angeles ghetto generates white backlash against Civil Rights Movement

1966

Black Panthers founded
Black militants embrace Black Power

NOW founded
Government creates affirmative action programs for women and minorities

1967

"Summer of Love"
Hippie gathering in Haight-Ashbury publicizes counterculture

1968

King assassinated
Nationwide rioting signals the end of the nonviolent Civil Rights Movement

Feminists picket Miss America Pageant
Feminists use media coverage to challenge sexist stereotypes

MyHistoryLab Connections

Visit www.myhistorylab.com for a customized Study Plan that will help you build your knowledge of *A Decade of Discord*.

Questions for Analysis

1. **What different views did Johnson and Goldwater offer on the role of the federal government in American society?**

   View the **Closer Look** *Competing Visions: The Federal Government, Friend or Foe?, p. 817*

2. **How did this test prevent African Americans from voting?**

   Read the **Document** *Voting Literacy Test (1965), p. 826*

3. **What impact did a politically active youth culture have?**

   Read the **Document** *The Report of the President's Commission on Campus Unrest, p. 828*

4. **Why did Malcolm X propose internationalizing the civil rights movement?**

   Watch the **Video** *Malcolm X, p. 830*

5. **How did competing views about the pill mirror earlier debates over female sexuality?**

   Watch the **Video** *Video Lecture: The Birth Control Pill: The Solution to the World's Problems or Sexual Chaos?, p. 834*

Other Resources from This Chapter

Read the **Document**

- *John F. Kennedy, Inaugural Address (1961), p. 813*
- *Fannie Lou Hammer, Voting Rights in Mississippi (1964), p. 814*
- *Rachael Carson, Silent Spring (1962), p. 818*
- *Martin Luther King Jr., "Letter from Birmingham City Jail" (1963), p. 821*
- *Letters from Mississippi Freedom Summer, p. 825*
- *Cesar Chavez, "He Showed Us the Way" (1978), p. 839*

View the **Closer Look**

- *Images as History: Birmingham, 1963, p, 823*
- *Competing Visions: Defining Black Power, p. 833*

View the **Image** *New Frontier Legislation, p. 812*

View the **Map** *Interactive Map: Impact of the Voting Rights Act of 1965, p. 827*

Watch the **Video**

- *Lyndon Johnson Presidential Campaign Ad: Little Girl vs. Mushroom Cloud, p. 816*
- *Video Lecture: Photographing the Civil Rights Movement, Birmingham, 1963, p. 822*
- *Martin Luther King Jr.'s Speech at the March on Washington, August, 1963, p. 824*

Righting a Nation Adrift

America in the 1970s and 1980s

The vision of the United States as a great and powerful nation suddenly seemed less assured in the 1970s. In 1973, a dispute between the U.S. and Arab nations led to an embargo that severely restricted oil imports. Gas stations across the nation posted signs like this one as they ran out of gas, dotting the American landscape with humiliating reminders that foreign nations could wreak havoc on the U.S. economy. Gas shortages also threatened the vision of America as a prosperous car culture, where it was the birthright of every citizen to work, live, and shop wherever they liked thanks to the freedom of movement that automobiles provided. To many Americans closed gas stations (which reappeared in 1979) were just one sign of a nation adrift. Domestic political scandals, a troubled economy, and lost international prestige made the future look dim.

Americans lost confidence in the federal government in the 1970s as the Watergate scandal and cover-up brought down President Richard Nixon, and the post–World War II boom times finally ended, leaving high inflation and unemployment. Economic woes and troubles abroad hampered the efforts of presidents Gerald Ford and Jimmy Carter to restore respect for the presidency. Americans did not agree over how to move the nation back onto the path of glory. Feminists and gays fought to extend the social justice campaigns of the 1960s, while the environmental movement focused America's attention on conserving its natural heritage. A new and powerful conservative coalition, however, formed around a competing vision that focused on protecting traditional values, limiting the role of the government in the economy, and flexing the nation's power overseas. In the 1980s, after two decades of grassroots activism, the conservative ascendancy was complete.

When Ronald Reagan, a committed conservative, became president in 1981, he refused to accept that America had entered an age of limits. Reagan rejected the liberal vision and diagnosed government as part of the problem, not the solution to the nation's economic woes. He also moved aggressively to restore America's image as a world power. An immensely popular president, Reagan restored the nation's confidence in the economy and the presidency, despite suffering political scandals of his own.

"Government is not the solution to our problem; government is the problem."
President RONALD REAGAN, 1981

Downturn and Scandal

Americans enjoyed unprecedented prosperity in the 1950s and 1960s, and few expected the bubble to burst. By the 1970s, however, periodic recessions returned, a shocking development for a nation that had grown accustomed to a steadily improving standard of living. The political repercussions were significant. Still reeling from the cultural and civil rights upheavals of the 1960s, the nation's new economic problems exacerbated the feeling that the country was adrift. The economic downturn, partly caused by turmoil overseas, coincided with a decade-long crisis of presidential leadership that began when political scandal enveloped the Nixon White House.

An Ailing Economy

An ailing economy created the sense of a nation adrift by the 1970s. In the 1960s Lyndon Johnson had tried to pay for both the Vietnam War (see Chapter 26) and the Great Society programs (see Chapter 27) without raising taxes. Heavy governmental spending created both a ballooning federal deficit and, by pumping so much cash into the economy, inflation. The end of the Vietnam War added rising unemployment to the list of economic woes. Returning veterans entered a job market hit hard by the cancellation of government defense contracts that triggered massive layoffs in the industrial sector.

Energy costs were also rising. Americans were six percent of the world's population, but consumed nearly 40 percent of global energy resources. Due to increased U.S. reliance on Middle Eastern oil, the unending strife in the region affected the daily lives of Americans. The United States had offered Israel strong financial and moral support ever since the United Nations created a homeland for the Jewish people in 1947 by partitioning Palestine into Jewish and Palestinian areas. Israel claimed territory in Palestine as its ancestral land, a view supported by the United States, which also believed that the world owed the Jewish people reparation for the horrors of the Holocaust. To Arab nations, however, the arrival of Jewish immigrants perpetuated the history of hated Western colonization in the Middle East. Wars between neighboring Arab nations and Israel ensued (detailed on **28.1**), and disputes over the fate of Palestinian refugees and Israeli land seizures continue to roil the region to this day.

Richard Nixon and subsequent presidents faced a thorny foreign policy dilemma in the Middle East. The U.S. government steadfastly supported Israel's right to exist, but given America's growing dependence on Middle Eastern oil, it could not afford to alienate oil-producing Arab nations. The Soviet push to form strong alliances in the Middle East also threatened to turn the oil-rich region into the new Cold War battlefield.

In 1973, Egypt and Syria (both armed with Soviet-provided weapons) attacked Israel on Yom Kippur (Judaism's holiest day) to regain territory lost to Israel in 1967. Nixon's decision to send military aid to Israel enraged the Arab world. In retaliation the Organization of the Petroleum Exporting Countries (OPEC), an international consortium of oil-producing nations that regulates the price and quantity of oil sold on the world market, announced an oil embargo of the United States. By this point the United States depended on the Middle East for 12 percent of the oil it consumed. The embargo lasted five months, enough time to ravage the American economy. OPEC finally lifted the embargo after Nixon persuaded Israel to withdraw from parts of Egyptian and Syrian territory seized during the Yom Kippur War.

In 1974, the nation entered its worst recession since the Great Depression. In typical periods of recession and depression, high unemployment went hand in hand with declining prices and wages. In the 1930s, pumping more federal money into the economy through the New Deal did not end the Depression, but it eased unemployment and stabilized prices, so farmers and businessmen could make a profit. During the financial crisis of the

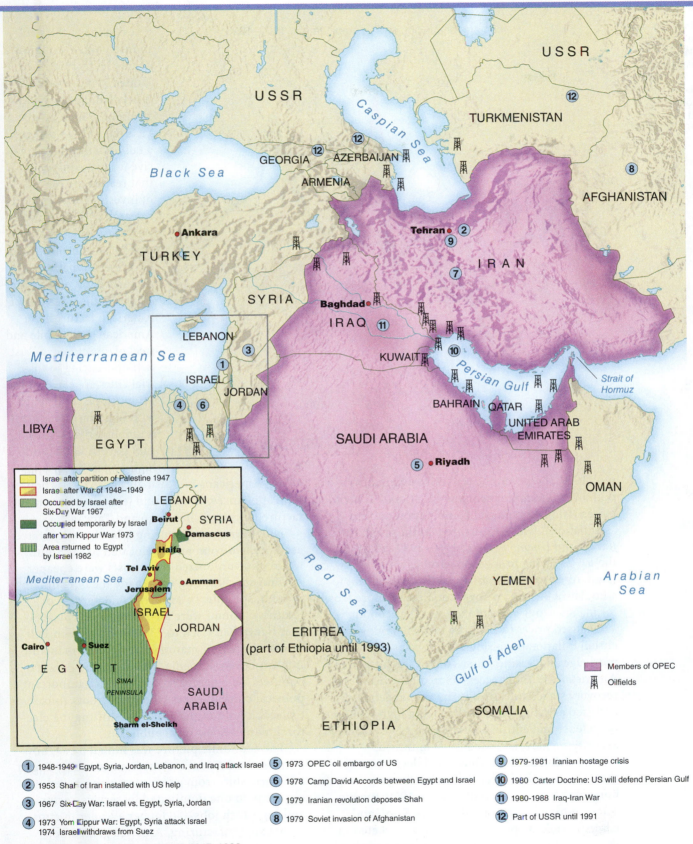

28.1 Middle East and Persian Gulf, 1947–1988
Dependence on Middle Eastern oil increased the importance of conflicts in this region for Americans.

Why did Israel's troubled relations with its neighbors concern the United States?

28.2 Inflation and Unemployment, 1960–1990

The combination of high unemployment and inflation created a phenomenon dubbed "stagflation" in the 1970s.

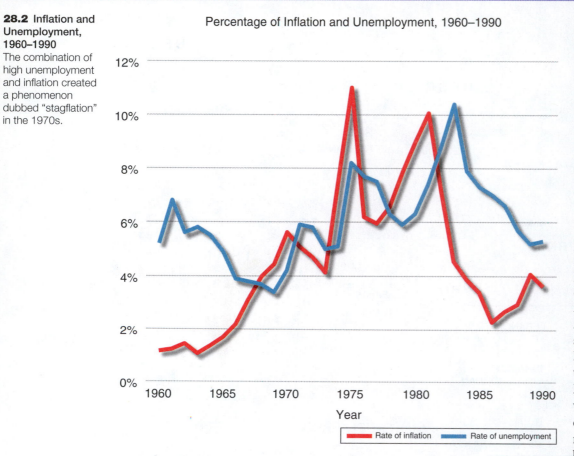

Percentage of Inflation and Unemployment, 1960–1990

Year

■ Rate of inflation   ■ Rate of unemployment

The decline in the steel industry was even more dramatic. In 1950, the United States produced nearly half of the world's steel. By 1980, it manufactured only 14 percent, a fall hastened by aggressive foreign competitors that reaped the rewards of investing heavily in research and innovation. New furnace technology, for instance, allowed Japanese competitors to produce a ton of steel for a third of the price it cost American factories. As American automobile and steel plants closed, a Rust Belt of decaying industrial cities appeared in the Midwest, places plagued with high unemployment, crumbling roads, bankrupt governments, and high welfare rolls. By the 1990s, Americans increasingly chose to buy household appliances, textiles, and television sets manufactured in places like Japan and Taiwan.

mid-1970s, however, the economy suffered from both high unemployment and inflation that kept prices rising, an unusual combination dubbed "stagflation," which is pictured on the graph *Inflation and Unemployment, 1960–1990* (**28.2**). In the 1970s, trying to solve one problem, unemployment, often worsened inflation. Tax cuts meant to stimulate a business recovery and create more jobs, for instance, put more money into the economy and caused prices to rise even further. Trying to curtail inflation by raising interest rates put home mortgage and business loans out of reach for many Americans. Without access to credit the business recovery stalled. Meanwhile the federal deficit skyrocketed as tax revenue declined, but high spending on defense and entitlement programs like Social Security, welfare, and Medicaid continued.

The rising unemployment had deep roots in the ailing auto and steel industries, long the backbone of the American economy. In 1970, the Big Three automakers, General Motors, Ford, and Chrysler, sold 89 percent of the cars marketed in the United States. Within ten years their market share dropped to 66 percent. Faced with higher gas prices, American consumers bought smaller, more fuel-efficient cars imported from Japan.

Northern manufacturing jobs also evaporated as American companies relocated to the South, where non-unionized labor costs were cheaper and air-conditioning now made the hot climate more hospitable. In 1960, only 18 percent of Southern homes were air-conditioned; by 1980 that figure had risen to 73 percent. A "Sun Belt" of new industrial manufacturing centers including San Diego, Phoenix, Houston, and Atlanta boomed. This demographic shift had important political consequences when grassroots conservatism took hold in the Sun Belt, shifting the electoral map in favor of Republicans.

The economic picture was not all bleak, however. In the 1970s, the American economy began a historic shift from a manufacturing-based economy to one dominated by service-sector and high-tech jobs. No longer a leader in auto or steel manufacturing, America gained new preeminence in high-tech fields like aerospace, electronics, and eventually computers. In the 1890s, Henry Ford had built his first car in his garage before revolutionizing the auto industry

What economic problems plagued the United States in the 1970s?

👁 **Watch** the **Video** *Video Lecture: The Rise and Fall of the Automobile Economy* (see Chapter 21). In 1976, Steven Jobs and Stephen Wozniak, 21 and 26 years old respectively, followed in Ford's footsteps by constructing their first personal computer in a family garage. The pair founded Apple Computers a year later, envisioning a machine that would transform daily life. The first Apple logo showed the seventeenth-century mathematician Sir Isaac Newton sitting under the apple that supposedly fell off a tree and hit him on the head, inspiring him to develop his theory of universal gravitational pull that revolutionized modern scientific thought. The subsequent, permanent logo just retained the apple. In 1976, the claim that computers could transform the world as much as Newton's theories seemed ludicrous. Yet within a year the computer age got underway when Apple released the first home computer designed for the general public. The computer revolution received another boost in 1980 when 29-year-old Bill Gates, the cofounder of an obscure start-up company called Microsoft, signed an agreement with International Business Machines (IBM) to provide operating software for its home computers. The deal made Gates a billionaire within two years.

Frustration at Home

Nixon initially embraced the same moderate course as Eisenhower, with whom he had served as vice president from 1953 to 1961. Like Eisenhower, Nixon billed himself as a fiscal conservative who was willing to accept popular social welfare programs like Social Security and Medicare. As the economic outlook worsened, however, Nixon instituted wage and price controls in 1971 to curb inflation, the most drastic government intervention in the economy since World War II.

Conservative outrage over his fiscal policies had little effect on Nixon, who intended to stay in the political center. He hoped to bolster the moderate wing of the Republican party by turning disgruntled Southerners, Northern blue-collar workers, and white suburbanites (Democrats who had voted for him in 1968; see Chapter 27), into lifelong Republicans. Called "the silent majority" these voters rejected some, but not all, of the liberal vision. The silent majority disliked Great Society programs that primarily aided minorities, but they still subscribed to the New Deal orthodoxy that made the government responsible for ensuring prosperity. Nixon's budget-cutting, therefore,

targeted social-welfare programs for minorities and the poor, measures that partially appeased fiscal conservatives without touching New Deal programs like Social Security that former Democrats and many moderate Republicans viewed as sacrosanct. Nixon also tried unsuccessfully to reduce the jumble of laws and programs that made welfare assistance to the poor expensive to administer. The poor viewed his proposal to guarantee all Americans a minimum income of $1,600 ($8,500 in today's dollars) as too low, while conservatives opposed it for redistributing income.

Nixon gained the loyalty of the silent majority by trying to tame the Supreme Court, which under the leadership of Chief Justice Earl Warren (see Chapter 27) had issued controversial rulings on school prayer and desegregation. When Warren retired in 1969, Nixon appointed Warren Burger to replace him, believing that Burger would influence his colleagues to offer a more restrained interpretation of the Constitution than Warren. Burger, however, had no intention of reducing the Court's commitment to school integration. The Court insisted that the North develop school busing programs to catch up with the South where, by 1971, 77 percent of black children attended school with white children.

The 1954 *Brown v. Board of Education* decision outlawing segregated schools had set off massive resistance throughout the South (see Chapter 25). In the 1970s, opposition to court-mandated integration moved northward as the silent majority found its collective voice and took to the streets. Busing sent black and white children to schools outside their neighborhoods, generating opposition in Northern, ethnic white enclaves where angry white parents objected to "big government" turning their children into "guinea pigs."

Boston became a hotbed of anti-busing fervor. On April 5, 1976, 200 white working-class Irish American teenagers began an adult-supervised anti-busing march in downtown Boston. Joseph Rakes, one of the teenage protesters, who brought along his family's American flag, later recalled feeling "blind anger" at busing policies that were destroying his close-knit South Boston community. "They took half the guys and girls I grew up with and said, 'You're going to school on the other side of town.' Nobody understood it at 15," Rakes explained. When Ted Landsmark, an African American lawyer on his way to a meeting, crossed the protesters' path, the students pounced on him.

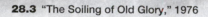

28.3 "The Soiling of Old Glory," 1976
The image of an anti-busing protester in Boston preparing to ram an African American lawyer with a flagpole underscored that deeply ingrained racial prejudices were more than just a Southern problem.

Boston Herald photographer Stanley Forman's Pulitzer-Prize winning photo "The Soiling of Old Glory" (**28.3**) showed Rakes poised to attack Landsmark with his flagstaff. In the photo Landsmark apparently struggles to free himself from the grip of another white man grabbing him from the rear. Contrary to the impression given by the photo, however, the man holding Landsmark was actually helping him to his feet after white youths had thrown him to the ground and beaten him. Rakes never hit Landsmark with the flagstaff. Yet when Landsmark, a seasoned civil rights activist, who had marched from Selma to Montgomery in 1965 (see Chapter 27), went to the hospital, he had doctors put a large bandage on his broken nose. Landsmark knew that the appearance of severe injuries would draw more press attention. The portrait of raw racial hatred captured in the photograph, and Landsmark's heavily bandaged face at

a press conference the following day, shocked white Boston and encouraged the city's leaders to initiate a sustained campaign to deescalate racial tensions. When the new school year began in September, *Time* magazine trumpeted the "Truce in Boston." By this time, however, the Supreme Court's stance had shifted, thanks to Nixon's more conservative appointments. After the Court ruled that independent suburban school districts did not have to participate in inner-city busing programs, accelerated "white flight" to the suburbs created a core of all-black urban schools ringed by suburban white schools in Boston and in other cities.

The Watergate Scandal

By reshaping the political landscape, Nixon won a landslide victory against antiwar Democrat George McGovern in 1972 (see Chapter 27). Yet rather

How does this photograph compare to the images of racial violence in the South seen in earlier chapters?

Read the **Document** *Boston Busing (1975)*

than ushering in an era of unchallenged Republican control, Nixon became embroiled in the Watergate scandal, an episode of presidential criminality that created a constitutional crisis, ended Nixon's political career, and helped the Democrats retake the White House in 1976.

On June 17, 1972, a night watchman caught five burglars breaking into the offices of the Democratic National Committee in a Washington, D.C., building complex called Watergate. The plan, financed by Nixon's reelection campaign and approved by White House staffers, called for the burglars to fix a broken telephone wiretap installed during a previous break-in so the Nixon campaign could listen to Democratic phone calls. After Nixon disavowed any previous knowledge of the plot, the story slid off the front pages, and he easily won re-election.

When the burglars went on trial in early 1973, however, one confessed to accepting a bribe to keep quiet about the White House's involvement in planning the break-in. In response the Justice Department and Senate launched two separate investigations. *Washington Post* reporters Carl Bernstein and Bob Woodward detailed the growing scandal in articles based on information from a secret informant whom they identified only by the nickname, Deep Throat (revealed in 2005 as William Mark Felt, the FBI's deputy director).

During one Senate committee hearing, Senator Howard Baker asked the key question: "What did the President know, and when did he know it?" Secret tapes that Nixon had made of all White House conversations promised to provide the answer. The showdown over gaining access to these tapes and what they revealed transformed the Watergate burglary into a constitutional crisis over whether the president was above the law.

Two competing visions of presidential power emerged. Nixon refused to turn over the tapes to the Justice Department or Congress, claiming that the constitutionally protected right of executive privilege meant he could keep advice from counselors private. Investigators argued that the president had no constitutional right to withhold evidence of corruption or abuse of power. Nixon next tried to use his authority to control the investigation. When Archibald Cox, who headed the Justice Department investigation, secured a court order for the tapes on Saturday, October 20, 1973, Nixon ordered Attorney General Elliot Richardson to fire Cox. Richardson and the deputy attorney general refused and resigned. The third-ranking official in the Justice Department finally fired Cox. Outrage greeted news of the "Saturday Night Massacre," and Nixon endured a cacophony of car horns sounding outside the White House day and night, where protesters urged passing motorists to "Honk for Impeachment."

After much delay and controversy, Nixon finally turned over highly edited versions of his taped White House conversations, enraging his critics even further. Liberal political cartoonists lampooned Nixon as a tyrant and a crook (see *Images as History: Watergate through Political Cartoons*, page 850). In July 1974, the House Judiciary Committee issued articles of impeachment against Nixon, charging him with obstruction of justice, abusing his presidential powers by ordering the CIA, FBI, and Internal Revenue Service (IRS) to harass his political enemies, and violating the Constitution by refusing to honor congressional subpoenas. The Supreme Court also unanimously ruled that Nixon could not withhold information pertaining to his own potential criminal wrongdoing.

On August 5, 1974, Nixon finally released the remaining tapes, and the nation heard the president authorize a cover-up plan. On June 23, 1972, Nixon had instructed the CIA to tell the FBI to end its Watergate investigation to protect "national security." Two days later, on August 8, 1974, to avoid impeachment proceedings almost certain to remove him from office, Nixon became the first president in U.S. history to resign, and Vice President Gerald Ford became president. "Our long national nightmare is over," the new president assured the nation.

"When the president does it that means that it is not illegal."
RICHARD NIXON in 1977, defending his actions as necessary for national security

"A government of laws was on the verge of becoming a government of one man."
Attorney general ELLIOT RICHARDSON

Read the Document *House Judiciary Committee's Conclusions on Impeachment (1974)*

What competing views of presidential power emerged during the Watergate crisis?

Images as History
WATERGATE THROUGH POLITICAL CARTOONS

Political cartoons have been a mainstay of political debate in America since the colonial era. "If the prime role of a free press is to serve as critic of government, cartooning is often the cutting edge of that criticism," stated Herb Block, who drew under the pseudonym Herblock. Political cartoonists like Herblock and Paul Conrad followed the long career of Richard Nixon from his early days as a communist-hunting congressman through his resignation as president. Their illustrations caricatured his face and shoulders, depicting a long beak-like nose, dark circles under his eyes, five o'clock shadow, and slumping shoulders.

Some conservative cartoonists defended Nixon, even as the Watergate scandal deepened. One caricature depicted the media as piranhas nipping at Nixon's heels as he tried to reach calmer waters, suggesting that he was the victim of a media feeding frenzy. When Nixon resigned, a Bert Whitman cartoon in the *Phoenix Gazette* showed the president exiting center stage, leaving behind spotlights that illuminated his foreign policy successes such as ending the Vietnam War and improving relations with China and the Soviet Union. To these conservative commentators Nixon's record as a strong leader in the world mattered more than his transgressions at home.

The cartoon, Herblock later noted, "comments not only on his situation at the time, but on his veracity and honesty—without using any words other than his own."

Nixon struggles to pull the two ends of a severed tape together, a reference to the severely edited tapes of White House conversations that Nixon had released to Watergate investigators.

By depicting Nixon with the word "not" in his mouth, Herblock transformed Nixon's 1973 statement, "I'm not a crook" into "I am a crook" in this 1974 cartoon.

Herblock, *Nixon Hanging Between the Tapes, Washington Post*, 1974

By 1973, the public knew that Nixon had instructed the FBI and IRS to harass people he considered political "enemies." The list included Paul Conrad, who drew political cartoons for the *Los Angeles Times*.

To prevent future presidents from using the FBI to spy on their domestic critics, the Foreign Intelligence Surveillance Act (1978) required secret judicial approval for any internal surveillance of U.S. citizens. After the terrorist attacks on September 11, 2001, Congress loosened these restrictions on monitoring Americans at home.

The cartoon title suggested that Nixon, rather than his opponents, destroyed his presidency.

Conrad satirized the president's paranoia by depicting Nixon as a despot sitting in the dark, creating "enemies lists" (which eventually included 30,000 people).

His Own Worst Enemy

Paul Conrad, *His Own Worst Enemy*, Los Angeles Times, 1973

What insights do these cartoons offer into the Watergate scandal?

View the **Closer Look** *Images as History: Watergate Through Political Cartoons*

A Crisis of Presidential Leadership

The Watergate scandal and the scars from the Vietnam War tested Americans' faith in the federal government. Congress moved to limit the powers of the president, and Americans disagreed over the direction to take in foreign policy post-Vietnam. The challenges were significant: dealing with renewed Soviet aggression, ensuring that support for Israel did not alienate oil-producing Arab nations, and improving relations with Central America.

A Weakened Presidency

When Gerald R. Ford became president, for the first time a man unelected as either president or vice president led the nation. Nixon had appointed Ford, then Republican House Minority leader, as his vice president in 1973, invoking the Twenty-Fifth Amendment to fill the office after disgraced Vice President Spiro Agnew resigned for having accepted bribes while governor of Maryland. During his 24 years in Congress, Ford built a reputation as an honest, fiscally conservative Republican and won the respect of legislators in both parties. "I'm a Ford, not a Lincoln," he said when he became vice president, distancing himself from both the elite who bought luxurious Lincoln cars and the political genius of the nation's sixteenth president.

Ford's modesty compared favorably with Nixon's obsessive quest for power. Believing that the nation wanted to turn the page quickly on the Watergate scandal, Ford announced that he was giving Nixon a "full, free, and absolute pardon" for any illegal acts that he might have committed as president. A long trial and possibly imprisoning the former president would only prolong the nation's agony, he believed. Ford, however, had misread the public's mood. His approval rating sank to 42 percent amid accusations that he was fulfilling the terms of a backroom deal made while Nixon was still president—a pardon in return for the presidency. Nixon went free, but over 70 others were eventually convicted of Watergate-related crimes. Ford never recovered from this loss of confidence in his leadership.

An emboldened Congress reined in presidential power. Nixon had accepted large donations from businessmen in return for favors and influence. In response Congress created a Federal Election Commission (FEC) in 1974 to monitor federal elections. Congress also limited campaign contributions by individuals and official political organizations and established a system of public funding for presidential elections. Opponents immediately challenged the constitutionality of these restrictions. In 1976, the Supreme Court struck down a provision that limited how much an individual could spend of his or her own money to win elected office, claiming that such restrictions (except for candidates who accepted matching federal funds) violated the First Amendment right to free speech. These efforts to curb influence-peddling through campaign donations had unintended consequences. Political action committees (PACs), which represented private interest groups, such as labor, business, and retirees, were allowed to donate more money than individuals, increasing their sway over the politicians they supported.

To repair public faith in the presidency, President Ford tried to shape a post-Vietnam foreign policy that restored America's image as an invincible superpower without reigniting fears that the nation was overextending its reach or behaving unethically. Exposés about how the United States was conducting the Cold War acquainted Americans with their government's willingness to support dictators around the world who pledged friendship to the United States over the Soviet Union. In 1974, *The New York Times* exposed the CIA's covert involvement in the overthrow of Salvador Allende, the democratically elected Marxist president of Chile. With aid from CIA operatives, anti-Soviet and pro-American General Augusto Pinochet seized power and established a brutal 16-year dictatorship that tortured, imprisoned, and killed dissenters. Congressional investigations also exposed CIA plots to assassinate leftist leaders in the Congo, Cuba, and the Dominican Republic.

To regain public confidence in how the government was waging the Cold War, Ford prohibited any government employee from engaging or conspiring in assassination plots. Complaints over

How did Congress and Ford respond to Nixon's wrongdoing?

human rights violations influenced him less. Ford refused to cut off U.S. aid to Pinochet and supported the military junta that seized power in Argentina in 1976.

Ford also tried to build on Nixon's foreign policy successes by retaining Henry Kissinger as secretary of state and national security advisor. Ford initially accepted Kissinger's view that détente, the policy of using diplomatic, economic, and cultural contacts to improve U.S. relations with China and the Soviet Union, would promote global stability by lowering the risk of nuclear war. Consequently Ford abided by the terms of the 1972 Strategic Arms Limitation Treaty, or **SALT I**, the first treaty between the Soviet Union and the United States that limited the deployment of intercontinental and submarine-launched ballistic missiles.

Nixon had also signed the 1972 Anti-Ballistic Missile (ABM) Treaty, in which the United States and the Soviet Union agreed to refrain from creating national missile defense systems. This treaty embraced the long-standing logic of **mutually assured destruction (MAD)**, the belief that the guarantee of a devastating nuclear counterattack would deter the United States and Soviet Union from ever employing their nuclear arsenals. By pledging to remain defenseless against a nuclear attack, each side hoped to dampen fears that it would ever launch a first strike against the other. Ford also joined with the Soviet Union and 31 other nations to sign the 1975 Helsinki Accords, which accepted the current East-West balance of power in Europe.

Ford's moderate course invited pounding criticism from the left and the right, ultimately spelling the demise of détente. Conservative critics, led by California Governor Ronald Reagan, lambasted Ford for "giving" away Eastern Europe to the Soviet Union. Liberal critics shared conservatives' concerns about Soviet treatment of dissidents. Bipartisan objections also arose over letting the Soviets maintain a larger arsenal of long-range and submarine-launched nuclear missiles than that of the United States. Over time Ford began to share these concerns that the Soviet Union was untrustworthy. Certain that the Soviets were continuing to build long-range intercontinental ballistic missiles, Ford heeded the advice of his hawkish defense secretary Donald Rumsfeld and poured money into the American missile program.

The Leadership Crisis Continues: Carter in the White House

As the 1976 presidential contest approached, Ford faced a strong challenge in the Republican primaries from 65-year-old Ronald Reagan, a former film actor who had just finished his second term as governor of California. Reagan's father had kept the family afloat during the Depression by working for the Works Project Administration, but some key adult experiences gradually transformed this son of the New Deal into a staunch conservative. During the Second Red Scare, Reagan became concerned about communism's influence in Hollywood, and he objected to paying nearly 70 percent of his film earnings in taxes. In 1962, he joined the Republican Party, enthusiastically supported Barry Goldwater in 1964, and became governor of California in 1966. In a close vote, Ford prevailed at the Republican convention, but Reagan vowed to "rise and fight again."

Ford's Democratic opponent was former Georgia Governor Jimmy Carter, a surprise choice, whom few Americans knew when he declared his candidacy. Carter's political ambitions even surprised his own mother. When he told her that he was running for president, she replied, "President of what?" Carter's Baptist faith and the image he cultivated of an uncorrupted Washington outsider who could restore honor to the White House attracted conservative Democrats who had voted for Nixon. "I will never lie to you," Carter assured voters.

Neither candidate generated much enthusiasm. The made-up campaign slogans in this political cartoon (**28.4**)—"Gerald R. Ford: a perfectly adequate guy for the seventies" and "Oh . . . Why Not? Ford in '76"—captured the general apathy to Ford's campaign. An equally lackluster campaigner, Carter benefited from the nation's ongoing economic woes, anger over Watergate, and Ford's misstep in pardoning Nixon. Carter managed to temporarily reassemble the New Deal

> ### "Don't Vote, It Only Encourages Them."
> A bumper sticker that reflected widespread voter apathy in the 1976 presidential election

What competing visions arose over Nixon's efforts to reshape U.S.-Soviet relations?

Watch the **Video** *Gerald Ford Presidential Campaign Ad (1976)*

coalition of white Southerners, urban blacks, and union
members to carry the election
by 297 to 240 electoral votes.
Less than 55 percent of the
electorate even bothered to
vote, however, a historic low
and disappointing follow-up to
the 1960s, when countless civil
rights activists had put their
lives on the line to secure
this right.

On his inauguration day
Carter chose to walk from
his swearing in on the Capitol steps to the White House
with his wife and family rather
than ride in a limousine, the
type of populist gesture that he
frequently made as president.
Ford had pardoned Nixon in an
attempt to heal wounds quickly.
Carter tried to remove another
source of festering discord by pardoning
10,000 Vietnam War draft resisters, many of
whom had fled to Canada, a move that enraged
conservatives but earned him the gratitude of liberal Democrats. Seeking to solidify liberal Democratic support, Carter moved quickly to build on
the liberal vision of Democrats John F. Kennedy
and Lyndon B. Johnson by creating the Department of Education and working with Congress to
establish a "Superfund" to clean up the nation's
most polluted areas. He also appointed the most
women and minorities to federal office of any
previous president.

Carter's outsider status and his tendency toward self-righteousness, however, hampered his
presidency. A hard worker, who rose early and
went to bed late, he pored over every memoran-
dum, even personally handling requests to use
the White House tennis court during his first six
months in office. The fiscally conservative Carter
had strong philosophical differences with liberal
Democrats who emphasized the advantages of
deficit-spending over balancing the federal budget. Carter believed that too much government
regulation was hampering the business recovery,
while liberal Democrats felt that regulation was
necessary to protect the public. The president
eventually prevailed, convincing Congress to
deregulate the trucking, communication, and
airline industries.

" DO YOU GET THE FEELING THIS CAMPAIGN LACKS A LITTLE SOMETHING? "

28.4 *Do You Get the Feeling This Campaign Lacks a Little Something?* Like Carter, Ford failed to generate much enthusiasm among the electorate in the 1976 presidential election.

Identifying rising oil costs as the main cause
of the nation's economic woes, Carter urged
Americans to consume less oil in a 1977 television
address that recalled Franklin D. Roosevelt's
famous fireside chats. As a fire crackled behind him, Carter, dressed in a cardigan sweater,
called the energy crisis "the moral equivalent of
war," which was the title of a famous essay by
nineteenth-century philosopher William James.
To discourage consumption, Carter proposed
ending the price controls that kept oil and gas
prices low and imposing higher federal taxes
on gasoline. To prevent price-gouging, he also
wanted oil and gas companies to pay higher taxes
on their profits. Carter tried to craft a vision
that would appeal to both laissez-faire adherents
who liked the idea of lifting price controls so the
market determined the price of oil, and liberals
who believed in government regulation to rein in
corporate profits and protect the environment.
The resulting energy law in 1978 compromised
between these conflicting visions. It lifted price
controls, raised the sales taxes on gas-guzzling
cars, and offered tax incentives for using alternative energy sources such as coal and solar heating.
The law did not, however, include a windfall profits tax on oil and gas company profits.

The country soon felt the effects of lifting
price controls without also raising taxes on oil

and gas company profits. In 1979, OPEC raised prices four times in five months, and revolution in Iran curtailed its oil exports. Images of motorists waiting for hours in line to buy gas, last seen during the 1973 oil embargo again dominated the news. The crisis reached its zenith on June 13, 1979, when over half of the nation's service stations ran out of gas. Meanwhile Exxon, an American company that imported oil from overseas, announced first quarter earnings of $1.9 billion in 1980, a record profit by an American corporation.

Carter renewed his call for a windfall-profit tax on oil and gas companies, hoping to use this revenue to fund public transportation, develop alternative energy sources, and help the poor pay for heating. To stimulate interest in energy conservation, Carter took to the airwaves to deliver an address soon dubbed the "malaise speech." America, he lamented, was enmeshed in a moral and spiritual crisis. The nation had gone from one that celebrated "hard work, strong families, close-knit communities, and our faith in God" to one that worshiped "self-indulgence and consumption." Carter's call for Americans to "seize control again of our national destiny" aroused only resentment over his sermonizing.

These two political cartoons, both drawn in 1980, encapsulated competing notions of where blame for the energy crisis lay. Bob Taylor, drawing for the *Dallas Times Herald*, focused on the nation's insatiable appetite for oil (**28.5**). He portrayed Uncle Sam as a drug addict willing to pay any price for his next fix of oil. "Hey, man . . . like I don't CARE what it's costing . . . I need it," a disheveled and stony-eyed Uncle Sam says as he prepares to inject a barrel of oil into his vein. By contrast John Milt Morris's "Profit-sharing plan!" indicted OPEC and American oil companies for price-gouging, viewing the consumer as a victim of their conspiracy to empty his pockets (**28.6**). A sign posted outside one gas station presented a third view by proclaiming "Higher prices, More Sass, Bad President, Out of Gas," putting the blame squarely on Carter's shoulders.

New Paths in Foreign Affairs

Carter had more success in foreign affairs than in domestic matters, although not without encountering opposition to his Wilsonian-inspired vision of America championing democracy worldwide. Constant meddling in the domestic affairs

28.5 *Hey, man … like I don't CARE what it's costing me*
This political caricature blamed Americans' oil addiction for the nation's energy problems.

28.6 *Profit Sharing Plan*
Expressing more sympathy for the average consumer, this caricature accused oil-producing nations and oil companies of creating artificial shortages to gouge consumers.

What different opinions surfaced about the root of America's energy problems?

👁 **Watch** the **Video** *Jimmy Carter, "Crisis of Confidence" (1979)*

of neighboring nations, he noted, had earned the United States the reputation as an imperial exploiter throughout Latin America. Liberal Democrats rejoiced when Carter resolved to make human rights and the spreading of democracy the centerpieces of his foreign policy.

The president's first major achievement was consistent with his desire to forge a new path in American diplomatic relations. Making amends for past American wrongdoing (see Chapter 19), Carter negotiated a treaty that returned the Panama Canal to Panama in 2000. The United States had controlled the Canal Zone since 1903, but by the 1970s, America's bigger submarines and ships did not fit through the canal, reducing its importance to national security and the economy. Three previous presidents had recognized these facts and opened negotiations, but Carter sealed the deal and won Senate ratification for the agreement in 1978.

Giving up control of the Panama Canal failed to dramatically improve relations between the United States and Latin America. Overtures to normalize relations with the Communist Cuban dictator Fidel Castro went nowhere. Carter also faced a severe test in Nicaragua, where civil war pitted the anti-communist dictator Anastasio Somoza against the Cuban-supported Sandinista rebels. When the Sandinistas prevailed, Carter offered them economic aid in the vain hope that he could dissuade them from creating a Cuban-like authoritarian communist state. Turning to Asia, Carter continued along the path forged by Nixon and established diplomatic relations with the People's Republic of China in 1979. This decision angered conservatives who viewed Taiwan, where the Nationalist government had fled after the Communist takeover of the mainland in 1949, as the rightful government of China. "To the Communists and those others who are hostile to our country," Reagan fumed, "President Carter and his supporters in the Congress seem like Santa Claus. They have given the Panama Canal away, abandoned Taiwan to the Red Chinese, and they're negotiating a SALT II treaty (with the Soviets) that could very well make this nation NUMBER TWO."

Ignoring these criticisms Carter signed the SALT II pact in June 1979, which capped missiles and bombers on each side. But as Reagan's comments revealed, American disaffection with détente ran deep. In the 1970s, Soviet-backed regimes took control of Angola, Somalia, Ethiopia,

> ## "An inordinate fear of communism has led us to embrace any dictator who joined in our fear."
>
> President JIMMY CARTER, making human rights a guiding principle in U.S. foreign policy

and Afghanistan, confirming skeptics' fears that détente had strengthened the enemy. Additional signs of Moscow's aggressive intentions came in 1977 when the Soviets began aiming new, highly accurate intermediate-range missiles (SS-20s) at Western Europe. Carter responded by securing NATO's authorization to install Pershing II missiles in Western Europe, which could reach Moscow in ten minutes.

Strained Soviet-American relations took another hit when the Soviet Union invaded Afghanistan in December 1979 to prop up its faltering Marxist government. The Soviets were eager to keep a friendly regime in power along their border, but the United States feared their ambitions might stretch into the oil-rich Middle East. Calling the invasion "the most serious threat to peace since the Second World War," Carter announced the Carter Doctrine, a declaration that the United States would use armed forces to stop any outside power from making inroads into the Persian Gulf region. He withdrew the SALT II treaty from the Senate, increased defense spending, cut off shipments of grain and technology to the Soviet Union, and announced that the United States would boycott the summer Olympics in Moscow. The Carter administration also sent aid to Muslim fundamentalist rebels battling the Soviets in Afghanistan, whose ranks included the Saudi-born Islamic militant Osama bin Laden. A wealthy recent college graduate dedicated to establishing an Islamic state in Afghanistan, bin Laden would later found al-Qaeda, an Islamic fundamentalist terrorist organization.

The Cold War had long held the attention of American presidents. The United States was just learning, however, to take conflicts in the Middle East as seriously. Carter hoped to lessen tension by negotiating an end to hostilities between Israel and Egypt. In 1978, he invited Egyptian President Anwar El Sadat and Israeli Prime Minister Menachem Begin to Camp David, a presidential mountain retreat in Maryland. Thirteen days of tense

Did Carter's dealings with the Soviet Union continue or undo initiatives undertaken by Nixon and Ford?

negotiations ended with the **Camp David Accords**. Israel agreed to give the Sinai Peninsula back to Egypt in 1982 (see 28.1). In return Egypt became the first Arab state to recognize Israel's right to exist. The United States rewarded each side with pledges of substantial military aid, support that continues to this day. Befriending Egypt neutralized the only credible military threat to Israeli security and brought a previous Soviet ally into the American fold, strengthening the American position in the Middle East.

If the Middle East gave Carter his greatest diplomatic victory, it also provided the low point of his presidency. In 1953, the United States had helped overthrow the left-leaning Iranian government and reinstated the reliably anti-communist Shah of Iran to ensure American access to Iranian oil. In 1979, radical Islamists overthrew the Shah, who fled the country. An Islamic cleric and revolutionary, the Ayatollah Ruhollah Khomeini, became the head of the world's first radical Islamist government. Khomeini's intense dark eyes, long snowy beard, and flowing robes made him appear dark and dangerous to Americans, who recoiled at his ferocious denunciations of the United States as "the Great Satan."

In October 1979, Carter made a fateful decision when he reluctantly agreed to let the ailing Shah of Iran, who was living in Mexico, into the United States for medical treatment. If the United States "turned our backs on the fallen Shah, it would be a signal to the world that the U.S. is a fair-weather friend," National Security Advisor Zbigniew Brzezinski told Carter. At 3:00 a.m. on November 4, 1979, the State Department received a telephone call from panicked officials in the American embassy in Teheran, the capital of Iran, reporting that a mob of Iranian university students had broken into the compound. The students proceeded to take embassy employees hostage. Khomeini had not ordered the hostage-taking, but he supported the students' demands that the United States return the Shah and his fortune to Iran to secure the hostages' release. His government, worried that the United States might try to return the Shah to power, wanted him in hand.

The **Iranian hostage crisis** became the defining event in Carter's presidency as Iranian revolutionaries held 52 Americans captive for 444 days. The media coverage was unprecedented, and most reporters viewed the crisis as a humiliating blow to America's honor. ABC News created a late-night show, "Nightline," that gave constant updates on "America Held Hostage" and repeatedly showed film footage of Iranian crowds chanting "Death to America" and the blindfolded captives. Frustration with Carter's inability to resolve the crisis caused his approval ratings to sink to 28 percent.

How to proceed was not clear, however, and Carter's key advisors offered him conflicting recommendations. Secretary of State Cyrus Vance focused on saving the hostages' lives and argued that the United States needed to negotiate patiently, no matter how long it took. National Security Advisor Brzezinski worried more about protecting America's image as a global superpower. He felt that the longer the crisis lasted, the weaker America appeared to the rest of the world, emboldening America's enemies. The Soviet

> ## "The release of the American hostages had become almost an obsession with me."
> President JIMMY CARTER comments on the Iran hostage crisis in his memoirs

invasion of Afghanistan a month into the hostage crisis seemingly corroborated Brzezinski's vision. *Choices and Consequences: Ending the Iranian Hostage Crisis* explores Carter's options and the repercussions of his decision to try to rescue the hostages.

Five months later Iraqi ruler Saddam Hussein launched an invasion of Iran to acquire its oil fields, and Khomeini finally decided to negotiate in earnest. Iran could no longer afford its diplomatic isolation, needing to reestablish its global trading networks to fend off the attack. After months of negotiations the United States agreed to give Iran $7.9 billion (the estimated value of the Shah's holdings in the United States) and pledged not to interfere in Iranian domestic affairs. Carter hoped to deliver the good news to the American people that the hostages were coming home before he left office on January 20, 1981. Instead, Khomeini waited until a few minutes after the new president Ronald Reagan was sworn into office to release the hostages, denying Carter a final triumph.

Choices and Consequences

ENDING THE IRANIAN HOSTAGE CRISIS

When Iranian students stormed the U.S. Embassy and took Americans hostage in 1979, President Carter faced a choice over whether to follow the advice of Secretary of State Cyrus Vance, who recommended patient negotiations, or National Security Advisor Zbigniew Brzezinski, who favored using force to end the crisis. For five months Carter brokered a compromise between these two positions by freezing Iranian financial assets in the United States, engaging in secret negotiations, and beefing up the American naval presence in the Arabian Sea. As Carter began his 1980 reelection bid, mounting public frustration along with concern that American inaction had encouraged the Soviet Union to invade Afghanistan, increased the pressure on Carter for decisive action.

Choices

1 Wait for Iran to tire of its diplomatic isolation, and then negotiate the hostages' release without alienating the rest of the Muslim world.

2 Make a show of strength by bombing Iranian oil refineries and military bases and mining harbors.

3 Use Special Forces to rescue the hostages.

Decision

When an Iranian negotiator told the administration that a diplomatic resolution was months away, Carter decided to act. In April, 1980, while Vance was out of town, Carter authorized a rescue mission by Special Forces.

Consequences

Swirling desert sands and a collision between American aircraft doomed the rescue mission in its first stages, further humiliating the United States. Vance immediately resigned, and in July the Shah died in Egypt, ending the question of returning him to Iran. When Iraq invaded Iran in September, seeking oil-rich territory, Khomeini decided to end Iran's diplomatic isolation. Winning concessions from the United States, Iran released the hostages on January 20, 1981, the day that Ronald Reagan was inaugurated president.

The ex-hostages arrive at Frankfurt, Germany on January 21, 1981, the day after their release.

Continuing Controversies

How important was the hostage crisis for the United States in the long-term?

Some say it was very important. The hostages' prolonged captivity branded Carter as inept and contributed to his re-election loss. To contain Iran, the United States supported Saddam Hussein during his eight-year war with Iran, again using a repressive Middle Eastern dictator to advance American interests. The hostage crisis also created a negative image of Islam in the United States that future Islamic terrorist attacks reinforced. The crisis was not so important, others counter, rejecting it as a major reason for Reagan's victory. In the 1980s, the failed Soviet invasion of Afghanistan, the Camp David Accords, and using a secular Iraq to contain Iranian influence protected U.S. economic interests in the region, diminishing the long-term significance of the hostage crisis.

What larger significance did Carter's advisors attach to the Iranian hostage crisis?

The Rights Revolution

Social turbulence did not cease with the end of the Vietnam War. Feminists and gay activists carried the 1960s' rights revolution into the 1970s and 1980s, striking at the heart of gender identity in American society. Meanwhile the environmental movement sought to reverse the toll of industrial pollution on the nation's natural habitats.

The Equal Rights Amendment and Abortion Controversies

Feminist political demands received unprecedented attention in the 1970s. To eradicate gender discrimination and sexual inequality at the workplace, feminist organizations lobbied for equal pay for equal work, an end to sexual harassment, and paid maternity leave. These bread-and-butter issues became even more pressing as the economic downturn of the 1970s forced more women into the workplace. The chart *Women and Work, 1900–2000* (**28.7**) shows the steady increase in the percentage of single and married women who worked outside the home over the second half of the twentieth century. Changing attitudes toward married women working and declining birthrates

28.7 Women and Work, 1900–2000 As more women entered the workforce, combating discrimination in the workplace became a major issue for the women's movement.

contributed to the increased female presence in the job market. Thanks to vacuum cleaners, gas and electric stoves, washing machines and dryers, women in the 1970s spent less time doing housework than their counterparts earlier in the century. Supermarkets, fast food, and prepackaged foods also simplified the tasks of shopping and cooking for a family. Nonetheless, working women faced challenges including the lack of affordable day care and the difficulty of convincing men to pitch in at home. On average women worked 15 hours (outside and inside the home) more a week than men. "You're on duty at work. You come home, and you're on duty," complained one wife. With one in two marriages ending in divorce, single-parenting often put more strains on working women with children. The most common reason couples gave for divorcing in the 1970s and 1980s: arguments over domestic responsibilities.

The feminist movement, however, faced challenges convincing working women that feminism provided the answer to the problems they faced balancing work and home life or advancing in the workplace. The press, one activist noted, portrayed the feminist as "a total weirdo—bra-burner, man-hater, lesbian, sickie!"—exaggerated stereotypes that threatened the movement's growth. Many women proved reluctant to publicly identify themselves as feminists, even if they privately supported the women's movement goals, fearing social stigmatization as unfeminine. Divisions within the women's movement created another major obstacle. Poor minority women often saw racial and ethnic prejudice as bigger obstacles to their economic advancement than gender discrimination, and regarded white, upper-middle-class feminists with suspicion. Feminism, in the words of one black woman, was "basically a family quarrel between White women and White men." Divisions between radicals and

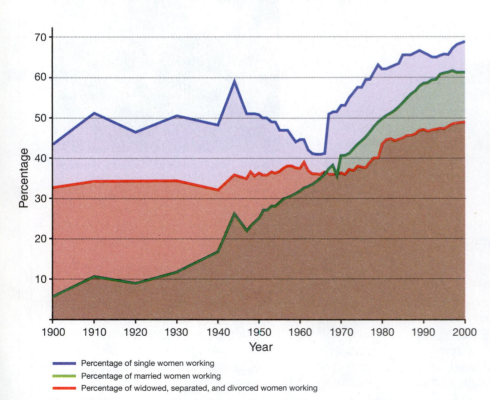

Legend:
Percentage of single women working
Percentage of married women working
Percentage of widowed, separated, and divorced women working

moderate feminists (see Chapter 27) also prevented women from speaking with one voice.

The feminist movement occasionally benefited from positive media coverage, as during made-for-television moments like the heavily hyped "battle of the sexes" in 1973 between tennis stars Billie Jean King and Bobby Riggs. Millions of Americans tuned in to watch King defeat Riggs, a self-proclaimed "male chauvinist pig" who argued that even a 55-year-old former tennis champion like himself could defeat the best female player in the world. Riggs announced his conversion to the feminist cause by shouting "equality for women" as he hit the final volley into the net. King's triumph advanced opportunities for women's professional sports. Feminist campaigning also led to the passage of Title IX of the 1972 Education Act, prohibiting gender discrimination in education. This law revolutionized high school and college sports by forcing administrators to create more teams and scholarships for female students.

Despite negative media portrayals and problems attracting working-class women, the feminist movement enjoyed other successes in the early 1970s. Cities established shelters for battered women and rape-crisis centers. Congress also passed the **Equal Rights Amendment (ERA)** in 1972, a proposal that congressional supporters had introduced regularly since 1923 that stated, "equality of rights under the law shall not be denied or abridged by the United States or by any State on account of sex." Within three years, 34 of the 38 states needed for ratification of the ERA had approved the measure.

This avalanche of change outraged cultural conservatives who charged that the ERA would destroy the American family. Phyllis Schlafly, a conservative Illinois lawyer with six children, led the anti-ERA crusade. Catapulting into the national spotlight, Schlafly helped forge the coalition among Catholics, Southerners, antifeminists, religious fundamentalists, and fiscal conservatives that pushed the Republican Party to the right throughout the 1970s. Feminists branded Schlafly a hypocrite, pointing out that she was a well-educated woman who had enjoyed a satisfying career in Republican politics before spearheading the anti-ERA campaign. "She's an extremely liberated woman," asserted Karen DeCrow, the president of the feminist National Organization for Women. *Competing Visions: Defining the Ideal Woman* (page 860) explores the debate over female gender identity in the 1970s. Schlafly's anti-feminist message resonated in the Southern and Mountain states, areas without strong local feminist organizations to offer a competing view of how gender discrimination adversely affected women in the workplace. In the end the anti-ERA forces prevailed. The ERA remained three states short when the deadline for approving the measure came in 1982, the first of many conservative political victories to come in the 1980s.

The rancor over legalized abortion, however, far surpassed the barbs exchanged over the ERA. Between 700,000 and 800,000 women a year sought illegal abortions, and botched procedures by incompetent practitioners working in unsanitary conditions killed 2,000–3,000 patients annually. The signs (**28.8**) in this 1970 St. Louis, Missouri protest march, held on the anniversary of the ratification of the Nineteenth Amendment, listed the right of legalized abortion as a key feminist demand. It remained the right of individual states to determine the legality

28.8 Women Marching for Equal Rights
These protesting feminists carried signs demanding legalized abortions, children's day care centers, passage of the Equal Rights Amendment, and more female candidates for political office.

How did the women participating in this protest march define female liberation?

Competing Visions
DEFINING THE IDEAL WOMAN

What did it mean to be a woman? Cultural conservatives answered "wife and mother;" feminists disagreed. In 1972, Gloria Steinem, founder of *Ms.*, a popular feminist magazine, argued that both women and men would be happier once freed from the straitjacket of culturally constructed gender roles. Conservative activist Phyllis Schlafly countered that gender identity was rooted in biology.

Gloria Steinem argued that women's liberation would benefit men as well as women.

I don't think most women want to pick up briefcases and march off to meaningless, depersonalized jobs…. We want to liberate men from those inhuman roles as well. We want to share the work and responsibility, and to have men share equal responsibility for the children. Probably the ultimate myth is that children must have fulltime mothers, and that liberated women make bad ones. The truth is that most American children seem to be suffering from too much mother and too little father.

Women now spend more time with their homes and families than in any other past or present society we know about. To get back to the sanity of the agrarian or joint family system, we need free universal day care. With that aid, as in Scandinavian countries, and with laws that permit women equal work and equal pay, man will be relieved of his role as sole breadwinner and stranger to his own children.

No more alimony. Fewer boring wives. Fewer childlike wives…. No more wives who fall apart with the first wrinkle because they've been taught that their total identity depends on their outsides. No more responsibility for another adult human being who has never been told she is responsible for her own life, and who sooner or later says some version of, "If I hadn't married you, I could have been a star." Women's Liberation really is Men's Liberation, too…. Colleague marriages, such as young people have now, with both partners going to law-school or the Peace Corps together, …. Communes; marriages that are valid for the child-rearing years only, there are many possibilities.

The point is that Women's Liberation is not destroying the American family. It is trying to build a human compassionate alternative out of its ruins.

Gloria Steinem

Phyllis Schlafly claimed that the "Positive Woman" embraced her distinctly female role.

The first requirement for the acquisition of power by the Positive Woman is to understand the differences between men and women…. She rejoices in the creative capability within her body and the power potential of her mind and spirit. She understands that men and women are different, and that those very differences provide the key to her success as a person and fulfillment as a woman.

The women's liberationist, on the other hand, is imprisoned by her own negative view of herself and of her place in the world around her…. Women must be made equal to men in their ability *not* to become pregnant and *not* to be expected to care for babies they may bring into the world. This is why women's liberationists are compulsively involved in the drive to make abortion and childcare centers for all women, regardless of religion or income, both socially acceptable, and government-financed…. The Positive Woman looks upon her femaleness and her fertility as part of her purpose, her potential, and her power. She rejoices that she has a capability for creativity that men can never have …

A Positive Woman cannot defeat a man in a wrestling match or boxing match, but she can motivate him, inspire him, encourage him, teach him, restrain him, reward him, and have power over him that he can never achieve over her with all his muscle…. The overriding psychological need of a woman is to love something alive. A baby fulfills this need in the lives of most women. If a baby is not available to fill that need, women search for a baby-substitute. This is the reason why women have traditionally gone into teaching and nursing careers. They are doing what comes naturally to the female psyche.

Phyllis Schlafly

Do Steinem and Schlafly offer realistic or clichéd depictions of women's lives, or a combination of both?

View the **Closer Look** *Competing Visions: Defining the Ideal Woman*

of abortion throughout the sixties and early seventies. California took the lead in changing what the *Los Angeles Times* called "Our Archaic Abortion Law" that only allowed a woman to end a pregnancy if her life was in danger. Bending to the popular will, then-California Governor Ronald Reagan reluctantly signed a bipartisan bill in 1967 that let women terminate pregnancies in cases of rape and incest and fetuses with severe physical and mental defects, a decision he later called a mistake.

Texas, however, still only allowed abortions if a pregnancy jeopardized a woman's life. Feminists felt that women, not male doctors, should have the right to make medical decisions about their own bodies. In 1970, Norma McCorvey, an unmarried, poor, pregnant 25-year-old, sued Texas under the pseudonym Jane Roe claiming that she had the right to a legal and safe abortion based on her constitutional "right to privacy." The Supreme Court dealt the feminist movement a stunning victory when it legalized abortion in its 1973 *Roe v. Wade* decision. The ruling came too late for McCorvey, who gave birth to a baby girl and gave her up for adoption as the case moved through the courts.

In rendering the *Roe v. Wade* decision, the Supreme Court ruled that the "right to privacy . . . is broad enough to encompass a woman's decision whether or not to terminate her pregnancy." The Court decision prohibited states from criminalizing abortion in the first trimester, but allowed them to regulate abortion in the second trimester and prohibit it during the third trimester when a fetus became viable. The Court, however, sidestepped a key question that would provoke much future controversy. "We need not resolve the difficult question of when life begins," the Court asserted. Critics argued that the Court had invented a right to privacy that did not exist in the Constitution. Supporters countered that court decisions over the last century had established this right. The debate soon seeped into national politics, when the Democrats assumed the mantle of the party dedicated to maintaining a woman's right to choose an abortion and the Republicans became predominantly against the right to abortion, a position that came to be known as "pro-life."

The vocabulary embraced by each side in the abortion debate revealed competing visions of what abortion meant. Supporters of legalized abortion called themselves "pro-choice," a label encapsulating their view that abortion was a question of personal liberty. In contrast "pro-life" forces believed that human life began at conception (not when a fetus was viable outside the womb); they therefore viewed abortion as tantamount to murder. Both sides employed the language of rights, the "rights of women" (pro-choice usage) squaring off against those of "unborn children" (pro-life term). The activist women facing off in this debate had different life experiences and conceptions of motherhood. Pro-life activists had often built their lives around children and the home and were outraged by their suspicion that pro-choice women had abortions "as a matter of convenience." Pro-choice activists tended to marry later, had more education, and were less religious. They usually wanted careers as well as children and refused to allow biology to dictate their life choices.

Twenty years after *Roe v. Wade* McCorvey changed her mind about abortion and became a born-again Christian, who joined the anti-abortion crusade. Her reversal illustrated the growing momentum of the pro-life movement, which used images of children, like the one affixed to the sign of this 1979 pro-life demonstrator protesting in Washington, D.C. (**28.9**), to emphasize the rights of children.

28.9 Pro-life Protest, 1979
Pro-life demonstrators who opposed legalized abortion put the focus on the right of unborn children to have a life rather than the right of women to control their own bodies.

In the twenty-first century, the pro-life movement took advantage of new ultrasound portraits of fetuses in the womb that showed beating hearts to underscore their argument that life began at conception. Unable to overturn the *Roe* decision directly, pro-life activists secured a ban on federal funding for abortions. Some states also required parental notification when minors sought abortions.

Gay Rights

The rights revolution also encompassed the gay and lesbian subcultures that existed in the shadows of mainstream society until the 1960s. Except for a few men and women who joined fledgling gay rights groups after World War II, most gay men and lesbians before the 1960s chose to live "in the closet," hiding their same-sex preferences from the world. Unlike blacks, women, and other minority groups, gay Americans did not have a long history of organizing to defend their rights. Heterosexual Americans uniformly disparaged gays as deviant and morally reprehensible. The American Psychiatric Association categorized homosexuality as a "mental disorder," a position it did not jettison until 1973. Taking the psychological stereotyping a step further, *Time* magazine viewed homosexuality as "a pernicious sickness." "If you were gay and you

accepted those societal norms, then you were at war with yourself," stated one college student as he recalled his own struggle to come to terms with his homosexuality. Exposure as a homosexual or lesbian could mean losing everything—job, spouse, friends, and social position.

In the 1960s the Civil Rights Movement and the hippie counterculture assault on sexual taboos inspired some gay people to "come out of the closet" and challenge the ways that American society ostracized them. The true awakening of the gay rights movement came during the **Stonewall riot** on June 28, 1969, when patrons frequenting the Stonewall Inn, a Greenwich Village male gay bar, fought back during a New York City police raid. This open defiance electrified the gay community, and the next morning a huge crowd gathered outside the Stonewall Inn, chanting "Gay Power," a modification of the "Black Power" slogan that black militants embraced (see Chapter 27). Energized gay men and lesbians founded the radical Gay Liberation Front in response to Stonewall, while hundreds of smaller gay rights groups sprouted up throughout the country. These organizations formed gay support groups on campuses, lobbied for antidiscrimination laws, marched in Gay Pride parades, and followed the "sit-in" model of the Civil Rights Movement by staging "kiss-ins" in restaurants. "We should have the same right to

28.10 AIDS Memorial Quilt, 1987
The panels of the AIDS Memorial Quilt portrayed the disease's victims as sons, brothers, and lovers with strong ties to their families and communities to challenge stereotypes of homosexuals as diseased pariahs.

How similar were the Gay Rights and Civil Rights Movements?   **Read** the **Document** *The Gay Liberation Front, Come Out (1970)*

express our affection publicly as heterosexuals have," asserted lesbian activist Barbara Gittings.

The increased visibility of the gay rights movement provoked a conservative response. In 1977, the deeply religious pop singer Anita Bryant, known to most Americans for her appearances in Florida orange juice television commercials, spearheaded a campaign to overturn a gay rights law in Dade County, Florida. Her victory galvanized forces on both sides of the gay rights debate.

Fundamentalist churches opposed legislation granting gays legitimacy, lobbying strongly for laws that prevented homosexuals from teaching in public schools. Gay rights groups ridiculed the notion that gay men, because they preferred men as sexual partners, were pedophiles. A more insidious challenge loomed ahead, however.

In 1981, the mainstream press began printing stories of a mysterious ailment sweeping through homosexual communities in New York and San Francisco. Acquired Immune Deficiency Syndrome (AIDS), a virus transmitted through the exchange of bodily fluids, ravaged the immune system of its victims. Acquiring AIDS was a virtual death sentence in the 1980s; the disease killed over 100,000 Americans by 1990. Because in the U.S. AIDS disproportionately struck homosexuals, the nation viewed the epidemic as more than a public health crisis.

The raging political debate over the status of homosexuals in America colored the competing visions about AIDS. Religious conservatives viewed AIDS as God's retribution against the "morally degenerate," ignoring evidence that AIDS could also strike the heterosexual population. (Thousands of hemophiliacs and other straight Americans for example, died after contracting AIDS from tainted blood transfusions.) Having just recently repudiated the notion that gay people were mentally ill, homosexuals now confronted fears that they were all diseased. AIDS patients told heartbreaking stories of losing their jobs, being turned away from hospital emergency rooms, and facing eviction from apartments by landlords who feared contamination. The gay community lobbied vigorously for increased federal funds to find a medical cure for the disease. Still, having fought so long to escape police harassment and end legal penalties for consensual homosexual acts, many gay activists were leery about urging homosexual men to modify their sexual behaviors. Larry Kramer chastised gay activists who "took the position that sexual promiscuity was the one freedom we had and that we had to fight to maintain it—even if it killed us. And it did kill us, a lot of us."

Kramer instead worked to popularize the "safe sex" message—no exchange of bodily fluids—that eventually gained currency in the gay community.

The two images shown here illustrate the competing visions within the gay community over how to best draw media attention to the mounting AIDS death toll. In 1987, the AIDS Memorial Quilt, the brainchild of San Francisco activist Cleve Jones, began touring the country after an inaugural unfurling on the National Mall in Washington, D.C. The nation's largest-ever public art endeavor, the quilt (28.10) made the individual stories of AIDS visible by allowing family and friends to create a square for a loved one, homosexual or heterosexual, lost to the disease. Squares were the size of a human grave, and they portrayed a mixture of embroidered personal remembrances and treasured possessions like jewelry.

Radical activists adopted a less poignant and more militant tone. Embracing the slogan "SILENCE = DEATH," the AIDS Coalition to Unleash Power (ACT-UP) staged its first "funeral" demonstration in 1987 to demand better medical treatment. Protesters lay down on a busy Wall Street intersection until police carried them away (28.11), employing the same civil disobedience tactics used by the Civil Rights Movement in the 1960s. ACT-UP also conducted phone "zaps" that barraged officials with calls on AIDS-related issues and barricaded the doors to the Food and Drug Administration to protest delays

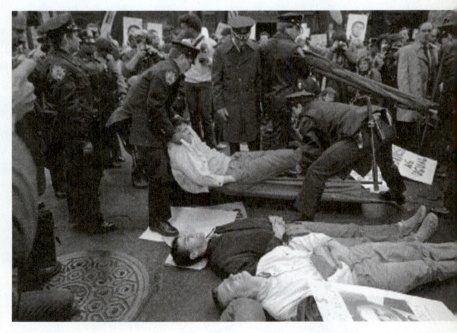

28.11 Act-Up Protestors Stage a Funeral Demonstration in Wall Street
Militant gay activists used civil disobedience to protest high prices and slow federal approval of life-saving anti-AIDS drugs. [*Source:* John Sotomayor/The New York Times/ Redux Pictures]

View the **Image** *Sign at a Gay Pride March*   What competing strategies did gay activists develop to publicize the AIDS crisis?

in approving AIDS-fighting drugs. *The New York Times* called ACT-UP, "rude, rash, effective." On September 14, 1989, seven ACT-UP members handcuffed themselves to the balcony of the New York Stock Exchange to protest the huge profits that Burroughs-Wellcome, a pharmaceutical company, had amassed selling AZT, the only drug then available to inhibit the progression of AIDS. Four days later, as a result of negative publicity, Burroughs-Wellcome dropped the price of AZT 20 percent. By 1996, a drug "cocktail" dramatically reduced AIDS-related deaths. A relentless safe-sex campaign and screening of donated blood also lowered the infection rate.

Environmentalism

On April 22, 1970, communities throughout the nation celebrated their first Earth Day. New York City crowds walked through a block-long plastic bubble to breathe pure air; demonstrators in Boston protested noise pollution; and population control advocates in Bloomington, Indiana, handed out free birth control pills. Earth Day made environmentalism visible, but the variety of causes that activists championed revealed the competing visions within the environmental movement. For New Left and counterculture environmentalists, eating organically produced food grown without pesticides became a symbolic way of purging the poison of mainstream American values out of their lives. Politicians interested in securing environmentally friendly legislation framed pollution as a straightforward health issue. To win widespread support for laws mandating lead-free gas and paint, they focused, for example, on how lead poisoning damaged children's brains. Traditional conservationist societies like the Sierra Club and Audubon Society concentrated on preserving pristine wild habitats from development. They supported expanding the National Park Service to safeguard wildness areas and provide recreational sanctuaries for over-taxed citizens living in the industrial world.

28.12 Environmental Disasters 1960-2010
Intense media coverage of man-made environmental disasters led to increased regulation of offshore drilling, nuclear energy, and the disposal of industrial waste.

Love Canal, 1978
When dumped chemical waste sickened residents. Congress created the "Superfund" requiring companies to clean up toxic waste sites.

Cuyahoga River Fire, 1969
Outrage over the heavily polluted river catching fire spurred clean water regulations and the creation of the EPA.

Santa Barbara Oil Spill, 1969
Offshore drilling was banned near coastlines after a drilling accident dumped 3 million gallons of oil into southern California waters.

Three Mile Island, 1979
Support for nuclear energy evaporated after a nuclear reactor leaked radioactive gas.

Exxon Valdez Oil Spill, 1989
Opposition intensified to drilling in the Arctic National Wildlife Refuge after a tanker ran aground, spilling 11 million gallons of oil.

Gulf of Mexico Oil Spill, 2010
In the nation's largest oil spill a blown-out offshore well leaked oil for 3 months, leading to inconclusive investigations into industry practices.

How did the nation respond to modern environmental disasters?

Presidential support for environmental reforms had begun during the Kennedy and Johnson administrations (see Chapter 27), and in the 1970s Nixon and Carter also increased federal environmental controls. New laws required the removal of asbestos (a cancer-causing building material) from schools. Companies had to reduce the amount of airborne toxins that their factories produced and clean up sites they had contaminated. Car manufacturers installed required catalytic converters that helped reduce automobile pollution by 75 percent. Meanwhile the consumer protection movement spearheaded by Ralph Nader led to the creation of a federal Consumer Product Safety Commission that could ban the sale of hazardous products, from cribs to cars. While the general public applauded changes that made their lives healthier and safer, blue-collar workers feared that new, expensive pollution controls on industry

28.13 Three Mile Island Nuclear Reactor Towers
America rejected nuclear power after the accident at the Three Mile Island nuclear power plant. That decision, coupled with limited federal support for solar and wind-generated power, increased the nation's dependence on overseas oil.

simply encouraged industrialists to move their factories overseas. "If you're hungry and out of work, eat an environmentalist," read one popular labor union bumper sticker.

Two well-publicized environmental scandals, however—one at Love Canal, a waterway near Niagara Falls, New York, and the other at Three Mile Island in Pennsylvania—convinced most Americans that their well-being depended on strict federal environmental regulation (**28.12**). After years of ignoring residents' complaints about rising levels of miscarriages and birth defects, New York State finally admitted in 1978 that the foul-smelling industrial waste dumped into the Love Canal contained deadly toxins that had polluted the area's ground and air. Congress responded by creating a Superfund to clean up dangerously polluted areas, spending $400 million over 20 years to restore the Love Canal region.

In 1979, the partial meltdown of a nuclear reactor at the Three Mile Island nuclear power plant in Pennsylvania caused nearly 100,000 panicked residents to flee when radioactive steam poured into the air. No one was hurt, but the government-sponsored clean-up took 14 years. Despite new, more stringent federal regulations for nuclear reactors, Americans equated the image of nuclear reactor towers with danger (**28.13**) and refused to accept new nuclear power plants in their neighborhoods despite a strong industry-wide safety record.

Not all Americans applauded new environmental regulation. A "Sagebrush Rebellion" arose in the West among conservatives demanding that the federal government return federally controlled lands to the states. Western miners, ranchers, and loggers chafed under new federal restrictions that limited their access to water, their ability to hunt predators, and their grazing rights on federal lands. Western votes helped Ronald Reagan win the presidency in 1980, and as president he listened sympathetically to their complaints about federal environmental policies. An avid outdoorsman who enjoyed riding horses at his California ranch, Reagan did not believe that the environment was in jeopardy. Emphasizing economic growth he loosened recently enacted pollution controls on industry and reduced the size and budget of the Environmental Protection Agency (EPA), an agency founded under Nixon's watch to enforce federal environmental regulations.

Which environmental visions prevailed in the 1970s and 1980s?

The Rise of the Right

Successful attacks on environmental regulation were just one component of a resurgent conservative coalition that emerged as the dominant force in American politics in the 1980s. Through right-leaning policy institutes, magazines, lobbying groups, and direct mail campaigns, conservatives spearheaded a powerful political movement whose vision Ronald Reagan championed when he entered the White House. A charismatic leader, Reagan's unrelenting optimism changed the national mood. The vision of a nation adrift evaporated as confidence in the economy and government rebounded.

The New Conservative Coalition

The emerging conservative coalition known as the New Right created alliances among groups with different concerns and views of what America and American government should be, reshaping the Republican Party in the process. Conservatives differed on whether a balanced budget or cutting taxes would guarantee prosperity. They disputed whether the government should actively promote conservative values or adopt a more libertarian approach that reduced governmental activity in all spheres. In the 1970s, the mix of ideas grew even more complicated, when neoconservatives, defectors from the liberal ranks, joined the conservative coalition. Seeking to explain his own political journey from the left to the right, Irving Kristol defined neoconservatives as "liberals who've been mugged by reality." Neoconservatives focused mostly on foreign affairs, urging the nation to cast off its Vietnam hangover and stand proud in the world again. Their insistence that America had the right to act unilaterally in world affairs soon prevailed over lingering noninterventionism in conservative thinking.

Former working-class and Southern Democrats also joined the emerging conservative coalition. Angry over court-ordered integration and busing, affirmative action programs that reserved jobs or school slots for minorities, and rising crime, these newcomers accepted the conservative orthodoxy of smaller government when it came to programs that primarily benefited minorities. Ethnic Northern whites in the Rust Belt resented their declining economic clout as industrial jobs evaporated, and they responded to Republican claims that "limousine liberal" elites were out of touch with working-class America. Finally the popularity of grassroots

conservative movements among burgeoning Sun Belt populations from Florida to Arizona completed the political realignment in the 1980s.

In the late 1970s, simmering resentment against increasing taxes exploded into open revolt. Big business and the well-to-do had long championed lower income and corporate taxes. Now the working class and middle class joined the tax revolt by demanding lower property taxes. Voters in California spearheaded the tax rebellion in 1978 when they approved Proposition 13. This ballot referendum, which reduced property taxes by 57 percent, caused drastic cuts in funding for public schools and universities. Voters in other states soon followed suit and increasingly found the Republican anti-tax message appealing.

The Republican Party also benefited from the rise of the **Religious Right**, conservative Christian groups that defended traditional values and supported right-wing political causes—the most sustained grassroots movement of the late twentieth century. Reagan saw the benefits of reaching out to the Religious Right, hoping to create a strong conservative coalition that would "attract those interested in the so-called 'social issues' and those interested in economic issues."

Protestant Fundamentalists had mobilized their ranks in the 1920s to end the teaching of evolution in Southern public schools. After the Scopes Trial (see Chapter 21), the mainstream media paid little attention to religious conservatives, but Fundamentalist radio stations, publishing houses, and revival meetings thrived in the South. Fundamentalists ended their self-imposed exile from mainstream politics in the 1950s when religious conservatives supported the nation's Cold War crusade against godless communism. The Supreme Court's 1962 ruling against school prayer (see Chapter 27) incensed Fundamentalists, as did Carter's attempts to revoke the tax-exempt status of religious schools that failed to integrate racially.

But politics alone does not explain why fundamentalism became a nationwide phenomenon in the 1970s, when nearly a quarter of the 50 million Protestant Americans described themselves as born-again Christians. In an era when sprawling suburbs and rancorous cultural debates created a sense of social fragmentation, close-knit Fundamentalist churches offered members cohesive communities, where people with similar values spoke the same language. The Fundamentalist vision of leading a morally upright life in keeping with divine will attracted white, middle-class suburbanites along with white, rural residents, creating a strong grassroots religious movement that cut across class and regional, if not racial, lines. Evangelical preachers, such as Pat Robertson, Jerry Falwell, Oral Roberts, Jimmy Swaggart, Robert Sculler, and Jim and Tammy Bakker, built media empires preaching that the Bible contained the literal truth to millions of television viewers—further popularizing the appeal of the Fundamentalist vision.

In the late 1960s, Nixon claimed to speak for the "silent majority" who objected to liberal policies in the privacy of their living rooms. In the 1980s, Republican politicians showered attention on the "moral majority," a well-organized network of politically active religious conservatives. In 1979, Falwell founded the Moral Majority, which he described as a "pro-life, pro-family, pro-morality, and pro-American" organization. The cover of Falwell's 1979 book, *America Can Be Saved*, showed him in front of a huge American flag, melding patriotism with religious fervor to create a vision of faith and conservative politics providing salvation to a nation adrift (**28.14**). The Moral Majority and other conservative religious groups registered two million new voters for the presidential contest of 1980. In the past Fundamentalists had distrusted Catholicism, but now, political concerns outweighed doctrinal differences. Fundamentalists formed a political alliance with

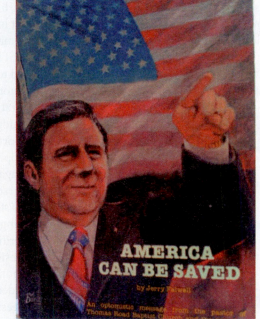

28.14 America Can Be Saved (1979)
The cover of Jerry Falwell's book illustrated the new connection between religious fundamentalism and political activism in the 1970s.

conservative Catholics, who shared their concerns about religious instruction in schools, abortion, and gay rights. Along with other members of the New Right, the Religious Right voted overwhelmingly for Reagan in the 1980 presidential election.

Setting a New Course: Reagan at Home

During the 1980 presidential campaign, Reagan focused voters' attention on the nation's economic woes by repeatedly asking "are you better off than you were four years ago?" Reagan's cheerfulness, humor, and athleticism offered a stark contrast to Carter's more drawn and weary demeanor. Memorizing his speeches and delivering them in a soothing baritone voice, Reagan's charisma helped him amass an almost worshipful following. His victory capped the rise of the New Right, a two-decade ascendancy that Watergate and Carter's election had interrupted. Reagan won the election by an impressive margin: 489 to 49 electoral votes. In his inaugural address he entreated the nation "to believe in our capacity to perform great deeds . . . after all, why shouldn't we believe that? We are Americans." Commentators likened Reagan's victory over the unpopular Carter in 1980 to Franklin D. Roosevelt's triumph over Herbert Hoover in 1932 (see Chapter 22). Each man created new coalitions that reshaped the political landscape; each inspired the country at a moment when it felt besieged.

Reagan entered the presidency passionate about cutting income and corporate taxes, reducing social welfare spending, and fighting communism. He immediately sent Congress a budget that cut spending for social programs, increased allocations for defense, and lowered taxes. Embracing the theory of supply-side economics, pro-business officials in the Reagan administration believed that letting entrepreneurs keep more of their profits would fuel economic growth, creating more and better-paying

View the **Closer Look** *Competing Visions: Two Presidential Views of America*

Why did the Religious Right thrive in the 1980s?

"Please tell me you're all Republicans."

A wounded President RONALD REAGAN to the emergency surgical team before they operated, 1981

jobs that generated enough tax revenue to offset the increases in military spending that Reagan proposed.

Liberal Democrats, however, suspected that Reagan had a more sinister reason for slashing taxes. Reagan, they charged, planned to starve the budget to force Congress to undertake even more draconian cuts in New Deal and Great Society social welfare programs that conservatives longed to abolish. Liberal Democrats derided his budget proposal as trickle-down economics, an approach discredited during the Hoover administration (see Chapter 22), when aid to the wealthy failed to create more jobs for the poor.

28.15 President Reagan Shot, 1981
The last photo shows Secret Service agent Jerry Parr shoving Reagan into his presidential limousine as a bullet hits him, but no one realized that Reagan had been shot until he reached the hospital.

Democrats in Congress were determined to fight Reagan's proposals. Then a nearly tragic turn of events gave Reagan an unexpected advantage. On March 30, 1981, a deranged 25-year-old named John Hinckley (seeking to impress teenage film actress Jodie Foster) shot Reagan, his press secretary James Brady, and two others outside a Washington hotel. After hearing a fire-cracker-like pop, news photographer Ron Edmonds took three quick photos (**28.15**): The first shows the president flinching as he hears shots; the second shows him turning to locate the source of the shooting; in the third, Secret Service agent Jerry Parr pushes Reagan into the presidential limousine as a bullet ricocheted off the car door and hit Reagan under his left armpit. Parr's quick-thinking is credited with saving Reagan's life—if Parr had not pushed the president down then the bullet would have likely hit him in the head. In the hospital, with a bullet lodged near his heart, Reagan maintained his trademark cheerfulness, telling his distraught wife, "Honey, I forgot to duck."

Americans rallied to his side, and when Reagan returned to work a month later, he presented his 70 percent approval ratings as evidence that the nation supported his budget proposal. It passed easily with bipartisan support from conservative Democrats. The top tax rate dropped from 70 percent to 50 percent, lowered again to 28 percent in 1986. Reagan's image as a resolute leader got another boost when he fired 11,000 striking air traffic controllers in August 1981, enforcing a ban on strikes by federal employees working in critical industries. Liberal critics lamented that the president's act sent a chilling message to organized labor, whose membership rolls and willingness to strike declined throughout the decade.

In 1984, Reagan easily won his reelection bid against Democrat Walter Mondale. Mondale energized the Democratic Party when he selected New York Congresswoman Geraldine Ferraro as his running mate, the nation's first female vice presidential candidate, but he made a key error by stating that he would raise taxes to close the deficit. Mondale expected Americans to reward him for his candor about the worrisome federal debt, but the nation was in no mood to fret. Reagan scored well with television campaign ads that centered on the theme "Morning Again in America." They featured scenes of small-town America where contented citizens celebrated marriages, schoolchildren pledged allegiance to the flag, and friends laughed together. "America is prouder, stronger, better. Why would we want to return to where we were less than four short years ago?" the voiceover asked. Many Americans agreed, and Reagan won every vote in the Electoral College except those from Mondale's home state of Minnesota and the District of Columbia, with a landslide total of 525 to 13.

Reagan remained relentlessly pro-business throughout his presidency. Driven to free private industry from government regulations that, in his view, restricted its growth, Reagan convinced Congress to deregulate the savings and loan industry. Once freed from strict government oversight, these banks lost huge amounts of depositors' money in speculative investments. In 1989, President George H. W. Bush, Reagan's successor, convinced Congress to bail them out at great cost to taxpayers rather than accept wide-scale bank failures that would certainly have sent the economy into a deep recession.

As the budget battles and savings and loan debacle revealed, Reagan's fiscal policies remained controversial. During his time in office, the federal debt nearly tripled (from $994 billion in 1981 to $2.6 trillion in 1988) as the hoped-for tax revenue failed to materialize and the military build-up continued unabated. After a serious recession in 1981–1983, the economy began to improve as inflation lessened and business activity picked up. The return of prosperity muted the impact of liberal criticism and helped Republicans argue that people at all class levels were doing better financially under Reagan's stewardship.

Democrats and Republicans offered competing visions on the economy throughout the 1980s. Democrats lamented the increased concentration of income in the hands of the top fifth of the population. "What I want to see above all is that this remains a country where someone can always get rich," Reagan stated in 1983. Chief executive officers (CEOs) of leading corporations had no reason for complaint. Their average salaries, adjusted for inflation, rose from $3 million to $12 million a year during Reagan's eight years in office, while outlays for subsidized housing dropped from $30 billion to $7 billion. In 1980, the average CEO made 40 times more than the average factory worker. By 1989, CEOs earned 93 times more. To Democrats Reagan's economic policies helped the rich get richer while the poor got poorer. Republicans countered that consumption was a better measurement of Americans' overall financial health than income distribution. In the 1980s, Americans went on a buying spree that rivaled the postwar boom of the 1950s, purchasing nearly 88 million cars, 63 million VCRs, and 62 million microwave ovens. Items previously available only to the wealthy, such as refrigerators and telephones, were found in nearly every American household by 1990. While the poorest Americans were not living as well as the richest, their

material circumstances were much improved when compared with those of previous generations.

Reagan spoke eloquently about cutting taxes and slashing welfare. He was decidedly less passionate about education, housing, health care, and the environment, often letting subordinates make key decisions in these areas. His hands-off management style differed vastly from Carter's micromanagement. Reagan rarely worked more than eight hours a day, enjoyed many vacations to his California ranch, and usually took an afternoon nap. "It's true that hard work never killed anyone, but I figure why take the chance?" he joked. Reagan's detractors viewed his detachment as senility and charged that he was just a figurehead. Supporters sometimes agreed that Reagan put his trust in the wrong hands. Over 100 members of his administration were indicted or forced to resign amid corruption charges, stemming in part from Reagan's lax oversight of his subordinates, who often acted without consulting him.

Foreign Policy Triumphs and Scandals

Reagan did more than reject the liberal economic vision; he also overturned the foreign policy initiatives set in place by his Republican predecessors. He changed the rules of the Cold War by abandoning MAD, the doctrine embraced by American and Soviet policymakers since the 1950s, as the basis for U.S. defense against the Soviet Union. Remaining defenseless against enemy nuclear weapons was an essential component of MAD. The ability to shoot down incoming missiles, the doctrine asserted, might encourage the enemy, who no longer feared its own destruction, to attack.

Reagan offered a competing view. "Let me share with you a vision of the future which offers hope," he declared in 1983, announcing the Strategic Defense Initiative (SDI). Challenging the view that vulnerability made America more secure, Reagan proposed building a missile shield that used lasers from space satellites to destroy incoming missiles. Publicly, he argued that his plan was compatible with the 1972 ABM treaty (which critics disputed), since he intended to share the technology with the Soviets. Privately, he expected the Soviet Union to go bankrupt trying to match the United States in building its own missile defenses.

Despite the billions spent on research, the SDI project failed. SDI nonetheless hurt the Soviet Union. A rapidly changing slate of elderly Soviet leaders responded to Reagan's challenge much as he expected. The new leaders increased military

Read the **Document** *Ronald Reagan, Speech at the Brandenburg Gate (1987)*

How did Democrats and Republicans differ on the state of the economy in the 1980s?

spending, ignoring the devastating consequences for Soviet citizens. In the 1980s, the Soviet Union spent between 15 and 17 percent of its GNP on defense, compared to 6.5 percent by the United States. Pervasive shortages meant that Soviet citizens spent hours in long lines outside poorly stocked stores, stoking discontent with communist rule.

Closer to home, Reagan looked for ways to destabilize communist and leftist regimes in the Caribbean and Central America, activities portrayed on the map, *American Intervention in Latin America, 1980–2000* (**28.16**). In Nicaragua he hoped to unseat the leftist Sandinistas. Sandinista aid to Marxist rebels battling the pro-American government in El Salvador confirmed Reagan's fears that communism was on the march in Central America, and he approved covert CIA assistance to the Contras, counterrevolutionary forces in Nicaragua that opposed the Sandinistas.

Congress had a different view of Central America. To continue the move away from direct interference in other nations' domestic affairs (a process begun by Ford and Carter), Congress prohibited the CIA and Department of Defense from funding any effort to overthrow the Sandinistas. National Security Council (NSC) Director Robert McFarlane and his assistant Marine Lt. Col. Oliver North convinced Reagan that these restrictions did not prevent the NSC from soliciting millions from Saudi Arabia and private donors

to aid the Contras. When Congress heard about these donations in 1984, it prohibited the government from using non-American funds to unseat the Sandinistas.

To thwart the regional expansion of communism, in October 1983 Reagan ordered U.S. troops to invade the tiny Caribbean island of Grenada. The president ostensibly dispatched U.S. forces to rescue American medical students trapped in Grenada, when a leftist government seized control. The troops' real mission was to remove a government seeking Cuban and Soviet military aid. By ordering troops into battle without consulting Congress, Reagan also used his powers as commander-in-chief (some argued unconstitutionally) to restore the strength of the presidency, badly diminished since Watergate.

Reagan supporters celebrated America's swift victory in Grenada, but critics viewed the event differently. They accused Reagan of using the Grenada invasion to distract Americans from more dismal news coming out the Middle East. Two days before the Grenada invasion, an Islamist suicide bomber had plowed a vehicle loaded with explosives into an unsecured barracks housing U.S. peacekeeping troops in Beirut, Lebanon, killing 241 servicemen. Iranian-backed Islamist terrorist groups (angry over U.S. support for Israel and Iraq, Iran's enemy) then increased their assaults against the United States by taking Americans hostage in Lebanon.

28.16 American Intervention in Latin America, 1980–2000 The United States continued to maintain Latin America as a sphere of influence in the 1980s.

How did Reagan's foreign policy initiatives break with policies set by Nixon and Carter?

Reagan's desires to end the Middle Eastern hostage crisis and halt the spread of communism in Central America led to the biggest political scandal of his administration. In the **Iran-Contra scandal**, Reagan administration officials sold arms to Iran to secure the hostages' release and then illegally used the proceeds to support the anti-Communist Contras in Nicaragua. The problems began in 1985 when Reagan asked his new NSC director John Poindexter and Oliver North to devise a covert plan to sell arms to Iran, which needed the weapons for its war with Iraq. As part of the secret agreement, the United States demanded that Iran secure the release of hostages held in Lebanon. After the deal went through, a few hostages were freed, but the arms-for-hostages deal backfired. Reagan's willingness to pay bribes to free American hostages encouraged militant Islamist groups to seize more over the next two years. Even more troubling, Poindexter and North secretly decided to divert profits from the arms sales to the Contras in Nicaragua—directly violating the congressional ban on aid to the anti-Communist rebels. When an American cargo plane carrying arms to the Contras crashed in 1986, their illegal action was exposed. Convicted of breaking the law, the pair won appeals based on legal technicalities and went free.

Poindexter and North claimed that Reagan knew nothing about their illegal diversion of funds to the Contras. "I made a very deliberate decision not to ask the president so I could insulate him," Poindexter testified before Congress. The public accepted this explanation, viewing Reagan as a hands-off administrator who could not always control his subordinates. With his approval rating dipping to below 50 percent, Reagan hoped to restore confidence in his leadership by improving relations with the Soviet Union.

The night before he became the Soviet leader in 1985, 54-year-old Mikhail Gorbachev admitted to his wife, "We can't go on living like this." Gorbachev was referring to both the ironclad Soviet control over the domestic economy and the government's long obsession with a possible American nuclear attack. Gorbachev embraced reform to save the Soviet Union, not destroy it. Eager to reduce Soviet outlays for defense so he could pump funds into the long-ignored economy, Gorbachev also moved to reduce tensions with the United States.

When Reagan and Gorbachev met in Washington, D.C., in December 1987, the pair took a historic step by signing the **Intermediate-Range Nuclear Forces Treaty** that approved the destruction of all U.S. and Soviet intermediate-range missiles in Europe. Past arms treaties had curtailed the growth of nuclear stockpiles. For the first time a U.S.-Soviet pact actually reduced nuclear arms. The thaw in relations continued when Gorbachev withdrew Soviet forces from Afghanistan in 1988 and reduced support for communist regimes throughout the world.

Like Carter, Reagan enjoyed his greatest successes and failures in the foreign policy arena. He rewrote the rules of the Cold War and achieved a new accommodation in U.S.-Soviet relations. The Iran-Contra scandal, however, brought back fears in some circles that the imperial presidency of the Nixon years had returned.

The Reagan Revolution

Reagan was a popular president, but supporters' claims of a "Reagan Revolution" appear exaggerated. Reagan lowered taxes for the wealthy and permanently curtailed the growth of the welfare state. He appointed right-leaning judges to the federal judiciary, including Sandra Day O'Connor as the first female Supreme Court justice. Cultural conservatives remained loyal to Reagan even though he offered little more than lip-service to their goals of outlawing abortion, returning prayer to public schools, or ending affirmative action.

As president Reagan always won applause when he proclaimed, "government is not the solution to our problem; government is the problem." Yet when he left office, the New Deal and Great Society were as vibrant and relevant as the day he entered the White House. Americans still expected the federal government to pay pensions, guarantee unemployment benefits, curb pollution, and help educate poor children. Rather than leaving an enduring institutional legacy, Reagan presided over a profound shift in political vision. His pro-business policies reinvigorated faith that an unfettered free market could make Americans prosperous, and his open alliance with the Religious Right brought discussion of issues that concerned cultural conservatives into the center of American political discourse. In foreign policy neoconservatives' interventionist ideas became influential in Republican circles. Finally, "Reagan succeeded in reviving national confidence at a time when there was a great need for inspiration. This was his great contribution as president," reporter Lou Cannon concluded. In a testament to Reagan's popularity, George H. W. Bush became the first vice president since Martin Van Buren (who followed the well-liked Andrew Jackson in 1837) to win election immediately after the president under whom he served completed his term.

How does Reagan's legacy compare to that left by Franklin D. Roosevelt?

1972

Congress passes ERA
Provokes heated debate over gender roles in American society

Watergate burglary
Sets in motion constitutional crisis over extent of presidential power

1973

OPEC oil embargo against the United States
Dramatizes American dependence on overseas oil exports

***Roe v. Wade* legalizes abortion**
Religious conservative coalition forms in opposition

1974

Nixon resigns
Gerald Ford, the first unelected vice president, becomes president

Ford pardons Nixon
Shakes public confidence in Ford's leadership

1977–1978

First home computer marketed
Computer revolution begins

Camp David Accords
Secures lasting peace between Egypt and Israel

CHAPTER REVIEW

Review Questions

1. What were the differences and similarities between the Watergate and Iran-Contra scandals?

2. How did concerns over human rights, communism, and the domestic economy influence foreign relations during the 1970s and 1980s?

3. How did Ronald Reagan's political vision differ from those embraced by his predecessors in the White House?

4. What competing visions animated debates over feminism, gay rights, and environmentalism?

5. Why did the New Right become so influential?

Key Terms

SALT I (1972) The first treaty between the Soviet Union and the United States that limited the deployment of intercontinental and submarine-launched ballistic missiles and the creation of missile-defense systems. **852**

Mutually assured destruction (MAD) The claim that the guarantee of a devastating nuclear counter-attack would deter the United States and Soviet Union from ever employing their nuclear arsenals. **852**

Camp David Accords (1978) Israel agreed to give the Sinai Peninsula back to Egypt; in return Egypt became the first Arab state to recognize Israel's right to exist. **856**

Iranian hostage crisis Defining event in Carter's presidency as Iranian revolutionaries held 52 Americans captive for 444 days. **856**

Equal Rights Amendment (ERA) A proposed constitutional amendment, which stated that "equality of rights under the law shall not be denied or abridged by the United States or by any State on account of sex." **859**

***Roe v. Wade* (1973)** Supreme Court decision that legalized abortion. **861**

Stonewall riot A 1969 battle between patrons of a Greenwich Village male gay bar and police that became the catalyst for the gay rights movement. **862**

Religious Right A collection of right-wing Christian groups that defended traditional values and supported conservative political causes. **866**

Iran-Contra scandal A law-breaking scheme that sold arms to Iran to secure the hostage's release and used the proceeds to support anti-Communists in Nicaragua. **871**

Intermediate-Range Nuclear Forces Treaty (1987) Approved the destruction of all U.S. and Soviet intermediate-range missiles in Europe. **871**

1979

Meltdown of nuclear reactor at Three Mile Island
Americans reject nuclear energy as an alternative to oil

Iranian hostage crisis begins
Carter's approval ratings plummet

1980–1981

AIDS epidemic begins
Stigmatizes gay people as diseased

President Reagan shot
Upsurge in popularity helps controversial budget plan pass

1983–1985

Reagan announces SDI
Challenges MAD doctrine

Iran-Contra scandal
Most serious presidential scandal since Watergate

1987–1988

ACT-UP stages first funeral demonstration
Puts pressure on government to fund anti-AIDS research

Intercontinental-Range Nuclear Forces Treaty signed
Spells the final phases of the Cold War

MyHistoryLab Connections

Visit www.myhistorylab.com for a customized Study Plan that will help you build your knowledge of *Righting a Nation Adrift*.

Questions for Analysis

1. **What role did the car industry play in the 20th century economy?**

   👁 **Watch** the **Video** *Video Lecture: The Rise and Fall of the Automobile Economy, p. 846*

2. **How does this campaign ad speak to the concerns of the silent majority?**

   👁 **Watch** the **Video** *Richard Nixon Presidential Campaign Ad (1968), p. 847*

3. **How did the integration of Boston's public schools compare to the experiences of the Little Rock Nine in 1957?**

   📖 **Read** the **Document** *Boston Busing (1975), p. 848*

4. **What different views did Carter and Reagan offer on the state of American society?**

   🔍 **View** the **Closer Look** *Competing Visions: Two Presidential Views of America, p. 867*

5. **How does this speech encapsulate Reagan's Cold War policy?**

   📖 **Read** the **Document** *Ronald Reagan, Speech at the Brandenburg Gate (1987), p. 869*

Other Resources from This Chapter

📖 **Read** the **Document**

- *House Judiciary Committee's Conclusions on Impeachment (1974), p. 849*
- *Roe v. Wade (1973), p. 861*
- *The Gay Liberation Front, Come Out (1970), p. 862*

🔍 **View** the **Closer Look**

- *Images as History: Watergate Through Political Cartoons, p. 850*
- *Competing Visions: Defining the Ideal Woman, p. 860*

🔍 **View** the **Image**

- *The Signing of the Camp David Accords (1978), p. 856*
- *Sign at a Gay Pride March, p. 863*

👁 **Watch** the **Video**

- *Gerald Ford Presidential Campaign Ad (1976), p. 852*
- *Jimmy Carter, "Crisis of Confidence" (1979), p. 854*
- *Video Lecture: Evangelical Religion and Politics, Then and Now, p. 866*
- *Ronald Reagan on the Wisdom of Tax Cuts, p. 868*

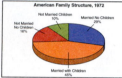

CHAPTER

29

Building a New World Order
The United States, 1989–2011

On the morning of September 11, 2001, 19 young Arab men boarded four planes on the East Coast. All belonged to the Islamic extremist organization known as al-Qaeda. Within half an hour after take-off, they stormed the cockpits of their planes with box cutters and mace, killed the American pilots, and installed their own pilots (who had each received flight instruction in private American aviation schools) to fly the planes into predetermined targets.

At 8:46 a.m. the first plane plowed into the North Tower of the World Trade Center in New York City, an internationally recognized landmark that symbolized American dominance over the world economy. Seventeen minutes later a second plane hit the South Tower. The nation now understood that what had first looked like a tragic accident was actually a coordinated attack against the United States. A third plane crashed into the Pentagon, headquarters of the U.S. Department of Defense, in Virginia, the building most closely associated with U.S. military might in the eyes of the world. Meanwhile passengers in the fourth hijacked plane reached the cockpit and prevented the terrorists from flying the plane into the Capitol, a worldwide symbol of democratic government. This plane instead crashed into a Pennsylvania field.

The blazing World Trade Center towers quickly crumbled, with the office workers and firefighters still inside the buildings as onlookers ran for cover. The skeletal ruins and mountains of debris became the burial site for thousands. One onlooker echoed the nation's sense of disbelief: "This is America. How can it happen in America? How?"

The 9/11 attacks, as they came to be known, reshaped the ongoing debate about America's role in the world and the best way to protect American citizens. Only 20 years earlier Americans had savored their victory in the Cold War as communist governments in Eastern Europe and the Soviet Union collapsed. When the Cold War ended, Americans believed that their nation would take the lead in creating a new world order even as they disputed how best to spread democracy, protect the U.S. economy, and flex the nation's military muscle. Enjoying prosperity for most of the 1990s, the country paid little attention to the new threat that loomed before the world's sole remaining superpower—terrorist strikes by anti-American Islamist extremists, such as al-Qaeda. Political debate instead centered on whether the liberal or conservative vision of government would prevail at home.

After 9/11 President George W. Bush moved with resolve to restore the image of America as a powerful and triumphant nation. He led the country into two wars: the first in Afghanistan; the second, far more controversial, in Iraq. In 2008, Americans provided a different sort of history-making moment by electing the first African American president of the United States. By then, the worst financial crisis since the Great Depression posed an additional challenge for the nation.

"None of us will ever forget this day, yet we go forward to defend freedom and all that is good and just in our world."

President GEORGE W. BUSH, speaking to the nation on the evening of September 11, 2001

"A Moment Rich with Promise"

On his inauguration day in 1989, George H. W. Bush announced that he had become president "at a moment rich with promise." The fall of communism throughout Eastern Europe and the Soviet Union within the next two years seemed to confirm this judgment. However, the end of the Cold War did not mean peace; the United States immediately fought two short wars in Panama and the Persian Gulf. Conflict also arose at home, as a huge federal deficit and simmering racial tensions that occasionally exploded into violence left some feeling that America's promise lay unfulfilled.

The Election of 1988

The son of a former Connecticut senator, George H. W. Bush served as a congressman, ambassador, Central Intelligence Agency (CIA) director, and vice president before becoming the Republican candidate for president in 1988. In this sense the decorated World War II pilot and former oilman was the ultimate insider, a man familiar with the corridors of power in Washington and the exclusive private clubs where financial deals were negotiated. A moderate Republican with a patrician style, Bush never projected the same charisma or the passion for conservative causes that had drawn voters to Ronald Reagan, the man he hoped to follow as president. Bush's campaign had to overcome these obstacles when he faced Massachusetts Democratic Governor Michael Dukakis in the presidential contest.

When Dukakis proposed increased spending on health care, education, and housing, the Bush team ridiculed the Democrat as a big-spending liberal and began calling him the governor of "Taxachusetts." In his stump speeches Bush also tapped into white peoples' fears of so-called black criminality by frequently mentioning Willie Horton, an African American prisoner who had taken advantage of a weekend furlough program in Massachusetts and gone on a crime rampage that included raping a white woman. Adding to his woes Dukakis made critical missteps, including one ill-advised photo-op during which he donned an oversized helmet and military jumpsuit to ride a tank (**29.1**). Most Americans felt that the photo made Dukakis look ridiculous, not presidential. By Election Day Bush had defined Dukakis as someone who would raise taxes and let criminals out of jail, and was

29.1 A Failed Photo-Op
Seeking to appear like a commander in chief, 1988 Democratic presidential candidate Michael Dukakis was instead ridiculed for riding around in a tank in a suit and tie.

How did George H. W. Bush prevail in the 1988 presidential election?

Read the **Document** *George H. W. Bush Inaugural Address (1989)*

unprepared to be commander in chief. He defeated Dukakis 426 to 111 in the Electoral College, capturing 53 percent of the popular vote.

Popular Revolts against Communism

When Bush became the 41st president of the United States in 1989, the former director of the CIA remained suspicious about Soviet Premier Mikhail Gorbachev's true motives for instituting internal reforms and reaching out to the United States (see Chapter 28). Officials worried that Gorbachev "was attempting to kill us with kindness," according to National Security Advisor Brent Scowcroft. Gorbachev was equally distrustful of Bush and his inner circle: "These people were brought up in the years of the Cold War and still do not have any foreign policy alternative." Caught off guard by the quick demise of communism in Eastern Europe, within a year Bush had changed his mind about Gorbachev "by 180 degrees."

In the first sign of the upheaval to come, Communist Hungary decided to take down the barbed wire fence between it and democratic Austria in May 1989. The East German government watched in dismay as thousands of its citizens drove to the Hungarian-Austrian border and then walked across to defect to the West. Turning to Moscow for help, East Germany received a surprising reply: "We can't do anything about it." A similarly uncharacteristic Soviet reaction greeted news that candidates from the democratic Polish workers' union Solidarity had won control of Poland's new bicameral Parliament, forming the first democratic government in postwar Eastern Europe. "This is entirely a matter to be decided by Poland," a Soviet official announced.

Soviet, Hungarian, and Polish leaders lifted restrictions on speech, voting, and economic activity to save their Communist regimes, unleashing a tide of popular revolt against Communist rule that soon overwhelmed them. Perhaps nowhere did the fall of communism come faster, and more unexpectedly, than in East Germany. On November 9, 1989, a botched news conference by a harried East German official triggered the destruction of the Berlin Wall. Instead of announcing a relaxation in rules governing travel between East and West Berlin, a confused East German official mistakenly told the press that starting immediately, East Germans could freely leave "through any of the border crossings." Electrified by the news that the wall was open, thousands of people gathered at armed crossing points, places where over 175 East Germans had been shot trying to cross over the last 28 years (see Chapter 24). When confused guards opened the gates, streams of East Germans poured across and joined with West Germans to rejoice atop the Berlin Wall.

Images as History: The Fall of the Berlin Wall (page 878) examines the media images that shaped Americans' reactions to this event. Further evidence of television's power to mold history came in the following days, as thousands of East Berliners headed for downtown department stores in West Berlin. Concrete walls had not prevented East Berliners from viewing American sitcoms (dubbed in German) showing the abundance of goods available in the West. Television-stoked desires for "work-saving gadgets, [well-stocked pantries], attractive surroundings and a touch of luxury," one reporter contended, helped bring the Berlin Wall down. Gorbachev's refusal to intervene with armed force was also critical. Within a year East and West Germany had reunified into one democratic nation, an American goal since the Cold War began in the late 1940s.

By the end of 1989, the Soviet Union no longer dominated Eastern Europe, losing territory that it had controlled since the end of World War II. One by one the individual states that formed the Soviet Union also demanded their independence, secession movements that Gorbachev tried to squash with economic embargos and, occasionally, troops. Desperate to stop the hemorrhaging, hard-line Communist insiders orchestrated a coup attempt in August 1990. They put President Gorbachev under house arrest in his vacation home and ringed the Soviet Parliament in Moscow with troops and tanks. Hesitating, the coup leaders lost the military's support, and the overthrow attempt failed. With the populace now demanding economic reforms and Communist Party officials blaming Gorbachev for losing control, he resigned as head of the Communist Party on August 24, 1990. Five days later the Soviet Communist Party itself was dissolved. By December 25, 1991, he was also no longer president as the Soviet Union ceased to exist, and all its member states, including Russia, became independent nations. After decades of trying to contain, weaken, and defeat the Soviet Union, the United States declared victory in the Cold War. "The Soviet Union did not simply lose the Cold War; the Western democracies won," Bush announced.

What role did ordinary citizens play in ending communism in East Germany and the Soviet Union?

Images as History

THE FALL OF THE BERLIN WALL

Photographs of Berlin had already punctuated key moments in the Cold War for Americans, including images of the 1948–1949 Berlin airlift and the wall's construction in 1961 to prevent East Berliners from defecting to West Berlin (see Chapter 24). Presidents John F. Kennedy and Ronald Reagan had made well-documented pilgrimages to the site, where they publicly denounced the Berlin Wall as a symbol of Communist oppression. Now, from the comfort of their living rooms, TV-viewing Americans watched as East and West Berliners climbed atop the wall throughout the night on November 9, 1989 to demand the reunification of their divided city.

The fall of communism in Europe reinforced American faith in the superiority of capitalism over communism, but some commentators urged the United States to undertake economic reforms at home to ensure that capitalism operated more fairly. What competing views do this photograph and political cartoon offer Americans about the importance of the Berlin Wall falling? What counter-arguments could critics offer?

After the evening celebrations East German guards reclaimed the top of the wall and impassively watched German civilians attack the graffiti-laden western side of the wall with chisels and hammers.

President Bush told the press that he had no desire "to dance on the wall," worried that any gloating might goad Gorbachev into sealing up the wall or prompt Soviet hardliners to overthrow Gorbachev.

Both reporters and ordinary people brought cameras to document this historic moment.

The image of one man destroying the wall piece-by-piece with his hammer resonated with Americans—it symbolized the ability of common people to make history and their desire to collect pieces of the wall as souvenirs.

Attacking the Berlin Wall with a Hammer

Would the fall of Communism usher in a better world? Many Americans believed so, but cartoonist Pat Oliphant offered a competing view by implying that free market capitalism did not always benefit everyone equally.

Pat Oliphant Questions the Triumph of Capitalism over Communism

The befuddlement of the hungry, homeless man dressed in rags suggests that there is no "we" in the United States—rich and poor view events like the fall of the Berlin Wall differently.

In the 1980s, the number of homeless people living and begging on the streets grew to a level not seen in urban America since the Progressive era.

Many Americans celebrated the fall of the Berlin Wall as a triumph of the nation's democratic, capitalist vision over a competing autocratic, anti-capitalist Communist one.

What symbolic importance did the fall of the Berlin Wall have?

View the **Closer Look** *Images as History: The Fall of the Berlin Wall*

The U.S. battle against communism was not over, however. On the other side of the world, the Chinese Communist regime made different choices when faced with a popular revolt. In April 1989, university students occupied Tiananmen Square in central Beijing to protest the removal of a high-ranking Communist official who had called for economic and political reforms. Behind closed doors Chinese Communist officials debated whether to end the demonstrations with troops or adopt a Gorbachev-like approach and accommodate some of the students' demands. On the morning of June 4, tanks appeared in Tiananmen Square, signaling that discussion within the inner circle had ended. Troops shot hundreds as they cleared the area of protesters. Two days later a lone man walking down the deserted Avenue of Eternal Peace made a solitary gesture of defiance by standing steadfast in the middle of the street as 17 tanks approached. When the lead tank swerved right to avoid hitting him, the man stepped right. When it swerved left, he stepped left. Finally the tanks stopped and the man jumped onto the first one, shouting to its driver, "Why are you here? My city is in chaos because of you." Associated Press photographer Jeff Widener captured this encounter in an award-winning photo seen on newspaper front-pages around the globe (**29.2**). Americans hailed "Tank Man," as he became known, for his inspirational defense of peace and human rights. No one in China, however, except for the bystanders who whisked him away and the Chinese authorities who probably executed him, ever knew of this encounter.

As the economic relationship between the United States and China changed, China's violent suppression of democracy movements provoked competing visions over how to proceed. In 1900, America wanted to sell China goods; by 1990, American companies increasingly outsourced manufacturing jobs to China, using cheap Chinese labor to satiate American consumers' demands for affordable goods. Some critics argued that by helping the Chinese government improve the standard of living for ordinary citizens, Americans were also bolstering the autocratic Communist regime. Others countered that recent events in Eastern Europe demonstrated that exposing Chinese citizens to Western values and goods would sow the seeds for an eventual democratic and capitalist revolution. A third faction worried that a prosperous and industrially strong China might replace the United States as the world's strongest power.

29.2 Standing Up for Democracy in China, 1989 Two days after the Chinese military brutally suppressed a popular rebellion in Tiananmen Square, a lone man stopped army tanks in their tracks; the world cheered his courageous stand.

Why did popular uprisings against communism in Europe and China have different outcomes?

Domestic Policy in the Bush Administration

The growing trade deficit with China (the United States bought more than it sold) was only one economic issue troubling Americans during the Bush years. "Read my lips: No new taxes," Bush had proclaimed during the 1988 campaign. Once in office, however, he reneged on his pledge by raising income taxes. Faced with the largest deficit in American history, the result of increased defense spending during the Reagan years without any corresponding tax increases and Bush's own decision to bail out the failing savings and loan industry in 1989 (see Chapter 28), he saw no other option. His decision angered many conservative Republicans, and some never forgave him. "Read My Lips: I Lied," ran one *New York Post* headline.

The combination of a huge deficit and an unfriendly Democratic majority in Congress discouraged Bush from proposing dramatic new domestic initiatives. A revolution of sorts nonetheless occurred when Bush signed the Americans with Disabilities Act, a 1990 civil rights law that prohibited discrimination against the disabled in employment, public accommodations, and telecommunications. The disabled gained unprecedented freedom of movement as legally required elevators, ramps, and sloped curbs became commonplace.

During the campaign Bush had courted the conservative wing of the Republican Party by promising to appoint like-minded judges. He fulfilled this pledge by nominating a conservative African American judge, Clarence Thomas, to the Supreme Court when Thurgood Marshall, the Court's first African American justice, retired. Controversy erupted, when Anita Hill, a former colleague, accused Thomas of sexual harassment, and Thomas responded by calling the televised confirmation hearings a "high-tech lynching." The Senate ultimately confirmed Thomas by a narrow majority in 1991. With workplace sexual harassment front-page news, an unprecedented number of women won congressional seats in the 1992 elections, including the first female African American senator, Carol Mosley Braun, a Democrat from Illinois.

While the Thomas hearings exposed gender discord, the 1991 Los Angeles riots brought simmering racial and ethnic tensions to the surface. In March a 78-mile car chase along Los Angeles freeways ended with white police brutally beating Rodney King, an African American, when he resisted arrest for speeding. A nearby resident captured the incident on film, but Americans differed on what the video revealed (**29.3**). Most blacks and some sympathetic whites saw a poorly trained and racist police force that harassed blacks, echoing complaints that had set off the Watts riots in 1965 (see Chapter 27).

29.3 Los Angeles Police Beat Motorist Rodney King, 1991 Many whites saw the police trying to control an unruly black man who had resisted arrest for speeding, but many blacks saw racist police brutality.

Which gender and racial issues dominated the headlines in the early 1990s?

Read the **Document** *William Julius Wilson, "The Urban Underclass"*

Others, including the jury (consisting of ten whites, one Latino, and one Asian American) that acquitted the officers, offered a competing vision. They saw over-worked police doing their job to protect law and order in a danger-ous neighborhood. The "not guilty" verdict set off four days of rioting in Los Angeles during which Latinos also took to the streets to air their frustra-tion with failing schools and entrenched poverty. Television networks con-tinuously aired footage of black youths assaulting a white truck driver, but paid little attention to the Asian-American–owned stores that blacks and Latinos ransacked as pay-back for allegedly having refused to serve or hire young men of color.

Map labels:

USSR
GEORGIA
AZERBAIJAN
ARMENIA
TURKEY
Black Sea
Caspian Sea
TURKMENISTAN
Kabul
AFGHANISTAN
Istanbul
Ankara
Tehran
PAKISTAN
Mosul
I R A N
Cyprus
Mediterranean Sea
SYRIA
Baghdad
IRAQ
Basra
Karachi
LEBANON
Damascus
Beirut
Jerusalem
Amman
ISRAEL
JORDAN
KUWAIT
QATAR
BAHRAIN
UNITED ARAB EMIRATES
Persian Gulf
Strait of Hormuz
EGYPT
SAUDI ARABIA
Riyadh
OMAN
Arabian Sea
Red Sea
PEOPLE'S DEMOCRATIC REPUBLIC OF YEMEN
YEMEN ARAB REPUBLIC
Aden

AFGHANISTAN: US airstrikes against al-Qaeda bases, 1988 US invades, 2001

PAKISTAN: Osama bin Laden's alleged hideout, 2003-2011 U.S. Special Forces kill Osama bin Laden, May 2, 2011

IRAN: Iraq-Iran War, 1980–88

KUWAIT: Iraq invades, 1990

SAUDI ARABIA: UN staging ground for Persian Gulf War, 1991

YEMEN: Al-Qaeda suicide bombers attack USS Cole, 2000

Legend:

Gulf War (1990-1991)
Allied air attacks
Area of ground combat
US battleships
US aircraft carriers

Iraq War (2003--)
US-led land campaign

Panama and the Persian Gulf War

Bush did not propose any new initiatives to address gender, racial, or ethnic inequities; his real inter-est lay in foreign affairs. As he contemplated the new role that the United States should assume in a post–Cold War world, Bush moved to address a festering problem close to home. His administration felt particularly uneasy about returning the Panama Canal in 2000 (see Chapter 28) to a Panamanian dic-tator who ruthlessly suppressed political opponents and oversaw lucrative drug-trafficking schemes. In December 1989, Bush launched Operation Just Cause, the largest American military campaign since the Vietnam War, to remove Manuel Noriega from power. The Panamanian invasion continued the na-tion's long tradition of maintaining Central America as a U.S. sphere of influence.

A crisis in the Middle East, however, offered Bush the opportunity to propose a new focus for U.S. foreign policy, now that the Cold War was

over. Bush faced the severest test of his admin-istration when Iraqi dictator Saddam Hussein, whose nation's oil fields supplied 11 percent of global oil exports, invaded the neighboring nation of Kuwait, a small country that provided 9 percent of the world's oil, on August 2, 1990 (**29.4**). The 1979 Carter Doctrine (see Chapter 28) had already established the oil-rich Persian Gulf as a region vital to national economic and strategic interests. Throughout the 1980s Iranian-financed terrorist attacks and hostage crises in Lebanon convinced the U.S. government that the fundamentalist Is-lamic government in Iran, not Iraq, posed the major threat in the Persian Gulf. During the eight-year Iraq-Iran War, the United States supplied Iraq with weapons and intelligence. Oil-rich Arab na-tions, including Saudi Arabia and Kuwait, had also lent Iraq billions of dollars to prevent Iranian revo-lutionary religious fervor from spreading to their kingdoms. When the war ended inconclusively in 1988 after nearly one million combatant deaths, Saddam demanded that Arab nations forgive Iraq's debt. He harbored particular animosity against

29.4 America and the Middle East, 1980–2003 The United States fought two major wars against Iraq, one in 1991 and the other beginning in 2003.

[Watch] the **Video** President George Bush's Early Response in the Persian Gulf War

What problems did the United States face in the Middle East from 1980–2003?

Kuwait, which he accused of exporting too much oil and depressing world oil prices, thereby hurting the Iraqi financial recovery from the war. When Kuwait refused his demands, Saddam declared that Kuwait had historically been part of Iraq and invaded.

After the Iraqi army easily overran Kuwait, President Bush rushed American troops and ships to Saudi Arabia. Operation Desert Shield, the president assured the public, was solely a defensive measure to prevent Iraq from attacking Saudi Arabia. After Saddam announced that he was annexing Kuwait, Bush began to question whether a purely defensive strategy was enough. Now in control of 20 percent of the world's oil, overnight Iraq became a major rival of Saudi Arabia, which had 26 percent of global oil supplies. With the president now contemplating war, General Colin Powell, chair of the Joint Chiefs of Staff, urged Bush to follow the rules of military engagement established in the Reagan years. The **Powell Doctrine** asserted that America should go to war only as a last resort when the president had full support from the nation and the international community, could employ overwhelming military force to win without serious loss of American life, and had a clear exit strategy.

To amass overwhelming military strength, Bush sent Secretary of State James Baker on a diplomatic tour to build an international coalition that eventually included 34 nations. Bush secured a United Nations (UN) resolution authorizing military action if Saddam did not withdraw by January 15, 1991. With Saudi Arabia agreeing to serve as the staging ground for the invasion, nearly 500,000 U.S. troops and 65 warships made their way to the Persian Gulf.

The Powell Doctrine called for more than overwhelming force; it also required enthusiastic support from the American people for an overseas military campaign. Bush faced stiff opposition from congressional Democrats, who argued that the president, a former Texas oilman, was primarily interested in protecting the lucrative profits of his former oil-business associates who imported oil from the Persian Gulf. Instead of war, Democrats promoted a competing vision that relied on economic sanctions to force Hussein to withdraw. Bush countered that Hussein's atrocities against his own people, notably his 1988 poison gas attacks against Kurdish villagers in northern Iraq, made him "worse than Hitler." Echoing Bush's claim, this political cartoon (**29.5**) showed Saddam holding a paper labeled "Kuwait takeover" as he looked into the mirror and asked Adolf Hitler's smiling reflection, "How'm I doing?" Bush, a decorated World War II veteran, reminded Americans that the world's failure to act when Hitler began his expansionist drive in 1938 had led to World War II. If an emboldened Saddam next attacked Saudi Arabia, he would control nearly half of the world's oil reserves. Bush also claimed that Saddam was actively trying to acquire nuclear weapons, and if he succeeded, he would be unstoppable. These arguments did not sway Democrats. With a vote split mostly along partisan lines, Congress voted to authorize war according to the terms spelled out in the UN resolution. When the UN deadline for withdrawal passed, the American-led UN coalition attacked Iraq the next day. Once the fighting started public debate ceased, and Americans rallied around the flag.

The Persian Gulf War unfolded in two phases. In the first phase U.S. forces bombed Iraqi installations in Kuwait

29.5 **"Mirror, Mirror on the Wall–How'm I doing?"**
This 1990 political cartoon supported President George H. W. Bush's claim that Iraqi dictator Saddam Hussein was a modern-day Hitler.

How did the Powell Doctrine influence Bush's preparations for war against Iraq in 1991?

Read the Document George Bush, Allied Military Action in the Persian Gulf (1991)

and major cities in Iraq for 39 days. In Kuwait the massive bombing terrified many poorly trained occupying Iraqi soldiers, and nearly one-quarter of the 400,000-man force deserted. A news team from the cable television news network CNN stayed in Baghdad, the capital of Iraq, throughout the bombing, and each night Americans watched their own nation's missiles streak across the sky and explode. The bombing destroyed Iraq's power grid, water treatment plants, radio and television stations, and roads—hampering its military activities but also leaving civilians without power or clean water.

With Iraqi defenses in shambles from the air attacks, the war's second phase began when ground troops attacked the Iraqi forces occupying Kuwait on February 23, 1991. General Norman Schwarzkopf led coalition forces during Operation Desert Storm, a massive assault that soundly defeated the Iraqi army within four days, pushing it out of Kuwait. When American soldiers crossed into Iraq, Bush abruptly halted the fighting. The war had lasted a total of 42 days.

the war beyond its original goal, Bush's approval ratings soared to 89 percent.

The UN peace agreement prohibited Saddam from rearming or acquiring nuclear weapons, restrictions enforced by UN inspectors who stayed in Iraq until 1998. The establishment of no-fly zones over Shiite and Kurdish areas stopped Saddam and his Sunni-dominated government from launching aerial attacks against these minorities within his own nation. The UN also instituted an oil embargo to prevent him from acquiring funds to reconstitute his nuclear weapons program. Critics charged that the embargo led to widespread food and medicine shortages among the civilian population, and failed to prevent Iraq from rearming. Instead of caring for his people, Saddam used the nation's meager cash flow to continue his lavish lifestyle and secured funds to amass a large arsenal of conventional weapons by illegally smuggling oil through Jordan, Turkey, Syria, and Egypt. When the UN initiated a "food-for-oil" program in 1996 that allowed Saddam to export some oil legally if he used the profits

---

"By God, we've kicked the Vietnam Syndrome once and for all."

An exultant President GEORGE H. W. BUSH at the end of the Persian Gulf War, 1991

American forces, Bush declared, had met their goal of ending Saddam's occupation of Kuwait and had no intention of conquering Iraq. The United States would henceforth rely on sanctions to curb Saddam, returning to the strategy of containment that had succeeded against the Soviet Union to win the Cold War. Neoconservatives embraced a competing vision. They viewed the war as an opportunity to remove Saddam from power. Bush advisors, including Secretary of Defense Dick Cheney, however, saw no advantage to staying in Iraq. They argued that it would be difficult, if not impossible, to bring together the nation's three different ethnic and religious groups (Sunnis, Shiites, and Kurds), each of which inhabited distinct regions, to form a democratic government. Abiding by the Powell Doctrine's emphasis on a clear exit strategy, Bush wanted to avoid a long, protracted war that could become a Vietnam-like quagmire. Having suffered relatively few casualties (148 battlefield deaths) and avoided widening

for humanitarian purposes, civilian conditions improved slightly.

Victory in the Persian Gulf War, along with the end of the Cold War, led to a revaluation of American foreign policy goals. After defeating Iraq Bush announced that the United States would build a "new world order," which he defined as playing an active global peacekeeping role dedicated to spreading democracy and prosperity. Some of his defense advisors encouraged the president to go even further to protect American dominance. In 1992, Cheney and his neoconservative aide, Paul Wolfowitz, asserted that the United States needed to respond immediately, and preemptively, to any foreign nation that challenged American military superiority or attempted to "overturn the established political and economic order." Bush never publicly embraced these neoconservative principles, but his son George W. Bush, the 43rd president of the United States, proved more receptive to these ideas.

What vision of American world leadership did neoconservatives promote?

Contested Visions of Government

 The Reagan years had redefined the American political landscape, shifting the political center away from New Deal and Great Society liberal assumptions that government could be a positive force in citizens' lives. To succeed in this changed political climate, a new breed of Democratic politician was needed—socially liberal but fiscally conservative. The most successful and most controversial "New Democrat" was William "Bill" Jefferson Clinton, who defeated George H. W. Bush in the 1992 presidential election and won reelection in 1996 against Kansas Senator Bob Dole. When Republican George W. Bush won the presidency in the heavily disputed 2000 election, he restored the conservative vision of low taxes and limited regulation that the political right had long championed.

Clinton's New Democrats

Clinton was relatively unknown when the 1992 presidential campaign began. While governor of Arkansas, at just 44 years of age, Clinton had chaired the Democratic Leadership Council, a group committed to shifting the Democratic Party to the political center by accepting market-based solutions to social problems and ending deficit spending. Exuding boundless energy and a vast knowledge of government, Clinton's magnetic personality and compassionate nature soon won him a dedicated following. "I feel your pain," became his mantra as he bear-hugged voters on the campaign trail. Clinton, one commentator noted, cultivated the image of "the president as the guy next door," who "struggles like the rest of us with his weight, his marriage, and his golf game."

Worried about the nation's finances, third-party candidate Ross Perot, a self-made Texas billionaire, entered the race and focused almost exclusively on how the federal deficit had ballooned under Bush. Winning 19 percent of the popular vote, Perot registered the best third-party showing since Theodore Roosevelt's run as the Progressive Party candidate in 1912. Clinton defeated Bush in the Electoral College, 370 to 168, but only 43 percent of the electorate voted for him.

Widely praised for his political skills, Clinton nonetheless stumbled badly during his first few weeks in office when he tried and failed to fulfill a campaign pledge to lift the ban against gays in the military. Proponents viewed the issue as a straightforward question of protecting civil rights; opponents countered that ignoring heterosexual soldiers' objections to serving alongside gay soldiers would undermine military discipline and hurt recruitment.

Clinton pleased no one with his compromise. Rather than lift the ban, he instituted a policy of **"Don't Ask, Don't Tell,"** which allowed closeted homosexuals and lesbians—gays who kept their sexual preferences hidden—to serve in the military.

Clinton's domestic agenda was ambitious, including a comprehensive plan to provide all Americans with health care. He delegated this major policy initiative to Hillary Rodham Clinton, his wife, an attorney with extensive experience in public service. Republicans successfully attacked the plan as "socialized medicine" that would deprive Americans of the freedom to choose their healthcare providers. The plan failed to win congressional approval. Clinton achieved a more modest victory with his tax proposals. Overcoming Republican opposition, he passed an economic stimulus package that offered tax incentives for job creation and increased taxes for large corporations and wealthy Americans—reversing Reagan's decision to lower taxes on the richest citizens.

Clinton also addressed economic problems caused by the recent globalization of the American economy. As late as 1970 most U.S. businesses manufactured strictly for the American market, and few stores stocked items made overseas. By the early 1980s, the United States exported and imported more goods than ever before. Exports rose from $43 billion in 1970 to $178 billion in 2000, while imports surged from $40 billion to $519 billion in 2000 (all figures adjusted for inflation). Importing more than it exported, the nation questioned whether this trade deficit hurt or helped the overall economy. American companies selling products at home now faced stiff competition from foreign manufacturers, while U.S. companies shifted production to places like China and Mexico where workers earned less. Globalization, however, also lowered costs for consumers and gave them a greater selection of products.

Clinton helped accelerate the trend toward globalization when he broke with organized labor to back the 1992 **North American Free Trade Agreement (NAFTA)**, a treaty that lifted trade barriers among the United States, Mexico, and Canada. Labor unions opposed NAFTA because they feared that it would encourage U.S. factories to relocate to Mexico, resulting in fewer jobs for American workers. American businesspeople liked NAFTA because it prohibited Mexican companies from manufacturing knock-offs of American products such as films, drugs, and clothing, essentially protecting their overseas and domestic markets by stopping the flow of counterfeit goods.

Clinton's emphasis on free trade reflected his desire to move the Democratic Party to the political center, but his Republican opponents cited his failed healthcare initiative as evidence that he subscribed to the same 1960s liberal vision that had spurred the creation of the Great Society (see Chapter 27). In the 1994 midterm elections, Georgia Congressman Newt Gingrich mobilized the New Right (see Chapter 28) with his call to end the "corrupt liberal welfare state." The Republicans captured both the House and the Senate for the first time since 1952. Gingrich's manifesto, "The Contract with America," envisioned smaller government, less regulation, term limits for members of Congress, welfare reform, and adding a balanced budget amendment to the Constitution. Little of this ambitious agenda was enacted, partly because Clinton stole some of Gingrich's thunder by undertaking his own program of welfare reform. Modifying legislation passed during the New Deal, he joined with Republicans and conservative Democrats in Congress to reduce the time that families (mostly single mothers) with dependent children could receive financial assistance. Clinton also tried to appeal to fiscal conservatives by balancing the federal budget for the first time in 30 years.

Clinton used his superior political skills not only to weaken the Republican resurgence but also to survive the scandals that plagued his presidency. In 1994, a special federal prosecutor, Kenneth Starr, began investigating charges that the president had participated in a fraudulent land deal during his tenure as Arkansas attorney general. During his investigation, Starr learned that President Clinton had engaged in a sexual relationship with a White House intern named Monica Lewinsky. Clinton was not the first president to have extramarital dalliances, but when giving testimony under oath on an unrelated matter, he denied the affair. Seven months later the president publicly acknowledged that he had lied as seen in this *New York Daily News* headline reporting his televised address to the nation (**29.6**). Republicans argued that Clinton's failure to tell the truth warranted impeachment. In 1998, the Republican-controlled House of Representatives completed the first stage of impeachment by voting that the president had lied under oath and obstructed justice. The Senate now had to decide whether these infractions met the constitutional test of "high crimes and misdemeanors" needed to remove a president from office. Ten Republican senators joined with Democrats in defeating the first charge of perjury by a vote of 55 to 45. The second charge of obstructing justice resulted in a 50 to 50 tie. Neither charge obtained the requisite two-thirds vote required to remove Clinton from the White House.

Clinton survived impeachment by cultivating the same "everyman" appeal that won him the presidency. "The essence of Clinton's success has been to persuade America that this scandal is about human weakness, not crime, and that at its core is not a string of felonies but a sin familiar to all—adultery," lamented conservative commentator Patrick Buchanan. The strong economy also helped keep Clinton's approval ratings near 60 percent throughout the ordeal.

29.6 Clinton's Sex Scandal When Clinton finally admitted to an "inappropriate relationship" with White House intern Monica Lewinsky, the lies he had previously told to cover it up led to his impeachment.

The Disputed Election of 2000

The election of 2000 again offered voters two competing notions of the role that the government should play in American society. Democrat Al Gore, then serving as vice president under Bill Clinton, ran against Republican George W. Bush, the son of former president George H. W. Bush. More liberal than Clinton, Gore was a well-known environmentalist whose pedantic manner often made him appear wooden. Bush was a born-again evangelical Christian who had cultivated a folksy persona while governor of Texas.

Reflecting the generally prosperous times, the two candidates put forward competing visions on how to spend the projected federal surplus. Calling it "the people's money," Bush proposed enormous tax cuts that he argued would fuel investment and economic growth. Rejecting the Democrat's emphasis on federal government activism, Bush vowed to create an "ownership society" where people had more control over their wealth, Social Security retirement accounts, health care, and property. Gore adhered to the traditional Democratic vision of using government regulation and federally funded programs to promote equity, environmental responsibility, and prosperity. He charged that Bush's tax cuts would disproportionately help the wealthy and starve federal programs for the poor. Gore proposed saving the surplus to prepare for the coming explosion in Social Security payments once the baby boom generation began retiring. Green Party candidate Ralph Nader, a consumer advocate who railed against corporate greed, and the conservative Patrick Buchanan, who ran on the Reform Party ticket, also entered the race.

In an age of machine-counted votes and instantaneous communication, Americans expected complete results on election night. However, with several states too close to call that evening, it took a few days before Gore emerged with 266 electoral votes, three short of the 270 required to win the presidency, to Bush's 246. All eyes now turned to Florida where a riveting 36-day drama unfurled over recounting ballots that vote-counting machines had rejected because voters had not completely punched the perforated box next to the candidate's name. Gore's team went to state court and won a hand recount in four primarily Democratic counties. Election inspectors, like the one pictured here (**29.7**), spent hours examining "hanging chads," partially punched boxes, to determine voters' intent. Arguing that time for a recount had run out, Republican Florida officials certified that Bush had won the state.

The battle now moved to the Supreme Court, where conservative justices accepted the Republican argument that the different standards used by inspectors to include or reject ballots violated the "equal protection" clause of the Fourteenth Amendment. As the map (**29.8**) shows, although Gore won the national popular vote, by winning Florida, Bush had the 271 electoral votes to win the election. Echoing the outraged Democratic response to the Supreme Court's decision to halt the recount, Justice John Paul Stevens wrote, "Although we may never know with complete certainty the identity of the winner of this year's Presidential election, the identity of the loser is perfectly clear. It is the Nation's confidence in the judge as an impartial guardian of the rule of law." Subsequent privately funded recounts undertaken by major news organizations all concluded that Bush had indeed won Florida.

The election results continued to rankle Democrats. Besides questioning poor ballot design and Supreme Court partisanship, Democrats charged that Florida Republicans had used shady tactics

29.7 Hanging Chads
A Florida election worker uses a magnifying glass to try to determine which candidate this voter had selected, reflecting the closeness of the 2000 presidential election.

Why was the 2000 presidential election so controversial?

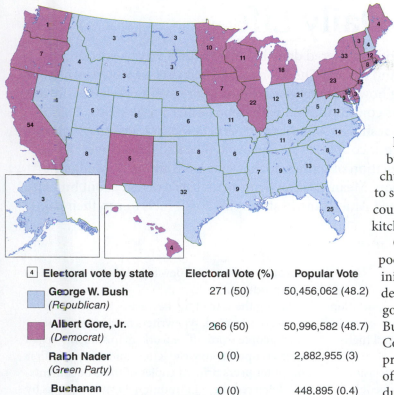

29.8 Presidential Election, 2000
A mere 537 votes in Florida decided the outcome of the 2000 presidential contest.

Electoral vote by state	Electoral Vote (%)	Popular Vote
George W. Bush (Republican)	271 (50)	50,456,062 (48.2)
Albert Gore, Jr. (Democrat)	266 (50)	50,996,582 (48.7)
Ralph Nader (Green Party)	0 (0)	2,882,955 (3)
Buchanan	0 (0)	448,895 (0.4)

initiatives that funded church-run community programs, arguing that local clergy understood their neighborhood problems better than government bureaucrats. Federal money flowed to churches offering after-school tutoring to students, transportation for the elderly, counseling for drug addicts, and soup kitchens for the homeless.

Critics saw little compassion for the poor in some of Bush's other economic initiatives. Ignoring the election's evidence that strong competing visions of governing continued to divide the nation, Bush relied on the Republican-controlled Congress to win swift congressional approval for the tax cuts and deregulation of financial markets that he had proposed during the campaign. Faced with the beginnings of a recession as overinflated stock prices collapsed, Bush and other conservative Republicans offered a new rationale for slashing taxes by an average of 15 percent. Over 40 percent of the tax cuts went to the wealthy, the people whose companies and investments would provide the jobs and capital to jump-start the economy, the president argued. When the short recession ended, Bush and his congressional supporters credited their tax cutting. Some economists suggested that the overinflated housing market was the real reason for the economic rebound. Home prices doubled between 1997 and 2005 as speculators bought and sold homes quickly to take advantage of rising prices. Low-interest loans encouraged homeowners to use their houses as collateral to borrow money, which they used to purchase consumer goods. For the moment the credit-fueled rise in housing prices infused cash into the economy, but the day of reckoning was ahead.

Despite his antigovernment philosophy Bush sometimes proved willing to strengthen the federal government's power. The bipartisan 2001 "No Child Left Behind" law tried to improve public schools by linking federal funding to student performance on annual standardized exams. Bush also dramatically increased the investigative powers of the Justice Department in the wake of the terrorist attack against the United States on September 11, 2001.

to disenfranchise African Americans, such as incorrectly claiming they were felons who could not vote. The post-election recriminations also targeted liberals who had rejected the centrist direction of the Democratic Party and voted for Nader. The Green Party candidate received 97,488 votes in Florida—a state that Bush won by a mere 537 votes.

Compassionate Conservatism

Bush entered office proclaiming that his administration would move away from the laissez-faire, antigovernment message championed by past Congressional Republican leaders like Gingrich. He instead embraced a new vision termed "**compassionate conservatism**," a philosophical approach to governing that emphasized using private industry, charities, and religious institutions, rather than the government, to provide community services. Adherents of compassionate conservatism argued that the poor quickly became dependent on government-run social welfare programs, losing the motivation and drive to improve themselves. As one Bush administration official put it, compassionate conservatives believed that "the government should encourage the effective provision of social services without providing the service itself." In keeping with this philosophy, the president championed faith-based

Transforming Daily Life

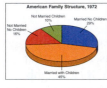

American Family Structure, 1972

Not Married Children 10%
Not Married No Children 16%
Married No Children 29%
Married with Children 45%

In the 1990s, computers altered daily life in countless ways, becoming essential to work and leisure. The Monica Lewinsky scandal broke on the Internet, revealing how the emergence of the World Wide Web transformed the way Americans communicated with one another in the 1990s. Demographic shifts also reshaped American society. Fewer heterosexual American couples married, while the desire of gay couples to wed provoked heated debate over the meaning of marriage. A sizable population of senior citizens emerged, and new immigrant communities formed across the nation. Meanwhile environmentalists worried about human-induced climate changes and entreated Americans to stop using fossil fuels to run their cars and factories.

The Computer Age

At key moments in American history, transportation or communication breakthroughs transformed daily life. The intercontinental railroad and federal highway system had quickened the movement of goods and people. Telegraphs, telephones, and televisions broke down the barrier of distance among people living in different regions. Thanks to these inventions Americans could speak directly to loved ones living elsewhere, learn instantaneously about events far from home, and laugh at the same jokes told on weekly television shows. In the 1990s, computer technology, especially personal computers and the Internet, again changed how Americans communicated, shopped, and received information.

First introduced in the 1980s (see Chapter 28), by the late 1990s millions of Americans spent hours a day at work or home typing on personal computers. The lucrative computer industry, fueled by the constant invention of ever-improving components and programs, supplanted the car and steel industry as the engine that drove prosperity. As manufacturing plants continued to close in the Midwest, areas where high-tech enterprises clustered, like Silicon Valley in northern California, boomed. Computer giants Microsoft (which produced the computer operating system Windows) and Apple became powerful corporations that employed highly educated workers and developed global markets for their products.

Going the way of the horse and buggy when cars were invented, typewriters became obsolete when people from office workers to students began using computers to write letters and essays. At first computer users printed copies of these documents and delivered them in traditional ways—such as by mailing letters or handing a teacher a completed assignment. By the end of the decade, however, more and more Americans relied on the Internet to deliver business and social correspondence electronically.

The Internet evolved from a primitive computer system designed in the 1960s to facilitate the exchange of data among geographically disparate military installations. The creation in the late 1980s of a computer network linking universities and five national supercomputer centers paved the way to providing instantaneous computer communication among civilians. When engineers in Switzerland developed the World Wide Web, a system for organizing electronic information, Internet use exploded. In 1994, six million Americans were connected to the Internet. By 2001, the 130 million Americans who surfed the web daily in offices, libraries, schools, or at home accounted for a quarter of all global Internet traffic.

Computers and the Internet quickly reshaped how Americans worked and played at the dawn of

> "When I took office [in 1993], only high energy physicists had ever heard of what is called the World Wide Web... Now even my cat has its own page.
> President BILL CLINTON, 1996

Which technological innovations of the twentieth century had the greatest impact on daily life?

View the **Image** ENIAC computer

the twenty-first century. Virtual business meetings now took place among geographically dispersed colleagues who looked into small cameras attached to their computers to converse with the people they saw on their screens. Office workers working in the same building sent a stream of e-mails to each other throughout the day, rather than telephoning or delivering a message in person. Many companies replaced paper records with computer databases that stored personal and commercial data.

Americans differed on the benefits that children derived from this new technology. A generation of youth hooked on computer games alarmed commentators who worried that their sedentary lifestyle was fueling an epidemic of childhood obesity. Others fretted that violent computer games desensitized children to real-world violence. Schools, however, quickly brought the Internet into the classroom. By simply typing a phrase into an Internet search engine, researchers of all ages gained instant access to information from libraries throughout the world. The Internet facilitated the spread of misinformation as well. Anyone could create a Web site, allowing virtual communities to form around almost any issue. A great resource for researching a medical condition, the Internet also helped terrorists publicize their causes and killings around the world.

The Internet reshaped commerce, becoming a virtual shopping mall and entertainment center as entrepreneurs rushed to market their wares. Shopping on the Internet, however, differed from taking a stroll down Main Street. The Internet-based company Amazon.com not only sold books more cheaply but built virtual communities in which readers posted their own reviews of books and sold used copies. The privacy and accessibility that the Internet afforded gave the pornography and gambling industries a boost, drawing millions of customers on a daily basis. To pay the credit card bills that they accumulated while shopping online, many Americans stopped sending checks through the mail and began using the Internet to pay their bills electronically. Droves of Americans stopped watching their favorite shows on TV when broadcast, preferring instead to watch them through the Internet when it was convenient.

The Changing Face of Families

In 1992, George H. W. Bush's vice president Dan Quayle attacked a popular television series *Murphy Brown* for positively portraying the unmarried

title character's decision to have a child. Quayle voiced the New Right's lament that marriage had lost ground to nontraditional family arrangements. The charts "American Family Structure, 1972" and "American Family Structure, 1998" (**29.9**) show that the composition of the American family had indeed changed radically in less than a generation. By 1998, 47 percent of American families lived in non-married households, both with and without children, compared to 26 percent in 1972. Gender roles within families also changed. In the traditional model of marriage, the husband worked and the wife stayed at home. By the end of the 1990s, most married couples worked outside the home.

Changing family structure prompted sometimes acrimonious debate between the New Right, who wanted to reverse these trends, and liberal Democrats, who championed the right of non-married partners to cohabitate and of single women to have children. Many people who considered themselves liberal on myriad economic and social issues, however, joined with the New Right in condemning same-sex or gay marriage. While many Americans were willing to tolerate same-sex couples living

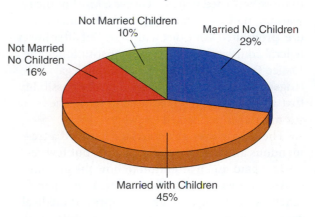

American Family Structure, 1972

- Not Married Children 10%
- Married No Children 29%
- Not Married No Children 16%
- Married with Children 45%

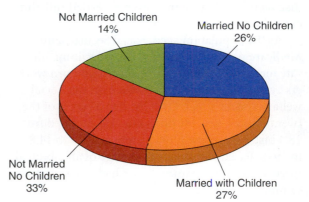

American Family Structure, 1998

- Not Married Children 14%
- Married No Children 26%
- Not Married No Children 33%
- Married with Children 27%

29.9 Changes in American Family Structure, 1972–1998 These graphs reveal that the percentage of married households with children dropped significantly by the end of the twentieth century.

What changes in family structure do these charts illustrate?

"Regardless of how you feel about marriage, it's wrong to treat people differently under the law."

An ad equating bans against gay marriage with past laws prohibiting interracial marriages

"I can marry a princess."

In a competing ad a young girl suggests that schools will promote legalized gay marriage

together, people on both ends of the political spectrum drew the line at same-sex marriages. In 1996, Congress passed the Defense of Marriage Act (DOMA), a law that defined marriage as a legal union between a man and a woman. Under this statute states that banned same-sex marriages did not have to accept legal marriages performed in other states, if a gay couple moved to their jurisdiction. In 2011, only Massachusetts, Connecticut, Vermont, New Hampshire, Iowa, Washington, D.C., and New York allowed same-sex marriages. Nine other states authorized "civil unions" between same-sex partners that granted them rights similar to those accorded married couples. Most of the remaining states, either through referendum or statute, prohibited same-sex marriage. But after lower federal courts ruled DOMA unconstitutional, the Justice Department stopped defending legal challenges to it in 2011. This opened up the possibility that all states would be required to recognize same-sex marriages performed elsewhere.

The debate over gay marriage received a tremendous amount of press exposure, but few reporters paid much attention to how the graying of America was altering family life. Life expectancy had increased thanks to improved medical care and decreasing poverty. Many middle-aged parents finished raising their children only to discover that their aging parents needed full-time caretaking.

As the population aged, Social Security and Medicare payments went up, but a declining birthrate meant that there were fewer native-born workers available to pay the taxes that kept this social welfare system afloat. Over the last 25 years of the twentieth century, the birth rate had declined from 18.4 births for every 1,000 people in 1970 to 14.8 in 1996. Faced with a labor shortage of able-bodied workers, the nation turned, as it had in the past, to immigrants to fill available jobs.

A Wave of Immigration

The massive wave of immigration that began after Congress eliminated national quotas in 1965 initiated another important social transformation. Between 1931 and 1965, around five million immigrants came to the United States. These numbers skyrocketed to 4.5 million in the 1970s; 7.3 million in the 1980s; and 9.1 million in the 1990s. Hundreds of thousands more entered the country illegally. Most of these immigrants came from Asia, Africa, and Latin America—only two million Europeans settled in the United States between 1980 and 2000. Some Americans satirically referred to the exploding Hispanic immigrant population in the Southwest as the *reconquista*, or reconquest of territory that Mexico had lost to the United States after the Mexican-American War of 1848 (see Chapter 11). Overall the United States attracted twice as many immigrants as all of the other nations in the world combined.

Competing claims about the economic benefits of immigration emerged, a debate explored more fully in *Competing Visions: The Economic Costs of Immigration*. The New Right also feared dire cultural consequences as the nation fragmented into permanent ethnic enclaves. "If America is to survive as 'one nation, one people' we need to call a 'time-out' on immigration, to assimilate the tens of millions who have lately arrived," exhorted Patrick Buchanan. To protect the nation's cultural cohesion, these right-leaning critics organized campaigns to make English the nation's official language.

Both Democrats and Republicans worried that immigrants, who were willing to work for less, took jobs away from native-born workers. Critics especially denounced illegal immigration, arguing that people who sneaked across the border often violated other laws as well. Illegal immigrants sent their

Competing Visions

THE ECONOMIC COSTS OF IMMIGRATION

To this day Americans continue to disagree about the economic costs of immigration. In the following passage Harvard economist George J. Borjas paints a pessimistic economic portrait. Tamar Jacoby disputes his claim that three decades of high immigration have hurt the U.S. economy. What factors does each emphasize to make a case?

George J. Borjas suggested that immigration affected socioeconomic groups differently in his 1996 article "The New Economics of Immigration: Affluent Americans Gain: Poor Americans Lose."

New research has established a number of points. The relative skills of successive immigrant waves have declined over much of the postwar period. In 1970, for example, the latest immigrant arrivals on average had 0.4 fewer years of schooling and earned 17 percent less than natives. By 1990 the most recently arrived immigrants had 1.3 fewer years of schooling and earned 32 percent less than natives ...

The large-scale migration of less-skilled workers has done harm to the economic opportunities of less-skilled natives Immigration may account for perhaps a third of the recent decline in the relative wages of less-educated native workers ...

The increasing welfare dependency in the immigrant population suggests that immigration may create a substantial fiscal burden on the most-affected localities and states ...

There exists a strong correlation between the skills of immigrants and the skills of their American-born children, so that the huge skill differentials observed among today's foreign-born groups will almost certainly become tomorrow's differences among American-born ethnic groups. In effect, immigration has set the stage for sizable ethnic differences in skills and socioeconomic outcomes, which are sure to be the focus of intense attention in the next century ...

Current immigration redistributes wealth from unskilled workers, whose wages are lowered by immigrants, to skilled workers and owners of companies that buy immigrants' services, and from taxpayers who bear the burden of paying for the social services used by immigrants to consumers who use the goods and services produced by immigrants.... Immigration changes how the economic pie is sliced up.... The harmful effects of immigration will not go away simply because some people do not wish to see them.

In her 2002 article "Too Many Immigrants," Tamar Jacoby argued that large-scale immigration benefited the United States economically.

The most commonly heard complaint about foreign workers is that they take jobs from Americans. Not only is this assertion untrue—nobody has found real evidence to support it—but cities and states with the largest immigrant populations (New York, Los Angeles, and others) boast far faster economic growth and lower unemployment than cities and states that do not attract immigrants. In many places, the presence of immigrants seems to reduce unemployment even among native-born blacks—probably because of the way immigrants stimulate economic growth.... Even if Borjas is right that a native-born black worker may take home $300 less a year as a result of immigration, this is a fairly small amount of money in the overall scheme of things. More to the point, globalization would have much the same effect on wages, immigrants or no immigrants ...

What about the costs imposed by immigrants, especially by their use of government services? It is true that many immigrants—though far from all—are poorer than native-born Americans, and thus pay less in taxes. It is also true that one small segment of the immigrant population—refugees—tends to be heavily dependent on welfare. As a result, states with large immigrant populations often face chronic fiscal problems.... [But] If we shift the lens to the federal level, and include the taxes that immigrants remit to the IRS, the calculation comes out very differently: immigrants pay in more than they take out.... 28 million immigrants form but a small part of the $12-trillion U.S. economy, and most of the fiscal costs and benefits associated with them are relatively modest. Besides, fiscal calculations are only a small part of the larger economic picture. How do we measure the energy immigrants bring—the pluck and grit and willingness to improvise and innovate?

Not only are immigrants by and large harder-working than the native-born, they generally fill economic niches that would otherwise go wanting.

View the **Closer Look** *Competing Visions: The Economic Costs of Immigration*

Are contemporary concerns about immigration similar or different from objections made earlier in the twentieth century?

29.10 Competing Views on Immigration Americans continue to debate whether immigrants are a burden or an asset.

children to school and received health care in hospitals, all at taxpayer expense, they charged. Unions and their supporters complained that undocumented workers could not join labor unions, making it more difficult to organize labor to improve working conditions and wages.

Champions of immigration, mostly from the political left, pointed to the nation's past success in assimilating immigrants and argued that immigrants took the low-paying jobs such as busboys, gardeners, and nannies that few Americans wanted. Countering claims that new immigrants failed to assimilate, advocates of immigration noted the high rate of interethnic marriages among second-generation immigrants. They also viewed complaints about multiculturalism as a racist attempt to protect the United States as a primarily white society. The different meanings attached to the word "benefits" in this political cartoon by Brian Fairrington (**29.10**) encapsulated the debate over whether immigrants drained the economy by seeking taxpayer-funded social services or contributed to overall prosperity by working for very little.

Climate Change

The computer revolution and shifting demographics were not the only factors changing American daily life. Scientists worried that accelerated climate change threatened to reshape the physical space that Americans inhabited and urged the nation to reverse human-induced environmental damage. They entreated Americans to switch from gas-guzzling cars like sport-utility

vehicles (SUVs) to automobiles that burned little or no fossil fuels. Americans, 4.5 percent of the global population, drove 24 percent of the world's 590 million cars. Ingrained driving habits, however, were hard to change.

Environmental scientists claimed that average temperatures had risen 1.8 degrees Fahrenheit over the last 100 years, a phenomenon called **global warming**. They attributed this climate shift to the widespread burning of fossil fuels (coal and oil) that pumped carbon dioxide into the air. Carbon dioxide was one of several greenhouse gases that trapped the sun's heat in the Earth's atmosphere. While the sun's rays were essential to human life, environmentalists blamed the rapidly rising levels of greenhouse gases for global warming.

This 2007 world map (**29.11**) shows which nations emitted the greatest amounts of carbon dioxide from burning fossil fuels. The United States, China, Russia, India, and Japan head the list. Developing nations in Africa with few cars or heavy industry emitted relatively little carbon dioxide. Besides emitting more total greenhouse gases than most other nations, the United States ranked tenth in the amount of greenhouse emissions per person.

Why did global warming matter? The quicker-than-normal melting of the Arctic ice cap, environmentalists warned, was causing sea levels to rise. If unchecked, rising waters would soon wash over sea-level lands throughout the world including the Mississippi Delta in the United States. Scientists also speculated that global warming affected rainfall patterns and storms, increasing droughts, wildfires, and hurricanes. Not everyone in the United States accepted these dire predictions. Some Americans questioned the scientific evidence linking climate change to human activity. Fluctuations in the earth's average temperature had occurred before, they argued, disputing the claim that permanent or catastrophic change in the atmosphere was underway. In 1997, the United States signed the Kyoto Protocol, an international agreement that set targets for reducing greenhouse emissions in industrial nations. In 2001, however, President George W. Bush argued that the agreement was flawed because it exempted China and relied on governmental controls, not market incentives, to develop "green" technology. The United States subsequently became the only nation besides Australia to sign, but not ratify, the treaty.

For Americans to reduce the amount of fossil fuels burned in cars and factories, lifestyles

What core arguments support and question the theory of global warming?

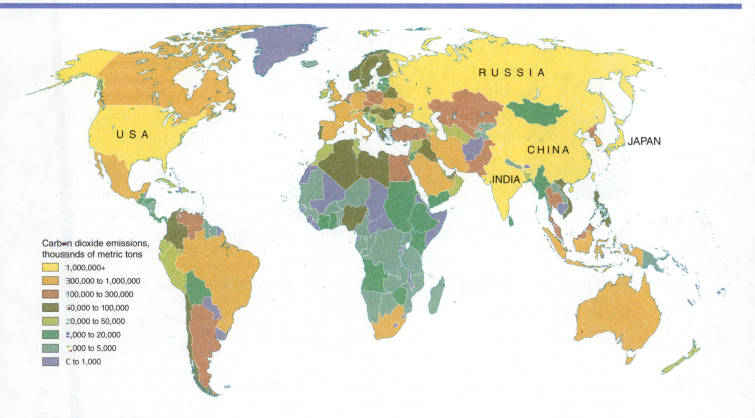

29.11 Global Carbon Dioxide Emissions
This 2007 map depicts the proportion of carbon dioxide gases emitted from burning fossil fuels (mostly in factories and cars) by each nation. The United States and China were the worst polluters, along with Japan, Russia, and India.

needed to change. Enjoying low gas prices few Americans felt compelled to invest time or money into developing "green" technology. National security concerns proved more effective in motivating the nation to re-examine its energy policy. The United States imported 65 percent of its oil, with Canada providing the largest share. After 9/11 a consensus emerged that the ongoing American presence in the Middle East (which provided 11 percent of the oil Americans consumed) bred resentment among Arab populations that helped Islamist terrorists recruit members.

Republicans and Democrats, however, disagreed over how to wean the nation off its dependence on foreign oil. The Bush administration championed bolstering oil production at home by lifting restrictions on drilling in the Arctic National Wildlife Refuge, a nationally protected wilderness in Alaska. This proposal enraged environmentalists and Democrats who worried that drilling accidents could contaminate this pristine area. They also feared losing valuable time in the battle against global warming by continuing, rather than ending, fossil fuel consumption.

"We are entering a period of consequences."

AL GORE, who won the 2007 Nobel Peace Prize for publicizing the global warming crisis

"Global warming—at least the modern nightmare version—is a myth."

British botanist DAVID BELLAMY

View the **Closer Look** *Competing Visions: Global Warming: Good Science or Media Hype?*

What accounts for the disparity in carbon dioxide emissions on this map?

New Threats in the Post–Cold War World

Middle East oil remained critical to the American economy throughout the 1990s and 2010s. Containing Iraqi leader Saddam Hussein presented an ongoing challenge for Presidents Bill Clinton and George W. Bush. Ethnic cleansing in Eastern Europe and Africa raised additional questions of how much responsibility America should assume to prevent massacres worldwide. When Islamic terrorists attacked U.S. targets overseas and at home, competing visions also arose over how to defend the nation from this new threat.

Ethnic Cleansing and Terrorism

In the 1990s, the nation faced a new foreign policy dilemma: when or whether to intercede on humanitarian grounds to stop massacres in parts of the world strategically unimportant to the United States. In 1992, images of a civil-war induced famine in Somalia, a country in East Africa, flooded American airwaves and newspapers. This image of a Somali woman and her starving child (**29.12**) echoed the Madonna and Child compositions used by Jacob Riis during the Gilded Age (see Chapter 17) and Dorothea Lange during the Depression (see Chapter 22) to rally popular support for aiding the poor. President George H. W. Bush responded to the public outcry by sending U.S. troops to help UN peacekeepers restore order, aid that incoming President Bill Clinton continued. Public opinion shifted dramatically in 1993, however, when news cameras captured the image of cheering Somalis dragging the corpse of an American soldier through the streets of Mogadishu, the capital city of Somalia, after rebel Somali warlords downed a U.S. helicopter (**29.13**). The

29.12 and 29.13 Competing Views of Civil Turmoil in Somalia, 1992 and 1993 Photographs like this one of a starving Somali woman and child prompted Americans to demand that the United States send troops to end the civil war responsible for the famine. A year later, angered by a photograph of Somali rebels dragging the corpse of an American soldier through the streets, Americans called for the return of U.S. troops. Both images encouraged Americans to view African nations as dysfunctional places where famine and fighting were endemic.

How did media coverage influence American views of Africa?

public now demanded an immediate withdrawal, and Clinton complied. The UN also withdrew its troops, and years of anarchy in Somalia followed. Reluctant to jeopardize American soldiers' lives again, Clinton proceeded cautiously in April 1994 when Hutus, the majority ethnic group in Rwanda, a nation in Central Africa, unleashed a 100-day genocidal rampage that killed 800,000 Tutsis, a minority ethic group. This time Clinton came under attack for failing to intervene decisively with force.

The photo of Somalis desecrating the corpse of an American soldier had other repercussions. Osama bin Laden, the Saudi exile who headed **al-Qaeda**, a fundamentalist Islamic terrorist organization, concluded that terrorist attacks against the United States would work, because Americans had no stomach for casualties. "One American pilot was dragged in the streets of Mogadishu [and] you left. ... the extent of your impotence and weaknesses became very clear," he jeered in 1996. Such pronouncements caused Paul Watson, the photojournalist who took the Pulitzer-prize winning image, to conclude that the "storm of outrage" over his photo taught terrorists that they could rely on publicity in the Western media to amplify the impact of their terrorist attacks.

During his first years in office, Clinton also had to respond to "ethnic cleansing," the intentional mass killing of one ethnic group by another, in the Balkans, a mountainous region of southeastern Europe. When Communist Yugoslavia dissolved in 1991, ethnic and religious differences provoked a civil war among Croatia, Bosnia, and Serbia, all former parts of Yugoslavia. Clinton resisted intervening until July 1995 when Serbian forces forced 25,000 Bosnian Muslim women and children to leave the town of Srebrenica, and murdered the 7,500 Muslim men and boys who remained behind. The United States participated in NATO air strikes of Serbian military positions and helped broker the 1995 Dayton Peace Accords, which settled disputed territorial boundaries and placed NATO troops (including Americans) on the ground as peacekeepers.

Preoccupied with humanitarian tragedies overseas, Americans paid less attention in the early 1990s to signs that the terrorist threat was moving closer to home. Many Arabs saw the United States and Israel as one, blaming both for taking away land that belonged to the Palestinians. Overseas hostage-takings and plane hijackings in the 1970s and 1980s kept the Arab-Israeli conflict in the news. In 1993, Kuwaiti and Iraqi-born terrorists exploded a massive car bomb in the parking garage of the World Trade Center, two towering skyscrapers in the heart of New York City's financial district that housed governmental agencies and companies involved in foreign trade. The explosion killed six people and created a six-story hole in the ground. The FBI captured the culprits easily when one tried to recover his deposit from a car rental agency for the van used in the attack. Reassured that law enforcement agencies had done their job and that the terrorists were inept, the public and government quickly forgot the incident.

But al-Qaeda, which maintained training bases in Afghanistan, resolved to try again. Determined to launch a *jihad*, or holy war against Western non-believers, bin Laden relied on his family's fortune and donations from Saudi Arabians to construct a clandestine terrorist network that recruited disciples from the Middle East, Asia, and Africa.

Not all terrorist threats during this period originated overseas. On April 19, 1995, Timothy McVeigh parked a rental truck filled with explosives in front of a federal building in Oklahoma City. The blast killed 168 people, including many children in a day care center, and wounded 800. McVeigh and his accomplice Terry Nichols viewed the attack as payback for the federal government's recent assaults against private paramilitary groups and their rural compounds filled with caches of weapons. Militia supporters like McVeigh rejected any legal restriction on their Second Amendment right to bear arms, citing gun laws as just one example of government tyranny. The bombing remained the deadliest terrorist attack against American civilians until 9/11.

Meanwhile al-Qaeda attacked U.S. targets overseas. Issuing a *fatwa*, or religious decree, declaring war against all Americans, bin Laden demanded that the United States remove its troops from Saudi Arabia (stationed there since the 1991 Persian Gulf War) and end its support of Israel. "It is more important for Muslims to kill Americans than other infidels," bin Laden declared. This pronouncement was more than rhetoric. In August 1998, al-Qaeda terrorists bombed the U.S. embassies in Nairobi, the capital of Kenya, and Dar es Salaam, a city in Tanzania. Clinton ordered an immediate retaliatory attack, and tomahawk cruise missiles rained down on eight al-Qaeda training camps in Afghanistan and on a pharmaceutical plant in Sudan, which was thought to have supplied bin Laden with chemical weapons.

His advisors presented Clinton with competing views over the next possible step. His antiterrorist advisor recommended continuing the bombing until the Taliban, Afghanistan's fundamentalist Islamic

29.14 The World Trade Center Collapses This photograph conveyed the panic that spread through lower Manhattan as rubble and smoke from the collapsing World Trade Center towers rained down on the streets.

government, turned bin Laden over to the United States. Pentagon officials opposed sustained bombing, worried that mounting civilian casualties would inflame anti-American sentiments throughout the Middle East. Assassinating bin Laden, others argued, would turn him into a martyr whose death fundamentalists would certainly avenge. Faced with these conflicting views, Clinton chose to rely on the CIA to thwart terrorist attacks against U.S. targets overseas. These covert agents uncovered several planned attacks but failed to prevent al-Qaeda from sending a small explosive-laden boat into the side of the *USS Cole*, a destroyer, which was anchored near the Middle Eastern

country of Yemen. The October 12, 2000, assault killed 17 sailors and injured 40. Clinton left office still waiting for verification that al-Qaeda was behind this attack. Incoming President George W. Bush received that confirmation, but had not settled on a response when al-Qaeda struck again on September 11, 2001.

9/11

On the morning of September 11, 2001, in an attack that became known as **9/11**, 19 terrorists operating from al-Qaeda cells inside the United States hijacked four planes. The terrorists, from Saudi Arabia, Egypt, Lebanon, and the United Arab Emirates, flew two planes into the World Trade Center towers, and a third into the Pentagon. The fourth plane crashed in Shanksville, Pennsylvania, after the passengers seized control of the cockpit, thwarting the terrorist plan to fly it into the Capitol. On this "day of terror," Americans watched in horror as the World Trade Center towers crumbled, causing rescue workers, victims, and onlookers to run for safety as the massive structures collapsed in a heap (**29.14**). A total of 2,973 people died in the attacks.

President Bush immediately announced that "we will make no distinction between the terrorists who committed these acts and those who harbor them." He issued an ultimatum to Afghanistan's Taliban government: turn over al-Qaeda members living there, including bin Laden, or face invasion. The Taliban refused. Receiving overwhelming support from Congress, the American people, and most foreign nations, the United States attacked Afghanistan on October 7, 2001. U.S. forces first bombed al-Qaeda training camps and arms depots, and then joined with the Northern Alliance, an Afghan rebel group, to drive the Taliban from power. The two-month conflict failed, however, to capture bin Laden, who had likely escaped into the mountains of neighboring Pakistan with help from Pakistani sympathizers.

Most Americans had supported the invasion, but many grew uneasy about how the Bush administration was conducting the war. These critics accused Bush of condoning torture by allowing CIA agents to use water-boarding, an interrogation tactic that simulated drowning, to try to extract information from captured al-Qaeda suspects held prisoner at the U.S. naval base in Guantánamo Bay in Cuba. The decision to incarcerate captured prisoners indefinitely at Guantánamo Bay, denying them the right to a fair trial, also aroused controversy.

How did the nation and government respond to the 9/11 attacks?

Read the **Document** *George Bush, Address to Congress (September 20, 2001)*

Responding to criticism that the nation's security agencies had failed to prevent the 9/11 attack, the president created the Department of Homeland Security, a new umbrella organization that housed the nation's intelligence-gathering and law enforcement agencies. He also secured congressional approval for the 2001 **Patriot Act**, which expanded the government's investigative and police powers. Critics soon attacked the law as an unconstitutional assault on civil liberties. This 2002 political cartoon by Pulitzer Prize winner Clay Bennett (**29.15**) exposed a familiar wartime dilemma—how to protect the nation against enemy agents operating on American soil while simultaneously safeguarding the privacy rights of Americans. In the cartoon determined federal workers remove planks from a couple's home to build a security fence, exposing their personal lives to public scrutiny. In the weeks after the 9/11 attacks, the FBI arrested hundreds of Arabs and Muslims in an effort to destroy any remaining al-Qaeda cells in the United States. Acting hastily, and often

on flimsy evidence, the FBI caught innocent people in its dragnet, and some spent months in jail before being released. Scores of Arab Americans, like Japanese Americans in World War II, hung American flags outside their businesses to counter suspicions that all Muslims were terrorists. In 2007, a federal court overturned the sections of the Patriot Act that made it easier for the government to secure search warrants as well as Internet and phone records.

The Iraq War

America's "war on terror" soon spread to Iraq. Containing Saddam Hussein's ambition to acquire weapons of mass destruction (nuclear, chemical, and biological weapons) had been an ongoing goal since the end of the 1991 Persian Gulf War. In 1998, the UN halted its weapons inspection program after Iraq refused to continue cooperating. President Clinton subsequently authorized Operation Desert Fox, a four-day

29.15 Security versus Privacy, 2002
This cartoon suggests that invading the privacy of Americans under the guise of increasing security worsened, rather than improved, their lives.

How do governmental efforts to prevent internal enemy attacks after 9/11 compare to those during World Wars I and II?

bombing campaign in December 1998 against 100 Iraqi military targets to destroy any weapons Saddam was hiding. Neoconservatives publicly urged Clinton to make removing Saddam a goal of American foreign policy. They had the chance to advance their views more forcefully once Bush appointed neoconservatives to key defense-related positions, including Secretary of Defense Donald Rumsfeld and Deputy Secretary of Defense Paul Wolfowitz.

This core of key neoconservative defense policy advisors included Vice President Dick Cheney. Reversing his previous stand when he had counseled the first President Bush to stop the Persian Gulf War without attacking Baghdad, Cheney, along with others, urged the president to attack Iraq while public concern about national security remained high. "Do we wait and hope he doesn't do what we know he is capable of, which is distributing weapons of mass destruction to anonymous terrorists, or do we take preemptive action?" asked neoconservative Richard Perle, chairman of the Defense Policy Board. These advisors championed **preemptive war**, the doctrine that the United States should use force to remove hostile regimes before they could pose a serious threat.

> ## "Our security will require all Americans to be forward-looking and resolute, to be ready for preemptive action when necessary to defend our liberty and to defend our lives."
>
> President GEORGE W. BUSH, announcing a shift in foreign policy from containment to preemption, 2002

State Department officials, especially Secretary of State Colin Powell, disagreed. They offered a competing vision that relied on the same Cold War–era containment policies that had eventually toppled the Soviet Union. Those urging restraint worried that a hostile fundamentalist Islamic government might replace Saddam's secular regime, fueling rather than dampening the terrorist threat against the United States. "Better the devil we know than the one we don't," one high-ranking intelligence official reasoned. *Choices and Consequences: Launching a Preemptive War* examines

the options before Bush as he made his decision to attack Iraq.

Having privately resolved to topple Saddam Hussein, Bush began laying the groundwork for sending American troops into Iraq. In September 2002, his administration announced a new national security strategy. The **Bush Doctrine** established the unilateral right to attack nations that harbored terrorists, to launch preemptive military strikes to prevent future attacks on the United States, and to replace autocratic governments with democratically elected ones. The inclusion of preemptive war was new, but other parts of the Bush Doctrine reiterated key principles announced by Bush's father when he defined a new post–Cold War direction for American foreign policy in 1992. Neoconservative Paul Wolfowitz played a key role in both administrations, devising a foreign policy that aggressively protected America's singular status as the world's strongest military power.

In building his case for war, the president repeatedly claimed that Saddam Hussein possessed weapons of mass destruction and had links to terrorist organizations, including al-Qaeda. By the summer of 2002, this rhetoric had convinced 54 percent of the American public of the falsehood that Saddam was responsible for the 9/11 attacks. To win support in the international community and at home, Bush sought both a UN resolution demanding that Iraq readmit weapons inspectors and a congressional joint resolution authorizing the use of force to enforce UN mandates and remove the "continuing threat" that Saddam posed. In arguing for war the administration pointed to secret correspondence between Iraq and Niger provided by Italian intelligence agents indicating that between 1999 and 2001 Saddam had made overtures to buy uranium oxide, material used to build a nuclear bomb, from Niger. Some CIA agents, including the envoy sent to Niger to investigate, privately doubted that Saddam had tried to buy uranium from Niger. This charge, however, convinced wavering Democrats to support the war. When the International Atomic Energy Agency announced that these incriminating letters were indeed forgeries, antiwar advocates charged that Bush had deliberately misled the country to build his case for war.

The Iraq War followed the same pattern as the 1991 Persian Gulf War—intense bombing followed by a ground invasion. The bombing campaign began on March 19, 2003, and within three weeks

Choices and Consequences

LAUNCHING A PREEMPTIVE WAR

In 2002, the Bush administration feared that Iraqi dictator Saddam Hussein had acquired, or was on the verge of acquiring, nuclear weapons and was developing chemical and biological weapons. President Bush worried that once Hussein acquired a sizeable arsenal, he would use it against his neighbors, including Israel, and help terrorists attack the United States. His advisors gave Bush three options about how to proceed.

Choices

| 1 Launch a preemptive war to remove Saddam from power. | 2 Work through the UN to impose economic sanctions and send weapons inspectors to Iraq. | 3 Support Iraqi exiles' plan to organize a coup that might trigger a mass uprising. |

Decision

In February 2002, Bush decided to fight. He announced that Saddam harbored weapons of mass destruction and had aided al-Qaeda. He made a half-hearted effort to work with the UN to reconstitute the weapons inspection program halted in 1998 and secured support from a handful of potential allies if the United States went to war. Announcing that Saddam had refused to cooperate adequately with UN weapons inspectors, the United States attacked Iraq on March 19, 2003.

Consequences

Active combat lasted three weeks and toppled Saddam. No weapons of mass destruction were found. Iraq elected a democratic government that struggled to contain ethnic and religious strife. U.S. forces came under daily attack until a surge of troops in 2008 weakened rebel insurgencies.

Looking for a coherent Iraq policy, Jack Ohman, *The Oregonian*, 2002

Continuing Controversies

Was the Iraq War justified?
Supporters of Bush's policies argued that removing Saddam benefited the Iraqi people and the world. Building a stable, democratic, and militarily weakened Iraq was necessary to protect American interests in the strategically and economically important Persian Gulf. The 9/11 attacks demonstrated that the United States must act aggressively and preemptively overseas to prevent future strikes on its own soil. Critics argued that Bush misled the American people by making false claims that Saddam possessed weapons of mass destruction and had ties to al-Qaeda. The war made America less secure by fanning anti-American sentiments in the Middle East that helped al-Qaeda recruit and diverted resources from the war in Afghanistan, where al-Qaeda was regrouping. Preemptive war set a dangerous precedent that lowered the threshold for going to war to simply feeling threatened by another nation.

What justifications and criticisms did the doctrine of preventative war arouse?

American troops were in Baghdad. On April 10, 2003, *USA Today* was one of many newspapers and television newscasts (**29.16**) showing an Iraqi crowd enlisting the aid of U.S. Marines to pull down a huge statue of Saddam. "The toppling of Saddam Hussein's statue in Baghdad will be recorded alongside the fall of the Berlin Wall as one of the great moments of liberty," Bush proclaimed. Although the event was initially seen as emblematic of Iraqi celebration over the fall of Saddam, subsequent reports suggested that American army personnel had staged the event in a square across from the hotel housing international journalists to create a positive iconic image of the war similar to the World War II image of U.S. Marines raising the flag on Iwo Jima (see Chapter 23). The controversy surrounding the picture mirrored Americans' debate over whether the war was based on lies or was, as Bush and his

supporters maintained, spreading democracy to the Middle East.

After active combat operations ceased, American troops faced a host of problems that kept them in Iraq. Widespread looting greeted the fall of Saddam Hussein, who eluded capture until December 13, 2003. He was held in prison, then put on trial and executed on December 30, 2006. Restoring law and order and creating a new democratic government proved difficult as Sunnis, Shiites, and Kurds divided along ethnic and religious lines. American soldiers caught up in the emerging civil war provided inviting targets for suicide bombers, while Iran and al-Qaeda penetrated Iraq to expand their influence in the region.

Controversy over the war continued at home, especially when scandalous photographs taken by soldiers at the American-run Abu Ghraib prison circulated in the mainstream media and on the Internet in 2004. While interrogating prisoners U.S. guards had taken photos of prisoners forced into humiliating sexual positions and being threatened with dogs. Other photos showed smiling American soldiers standing beside beaten and bloody corpses. As with the 1968 My Lai massacre in Vietnam (see Chapter 26), Americans held strong competing visions on what they felt the photos represented. Some saw rogue soldiers acting on their own; others blamed the president for authorizing brutal interrogating techniques on suspected terrorists. Another group sidestepped the moral question and instead debated whether torture produced valuable information or simply encouraged suspects to say what interrogators wanted to hear.

29.16 "Baghdad Falls," April 10, 2003
Initial news reports spoke of jubilant crowds cheering as U.S. Marines helped them pull down a statue of Saddam Hussein, but later reports suggested that the army had staged the incident.

What accomplishments and setbacks did the United States experience in the Iraq War?

The Election of 2008

In 2004, Bush won reelection against Democratic challenger Massachusetts Senator John Kerry, a Vietnam War veteran whose record both as a decorated officer and peace activist came under Republican attack during the campaign. Despite the growing unpopularity of the war in Iraq, the fresh memories of 9/11 bolstered Bush's argument that only he could adequately protect the nation against terrorism. In a close election Bush won the popular vote by only 3 percent and captured the Electoral College 286 to 252.

By 2008, however, the president's approval rates had sunk to historic lows—only Truman and Nixon had polled lower. These lows reflected the nation's unease with its seemingly permanent presence in Iraq and recoil at the White House's initial failure to react when Hurricane Katrina devastated New Orleans' predominantly black neighborhoods in 2005. In the 2008 presidential contest, Democratic and Republican candidates both repudiated the Bush administration and ran campaigns that promised change.

The election soon assumed historic dimensions when Hillary Rodham Clinton, the former First Lady and now a senator from New York, announced her candidacy. Clinton had a long record of public service dedicated to healthcare issues, but her initial support for the war in Iraq angered antiwar Democrats. First-term Illinois Senator Barack Obama, the 47-year-old son of a white woman from Kansas and an African father, astutely campaigned on his own consistent opposition to the war. When the crowded Democratic field narrowed to Clinton and Obama, the 2008 election was guaranteed to make history. For the first time either a woman or an African American would head the national Democratic ticket. At the end of a bruising primary battle, Obama prevailed to become the Democratic nominee.

In the general election Obama faced Republican John McCain, a former Navy pilot whom the Communist Vietnamese had held captive for six years during the Vietnam War. The 72-year-old senator from Arizona had a reputation as a maverick for occasionally breaking ranks with fellow Republicans. Hoping to make some history of his own, and perhaps woo Clinton supporters, McCain selected Alaska Governor Sarah Palin as his running mate—only the second time that a woman had received this honor.

Obama pledged to end the war in Iraq quickly and roll back the Bush-era tax cuts for the wealthy, while McCain supported both. Debate over the Iraq War faded when a cascade of bank and insurance company failures sent the stock market into a tailspin. In the midst of the crisis, economists offered the following explanation for the downturn that future investigations may or may not confirm. During the last five years, as housing prices rose dramatically and Congress deregulated the banking and financial industries, banks had made numerous risky loans that let people purchase homes they could not afford, and Wall Street brokers had invested heavily in mortgage-backed securities. When housing prices started declining in summer 2007, the dominos began to fall. Bank foreclosures on people who could not pay their mortgages increased, and even more ominously, the declining value of mortgage-backed securities threatened to bankrupt leading Wall Street firms, wiping out many Americans' retirement investments. To stabilize the mortgage market, the government took over two leading lenders, Freddie Mac and Fannie Mae. Treasury Secretary Henry Paulson refused to intervene when Lehman Brothers, a major investment firm, went bankrupt in September 2008. This bankruptcy shocked the financial sector. Credit markets froze as banks stopped lending and investors began moving money from stocks and bonds to U.S. Treasury notes.

By mid-September the Bush administration decided that an infusion of $700 billion was needed to unfreeze the credit markets and stop the stock market's freefall. Enraged House Republicans revolted. In their view the government "bail-out" used taxpayer money to reward bad behavior. Many Democrats accepted the competing view that the government would recoup this money when the economy and value of these investments improved. Congress eventually authorized the funds, which Paulson used to infuse capital directly into banks rather than buying low-valued assets. What happened to this money became a major political question, still unanswered.

Obama was a captivating orator who drew thousands to his rallies. Even Hillary Clinton campaigned for him. Obama drew enthusiastic support from whites and blacks; young and old; Hispanic and Asian.

> "[I]t is that American spirit—that American promise—that pushes us forward even when the path is uncertain."
>
> BARACK OBAMA, accepting the 2008 presidential Democratic nomination

29.17 "Obamanania" Almost overnight Barack Obama became an American icon, a boon to Washington, D.C.-area gift shops selling souvenirs to the 2 million people who braved freezing temperatures to see Obama inaugurated as the nation's 44th president on January 20, 2009.

Exuding confidence, calm, and charm, Obama amassed an inspired following who put his likeness on posters, vans, t-shirts, bridges, boats, and even tattoos. The image of Obama on the souvenir mugs in this photo (**29.17**) came from an iconic poster by artist Shepard Fairey. The mugs paired Obama's silhouette with the campaign's catchphrase: "Change we can believe in." By contrast, Fairey's poster carried the single word "Hope," a message that detractors modified into "Nope" on their own tee-shirts and bumper stickers.

An intensely disciplined candidate, Obama stuck to a clear message of economic reform. The McCain campaign was more erratic, one day highlighting economics; the next portraying Obama as the heir to sixties-era radicalism. Thanks to support from swing voters (those without strong ideological convictions), momentum for Obama built throughout the fall. On November 4, 2008, he became the first African American president of the United States by winning a decisive victory: 365 to 173 electoral votes, and 53 percent of the popular vote.

Troubled Times

Obama's emphasis on change during the campaign raised liberals' expectations that he would move quickly to regulate Wall Street, enact universal health care, end the ban on gays in the military, and withdraw from Iraq and Afghanistan. Conservatives, however, adamantly opposed enlarging the role and cost of government. Within this highly contentious partisan environment, Obama found himself under attack from the right and left.

The economic crisis posed the most immediate challenge for Obama. With the Democrats controlling both the House and Senate, he quickly secured passage of a massive government spending bill to stimulate the economy. Republicans (including many who had supported Bush's deficit spending) vehemently opposed increasing the national debt. When the economy failed to rebound quickly, two competing views on the stimulus spending emerged. The Obama administration asserted that the infusion of government money prevented another Great Depression by staving off the collapse of the nation's financial institutions and averting massive layoffs. Republicans countered that ineffective government interference stymied the recovery, leaving taxpayers with a bill that would take generations to pay off.

Liberals urged Obama to hold Wall Street accountable for the misdeeds that caused the economic meltdown, and Congress did strengthen regulatory oversight of financial institutions. Americans increasingly, however, directed their anger over the ongoing economic crisis at Washington. Concerns about the escalating debt and federal power energized

How did past civil rights activism help make Obama's election possible?

○ Watch the Video *Video Lecture: The Connection Between Obama and Lincoln*

grassroots conservatives, who used social networking media to draw crowds to their initial demonstrations. The spectacular rise of the Tea Party movement had begun, named to evoke the revolutionary spirit of the 1774 Boston Tea Party. Support from conservative television pundits and high-profile politicians like Sarah Palin also fueled the movement's growth.

By actively opposing the president's health insurance reform initiative, the Tea Party solidified its influence within Republican circles. In pushing for health-care reform, Obama hoped to succeed where Truman and Clinton had failed. J.R. Rose's 2009 political cartoon aptly captured the political divide that characterized this rancorous debate (**29.18**). To marshal support, Obama cited the many uninsured (16 percent of the population, or 47 million people), rising health-care and insurance costs, and troubling industry practices such as lifetime limits on coverage. Opting for a reform of private health insurance practices rather than the single-payer government-run system liberals favored, Obama angered his base and did little to assuage conservatives. Health insurance reform legislation passed in 2010 without receiving a single Republican vote amid liberal criticism that the law did too little. The law's requirement that all Americans purchase health insurance became a flashpoint for conservatives and independents worried about intrusive governmental power. States immediately challenged the constitutionality of this mandate. The mixed rulings in federal district courts suggested that the Supreme Court would ultimately determine whether Obama's attempt to establish universal healthcare would prevail.

Sweeping Republican victories in the 2010 mid-term elections included Tea Party candidates who vowed to curb the power of government by repealing the healthcare law, cutting the federal budget, and making Bush-era tax cuts permanent. Focused on fiscal issues, Tea Party activists had less interest in championing conservatives' traditional social and cultural agenda. Instead of rallying supporters to reverse the 2010 repeal of the military's "Don't Ask, Don't Tell" policy that prevented gay servicemen from openly acknowledging their sexual orientation, the Tea Party used its influence within the Republican

Party to demand a permanent reduction in the size and scope of the federal budget.

Liberal disenchantment with Obama stemmed mainly from his foreign policy decisions, especially escalating the war in Afghanistan and continued operation of the Guantanamo Bay prison. Obama prohibited the use of water-boarding, but reaffirmed the Bush-era policy of holding prisoners indefinitely without charges. Sending an additional 30,000 troops to Afghanistan in October 2009, Obama tried to reassure his liberal base by setting a tentative withdrawal date of 2014 from Afghanistan. Obama satisfied Americans of all political persuasions when he announced on May 2, 2011 that U.S. Special Forces had tracked down and killed Osama bin Laden in his Pakistani hideout. Documents recovered during the raid provided crucial intelligence that allowed Obama to claim that the United States for the moment had the upper-hand in the war on terror. He also moved decisively to draw down forces in Iraq. An influx of U.S. troops in 2008 had reduced insurgent attacks, both improving the public's views of the Iraq War and strengthening Obama's claim that the war had been won. In October 2011 Obama announced that the U.S. military would leave Iraq by year's end. "After nearly nine years, America's war in Iraq will be over," he announced, a decision supported by 75% of Americans.

29.18 A Vigorous Debate. During the year-long debate over health insurance reform Democrats and Republicans articulated competing visions of the role that the federal government should play in American society.

1989

Fall of the Berlin Wall
Symbolizes demise of communism in Eastern Europe

Chinese students occupy Tiananmen Square
Communist government violently suppresses pro-democracy movement

1991

Persian Gulf War
United States announces intention to build "a new world order"

Soviet Union ceases to exist
United States declares victory in the Cold War

1998

UN withdraws weapon inspectors from an uncooperative Iraq
Growing U.S. alarm over Saddam's drive to acquire nuclear weapons

President Bill Clinton impeached
Cleared of charges, but scandal mars Clinton's second term

2000

al-Qaeda strikes *USS Cole* near Yemen
Precursor to 9/11 attacks inside the United States

George W. Bush elected president
Controversy over disputed recount in Florida divides the nation

CHAPTER REVIEW

Review Questions

1. What values and ideas shaped key American foreign policy decisions in this period?

2. What controversies emerged over immigration and gay marriage?

3. How did liberals and conservatives modify their long-standing visions of the role government should play?

4. How did the media shape American attitudes about world events?

5. How did the United States reconcile its domestic values with its new imperialistic ventures in the world from 1989–2009?

Key Terms

Powell Doctrine General Colin Powell's assertion that the nation should go to war only as a last resort when the president had full support from the nation and the international community, could employ overwhelming military force to win without serious loss of American life, and had a clear exit strategy. **882**

"Don't Ask, Don't Tell" The policy instituted during the Clinton era that allowed closeted homosexuals and lesbians, gays who kept their sexual preferences hidden, to serve in the military. **884**

North American Free Trade Agreement (NAFTA) A 1992 treaty that lifted trade barriers among the United States, Mexico, and Canada. **885**

"compassionate conservatism" A philosophical approach to governing that emphasized using private industry, charities, and religious institutions, rather than the government, to provide community services. **887**

global warming The scientific theory that widespread burning of fossil fuels emitted greenhouse gases into the atmosphere that caused average global temperatures to rise. **892**

al-Qaeda A fundamentalist Islamic terrorist organization led by Saudi exile Osama bin Laden. **895**

9/11 September 11, 2001, was the day of al-Qaeda attacks on the United States; terrorists hijacked four planes and flew two into the World Trade Center towers and one into the Pentagon; one crashed on a field in Shanksville, Pennsylvania. **896**

Patriot Act A controversial 2001 law that greatly expanded the government's investigative and police powers. **897**

preemptive war The notion that the United States should remove hostile regimes with force before they could pose a serious threat. **898**

Bush Doctrine Established the unilateral right to attack nations that harbored terrorists, to launch preemptive military strikes to prevent future attacks on the United States, and to replace autocratic governments with democratically elected ones. **898**

2001

al-Qaeda launches 9/11 attacks
United States begins "war on terror" overseas and at home

Congress passes the Patriot Act
Americans debate whether law protects nation or violates civil liberties

2003

Iraq War begins
Preemptive war puts U.S. troops in Iraq indefinitely

2008

Economic downturn begins
Economists predict worst financial crisis since the Great Depression

Barack Obama elected president
First African American elected president

2010

Tea Party emerges
Grassroots conservative movement emphasizes limited government

Health insurance overall
Establishes universal healthcare system

MyHistoryLab Connections

Visit www.myhistorylab.com for a customized Study Plan that will help you build your knowledge of *Building a New World Order*.

Questions for Analysis

1. Why does Wilson conclude that class matters more than race in explaining urban poverty?

 Read the **Document** *William Julius Wilson, The Urban Underclass, p. 880*

2. How did the president justify military action against Iraq in 1991?

Read the **Document** *George Bush, Allied Military Action in the Persian Gulf (1991), p. 882*

3. What are the competing views on global warming?

View the **Closer Look** *Competing Visions: Global Warming: Good Science or Media Hype?, p. 893*

4. What new vision of America's role in the world followed 9/11?

Read the **Document** *George W. Bush, National Security Strategy of the United States of America (2002), p. 898*

5. What is the historical significance of electing the nation's first African American president?

Watch the **Video** *Video Lecture: The Historical Significance of the 2008 Election, p. 901*

Other Resources from This Chapter

Read the **Document**

- *George H. W. Bush Inaugural Address (1989), p. 876*
- *Articles of Impeachment Against William Jefferson Clinton, p. 885*
- *George Bush, Address to Congress (September 20, 2001), p. 896*

View the **Closer Look**

- *Images as History: The Fall of the Berlin Wall, p. 878*
- *Competing Visions: The Economic Costs of Immigration, p. 891*

View the **Image** *ENIAC computer, p. 888*

Watch the **Video**

- *President George Bush's Early Response in the Persian Gulf War, p. 881*
- *Bill Clinton Sells Himself to America: Presidential Campaign Ad (1992), p. 884*
- *Video Lecture: The Connection Between Obama and Lincoln, p. 902*

Appendix

- **The Declaration of Independence**

- **The Articles of Confederation**

- **The Constitution of the United States of America**

- **Amendments to the Constitution**

- **Presidential Elections**

- **Presidents and Vice Presidents**

For additional reference material, go to

www.pearsonamericanhistory.com

For the on-line appendix, click on Pearson American History Study Site.

The on-line appendix includes the following:

The Declaration of Independence

In Congress, July 4, 1776

The Unanimous Declaration of the Thirteen United States of America

When, in the course of human events, it becomes necessary for one people to dissolve the political bonds which have connected them with another, and to assume, among the powers of the earth, the separate and equal station to which the laws of nature and of nature's God entitle them, a decent respect to the opinions of mankind requires that they should declare the causes which impel them to the separation.

We hold these truths to be self-evident: That all men are created equal; that they are endowed by their Creator with certain unalienable rights; that among these are life, liberty, and the pursuit of happiness; that, to secure these rights, governments are instituted among men, deriving their just powers from the consent of the governed; that whenever any form of government becomes destructive of these ends, it is the right of the people to alter or to abolish it, and to institute new government, laying its foundation on such principles, and organizing its powers in such form, as to them shall seem most likely to effect their safety and happiness. Prudence, indeed, will dictate that governments long established should not be changed for light and transient causes; and accordingly all experience hath shown that mankind are more disposed to suffer, while evils are sufferable, than to right themselves by abolishing the forms to which they are accustomed. But when a long train of abuses and usurpations, pursuing invariably the same object, evinces a design to reduce them under absolute despotism, it is their right, it is their duty, to throw off such government, and to provide new guards for their future security. Such has been the patient sufferance of these colonies; and such is now the necessity which constrains them to alter their former systems of government. The history of the present King of Great Britain is a history of repeated injuries and usurpations, all having in direct object the establishment of an absolute tyranny over these states. To prove this, let facts be submitted to a candid world.

He has refused his assent to laws, the most wholesome and necessary for the public good.

He has forbidden his governors to pass laws of immediate and pressing importance, unless suspended in their operation till his assent should be obtained; and, when so suspended, he has utterly neglected to attend to them.

He has refused to pass other laws for the accommodation of large districts of people, unless those people would relinquish the right of representation in the legislature, a right inestimable to them, and formidable to tyrants only.

He has called together legislative bodies at places unusual, uncomfortable, and distant from the depository of their public records, for the sole purpose of fatiguing them into compliance with his measures.

He has dissolved representative houses repeatedly, for opposing, with manly firmness, his invasions on the rights of the people.

He has refused for a long time, after such dissolutions, to cause others to be elected; whereby the legislative powers, incapable of annihilation, have returned to the people at large for their exercise; the state remaining, in the mean time, exposed to all the dangers of invasions from without and convulsions within.

He has endeavored to prevent the population of these states; for that purpose obstructing the laws for naturalization of foreigners; refusing to pass others to encourage their migration hither, and raising the conditions of new appropriations of lands.

He has obstructed the administration of justice, by refusing his assent to laws for establishing judiciary powers.

He has made judges dependent on his will alone, for the tenure of their offices, and the amount and payment of their salaries.

He has erected a multitude of new offices, and sent hither swarms of officers to harass our people and eat out their substance.

He has kept among us, in times of peace, standing armies, without the consent of our legislatures.

He has affected to render the military independent of, and superior to, the civil power.

He has combined with others to subject us to a jurisdiction foreign to our constitution, and unacknowledged by our laws, giving his assent to their acts of pretended legislation:

For quartering large bodies of armed troops among us;

For protecting them, by a mock trial, from punishment for any murder which they should commit on the inhabitants of these states;

For cutting off our trade with all parts of the world;

For imposing taxes on us without our consent;

For depriving us, in many cases, of the benefits of trial by jury;

For transporting us beyond seas, to be tried for pretended offenses;

For abolishing the free system of English laws in a neighboring province, establishing therein an arbitrary government, and enlarging its boundaries, so as to render it at once an example and fit instrument for introducing the same absolute rule into these colonies.

For taking away our charters, abolishing our most valuable laws, and altering fundamentally the forms of our governments;

For suspending our own legislatures, and declaring themselves invested with power to legislate for us in all cases whatsoever.

He has abdicated government here, by declaring us out of his protection and waging war against us.

He has plundered our seas, ravaged our coasts, burned our towns, and destroyed the lives of our people.

He is at this time transporting large armies of foreign mercenaries to complete the works of death, desolation, and tyranny already begun with circumstances of cruelty and perfidy scarcely paralleled in the most barbarous ages, and totally unworthy the head of a civilized nation.

He has constrained our fellow-citizens, taken captive on the high seas, to bear arms against their country, to become the executioners of their friends and brethren, or to fall themselves by their hands.

He has excited domestic insurrection among us, and has endeavored to bring on the inhabitants of our frontiers the merciless Indian savages, whose known rule of warfare is an undistinguished destruction of all ages, sexes, and conditions.

In every stage of these oppressions we have petitioned for redress in the most humble terms; our repeated petitions have been answered only by repeated injury. A prince, whose character is thus marked by every act which may define a tyrant, is unfit to be the ruler of a free people.

Nor have we been wanting in our attentions to our British brethren. We have warned them, from time to time, of attempts by their legislature to extend an unwarrantable jurisdiction over us. We have reminded them of the circumstances of our emigration and settlement here. We have appealed to their native justice and magnanimity; and we have conjured them, by the ties of our common kindred, to disavow these usurpations, which would inevitably interrupt our connections and correspondence. They, too, have been deaf to the voice of justice and of consanguinity. We must, therefore, acquiesce in the necessity which denounces our separation, and hold them, as we hold the rest of mankind, enemies in war, in peace friends.

We, therefore, the representatives of the United States of America, in General Congress assembled, appealing to the Supreme Judge of the world for the rectitude of our intentions, do, in the name and by the authority of the good people of these colonies, solemnly publish and declare, that these United Colonies are, and of right ought to be, FREE AND INDEPENDENT STATES; that they are absolved from all allegiance to the British crown, and that all political connection between them and the state of Great Britain is, and ought to be, totally dissolved; and that, as free and independent states, they have full power to levy war, conclude peace, contract alliances, establish commerce, and do all other acts and things which independent states may of right do. And for the support of this declaration, with a firm reliance on the protection of Divine Providence, we mutually pledge to each other our lives, our fortunes, and our sacred honor.

John Hancock

Button Gwinnett	Francis Lightfoot Lee	Jno. Witherspoon
Lyman Hall	Carter Braxton	Fras. Hopkinson
Geo. Walton	Robt. Morris	John Hart
Wm. Hooper	Benjamin Rush	Abra. Clark
Joseph Hewes	Benja. Franklin	Josiah Bartlett
John Penn	John Morton	Wm. Whipple
Edward Rutledge	Geo. Clymer	Saml. Adams
Thos. Heyward, Junr.	Jas. Smith	John Adams
Thomas Lynch, Junr.	Geo. Taylor	Robt. Treat Paine
Arthur Middleton	James Wilson	Elbridge Gerry
Samuel Chase	Geo. Ross	Step. Hopkins
Wm. Paca	Caesar Rodney	William Ellery
Thos. Stone	Geo. Read	Roger Sherman
Charles Carroll of Carrollton	Tho. M'kean	Sam'el Huntington
George Wythe	Wm. Floyd	Wm. Williams
Richard Henry Lee	Phil. Livingston	Oliver Wolcott
Th. Jefferson	Frans. Lewis	Matthew Thornton
Benj. Harrison	Lewis Morris	
Thos. Nelson, Jr.	Richd. Stockton	

The Articles of Confederation

Between the States of New Hampshire, Massachusetts Bay, Rhode Island and Providence Plantations, Connecticut, New York, New Jersey, Pennsylvania, Delaware, Maryland, Virginia, North Carolina, South Carolina, Georgia

ARTICLE 1

The stile of this confederacy shall be "The United States of America."

ARTICLE 2

Each State retains its sovereignty, freedom and independence, and every power, jurisdiction, and right, which is not by this confederation expressly delegated to the United States, in Congress assembled.

ARTICLE 3

The said states hereby severally enter into a firm league of friendship with each other for their common defence, the security of their liberties and their mutual and general welfare; binding themselves to assist each other against all force offered to, or attacks made upon them, or any of them, on account of religion, sovereignty, trade, or any other pretence whatever.

ARTICLE 4

The better to secure and perpetuate mutual friendship and intercourse among the people of the different states in this union, the free inhabitants of each of these states, paupers, vagabonds, and fugitives from justice excepted, shall be entitled to all privileges and immunities of free citizens in the several states; and the people of each State shall have free ingress and regress to and from any other State, and shall enjoy therein all the privileges of trade and commerce, subject to the same duties, impositions, and restrictions, as the inhabitants thereof respectively; provided, that such restrictions shall not extend so far as to prevent the removal of property imported into any State, to any other State of which the owner is an inhabitant; provided also, that no imposition, duties, or restriction, shall be laid by any State on the property of the United States, or either of them.

If any person guilty of, or charged with treason, felony, or other high misdemeanor in any State, shall flee from justice and be found in any of the United States, he shall, upon demand of the governor or executive power of the State from which he fled, be delivered up and removed to the State having jurisdiction of his offence.

Full faith and credit shall be given in each of these states to the records, acts, and judicial proceedings of the courts and magistrates of every other State.

ARTICLE 5

For the more convenient management of the general interests of the United States, delegates shall be annually appointed, in such manner as the legislature of each State shall direct, to meet in Congress, on the 1st Monday in November in every year, with a power reserved to each State to recall its delegates, or any of them, at any time within the year, and to send others in their stead for the remainder of the year.

No State shall be represented in Congress by less than two, nor by more than seven members; and no person shall be capable of being a delegate for more than three years in any term of six years; nor shall any person, being a delegate, be capable of holding any office under the United States, for which he, or any other for his benefit, receives any salary, fees, or emolument of any kind.

Each State shall maintain its own delegates in a meeting of the states, and while they act as members of the committee of the states.

In determining questions in the United States, in Congress assembled, each State shall have one vote.

Freedom of speech and debate in Congress shall not be impeached or questioned in any court or place out of Congress: and the members of Congress shall be protected in their persons from arrests and imprisonments, during the time of their going to and from, and attendance on Congress, except for treason, felony, or breach of the peace.

ARTICLE 6

No State, without the consent of the United States, in Congress assembled, shall send any embassy to, or receive any embassy from, or enter into any conference, agreement, alliance, or treaty with any king, prince, or state; nor shall any person, holding any office of profit or trust under the United States, or any of them, accept of any present, emolument, office or title, of any kind whatever, from any king, prince, or foreign state; nor shall the United States, in Congress assembled, or any of them, grant any title of nobility.

No two or more states shall enter into any treaty, confederation, or alliance, whatever, between them, without the consent of the United States, in Congress assembled, specifying accurately the purposes for which the same is to be entered into, and how long it shall continue.

No State shall lay any imposts or duties which may interfere with any stipulations in treaties entered into by the United States, in Congress assembled, with any king, prince, or state, in pursuance of any treaties already proposed by Congress to the courts of France and Spain.

No vessels of war shall be kept up in time of peace by any State, except such number only as shall be deemed necessary by the United States, in Congress assembled, for the defence of such State or its trade; nor shall any body of forces be kept up by any State, in time of peace, except such number only as, in the judgment of the United States, in Congress assembled, shall be deemed requisite to garrison the forts necessary for the defence of such State; but every State shall always keep up a well regulated and disciplined militia, sufficiently armed and accoutred, and shall provide, and constantly have ready for use, in public stores, a due number, of field pieces and tents, and a proper quantity of arms, ammunition and camp equipage.

No State shall engage in any war without the consent of the United States, in Congress assembled, unless such State be actually invaded by enemies, or shall have received certain advice of a resolution being formed by some nation of Indians to invade such State, and the danger is so imminent as not to admit of a delay till the United States, in Congress assembled, can be consulted; nor shall any State grant commissions to any ships or vessels of war, nor letters of marque or reprisal, except it be after a declaration of war by the United States, in Congress assembled, and then only against the kingdom or state, and the subjects thereof, against which war has been so declared, and under such regulations as shall be established by the United States, in Congress assembled, unless such States be infested by pirates, in which case vessels of war may be fitted out for that occasion, and kept so long as the danger shall continue, or until the United States, in Congress assembled, shall determine otherwise.

ARTICLE 7

When land forces are raised by any State for the common defence, all officers of or under the rank of colonel, shall be appointed by the legislature of each State respectively, by whom such forces shall be raised, or in such manner as such State shall direct; and all vacancies shall be filled up by the State which first made the appointment.

ARTICLE 8

All charges of war and all other expences, that shall be incurred for the common defence or general welfare, and allowed by the United States, in Congress assembled, shall be defrayed out of a common treasury, which shall be supplied by the several states, in proportion to the value of all land within each State, granted to or surveyed for any person, as such land and the buildings and improvements thereon shall be estimated according to such mode as the United States, in Congress assembled, shall, from time to time, direct and appoint.

The taxes for paying that proportion shall be laid and levied by the authority and direction of the legislatures of the several states, within the time agreed upon by the United States, in Congress assembled.

ARTICLE 9

The United States, in Congress assembled, shall have the sole and exclusive right and power of determining on peace and war, except in the cases mentioned in the 6th article; of sending and receiving ambassadors; entering into treaties and alliances, provided that no treaty of commerce shall be made, whereby the legislative power of the respective states shall be restrained from imposing such imposts and duties on foreigners as their own people are subjected to, or from prohibiting the exportation or importation of any species of goods or commodities whatsoever; of establishing rules for deciding, in all cases, what captures on land or water shall be legal, and in what manner prizes, taken by land or naval forces in the service of the United States, shall be divided or appropriated; of granting letters of marque and reprisal in times of peace; appointing courts for the trial of piracies and felonies committed on the high seas, and establishing courts for receiving and determining, finally, appeals in all cases of captures; provided, that no member of Congress shall be appointed a judge of any of the said courts.

The United States, in Congress assembled, shall also be the last resort on appeal in all disputes and differences now subsisting, or that hereafter may arise between two or more states concerning boundary, jurisdiction or any other cause whatever; which authority shall always be exercised in the manner following: whenever the legislative or executive authority, or lawful agent of any State, in controversy with another, shall present a petition to Congress, stating the matter in question, and praying for a hearing, notice thereof shall be given, by order of Congress, to the legislative or executive authority of the other State in controversy, and a day assigned for the appearance of the parties by their lawful agents, who shall then be directed to appoint, by joint consent, commissioners or judges to constitute a court for hearing and determining the matter in question; but, if they cannot agree, Congress shall name three persons out of each of the United States, and from the list of such persons each party shall alternately strike out one, in the petitioners beginning, until the number shall be reduced to thirteen; and from that number not less than seven, nor more than nine names, as Congress shall direct, shall, in the presence of Congress, be drawn out by lot; and the persons whose names shall be drawn, or any five of them, shall be commissioners or judges to hear and finally determine the controversy, so always as a major part of the judges who shall hear the cause shall agree in the determination; and if either party shall neglect to attend at the day appointed, without shewing reasons which Congress shall judge sufficient, or, being present, shall refuse to strike, the Congress shall proceed to nominate three persons out of each State, and the secretary of Congress shall strike in behalf of such party absent or refusing; and the judgment and sentence of the court to be appointed, in the manner before prescribed, shall be final and conclusive; and if any of the parties shall refuse to submit to the authority of such court, or to appear or defend their claim or cause, the court shall nevertheless proceed to pronounce sentence or judgment, which shall, in like manner, be final and decisive, the judgment or sentence and other proceedings being, in either case, transmitted to Congress, and lodged among the acts of Congress for the security of the parties concerned: provided, that every commissioner, before he sits in judgment, shall take an oath, to be administered by one of the judges of the supreme or superior court of the State where the cause shall be tried, "well and truly to hear and determine the matter in question, according to the best of his judgment, without favor, affection, or hope of reward": provided, also, that no State shall be deprived of territory for the benefit of the United States.

All controversies concerning the private right of soil, claimed under different grants of two or more states, whose jurisdictions, as they may respect such lands and the states which passed such grants, are adjusted, the said grants, or either of them, being at the same time claimed to have originated antecedent to such settlement of jurisdiction, shall, on the petition of either party to the Congress of the United States, be finally determined, as near as may be, in the same manner as is before prescribed for deciding disputes respecting territorial jurisdiction between different states.

The United States, in Congress assembled, shall also have the sole and exclusive right and power of regulating the alloy and value of coin struck by their own authority, or by that of the respective states; fixing the standard of weights and measures throughout the United States; regulating the trade and managing all affairs with the Indians not members of any of the states; provided that the legislative right of any State within its own limits be not infringed or violated; establishing and regulating post offices from one State to another throughout all the United States, and exacting such postage on the papers passing through the same as may be requisite to defray the expences of the said office; appointing all officers of the land forces in the service of the United States, excepting regimental officers; appointing all the officers of the naval forces, and commissioning all officers whatever in the service of the United States; making rules for the government and regulation of the said land and naval forces, and directing their operations.

The United States, in Congress assembled, shall have authority to appoint a committee to sit in the recess of Congress, to be denominated "a Committee of the States," and to consist of one delegate from each State, and to appoint such other committees and civil officers as may be necessary for managing the general affairs of the United States, under their direction; to appoint one of their number to preside; provided that no person be allowed to serve in the office of president more than one year in any term of three years; to ascertain the necessary sums of money to be raised for the service of the United States, and to appropriate and apply the same for defraying the public expences; to borrow money or emit bills on the credit of the United States, transmitting, every half year, to the respective states, an account of the sums of money so borrowed or emitted; to build and equip a navy; to agree upon the number of land forces, and to make requisitions from each State for its quota, in proportion to the number of white inhabitants in such State; which requisitions shall be binding; and, thereupon, the legislature of each State shall appoint the regimental officers, raise the men, and cloathe, arm, and equip them in a soldier-like manner, at the expence of the United States; and the officers and men so cloathed, armed, and equipped, shall march to the place appointed and within the time agreed on by the United States, in Congress assembled; but if the United States, in Congress assembled, shall, on consideration of circumstances, judge proper that any State should not raise men, or should raise a smaller number than its quota, and that any other State should raise a greater number of men than the quota thereof, such extra number shall be raised, officered, cloathed, armed, and equipped in the same manner as the quota of such State, unless the legislature of such State shall judge that such extra number cannot be safely spared out of the same, in which case they shall raise, officer, cloathe, arm, and equip as many of such extra number as they judge can be safely spared. And the officers and men so cloathed, armed, and equipped, shall march to the place appointed and within the time agreed on by the United States, in Congress assembled.

The United States, in Congress assembled, shall never engage in a war, nor grant letters of marque and reprisal in time of peace, nor enter into any treaties or alliances, nor coin money, nor regulate the value thereof, nor ascertain the sums and expences necessary for the defence and welfare of the United States, or any of them: nor emit bills, nor borrow money on the credit of the United States, nor appropriate money, nor agree upon the number of vessels of war to be built or purchased, or the number of land or sea forces to be raised, nor appoint a commander in chief of the army or navy, unless nine states assent to the same; nor shall a question on any other point, except for adjourning from day to day, be determined, unless by the votes of a majority of the United States, in Congress assembled.

The Congress of the United States shall have power to adjourn to any time within the year, and to any place within the United States, so that no period of adjournment be for a longer duration than the space of six months, and shall publish the journal of their proceedings monthly, except such parts thereof, relating to treaties, alliances or military operations, as, in their judgment, require secrecy; and the yeas and nays of the delegates of each State on any question shall be entered on the journal, when it is desired by any delegate; and the delegates of a State, or any of them, at his, or their request, shall be furnished with a transcript of the said journal, except such parts as are above excepted, to lay before the legislatures of the several states.

ARTICLE 10

The committee of the states, or any nine of them, shall be authorized to execute, in the recess of Congress, such of the powers of Congress as the United States, in Congress assembled, by the consent of nine states, shall, from time to time, think expedient to vest them with; provided, that no power be delegated to the said committee for the exercise of which by the articles of confederation, the voice of nine states, in the Congress of the United States assembled, is requisite.

ARTICLE 11

Canada acceding to this confederation, and joining in the measures of the United States, shall be admitted into and entitled to all the advantages of this union; but no other colony shall be admitted into the same, unless such admission be agreed to by nine states.

ARTICLE 12

All bills of credit emitted, monies borrowed and debts contracted by, or under the authority of Congress before the assembling of the United States, in pursuance of the present confederation, shall be deemed and considered as a charge against the United States, for payment and satisfaction whereof the said United States and the public faith are hereby solemnly pledged.

ARTICLE 13

Every State shall abide by the determinations of the United States, in Congress assembled, on all questions which, by this confederation, are submitted to them. And the articles of this confederation shall be inviolably observed by every State, and the union shall be perpetual; nor shall any alteration at any time hereafter be made in any of them, unless such alteration be agreed to in a Congress of the United States, and be afterwards confirmed by the legislatures of every State.

These articles shall be proposed to the legislatures of all the United States, to be considered, and if approved of by them, they are advised to authorize their delegates to ratify the same in the Congress of the United States; which being done, the same shall become conclusive.

The Constitution of the United States of America Preamble

PREAMBLE

We the People of the United States, in Order to form a more perfect Union, establish Justice, insure domestic Tranquility, provide for the common defence, promote the general Welfare, and secure the Blessings of Liberty to ourselves and our Posterity, do ordain and establish this Constitution for the United States of America.

ARTICLE 1

Section 1

All legislative Powers herein granted shall be vested in a Congress of the United States, which shall consist of a Senate and House of Representatives.

Section 2

The House of Representatives shall be composed of Members chosen every second Year by the People of the several States, and the Electors in each State shall have the Qualifications requisite for Electors of the most numerous Branch of the State Legislature.

No Person shall be a Representative who shall not have attained to the Age of twenty five Years, and been seven Years a Citizen of the United States, and who shall not, when elected, be an inhabitant of that State in which he shall be chosen.

Representatives and direct Taxes shall be apportioned among the several States which may be included within this Union, according to their respective Numbers, *which shall be determined by adding to the whole Number of free Persons, including those bound to Service for a Term of Years, and excluding Indians not taxed, three fifths of all other Persons.** The actual Enumeration shall be made within three Years after the first Meeting of the Congress of the United States, and within every subsequent Term of ten Years, in such Manner as they shall by Law direct. The Number of Representatives shall not exceed one for every thirty Thousand, but each State shall have at Least one Representative; *and until such enumeration shall be made, the State of New Hampshire shall be entitled to chuse three, Massachusetts eight, Rhode-Island and Providence Plantations one, Connecticut five, New York six, New Jersey four, Pennsylvania eight, Delaware one, Maryland six, Virginia ten, North Carolina five, South Carolina five, and Georgia three.*

When vacancies happen in the Representation from any State, the Executive Authority thereof shall issue Writs of Election to fill such Vacancies.

The House of Representatives shall chuse their Speaker and other Officers; and shall have the sole Power of Impeachment.

Section 3

The Senate of the United States shall be composed of two Senators from each State, chosen by the Legislature thereof, for six Years; and each Senator shall have one Vote.

Immediately after they shall be assembled in Consequence of the first Election, they shall be divided as equally as may be into three Classes. The Seats of the Senators of the first Class shall be vacated at the Expiration of the second Year, of the second Class at the Expiration of the fourth Year, and of the third Class at the Expiration of the sixth Year so that one third may be chosen every second Year; and if Vacancies happen by Resignation, or otherwise, during the Recess of the Legislature of any state, the Executive thereof may make temporary Appointments until the next Meeting of the Legislature, which shall then fill such Vacancies.

No Person shall be a Senator who shall not have attained to the Age of thirty Years, and been nine Years a Citizen of the United States, and who shall not, when elected, be an Inhabitant of that State for which he shall be chosen.

The Vice President of the United States shall be President of the Senate, but shall have no Vote, unless they be equally divided.

The Senate shall chuse their other Officers, and also a President pro tempore, in the Absence of the Vice President, or when he shall exercise the Office of President of the United States.

The Senate shall have the sole Power to try all Impeachments. When sitting for that Purpose, they shall be on Oath or Affirmation. When the President of the United States is tried the Chief Justice shall preside: And no Person shall be convicted without the Concurrence of two thirds of the Members present.

Judgment in Cases of Impeachment shall not extend further than to removal from Office, and disqualification to hold and enjoy any Office of honor, Trust or Profit under the United States: but the Party convicted shall nevertheless be liable and subject to Indictment, Trial, Judgment and Punishment, according to Law.

---

*Passages no longer in effect are printed in italic type.

Section 4

The Times, Places and Manner of holding Elections for Senators and Representatives, shall be prescribed in each State by the Legislature thereof; but the Congress may at any time by Law make or alter such Regulations, except as to the Places of chusing Senators.

The Congress shall assemble at least once in every Year, *and such Meeting shall be on the first Monday in December, unless they shall by Law appoint a different Day.*

Section 5

Each House shall be the Judge of the Elections, Returns and Qualifications of its own Members, and a Majority of each shall constitute a Quorum to do Business; but a smaller Number may adjourn from day to day, and may be authorized to compel the Attendance of absent Members, in such Manner, and under such Penalties as each House may provide.

Each House may determine the Rules of its Proceedings, punish its Members for disorderly Behaviour, and, with the Concurrence of two thirds, expel a Member.

Each House shall keep a Journal of its Proceedings, and from time to time publish the same, excepting such Parts as may in their Judgment require Secrecy; and the Yeas and Nays of the Members of either House on any question shall, at the Desire of one fifth of those Present, be entered on the Journal.

Neither House, during the Session of Congress, shall, without the Consent of the other, adjourn for more than three days, nor to any other Place than that in which the two Houses shall be sitting.

Section 6

The Senators and Representatives shall receive a Compensation for their Services, to be ascertained by Law, and paid out of the Treasury of the United States. They shall in all Cases, except Treason, Felony and Breach of the Peace, be privileged from Arrest during their Attendance at the Session of their respective Houses, and in going to and returning from the same; and for any Speech or Debate in either House, they shall not be questioned in any other Place.

No Senator or Representative shall, during the Time for which he was elected, be appointed to any civil Office under the Authority of the United States, which shall have been created, or the Emoluments whereof shall have been encreased during such time, and no Person holding any Office under the United States, shall be a Member of either House during his Continuance in Office.

Section 7

All Bills for raising Revenue shall orginate in the House of Representatives; but the Senate may propose or concur with Amendments as on other Bills.

Every Bill which shall have passed the House of Representatives and the Senate, shall, before it become a Law, be presented to the President of the United States; If he approve he shall sign it, but if not he shall return it, with his Objections to the House in which it shall have originated, who shall enter the Objections at large on their Journal, and proceed to reconsider it. If after such Reconsideration two thirds of that House shall agree to pass the Bill, it shall be sent, together with the Objections, to the other House, by which it shall likewise be reconsidered, and if approved by two thirds of that House, it shall become a Law. But in all such Cases the Votes of both Houses shall be determined by yeas and Nays, and the Names of the Persons voting for and against the Bill shall be entered on the Journal of each House respectively. If any Bill shall not be returned by the President within ten Days (Sundays excepted) after it shall have been presented to him, the Same shall be a Law, in like Manner as if he had signed it, unless the Congress by their Adjournment prevent its Return, in which Case it shall not be a Law.

Every Order, Resolution, or Vote to which the Concurrence of the Senate and House of Representatives may be necessary (except on a question of Adjournment) shall be presented to the President of the United States; and before the Same shall take Effect, shall be approved by him, or being disapproved by him, shall be repassed by two thirds of the Senate and House of Representatives, according to the Rules and Limitations prescribed in the Case of a Bill.

Section 8

The Congress shall have Power To lay and collect Taxes, Duties, Imposts and Excises, to pay the Debts and provide for the common Defence and general Welfare of the United States; but all Duties, Imposts and Excises shall be uniform throughout the United States;

To borrow Money on the credit of the United States;

To regulate Commerce with foreign Nations, and among the several States, and with the Indian Tribes;

To establish an uniform Rule of Naturalization, and uniform Laws on the subject of Bankruptcies throughout the United States;

To coin Money, regulate the Value thereof, and of foreign Coin, and fix the Standard of Weights and Measures;

To provide for the Punishment of counterfeiting the Securities and current Coin of the United States;

To establish Post Offices and post Roads;

To promote the Progress of Science and useful Arts, by securing for limited Times to Authors and Inventors the exclusive Right to their respective Writings and Discoveries;

To constitute Tribunals inferior to the supreme Court;

To define and punish Piracies and Felonies committed on the high Seas, and Offences against the Law of Nations;

To declare War, grant Letters of Marque and Reprisal, and make Rules concerning Captures on Land and Water;

To raise and support Armies, but no Appropriation of Money to that Use shall be for a longer Term than two Years;

To provide and maintain a Navy;

To make Rules for the Government and Regulation of the land and naval Forces;

To provide for calling forth the Militia to execute the Laws of the Union, suppress Insurrections and repel Invasions;

To provide for organizing, arming, and disciplining, the Militia, and for governing such Part of them as may be employed in the Service of the United States, reserving to the States respectively, the Appointment of the Officers, and the Authority of training the Militia according to the discipline prescribed by Congress;

To exercise exclusive Legislation in all Cases whatsoever, over such District (not exceeding ten Miles square) as may, by Cession of particular States, and the Acceptance of Congress, become the Seat of the Government of the United States, and to exercise like Authority over all Places purchased by the Consent of the Legislature of the State in which the Same shall be, for the Erection of Forts, Magazines, Arsenals, dock-Yards, and other needful Buildings;—And

To make all Laws which shall be necessary and proper for carrying into Execution the foregoing Powers, and all other Powers vested by this Constitution in the Government of the United States, or in any Department of Officer thereof.

Section 9

The Migration or Importation of such Persons as any of the States now existing shall think proper to admit, shall not be prohibited by the Congress prior to the Year one thousand eight hundred and eight, but a Tax or duty may be imposed on such Importation, not exceeding ten dollars for each Person.

The Privilege of the Writ of Habeas Corpus shall not be suspended, unless when in Cases of Rebellion or Invasion the public Safety may require it.

No Bill of Attainder or ex post facto Law shall be passed.

No Capitation, or other direct, Tax shall be laid, unless in Proportion to the Census or Enumeration herein before directed to be taken.

No Tax or Duty shall be laid on Articles exported from any State.

No Preference shall be given by any Regulation of Commerce or Revenue to the Ports of one State over those of another: nor shall Vessels bound to, or from, one State, be obliged to enter, clear, or pay Duties in another.

No Money shall be drawn from the Treasury, but in Consequence of Appropriations made by Law; and a regular Statement and Account of the Receipts and Expenditures of all public Money shall be published from time to time.

No Title of Nobility shall be granted by the United States: And no Person holding any Office of Profit or Trust under them, shall, without the Consent of the Congress, accept of any present, Emolument, Office, or Title, of any kind whatever, from any King, Prince, or foreign State.

Section 10

No State shall enter into any Treaty, Alliance, or Confederation; grant Letters of Marque and Reprisal; coin Money; emit Bills of Credit; make any Thing but gold and silver Coin a Tender in Payment of Debts; pass any Bill of Attainder, ex post facto Law, or Law impairing the obligation of Contracts, or grant any Title of Nobility.

No State shall, without the Consent of the Congress, lay any Imposts or Duties on Imports or Exports, except what may be absolutely necessary for executing its inspection Laws: and the net Produce of all Duties and Imposts, laid by any State on Imports or Exports, shall be for the Use of the Treasury of the United States; and all such Laws shall be subject to the Revision and Controul of the Congress.

No State shall, without the Consent of Congress, lay any Duty of Tonnage, keep Troops, or Ships of War in time of Peace, enter into any Agreement or Compact with another State, or with a foreign Power, or engage in War, unless actually invaded, or in such imminent Danger as will not admit of delay.

ARTICLE II

Section 1

The executive Power shall be vested in a President of the United States of America. He shall hold his Office during the Term of four Years, and, together with the Vice President, chosen for the same Term, be elected, as follows:

Each State shall appoint, in such Manner as the Legislature thereof may direct, a Number of Electors, equal to the whole Number of Senators and Representatives to which the State may be entitled in the Congress: but no Senator or Representative, or Person holding an Office of Trust or Profit under the United States, shall be appointed an Elector.

The Electors shall meet in their respective States, and vote by Ballot for two Persons, of whom one at least shall not be an Inhabitant of the same State with themselves. And they shall make a List of all the Persons voted for, and of the Number of Votes for each; which List they shall sign and certify, and transmit sealed to the Seat of the Government of the United States, directed to the President of the Senate. The President of the Senate shall, in the Presence of the Senate and House of Representatives, open all the Certificates, and the Votes shall then be counted. The Person having the greatest Number of Votes shall be the President, if such Number be a Majority of the whole number of Electors appointed; and if there be more than one who have such Majority, and have an equal Number of Votes, then the House of Representatives shall immediately chuse by Ballot one of them for President; and if no Person have a Majority, then from the five highest on the List the said House shall in like Manner chuse the President. But in chusing the President, the Votes shall be taken by States, the Representation from each State having one Vote; A quorum for this Purpose shall consist of a Member or Members from two thirds of the States, and a Majority of all the States shall be necessary to a Choice. In every Case, after the Choice of the President, the Person having the greatest Number of Votes of the Electors shall be the Vice President. But if there should remain two or more who have equal Votes, the Senate shall chuse from them by Ballot the Vice President.

The Congress may determine the time of chusing the Electors, and the Day on which they shall give their Votes; which Day shall be the same throughout the United States.

No person except a natural born Citizen, *or a Citizen of the United States, at the time of the Adoption of this Constitution,* shall be eligible to the Office of President; neither shall any Person be eligible to that Office who shall not have attained to the Age of thirty five Years, and been fourteen Years a Resident within the United States.

In Case of the Removal of the President from Office, or of his Death, Resignation, or Inability to discharge the Powers and Duties of the said Office, the Same shall devolve on the Vice President, and the Congress may by Law provide for the Case of Removal, Death, Resignation or Inability, both of the President and Vice President, declaring what Officer shall then act as President, and such Officer shall act accordingly, until the Disability be removed, or a President shall be elected.

The President shall, at stated Times, receive for his Services, a Compensation, which shall neither be encreased nor diminished during the Period for which he shall have been elected, and he shall not receive within that period any other Emolument from the United States, or any of them.

Before he enter on the Execution of his Office, he shall take the following Oath or Affirmation:—"I do solemnly swear (or affirm) that I will faithfully execute the Office of President of the United States, and will to the best of my Ability, preserve, protect and defend the Constitution of the United States."

Section 2

The President shall be Commander in Chief of the Army and Navy of the United States, and of the Militia of the several States, when called into the actual Service of the United States; he may require the Opinion, in writing, of the principal Officer in each of the executive Departments, upon any Subject relating to the Duties of their respective Offices, and he shall have Power to grant Reprieves and Pardons for Offences against the United States, except in Cases of Impeachment.

He shall have Power, by and with the Advice and Consent of the Senate, to make Treaties, provided two thirds of the Senators present concur; and he shall nominate, and by and with the Advice and Consent of the Senate, shall appoint Ambassadors, other public Ministers and Consuls, Judges of the supreme Court, and all other Officers of the United States, whose Appointments are not herein otherwise provided for, and which shall be established by Law: but the Congress may by Law vest the Appointment of such inferior Officers, as they think proper in the President alone, in the Courts of Law, or in the Heads of Departments.

The President shall have Power to fill up all Vacancies that may happen during the Recess of the Senate, by granting Commissions which shall expire at the End of their next Session.

Section 3

He shall from time to time give to the Congress Information of the State of the Union, and recommend to their Consideration such Measures as he shall judge necessary and expedient; he may, on extraordinary Occasions, convene both Houses, or either of them, and in Case of disagreement between them, with Respect to the Time of Adjournment, he may adjourn them to such Time as he shall think proper; he shall receive Ambassadors and other public Ministers; he shall take Care that the Laws be faithfully executed, and shall Commission all the officers of the United States.

Section 4

The President, Vice President and all civil Officers of the United States, shall be removed from Office on Impeachment for, and Conviction of, Treason, Bribery or other high Crimes and Misdemeanors.

ARTICLE III
Section 1

The judicial Power of the United States, shall be vested in one supreme Court, and in such inferior Courts as the Congress may from time to time ordain and establish. The Judges, both of the supreme and inferior Courts, shall hold their offices during good Behaviour, and shall, at stated Times, receive for their Services, a Compensation, which shall not be diminished during their Continuance in Office.

Section 2

The judicial Power shall extend to all Cases, in Law and Equity, arising under this Constitution, the Laws of the United States, and Treaties made, or which shall be made, under their Authority;—to all Cases affecting Ambassadors, other public Ministers and Consuls;—to all Cases of admiralty and maritime Jurisdiction;—to Controversies to which the United States shall be a Party;—to Controversies between two or more States;—between a State and Citizens of another State;—between Citizens of different States;—between Citizens of the same State claiming Lands under Grants of different States, and between a State, or the Citizens thereof, and foreign States, Citizens or Subjects.

In all Cases affecting Ambassadors, other public Ministers and Consuls, and those in which a State shall be Party, the supreme Court shall have original Jurisdiction. In all the other Cases before mentioned, the supreme Court shall have appellate Jurisdiction, both as to Law and Fact, with such Exceptions, and under such Regulations as the Congress shall make.

The Trial of all Crimes, except in Cases of Impeachment, shall be by Jury; and such Trial shall be held in the State where the said Crimes shall have been committed, but when not committed within any State, the Trial shall be at such Place or Places as the Congress may by Law have directed.

Section 3

Treason against the United States, shall consist only in levying War against them, or in adhering to their Enemies, giving them Aid and Comfort. No person shall be convicted of Treason unless on the Testimony of two Witnesses to the same overt Act, or on Confession in open Court.

The Congress shall have Power to declare the Punishment of Treason, but no Attainder of Treason shall work Corruption of Blood, or Forfeiture except during the Life of the Person attainted.

ARTICLE IV
Section 1

Full Faith and Credit shall be given in each State to the public Acts, Records, and judicial Proceedings of every other State. And the Congress may by general Laws prescribe the Manner in which such Acts, Records and Proceedings shall be proved, and the Effect thereof.

Section 2

The Citizens of each State shall be entitled to all Privileges and Immunities of Citizens in the several States.

A Person charged in any State with Treason, Felony, or other Crime, who shall flee from Justice, and be found in another State, shall on Demand of the executive Authority of the State from which he fled, be delivered up, to be removed to the State having Jurisdiction of the Crime.

No Person held to Service or Labour in one State, under the Laws thereof, escaping into another, shall, in Consequence of any Law or Regulation therein, be discharged from such Service or Labour, but shall be delivered up on Claim of the Party to whom such Service or Labour may be due.

Section 3

New States may be admitted by the Congress into this Union; but no new State shall be formed or erected within the Jurisdiction of any other State; nor any State be formed by the Junction of two or more States, or Parts of States, without the Consent of the Legislatures of the States concerned as well as of the Congress.

The Congress shall have Power to dispose of and make all needful Rules and Regulations respecting the Territory or other Property belonging to the United States; and nothing in this Constitution shall be so construed as to Prejudice any Claims of the United States, or of any particular States.

Section 4

The United States shall guarantee to every State in this Union a Republican Form of Government, and shall protect each of them against Invasion; and on Application of the Legislature, or of the Executive (when the Legislature cannot be convened) against domestic violence.

ARTICLE V

The Congress, whenever two thirds of both Houses shall deem it necessary, shall propose Amendments to this Constitution, or, on the Application of the Legislatures of two thirds of the several States, shall call a Convention for proposing Amendments, which, in either Case, shall be valid to all Intents and Purposes, as Part of this Constitution, when ratified by the Legislatures of three fourths of the several States, or by Conventions in three fourths thereof, as the one or the other Mode of Ratification may be proposed by the Congress; Provided that *no Amendment which may be made prior to the Year One thousand eight hundred and eight shall in any Manner affect the first and fourth Clauses in the Ninth Section of the first Article; and that no State, without its Consent, shall be deprived of its equal Suffrage in the Senate.*

ARTICLE VI

All Debts contracted and Engagements entered into, before the Adoption of this Constitution, shall be as valid against the United States under this Constitution, as under the Confederation.

This Constitution, and Laws of the United States which shall be made in Pursuance thereof; and all Treaties made, or which shall be made, under the Authority of the United States, shall be the supreme Law of the Land; and the Judges in every State shall be bound thereby, any Thing in the Constitution or Laws of any State to the Contrary notwithstanding.

The Senators and Representatives before mentioned, and the Members of the several State Legislatures, and all executive and Judicial Officers, both of the United States and of the several States, shall be bound by Oath or Affirmation, to support this Constitution; but no religious Test shall ever be required as a Qualification to any Office of public Trust under the United States.

ARTICLE VII

The Ratification of the Conventions of nine States, shall be sufficient for the Establishment of this Constitution between the States so ratifying the Same.

Done in Convention by the Unanimous Consent of the States present the Seventeenth Day of September in the Year of our Lord one thousand seven hundred and Eighty seven and of the Independence of the United States of America the Twelfth* IN WITNESS whereof We have hereunto subscribed our Names,

---

*The Constitution was submitted on September 17, 1787, by the Constitutional Convention, was ratified by the Convention of several states at various dates up to May 29, 1790, and became effective on March 4, 1789.

George Washington
President and Deputy from Virginia

Delaware
George Read
Gunning Bedford, Jr.
John Dickinson
Richard Bassett
Jacob Broom

Maryland
James McHenry
Daniel of St. Thomas Jenifer
Daniel Carroll

Virginia
John Blair
James Madison, Jr

North Carolina
William Blount
Richard Dobbs Spraight
Hugh Williamson

South Carolina
John Rutledge
Charles Cotesworth
  Pinckney
Charles Pinckney
Pierce Butler

Georgia
William Few
Abraham Baldwin

New Hampshire
John Langdon
Nicholas Gilman

Massachusetts
Nathaniel Gorham
Rufus King

Connecticut
William Samuel Johnson
Roger Sherman

New York
Alexander Hamilton

New Jersey
William Livingston
David Brearley
William Paterson
Jonathan Dayton

Pennsylvania
Benjamin Franklin
Thomas Mifflin
Robert Morris
George Clymer
Thomas FitzSimons
Jared Ingersoll
James Wilson
Gouverneur Morris

Amendments to the Constitution

AMENDMENT I

Congress shall make no law respecting an establishment of religion, or prohibiting the free exercise thereof; or abridging the freedom of speech, or of the press; or the right of the people peaceably to assemble, and to petition the Government for a redress of grievances.

AMENDMENT II

A well regulated Militia being necessary to the security of a free State, the right of the people to keep and bear Arms, shall not be infringed.

AMENDMENT III

No Soldier shall, in time of peace be quartered in any house, without the consent of the Owner, nor in time of war, but in a manner to be prescribed by law.

AMENDMENT IV

The right of the people to be secure in their persons, houses, papers, and effects, against unreasonable searches and seizures, shall not be violated, and no Warrants shall issue, but upon probable cause, supported by Oath or affirmation, and particularly describing the place to be searched, and the persons or things to be seized.

AMENDMENT V

No person shall be held to answer for a capital, or otherwise infamous crime, unless on a presentment or indictment of a Grand Jury, except in cases arising in the land or naval forces, or in the Militia, when in actual service in time of War or public danger; nor shall any person be subject for the same offense to be twice put in jeopardy of life or limb; nor shall be compelled in any criminal case to be a witness against himself, nor be deprived of life, liberty, or property, without due process of law; nor shall private property be taken for public use, without just compensation.

AMENDMENT VI

In all criminal prosecutions, the accused shall enjoy the right to a speedy and public trial, by an impartial jury of the State and district wherein the crime shall have been committed, which district shall have been previously ascertained by law, and to be informed of the nature and cause of the accusation; to be confronted with the witnesses against him; to have compulsory process for obtaining witnesses in his favor, and to have the Assistance of Counsel for his defence.

AMENDMENT VII

In Suits at common law, where the value in controversy shall exceed twenty dollars, the right of trial by jury shall be preserved, and no fact tried by a jury, shall be otherwise reexamined in any Court of the United States, than according to the rules of the common law.

AMENDMENT VIII

Excessive bail shall not be required, nor excessive fines imposed, nor cruel and unusual punishments inflicted.

AMENDMENT IX

The enumeration in the Constitution, of certain rights, shall not be construed to deny or disparage others retained by the people.

AMENDMENT X*

The powers not delegated to the United States by the Constitution, nor prohibited by it to the States, are reserved to the States respectively, or to the people.

AMENDMENT XI
[ADOPTED 1798]

The Judicial power of the United States shall not be construed to extend to any suit in law or equity, commenced or prosecuted against one of the United States by Citizens of another State, or by Citizens or Subjects of any Foreign State.

AMENDMENT XII
[ADOPTED 1804]

The Electors shall meet in their respective states, and vote by ballot for President and Vice President, one of whom, at least, shall not be an inhabitant of the same state with themselves; they shall name in their ballots the person voted for as President, and in distinct ballots the person voted for as Vice President, and they shall make distinct lists of all persons voted for as President, and of all persons voted for as Vice President, and of the number of votes for each, which lists they shall sign and certify, and transmit sealed to the seat of the government of the United States, directed to the President of the Senate;—The President of the Senate shall, in the presence of the Senate and House of Representatives, open all the certificates and the votes shall then be counted;—The person having the greatest number of votes for President, shall be the President, if such number be a majority of the whole number of Electors appointed; and if no person have such majority, then

---

*The first ten amendments (the Bill of Rights) were ratified and their adoption was certified on December 15, 1791.

from the persons having the highest numbers not exceeding three on the list of those voted for as President, the House of Representatives shall choose immediately, by ballot, the President. But in choosing the President, the votes shall be taken by states, the representation from each state having one vote; a quorum for this purpose shall consist of a member or members from two-thirds of the states, and a majority of all the states shall be necessary to a choice. And if the House of Representatives shall not choose a President whenever the right of choice shall devolve upon them, before the fourth day of March next following, then the Vice President shall act as President, as in the case of the death or other constitutional disability of the President.—The person having the greatest number of votes as Vice President, shall be the Vice President, if such number be a majority of the whole number of Electors appointed, and if no person have a majority, then from the two highest numbers on the list, the Senate shall choose the Vice President; a quorum for the purpose shall consist of two-thirds of the whole number of Senators, and a majority of the whole number shall be necessary to a choice. But no person constitutionally ineligible to the office of President shall be eligible to that of Vice President of the United States.

AMENDMENT XIII
[ADOPTED 1865]

Section 1

Neither slavery nor involuntary servitude, except as a punishment for crime whereof the party shall have been duly convicted, shall exist within the United States, or any place subject to their jurisdiction.

Section 2

Congress shall have power to enforce this article by appropriate legislation.

AMENDMENT XIV
[ADOPTED 1868]

Section 1

All persons born or naturalized in the United States, and subject to the jurisdiction thereof, are citizens of the United States and of the State wherein they reside. No State shall make or enforce any law which shall abridge the privileges or immunities of citizens of the United States; nor shall any State deprive any person of life, liberty, or property, without due process of law; nor deny to any person within its jurisdiction the equal protection of the laws.

Section 2

Representatives shall be apportioned among the several States according to their respective numbers, counting the whole number of persons in each State, excluding Indians not taxed. But when the right to vote at any election for the choice of electors for President and Vice President of the United States, Representatives in Congress, the Executive and Judicial officers of a State, or the members of the Legislature thereof, is denied to any of the male inhabitants of such State, being twenty-one years of age, and citizens of the United States, or in any way abridged, except for participation in rebellion, or other crime, the basis of representation therein shall be reduced in the proportion which the number of such male citizens shall bear to the whole number of male citizens twenty-one years of age in such State.

Section 3

No person shall be a Senator or Representative in Congress, or elector of President and Vice President, or hold any office, civil or military, under the United States, or under any State, who, having previously taken an oath, as a member of Congress, or as an officer of the United States, or as a member of any State legislature, or as an executive or judicial officer of any State, to support the Constitution of the United States, shall have engaged in insurrection or rebellion against the same, or given aid or comfort to the enemies thereof. But Congress may by a vote of two-thirds of each House, remove such disability.

Section 4

The validity of the public debt of the United States, authorized by law, including debts incurred for payment of pensions and bounties for services in suppressing insurrection or rebellion, shall not be questioned. But neither the United States nor any State shall assume or pay any debt or obligation incurred in aid of insurrection or rebellion against the United States, or any claim for the loss or emancipation of any slave; but all such debts, obligations and claims shall be held illegal and void.

Section 5

The Congress shall have power to enforce, by appropriate legislation, the provisions of this article.

AMENDMENT XV
[ADOPTED 1870]

Section 1

The right of citizens of the United States to vote shall not be denied or abridged by the United States or by any State on account of race, color, or previous condition of servitude.

Section 2

The Congress shall have power to enforce this article by appropriate legislation.

AMENDMENT XVI

[ADOPTED 1913]

The Congress shall have power to lay and collect taxes on incomes, from whatever source derived, without apportionment among the several States, and without regard to any census or enumeration.

AMENDMENT XVII

[ADOPTED 1913]

The Senate of the United States shall be composed of two Senators from each State, elected by the people thereof, for six years; and each Senator shall have one vote. The electors in each State shall have the qualifications requisite for electors of the most numerous branch of the State legislatures.

When vacancies happen in the representation of any State in the Senate, the executive authority of such State shall issue writs of election to fill such vacancies: Provided, That the legislature of any State may empower the executive thereof to make temporary appointments until the people fill the vacancies by election as the legislature may direct.

This amendment shall not be so construed as to affect the election or term of any Senator chosen before it becomes valid as part of the Constitution.

AMENDMENT XVIII

[ADOPTED 1919, REPEALED 1933]

Section 1

After one year from the ratification of this article the manufacture, sale, or transportation of intoxicating liquors within, the importation thereof into, or the exportation thereof from the United States and all territory subject to the jurisdiction thereof for beverage purposes is hereby prohibited.

Section 2

The Congress and the several States shall have concurrent power to enforce this article by appropriate legislation.

Section 3

This article shall be inoperative unless it shall have been ratified as an amendment to the Constitution by the legislatures of the several States, as provided in the Constitution, within seven years from the date of the submission hereof to the States by the Congress.

AMENDMENT XIX

[ADOPTED 1920]

The right of citizens of the United States to vote shall not be denied or abridged by the United States or by any State on account of sex.

Congress shall have power to enforce this article by appropriate legislation.

AMENDMENT XX

[ADOPTED 1933]

Section 1

The terms of the President and Vice President shall end at noon on the 20th day of January, and the terms of Senators and Representatives at noon on the 3d day of January, of the years in which such terms would have ended if this article had not been ratified and the terms of their successors shall then begin.

Section 2

The Congress shall assemble at least once in every year, and such meeting shall begin at noon on the 3d day of January, unless they shall by law appoint a different day.

Section 3

If, at the time fixed for the beginning of the term of the President, the President elect shall have died, the Vice President elect shall become President. If a President shall not have been chosen before the time fixed for the beginning of his term, or if the President elect shall have failed to qualify, then the Vice President elect shall act as President until a President shall have qualified; and the Congress may by law provide for the case wherein neither a President elect nor a Vice President elect shall have qualified, declaring who shall then act as President, or the manner in which one who is to act shall be selected, and such person shall act accordingly until a President or Vice President shall have qualified.

Section 4

The Congress may by law provide for the case of the death of any of the persons from whom the House of Representatives may choose a President whenever the right of choice shall have devolved upon them, and for the case of the death of any of the persons from whom the Senate may choose a Vice President whenever the right of choice shall have devolved upon them.

Section 5

Sections 1 and 2 shall take effect on the 15th day of October following the ratification of this article.

Section 6

This article shall be inoperative unless it shall have been ratified as an amendment to the Constitution by the legislatures of three fourths of the several States within seven years from the date of its submission.

AMENDMENT XXI

[ADOPTED 1933]

Section 1

The eighteenth article of amendment to the Constitution of the United States is hereby repealed.

Section 2

The transportation or importation into any State, Territory, or possession of the United States for delivery or use therein of intoxicating liquors in violation of the laws thereof, is hereby prohibited.

Section 3

This article shall be inoperative unless it shall have been ratified as an amendment to the Constitution by conventions in the several States, as provided in the Constitution, within seven years from the date of the submission hereof to the States by the Congress.

AMENDMENT XXII

[ADOPTED 1951]

Section 1

No person shall be elected to the office of the President more than twice, and no person who has held the office of President, or acted as President, for more than two years of a term to which some other person was elected President shall be elected to the office of the President more than once. But this Article shall not apply to any person holding the office of President when this Article was proposed by the Congress, and shall not prevent any person who may be holding the office of President, or acting as President, during the term within which this Article becomes operative from holding the office of President or acting as President during the remainder of such term.

Section 2

This article shall be inoperative unless it shall have been ratified as an amendment to the Constitution by the legislatures of three-fourths of the several States within seven years from the date of its submission to the States by the Congress.

AMENDMENT XXIII

[ADOPTED 1961]

Section 1

The District constituting the seat of Government of the United States shall appoint in such manner as the Congress shall direct:

A number of electors of President and Vice President equal to the whole number of Senators and Representatives in Congress to which the District would be entitled if it were a State, but in no event more than the least populous State; they shall be in addition to those appointed by the States, but they shall be considered, for the purposes of the election of President and Vice President, to be electors appointed by a State; and they shall meet in the District and perform such duties as provided by the twelfth article of amendment.

Section 2

The Congress shall have power to enforce this article by appropriate legislation.

AMENDMENT XXIV

[ADOPTED 1964]

Section 1

The right of citizens of the United States to vote in any primary or other election for President or Vice President, for electors for President or Vice President, or for Senator or Representative in Congress, shall not be denied or abridged by the United States or any state by reason of failure to pay any poll tax or other tax.

Section 2

The Congress shall have the power to enforce this article by appropriate legislation.

AMENDMENT XXV

[ADOPTED 1967]

Section 1

In case of the removal of the President from office or his death or resignation, the Vice President shall become President.

Section 2

Whenever there is a vacancy in the office of the Vice President, the President shall nominate a Vice President who shall take the office upon confirmation by a majority vote of both houses of Congress.

Section 3

Whenever the President transmits to the President pro tempore of the Senate and the Speaker of the House of Representatives his written declaration that he is unable to discharge the powers and duties of his office, and until he transmits to them a written declaration to the contrary, such powers and duties shall be discharged by the Vice President as Acting President.

Section 4

Whenever the Vice President and a majority of either the principal officers of the executive departments or of such other body as Congress may by law provide, transmit to the President pro tempore of the Senate and the Speaker of the House of Representatives their written declaration that the President is unable to discharge the powers and duties of his office, the Vice President shall immediately assume the powers and duties of the office as Acting President.

Thereafter, when the President transmits to the President pro tempore of the Senate and the Speaker of the House of Representatives his written declaration that no inability exists, he shall resume the powers and duties of his office unless the Vice President and a majority of either the principal officers of the executive department or of such other body as Congress may by law provide, transmit within four days to the President pro tempore of the Senate and the Speaker of the House of Representatives their written declaration that the President is unable to discharge the powers and duties of his office. Thereupon Congress shall decide the issue, assembling within 48 hours for that purpose if not in session. If the Congress, within 21 days after receipt of the latter written declaration, or, if Congress is not in session, within 21 days after Congress is required to assemble, determines by two-thirds vote of both houses that the President is unable to discharge the powers and duties of his office, the Vice President shall continue to discharge the same as Acting President; otherwise, the President shall resume the powers and duties of his office.

AMENDMENT XXVI
[ADOPTED 1971]

Section 1

The right of citizens of the United States, who are 18 years of age or older, to vote shall not be denied or abridged by the United States or any state on account of age.

Section 2

The Congress shall have the power to enforce this article by appropriate legislation.

AMENDMENT XXVII
[ADOPTED 1992]

No law, varying the compensation for the services of the Senators and Representatives shall take effect, until an election of Representatives shall have intervened.

Presidential Elections

Year	Candidates	Parties	Popular Vote	Electoral Vote	Voter Participation
1789	**George Washington**		*	69	
	John Adams			34	
	Others			35	
1792	**George Washington**		*	132	
	John Adams			77	
	George Clinton			50	
	Others			5	
1796	**John Adams**	**Federalist**	*	71	
	Thomas Jefferson	Democratic-Republican		68	
	Thomas Pinckney	Federalist		59	
	Aaron Burr	Dem.-Rep.		30	
	Others			48	
1800	**Thomas Jefferson**	**Dem.-Rep.**	*	73	
	Aaron Burr	Dem.-Rep.		73	
	John Adams	Federalist		65	
	C. C. Pinckney	Federalist		64	
	John Jay	Federalist		1	
1804	**Thomas Jefferson**	**Dem.-Rep.**	*	162	
	C. C. Pinckney	Federalist		14	
1808	**James Madison**	**Dem.-Rep.**	*	122	
	C. C. Pinckney	Federalist		47	
	George Clinton	Dem.-Rep.		6	
1812	**James Madison**	**Dem.-Rep.**	*	128	
	De Witt Clinton	Federalist		89	
1816	**James Monroe**	**Dem.-Rep.**	*	183	
	Rufus King	Federalist		34	
1820	**James Monroe**	**Dem.-Rep.**	*	231	
	John Quincy Adams	Dem.-Rep.		1	
1824	**John Quincy Adams**	**Dem.-Rep.**	108,740 (31%)	84	26.9%
	Andrew Jackson	Dem.-Rep.	153,544 (44%)	99	
	William H. Crawford	Dem.-Rep.	40,856 (12%)	41	
	Henry Clay	Dem.-Rep.	47,531 (14%)	37	
1828	**Andrew Jackson**	**Democratic**	647,286 (56.0%)	178	57.6%
	John Quincy Adams	National Republican	508,064 (44.0%)	83	
1832	**Andrew Jackson**	**Democratic**	688,242 (54.2%)	219	55.4%
	Henry Clay	National Republican	473,462 (37.4%)	49	
	John Floyd	Independent		11	
	William Wirt	Anti-Mason	101,051 (7.8%)	7	

Year	Candidates	Parties	Popular Vote	Electoral Vote	Voter Participation
1836	**Martin Van Buren**	**Democratic**	**762,198 (50.8%)**	**170**	57.8%
	William Henry Harrison	Whig	549,508 (36.6%)	73	
	Hugh L. White	Whig	145,342 (9.7%)	26	
	Daniel Webster	Whig	41,287 (2.7%)	14	
	W. P. Magnum	Independent		11	
1840	**William Henry Harrison**	**Whig**	**1,274,624 (53.1%)**	**234**	80.2%
	Martin Van Buren	Democratic	1,127,781 (46.9%)	60	
	J. G. Birney	Liberty	7069	—	
1844	**James K. Polk**	**Democratic**	**1,338,464 (49.6%)**	**170**	78.9%
	Henry Clay	Whig	1,300,097 (48.1%)	105	
	J. G. Birney	Liberty	62,300 (2.3%)	—	
1848	**Zachary Taylor**	**Whig**	**1,360,967 (47.4%)**	**163**	72.7%
	Lewis Cass	Democratic	1,222,342 (42.5%)	127	
	Martin Van Buren	Free-Soil	291,263 (10.1%)	—	
1852	**Franklin Pierce**	**Democratic**	**1,601,274 (50.8%)**	**254**	69.6%
	Winfield Scott	Whig	1,386,580 (43.9%)	42	
	John P. Hale	Free-Soil	155,825 (5.0%)	—	
1856	**James Buchanan**	**Democratic**	**1,832,955 (45.3%)**	**174**	78.9%
	John C. Frémont	Republican	1,339,932 (33.1%)	114	
	Millard Fillmore	American	871,731 (21.6%)	8	
1860	**Abraham Lincoln**	**Republican**	**1,865,593 (39.8%)**	**180**	81.2%
	Stephen A. Douglas	Democratic	1,382,713 (29.5%)	12	
	John C. Breckinridge	Democratic	848,356 (18.1%)	72	
	John Bell	Union	592,906 (12.6%)	39	
1864	**Abraham Lincoln**	**Republican**	**2,213,655 (55.0%)**	**212**[†]	73.8%
	George B. McClellan	Democratic	1,805,237 (45.0%)	21	
1868	**Ulysses S. Grant**	**Republican**	**3,013,421 (53%)**	**214**	78.1%
	Horatio Seymour	Democratic	2,706,829 (47%)	80	
1872	**Ulysses S. Grant**	**Republican**	**3,597,132 (55.6%)**	**286**	71.3%
	Horace Greeley	Dem.; Liberal Republican	2,834,761 (43.8%)	66[‡]	
1876	**Rutherford B. Hayes**[§]	**Republican**	**4,036,572 (48.0%)**	**185**	81.8%
	Samuel J. Tilden	Democratic	4,284,020 (51.0%)	184	
1880	**James A. Garfield**	**Republican**	**4,454,416 (48.5%)**	**214**	79.4%
	Winfield S. Hancock	Democratic	4,444,952 (48.1%)	155	
1884	**Grover Cleveland**	**Democratic**	**4,874,986 (48.5%)**	**219**	77.5%
	James G. Blaine	Republican	4,851,981 (48.2%)	182	
1888	**Benjamin Harrison**	**Republican**	**5,439,853 (47.9%)**	**233**	79.3%
	Grover Cleveland	Democratic	5,540,309 (48.6%)	168	

Year	Candidates	Parties	Popular Vote	Electoral Vote	Voter Participation
1892	**Grover Cleveland**	**Democratic**	**5,556,918 (46.1%)**	**277**	**74.7%**
	Benjamin Harrison	Republican	5,176,108 (43.0%)	145	
	James B. Weaver	People's	1,041,028 (9%)	22	
1896	**William McKinley**	**Republican**	**7,104,779 (51.1%)**	**271**	**79.3%**
	William Jennings Bryan	Democratic People's	6,502,925 (47.7%)	176	
1900	**William McKinley**	**Republican**	**7,207,923 (51.7%)**	**292**	**73.2%**
	William Jennings Bryan	Dem.-Populist	6,358,133 (45.5%)	155	
1904	**Theodore Roosevelt**	**Republican**	**7,623,486 (57.9%)**	**336**	**65.2%**
	Alton B. Parker	Democratic	5,077,911 (37.6%)	140	
	Eugene V. Debs	Socialist	402,400 (3.0%)	—	
1908	**William H. Taft**	**Republican**	**7,678,908 (51.6%)**	**321**	**65.4%**
	William Jennings Bryan	Democratic	6,409,104 (43.1%)	162	
	Eugene V. Debs	Socialist	402,820 (2.8%)	—	
1912	**Woodrow Wilson**	**Democratic**	**6,296,547 (41.9%)**	**435**	**58.8%**
	Theodore Roosevelt	Progressive	4,118,571 (27.4%)	88	
	William H. Taft	Republican	3,486,720 (23.2%)	8	
	Eugene V. Debs	Socialist	900,672 (6.0%)	—	
1916	**Woodrow Wilson**	**Democratic**	**9,129,606 (49.4%)**	**277**	**61.6%**
	Charles E. Hughes	Republican	8,538,221 (46.2%)	254	
	A. L. Benson	Socialist	585,113 (3.2%)	—	
1920	**Warren G. Harding**	**Republican**	**16,152,200 (60.4%)**	**404**	**49.2%**
	James M. Cox	Democratic	9,147,353 (34.2%)	127	
	Eugene V. Debs	Socialist	917,799 (3.4%)	—	
1924	**Calvin Coolidge**	**Republican**	**15,725,016 (54.0%)**	**382**	**48.9%**
	John W. Davis	Democratic	8,386,503 (28.8%)	136	
	Robert M. La Follette	Progressive	4,822,856 (16.6%)	13	
1928	**Herbert Hoover**	**Republican**	**21,391,381 (58.2%)**	**444**	**56.9%**
	Alfred E. Smith	Democratic	15,016,443 (40.9%)	87	
	Norman Thomas	Socialist	267,835 (0.7%)	—	
1932	**Franklin D. Roosevelt**	**Democratic**	**22,821,857 (57.4%)**	**472**	**56.9%**
	Herbert Hoover	Republican	15,761,841 (39.7%)	59	
	Norman Thomas	Socialist	884,781 (2.2%)	—	
1936	**Franklin D. Roosevelt**	**Democratic**	**27,751,597 (60.8%)**	**523**	**61.0%**
	Alfred M. Landon	Republican	16,679,583 (36.5%)	8	
	William Lemke	Union	882,479 (1.9%)	—	
1940	**Franklin D. Roosevelt**	**Democratic**	**27,244,160 (54.8%)**	**449**	**62.5%**
	Wendell L. Willkie	Republican	22,305,198 (44.8%)	82	
1944	**Franklin D. Roosevelt**	**Democratic**	**25,602,504 (53.5%)**	**432**	**55.9%**
	Thomas E. Dewey	Republican	22,006,285 (46.0%)	99	

Year	Candidates	Parties	Popular Vote	Electoral Vote	Voter Participation
1948	**Harry S Truman**	**Democratic**	**24,105,695 (49.5%)**	**304**	**53.0%**
	Thomas E. Dewey	Republican	21,969,170 (45.1%)	189	
	J. Strom Thurmond	State-Rights Democratic	1,169,021 (2.4%)	38	
	Henry A. Wallace	Progressive	1,157,326 (2.4%)	—	
1952	**Dwight D. Eisenhower**	**Republican**	**33,778,963 (55.1%)**	**442**	**63.3%**
	Adlai E. Stevenson	Democratic	27,314,992 (44.4%)	89	
1956	**Dwight D. Eisenhower**	**Republican**	**35,575,420 (57.6%)**	**457**	**60.6%**
	Adlai E. Stevenson	Democratic	26,033,066 (42.1%)	73	
	Other	—	—	1	
1960	**John F. Kennedy**	**Democratic**	**34,227,096 (49.9%)**	**303**	**64%**
	Richard M. Nixon	Republican	34,108,546 (49.6%)	219	
	Other	—	—	15	
1964	**Lyndon B. Johnson**	**Democratic**	**43,126,506 (61.1%)**	**486**	**61.7%**
	Barry M. Goldwater	Republican	27,176,799 (38.5%)	52	
1968	**Richard M. Nixon**	**Republican**	**31,785,480 (44%)**	**301**	**60.6%**
	Hubert H. Humphrey	Democratic	31,275,166 (42%)	191	
	George Wallace	American Indep.	9,906,473 (14%)	46	
1972	**Richard M. Nixon**	**Republican**	**46,740,323 (60.7%)**	**520**	**55.2%**
	George S. McGovern	Democratic	28,901,598 (37.5%)	17	
	Other	—	—	1	
1976	**Jimmy Carter**	**Democratic**	**40,828,587 (50.0%)**	**297**	**53.5%**
	Gerald R. Ford	Republican	39,147,613 (47.9%)	241	
	Other	—	1,575,459 (2.1%)	—	
1980	**Ronald Reagan**	**Republican**	**43,901,812 (50.7%)**	**489**	**52.6%**
	Jimmy Carter	Democratic	35,483,820 (41.0%)	49	
	John B. Anderson	Independent	5,719,437 (6.6%)	—	
	Ed Clark	Libertarian	921,188 (1.1%)	—	
1984	**Ronald Reagan**	**Republican**	**54,455,075 (59.0%)**	**525**	**53.3%**
	Walter Mondale	Democratic	37,577,185 (41.0%)	13	
1988	**George H. W. Bush**	**Republican**	**48,886,097 (53.4%)**	**426**	**50.3%**
	Michael S. Dukakis	Democratic	41,809,074 (45.6%)	111	
1992	**William J. Clinton**	**Democratic**	**44,908,254 (43%)**	**370**	**55.1%**
	George H. W. Bush	Republican	39,102,343 (37.5%)	168	
	Ross Perot	Independent	19,741,065 (18.9%)	—	
1996	**William J. Clinton**	**Democratic**	**45,590,703 (50%)**	**379**	**49%**
	Robert Dole	Republican	37,816,307 (41%)	159	
	Ross Perot	Reform	7,866,284 (8%)	—	
2000	**George W. Bush**	**Republican**	**50,456,062 (47.88%)**	**271**	**49.3%**
	Al Gore	Democratic	50,996,582 (48.39%)	266‖	
	Ralph Nader	Green	82,955 (2.72%)	—	
	Other		834,774 (less than 1%)	—	

Year	Candidates	Parties	Popular Vote	Electoral Vote	Voter Participation
2004	**George W. Bush**	**Republican**	**60,934,251 (51.0%)**	**286**	**55.6%**
	John F. Kerry	Democratic	57,765,291 (48.0%)	252	
	Ralph Nader	Independent	405,933 (less than 1%)	—	
2008	**Barack H. Obama**	**Democratic**	**69,456,897**	**365**	**56.8%**
	John McCain	Republican	59,934,814	173	
	Ralph Nader	Independent	738,475	0	

*Electors selected by state legislatures.

†Eleven secessionist states did not participate.

‡Greeley died before the electoral college met. His electoral votes were divided among the four minor candidates.

§Contested result settled by special election.

‖One District of Columbia Gore elector abstained.

Presidents and Vice Presidents

	President	Vice President	Term
1.	George Washington	John Adams	1789–1793
	George Washington	John Adams	1793–1797
2.	John Adams	Thomas Jefferson	1797–1801
3.	Thomas Jefferson	Aaron Burr	1801–1805
	Thomas Jefferson	George Clinton	1805–1809
4.	James Madison	George Clinton (d. 1812)	1809–1813
	James Madison	Elbridge Gerry (d. 1814)	1813–1817
5.	James Monroe	Daniel Tompkins	1817–1821
	James Monroe	Daniel Tompkins	1821–1825
6.	John Quincy Adams	John C. Calhoun	1825–1829
7.	Andrew Jackson	John C. Calhoun	1829–1833
	Andrew Jackson	Martin Van Buren	1833–1837
8.	Martin Van Buren	Richard M. Johnson	1837–1841
9.	William H. Harrison (d. 1841)	John Tyler	1841
10.	John Tyler	—	1841–1845
11.	James K. Polk	George M. Dallas	1845–1849
12.	Zachary Taylor (d. 1850)	Millard Fillmore	1849–1850
13.	Millard Fillmore	—	1850–1853
14.	Franklin Pierce	William R. King (d. 1853)	1853–1857
15.	James Buchanan	John C. Breckinridge	1857–1861
16.	Abraham Lincoln	Hannibal Hamlin	1861–1865
	Abraham Lincoln (d. 1865)	Andrew Johnson	1865
17.	Andrew Johnson	—	1865–1869
18.	Ulysses S. Grant	Schuyler Colfax	1869–1873
	Ulysses S. Grant	Henry Wilson (d. 1875)	1873–1877
19.	Rutherford B. Hayes	William A. Wheeler	1877–1881
20.	James A. Garfield (d. 1881)	Chester A. Arthur	1881
21.	Chester A. Arthur	—	1881–1885
22.	Grover Cleveland	Thomas A. Hendricks (d. 1885)	1885–1889
23.	Benjamin Harrison	Levi P. Morton	1889–1893
24.	Grover Cleveland	Adlai E. Stevenson	1893–1897
25.	William McKinley	Garret A. Hobart (d. 1899)	1897–1901
	William McKinley (d. 1901)	Theodore Roosevelt	1901
26.	Theodore Roosevelt	—	1901–1905
	Theodore Roosevelt	Charles Fairbanks	1905–1909
27.	William H. Taft	James S. Sherman (d. 1912)	1909–1913
28.	Woodrow Wilson	Thomas R. Marshall	1913–1917
	Woodrow Wilson	Thomas R. Marshall	1917–1921
29.	Warren G. Harding (d. 1923)	Calvin Coolidge	1921–1923
30.	Calvin Coolidge	—	1923–1925

	President	Vice President	Term
	Calvin Coolidge	Charles G. Dawes	1925–1929
31.	Herbert Hoover	Charles Curtis	1929–1933
32.	Franklin D. Roosevelt	John N. Garner	1933–1937
	Franklin D. Roosevelt	John N. Garner	1937–1941
	Franklin D. Roosevelt	Henry A. Wallace	1941–1945
	Franklin D. Roosevelt (d. 1945)	Harry S Truman	1945
33.	Harry S Truman	—	1945–1949
	Harry S Truman	Alben W. Barkley	1949–1953
34.	Dwight D. Eisenhower	Richard M. Nixon	1953–1957
	Dwight D. Eisenhower	Richard M. Nixon	1957–1961
35.	John F. Kennedy (d. 1963)	Lyndon B. Johnson	1961–1963
36.	Lyndon B. Johnson	—	1963–1965
	Lyndon B. Johnson	Hubert H. Humphrey	1965–1969
37.	Richard M. Nixon	Spiro T. Agnew	1969–1973
	Richard M. Nixon (resigned 1974)	Gerald R. Ford	1973–1974
38.	Gerald R. Ford	Nelson A. Rockefeller	1974–1977
39.	Jimmy Carter	Walter F. Mondale	1977–1981
40.	Ronald Reagan	George H. W. Bush	1981–1985
	Ronald Reagan	George H. W. Bush	1985–1989
41.	George H. W. Bush	J. Danforth Quayle	1989–1993
42.	William J. Clinton	Albert Gore, Jr.	1993–1997
	William J. Clinton	Albert Gore, Jr.	1997–2001
43.	George W. Bush	Richard Cheney	2001–2005
	George W. Bush	Richard Cheney	2005–2009
44.	Barack H. Obama	Joseph R. Biden, Jr.	2009–

Glossary

9/11 (p. 896) September 11, 2001, was the day of al-Qaeda attacks on the United States; terrorists hijacked four planes and flew two into the World Trade Center towers and one into the Pentagon; one crashed on a field in Shanksville, Pennsylvania.

agent orange (p. 790) A defoliant that stripped trees of their leaves to expose Vietcong hideouts and killed crops.

Alcatraz Proclamation (p. 839) Sardonic statement issued by Indian activists, who occupied the island of Alcatraz and described it as the perfect site for an Indian reservation because it lacked running water, sanitation, schools, mineral resources, and productive soil.

Allies (World War I) (p. 594) A group of fighting partners including initially Britain, France, Belgium, and Russia, and eventually totalling eighteen nations, with Italy and the United States.

Allies (World War II) (p. 688) Name for powers fighting Germany, eventually including the United States, Britain, France, and the Soviet Union.

al-Qaeda (p. 895) A fundamentalist Islamic terrorist organization led by Saudi exile Osama bin Laden.

American Expeditionary Forces (p. 612) Two million American soldiers who fought overseas under the command of General John J. Pershing.

American Federation of Labor (AFL) (p. 678) A craft-based organization that accepted only skilled workers, like carpenters or cigar makers, who practiced a trade.

Angel Island (p. 581) Immigration processing station in the San Francisco Bay for Asian immigrants.

Axis (p. 688) Name for nations fighting the Allies, including Germany, Italy, and Japan.

baby boom generation (p. 750) The 76.4 million Americans born between 1946 and 1964.

Battle of Little Bighorn (p. 456) Lt. Col. George A. Custer and the Seventh Cavalry are wiped out by a force of Cheyenne, Sioux, and Arapaho warriors on June 25, 1876; hardens white attitudes toward Native Americans.

Bay of Pigs operation (1961) (p. 747) Failed attempt to use an amphibious invasion by Cuban exiles to overthrow the Cuban dictator Fidel Castro.

Beats (p. 763) Members of the bohemian communities of poets, novelists, and artists that flourished in New York's Greenwich Village and San Francisco's North Beach and who rejected middle-class suburban values.

Berlin airlift (1948–1949) (p. 726) Americans and British used planes to resupply West Berlin to stymie the Soviet blockade of the city.

Birmingham campaign (p. 821) Civil rights effort to desegregate Birmingham, Alabama, where shocking images of police brutality prompted Kennedy to push for a federal civil rights act.

Black Codes (p. 413) Laws designed by the ex-Confederate states to sharply limit the civil and economic rights of freedmen and create an exploitable workforce.

Black Panthers (p. 832) Militant civil rights group dedicated to armed self-defense, racial pride, and inner-city renewal.

Black Power (p. 832) A call for blacks to unite politically and economically in black-only organizations to protect their racial identity as they fought for equality.

blacklist (p. 483) A list of workers that employers in a particular town or industry refused to hire because they were considered troublemakers.

Bonus March (p. 660) A two-month-long demonstration by forty thousand impoverished World War I veterans in Washington, D.C., that ended violently when the army expelled the protesters.

***Brown v. Board of Education* (1954) (p. 766)** Supreme Court decision that segregated schools violated the equal protection clause of the Fourteenth Amendment.

"Buffalo Bill's Wild West" (p. 462) A circuslike production begun in 1883 that helped create a romantic and mythological view of the West in the American imagination.

Bush Doctrine (p. 898) Established the unilateral right to attack nations that harbored terrorists, to launch preemptive military strikes to prevent future attacks on the United States, and to replace autocratic governments with democratically elected ones.

Camp David Accords (1978) (p. 856) Israel agreed to give the Sinai Peninsula back to Egypt; in return Egypt became the first Arab state to recognize Israel's right to exist.

Carpetbagger (p. 418) White Southerners' derogatory term for Northerners who came south after the war to settle, work, or aid the ex-slaves. It falsely suggested they were penniless adventurers who came south merely to get rich.

"cash and carry" (p. 687) A policy that required belligerent nations to pay cash for goods and transport them on their own ships.

central business districts (p. 511) Sections of cities devoted exclusively to commercial enterprises such as banks, department stores, and the offices of corporations, accountants, lawyers, and other professions.

Central Powers (p. 594) Initially Germany and Austria-Hungary; expanded by 1915 to include the Ottoman Empire and Bulgaria.

Chinese Exclusion Act (p. 484) An 1882 law barring Chinese immigration to the United States for ten years. Renewed several times. It remained in effect until 1943.

City Beautiful Movement (p. 508) A movement begun in the 1880s that advocated comprehensive planning and grand redesign of urban space to eliminate pollution and overcrowding.

civil disobedience (p. 772) A strategy of nonviolence used by demonstrators to protest a law or a policy considered unjust.

Civil Rights Act of 1875 (p. 426) Passed by Congress in 1875, it required state governments to provide equal access in public facilities such as schools and to allow African Americans to serve on juries. In 1883 the U.S. Supreme Court ruled it unconstitutional.

Civil Rights Act of 1964 (p. 826) Legislation that banned segregation in businesses and places open to the public (such as restaurants and public schools) and prohibited discrimination in employment on the basis of race, religion, ethnicity, or sex.

Clayton Anti-Trust Act (1914) (p. 539) The act prohibited interlocking company directories and exempted trade unions from prosecution under the 1890 Sherman Anti-Trust Act.

Cold War (p. 721) A full-scale ideological and military conflict between the United States and the Soviet Union and their allies that led to several hot wars around the globe, although the Americans and Soviets, fearful of a nuclear showdown, never fought each other directly.

Committee on Public Information (p. 605) Government agency that controlled the flow of information and shaped public opinion about the war with posters, Four-Minute Men, pamphlets, and films.

company town (p. 524) A town built and owned by a corporation and rented to its employees, reflecting both the corporation's desire to help their workers and to control them.

"compassionate conservatism" (p. 887) A philosophical approach to governing that emphasized using private industry, charities, and religious institutions, rather than the government, to provide community services.

Compromise of 1877 (p. 427) Resolution of the disputed presidential election of 1876 that handed victory to Republican Rutherford B. Hayes over Democrat Samuel J. Tilden. Democrats agreed to the deal in exchange for patronage and the continued removal of federal troops from the South.

Congress of Industrial Organizations (CIO) (p. 678) A brand-new type of labor organization that organized workers within an entire industry rather than by their trade orientation.

conscientious objectors (p. 609) Those who opposed participating in military service because of religious, philosophical, or political belief.

conservationist (p. 540) An environmentalist who wanted to meet present economic needs and conserve natural resources for future generations.

conspicuous consumption (p. 515) A term used to describe lavish displays of wealth by the rich, including construction of opulent mansions and hosting lavish balls.

containment (p. 722) The label affixed to multiple American foreign policy initiatives meant to prevent the Soviet Union from expanding its influence around the globe.

corporation (p. 472) Businesses owned by people who buy shares of stock in the company.

Coxey's Army (p. 523) A protest march from Ohio to Washington, D.C., in 1894 organized by Jacob Coxey to publicize demands for the federal government to alleviate the suffering brought on by the Panic of 1893.

Cuban Missile Crisis (1962) (p. 747) A showdown between the United States and the Soviet Union over Khrushchev's decision to place Soviet missiles aimed at America in Communist Cuba.

Dawes Plan (1924) (p. 651) International agreement that loaned Germany $200 million in gold to pay a reduced reparation bill and gave Germany more time to meet its debt.

Dawes Severalty Act (p. 458) 1887 law that started the breakup of reservations by offering Native Americans allotments of 160 acres of reservation land to encourage them to become independent farmers.

depression (p. 481) A contraction of economic growth, widespread business failure, and high rates of unemployment lasting several years.

deserving poor (p. 676) Needy Americans who were legitimately entitled to public support, a category open to differing interpretations.

détente (p. 802) Relaxing Cold War tensions by using diplomatic, economic, and cultural contacts to improve U.S. relations with China and the Soviet Union.

domino theory (p. 781) The fear that a communist Vietnam would open the door to a complete communist takeover of Southeast Asia.

"Don't Ask, Don't Tell" (p. 884) The policy instituted during the Clinton era that allowed closeted homosexuals and lesbians, gays who kept their sexual preferences hidden, to serve in the military.

double-victory campaign (p. 699) Civil rights call for victory against both fascism overseas and racial prejudice at home.

Dust Bowl (p. 670) Drought and soil erosion caused massive dust storms across southern and plains states throughout the thirties.

Eighteenth Amendment (1919) (p. 633) Constitutional amendment that banned the sale, manufacture, and transportation of intoxicating liquors.

Equal Rights Amendment (ERA) (p. 859) A proposed constitutional amendment, which stated that "equality of rights under the law shall not be denied or abridged by the United States or by any State on account of sex."

Espionage Act (1917) (p. 606) Legislation that made it a crime to obstruct military recruitment, to encourage mutiny, or to aid the enemy by spreading lies.

ethnic enclaves (p. 501) Urban neighborhoods in New York City dominated by one particular immigrant group, often leading to names such as Little Germany and Little Italy.

Eugenicists (p. 646) Those who wanted to improve the human race by controlling its hereditary qualities.

Exodusters (p. 444) More than twenty thousand ex-slaves who in 1879 left violence and poverty in the South to take up farming in Kansas.

Fair Deal (p. 754) Truman's proposals for national health care, public housing, education, and public works projects.

farmers' alliances (p. 519) Organizations in the 1870s and 1880s dedicated to helping farmers struggling with rising costs and falling crop prices by advocating farmer cooperatives and laws to regulate banks and railroads.

fascist state (p. 686) A type of dictatorial regime that arose in Germany, Italy, and Spain that glorified the state over the individual.

Federal Reserve Act (1913) (p. 539) The act creating a federally run Federal Reserve to serve as a "banker's bank" that held a portion of bank funds in reserve to help member banks in time of crisis, set rates for business loans, and issued a new national paper currency.

Federal Trade Commission (1914) (p. 539) A federal agency with the power to order companies to cease unfair trading practices whose decisions were subject to court review.

Fifteenth Amendment (p. 421) Constitutional amendment passed by Congress in 1869 providing an explicit constitutional guarantee for black suffrage.

First Red Scare (1919–1920) (p. 634) Period when the Justice Department arrested and deported alien anarchists and Communists suspected of trying to destroy American democracy and capitalism.

Fourteen Points (p. 601) Speech by Woodrow Wilson to Congress on January 8, 1918, that outlined a postwar world dominated by democracy, free trade, disarmament, self-determination, resolved territorial disputes in Europe, and a league of nations to mediate future international crises.

Fourteenth Amendment (p. 417) Drafted by Congress in June 1866, it defined citizenship to include African Americans, guaranteed equal protection before the law, and established the federal government as the guarantor of individual civil rights.

Freedmen's Bureau (p. 408) Relief agency for the war-ravaged South created by Congress in March 1865. It provided emergency services, built schools, and managed confiscated lands.

Freedom Rides (p. 819) Interstate bus journeys by black and white activists who entered segregated bus facilities together throughout the South.

Freedom Summer, 1964 (p. 825) Multipronged attack on white supremacy in Mississippi that included a voter registration drive and the creation of Freedom Schools.

Frontier Thesis (p. 464) Historian Frederick Jackson Turner's 1893 theory that extolled the positive role the frontier had played in shaping the American character and consequently American institutions.

fundamentalism (p. 636) An evangelical Christian theology that viewed the Bible as an authentic, literal recounting of historical events and the absolute moral word of God.

Geneva Accords (1954) (p. 782) Called for a temporary partition of Vietnam along the seventeenth parallel, with the Vietminh in the north and the French in the south, and a general election in two years to reunify the country under one government.

Gentlemen's Agreement (1907–1908) (p. 581) Japanese agreement to deny passports to Japanese workers intending to immigrate to the United States.

Gilded Age (p. 498) The name for the period 1877–1900 that suggested the amazing achievements of the period were like a thin gold layer that covered many unresolved social problems.

global warming (p. 892) The scientific theory that widespread burning of fossil fuels emitted greenhouse gases into the atmosphere that caused average global temperatures to rise.

Grange (p. 449) Originally founded in the fall of 1867 by Oliver H. Kelley as a social and educational society for farmers, it became a major political force in the Midwest in the mid-1870s.

Great Depression (p. 659) The most devastating and longest economic crisis in American history that lasted from 1929 to 1939.

Great Plains (p. 443) Vast open territory stretching east to west from present-day Missouri to the Rocky Mountains, and north to south from North Dakota to Texas.

Great Society (p. 816) President Johnson's wide-ranging social welfare reforms intended to make the amenities of modern life—a decent standard of living, education, health care, and clean water—available to all Americans.

Gulf of Tonkin Resolution (1964) (p. 787) Gave Johnson permission "to take all necessary measures to repel any armed attack against the forces of the United States and to prevent further aggression" in Vietnam.

Harlem Renaissance (p. 634) An outpouring of African American artistic expression in the 1920s and 1930s.

Haymarket Riot (p. 494) A violent incident touched off when a bomb exploded amid a group of policemen as they broke up a peaceful labor rally in Chicago's Haymarket Square on May 4, 1886.

hippies (p. 829) Youthful social rebels who renounced material acquisition and used drugs to explore their inner spiritual selves.

Ho Chi Minh Trail (p. 789) A 600-mile North Vietnamese supply route that ran along the western border of Vietnam through neighboring Laos and Cambodia.

holding company (p. 477) A huge corporation that bought and ran other corporations by purchasing their stock.

Hollywood blacklist (p. 739) A list of individuals with suspected past or present communist ties whom film studios refused to hire.

Holocaust (p. 708) German-engineered World War II extermination of Jews and other peoples that Germans considered inferior.

Homestead Act (p. 440) Passed in 1862, it provided 160 acres of free land to any settler willing to live on it and improve it for five years; promoted massive westward migration.

horizontal integration (p. 476) Business organization where one company buys many other companies producing the same product to eliminate competition and achieve greater efficiency.

Immigration Act of 1924 (p. 634) Law that allowed unrestricted immigration from the Western Hemisphere, curtailed all Asian immigration, and used quotas to control how many immigrants emigrated from individual European nations.

imperialism (p. 562) The late nineteenth-century term for colonizing foreign nations and lands, relying primarily on business, political, and military structures rather than settlers to rule colonized peoples and exploit their resources.

Industrial Workers of the World (IWW) (p. 543) This group envisioned "one big union" that welcomed all workers regardless of sex, race, ethnicity, or skill, which would one day take over all means of production.

initiative (p. 553) Provided a way, usually by gathering signatures on petitions, for the electorate to introduce legislation before state legislatures.

Intermediate-Range Nuclear Forces Treaty (1987) (p. 871) Approved the destruction of all U.S. and Soviet intermediate-range missiles in Europe.

internment camps (p. 695) Camps in the United States that held people of Japanese descent under armed guard in isolated areas.

interventionists (p. 686) Those advocating direct engagement in overseas conflicts.

Iran-Contra scandal (p. 871) A law-breaking scheme that sold arms to Iran to secure the hostage's release and used the proceeds to support anti-Communists in Nicaragua.

Iranian hostage crisis (p. 856) Defining event in Carter's presidency as Iranian revolutionaries held 52 Americans captive for 444 days.

iron curtain (p. 722) Winston Churchill's characterization of the military and ideological barrier erected by the Soviet Union that separated Western and Eastern Europe into free and dominated halves.

Kellogg-Briand Pact (1928) (p. 649) Treaty that renounced aggressive war as an instrument of national policy.

Kennedy and Nixon debate (p. 761) The 1960 first televised presidential election debate watched by nearly 77 million Americans, or 60 percent of the adult population.

Knights of Labor (p. 490) A labor organization founded in 1869 that in the 1880s accepted workers of all trades and backgrounds and became the world's largest industrial union.

Korean War (1950–1953) (p. 729) The United States fought Communist North Koreans and Chinese to a stalemate, frustrating Americans, who had to learn to accept only a partial victory.

Ku Klux Klan (p. 422) The best-known of the many secret white terrorist organizations. It arose in the South in 1866 and targeted freedmen and symbols of black self improvement and independence and played a key role in reestablishing white supremacy by the late 1870s.

laissez-faire (p. 490) (French for "let do" or leave alone) A philosophy that argued that the government should impose no restraints on business.

League of Nations (p. 616) An international collective security organization composed of member nations where member nations agreed to mediate future international disputes to prevent wars and work together to improve global human conditions.

Lend-Lease (p. 689) A policy that circumvented "cash and carry" by loaning rather than selling arms to the Allies.

Levittowns (p. 758) Planned suburban communities where developers standardized every part of the construction process.

Little Rock Nine (p. 771) Nine black teenagers who integrated Central High School in Little Rock, Arkansas, in 1957 and became the focus of a national crisis that required the intervention of federal troops to resolve.

Lochner v. New York **(1905) (p. 544)** A Supreme Court ruling that unless long work hours directly jeopardized workers' health, the government could not abridge an employee's freedom to negotiate his own work schedule with his employer.

Long Drive (p. 449) The annual cattle drives of more than 1,000 miles from Texas to the Great Plains that started in 1866 and established the ranching industry in the West.

"long telegram" (p. 722) An influential 5,000-word missive by diplomat George F. Kennan that outlined why America needed to develop an aggressive foreign policy aimed at containing Soviet expansionist impulses.

Ludlow Massacre (1914) (p. 544)   Colorado state troops set a striking miners' camp ablaze, killing thirteen women and children, an act that outraged laborers throughout the nation.

Lusitania **(p. 598)**   British passenger ship sunk by a German U-boat on May 7, 1915, an attack that killed 1,198 passengers, including 128 Americans.

Manhattan Project (p. 712)   Code-named secret U.S. government research program to produce the atomic bomb.

March on Washington, 1963 (p. 824)   Massive demonstration in the nation's capital that demanded passage of a federal civil rights act and more economic opportunities.

Marshall Plan (1948–1952) (p. 724)   Aimed to restore Europeans' faith in capitalism by sending $13 billion ($119 billion in today's dollars) overseas to rebuild Europe's ruined roads, bridges, factories, and farms.

McCarthyism (p. 739)   The government's anti-communist crusade named for Senator Joseph McCarthy from Wisconsin, who, along with the House Committee on Un-American Activities (HUAC), spearheaded numerous governmental investigations into communist activities, many of them spurious.

Meat Inspection Act (1906) (p. 552)   Law gave federal inspectors the authority to condemn meat unfit for consumption and established federal sanitary standards for meatpacking plants.

"Migrant Mother" (p. 673)   Dorothea Lange's 1936 photograph of a destitute woman, which became an iconic portrait of Depression-era suffering.

military-industrial complex (p. 755)   Eisenhower's term for the close ties between the defense industry and the Pentagon that might unduly influence government policy.

Mississippi Plan (p. 426)   Campaign of violence and intimidation waged by armed groups of whites closely allied with the Democratic Party that drove Republicans from power in the Mississippi state elections of 1874. Copied by other Southern states.

Modernism (p. 636)   A liberal Christian theology embraced in many urban areas that emphasized the ongoing revelation of divine truth.

monopoly (p. 474)   The control of an industry or market by one corporation.

Montgomery Bus Boycott (1955–1956) (p. 768)   A year-long bus boycott that brought a new leader, Martin Luther King Jr., and a new strategy of nonviolent protest to the forefront of the Civil Rights Movement.

Mormons (p. 445)   A religious sect founded in upstate New York in 1830. Driven by persecution they headed west in 1846 and settled in a valley in Utah near the Great Salt Lake.

Muckrakers (p. 553)   Progressive Era term for investigative journalists who wrote exposés on government and business corruption.

Muller v. Oregon **(1908) (p. 546)**   The Supreme Court upheld maximum hour laws for female workers because protecting women's reproductive health served the public good.

Munich Conference (1938) (p. 687)   Hoping to avoid war, Britain and France agreed to let Germany occupy the Sudetenland, a German-speaking part of Czechoslovakia.

mutually assured destruction (MAD) (p. 852)   The claim that the guarantee of a devastating nuclear counter-attack would deter the United States and Soviet Union from ever employing their nuclear arsenals.

My Lai (p. 799)   A Vietnamese village where American soldiers massacred 500 civilians in 1968.

Nation of Islam (p. 830)   African American sect that rejected integration as the path to salvation for the black community and instead wanted to establish a separate black nation.

National Organization for Women (NOW) (p. 834)   An organization dedicated to securing equal rights for women in employment, education, and politics.

Neutrality Acts (p. 687)   A series of laws from 1935 to 1939 which restricted arms sales, loans, and transport of goods with nations at war.

New Deal (p. 662)   An avalanche of legislation from 1933 to 1938 intended to promote economic recovery, reform American capitalism, and offer security to ordinary Americans.

New Deal coalition (p. 679)   A political partnership formed in the midthirties among liberals, trade unionists, Catholics, and northern blacks that redrew the nation's political map.

New Frontier (p. 813)   Kennedy's legislative program that proposed raising the minimum wage, reducing overcrowding in schools, and providing health care for the elderly.

New Left (p. 828)   A small, but highly visible, coalition of left-leaning student-based organizations that attacked racial discrimination, poverty, and the war in Vietnam.

New Negro (p. 642)   Spirit of black racial pride and militancy that set a younger generation of African American artists and civil rights leaders apart from their predecessors.

New South (p. 428)   Optimistic phrase white Southerners used to describe the post-Reconstruction South, reflecting the South's development of a new system of race relations based on segregation and white supremacy and pointing to a profound economic transformation that swept across the region.

New Woman (p. 513)   A phrase used to describe young women in the 1890s and early 1900s that reflected their rising levels of education, economic independence, and political and social activism.

Nineteenth Amendment (p. 605)   Constitutional amendment that granted women the right to vote; it was ratified August 26, 1920.

non-interventionists (p. 686)   Those urging the nation to stay out of overseas conflicts.

North American Free Trade Agreement (NAFTA) (p. 885)   A 1992 treaty that lifted trade barriers among the United States, Mexico, and Canada.

North Atlantic Treaty Organization (NATO) (p. 722)   A post-World War II military alliance between the United States and Western European powers.

nuclear fallout (p. 734)   The deadly pollution that descends through the air after a nuclear bomb explosion.

Open Door Policy (p. 579)   A U.S.-sponsored nonbinding international agreement that kept the Chinese market open to all foreign nations.

Organization of the Petroleum Exporting Countries (OPEC) (p. 844)   An international consortium of oil-producing nations that regulated the price and quantity of oil exported to the world market.

Panama Canal (p. 584)   A manmade waterway through Panama completed in 1914 to link the Pacific and Atlantic oceans.

Panic of 1873 (p. 424)   A financial panic on Wall Street that touched off a national economic recession causing financial houses, banks, and businesses to fail. Hundreds of thousands of workers lost their jobs.

Patriot Act (p. 897)   A controversial 2001 law that greatly expanded the government's investigative and police powers.

Peace Corps (p. 813)   Government agency that President Kennedy established to send recent college graduates to work on humanitarian projects overseas in developing nations.

peace movement (p. 790)   A loose coalition of anti-Vietnam war activists that included pacifists, students, professors, clergy, hippies, civil rights activists, and middle-class liberals.

Pearl Harbor (p. 690)   A U.S. naval base in Hawaii that the Japanese attacked on December 7, 1941.

People's Party (p. 517) A third party effort launched in 1890 by a coalition of farmer organizations, reformers, and labor unions and dedicated to curbing corporate power and increasing the voice of the masses in politics.

Platt Amendment (p. 572) Granted the United States the right to maintain a naval base at Guantánamo Bay, to intervene militarily in Cuban domestic affairs, and a privileged trading relationship with Cuba. The Cuban government also needed permission from the United States before entering into treaties with other nations.

political machines (p. 500) Powerful urban political organizations that mobilized large blocs of working-class and immigrant voters and often engaged in corrupt and illegal activity.

Powell Doctrine (p. 882) General Colin Powell's assertion that the nation should go to war only as a last resort when the president had full support from the nation and the international community, could employ overwhelming military force to win without serious loss of American life, and had a clear exit strategy.

preemptive war (p. 898) The notion that the United States should remove hostile regimes with force before they could pose a serious threat.

preservationist (p. 539) An environmentalist who championed preserving nature in its unspoiled state.

Proposition 13 (1978) (p. 866) Referendum in California that dramatically reduced property taxes, spearheading grassroots tax rebellion nationwide.

Pullman strike (p. 524) A bitter strike that began on May 11, 1894, at the Pullman Palace Car Company and soon spread nationwide, paralyzing the railroad system. President Cleveland sent in federal troops and broke the strike.

Pure Food and Drug Act (1906) (p. 552) Law levied federal fines for mislabeling food or medicine.

recall (p. 553) Used special elections to remove unpopular officials from office before their term expired.

reconcentration (p. 565) Spanish policy that herded Cuban peasants off their farms into heavily fortified cities followed by systematic destruction of the crops that fed the rebel armies.

Redeemers (p. 426) Name for white Southern political leaders who successfully returned their states to white Democratic rule in the mid-1870s. The name was intended to depict these leaders as saviors of Southern society from rule by freedmen, scalawags, and carpetbaggers.

referendum (p. 553) Legislative proposal on the ballot enabling the voting public to decide whether a measure becomes law.

Religious Right (p. 866) A collection of right-wing Christian groups that defended traditional values and supported conservative political causes.

robber barons (p. 476) A pejorative name for big business leaders that suggested they grew rich by devious business practices, exploitation of workers, and political manipulation.

Roe v. Wade (1973) (p. 861) Supreme Court decision that legalized abortion.

Roosevelt Corollary (1904) (p. 587) Corollary to the 1823 Monroe Doctrine that announced the U.S. intention to act as an "international police power" in Latin America.

Rough Riders (p. 570) A volunteer unit of cowboys, Ivy League athletes, city police officers, and Pawnee scouts led by Theodore Roosevelt that gained fame by charging up the San Juan Heights during the Spanish-American War.

Rust Belt (p. 845) Decaying industrial cities in the Midwest, places plagued with high unemployment, crumbling roads, bankrupt governments, and high welfare rolls.

SALT I (1972) (p. 852) The first treaty between the Soviet Union and the United States that limited the deployment of intercontinental and submarine-launched ballistic missiles and the creation of missile-defense systems.

Sand Creek Massacre (p. 454) A massacre of some two hundred Cheyenne Indians on November 29, 1864, in Colorado by a military outfit known as the Colorado Volunteers under Colonel John M. Chivington.

Scalawag (p. 418) White Southerners' derogatory term for fellow whites considered traitors to their region and race for joining the Republican Party and cooperating with Reconstruction policy.

Schlieffen Plan (p. 596) A military plan that called for Germany to attack and quickly defeat France while the cumbersome Russian army mobilized.

scientific management (p. 543) The effort to use scientific knowledge to secure maximum output and profit.

Second Red Scare (p. 737) Widespread effort to root out Communist spies after World War II that lasted for nearly a decade.

Sedition Act (1918) (p. 606) Legislation that went even further than the Espionage Act by prohibiting anyone from uttering, writing, or publishing "any abusive or disloyal language" concerning the flag, constitution, government, or armed forces.

self-determination (p. 601) Giving people a voice in selecting their own government.

settlement houses (p. 505) Institutions established in cities beginning in the 1880s that were dedicated to helping the poor by providing a wide range of social and educational services.

Seventeenth Amendment (1913) (p. 553) A constitutional amendment that enabled voters, rather than state legislatures, to elect federal senators.

Share Our Wealth (p. 674) Louisiana Senator Huey Long's plan to redistribute money from the rich to the poor.

Sherman Anti-Trust Act (p. 477) Authorized the Justice Department to prosecute any illegal contract, combination, or conspiracy among corporations that eliminated competition or restrained free trade.

silent majority (p. 801) Nixon's term for the large number of Americans who supported the war quietly in the privacy of their homes.

sit-down strike (p. 679) Workers occupy a factory to paralyze production lines and prevent strikebreakers or management from entering the building.

sit-ins (p. 772) Nonviolent demonstrations where civil rights protesters employed the tactic of civil disobedience to occupy seats at whites-only lunch counters.

Sixteenth Amendment (1913) (p. 539) The constitutional amendment authorizing federal income taxes.

social Darwinism (p. 488) The belief that the principles of evolution, which Darwin had observed in nature, also applied to society. Advocates argued that individuals or groups achieve advantage over others as the result of biological superiority, an idea expressed as "survival of the fittest."

Social Gospel (p. 534) The religious belief that Christians had a responsibility to create an ethically sound and morally upright society.

socialism (p. 484) A theory that rejected capitalism and advocated common ownership of property and social and economic equality.

Southeast Asian Treaty Organization (SEATO) (p. 783) 1954 alliance among the United States, Britain, France, Australia, New Zealand, Thailand, the Philippines, and Pakistan who pledged to "meet common danger" in Southeast Asia together.

Southern Christian Leadership Conference (SCLC) (p. 770) Civil rights organization founded by Martin Luther King Jr. that used black churches to devise a new nonviolent strategy of direct action.

Spanish Influenza (p. 614) A lethal flu virus that killed millions worldwide in 1918.

sphere of influence (p. 579) The term used to describe the exclusive political and trading rights that a foreign nation enjoyed within another nation's territory.

Spirit of St. Louis (p. 630) The plane that Charles Lindbergh piloted on the first-ever nonstop solo flight from New York to Paris on May 21, 1927.

Stock market crash of 1929 (p. 657) A ten-day period beginning on October 20, 1929, when the value of stocks plummeted as panicked investors sold off their stock in droves. This moment is usually considered the official start of the Depression.

Stonewall riot (p. 862) A 1969 battle between patrons of a Greenwich Village male gay bar and police that became the catalyst for the gay rights movement.

Strategic Defense Initiative (SDI) (p. 869) Reagan's proposal to build a missile shield that used lasers from space satellites to destroy incoming missiles.

Student Nonviolent Coordinating Committee (SNCC) (p. 775) Student-run civil rights organization founded in 1960.

suburbs (p. 511) Middle- and upper-class residential communities established just beyond a city's boundary but connected to the urban center by mass transit.

supply-side economics (p. 867) Reagan administration theory that letting entrepreneurs keep more of their profits would fuel economic growth, job creation, and more tax revenue to offset military spending.

Taft-Hartley Act (1947) (p. 753) Law that abolished the closed shop, banned so-called sympathy boycotts, and required that all union officers sign affidavits certifying that they were not members of the Communist Party.

Teller Amendment (p. 568) Congressional promise "to leave the government and control of the [Cuban] Island to its people" at the end of the Spanish-American War.

Ten Percent Plan (p. 408) Pardoned all Southerners (except highranking military officers and Confederate officials) who took an oath pledging loyalty to the Union and support for emancipation. As soon as 10 percent of a state's voters took this oath, they could call a convention, establish a new state government, and apply for congressional recognition.

tenements (p. 502) Multiple family dwellings of four to six stories housing dozens of families that became the most common form of housing for poor city dwellers by the 1860s.

Tet Offensive (1968) (p. 792) A massive, coordinated Communist assault against more than 100 cities and towns in South Vietnam.

The Jazz Age (p. 642) Nickname for the twenties that reflected the popularity of jazz music.

transcontinental railroad (p. 440) A line spanning the continental United States. Congress helped the Union Pacific and Central Pacific railroads build it by providing land grants, cash incentives, and loans.

trans-Mississippi West (p. 440) The region of the United States west of the Mississippi River.

Treaty of Paris (1898) (p. 571) Agreement that ended the Spanish-American War, with Spain relinquishing its claim to Cuba and the United States receiving Puerto Rico and Guam. In return for $20 million, Spain turned the Philippines over to the United States.

Truman Doctrine (p. 724) A foreign policy initiative that gave the United States an active role in stopping the global spread of communism by supporting "free peoples who are resisting attempted subjugation by armed minorities or by outside pressures."

trust (p. 476) A legally binding deal bringing many companies in the same industry under the direction of a board of "trustees."

trust-busting (p. 536) Governmental action to dissolve monopolies.

Twenty-First Amendment (1933) (p. 634) Constitutional amendment that repealed the Eighteenth Amendment.

U-boat (p. 597) New in World War I, a German submarine that launched surprise torpedo attacks against Allied merchant and naval ships.

Universal Negro Improvement Association (UNIA) (p. 638) Organization founded by Marcus Garvey to spread his message of racial pride, economic self-sufficiency, and returning to Africa.

Versailles Peace Treaty (1919) (p. 616) The controversial treaty that ended World War I by requiring Germany to pay reparations and disarm.

vertical integration (p. 476) Business organization where one company controls the main phases of production of a product, from acquiring raw materials to retailing the finished goods.

Vietcong (p. 783) Slang term for South Vietnamese communists.

Vietminh (p. 780) The term initially used to describe all Vietnamese communists, and used after 1954 solely for North Vietnamese communists.

Vietnamization (p. 801) A Nixon administration policy that turned the bulk of the ground fighting over to the South Vietnamese Army.

Volstead Act (1919) (p. 633) Law that established criminal penalties for manufacturing, transporting, or possessing alcohol.

Voting Rights Act of 1965 (p. 827) Legislation that prohibited literacy tests and poll taxes and authorized the use of federal registrars to register voters if states failed to respect the Fifteenth Amendment.

Wade-Davis Bill (p. 408) A Reconstruction program designed to punish Confederate leaders and permanently destroy the South's slave society.

war bonds (p. 606) Short-term loans that individual citizens made to the government that financed two-thirds of the U.S. World War I costs.

Warren Court (p. 813) Supreme Court that brought about a legal revolution in the United States by permanently altering American schools, politics, the criminal justice system, and cultural norms.

Washington Conference (1921–1922) (p. 647) Meeting of world powers that resulted in agreements that limited naval arms, reaffirmed America's Open Door policy that kept Chinese trade open to all, and secured pledges of cooperation among the world's leading military powers.

Watergate scandal (1972) (p. 806) A botched Republican-engineered break-in of the Democratic National Committee headquarters in Washington, D.C. that forced Nixon to resign in 1974.

welfare capitalism (p. 541) The notion of using benefits to gain workers' loyalty, improve worker morale, and weaken interest in unions.

Western Front (p. 596) Complex system of trenches and earthworks that ran for 460 miles from the North Sea to Switzerland that pitted Germany against Belgium, France, Britain, and the United States.

"the white man's burden" (p. 575) The Anglo-Saxon quest to better the lives of so-called racially inferior peoples by spreading Western economic, cultural, and spiritual values and institutions.

women's suffrage (p. 512) The effort to obtain voting rights for women that eventually gained passage of the Nineteenth Amendment (1920).

Wounded Knee Massacre (p. 461) U.S. soldiers open fire on a group of Sioux Indians on December 29, 1890, killing between two hundred and three hundred.

yellow press (p. 565) Tabloid journalists and newspapers that reported sensationalist stories with a strong emotional component during the Spanish-American War.

Zimmermann Telegram (p. 600) German foreign minister Arthur Zimmermann offered to help Mexico recover Texas, New Mexico, and Arizona if Mexico would start a borderland war with the United States and ask Japan to join them.

zoot-suiters (p. 701) Name given to Mexican American youths who wore oversize suits.

Credits

Negative no. 80433d; **p. 518:** The Granger Collection, NYC—All rights reserved; **p. 521:** The Granger Collection, NYC—All rights reserved; **p. 522:** The Saturday Globe July 9th, 1892; **p. 523:** Ohio Historical Society; **p. 524:** ICHi-38519; Manufacturing Town of Pullman and Car Works; Pullman (Ill.), 1881; Creator-unknown./Chicago History Museum;**p. 525:** The Granger Collection, NYC—All rights reserved; **p. 526:** Library of Congress Prints and Photographs Division; **p. 528:** (top left) The Granger Collection, NYC—All rights reserved; (top left center) The Granger Collection, NYC—All rights reserved; (top right center) Collection of The New York Historical Society, Box1.f 10. Negative no. 80433d; (top right) The Granger Collection, NYC—All rights reserved; **p. 529:** (top left) Ohio State University Cartoon Research Library; (top left center) Jacob A. Riis "Italian Mother and Her Baby in Jersey Street", in the home of an Italian rag-picker, Jersey Street, circa 1890. Museum of the City of New York, The Jacob A. Riis Collection (#157); (top right center) Bettmann/CORBIS; (top right) ICHi-51283; Hull House-map of Nationalities in Chicago; Chicago (Ill.); n.d.; Creator-Hull House. Chicago History Museum.

CHAPTER 18

p. 530: (top left) Brown Brothers, Sterling, PA; (upper center left) Library of Congress Prints and Photographs Division[LC-USZC4-435]; (center left) Library of Congress Prints and Photographs Division[LC-DIG-nclc-05436]; (lower center left) Library of Congress Prints and Photographs Division[LC-DIG-nclc-01455]; (bottom left) The Granger Collection, NYC—All rights reserved; **pp. 530–531:** Victor Joseph Gatto/Museum of the City of New York; **p. 533:** Brown Brothers, Sterling, PA; **p. 535:** Library of Congress Prints and Photographs Division[LC-USZC4-435]; **p. 536–537:** Library of Congress Prints and Photographs Division[LC-USZC4-435]; **p. 539:** Bettmann/CORBIS; **p. 540:** Library of Congress Prints and Photographs Division[LC-USZ62-111138]; **p. 541:** Library of Congress Prints and Photographs Division[LC-DIG-nclc-05436]; **p. 542:** From the Collection of the Henry Ford Museum;**p. 544:**Library of Congress Prints and Photographs Division[LC-DIG-nclc-05436]; **p. 545:** Joseph Lochner/National Geographic Stock; **p. 546:** (top left) Library of Congress Prints and Photographs Division[LC-DIG-nclc-01455]; (center left) Kansas State Historical Society; (center) Bettmann/CORBIS; **p. 548:** Trade Catalog Collection. Baker Library Historical Collections. Harvard Business School; **p. 550:** Library of Congress Prints and Photographs Division[LC-DIG-nclc-01455]; **p. 551:** (top center) "Lewis W. Hine/Library of Congress Prints and Photographs Division[LC-DIG-nclc-03487]"; (bottom center) "Lewis Wickes Hines/Library of Congress Prints and Photographs Division[LC-DIG-nclc-04928]"; **p. 553:** (top left) Advertising Ephemera Collection. Baker Library Historical Collections. Harvard Business School; (center) Advertising Ephemera Collection. Baker Library Historical Collections. Harvard Business School. olvwork88222; **p. 555:** Library of Congress Prints and Photographs Division[LC-USZC4-8176]; **p. 557:** The Granger Collection, NYC—All rights reserved; **p. 558:** (top left) Library of Congress Prints and Photographs Division[LC-USZC4-435]; (top left center) Bettmann/CORBIS; (top right center) Joseph Lochner/National Geographic Stock; (top right) Advertising Ephemera Collection. Baker Library Historical Collections. Harvard Business School; **p. 559:** (top left) Library of Congress Prints and Photographs Division[LC-DIG-nclc-01455]; (top left center) Victor Joseph Gatto/Museum of the City of New York; (top right center) Library of Congress Prints and Photographs Division[LC-USZC4-8176]; (top right) From the Collection of the Henry Ford.

CHAPTER 19

p. 560: (upper center left) The Granger Collection, NYC—All rights reserved; (center left) Harvard University Widener Library; (lower center left) Bettmann/CORBIS; (bottom left) Bettmann/CORBIS; **pp. 560-561:** ICHi-08428; Destruction of the Battleship Maine in Havana Harbor in the Spanish-American War; Havana (Cuba); 1898 Feb. 15; Creator-Kurz & Allison/Chicago History Museum; **p. 565:** The Granger Collection, NYC—All rights reserved; **p. 567:** (center right) Fredric Remington; (bottom right) Library of Congress Prints and Photographs Division; **p. 570:** The Granger Collection, NYC—All rights reserved; **p. 571:** Grant Hamilton/Andy Moursund/www.georgetownbookshop.com; **p. 572:** CORBIS All Rights Reserved; **p. 573:** (top left) Harvard University Widener Library; (bottom right) HarpWeek, LLC; **p. 574:** Harvard University Widener Library; **p. 575:** Library of Congress Prints and Photographs Division[LC-USZC2-102]; **p. 576:** Library of Congress Prints and Photographs Division[LC-USZ62-91465]; **p. 578:** National Archives and Records Administration; **p. 579:** Bettmann/CORBIS; **p. 582:** Bettmann/CORBIS; **p. 583:** Science Museum/SSPL/The Image Works; **p. 584:** By permission of the Marcus Family/Library of Congress Prints and Photographs Division[LC-USZC4-14985]; **p. 585:** Map of the Panama Canal from the Atlantic to the Pacific Ocean, 1913 (litho), American School, (20th century)/Private Collection/Peter Newark American Pictures/The Bridgeman Art Library International; **p. 586:** Bettmann/CORBIS; **p. 587:** The Granger Collection, NYC—All rights reserved; **p. 588:** Brown Brothers; **p. 590:** (top left center) ICHi-08428; Destruction of the Battleship Maine in Havana Harbor in the Spanish-American War; Havana (Cuba); 1898 Feb. 15; Creator-Kurz & Allison/Chicago History Museum; (top right center) Harvard University Widener Library; **p. 591:** (top left) Bettmann/CORBIS; (top left center) Bettmann/CORBIS; (top right center) Bettmann/CORBIS; (top right) Map of the Panama Canal from the Atlantic to the Pacific Ocean, 1913 (litho), American School, (20th century)/Private Collection/Peter Newark American Pictures/The Bridgeman Art Library International.

CHAPTER 20

p. 592: (top left) Brown Brothers, Sterling, PA; (upper center left) Library of Congress Prints and Photographs Division[LC-USZC4-10218]; (lower center left) Library of Congress Prints and Photographs Division[LC-USZC4-14985]; (bottom left) © (Photographer)/CORBIS All Rights Reserved; **pp. 592–593:** Library of Congress Prints and Photographs Division[LC-USZC4-1129]; **p. 594:** Brown Brothers, Sterling, PA; **p. 598:** Brown Brothers, Sterling, PA; **p. 599:** Bain News Service/Historical/CORBIS; **p. 600:** By permission of the Marcus Family; **p. 602:** Library of Congress Prints and Photographs Division[LC-USZC4-10218]; **p. 603:** © 2011 The Jacob and Gwendolyn Lawrence Foundation, Seattle/Artists Rights Society (ARS), New York; **p. 605:** Bettmann/CORBIS; **p. 607:** (center) The Granger Collection, NYC—All rights reserved; (bottom right) Library of Congress Prints and Photographs Division[LC-USZC4-9659]; **p. 608:** (top left) National Archives and Records Administration; (top right) National Archives and Records Administration; **p. 610:** Bettmann/CORBIS; **p. 611:** (bottom left) Library of Congress Prints and Photographs Division; (bottom right) Library of Congress Prints and Photographs Division; **p. 614:** (top) National Archives and Records Administration; (bottom left) U.S. Naval Historical Center Photograph; **p. 619:** (bottom left) Bettmann/CORBIS; (bottom right) Bettmann/CORBIS; **p. 620:** Bettmann/CORBIS; **p. 621:** John Steuart Curry (American, 1897–1946) Parade to War, Allegory, 1938. Gift of Barnett Banks, Inc., AG.1991.4.1/Cummer Museum and Gardens; **p. 622:** (top left center) Library of Congress Prints and Photographs Division[LC-USZC4-1129]; (top right center) Bain News Service/Historical/CORBIS; (top right) The Granger Collection, NYC—All rights reserved; **p. 623** (top left) © 2011 The Jacob and Gwendolyn Lawrence Foundation, Seattle/Artists Rights Society (ARS), New York; (top left center) National Archives; (top right center) Bettmann/CORBIS; (top right) Bettmann/CORBIS.

CHAPTER 21

p. 624: (top left) "The Dolph Briscoe Center for American History, The University of Texas"; (upper center left) Bettmann/CORBIS; (center left) © Bettmann/CORBIS; (lower center left) Courtesy of the Library of Congress; (bottom left) Library of Congress Prints and Photographs Division[LC-DIG-ppmsca-03639]; **p. 625:** Underwood & Underwood/Bettmann Premium/CORBIS; **p. 626,**" The Dolph Briscoe Center for American History, The University of Texas"; **p. 627:** © Terry Donnelly; **p. 630:** The Granger Collection, NYC—All rights reserved; **p. 631:**Underwood & Underwood/CORBIS; **p. 632:** Bettmann/CORBIS; **p. 633:** Library of Congress Prints and Photographs Division[LC-USZC4-2862];

CHAPTER 22

CHAPTER 23

CHAPTER 24

CHAPTER 25

Pictures/Getty Images; **p. 757:** Loomis Dean//Time Life Pictures/Getty Images; **p. 759:** Bettmann/CORBIS; **p. 760:** Frank Driggs Collection/Getty Images; **p. 761:** (bottom left) Bettmann/CORBIS; (bottom right) Cedil Stoughton/John F. Kennedy Presidential Library and Museum; **p. 763:** Frank Driggs Collection/Getty Images; **p. 764:** (top)"The Metropolitan Museum of Art/Art Resource, NY/© 2011 The Pollock-Krasner Foundation/Artists Rights Society (ARS), New York."; (center) "Courtesy Center for Creative Photography, University of Arizona © 1991 Hans Namuth Estate"; **p. 765:** Bruce Davidson/Magnum Photos; **p. 766:** Library of Congress Prints and Photographs Division[LC-DIG-ppmsca-08092]; **p.767:** (center) The Chicago Defender; (bottom center) Bettmann/CORBIS; **p. 769:** AP Photo/Gene Herrick; **p. 771:** "© Ernest C. Withers Trust, courtesy Withers Family Trust"; **p. 775:** Photograph by Fred Blackwell; **p. 776:** (top left) Bettmann/CORBIS; (top left center) Bettmann/CORBIS; (top right center) "The Metropolitan Museum of Art/Art Resource, NY/© 2011 The Pollock-Krasner Foundation/Artists Rights Society (ARS), New York."; (top right) Bettmann/CORBIS; **p. 777:** (top left) Bruce Davidson/Magnum Photos; (top left center) Library of Congress Prints and Photographs Division[LC-DIG-ppmsca-08092]; (top right center) Frank Driggs Collection/Getty Images; (top right) Photograph by Fred Blackwell.

CHAPTER 26

p. 778: (top left) Malcolm Browne/AP Photo; (upper center left) Larry Burrows/Time Life Pictures/Getty Images; (lower center left) Library of Congress Prints and Photographs Division[LC-USZ62-129641]; (bottom left) Bettmann/CORBIS; **pp. 778–779:** Bernie Boston/The Washington Post/Getty Images; **p. 780:** Malcolm Browne/AP Photo; **p. 781:** Hulton-Deutsch Collection/CORBIS; **p. 782:** Library of Congress Prints and Photographs Division[LC-USZ62-129714]; **p. 785:** AP Photo/Malcolm Browne; **p. 786:** Lyndon Baines Johnson Library Collection; **p. 787:** © David Levine; **p. 788:** CORBIS; **p. 789:** (top left) Larry Burrows/Time Life Pictures/Getty Images; (bottom right) Trong Thanh/Doug Niven/Another Vietnam; **p. 790:** Larry Burrows/Time Life Pictures/Getty Images; **p. 792:** Universal Uclick; **p. 794:** AP Photo/Eddie Adams; **p. 795:** Larry Burrows/Time Life Pictures/Getty Images; **p. 796:** Library of Congress Prints and Photographs Division[LC-USZ62-129641]; **p. 797:** Library of Congress Prints and Photographs Division[LC-USZ62-129641]; **p. 799:** Ronald S. Haeberle//Time Life Pictures/Getty Images; **p. 800:** Bettmann/CORBIS; **p. 801:** Bettmann/CORBIS; **p. 804:** Howard Ruffner/Time & Life Images/Getty Images; **pp. 806-807:** Bettmann/CORBIS; **p. 808:** (top left) Hulton-Deutsch Collection/CORBIS; (top right center) Lyndon Baines Johnson Library Collection; **p.809:** (top left) Larry Burrows/Time Life Pictures/Getty Images; (top left center) Ronald S. Haeberle//Time Life Pictures/Getty Images; (top right center) Howard Ruffner/TIME & LIFE Images/Getty Images; (top right) Bettmann/CORBIS.

CHAPTER 27

p. 810: (top left) Hank Walker//Time Life Pictures/Getty Images; (upper center left) Charles Moore/Black Star; (lower center left) Robert Altman Photography; (bottom left) "A 1967 Herblock Cartoon. copyright by The Herb Block Foundation"; **pp. 810-811:** Santi Visalli Inc./Getty Images; **p. 812:** Hank Walker//Time Life Pictures/Getty Images; **p. 815:** Bettmann/CORBIS; **p. 816:** (all) Democratic National Committee; **p. 817:** (all) Democratic National Committee; **p. 819:** Charles Moore/Black Star; **p. 820:** Bettmann/CORBIS; **p. 822:** Charles Moore/Black Star; **p. 823:** Charles Moore/Black Star; **p. 824:** CORBIS; **p. 825:** MPI/Archive Photos/Getty Images; **p. 827:** 1976 Matt Herron/Take Stock/ The Image Works; **p. 828:** Robert Altman Photography; **p. 829:** Robert Altman Photography; **p. 830:** Bob Gomel/Time Life Pictures/Getty Images; **p. 831:** AP Photo; **p. 832:** Library of Congress Prints and Photographs Division[LC-USZC4-1564]; **p. 833:** (center background) David J. & Janice L. Frent Collection/CORBIS; **p. 835:** AP Photo; **p. 836:** (top left) The Herb Block Foundation; (bottom left) Steve Schapiro; **p. 837:** "A 1967 Herblock Cartoon. copyright by The Herb Block Foundation"; **p. 838:** AP Photo; **p. 839:** Walter P. Reuther Library/Wayne State University; **p. 840:** (top left) Bettmann/CORBIS; (top left center) Bettmann/CORBIS; (top right center) Charles Moore/Black Star; (top right) MPI/Archive Photos/Getty Images; **p. 841:** (top left) 1976 Matt Herron/Take Stock/ The Image Works; (top left center) Robert Altman Photography; (top right center) Library of Congress Prints and Photographs Division[LC-USZC4-1564]; (top right) AP Photo.

CHAPTER 28

p. 842: (top left) A 1974 Herblock Cartoon, copyright by the Herb Block Foundation; (upper center left) Courtesy The Gallery on Greene; (lower center left) Bettmann/CORBIS; (bottom left) Cindy Elgrably; **pp. 842–843:** H. Armstrong Roberts/ClassicStock/Corbis; **p. 844:** A 1974 Herblock Cartoon, copyright by the Herb Block Foundation; **p. 848:** "The Soiling of Old Glory" - Pulitzer Prize 1976. www.stanleyformanphoto.com; **p. 850:** (top right) A 1974 Herblock Cartoon, copyright by the Herb Block Foundation; (bottom right) Paul Conrad/© Tribune Media Services, Inc.; **p. 851:** Courtesy The Gallery on Greene; **p. 853:** Courtesy The Gallery on Greene; **p. 854:** (bottom left) Reprinted with Permission by The Dallas Morning News; (bottom right) Courtesy of Lee Phillips, the artist's daughter; **p. 857:** © Sygma/Corbis; **p. 858:** Bettmann/CORBIS; **p.859:** Bettmann/CORBIS; **p. 860:** (bottom left) Bettmann/CORBIS; (bottom right) AP Photo; **p. 861:** Bettmann/CORBIS; **p. 862:** Hisham Ibrahim/Corbis; **p. 863:** John Sotomayor/The New York Time/Redux Pictures; **p. 865:** W. Cody/CORBIS; **p. 866:** Cindy Elgrably; **p. 867:** Cindy Elgrably; **p. 868:** AP Photo/Ron Edmonds; **p. 872:** (top left) AP Photo; (top left center) H. Armstrong Roberts/ClassicStock/Corbis; (top right center) Paul Conrad/© Tribune Media Services, Inc.; **p. 873:** (top left) W. Cody/CORBIS; (top left center) Hisham Ibrahim/Corbis; (top right) John Sotomayor/The New York Time/Redux Pictures.

CHAPTER 29

p. 874: (top left) David Brauchli/ Reuters/Corbis; (upper center left) Robert King/Staff/Getty Images News/Getty Images; (bottom left) Susan Meiselas/Magnum Photos; **pp. 874-875:** © Sean Adair/Reuters/CORBIS; **p. 876:** (top left) David Brauchli/Reuters/Corbis; (bottom) AP Photo/Michael Samojeden; **p. 878:** (top right) David Brauchli/ Reuters/Corbis; (bottom center) OLIPHANT © Universal Press Syndicate; **p. 879:** AP Photo/Jeff Widener, File; **p. 880:** CNN/Getty Images; **p. 882:** From the Best Cartoons of the Year, 1991 edition by Charles Brooks ©1991 by Charles Brooks used by permission of the publisher, Pelican Publishing Company, Inc.; **p. 884:** Robert King/Staff/Getty Images News/Getty Images; **p. 885:** Najlah Feanny/Corbis; **p. 886:** Robert King/Staff/Getty Images News/Getty Images; **p. 892:** © 2003 Brian Fairrington and PoliticalCartoons.com; **p. 894:** (top left) Susan Meiselas/Magnum Photos; (bottom left) Andrew Holbrooke/Corbis; (bottom right) Paul Watson/Toronto Star; **p. 896:** Susan Meiselas/Magnum Photos; **p. 897:** Clay Bennett/(c)2001 The Christian Scienc Monitor (www.CSMonitor.com). Reprinted with Permission; **p. 899:** The Permissions Group, Inc./ Ohman/TMS Reprint; **p. 900:** USA Today; **p. 902:** © MOLLY RILEY/Reuters/Corbis; **p. 903:** John R. Rose, Byrd Newspapers of Va; **p. 904:** (top left) David Brauchli/Reuters/Corbis; (top left center) From the Best Cartoons of the Year, 1991 edition by Charles Brooks © 1991 by Charles Brooks used by permission of the publisher, Pelican Publishing Company, Inc; (top right center) Najlah Feanny/Corbis; (top right) Robert King/Staff/Getty Images News/Getty Images; **p. 905:** (top left) © Sean Adair/Reuters/CORBIS; (top left center) USA Today; (top right center) © MOLLY RILEY/Reuters/Corbis; (top right) John R. Rose, Byrd Newspapers of Va.

Index

A

Abstract Expressionism, 764
Abu Graib prison, 900
Acquired Immune Deficiency Syndrome (AIDS), 863–864
Adams, Eddie, 794
Adams, Henry, 444
Addams, Jane, 508, 534, 549, 556
The Adventures of Huckleberry Finn (Twain), 462
The Adventures of Tom Sawyer (Twain), 462
African Americans
  as cowboys, 450
  freedom of movement for, 409
  migration during World War I of, 603–604
  New Deal for, 679–680
  during Phillippine-American War, 577–578
  during Progressive Era, 555–556
  racists hostilities from white workers, 484
  westward migration of, 444–445
  women, workplace and, 486
  World War I and, 609
  World War II and, 699–701
African American women, voting rights of, 644
Agricultural Adjustment Act (AAA) of 1933, 570, 680
Agricultural Marketing Act (1929), 657
Agriculture
  hard times for farmers (1860–1900), 448–449
  New Deal policies, 670–671
  ranching, 449–450
Aguinaldo, Emilio, 575–578
Alger, Horatio, 488
Ali, Muhammad, 830–831
Allen, Frederick Lewis, *625*
Allies, 688
Allies (World War II), 716
Al-Qaeda, 874, 895, 904
Altgeeld, Richard, 525
American Civil Liberties Union (ACLU) 635, 636
American Federation of Labor (AFL), 678, 682, 753

American Progress (Gast), 439, *439*
American Protective Association (APA), 506
American Railway Union (ARU), 524
Americans with Disabilities Act (1990), 880
Amnesty Act, 423
Anarchists, 634–635
Anderson, Archer, 429
Anderson, Sherwood, 632
Angel Island, 581–582
Anson, Adrian "Cap," 514
Anti-Saloon League, 547, 634
Appeasement, 686–688
Apple Computer, 847
Arabic (ship), 598
Armour, Philip, 476
Armstrong, Louis, 642
Arthur, Chester A., 498
Auto industries, 836
Axis powers, 688, 716

B

Babcock, Orville E., 423
Baby boom generation, 750, 758, 776
Baker, Ella, 774
Baker, Ray Stannard, 536
Bakker, Jim and Tammy, 867
Baldwin, James, 830
Baldwin, Roger, 635
Barton, Clara, 486
Baseball, 514
  radio and, 630
Bataan Death March, 693–694
Bates, Daisy, 771, 772
Bay of Pigs operation, 744–747, 748
Beals, Melba Pattillo, 772
Beats/beatniks, 763–764
Begin, Menachem, 855–856
Beitler, Lawrence, 638
Belknap, William W., 423
Bell, Alexander Graham, 471
Bellamy, David, 893
Bellamy, Edward, 490
Bennett, Clay, 897
Berle, Adolf, 662
Berlin Airlift, 726–727, 748
Berlin, Irving, 515

Berlin Wall, 743–744, 745
  fall of, 878
Berman, Alexander, 522
Bernstein, Carl, 849
Bicycling, 513
Big business
  emergence of, 470–477
  modern practices of, 472–473
  railroads, 472
  reasons for fearing, 491
  reining in, 535–540
  rising concern over power of, 473–474
bin Laden, Osama, 903
Birmingham campaign, 821–824, 840
Birth control, 646
Black Codes, 413–415, *415*, 436
"Black Friday" scandal, 423
Black, Hugo, 696
Blacklists, 483, 496
Blackmore, William, 453
Black Panthers, 832–834
Black Power, 832–834, 840
Black Thursday, 658
Blair, Francis, 420
Bloody Sunday assault, 826–827
Bonus March, 660, 661, 682
Borjas, George J., 891
Bourke-White, Margaret, 680
Boxer Rebellion, 580
Bradford, Susan, 409
Brady, James, 868
Brain Trust, 662
Brandeis, Louis, 546
Brando, Marlon, 762
Braun, Carol Mosley, 880
Bread Line–No One Has Starved (Marsh), 660, *660*
Brest-Litovsk Treaty, 601
Brooklyn Bridge, 498, *499*
Browne, Malcom, 784, 785
Brown, Helen Gurley, 834
Brown v. Board of Education (1954), 766, 770, 776, 813, 847
Bryant, Roy, 768
Bryan, William Jennings, 525–527, 537, 572, 573, 588–589, 596, 636
Brzezinski, Zbigniew, 856, 857

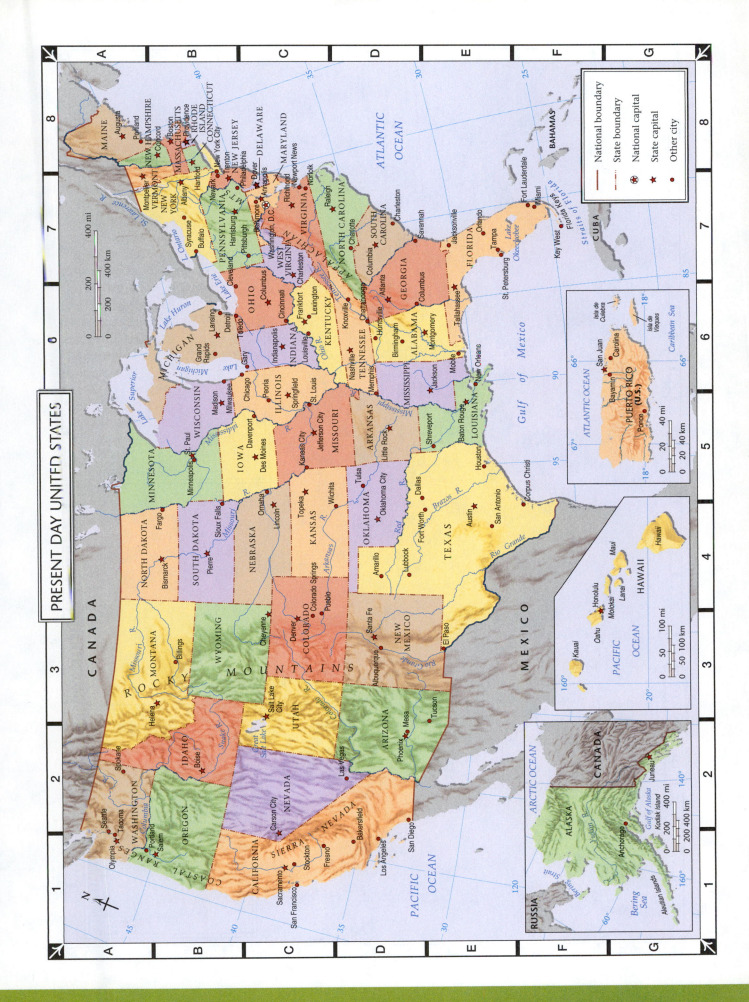

PRESENT DAY UNITED STATES

M-1

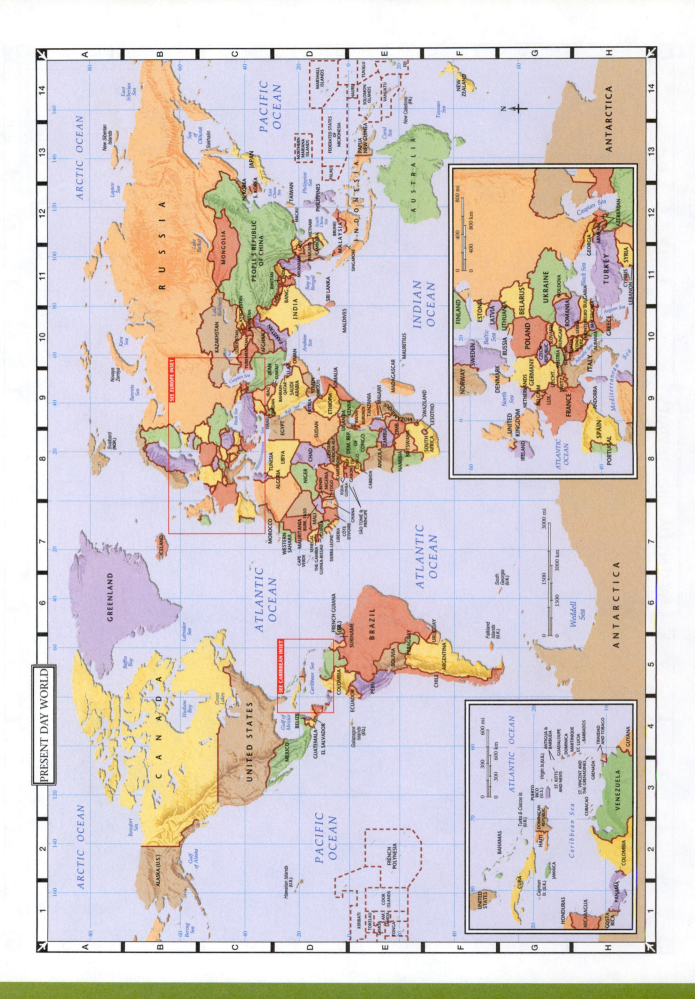

PRESENT DAY WORLD